The Family in Social Context

The Family in Social Context

Fourth Edition

GERALD R. LESLIE

New York OXFORD UNIVERSITY PRESS 1979

See page 639 for photo credits.
Library of Congress Cataloging in Publication Data
Leslie, Gerald R
The family in social context.
Includes index.
1. Family—United States. 2. Family. I. Title.
HQ535.L4 1979 301.42 78-17768 ISBN 0-19-502423-0

Third printing, 1980

Printed in the United States of America

Preface

The fourth edition of this book is the product of 30 years' experience in teaching courses on the family at several major universities. It contains materials and emphases that the author has found especially useful in bringing understanding to students. The purpose of a textbook, after all, is to make learning more efficient and pleasurable for both instructors and students.

It is a big book, including most of the material usually covered in courses offered under titles such as the Modern Family, the Sociology of the Family, and Marriage and the Family. Not all instructors will be able to cover all of it in one term. They should, however, find ample material to get into their courses the specific emphases they want. Moreover, by assigning the whole book to be read, they can give their students what often requires a textbook and a book of readings combined.

One feature of the book is unusually extensive coverage of cross-cultural and historical material. With the trend toward inclusion of more such material in family courses, many instructors will want to spend considerable time on Parts I and II. Those instructors who do not emphasize the family systems of other societies will want to move more quickly to Part III, Contemporary American Families.

Several features are new to this edition. The chapter on Alternative Life Styles has been merged with the chapter on Utopian Family Experiments, reflecting the decline of the youth counterculture. This change puts the upheaval of the late 1960s and early 1970s into better historical and social perspective. There is a separate section on marital power, and a new section on violence between spouses and against children. The marital, work, and parental expectations of men and women receive systematic treatment, including planned childlessness. Delays in the time of marriage, increasing divorce rates, and the nature and problems of one-parent families are analyzed.

The last eight chapters of the book continue to be organized in a life-cycle framework, providing a wealth of detail on the functioning of contemporary families from adolescence through old age. Some instructors will interpret these materials in strictly institutional terms; some will use a more functional approach. The needs of both groups should be met fully.

Finally, the book continues to avoid confusing profundity with obscurantism. It assumes that the conceptual apparatus essential to an understanding of the field can be employed in a clear and simple writing style to make learning a pleasure.

Gainesville, Florida G. R. L.
January 1978

Contents

I Cross-Cultural Perspectives

II Historical and Theoretical Perspectives

III Contemporary American Families

IV The Family Life Cycle

I
Cross-Cultural Perspectives

I
The Nature of the Family

The family is, as far as we know, the toughest institution we have. It is, in fact, the institution to which we owe our humanity. We know no other way of making human beings except by bringing them up in a family. Of course this does not mean that widows cannot bring up children; but the widowed mother brings up her children to know that their father is dead, that they had a father, and that the children next door have a father. The model is still there. And of course this holds for the widower as well. But we know no other way to bring children up to be human beings, able to act like men and women, and able to marry other men and women and bring up children, except through the family.[1]

The paragraph above was written by one of America's most respected social scientists a generation ago. Many people today ask whether it is still true; whether the family is the toughest institution we have; and whether the only way to raise children successfully is in families. Although this book will do far more than simply answer these questions, it will attempt to answer them in the context of both several thousand years of human experience and in the context of the seemingly revolutionary changes of recent years.

It is a large task. Even if we exclude analyses of the family in genetic, embryological, anatomical, and physiological terms, to say nothing of legal, economic, and political ones, and confine our analysis to the family as a social institution, we still must consider human-kind's experience

1. Margaret Mead, "The Impact of Cultural Changes on the Family," *The Family in the Urban Community*, Detroit: The Merrill-Palmer School, 1953, p. 4.

over several thousand years and over the entire world. We must analyze the family in its total social context.

SOCIETY AND THE SOCIAL CONTEXT

Conventionally, the term *society* has been used to refer to substantial collections of people living in near isolation from other such collections, having definite geographic boundaries, and enacting distinctive cultures. The term is easy to apply to preliterate peoples, but more difficult to apply to modern industrial nations where there is less isolation and where cultural boundaries and national boundaries do not always coincide.

Anthropologists estimate that there have been 4000 separable societies in the world since the dawn of human experience.[2] These range from preliterate societies of fewer than 400 people to modern societies of over 800 million. Not even a majority of these societies has been systematically studied. The most adequate analysis has been done by Murdock who compiled the Ethnographic Atlas of 1170 carefully selected societies.[3] Among those 1170 societies, some are known through history and some exist now, some are preliterate and some are civilized societies.

Few people, except social scientists, know that there have been so many societies. Moreover, when they become aware of this tremendous range of human groups many people wonder how relevant the experience of small preliterate societies in the mid-Pacific, the Andes, or Africa is to the problem of complex societies such as the United States. They wonder whether the experience of 178 people isolated and virtually without material possessions should be compared with the customs of a society of 215 million people who have created an automated, computerized economy and one in which the arts and humanities flourish.

The problems of comparing societies are complex and we need not get into them here. Suffice it to say that anthropologists believe that it is legitimate and useful to compare large and small societies when the purpose is to try to understand the full range of solutions to universal human problems. Regardless of the size or technological advancement, each society's customs and institutions constitute an independent solution to the problem of ensuring survival. The family system of a society

2. George P. Murdock, "World Ethnographic Sample," *American Anthropologist* 59 (Aug. 1957), pp. 664–87.

3. George P. Murdock, *Ethnographic Atlas*, Pittsburgh: University of Pittsburgh Press, 1967.

of 178 people might not be practical in the United States, but it does represent another means of coping with the same general human problems that we face. Moreover, if we see that the majority, or even a significant minority, of societies have family systems that differ significantly from our own, it becomes more difficult for us to believe that our own system is divinely ordained or even inherently superior.[4]

Social Institutions

The concept of social institutions will appear throughout this book, for social scientists are much concerned with the institutional aspects of the family. At this point our task is to discuss briefly the major social institutions and to place the family institution within the context of the society's larger institutional structure.

Sociologists use the term *institution* in a different and more technical way than does the average person. Sociologists view institutions as systems of social norms. Norms are society's rules of conduct for its members. Norms range from the formal—each person may have only one spouse—to the informal—letting father have the largest piece of pie. The number of such rules, or customary behaviors, is exceedingly large and covers almost every aspect of life. Growing up in a society means learning its norms so that as an adult one will be able to function successfully with other similarly socialized people.

Although most people may not be aware of it, norms are organized into patterns. In the family, for example, there are norms that specify which persons are eligible to marry, how many spouses they may have, who is eligible to marry whom, when they should marry, who should be the boss in the family, where they should live, what the division of labor should be, the proper attitudes toward children and oldsters, and so on. Detailed examination of the normative system controlling family behavior will appear in subsequent chapters.

In all societies, complex normative patterns appear in certain basic areas. There is always a normative system governing the legitimate use of power in the society. We call this system of norms government. Similarly, another normative system defines the production, distribution, and

4. The tendency of people to regard their own ways of doing things as the best is, of course, the concept of ethnocentrism. Ethnocentrism serves the valuable function of promoting loyalty to one's own society and its institutions but it makes it difficult for us to see the relativity of cultural practices. The principle of cultural relativity holds that the functions and meaning of practices can be understood only in the context of the larger culture in which they are found—not in the context of our values and practices.

consumption of goods and services: the economic institution. A third normative system regulates our relation to the supernatural: the religious institution. The educational institution is concerned with the transmission of values, attitudes, knowledge, and skills from one generation to the next. And there are always rules regulating adult sex relationships and procreation: the family institution.

> In every known society, at least some persons consider themselves kin of at least some other persons, living and dead. The way in which kinship is expressed and the kinds of behavior which follow from the recognition of this relationship vary from culture to culture.
>
> PHILIP K. BOCK, *Modern Cultural Anthropology: An Introduction*, New York: Alfred A. Knopf, 1969, pp. 87–88

All societies have these major institutions: family, government, economic system, education, and religion. The content of a society's institutions determines in large measure its character. Understanding these basic institutions leads to understanding of the society.[5]

The institutions of a society are related to one another. Government, for example, impinges upon the family in many ways. The authority wielded within the family may well stand in some inverse relation to the power vested in the government: when the government is weak the family may exercise considerable control of individual behavior and vice versa. Government may provide a host of services to families and their members or it may require that families be largely self-sufficient.

Moreover, the interrelations among a society's institutions may vary over time. There was a time in our history when there was relatively little differentiation among the major institutions: when the family performed many of what today are the functions of government, religion, and the schools. Later on, Western religious institutions became powerful and restricted and controlled family life. Still other changes saw government come to exercise great regulatory power, and current interrelations between the family and the economy have much to do with the nature of present-day family problems. One social institution can be understood only in the context of its relations with other institutions.

5. Unfortunately, sociologists occasionally use the term *institution* not only in its technical sense but also in its lay usage. Thus people refer to prisons and hospitals as institutions. Actually institutionalization is a process, going on in many areas of life simultaneously.

Functional Requisites for Societal Survival

The fact that certain institutions are found in all known societies suggests that societies may not be able to exist without them. Or, to put it differently, the major social institutions play a very large role in accomplishing those basic functions which are essential to a society's survival.

Apparently there are certain minimum tasks that must be performed in all societies. Unless they are performed adequately, the society would cease to exist. An analogy may help to make the point. We might hypothesize that a quality-control department is essential to the survival of a manufacturing company. A company might survive if it occasionally put out defective merchandise, but if much of its product were defective, customers would take their business elsewhere and the company would go bankrupt. Perhaps the only way to prevent this from happening is to have a quality-control department to make sure that the company's product uniformly meets predetermined standards.

Notice that we are not saying that the conscious purpose of a quality-control department is to keep a company in business. Nor are we saying that a company could not be established and operate without a quality-control department. We are saying that, in the long run, a company that does not develop effective means of quality control is likely not to be able to meet the competition and, hence, is likely not to survive.

So it is with societies. To speak of there being functional requisites to a society's survival does not mean that each society is aware that certain tasks must be performed and that it consciously creates arrangements to provide for them. Nor is it to say that there have never been societies in which these tasks were not properly provided for. It is to say that if such societies existed, they have long since ceased to exist.

Social scientists, from their studies of societies, have concluded that there are certain minimum conditions that must be met. These functional requisites that are met principally through a society's major institutions include the following: (1) provision for the continued adequate biologic functioning of the members of the society; (2) provision for the reproduction of new members of the society; (3) provision for the adequate socialization of new members of the society; (4) arrangements for the production and distribution of goods and services; (5) provision for the maintenance of order within the group and with outsiders, and (6) the meaning of life must be defined and the motivation for group and individual survival must be maintained.

Continued Biologic Functioning. In our analysis of human social life, we should never forget that we are biological organisms who share problems of survival with all other animal species. Our survival depends upon provision of the basic necessities of food, clothing, and shelter. Without these we could not remain healthy—and the maintenance of health is a part of this requisite to societal survival. People must be relatively healthy also to reproduce successfully, and reproduction is a part of the maintenance of biologic functioning. The provision of food, clothing, and shelter of course implies that there must be an organized pattern of work. Food, clothing, and shelter must be produced and distributed, according to some notion of equity, among the society's members. Except in the simplest societies, the provision for continued biologic functioning does not stop at this rudimentary level. In societies above the subsistence level, the basic necessities are elaborated into standards of nutrition, comfort, style, medical care, family planning, and so on. But whatever the level at which the society operates, certain minimum provisions in this area are essential to survival.

Two institutions are deeply involved in meeting this functional requisite for societal survival. The production and distribution of goods and services occurs through the economic system. The usual consumption unit for goods and services is the family. Moreover, the family is the unit of reproduction and the primary source of care for ailing persons. It is no accident that the meeting of functional requisites is accomplished significantly through social institutions. Institutions develop originally in response to societies' needs to survive.

Adequate Reproduction. That the various functional requisites are interrelated has been shown by our reference to reproduction when talking primarily about continued biologic functioning. The problem of replacement of members of the society is so fundamental, however, that it deserves separate discussion.

Unless a society provides for an adequate number of children to be born and cared for, the population will dwindle and eventually disappear. All societies have normative systems which regulate child-bearing and child-rearing. These societal rules define who is qualified to bear children, when reproduction may begin, how many children should be born, how the children should be cared for, and so on. These norms make up part of the institution of the family.

Even in this area, which seems to fall squarely within the institutional sphere of the family, other institutions are involved. The educational system shares with the family the care and training of the young. The replacement of societal members may occur also through recruitment from other societies. This process sometimes assumes large proportions through immigration. Immigrants require resocialization into the normative system of the new society, again involving the educational institution. No society for long, however, depends upon immigration to provide new members. New adults are not so dependable a source of replacement as are infants born into the society, and infants are not faced with conflicts between two normative systems. In all societies, the replacement of members occurs primarily through reproduction.

Socialization of New Members. The term *socialization* encompasses learning the values, attitudes, knowledge, skills, and techniques which a society possesses—in short, it involves learning the culture. A very important part of the culture is the normative system, including the major institutions. Socialization molds the child's biological potential into the pattern of functioning that we call human personality.

Socialization covers all learning, including the indirect and unanticipated learning that occurs whenever the child observes parents or others in interaction. Thus the child learns socially disapproved as well as approved behaviors and masters the nuances which are not taught in school, in college, or in apprenticeship.

No society allows socialization to proceed according to chance. The family institution includes norms defining proper parental behavior. It defines what parents properly may teach children and what they may not. Beyond the familial contribution, and intertwined with it, there always lies a body of knowledge and practice shared by the society at large which the society transmits to all new members. For unless the members of a society share a common core of values, beliefs, and practices, the organization of the society cannot be maintained.

The organization of the socialization process outside the family is, of course, what we call the educational institution. It may be rudimentary and nonspecialized, involving only a few wise elders passing on the ancient lore and youngsters working in informal apprenticeship with adults, or it may be highly organized and complex, including nursery schools, schools, colleges, and graduate schools.

Socialization does not cease when adulthood is reached. The socialization of the young is so dramatic that most of our attention has focused upon it. The early Freudian emphasis in psychology concentrated attention upon the development of personality during the first few years of life. We are realizing more and more, however, that learning occurs throughout life. College seniors have only begun to prepare for their occupational roles, and it takes considerable learning to transform them into the mature, poised, knowledgeable, self-confident leaders they may be as middle-aged adults. Similarly, becoming a husband or wife and a parent involves learning attitudes, sentiments, and skills that are not learned in school. Even becoming old involves complicated learning that the young and middle-aged cannot appreciate. The need for society to socialize its members may be most dramatic in the early years of life, but the continued functioning of a society is equally dependent upon the continued socialization of its adult members.

Production and Distribution of Goods and Services. All known societies have norms defining what goods shall be produced, how, and by whom. At bottom is the problem of ensuring the survival of individuals. But the regulation of economic activity does not stop here. All societies elaborate their regulations to provide for a division of labor among the members of the society. The economic and family institutions become intertwined, for there is always a division of labor between the sexes and between adults and children. The definition of man's work and woman's work both is derived from the family and is further influenced by it. The division of labor among age groups similarly is partly a family and partly an economic matter. Further, the production of goods results in the accumulation of property and necessitates rules for transmitting property from one generation to the next. Such rules again are involved in both the family and the economic system.

The adequate functioning of these various sets of norms ensures that the necessary goods will be produced, that they will be distributed in predictable fashion, and that competition among the members of the society will be limited and controlled.

Maintenance of Order. The rules which maintain order within societies range from informal customs to legally enforced codes. All societies have such customs and codes to govern relationships among members of the society and between members of the society and outsiders.

This is the general area involving the legitimate use of power and force through what we call government. Through organizations ranging from a few tribal elders to large nation states, societies regulate behavior in the interests of the group. Police forces, regulatory commissions, courts, prisons, and the like are representative of the enforcement apparatus. Such apparatus usually is conspicuous in the society, and people remain quite aware of the potential threats thus presented.

Yet it is inherent in social organization that the threat of force is a far more effective deterrent to deviation from approved behavior than is the actual use of force. In fact, the need to use force on any great scale is symptomatic of ineffective social organization. Even in the most complex society with the most elaborate regulatory and enforcement agencies, there cannot be enough police and other officers to force people to conform. Imagine, for example, what would happen if most citizens did not habitually obey traffic laws or voluntarily abstain from stealing. The vast majority of violators would go unapprehended, and those who were caught would overflow the jails and swamp the courts. The threat of force is effective only if it does not often have to be used, and all societies depend primarily upon other means for securing conformity.

The primary technique for gaining conformity in all societies is the thorough socialization of individuals. Socialization normally produces persons who have so thoroughly learned the official and unofficial norms that not only do they not want to violate them but it does not often occur to them that they might do so. It is common knowledge, for example, that small children take things that don't belong to them. Five-year-olds pick up attractive items in a store with little guilt because they have not yet learned how much other people disapprove. A few years later, they may still steal small items they want, but now with furtiveness and guilt. By the time they reach adulthood, they ordinarily do not have to be watched and they now help teach other younger persons that stealing is reprehensible. The word *conscience* is used to refer to this internalization of norms within the personality.

Here, again, the family institution and the political institution interpenetrate. Parents and siblings, aided by the formal educational system, teach conformity to the norms, which the political system has the official responsibility for enforcing. Without effective cooperation among the institutions, order would soon break down and the society would disintegrate.

Maintaining Motivation for Survival. To some degree the adequate performance of all of the preceding functional requisites depends upon this last one. There is a universal human problem of ascribing meaning to life itself and providing people with motivation for survival.

The rationale for valuing existence varies among societies, but some rationale always is provided. In one society the purpose of life may be to provide for worship of the Almighty. In a second, the goal may be continuation of the family line. Alternative and overlapping goals in life might include the appreciation of nature, the destruction of enemies, and hedonistic enjoyment. Some combination of goals is often found.

The religious institution is deeply involved in this area. One of the functions of religion is to define and strengthen ultimate values and to define relationships with the supernatural. The interpenetration of the religious and the family institution in this connection is obvious. In relatively undifferentiated societies it may be the father, himself, who serves as priest. In more complex societies, it is still likely to be the family that guides the young into the formal religious organizations and which complements the instruction of the church with family devotions and home worship. This complementariness is well illustrated by holidays such as Christmas and Easter, Chanukah and Yom Kippur, in which family, church, and synagogue are deeply involved.

The functional requisites for societal survival are the minimum conditions for its continued existence. We have emphasized the family's involvement in these tasks and the overlapping of the roles of the family with those of other institutions.

THE NATURE OF FAMILY ORGANIZATION

The family is sometimes called the basic social institution. For, although the major institutions are found in all societies, their relative importance and the clarity with which they are defined varies from one society to another. The family is always a conspicuous feature of social organization. The family is always easy to locate, is in the constant awareness of people, and is deeply involved in the performance of the functional requisites. These are sweeping generalizations. They are true enough—but not without qualification. There follow several hundred pages of qualifications!

The Nuclear Family

Not only is the family universal, but a specific form of it—the nuclear family—comes close to being a cultural universal.[6] Americans easily understand the nuclear family because in our society the nuclear family is virtually synonymous with the family in general. The United States has the nuclear family as the basic residential family unit.

The term *nuclear family* refers simply to two adults of opposite sex, living in a socially approved sex relationship, and their own or adopted children. It is the familiar unit of mother, father, and children. Data from societies all over the world point overwhelmingly to the central role which the nuclear family plays in human experience.

6. George P. Murdock, *Social Structure*, New York: The Macmillan Company, 1949, Ch. 1.

One indication of the significance and utility of a scientific generalization is the amount of research and writing stimulated by it, which activity seeks to test, expand, and qualify the generalization. By this test, Murdock's generalization that the nuclear family is a distinct functional unit in all societies must be one of the most seminal contributions to twentieth-century social science. Virtually all work in this area for the past twenty-five years has used Murdock's analysis as a starting point.

Some scholars argue that there are exceptions to the universality of the nuclear family, but their evidence for exceptions is less impressive than Murdock's evidence for universality. The challengers generally use data from groups that do not constitute independent societies, and which partial exceptions typically fail to endure for as long as two full generations even where they do occur.[7] One of their favorite illustrations is the

---

> . . . Whatever the degree of intensity with which kinship ties are utilized to forge social bonds, no society so far has managed to dispense with an irreducible minimum of kinship-based social relationships. And until Huxley's *Brave New World* is realized and bottles are substituted for mothers, they are unlikely ever to be dispensed with. . . .
>
> ROBIN FOX, *Kinship and Marriage*, Baltimore: Penguin Books, 1967, p. 16

Nayar of Malabar. The Nayar, for a while, had an arrangement in which the husband lived with his sister's family and visited his wife only at night for sexual purposes. The Nayar are not a separate society, however. They are a caste in the south of India. Moreover, this custom has not survived even among the Nayar who are tending toward the nuclear family as a prominent residential unit.[8] A second alleged exception, the Kibbutzim of modern Israel are not a separate society either, and they, too, give increasing prominence to the nuclear family.

7. These arguments appear most clearly in the work of Reiss. See Ira L. Reiss, *Family Systems in America*, New York: Holt, Rinehart and Winston, 1976. See also Lewellyn Hendrix, "Nuclear Family Universals: Fact and Faith in the Acceptance of an Idea," *Journal of Comparative Family Studies* 6 (Autumn 1975), pp. 125–38; Gary R. Lee, *Family Structure and Interaction: A Comparative Analysis*, Philadelphia: Lippincott, 1977; and Betty Yorburg, "The Nuclear and the Extended Family: An Area of Conceptual Confusion," *Journal of Comparative Family Studies* 6 (Spring 1975), pp. 5–14.
8. See Joan P. Mencher, "The Nayars of South Malabar," in Meyer F. Nimkoff, *ed.*, *Comparative Family Systems*, Boston: Houghton Mifflin, 1965, pp. 163–91.

More significant than these cases for understanding family structure are the facts that nuclear families often are incomplete, and often are incorporated into larger families. In any society, some nuclear families contain only one adult and some contain more than two adults. Similarly there may or may not be children present. If the husband has died or been divorced, the wife may continue the family alone and vice versa. Or there may be a grandparent or unmarried brother or sister living with the family. Either the married couple may have had no children, or they may have children who have grown and gone. The important thing about these exceptions is that they are exceptions. People who live temporarily in expanded or contracted nuclear families prepare the children to form intact nuclear families when they grow into adulthood.

A study of four-, five-, and six-year-old American and Japanese children shows that children need not be reared by both parents to learn the different roles that men and women customarily play. The youngsters, whose fathers are absent, see fathers as breadwinners, leaders, and decision makers even though their own mothers assume these roles. They learn the appropriate adult roles from brothers and sisters, other relatives, the mass media, and through school experiences. The investigators speculate that these children in adulthood will be more comfortable with conventional than with deviant family roles.

Paraphrased from HEW News Release, December 18, 1972, describing research by Joan Aldous and Takeji Kamido

---

In many societies, nuclear families exist as parts of larger kinship units. Even where the nuclear family is embedded in a network of grandparents, grandchildren, cousins, uncles, and so on, however, it tends to be a distinct unit and to have its own private quarters. Moreover, the nuclear family ordinarily is the smallest kinship unit which is treated as a separate unit by the rest of the society.

Before proceeding further, it may be helpful to distinguish the family from marriage. We reserve *marriage* not for the married couple itself but for the complex of customs which regulates the relationship between husband and wife and provides for the creation of a family. Marriage specifies the appropriate way of establishing a relationship, the normative structure for ordering it, and often includes provision for terminating it.

The Family of Orientation and the Family of Procreation. To view

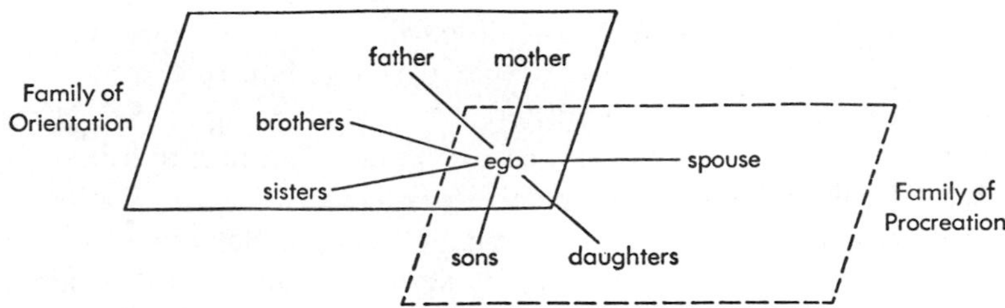

Figure 1.1. Diagram of the families of orientation and procreation

the nuclear family as a set of parents and their children is to view it in static, cross-sectional fashion. It describes the nuclear family at any given point in time but it fails to describe the experience in the nuclear family of any given person.

Normally, during his or her lifetime, each person is a member of two different, overlapping nuclear families. He or she is born into a nuclear family composed of self, siblings (brothers and sisters), and parents. This family is called the *family of orientation.* At marriage the individual leaves the family of orientation to create a new family composed of self, spouse, and their children. This new nuclear family in which the individual lives as an adult is called the *family of procreation.* The families of orientation and procreation are diagrammed in Figure 1.1. The word *ego,* the Latin word for "self," is used to stand for any individual.

The term *nuclear family* refers either to the family of orientation or to the family of procreation. Note that ego is the only person who is a member of both of these nuclear families. If we were to diagram the nuclear families of each other member of ego's nuclear families (mother, spouse, or sibling), the same thing would be true. Each pair of nuclear families would have only one member in common. This has much to do with the complexity of kinship structure.

Nuclear Family Functions. If we look at the common characteristics of nuclear families in various societies, we see that they parallel closely the functional requisites for societal survival. We find that (1) the marriage relationship always provides for meeting the sex needs of adults; (2) the nuclear family is the unit of reproduction; (3) the nuclear family is a unit of common residence; (4) the nuclear family is the primary unit of economic cooperation; and (5) the nuclear family has important responsibility for the socialization of children.

> As far as we know there is no biological instinct that makes a man into a good father. It is necessary to persuade him to want to be a father, and each society uses different means of doing so. Sometimes he is persuaded to be a father because he needs an heir to inherit his land. The French-Canadians used to persuade him to be a father by not giving bachelors hunting or fishing licenses. Sometimes he was persuaded to be a father through a system of ancestor worship in which a man lacking children to worship him after death had no proper existence in the next world.
>
> There have been all varieties of inducements, and they all tend to break down. The real variation through history has been in what has been done with the role of fathers. What has been done with mothers has been extremely monotonous on the whole, and heavily determined biologically, although it has varied, of course, with the invention of baby carriages and feeding bottles and things of that sort.
>
> MARGARET MEAD, "The Impact of Cultural Changes on the Family," in *The Family in the Urban Community*, Detroit: The Merrill-Palmer School, 1953, pp. 3–4

1. The nuclear family, through the marital relationship, always provides for meeting the sex needs of its adult members. Sex is a powerful impulse that is nowhere permitted expression without regulation; unregulated sexual expression would threaten the cooperative relationships necessary within the family and society. Neither do societies deny regular sexual gratification to any sizable proportion of their adult members. Some adults, or even defined groups of adults, may remain celibate, but what evidence is available suggests that whenever sexual access is denied to a sizable segment of men or women the society is likely to become unstable and major social change will occur.

It would be a mistake, however, to assume that the availability of sex within marriage accounts for the existence of marriage. In our own society, before the recent liberalization of sexual attitudes, this might have seemed true. Even today, a large proportion of American youth have difficulty establishing satisfactory sex relationships before marriage. Many other societies, however, grant considerable sex freedom to unmarried adolescents and young adults, imposing more restrictions upon the availability of sex partners after a person is married than before. If sex were the only, or even the chief, reason for marriage, we would expect persons in these societies to resist marriage. Such is not the case.

People marry just as predictably in these societies as in our own. Most societies assign full adult status only to married people, and adult functioning, because of the sexual division of labor, is more difficult for the single person. We need to look to the full patterns of relationships between men and women to account for the universality of marriage.

2. The relationship between husband and wife is expected to produce children. Even today, when societies are becoming conscious of overpopulation, the expectation is that most marriages will produce at least one child. The fact that all societies place high value upon having children testifies to the necessity of children to the society's survival. Generally, all children are loved and cared for, but distinctions may be made among them. Male children, for example, often are preferred to female children, with occasional female infanticide being found. In all societies the reproductive function of the nuclear family is emphasized.

It even appears that some societies make the sex relationship between husband and wife contingent upon reproduction rather than the other way around. The Banaro of New Guinea, for example, forbid the husband to have intercourse with his wife until after she has borne a child by another man chosen for the purpose. The husband is granted sexual access to the wife only after her ability to produce children has been established.

3. In most societies, the residential kin group is not limited to the nuclear family. It may include grandparents and grandchildren. There may be brothers and their wives, sisters and their husbands. There may also be siblings, aunts, nephews, and so on. A residential kin group may be larger than the nuclear family. Always included with a residential kin group, however, and identifiable within it, is the nuclear family.

Where larger residential kin units are found, there may be common facilities, such as cooking space, dining space, and space for relaxation, but there are usually separate dwellings or apartments also. Each nuclear family ordinarily has some private quarters.

4. Economic cooperation within the nuclear family, along with the sex relationship between the father and mother, binds it together. This cooperation is rooted in biological differences between the sexes and is reinforced by the culturally defined division of labor. Males everywhere are generally physically more powerful, while women with children have their freedom of movement hampered by pregnancy and nursing. All societies have developed a sex division of labor which assigns much of the heavier work and most of the roaming to men. Women are as-

signed more household tasks and the routine caring for children. Neither the man nor the woman can function at full efficiency without the services of the other.[9]

All societies also have a division of labor by age, assigning certain lighter tasks to children. Our own urban industrial society has restricted such childhood tasks severely, but even here there exist tasks ranging from mowing the lawn to walking the dog, and from going to the grocery to baby-sitting with younger siblings. In most agriculture-oriented societies, the economic contribution of children is more obvious and greater. This division of labor continues into subsequent stages of the family life-cycle when the dependency patterns may become reversed. One day the parents will need support, and their adult children will be in a position to provide it. Both across sex lines and generational levels, economic cooperation helps to account for the importance of the nuclear family.

5. Even in highly specialized societies, the nuclear family has responsibility for the care and socialization of children during their early years. The facts of parturition and nursing determine that there will be earlier and more intense contact with the mother. Ordinarily she assumes most of the responsibility for physical care of the infant and only gradually does the father become involved in training the child. The training ultimately is much more complex than mere physical care and requires the combined efforts of both parents. Only the father can transmit to his sons the skills required of adult males in the society, and only the mother can provide comparable training for her daughters. Boys and girls learn from both of their parents how to interact with members of the opposite sex. The more elaborate the society, the more agencies are likely to share in this socialization, but in all societies the nuclear family plays an important role in it.

The nuclear family almost everywhere is characterized by sexual, reproductive, residential, economic, and socialization functions. Groups and agencies outside the family often share in the fulfillment of these tasks but never to the exclusion of the nuclear family. No society has yet found a satisfactory substitute for the nuclear family.

9. The women's liberation movement argues that conditions of modern life have removed most of the necessity for a sex-based division of labor. For critiques of this topic, see Joel Aronoff and William D. Crano, "A Re-examination of the Cross-cultural Principles of Task Segregation and Sex Role Differentiation in the Family," *American Sociological Review* 40 (Feb. 1975), pp. 12–20; and Gerald Marwell, "Why Ascription? Parts of a More or Less Formal Theory of the Functions and Dysfunctions of Sex Roles," *American Sociological Review* 40 (Aug. 1975), pp. 445–55.

Kinship Organization

The nature of Western family organization makes it easy for American students to grasp the concept of the nuclear family. To a large extent the nuclear family is exemplified by the family in the United States. This same family structure is a handicap, however, when it comes to understanding kinship organization throughout most of the rest of the world. For in most societies, nuclear families do not exist in relative isolation from other kin units. Most societies have additional forms of family or kinship organization. Nuclear families may be combined through plural marriage or through extension of the parent-child relationship into composite families. In addition, the means of tracing descent often produce larger kinship units known variously as lineages, moieties, clans, and so on. None of these other forms of kinship organization is universal. It is important, however, to emphasize, along with the primacy of the nuclear family, that most societies have a kinship organization more elaborate and complex than ours.

The Family as a Social Group

So far we have emphasized the family as a social institution; as a normative system. It consists of more or less formal rules and regulations concerning the conduct of a major aspect of life. The family institution is not limited to the particular form given to it by a particular group of people, by the Jones family, say, or the Kowalskis. The family institution does not come into existence with the Joneses or the Kowalskis, and it does not die with them. The family as an institution is an abstraction or, rather, a series of abstractions from behavior. By observing the behavior of a sufficiently large and representative group of people in a society and by studying its official codes, we can state that the family institution of that society has certain features. This form of analysis provides a powerful tool for understanding human behavior.

There is yet another way of viewing families and their behavior. It focuses upon the specific groups of people through whom the family institution is enacted and transmitted to subsequent generations. The distinction is not completely clear-cut: it is a matter of emphasis. The nuclear family, for example, is an institutional form—a series of prescriptions and proscriptions—about the relationships among its members and also refers to a specific group of people—mother, father, sons, and daughters.

In addition to the nuclear family there are a number of fairly common family groups in the United States. People who think that it is desirable to live in independent nuclear families sometimes live in different circumstances. To understand the operation of our nuclear family system fully, it is necessary to have an awareness of some of these variations.[10]

The Household. A household is simply a group of people who share a common dwelling. Normally a group united by ties of marriage, blood, or adoption forms the core of a household. There are many nuclear families that have unmarried relatives or aged parents living with them. A household may also comprise an unmarried brother and sister who live together. Even several bachelors living together constitute a household. A household often is a family group but it need not be: it may be an unrelated group of people who share the customary living arrangements of a family group.[11]

Primary Family. A primary family consists of the head of a household and all other persons in the household who are related to him or her. In the normal course of events, the head of the household is a parent and the related persons are the spouse and children.

Secondary Family. A secondary family comprises two or more persons who are related to one another and who live with a primary family to whom they are not related. A servant couple provides one illustration, and a pair of married college students living in a professor's home provides another.

Subfamily. A subfamily is a married couple with or without children, or one parent with one or more children under 18 years of age, related to and living with a primary family. Young married couples living with one set of parents, or a widowed wife and her children who have returned to the parental home, provide illustrations.

These definitions are essentially those of the United States Census and they are given here because the Census is the primary source of statistical information about the structure of families and the living arrangements of families and unrelated individuals in the United States. Summary figures from the Census for the year 1975 are shown in Table 1.1.

10. See Donald W. Ball, "The 'Family' as a *Sociological* Problem: Conceptualization of the Taken-for-Granted as Prologue to Social Problems Analysis," *Social Problems* 19 (Winter 1972), pp. 295–307.

11. For analyses of recent changes in the composition of American family groups, see Paul C. Glick, "A Demographer Looks at American Families," *Journal of Marriage and the Family* 37 (Feb. 1975), pp. 15–26; and Frances E. Kobrin, "The Primary Individual and the Family: Changes in Living Arrangements in the United States Since 1940," *Journal of Marriage and the Family* 38 (May 1976), pp. 233–39.

Table 1.1. Households, families, subfamilies, married couples, and unrelated individuals in the United States, 1975

Type of Unit	*1975*
Households	71,120,000
Families	
Primary families	55,563,000
Secondary families	149,000
Subfamilies	1,349,000
Married couples	47,547,000
Unrelated individuals	19,100,000

Source: U.S. Bureau of the Census, *Statistical Abstract of the United States: 1977* (Washington, D.C.), p. 39.

When one focuses on the family as a social group, attention is directed inward toward the relationships within the family unit. It may be some exaggeration to say that institutional analyses emphasize relationships between the family and other aspects of the society while group analyses are more social psychological, focusing upon the emotional dynamics within the family. But a difference in emphasis, at least, is there. Both institutional and social psychological analyses will be used throughout this book.

SUMMARY

No one knows just how many human societies there are and have been, for societal boundaries often are difficult to define. There are, however, at least 4000 identifiable societies, ranging from preliterate to modern. The culture of each of these societies constitutes an independent solution to the common human problem of group living. Study of these societies will help us to understand our own society and our own family system.

The term *institution* is used by social scientists to refer to complex systems of social norms organized about the preservation of basic societal values. All societies have certain basic institutions—government, an economic system, an educational system, a religious institution, and the family. The institutions in a society are interrelated. Each impinges upon the others and the relationships among them change over time.

Institutions play major roles in performing the tasks essential for the society's survival. Such tasks are called functional requisites. Functional requisites include provision for (1) continued adequate biological functioning; (2) reproduction; (3) the socialization of new members of the society; (4) the production and distribution of goods and services; (5) the maintenance of order within the group; and (6) maintenance of the motivation for individual and group survival. The family plays an important role in the performance of each of these essential tasks, sharing the responsibility differentially with the other major institutions.

The nuclear family, composed of a married pair and their offspring, is a family unit of special importance. Normally people are members of two such units during their lifetimes, the family of orientation and the family of procreation. The nuclear family (1) provides regular sexual outlet for adults; (2) is the unit of procreation; (3) is the basic unit of economic cooperation; (4) maintains a common residence; and (5) has basic responsibility for the indoctrination of the young.

In most societies, nuclear families are organized into larger kinship units. This may be accomplished either through the practice of plural marriage or through the extension of the parent-child relationship. The means of tracing descent, through lineages, clans, and the like, often encourage larger family units also. Adequate understanding of social structure requires analysis of the whole of kinship organization, not just of the nuclear family.

When the family is viewed as a social institution, the norms governing family forms and functions are emphasized. There is yet another important way of analyzing family patterns, however. Families are also social groups. Institutions consist of social norms while groups consist of people in interaction. When one focuses upon the family as a social group, attention is directed more toward its internal functioning than toward its relationships with other aspects of the society. There are many ways to classify family groups but one of the most useful ways is to follow the usages of the Bureau of the Census. The Census classifies family groups into primary families, secondary families, subfamilies, and married couples. It also distinguishes families from households, and counts individuals living apart from any family groups.

SUGGESTED READINGS

Bernard, Jessie, *The Future of Motherhood*, New York: Penguin, 1974. A leading scholar examines the past, present, and future of motherhood in the U.S. and the world. Fascinating reading.

Burr, Wesley R., *Theory Construction and the Sociology of the Family*, New York: John Wiley and Sons, 1973. A sophisticated and technical volume analyzing the process by which sociologists construct theories of family behavior. Good preparation for advanced study in the field.

Carter, Hugh, and Glick, Paul C., *Marriage and Divorce: A Social and Economic Study*, Cambridge, Mass.: Harvard University Press, 1976. A monograph of the American Public Health Association, this book contains a wealth of information about the structure and functioning of American families.

Christensen, Harold T., and Johnsen, Kathryn P., *Marriage and the Family*, New York: The Ronald Press Company, 1971. Written as a functional textbook in preparation for marriage and family life, this analysis is both current and theoretically sophisticated.

Clayton, Richard R., *The Family, Marriage, and Social Change*, Lexington, Mass.: Heath, 1975. A comprehensive sociological analysis of the family. Written as a textbook for college courses on the family.

Ferriss, Abbott L., *Indicators of Change in the American Family*, New York: Russell Sage Foundation, 1970. The first systematic attempt to use data collected over periods of time to trace changes in the functioning of American families.

Nye, F. Ivan, and Berardo, Felix M., *eds., Emerging Conceptual Frameworks in Family Analysis*, New York: The Macmillan Company, 1966. Systematic analysis of eleven different theoretical approaches to the analysis of family data. Includes anthropological, psychoanalytic, economic, legal, and religious approaches.

Streib, Gordon F., *ed., The Changing Family: Adaptation and Diversity*, Reading, Massachusetts: Addison-Wesley Publishing Company, 1973. A discriminating collection of essays on both the positive and negative aspects of newer forms of family organization. Enjoyable reading.

Wakil, S. Parvez, *ed., Marriage and Family: Canadian Perspectives*, Toronto, Ontario, Canada: Butterworth, 1975. A comprehensive collection of essays on the family system in Canada. Good antidote to the parochialism of most treatments of the family in the U.S.

FILMS

Beginnings of Conscience (McGraw-Hill Book Company, Text-film Division, 1221 Avenue of the Americas, New York, N.Y. 10020), 16 minutes. The social conscience which James Bruce, the adult, manifests is traced back to his socialization as a child. The conscience which he gradually develops in childhood through the experiencing of such social sanctions as force, exclusion, and ridicule later functions almost automatically in adulthod to make him a social being.

A Cross-Cultural Approach to the Acquisition of Sex Roles and Social Standards (Harper and Row Media, 10 East 53rd Street, New York, N.Y.

10022), 25 minutes. Children in Guatemala, Kenya, and Japan learn sex role standards through observation, imitation, praise, and punishment.

Excited Turkeys (Grove Press Film Division, 80 University Place, New York, N.Y. 10003), 10 minutes. Focuses on the traditional Thanksgiving dinner to examine the "apple pie" family. Studies the myths that Americans have created about their cultural and rational identity.

The Family: Lifestyles of the Future (Document Associates, 880 Third Avenue, New York, N.Y. 10022), 20 minutes, color. Margaret Mead narrates an examination of traditional values and current unconventional forms of family life. Concludes that there will be diversity in family forms in the future.

A House, a Wife, and a Singing Bird (available through Oklahoma State University Audio-Visual Center, Stillwater, Okla. 74074), 30 minutes, color. A wise man tells a youth that old men dream dreams but it is the young men who make them come true, and to be happy, a man must have a wife, a house, and a singing bird. Shows the young Indonesian searching for a place to live, ways that people make a living, customs, and finally the marriage ceremony.

Windy Day (Grove Press Film Division, 80 University Place, New York, N.Y. 10003), 12 minutes. An animated film featuring the voices of two young girls deals with the responses of children to romance, marriage, and adulthood. The children muse about their parents getting married, growing old, and dying.

QUESTIONS AND PROJECTS

1. Explain how we can learn about the American family system from knowledge of the family systems of preliterate societies.
2. Define the concept *social institution.* How are institutional patterns inferred from behavior?
3. Name the basic social institutions and give a brief definition of each. In what ways are the various institutions of a society interrelated? Illustrate.
4. Define the term *functional requisites.* Have there ever been societies that did not provide for meeting the functional requisites? If so, what happened to them?
5. Show, through illustration, how the family is involved in meeting each of the functional requisites.
6. Why is the family sometimes called the *basic social institution?*
7. Define the term *nuclear family.* Does the fact that some members of a society do not live in nuclear units detract from the importance of the nuclear family? Why or why not?

8. Distinguish between the family and marriage. What is the relationship between the two?
9. What is the family of orientation? The family of procreation? Draw a diagram indicating the relationship between them.
10. What are the principal functions of the nuclear family? Illustrate each.
11. What is meant by the family "as a social group"? How is the family as a social group different from the family as an institution?
12. Define each of the following terms: *household; primary family; secondary family; subfamily*.

2

The Family in World Perspective

The Book of Genesis had it wrong. "In the beginning God created Eve," says Johns Hopkins Medical Psychologist John Money. What he means is that the basic tendency of the human fetus is to develop as a female. If the genes order the gonads to become testicles and put out the male hormone androgen, the embryo will turn into a boy; otherwise it becomes a girl. "You have to add something to get a male," Money notes. "Nature's first intention is to create a female."

Nature may prefer women, but virtually every culture has been partial to men. That contradiction raises an increasingly pertinent question (as well as the hackles of militant feminists): Are women immutably different from men? Women's Liberationists believe that any differences—other than anatomical—are a result of conditioning by society. The opposing view is that all of the differences are fixed in the genes. . . .

The idea that genetic predispositions exist is based on three kinds of evidence. First, there are the "cultural universals" cited by Margaret Mead. Almost everywhere, the mother is the principal caretaker of the child, and male dominance and aggression are the rule. . . . Then there is the fact that among most ground-dwelling primates, males are dominant and have as a major function the protection of females and offspring. Some research suggests that this is true even when the young are raised apart from adults, which seems to mean that they do not learn their roles from their society.

Finally, behavioral sex differences show up long before any baby could possibly perceive subtle differences between his parents or know which parent he is expected to imitate. . . . Physical differences appear even before birth. The heart of the female fetus often beats faster and girls develop more rapidly. . . . Recent research hints that there may even be sex differences in the brain. . . . In fact, newborn girls do show different responses in some situations. They react more strongly to the removal of a blanket and more quickly to touch and pain. . . . Twelve-week-old girls gaze longer at photographs of faces than at geometric figures. . . .[1]

The quotation above bears upon one of the major family issues of the late twentieth century; the degree to which family patterns are biologically or culturally determined. The evidence for biological determinism is far from complete or convincing, and it will be many years before scientists are able to unravel the puzzle satisfactorily.[2] In the meantime, we do know that, whatever the biological facts, there has been, and generally still is, a pervasive cultural bias leading to the masculine domination of societies. At the same time, the past few decades have seen a startling and almost worldwide change in concepts of appropriate man-woman relationships.

COMPOSITE FAMILY FORMS

The nuclear family is the basic building block in family structure. In most societies, nuclear families are combined into larger units in one of two ways. They are combined through plural marriage or through extension of the parent-child relationship. Nuclear families combined through plural marriage are called *polygamous families,* and those combined through the parent-child relation are called *extended families.*

Polygamous Families

Many Americans hear the word "polygamy," and think of the sexual aspects of marriage. We are likely to imagine polygamy as one long sexual orgy. Nothing could be further from the truth.

In the first place, polygamous marriage is based upon more than extension of the sexual privilege. Most societies grant sexual privileges with persons to whom the individual is not and probably never will be married. Moreover, marriage involves more than just an approved sex relationship. In marriage there is also the expectation of reproduction, common residence, and economic cooperation. To understand polygamy it is necessary to emphasize these latter aspects of marriage.

1. From *Time,* The Weekly Newsmagazine, March 20, 1972, p. 43; copyright Time Inc., 1972. Reprinted by permission.
2. John Money and Anke A. Ehrhardt, *Man and Woman, Boy and Girl,* Baltimore: The Johns Hopkins University Press, 1973.

One common error is to assume that polygamy is forced upon unenthusiastic women by lecherous men. Actually, polygamous societies are not like that. Where polygamy is fully institutionalized, women may be as involved in its perpetuation as men are, and some men are pressured by their wives into taking additional marriage partners.

Perhaps an analogy will help make the point. In the United States, women have been known to pressure their husbands to acquire possessions and other status symbols which the wives can use to raise their status with other wives. A woman may urge her husband, for example, to acquire a larger house, more automobiles, domestic help, a new fur coat for her, or perhaps to take her on a lavish, expensive vacation. In a polygamous society, a woman might similarly urge her husband to take a second wife. After all, the reasoning goes, what kind of man is it who cannot afford a second wife? If he truly loved her, he would get another wife to help her with her domestic duties. The first wife in polygamous societies often occupies a preferential position and the second wife may be something of a servant as well. Moreover, a second wife might serve the useful function of periodically relieving the first wife of sexual duty.

For his part, we might imagine the husband saying to his wife, "But I can't afford another wife. Sure Jones got his wife another wife, but he makes more money than I do." As for sex, it is sexual privilege that is pleasurable—not sexual duty. The most ardent Don Juan might give up seduction if he knew he had to sleep twice a week with each of his conquests. Under polygamy, the husband normally is required to treat his wives equally, to live with them in rotation, and to have sexual intercourse with them. Nothing dulls the sexual appetite more than obligation. A twenty-year-old man might not think that he would be too oppressed by such a burden. But twenty-year-old men can afford extra wives about as regularly as twenty-year-old men can afford large houses and fur coats. The forty- or fifty-year-old man who can afford the extra wife may not be quite so confident of his sexual prowess.

This was an analogy, of course, and it should not be pressed too far. The basic points are: First, polygamy involves more than sex. It is intimately tied up with economic functioning and status considerations. Second, where polygamy exists it is likely to be supported by women as well as by men. And, third, polygamy is a normative system involving a series of obligations upon men and women. People in polygamous societies may react to those obligations much as we react to the obligations in our monogamous system.

So far, we have used *polygamy* in its lay sense. Technically, polygamy is the general term used to refer to all marriage forms that involve the taking of plural spouses. Under polygamy, the spouses may be either husbands or wives. Polygamy is subdivided into two types, *polygyny* and *polyandry*. Polygyny is more common, involving plural wives. Polyandry, the taking of plural husbands, is rare.

Polygyny. Again, because of our own cultural biases, it is not too difficult for most Americans to imagine polygynous societies. We may misunderstand polygyny, but at least we can imagine it. Polygyny further subdivides into two basic types, *sororal* and *nonsororal*. The Latin word *soror* means sister. Under sororal polygyny the wives are sisters. Under nonsororal polygyny, the wives may be unrelated.

To most Americans, the best known sororal polygynous society may be that of the Hebrews. Students will remember the story of Jacob, Rachel, and Leah. Jacob wished to marry Rachel, the younger daughter of Laban. Jacob worked for seven years to earn the "bride price" for Rachel, only to be told that the younger daughter could not be married until the elder daughter was married. So Jacob took Leah and worked another seven years for Rachel.

Sororal polygyny is widespread over the world. Polygyny does produce problems of adjustment for the people who practise it (as does any form of marriage), and sororal polygyny seems to minimize some problems. Co-wives who are sisters are more likely to get along with one another than are co-wives who are not sisters. Having grown up together, they are likely to have similar values, attitudes, and ways of doing things. Jealousy is also less likely than between unrelated women. This situation is often reflected in housing arrangements. The separation of the dwellings of the co-wives is likely to be more marked if they are not sisters.

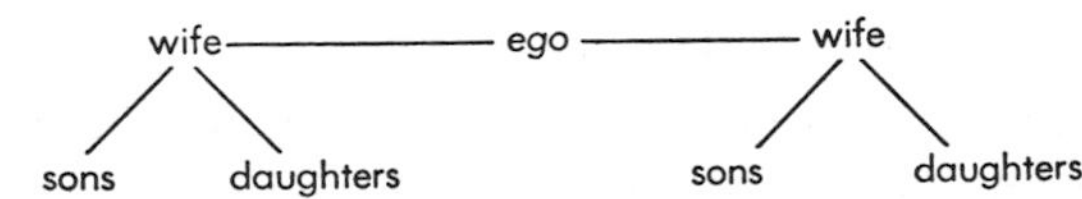

Figure 2.1. Diagram of independent, polygynous family

A special form of sororal polygyny is the *sororate*, in which there is a cultural rule specifying that the preferred mate for a widower is the sister of his deceased wife. Under the sororate, the marriages are successive rather than concurrent.

Many societies practise both sororal and nonsororal polygyny. The Mormons and the Crow Indians in the early United States are examples. The breakdown of Mormon polygyny often is attributed to the fact that the Mormons permitted unrelated wives to live in close contact and to the fact that Mormon husbands often showed preference for the most recent wife.

> The majority isolate themselves in small rural communities. Others live in metropolitan areas, their way of life known to their neighbors. And a few in recent months have dared to state in public that they practice polygamy. . . .
>
> State and federal officials estimate that there are 25,000 to 35,000 Americans practicing polygamy. Most are in Utah, Arizona, Idaho, Nevada and Montana, or across the borders in Mexico and Canada.
>
> Prosecution of polygamists is rare now, but evidence of their existence is easy to gather. They list up to 25 children on tax returns. Brothers and sisters a few months apart in age sit together in classrooms. . . .
>
> Associated Press, May 25, 1975

Murdock has prepared estimates of the incidence of polygyny for one sample of 250 societies and for an expanded sample of 565 societies. Polygyny was found in 75 percent of the first sample of societies and in 81 percent of the second.[3]

Where it exists, polygyny usually is accorded higher status than is monogamy. Yet, even where polygyny is preferred, it tends to be practised only by a small segment of the population. In some instances the right to take multiple wives is limited to ruling families or to high-status persons. But even where such restrictions do not exist, most persons in polygynous societies remain monogamous. There are at least two reasons for this: (1) the economic factor, and (2) the sex ratio.

1. The existence of polygyny implies relatively high living standards. It means that one man must be capable of supporting at least two women and their children. Even where the highest living standards prevail, not many men can afford this. Most men in the United States, for example, could not afford two wives even if it were permitted. Thus, as an economic necessity most men in polygynous societies have only one wife. Only the very wealthy are likely to afford more than one.

3. George P. Murdock, *Social Structure*, New York: The Macmillan Company, 1949, p. 28, and "World Ethnographic Sample," *American Anthropologist* 59 (Aug. 1957), p. 686.

2. The second factor which exerts a push in the direction of monogamy is biological. In all societies the sex ratio hovers about one hundred. The sex ratio is the number of men per one hundred women in the society. The denominator of the fraction usually is not stated. If, for example, there are 110 men for every 100 women, the sex ratio is 110. If there are 97 men for every 100 women the sex ratio is 97, and so on.

There are *primary*, *secondary*, and *tertiary* sex ratios. The primary sex ratio is the ratio at conception and is variously estimated to range from 120 to 150. Mortality rates are higher among male fetuses than among female fetuses and, by birth, the ratio is down to 105 or 106. The sex ratio at birth is the secondary sex ratio. Males continue to have higher mortality rates during childhood and by adulthood, the sex ratio in most societies (the tertiary sex ratio) is around 100.

As indicated in Chapter 1, all societies afford marriage and regular sexual intercourse to most adults. Since there are approximately equal numbers of men and women, monogamy for most people is the only circumstance possible. For every man who has three wives, there may be two men who will have none. The number of males might be held in check through male infanticide, but children, and particularly male infants, tend to be highly valued. The result is that polygyny is found in many places over the world but it is not common even where preferred. Polygyny is more widely valued but monogamy is more widely practised.

Polyandry. For most people in our society, polyandry is difficult to imagine. As a matter of fact, polyandry is difficult to imagine outside of our society too, and is very rare. Murdock found only 4 societies out of 565 to practise it—less than 1 percent.[4]

Polyandry also is divided into two types: fraternal, where the husbands are brothers; and nonfraternal, where the husbands may be unrelated. When nonfraternal polyandry is practised, the husbands are likely to have separate dwellings. The Todas, in Southern India, practise fraternal polyandry,[5] and the Marquesan Islanders practise nonfraternal polyandry.[6]

A special variant of taking brothers as husbands is the custom of *levirate*. The levirate is a cultural norm specifying that the preferred mate

4. Murdock, "World Ethnographic Sample," *loc. cit.* See also John F. Peters and Chester L. Hunt, "Polyandry Among the Yanomama Shirishana," *Journal of Comparative Family Studies* 6 (Autumn 1975), pp. 197–207.

5. His Royal Highness, Prince Peter of Greece and Denmark, "The Tibetan Family System," in Meyer F. Nimkoff, *ed., Comparative Family Systems*, Boston: Houghton Mifflin, 1965, pp. 192–208.

6. Murdock, "Sample," pp. 675–86.

for a widow is the brother of her deceased husband, as among the ancient Hebrews. In a polygynous society where the brother is married, the widow often becomes a secondary spouse to him. The caution should be added that the terms *levirate* and *sororate* are appropriate only when there is a societal preference and resulting social pressure for the arrangement to be followed. The terms do not apply to societies like our own, where such marriages occur occasionally but are not the general practice.

Polyandry creates one problem that polygyny does not: that of determining paternity. Obviously the biological father generally remains unknown. The customs of the Todas are instructive in this respect. First of all, there is no great emotional investment on the part of the husbands in establishing paternity. For legal and ceremonial purposes, paternity is established through a ceremony in which one of the husbands presents a toy bow and arrow to the pregnant wife. That husband becomes the father of the child. During subsequent pregnancies, the rite may be repeated by other husbands if they wish to become fathers. Thus, the social status of father has no necessary connection with the biological fact of having sired a child.

There are so few cases of polyandry that only tentative explanations for it have been developed. It appears that polyandry is associated with extreme societal poverty; that it is found in societies existing very close to the minimum subsistence level. We can't say that poverty causes polyandry, because there are many poverty-ridden societies which are not polyandrous. A true cause-and-effect relationship exists only where the alleged cause invariably is followed by the supposed effect.

As an adjustment to poverty, polyandry has certain advantages. If the level of living were so low that a man could not produce sufficient food for a wife and children, he might be able to have a wife and children by sharing their support with other men. Polyandry also keeps the birth rate low and, thus, keeps the population in check. The reproductive potential for any society is set by the number of females who have the opportunity for sexual outlet. Since each woman can produce only one child every nine months, it does not matter how many husbands are involved. The polyandrous society thus can provide sexual outlet for a large number of males and still keep the birth rate low. There is some evidence of a tendency in polyandrous societies to keep the sex ratio in proper balance through ritual female infanticide. His Royal Highness Prince Peter of Greece and Denmark, a foremost student of the Tibetan family system, believes that fraternal polyandry among the Tibetans is a device for keeping the family property intact. Polyandry permits all the brothers to continue living on the land and permits them to transfer it intact to the next generation. Such an explanation, of course, is consistent with the idea of an association between poverty and polyandry.

Group Marriage. Continuing debate over whether or not group marriage exists illustrate a startling fact about our own society and its kinship system. We are accustomed to thinking of our society as complex and of other societies as being much less so. In fact, we often use value-laden adjectives such as "simple" and "primitive" to describe preliterate societies. In some respects, our society *is* complex. Its technology and probably its economic and political institutions are intricate and involved. But when we come to family and kinship, the institutions of many so-called simple societies are more complex than our own. It appears, literally, that persons reared in our relatively simple system, and handicapped by a language associated with such simplicity of kinship, are unable to conceptualize adequately the marital, family, and kinship customs of many other societies.

Western anthropologists use the term *group marriage* to refer to a situation in which a group of men and a group of women are married in common to one another. And they cannot agree on whether or not such practices exist. Murdock says that group marriage "appears never to exist as a cultural norm."[7] He acknowledges, however, that among the Kaingang of Brazil,[8] 8 percent of all recorded marriages over a period of 100 years were group marriages. Linton describes the Marquesan Islanders as practising group marriage.[9] The Dieri of Australia and the Chukchee of Siberia also have been reported to practise group marriage.

In fact, it appears that the categories of polygyny, polyandry, and group marriage are inadequate to describe the marriage forms in some preliterate societies. Both polygyny and polyandry and combinations of them exist in some societies. In addition, there may be the sharing of sexual privileges without the common residence and economic cooperation which we regard as essential to true marriage. Whether or not group marriage exists seems almost a question of semantics. It may be that the answer is less significant than the fact that we are ill equipped to understand fully the complex kinship institutions of many societies.

Polygamy and the Economy. Monogamy, polygyny, and polyandry

7. *Social Structure,* p. 24.
8. Jules Henry, *Jungle People,* New York: Vintage Books, 1964, p. 45. Henry uses the term "joint marriage" instead of the term "group marriage."
9. Ralph Linton, *The Study of Man,* New York: D. Appleton-Century, 1936, pp. 181–82.

are widely scattered over the world. Moreover, what associations have been discovered between them and other aspects of social structure are far from perfect. There are certain very rough relationships between the type of marriage and the economic situation in the society. The following tentative generalizations may be hazarded. First, when small family units are as efficient as large ones, monogamy may be favored. Second, where women have relatively little economic contribution to make, polyandry may be preferred. Finally, where large family units are advantageous and one man can support several women, polygyny may be favored.[10] In pastoral societies, keeping herds and flocks, one man and his sons may be able to shepherd enough animals to keep several women busy processing meat, hides, and milk, and operating the household.

Extended Families

The second mode of combining nuclear families into larger units is through the parent-child relationship. Such combination produces residential units of three or more generations—at least grandparents, parents, and children. Extended families may be compounded of either monogamous or polygamous families. Families need not be either polygamous or extended; they can be both. A simple diagram of a three-generation extended family is given in Figure 2.2. For simplicity, a monogamous family is shown. Note that there are three separate nuclear families—the families of procreation of ego's father, of ego, and of ego's brother. These are dependent nuclear families in contrast with the independent

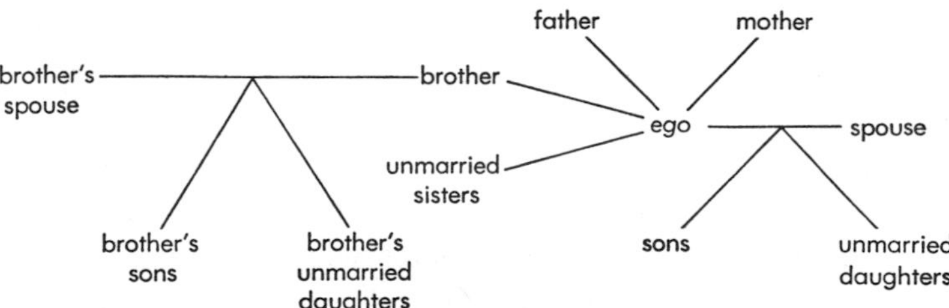

Figure 2.2. Diagram of three-generation extended, patrilocal, monogamous family

10. For an analysis of how demographic conditions limit opportunities to maintain extended family households, see Karen K. Petersen, "Demographic Conditions and Extended Family Households: Egyptian Data," *Social Forces* 46 (June 1968), pp. 531–37.

polygynous family diagrammed in Figure 2.1. Nuclear families or polygamous two-generation families are called independent. The nuclear families included in an extended family unit are referred to as dependent families.

Consanguine and Conjugal Family Types. In structuring kinship, priority tends to be assigned either to marital ties or to blood ties. When priority is given to marital ties, the system is called *conjugal.* Our own family system is a conjugal one. Independent nuclear or polygamous family systems ordinarily are conjugal systems.

In contrast, extended family systems emphasize blood ties–those between parents and children or between brothers and sisters–over marital ties. These are *consanguine* systems. In a conjugal system, a man may leave his parents and "cleave unto his wife." In a consanguine system, the wife (or husband) is an outsider whose wishes and needs must be subordinated to the continuity and welfare of the extended kin group.

Conjugal families, including only two generations, are transitory in character. They disintegrate with the death of the parents. The family of orientation of the offspring ceases to exist and the family of procreation comes into being. The family of procreation creates a new family of orientation for its offspring and in turn will disappear with the death of the new parents. Thus, conjugal families are short lived. With their short duration and the drastic break from one generation to the next, they are not good vehicles for the maintenance of family traditions or for keeping family property intact over the generations. On the other hand, since conjugal families involve relatively few people, there may be little need for roles to be prescribed in great detail. There may be more improvisation permitted on the role of husband, daughter, and so on. We pride ourselves, in the United States, on the opportunities for personal development and personal fredom that our system provides. At the same time, many of us know little about our great grandparents, and few of us hold substantial family property.

In contrast, consanguine families are immortal. The continued existence of the family does not depend upon any one person or any couple. At marriage, one of the spouses remains with the family of orientation and is joined by husband or wife. The couple raise their children in a large family setting, and, even if the mother or father should die prematurely, there are other kin present to absorb the several facets of the parental role. Eventually when the grandparents retire or die, control and property pass without great fanfare to the next generation.

The advantages and limitations of the consanguine family are the reverse of those of the conjugal family. Whereas the conjugal family tends to produce the splitting of family property at each generation, the consanguine family permits it to be transmitted intact. Since consanguine families ideally involve a sizable number of persons spread over at least three generations, the role behaviors for each family member at each stage in life are laid down in considerable detail. One is under pressure to enact the roles of son, elder brother, husband, father, and eventually grandfather, as they have been traditionally enacted. Whether one is well suited temperamentally to playing these roles has little to do with it. Instead of the personal freedom emphasized in a conjugal family system, emphasis is placed upon the faithful performance of prescribed roles.

A widely discussed variant of the extended family deserves brief mention here. This is the so-called *joint family* of India.[11] The joint family is the traditional Indian family in which adult brothers live together with their respective families of procreation. In addition to maintaining a common residence, they hold property in common and assume joint responsibility for the education of younger siblings.

This Indian joint family actually is characteristic of just one stage in the life-cycle, with persons typically passing through several stages during their lifetime. The process begins when the sons remain in the parental home following their marriage. While the father is alive, the Indian family does not differ significantly from other extended families. Following the father's death, the true joint family comes into existence when the brothers keep the extended household intact. This joint family is preserved until all of the younger siblings are educated and married, at which time the brothers split off their families of procreation and divide the family property between them. Thus, for a time, nuclear units exist separately. Soon, however, the sons of the brothers are ready for marriage and the process begins again.

11. M. S. Gore, "The Traditional Indian Family," in Meyer F. Nimkoff, *ed., Comparative Family Systems,* Boston: Houghton Mifflin, 1965, pp. 209–31. See also George H. Conklin, "Emerging Conjugal Role Patterns in a Joint Family System: Correlates of Social Change in Dharwar, India," *Journal of Marriage and the Family* 35 (Nov. 1973), pp. 742–48; Ann Baker Cottrell, "Outsiders' Inside View: Western Wives' Experiences in Indian Joint Families," *Journal of Marriage and the Family* 37 (May 1975), pp. 400–407; A. A. Khatri, "The Adaptive Extended Family in India Today," *Journal of Marriage and the Family* 37 (Aug. 1975), pp. 633–42; and G. N. Ramu, "Urban Kinship Ties in South India: A Case Study," *Journal of Marriage and the Family* 36 (Aug. 1974), pp. 619–27.

Composite Families and the Economy

In Murdock's analysis of 250 societies, he found that approximately one-fourth had the nuclear family only, another one-fourth had polygamous but not extended families, and about one-half had extended family systems, which could be either monogamous or polygamous. Nimkoff and Middleton subsequently analyzed data from 549 of the cultures included in the World Ethnographic Sample.[12] They correlated the type of family system with certain economic factors, particularly the subsistence pattern and the amount of family property. Still more recently, Osmond,[13] and Blumberg and Winch[14] analyzed data from the *Ethnographic Atlas* and related familial complexity to societal complexity.

The results of these studies lead to the following tentative generalizations. First, the independent nuclear family is found at both ends of the economic scale. It predominates in societies with primitive hunting and gathering economies where the food supply is uncertain, and also in modern industrial societies. Second, the extended family predominates in agricultural economies and reaches its fullest development in farming economies that combine agriculture with animal husbandry. Finally, independent nuclear families and extended families occur with about equal frequency in societies which depend on hunting and fishing, in societies that depend primarily upon animal husbandry, or where animal husbandry exists along with fishing. Thus, the independent nuclear family is found both at the top and at the bottom of the scale, with extended family systems being more prevalent in the middle.

FAMILY STRUCTURE AND THE REGULATION OF SEX

All societies regulate sexual behavior. They all provide regular sexual outlet for most adults, but nowhere is the selection of partners simply a

12. Meyer F. Nimkoff and Russell Middleton, "Types of Family and Types of Economy," *American Journal of Sociology* 66 (Nov. 1960), pp. 215–25. See also Hsien-Jen Chu and J. Selwyn Hollingsworth, "A Cross-Cultural Study of the Relationship Between Family Types and Social Stratification," *Journal of Marriage and the Family* 31 (May 1969), pp. 322–27.

13. Marie W. Osmond, "A Cross-Cultural Analysis of Family Organization," *Journal of Marriage and the Family* 31 (May 1969), pp. 302–10.

14. Rae L. Blumberg and Robert F. Winch, "Societal Complexity and Familial Complexity: Evidence for the Curvilinear Hypothesis," *American Journal of Sociology* 77 (March 1972), pp. 898–920.

personal choice. Instead there are obligations, alternatives, possibilities, discouragements, and prohibitions. Moreover, these prescriptions and proscriptions are intricately bound up with family and kinship.

As with the more complicated combinations of plural marriage, intercultural variation in the regulation of sexual behavior is difficult for many Americans to put in proper perspective. Our own society is one of a very few that traditionally have completely prohibited sexual intercourse outside of marriage. Murdock estimates the proportion of such societies in the world to be less than 5 percent.[15] People who have grown up in such a society are prone to make moralistic judgments about patterns that provide for a range of sex partners both before and after marriage. It is well to keep in mind that patterns different from our own can be understood only in the larger social context in which they are found.

In the United States and much of the rest of the Western world sex itself has been the focus of regulation. Sex is still frequently seen as a necessary evil. It is not so in most other societies. Most commonly, sexual regulation is part of the broader regulation of marriage, reproduction, kinship, and social status. What we encounter in most of the world is a series of permissions and restrictions in relation to these other phenomena.

Premarital Sex Relationships

The marriage relationship is one of the major foci of sexual regulation. Most societies see nothing inconsistent between the regulation of sex in marriage and considerable sex freedom before marriage; consequently complete premarital chastity is a minority pattern over the world. In some societies there is almost complete freedom of premarital sexual relationships, with boys and girls allowed to take and to change partners at will. Surprisingly, the incidence of pregnancies appears to be quite low. Some writers attribute this to the relative youthfulness and undeveloped fecundity of the persons involved. In some cases birth control techniques may be employed, but it is difficult to gather data on this. Generally when pregnancy does occur it is not the tragedy that a premarital pregnancy in our society might be. It may even be that the girl's marriageability will be enhanced by her own proven ability to have children.

Murdock found premarital sex relationships to be fully approved in 65 societies, to be conditionally approved in 43, to be mildly disapproved in

15. *Social Structure*, p. 264.

6, and to be forbidden in 44.[16] In some societies where complete premarital freedom is not sanctioned, intercourse with selected persons—such as cross cousins,[17] who are potential marriage partners—is permitted. In sum, about 70 percent of the societies for whom data are available permit premarital intercourse. In most of the others, the taboo falls particularly upon females and seems to be based upon the necessity to prevent pregnancies. In most societies it is less of a moral issue than with us.

Social Status and Sex Relationships

The rules of *endogamy* and *exogamy* are two conspicuous examples of the relation between sexual regulation and social status. Technically, endogamy and exogamy define potential marriage partners and, indirectly, sexual partners. Endogamy requires a person to select a marriage partner from within the tribe, community, social class, nationality, race, or other grouping. Such requirements exist in virtually all societies and often have strong sanctions attached to them. Conversely, exogamy requires a person to select a marriage partner from outside certain groups. Exogamous requirements appear to result from extensions of the incest taboos which prohibit sex relationships with close kin.

Exceptions to existing sexual regulations sometimes are made for high-status persons. The custom of *jus primae noctis* in medieval times and in some preliterate societies has received considerable public attention. Under *jus primae noctis*, the feudal lord, a priest, chief, or other high-status male selected for the purpose is entitled and obligated to have the first sexual intercourse with each bride. This custom has been interpreted to reinforce the head-man's proprietary interest in the persons and property of his subjects and as a means of offering proof to the society that a bride is virginal.[18] Exceptions to prevailing incest taboos are also known to have existed for members of royal families in some societies.

16. *Ibid.*, p. 265.

17. Cross cousins are the children of a father's sister or of a mother's brother. In many societies, cross cousins are preferred marriage partners. Parallel cousins are the children of a father's brother or of a mother's sister.

18. This is another practice regularly misinterpreted by many Westerners. Many of us think of *jus primae noctis* as a highly erotic situation and as an uncomplicated privilege of rank. It is sobering to realize that privilege tends to shade off into duty and that the lord or chief may not be free to take only the brides attractive to him.

Kinship and Sexual Regulation

Sexual freedom before marriage does not necessarily mean sexual freedom in marriage, for most societies regulate closely the sexual behavior of married people. Most societies forbid intercourse between a married man and an unrelated woman. At the same time, however, few societies are as restrictive as ourselves in allowing intercourse only between spouses.

Most societies recognize some "privileged relationships" both before marriage and for married persons that give the person legitimate sexual outlet with certain classes of kin. Before marriage, the most common privileged relationship is with cross cousins where they are preferred marriage partners. In Murdock's 250 societies, 11 allow intercourse with a father's sister's daughter and 14 with a mother's brother's daughter.[19]

Within marriage a comparable situation exists, particularly where the levirate and sororate are found. The privileged relationships are with the siblings-in-law who are potential spouses. Nearly two-thirds of the sample societies permit intercourse with brothers-in-law or sisters-in-law.

In many societies there is an assumption that men, particularly, suffer if denied sex for very long. The assumption for women is less explicit, the argument sometimes being that women do not experience sexual frustrations comparable to those of men. In some societies, also, there are taboos upon intercourse during menstruation, pregnancy, and during a lactation period that may last for three or four years. Granting sexual access to other female relatives often is rationalized as a means of relieving the sexual frustration that would be experienced during these periods.

This logic has been institutionalized in a few societies in the custom of *sexual hospitality*. The custom is found in societies in which men travel and are away from their wives during their travel. When they stop with a family for the night, it is obligatory upon the host to provide a sleeping partner, just as he provides food and shelter. It is generally equally obligatory upon the guest to accept the sexual partner, just as he accepts food. Students' interpretations of sexual hospitality should be made in full awareness that the partner proffered may not be a luscious young girl but may be one's obese aunt or even a toothless grandmother.[20]

19. Murdock, *Social Structure*, p. 268.

20. Appreciation of the customs of one composite people practising sexual hospitality may be gained from the pair of novels by Hans Ruesch, *Top of the World* (Pocket Books, 1959), and *Back to the Top of the World*, New York: Charles Scribner's Sons, 1973. These fascinating novels are anthropologically sound.

The regulation of sexual behavior in and out of marriage is part of the regulation of family behavior. Sexual regulation cannot be understood apart from the larger normative system of which it is a part. Moreover, understanding of the larger system requires understanding of its constituent parts. One set of sexual regulations having great significance for family structure has yet to be discussed.

THE STRUCTURAL IMPLICATIONS OF INCEST TABOOS

An important factor in the analysis of family structure is the understanding of the nature and effects of incest taboos. The term *incest* refers to the prohibition of sexual intercourse with close blood relatives. Such taboos exist in all known societies.

Sexual intercourse between members of the nuclear family always is taboo except between husband and wife. No society regularly permits intercourse between father and daughter, mother and son, or brother and sister. Virtually all societies also proscribe sex relationships with adoptive parents, adoptive children, stepchildren, godparents and godchildren—persons who occasionally stand in lieu of regular members of the nuclear family. Not only are such relationships prohibited, but most people react to incestuous relationships with aversion and disgust.

As with most rules, there are a few exceptions. It is known, for example, that intermarriage of brothers and sisters has been permitted or required in certain royal families. Among the ancient Egyptians of the Ptolemaic period, among the Inca Indians, and within the old Hawaiian aristocracy, brother-sister marriage occurred within royal families. The practice generally is interpreted as a device for keeping property and power within the family. Murdock also reports that the Dobus, a Melanesian people, regard intercourse with one's mother after the father's death as a private sin but not as a public offense.[21] The Balinese permit twins to marry on the assumption that they have already been too intimate in the womb. And an African people, the Thonga, are reputed to permit father-daughter incest in extraordinary preparation for a great hunt. These exceptions, of course, do not apply to whole societies and their very nature emphasizes the universality of incest taboos.

There are two instances reported of societies where incestuous relationships within the nuclear family may have been more widespread.

21. *Social Structure,* p. 13.

Slotkin claims that father-daughter, mother-son, and brother-sister incest all were generally permitted in ancient Persia.[22] Middleton also believes that brother-sister marriage in Roman Egypt occurred among commoners as well as within the royal family.[23] He interprets these marriages as a device for keeping property within the family. Unfortunately, it is not possible to gather additional data concerning these possible exceptions. Comparable situations apparently do not exist in any contemporary society. Suffice it to say that even should these two interpretations prove valid, the prohibition of sexual intercourse within the nuclear family is the most nearly universal social custom.

Discontinuity in the Nuclear Family

A primary effect of incest taboos is to make the nuclear family discontinuous. Sons and daughters are forced to go outside the nuclear family to find mates, resulting in a break between the family of orientation and the family of procreation. Were this not true, the nuclear family would be immortal. Brothers would marry their sisters and property, traditions, and folkways would be transmitted undisturbed from generation to generation. Kinship structure would be simple. Except for distinctions by age and sex, no other differentiation would be necessary.

The selection of mates from outside the nuclear family produces a continuous overlapping of nuclear families. The nuclear family experience of any two persons, over their lifetimes, is different. Each person becomes related biologically to an ever-expanding number of people. This is illustrated in Figure 2.3.

The terms "primary," "secondary," and "tertiary" relatives describe the degree of relationship between a person and the ever-expanding circle of relatives.[24] Primary relatives are the members of ego's nuclear families—mother, father, brothers, sisters, spouse, sons, and daughters—seven categories in all. Secondary relatives are composed of the primary relatives of ego's primary relatives—33 categories in all. Tertiary relatives are the primary relatives of ego's secondary relatives—151 different categories. Note that these are categories of relatives and that most categories may include several people. Some perspective on these degrees of rela-

22. J. S. Slotkin, "On a Possible Lack of Incest Regulations in Old Iran," *American Anthropologist* 49 (Oct.-Dec. 1947), pp. 612–15.

23. Russell Middleton, "Brother-Sister and Father-Daughter Marriage in Ancient Egypt," *American Sociological Review* 27 (Oct. 1962), pp. 603–11.

24. A. R. Radcliffe-Brown, "The Study of Kinship Systems," *Journal of the Royal Anthropological Institute* 71 (1941), p. 2.

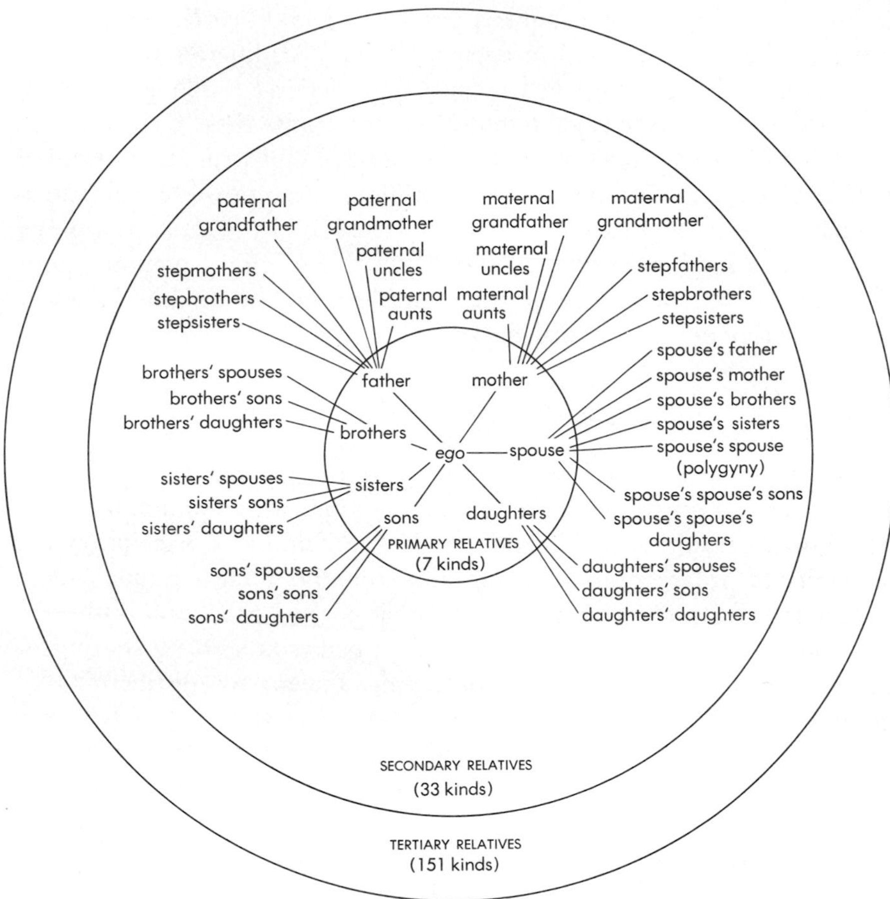

Figure 2.3. Diagram of maximum number of kinds of primary, secondary, and tertiary relatives, polygamous marriage

tionship may be gained by realizing that first cousins, generally recognized relatives in our own society, are tertiary relatives.

Where we stop tracing relationship, biologically, is purely arbitrary. It is obvious that even by the time we trace relationships out three degrees we have included so many categories, to say nothing of the larger number of people, that we cannot possibly have close social relationships with all of them. How many of us can name even one person who belongs to each of the 151 different categories of tertiary relatives?

Because of the ever-expanding number of biological kin, all societies select certain categories of kin for recognition and ignore others. All societies have *social* definitions establishing priorities with certain biological kin. Family relationships are social relationships that include norms governing the sharing of affection, economic cooperation, and the provision of mutual aid in time of need. There isn't enough affection to scatter indiscriminately over several hundred people, and to be entitled to aid from several hundred people is tantamount to receiving aid from no one. The satisfactory performance of family duties requires a group of kin of manageable size with whom orderly relationships may be maintained. To reduce the number of biologically related kin to a manageable social group, all societies have *rules of descent.*

Rules of Descent

Rules of descent are social definitions that determine for individuals who, among the myriad of biological kin, they consider themselves related to. Rules of descent define the family as a social group in contrast to the family as a biological group.

There are four general rules of descent. We shall take them in order of the frequency of their appearance.

Patrilineal descent is the most common form. Under patrilineal descent, the person is assigned at birth to a group of kin who are related through males only. To put it technically, descent is traced through the male lineage. The most important ties are those from father to son to grandson. A wife typically marries into her husband's family and their children become members of the husband's family but not of the family into which the wife was born.

Such unilineal systems of descent obviously are not in accord with the facts of biological relationship. Relationship to biological kin on the father's side is affirmed while relationship to the mother's biological kin is ignored. Some early anthropologists believed that patrilineal descent meant that the people were ignorant of the ties to the maternal kin. This is not true, however. Neither is patrilineal descent confined to preliterate peoples. Patrilineal descent has a long history in Eastern and Western civilizations. Unilineal systems of descent do not mean that people deny their biological relationship to the opposite lineage. They do mean that systems of descent are means of defining social relationships and that family structure, while rooted in the facts of biological relationship, is not limited by them. Family structure is social structure.

The second most common system of descent is called *bilateral.* It involves tracing relationships through two sides of the family—through the mother's biological kin and the father's biological kin equally. The size of the kin group is regulated by limiting it to close relatives on each side. Such a system of tracing social relationships is in accord with the facts of biological relationship. Because it is the system of descent used in our own society, it makes sense to most Americans.

Matrilineal descent is the obverse of patrilineal descent. It traces relationship through females and the female line, discarding the father's relatives. Matrilineal descent is less common. As we shall see, descent, residence, inheritance—indeed virtually all family phenomena—are more frequently determined through males than through females.

The fourth system, *double descent*, is useful simply to provide insight into how complicated kinship systems can and do get. It is not common. Where double descent exists, each person at birth is assigned to two kin groups, one traced through paternal relatives and one through maternal relatives. He or she becomes a member of the father's patrilineal group and a member of the mother's matrilineal kin group. There are, in the world, even more complex systems in which relationships are traced differently for sons and daughters and which zigzag between the sexes, from generation to generation.[25]

The rules of descent select from the ever-expanding group of biological kin those with whom social relationships are to be maintained. Associated with rules of descent are rules of inheritance.

Rules of Inheritance

Inheritance patterns are more complex than systems of descent and have been studied less thoroughly. They are complicated by the facts that some possessions such as clothing, ornaments, and tools are used only by members of one sex while other possessions, such as money, are transmitted to either sex. Through most of human history and over much of the world, inheritance rights have centered on land, dwellings, animals, and generally, the means of production. If such property passes to the heir or heirs through males, the rule is said to be *patrilineal;* if the route is through females (from a man to his sister's son) then it is *matrilineal.*

Inheritance patterns are further complicated because men and women may or may not inherit equally, and even within the same sex siblings may or may not inherit equally. More often than not, the inheritance of

25. Students who wish to read more on this system of descent are referred to Margaret Mead, *Sex and Temperament in Three Primitive Societies*, New York: Mentor Books, 1950, pp. 119–63.

major property is through males to other males. The inheritance rights of women often are circumscribed and sometimes nonexistent.

The inheritance rights of males may vary with birth order. If all sons do not inherit equally, the most likely situation is for the eldest son to inherit all or a disproportionate part of the property. This arrangement is known as *primogeniture*. Less commonly found is *ultimogeniture*, where the youngest son is favored.

Rules of Residence

The nuclear family is virtually everywhere a residential unit. At marriage the husband and wife take up residence together. Since they come from different families of orientation, one or the other or both must move at marriage. The alternatives available, in relation to their respective families, are few: they can locate with the husband's family of orientation, with the wife's family, away from both families, or in some combination of these. All societies have developed norms to determine which alternative shall be followed. These norms are called rules of residence.

The most common rule is *patrilocal*. Under patrilocal residence the bride leaves her family of orientation and sets up housekeeping with her husband in the same dwelling with, or adjacent to, his family of orientation. Note that patrilocal residence does not refer to the wife's going to live with the husband but to her going to live with the husband's family. Patrilocal residence is common over the world. A special variant of patrilocal residence is *matri-patrilocal*, where residence is with the bride's family of orientation for a prescribed period after which the couple take up permanent residence with the groom's family. The couple may live with the bride's family for one year or until the first child is born.

Matrilocal residence involves the husband leaving his family of orientation to take up residence with his bride in the locale of her family of orientation. Closely related to matrilineal descent and inheritance is another rule of residence known as *avunculocal*. Under avunculocal residence, the couple take up residence with the maternal uncle of the groom. Thus, the residence rule is built around males of the female line. Few societies have avunculocal residence.

Under bilocal residence, the couple is permitted to choose whether they will locate with the husband's or the wife's kin. The strength of the personal ties between the couple and their parents, the relative wealth of the parents and their power in the community, and the need for assistance from the young couple may be determining factors.

Note that the rules of residence discussed so far, all favor the development of extended families. All create units of at least three generations. They also put one of the spouses into a favored position. The spouse who stays with his or her family is surrounded by kin sympathetic to his or her cause in disputes with the other spouse. The spouse who has to move, in contrast, is relocated among relative strangers and somewhat isolated from the support of kin. Thus the rule of residence may influence the distribution of power between the spouses in marriage.

The final rule of residence is *neolocal.* As the term implies, this rule involves the establishment of a new residence, apart from both families of orientation. This is the only rule which militates against the development of extended family units and encourages isolation of the nuclear family. This is the rule followed in our society.

It is probably apparent that there are certain logical associations among patrilineal descent, patrilineal inheritance, and patrilocal residence, and among matrilineal descent, matrilineal inheritance, and matrilocal residence. Murdock concluded that patrilocal residence is associated with polygyny, warfare, slavery, and an economy which depends upon the chase rather than upon collecting. Matrilocal residence is favored by the development of agriculture in a previously hunting and gathering economy and by the ownership of land by women. Bilocal residence is accompanied by a migratory life in unstable bands and, at a higher economic level, by approximate equality of the sexes in the ownership of property. Finally, neolocal residence is associated with approximately equal economic contributions by men and women, monogamy, extensive poverty, and individualism.

Murdock also assigns priority to rules of residence in determining systems of descent and inheritance. He concludes that rules of residence are likely to be affected first by changes in the economic base and by technological development. As the residential kin group alters, changes gradually come about in the means of tracing relationships.[26]

One final set of associations with rules of residence deserves mention. The phenomenon known as *bride price* exists in approximately two-thirds of the societies for whom data are available. Bride price refers to a payment of money or goods to the bride's family at marriage, to the exchange of one of the husband's female relatives for the bride, or to a

26. See Robert E. Mitchell, "Residential Patterns and Family Networks (I)," *International Journal of Sociology of the Family* 2 (Sept. 1972), pp. 212–24.

period of work-service for the bride. The payment of bride price is associated with rules of residence that remove the bride most drastically from her family of orientation.

Libya's oil boom may be pricing some of its women out of the marriage market. Fathers used to demand a fee of about $3,500 in cash with a camel, sheep and some gold coins thrown in for marrying off their daughters.

But in a society fueled by oil, the groom's family in a "low bracket" transaction now plunks down the equivalent of $12,000 in cash and a new car in addition to the customary camel and a sheep or two. In the upper brackets, gifts of $35,000 in cash are not unusual. . . .

Associated Press, Sept. 7, 1975

Some early students of kinship interpreted bride price as outright purchase of the wife, as one would purchase cattle or other property. Such interpretation appears erroneous and to miss the true functions of bride price. There appear to be essentially two functions. First, the bride price offers recompense to the bride's family for loss of her services. Particularly when the bride's and groom's families live in different communities and patrilocal residence is followed, the bride's family's economic loss may be very real. Second, the bride price is insurance against maltreatment of the bride by the husband or his family. The sum involved usually is substantial and if the bride is unjustly divorced or forced to return to her parental home because of mistreatment, her family generally retains possession of the bride price. True wife-purchase appears to be rare.

Authority Patterns in the Family

Strictly speaking, the distribution of authority between husband and wife does not derive directly from the incest taboos. The relationships between family authority patterns and rules of descent and residence, however, make brief discussion of them relevant here. We may describe three principal types as patriarchal, matriarchal, and equalitarian.

A *patriarchal* system is one in which power and authority are vested in males, with the eldest male usually wielding arbitrary power. Patriarchal systems have been common through history and over the world. The ancient Hebrews, Greeks, and Romans; the Hindus and Mohammedans; and the Chinese and Japanese provide a few examples.

Patrilineal descent, patrilineal inheritance, patrilocal residence, and primogeniture all are associated with male dominance. In addition, polygyny, a double standard of sexual morality, masculine privilege in divorce, the arrangement of children's marriages by adults, and a low status for women are frequent accompaniments of patriarchy. We do not have quantitative data to indicate what proportion of the world's societies are and have been strong patriarchies, but abundant descriptive data exist. Few would question that male dominance is the rule rather than the exception.

Logically, a *matriarchal* family type is very simple; matriarchy should involve the complete vesting of power in females. Except in the comic strips, however, and in D-grade Hollywood movies, true matriarchies are never found. The fabled Amazon women are just that—a fable. Even in societies organized about women, in societies which follow matrilineal descent, inheritance, and residence, power tends to be held by males in the female lineage. Power usually is held by the women's brothers—from the viewpoint of ego, by the maternal uncle. Male dominance, or a tendency toward it, appears to be nearly universal. A minority of societies are organized around the female lineage, but even then, power, status, and property tend to be held by males.

One common feature of human existence which has put women into positions of power is the tendency for women to outlive men. Men are physically stronger, but women live longer. Patriarchal societies often accord high status to older people, and sons usually are trained to respect their mothers. When the father dies first, the son who assumes power may continue to defer to his mother, thus creating by default a degree of female dominance in the society.

The third logical type, the equalitarian family, implies equal distribution of power and authority between husband and wife.[27] This arrangement is in accord with some of the basic facts of human existence. Few fair-minded people would question that, except perhaps for brute

27. Most of the concepts employed in this chapter—patriarchal, matrilineal, neolocal, polygymous, authoritarian, and so on—are *ideal types*. See Max Weber, *The Methodology of the Social Sciences,* translated and edited by Edward A. Shils and Henry A. Finch, Chicago: The Free Press, 1949. Ideal types are concepts created by taking one or more characteristics typical of a phenomenon and accentuating those characteristics to their logical maximum or reducing them to their logical minimum. They are not accurate descriptions of reality, but represent logical exaggerations of reality. There is no such thing, for example, as a patriarchal society, if we mean by that a society in which all power is vested in males. There are only societies in which considerable power is held by males. Ideal types are logically extreme standards against which reality is measured. As long as we are careful to avoid the fallacy of *reification*, of confusing the concept with reality, ideal types are useful analytic devices.

strength, there are many women in any society who are as strong, intelligent, clever, and ambitious as their husbands. Even in the most patriarchal societies, strong wives probably have dominated weak husbands. One of the traditional ways of writing "wife" in Chinese characters was to show a woman's hand holding onto a man's ear. The equalitarian family simply represents institutionalization of this situation. The Western family, and particularly the family in the United States, has been tending for many decades toward an equalitarian form.

Extension of Incest Taboos Outside the Nuclear Family

All societies taboo all cross-sex relationships within the nuclear family, but no society stops there. Some additional kin are always tabooed. Interestingly, however, there is no one class of kin outside the nuclear family from which it is not acceptable to choose a sex partner in some society. First cousins, aunts, nephews, and so on, are taboo in some societies but not in others. At first glance, there does not appear to be much rhyme or reason to these extensions.

Obviously the taboos are not extended strictly in accord with biological relationship. In most societies, intercourse is permitted with some fairly close blood relatives and prohibited with more distant ones. The key to these extensions is the family as a social group rather than the family as a biological group. Those groups who are prohibited tend to be those whom the system of descent defines as closely related. Thus the *extension* of incest taboos tends to be rooted more in sociology than in biology.

A peculiar feature of incest taboos is their strength and the attitudes which surround them. A peculiar horror attaches to their violation; scarcely can a more heinous offense be imagined. The repugnance is greatest at incest within the nuclear family and becomes less strong as one moves outward from the nuclear family along the socially defined lines of kinship.

The Enforcement of Incest Taboos

The basic technique upon which most societies depend for the enforcement of incest taboos is to instill them so thoroughly in the society's members that violations become virtually inconceivable. The learning of the incest taboos is a basic part of socialization. It is commonplace in American society that many small children are relatively free in acting upon their sexual impulses and indiscriminate in their choice of partners.

It is not unusual, for example, for young brothers and sisters to join in sex play. By adulthood, however, the taboos have been so thoroughly learned that aversion, bordering upon physical illness, may be the response to any prospect of sexual intercourse within the nuclear family. Adult brothers and sisters may sleep in adjoining bedrooms and appear before one another in states of partial undress without arousing any sexual response in either person. This internalization of the taboos within personality is far more effective than any external restraints might be and is the primary mechanism upon which most societies depend.

Not all societies, however, depend upon internalization alone. In some societies there are, in addition, patterns of avoidance behavior between persons who are tabooed but between whom intercourse might occur. At puberty, for example, the norms may prescribe that brother and sister shall no longer be alone together. If the sister enters a room and only her brother is present, he may be required to leave. Similarly, the norms may provide that a man may not look directly upon his mother-in-law. Whenever they are together, he may be required to keep his face turned away. Murdock found the relationship between a man and his mother-in-law and between a father and his son's wife to be classic avoidance relationships.

Avoidance relationships appear not to be depended upon by any society to the exclusion of internalization of incest taboos, but rather as supplements thereto where the internalization process is not wholly effective. A man's relationships with his mother-in-law or his son's wife, for example, are not likely to be so strongly tabooed as those with his sister or daughter. Avoidance relationships also are quite effective, up to a point. People who cannot be alone together or who cannot look at one another ordinarily are not in great danger of sexual involvement. The superiority of internalization of the taboos as a means of control is that it continues to be effective even when the situational restraints are removed.

Indoctrination of people with social norms is never perfect, and violations of the incest taboos occur in all societies. The few violations appear to be exceptions which validate the rule. Kinsey reports that violations in our society are so rare that it would be misleading to mention specific figures.[28] Weinberg studied 203 cases of incest known to the authorities in Illinois,[29] and reports that the detected incidence of incest

28. Alfred C. Kinsey, Wardell B. Pomeroy, and Clyde E. Martin, *Sexual Behavior in the Human Male,* Philadelphia: W. B. Saunders, 1948, p. 558.
29. S. Kirson Weinberg, *Incest Behavior,* New York: Citadel Press, 1955, p. 39.

in the United States in 1920 was 1.9 offenders per 1 million population, and in 1930 was 1.1.

These detected figures probably underestimate the actual incest rates. True rates are probably considerably higher; certainly the experience of social workers and clinicians would indicate so. It is significant, however, that great effort is made to suppress knowledge of specific cases of incest. The maintenance of the taboo is too crucial to the larger society to permit open discussion of violations which do occur.

Explanation of Incest Taboos

People have long sought an adequate explanation of the universality of incest taboos. Dozens of explanations have been proposed, most of them so bizarre that no discussion of them need be given. Of the many proposed explanations, only a few have more than superficial plausibility. Upon detailed examination most of those also prove inadequate. We will examine four of the commonly accepted explanations before arriving at the one which appears most plausible.[30]

Alleged Harmful Effects of Inbreeding. One explanation attributes the taboo between blood relatives to the adverse effects of inbreeding upon the quality of the population. It is claimed that inbreeding leads to deterioration of the stock (perpetuation of hemophilia within inbred European families is used as an illustration) and recognition of this fact has led people everywhere to prohibit such relationships.

This explanation has appeal, for inbreeding does tend to bring genetic deficiencies into expression. Most human genetic deficiencies are carried as recessive genes and do not produce harmful effects when the carrier is mated with a person who does not carry the same recessive gene. The odds are much greater that a closely related person also carries the harmful recessive gene and that if these closely related persons are mated, the defect will appear in their offspring.

There are several problems with this logic, however. For one thing, this logic might be reversed to promote biological improvement of the species. Inbreeding is precisely what is used in animal husbandry to produce steers which yield more and higher quality beef, chickens which contain more white meat, faster race horses, and so on. If people were completely rational, they might promote inbreeding within certain lines along with prohibiting it in others. It can be argued that until recently, if even now, we did not have sufficient knowledge of human genetics to

30. The following section follows closely Murdock, *Social Structure*, pp. 289–301.

make such selective regulation possible. Granting this argument, it appears unlikely that vastly improved knowledge of genetics would have much influence upon incest taboos.

A more serious difficulty with this explanation is that it assumes a rationality which in some cases is literally impossible. Until recently, at least, some preliterate peoples lacked adequate knowledge of the reproductive process, occasionally being unaware of the role of the father in procreation. The Arunta and the Trobriand Islanders are illustrations. Incest taboos are no less complex and are just as strong in these societies who could not possibly connect genetic problems to inbreeding.

Still another problem is that incest taboos in most societies do not coincide with the closeness of biological relationship. Distant biological relatives may be prohibited while procreation with closer relatives is permitted. Thus, we must conclude that while the prohibition of inbreeding has some salutary effects in some instances, the total weight of evidence is against this explanation for most of the incest taboos.

Alleged Instinct Against Inbreeding. The internalization of norms against inbreeding among most people is so effective that revulsion against incestuous relations seems almost to be a part of the biological structure of the organism. This fact led some writers to posit the existence of an instinct against incest.

Early in the twentieth century, the concept of instinct was seized upon to explain a tremendous variety of human behaviors ranging from simple autonomic reflexes to complex and variable patterns of behavior such as parenthood and war. Gradually, however, the absurdity of postulating hundreds of human instincts became apparent.[31] It was concluded that the term *instinct* has utility only to refer to complex patterns of behavior which are biologically fixed for the species and which cannot be explained as a product of learning.

The concept of instinct cannot explain incest taboos. In the first place, violations of the taboos occur. If there were an instinct operating, violations could not take place unless some people were born without the instinct, an implausible assumption. Second, incest taboos are highly variable. It makes no sense biologically to claim that instincts prohibit intercourse with first cousins in one group and not in another. Third, if there were an instinct against incest, there would be no need for the widespread horror of incest. A biological mechanism operates automatically without need for buttressing emotional reactions. The instinct explanation has been generally discarded by biological and by social scientists.

31. Luther L. Bernard, *Instinct: A Study in Social Psychology*, New York: Holt, 1924.

Familiarity Breeds Disinterest. Edward Westermarck explained incest taboos by the fact that continued close association between persons of opposite sex lessens their sexual attraction for one another.[32] That some lessening of interest does occur with continued close association seems to be a fact. Virtually all husbands and wives recognize it even in a context where sexual participation is expected. Recently in the kibbutzim of Israel it has been found that among children reared together where there are few taboos upon nudity and where sexual interest might be expected to develop, it does not. In ancient Egypt where royal brother and sister were expected to marry, it was usual to separate them in childhood and to keep them apart until adulthood so that they would be sexually attracted to one another.

The problem is not with the facts themselves as with the facts as an explanation of incest taboos. The effects of growing up together cannot explain the frequent extension of incest taboos to kin who are not members of the household and with whom one might not have continuing close association. In the reverse situation, preferential mate selection (the levirate, sororate, and cross-cousin marriage) often calls for marriage with persons with whom one has been associated long and intimately.

There is also reason for questioning the facts. We know that there are many exceptions to the rule and that some persons are attracted sexually to other members of their own nuclear families. The logic of lessened sexual attraction would not explain why sex relationships should be prohibited in those cases where attraction does exist.

Frustrations in the Oedipal Involvement. Another explanation has come out of psychoanalytic theory. Freud developed the notion of universal sexual attraction of a boy to his mother from Sophocles' *Oedipus Rex,* in which the son, Oedipus, unknowingly slays his father and marries his mother. When he learns what he has done, he is overwhelmed with guilt and blinds himself. In psychoanalytic theory, this became the universal situation where the child's sexual attraction to the parent of opposite sex must be repressed because of the harm that would be done to the child should the parent of the same sex become aware of the incestuous desires. The repression is only partly successful, and the horror which is attached to violations of the incest taboos is interpreted as reaction formation against the partly repressed impulses.

This psychoanalytic interpretation makes sense in the context of Western family organization but not in societies with radically different family organization. Malinowski attempted to test the notion of a

32. Edward Westermarck, *The History of Human Marriage,* New York: Allerton Book Company, 1922, Vol. 2, p. 192.

universal Oedipal complex through study of the Trobriand Islanders, a matrilineal society in which the role of paternity was not understood and in which the maternal uncle performed most of the functions associated with the father role in Western society. He found that the child's hostility was directed toward the uncle rather than toward the father and that the basis for hostility was not sexual jealousy but resentment against authority. Thus, the Oedipus complex is not a universal phenomenon but is a product of middle-class family structure in Western society.[33]

The Oedipus hypothesis is inadequate in other respects. It does not account for the universal extension of taboos beyond the nuclear family. Nor does it account for variability in the definitions of which relatives are taboo. Psychoanalysis usefully focused attention upon the dangers of sexual conflict within the nuclear family but by itself it did not provide an adequate explanation of incest taboos.

An Eclectic Explanation. The term *eclecticism* refers to the combination of elements of existing theories into a new, more comprehensive theory. Murdock has proposed an eclectic theory of incest taboos which provides the most satisfactory explanation of them to date. In so doing, he draws upon contributions from sociology, cultural anthropology, psychoanalysis, and behavioristic psychology.[34]

The explanation begins by assuming, with the psychoanalysts, that immature sexual responses, or at least responses which adults interpret as sexual, are made by the infant toward its parents as part of responses to feeding, protection, and general care. These incipient responses meet with rebuffs and frustration both because of lack of interest by parents and because of the threats which are inherent in such behavior.

The parents, as sexually experienced adults, feel some sexual attraction toward their children. Having been indoctrinated with restraints upon sexual behavior with children and within the nuclear family, the parents react with guilt and anxiety. Their anxiety is heightened because each parent would be threatened by the other's sexual attraction to one of the children. As a consequence, both parents strongly discourage their children from making any sexual overtures.

The explanation of the cultural sanctioning of these tendencies within families comes from sociology. The family is the basic unit of reproduc-

33. Bronislaw Malinowski, *Sex and Repression in Savage Society*, New York: Harcourt, Brace, 1927.

34. *Social Structure*, pp. 292–300. For other analyses of the incest taboos, see Christopher Bagley, "Incest Behavior and Incest Taboo," *Social Problems* 16 (Spring 1969), pp. 505–19; and Richard L. Means, "Sociology, Biology, and the Analysis of Social Problems," *Social Problems* 15 (Fall 1967), pp. 200–212.

tion, economic cooperation, and socialization. Sexual rivalry within the group would jeopardize its efficient functioning and its existence. Fathers competing with sons for the mother and the daughters, and mothers competing with daughters for the father and brothers would tear the group apart. Thus the self-interest of individuals and the societal interest are consistent with one another. Sexual restraints within the family receive normative support from the society at large.

Kingsley Davis points out, further, that should inbreeding occur, the resulting confusion of statuses would be unbelievable. As he says, "The incestuous child of a father-daughter union . . . would be a brother of his own mother, i.e. the son of his own sister; a stepson of his own grandmother; possibly a brother of his own uncle; and certainly a grandson of his own father."[35] All family systems provide definitions of proper behavior between various family members; these definitions would break down in the face of widespread inbreeding.

The extension of incest taboos beyond the nuclear family is explained through the psychological concept of "stimulus generalization." According to this principle, any response elicited by a stimulus will be elicited by other stimuli in direct proportion to their similarity to the original stimulus. Thus, if the mother is tabooed, other women will be tabooed in proportion to their perceived similarity to her. Where maternal aunts are called by the same kinship terms as the mother (as they sometimes are), where they live in the same household, and where the sororate exists, the maternal aunts are likely to be tabooed also.

There still remains the problem of why the taboos are extended further in some cases than in others, both within and among societies. Suffice it to say that anthropologists have determined that kinship systems have both a history and a structure that is somewhat self-limiting. To explain why a particular society has an irregular extension of incest taboos, it is necessary to know both its historical connections with other societies and the particular directions of change which are facilitated and restricted by its existing kinship structure.

SUGGESTED READINGS

Since Chapters 2 and 3 form a single unit, the summary, suggested readings, films, and study questions and projects will be found at the end of Chapter 3.

35. Kingsley Davis, "Legitimacy and the Incest Taboo," in Norman W. Bell and Ezra F. Vogel, *eds., A Modern Introduction to the Family*, Glencoe, Illinois: The Free Press, 1960, p. 401.

TEA

3
Worldwide Trends in Family Patterns

The analyses in Chapter 2 have given us a broad picture of human family experience throughout the world. What that analysis lacks, however, is attention to changes that have been occurring over the past few decades. In this chapter, we begin by describing efforts to find universal evolutionary stages through which family systems have progressed. In the light of failure of that effort, we turn to analysis of current world trends in family patterns, concluding with description of the women's movement.

EVOLUTIONARY THEORY

The publication of two books in 1861 might be taken to establish an arbitrary beginning of sociological interest in the family. One, *Das Mutterrecht,* was written by a Swiss jurist, J. J. Bachofen; the other, *Ancient Law,* was written by the anthropologist Sir Henry Sumner Maine. The two books proposed quite different theories of the development of family organization, but both attempted to trace the evolution of family structure from its beginnings in primitive promiscuity to the final form of permanent monogamy.

Most early writers did not state directly that man lived originally in a promiscuous horde, but believed that such a condition could be inferred from the widespread "promiscuous" mating discovered among preliterate peoples. What appeared to be promiscuity to anthropologists, ship captains, and missionaries was not that at all, but only forms of sexual regulation different from Western ones. Nevertheless this ethnocentric interpretation of preliterate sexual behavior prevailed, and the assumption of original human promiscuity was widespread.

From this beginning, many writers reasoned that family systems everywhere passed through a series of stages eventuating in Western-style monogamy. From an hypothesized original promiscuity Sumner believed that the next stage might have been a more or less durable informal monopoly of one or more women by a man. This stage he called *monandry*. From monandry, the next stage probably was group marriage. Group marriage developed into polyandry, and polyandry into polygyny. The stage of monogyny, one wife plus additional consorts, preceded the final development of monogamy.[1]

There were many variants of the evolutionary scheme. Bachofen assumed an original promiscuity and, along with it, an actual supremacy of women which resulted in the development of a matriarchal, matrilineal society.[2] Gradually, he says, women lost their power and the final stage of the patriarchate emerged. A contrary view was proposed by Maine who secured his data from ancient legal codes.[3] Not surprisingly, since the societies he studied were strongly patriarchal, he concluded that the human family has been basically patriarchal.

These theories have only historical interest today. Sophisticated anthropological study has rendered implausible the proposition that families everywhere have passed through similar stages or that there is any unilinear trend toward the monogamous family. The question of family origins is lost in prehistory, and social scientists have ceased to pursue a problem upon which data can never be brought to bear.

CURRENT WORLD TRENDS

Most sociologists trace major changes in the American family to the Industrial Revolution and the consequent urbanization of society. They believe that industrialization was instrumental in transforming the authoritarian, large, stable, rural family system into a more equalitarian, relatively isolated, unstable, nuclear family. They ask whether there

1. William Graham Sumner and Albert G. Keller, *The Science of Society*, Vol. 3, New Haven: Yale University Press, 1927.
2. J. J. Bachofen, *Das Mutterrecht*, Stuttgart, Germany, 1861.
3. Sir Henry Sumner Maine, *Ancient Law*, London: Murray, 1861.

may not be a causal connection between industrialization and the nuclear family.

The logic of this position is simple. In an agricultural society, family members work together as an economic unit. Sons become apprenticed to fathers and eventually inherit the land. There is a clear division of labor between men and women but the division of labor among men is minimal. A person's status in the community is clearly fixed by the family into which the person is born. Large families are advantageous. With industrialization, all of this changes. Work is removed from home to factories. The division of labor becomes complex and schools, not fathers, teach many occupational skills. The use of specialized occupational skills requires that young people move away to the cities. Occupational success produces mobility upward in the social class structure and further isolates parents and children from grandparents. Property becomes intangible and ties to the land are lost. Thus, the argument runs, industrialization changes extended family systems into nuclear systems.

The argument is persuasive. It accords with the American experience; it is consistent with current happenings in other areas of the world. In order to provide some test of the argument, Goode assembled family data covering roughly the past fifty years in the West, in Arabic Islam, in sub-Saharan Africa, in India, China, and Japan.

Goode concluded that "the alteration appears to be in the direction of some type of conjugal family pattern—that is toward fewer kinship ties with distant relatives and a greater emphasis on the nuclear family unit of couple and children."[4] Note that Goode does not say that all family systems are becoming more like ours. He says that the trend is toward *some type* of conjugal system. In fact, Goode's study indicates that the problem is more complicated than whether other family systems are becoming more like ours. He adds the following cautions.

1. Even if the family systems in diverse areas of the world are moving *toward* similar patterns, they *begin* from very different points, so that the trend in one family trait may differ from one society to another—for example, the divorce or illegitimacy rate might be dropping in one society but rising in another.
2. The elements within a family system may each be altering at different rates of speed. . . .
3. Just *how* industrialization or urbanization affects the family system or how the family system facilitates or hinders these processes is not clear.

4. William J. Goode, *World Revolution and Family Patterns*, New York: The Free Press, 1963.

4. It is doubtful that the amount of change in family patterns is a simple function of industrialization; more likely, ideological and value changes, partially independent of industrialization, also have some effect on family action.
5. Some beliefs about how the traditional family system worked may be wrong.
6. Correlatively, it is important to distinguish *ideal* family patterns from real family behavior and values. . . .[5]

Zelditch, in an independent analysis of the relation between industrialization and family change, reaches similar conclusions. He states that any kind of nonsubsistence expanding economy, or even political changes can destroy the authority structure on which the extended family depends.[6] He summarizes the conditions for change as:

1. any change by which kinship and occupational structures become differentiated.
2. where income and status come to depend upon factors not controlled by the extended family.
3. where sons begin to contribute more status and income to the family than do their fathers.
4. where the self interests of family members are not identified with continuity of the family.

These conditions, he says, produce a trend toward the conjugal family whether or not industrialization is involved. In a few generations, all that is left may be a sense of personal obligation and affection toward kin. Gradually these sentiments are restricted to fewer and fewer kin, and more and more the relatives included are bilateral.

That there is no simple cause-and-effect relationship between industrialization and the nuclear family is clear. Nuclear family systems are found in primitive, nonindustrialized societies as well as in modern ones. Nor is it clear that it is simply industrialization which is producing the changes that are evident in much of the world.[7] Goode points out that

5. *Ibid.*, pp. 1–2.
6. Morris Zelditch, Jr., "Cross-Cultural Analyses of Family Structure," in Harold T. Christensen, *ed.*, *Handbook of Marriage and the Family*, Chicago: Rand McNally, 1964, p. 496.
7. George H. Conklin, "The Extended Family as an Independent Factor in Social Change: A Case From India," *Journal of Marriage and the Family* 36 (Nov. 1974), pp. 798–804; Greer Litton Fox, "Love Match and Arranged Marriage in a Modernizing Nation: Mate Selection in Ankara, Turkey," *Journal of Marriage and the Family* 37 (Feb. 1975), pp. 180–93; Herman Lantz, Margaret Britton, Raymond Schmitt, and Eloise C. Snyder, "Pre-Industrial Patterns in the Colonial Family in America: A Content Analysis of Colonial Magazines," *American Sociological Review* 33 (June 1968), pp. 413–26; V. V.

we cannot assume that non-Western family systems were similar to Western family systems at some undefined historical period just before industrialization.

Goode also emphasizes the role of ideological changes—changes in values—that are helping to transform non-Western family systems. He sees all family systems as containing points of strain—features which make them vulnerable to change. Consanguine extended family systems have subjugated women and subordinated the young to their elders. Among women and the young and among intellectuals, radical ideologies have been emerging concurrent with and even prior to industrialization.

One such new ideology is that of economic progress, the notion that technological development and the production of wealth is more important than the preservation of traditional customs. A second ideology is that of individualism, the notion that personal welfare is more important than family continuity. A third emerging ideology is that of equalitarianism, the notion that women should have equal rights with men. Taken together, these emerging values may be as instrumental in producing family change as are the effects of industrialization.

It remains now only to summarize the general changes involved in the widespread trend toward some variant of the conjugal, nuclear family. The changes include trends toward: (1) free choice of spouse, (2) more equal status for women, (3) equal rights of divorce, (4) neolocal residence, (5) bilateral kin, and (6) the equality of individuals against class or caste barriers.

Free Choice of Spouse

Extended family systems and the arrangement of marriages by parents have long been associated. Love as a basis for marriage is discouraged because affection between a young couple cannot be permitted to conflict with its obligations to the family group. The spouse who moves at marriage often is subordinated to members of the new family until he or she has been so completely socialized into the new family that opposition to its customs has been completely eliminated. Most often, of course, it is

---

Prakasa Rao and V. Nandini Rao, "Arranged Marriages: An Assessment of the Attitudes of the College Students in India," *Journal of Comparative Family Studies* 7 (Autumn 1976), pp. 433–53; P. K. Roy, "Industrialization and 'Fitness' of Nuclear Family: A Case Study in India," *Journal of Comparative Family Studies* 5 (Spring 1974), pp. 74–86; and Rudy R. Seward, "The Colonial Family in America: Toward a Socio-Historical Restoration of Its Structure," *Journal of Marriage and the Family* 35 (Feb. 1973), pp. 58–70.

the woman who moves at marriage and who is at greatest disadvantage.

The conditions of urban living often include separation from both families of orientation so that the ability of the new spouse to get along with in-laws is no longer so important. Instead, the relationship between husband and wife assumes greatest importance. Probably in all times and places certain men and women have been attracted to one another, but, whereas extended family systems exclude such attraction as bases for marriage, conjugal family systems often make romantic love the primary basis for marriage. Until recently, the encouragement of romantic love and the right to choose one's own marital partner were not widespread in non-Western countries. Now they are spreading rapidly.

Toward Equal Status for Women

Patrilineal descent and patrilocal residence have been associated with patriarchy and the subordination of women. Polygyny has been widespread, with some women assigned the status of secondary wives. The custom of concubinage in which women have approved status as additional sex partners but not the full legal and other rights of wives also has been widespread. Then there are the more informal, socially disapproved situations where wealthy and influential men have had mistresses who had no rights at all.

The emerging right of women to choose their husbands is doing much to change this. When men must compete for women, inevitably women gain a certain power. Coupled with this is the fact that education for women is spreading rapidly. Women take jobs in the expanding economy and often their salary approaches that of men. The cities, moreover, offer independent living opportunities for women who cannot marry men on terms that are satisfactory to them.

Goode points out that while the philosophy of equal rights for women receives more verbal acceptance in upper social-class levels, the equal rights are more effective at lower-class levels.[8] Upper-class men may believe that they should grant equal rights to women but their own wealth and power lead them to expect deference from their wives. Lower-class men, on the other hand, have less power over their wives because of the greater economic contribution lower-class wives make to the family. Goode also warns that no family system now grants full equality to

8. *Op. cit.*, pp. 21–22, 372.

women and none is likely to do so as long as the daily work involving house and children is regarded as woman's responsibility.[9]

Equal Rights of Divorce

The modern term *divorce* is somewhat misleading when applied to many non-Western and ancient societies. What has often been found among them might be more usefully referred to as the husband's right of repudiation of the wife. The distinction is important. Divorce may be secured only on specified grounds and with some official body such as the courts determining the equity of the matter. In many non-Western and ancient societies, however, the husband or his family has been the sole judge. With no more ceremony than telling the wife before witnesses, or handing her a slip of paper, a so-called bill of divorcement, the husband could end the marriage. The wife often had no recourse and no corresponding rights.

Women in many countries now are demanding protection against unjust repudiation by the husband or his family—that husbands be permitted divorce only for cause. Similarly, they demand equal rights; that the same or comparable grounds for the divorce of a wife should also be grounds for the divorce of a husband. Again the caution should be added that divorce rights in many societies still favor the husband. There is a *trend only* toward equal divorce rights for women.

Neolocal Residence

Patrilocal residence has been common over the world. Even matrilocal residence, also reflecting extended family organization, has been more common than neolocal residence. As urbanization and industrialization proceed, more and more families of procreation find their residences being determined by the location of the husband's job. By default, if not by design, neolocal residence is becoming more common. In some cases, nuclear families plan for decades eventually to return to their extended families. Sometimes they do; often they do not.

9. For vigorous protest against this state of affairs, see Kate Millett, *Sexual Politics*. New York: Doubleday, 1970; and Robin Morgan, *ed.*, *Sisterhood Is Powerful*, New York: Random House, 1970.

Bilateral Kindred

Technically, *kindred* refers to a bilateral kin group. Even where formal unilineages exist, social and geographical mobility and neolocal residence lead to weakening of ties with extended kin. Tasks formerly performed by the lineage either are assumed by the conjugal family or by public and private agencies—police, courts, welfare agencies, and so on. Gradually, ties with kin are reduced to a smaller and smaller group, typically drawn from both the husband's and the wife's lineages. Whether ties are maintained with any kin at all comes to depend upon affection for those kin rather than upon obligation to them.

Equality of Individuals Against Caste or Class Barriers

The trends toward free mate choice, equality for women, and equal divorce rights are part of a larger ideological change. A pervasive philosophy of individualism appears to be spreading over much of the world—a philosophy which militantly asserts the importance of the person over the continuity of the group. This is a radical philosophy. The worth of the individual comes to be more important than inherited wealth or ethnic group. The individual's status comes to be evaluated not so much by the lineage into which he or she was born as by their own accomplishments. The status of the family, then, must be determined for each generation anew.

In closing this section, a few cautions are in order. First, the trends described are just that—trends. It would be a mistake to conclude that extended family systems the world over have broken down. Most societies in the world today have unilineal descent, extended families, and male domination. The trends toward conjugal family systems, widespread as they are, generally are confined to urbanized, industrialized regions. The great masses of population in the hinterlands of countries like China and India, to say nothing of preliterate societies, are relatively unaffected. Moreover, these changes, where they appear, often are viewed as social problems, as symptoms of the breakdown of time-honored ways. Men and women, young and old are pitted against one another. One should not construct a stereotype of societies emerging from the darkness of autocratic extended families into the light of conjugal systems held together by ties of affection.

Finally, we should remember how little we know of the cause-and-effect relations underlying these trends. That urbanization and industrialization are involved is obvious; that urbanization and industrialization alone cannot account for the trends is equally obvious. Ideological factors—individualism, democracy, economic progress—are involved and appear to be both cause and effect. To some degree, the ideals, the technology, and the family system are being exported to the rest of the world from the West. But other societies cannot be seen properly as following the West. Other societies, exposed to technological and ideological change, will incorporate the effects of those changes in ways unique to themselves. Each society has a history and a present structure into which change must be incorporated. Other societies, even if they are profoundly altered by it, will adapt the conjugal family system to their own needs.

THE WOMEN'S MOVEMENT

Although trends such as free choice of spouse, equal rights for women, and equal rights of divorce are revolutionary in much of the world, they appear strangely archaic in contemporary American society. The United States has an organized women's rights movement that began more than a century ago, which has drastically altered relationships between men and women, and which has assumed new vitality over the past 15 years. The final section of this chapter will summarize the history of the women's movement in the United States, assess its present status, and lay the groundwork for analysis of issues pertaining to the status of women in subsequent chapters.

History of the Movement

In 1848, the catch-phrase was "women's rights" rather than "women's liberation," but like the revitalized movement that was to emerge more than a century later, the women's rights movement grew out of a larger civil rights struggle, the Abolitionist movement. Elizabeth Cady Stanton and Lucretia Mott led the effort which produced the Women's Rights Convention at Seneca Falls, New York, and which laid down the basic proposition that, "Men and women are born equally free and independent members of the human race, equally endowed with intelligence and ability, and equally entitled to the free exercise of their individual rights and liberty." The convention demanded the right of women to vote, equal educational and occupational opportunities, and the elimination of legal discrimination against women. The achievement of these goals was slow in coming and, to this day, only one of them has been completely attained. A variety of organizations—the Women's Trade Union League, the General Federation of Women's Clubs, and the Women's Christian Temperance Union—joined forces to press for women's suffrage.[10] In 1920, the Nineteenth Amendment to the Constitution became effective, and women gained the vote.

Popular writing often claims that the women's movement went into eclipse following 1920,[11] but that is oversimplification. The movement became fragmented and torn by conflict, and the more conservative faction won out until the early 1960s. The radical faction, represented by the National Women's Party founded in 1916, espoused a philosophy of "identical rights" and proposed, in 1923, an equal rights amendment to the U.S. Constitution. The proposed amendment read, "Men and women shall have equal rights throughout the United States, and every place subject to its jurisdiction. Congress shall have power to enforce this article by appropriate legislation." The amendment received little support, and in part because of its identification with the amendment, the National Women's Party also failed to gain widespread support.

The conservative wing of the women's rights movement, after 1920, promoted a concept of "equivalent rights" for women, which held that women are equal to but different from men. That difference, it was held, should be recognized through protective legislation for women establishing minimum wage levels, providing meal and rest periods, limiting the number of hours worked, limiting the loads to be lifted, and so on. The Women's Bureau in the U.S. Department of Labor was created in 1920 and, for the next 40 years, promoted such policies. It was supported by the influential League of Women Voters.

The Revolution of the 1960s

Reaction against the conservatism of the women's rights movement following World War I was symbolized by the publication of Betty Friedan's *The Feminine Mystique* in 1963.[12] Friedan argued that women have been trapped into believing that housewifery and childrearing bring deep and lasting satisfaction when actually they consist of the

10. Jo Freeman, "The Origins of the Women's Liberation Movement," *American Journal of Sociology* 78 (Jan. 1973), pp. 792–811.
11. Marlene Dixon, "Why Women's Liberation—2?" in Milton Mankoff, *ed., The Poverty of Progress: The Political Economy of American Social Problems,* New York: Holt, Rinehart and Winston, 1972, p. 251.
12. New York: Dell Publishing Company.

most menial and humdrum tasks. Women, she said, should use their talents in creative endeavor in the occupational world just as men do.

In the early 1960s, many women who shared Friedan's views allied themselves with the civil rights movement and with the emerging radical left, thinking that those who sought equality for blacks and other minorities would also support equality for women. They were disillusioned upon finding that sexism pervaded these movements. One woman activist stated that, "Civil rights has always been a very male-dominated movement. Most radical organizations saw to it that the 'chicks' operated the mimeograph machines and scampered out for coffee while the men ran the show."[13] The most devastating "put down" of women has been attributed to Stokely Carmichael of SNCC who is reputed to have stated that "the only position for women in the movement is prone."

In the long run, the support of the federal government for the movement may prove more significant than the efforts of any private groups. In 1964, while Congress was debating the banning of racial discrimination in employment as part of the Civil Rights Act of 1964, an amendment was introduced forbidding discrimination by sex also. Although it was apparently intended as a joke and as a delaying tactic, the Act as finally passed did forbid such discrimination. For several years, federal administrators did not take the sex discrimination ban seriously, but by the early 1970s, firms receiving federal contracts and universities receiving federal funds came under heavy pressure to develop "affirmative action" programs to employ women in appropriate numbers in responsible and high paid positions. Additional pressure was applied through the Equal Employment Opportunity Act of 1972. The need for such remedial action had been documented in 1965 in the report of the President's Commission on the Status of Women which showed that working women earn roughly half as much as men, and that the ratio of women in professional and executive positions has been dropping recently.

The year 1966 saw the formation of NOW (National Organization for Women), with Betty Friedan as its first president. The goals of NOW include, ". . . a sex-role revolution for men and women which will restructure all our institutions: childrearing, education, marriage, the family, medicine, work, politics, the economy, religion, psychological theory, human sexuality, morality and the very evolution of the race."[14] Friedan insists that the name, National Organization *for* Women,

13. *Time*, Aug. 31, 1970, p. 17.
14. Betty Friedan, "Up From the Kitchen Floor," *The New York Times Magazine*, March 4, 1973, p. 30.

rather than National Organization of Women reflects her realization that men should be included as equal members. She states, further, that she never visualized women as an oppressed class fighting to wrest power away from men.

Nevertheless, meetings of local chapters of NOW often were "consciousness-raising" quasi-therapy sessions in which participants were encouraged to ventilate their feelings about the frustrations that women face in a male-dominated society and, specifically, their mistreatment at the hands of men. That NOW was not wholly receptive to such man-hating is suggested by the early appearance of radical splinter groups such as WITCH (Women's International Terrorist Conspiracy from Hell) and SCUM (Society for Cutting Up Men). By 1970, lesbianism had become a major issue, and Friedan believes that a small group of radical lesbians set out to take control of NOW.

From the outside, it appears that the Women's Liberation Movement was blessed, or cursed, with a number of potentially very strong leaders, sincere in their own conceptions of how the movement might become most influential. In addition to Friedan, Ti Grace Atkinson, Gloria Steinem, Robin Morgan, and Kate Millett were some of the more prominent ones. The issue of whether the movement should adopt the rhetoric of sex-class warfare, based upon the hatred of men, undoubtedly helped curtail the growth of the movement. In 1968, for example, when NOW first advocated repeal of all abortion laws, a substantial proportion of its members resigned. In 1973, a NOW resolution in support of lesbianism threatened another major break in the ranks.

Although accurate membership figures are not available, it is clear that NOW has quite a limited membership base. Estimates indicate that it had only from 3000 to 5000 members in 1970, and from 8000 to 15,000 members in 1973.[15] Moreover, most of the members are white middle-class women. Efforts to recruit sizable numbers of black women have failed miserably. As a worker for the Southern Christian Leadership Council in Atlanta put it, "[Black women are] just begining to get the kind of good treatment as women that white women have always had—they don't want to give it up too fast. Black men have just gotten enough money to take them to nice places, and women like it.[16]

In 1970, another development gave added strength to the Women's Liberation Movement; a woman's political caucus was founded. The

15. *Time, op. cit.*, p. 17; Jo Freeman, *op. cit.*, p. 799; and Betty Friedan, "Up From the Kitchen Floor," p. 34.
16. *Time*, ibid., p. 21.

caucus's influence was evident at the 1972 national political conventions where there were large increases in the women delegates. There was also a 20 percent increase in the women elected to public office that year. In 1973, the first National Women's Political Caucus met with 1200 participants representing 30,000 members in all 50 states. The Caucus, learning from NOW's struggles, downplayed the issue of lesbianism and re-dedicated itself to broad social objectives, not to narrowly feminist ones. The Caucus approved of two basic goals: the election and appointment of more women to public office; and improvement of the situation of minorities and the poor through legislation.

The Equal Rights Amendment

Congress in 1972 showed special interest in an equal rights amendment to the Constitution, almost 50 years after one was first proposed. On May 22, 1972, five months after the House had acted, the Senate authorized an amendment which has three basic provisions: (1) equality of rights under the law shall not be denied or abridged by the United States or by any state on account of sex; (2) the Congress shall have the power to enforce, by appropriate legislation, the provisions of this article; and (3) this amendment shall take effect two years after ratification.

Before the amendment can take effect, it must receive the approval of three-fourths (38) of the legislatures of the 50 states. Moreover, those approvals must be secured within seven years of the date of approval by Congress, or by May 22, 1979. In view of the case with which congressional approval was secured, many people predicted early ratification by the states, and 22 of them ratified it before the end of 1972. By early 1973, however, serious opposition had surfaced, and 13 state legislatures voted disapproval. A national movement, called Stop ERA, emerged under Phyllis Schlafly to argue that ERA would deprive women of major rights and protections such as the right to financial support by their husbands, the right to Social Security benefits that widows receive from their husbands' jobs, the right to alimony and child support in the event of divorce, and exemption from military service.

It is impossible to tell whether the amendment will receive ratification. The early wave of support for it has dissipated, and ratification becomes less likely as time goes by. The battle lines are rather clearly drawn. The President of the United States supports it, the chairmen of both major political parties have called for ratification, the citizens' lobby Common Cause supports it, as do NOW, the National Women's

Political Caucus, and the League of Women Voters. Opposed to it is the AFL-CIO which argues that state labor laws on wages, hours, and conditions of employment for women would be invalidated. The Roman Catholic Church takes no position on the amendment, but many Catholic lay groups, including the powerful National Council of Catholic Women, oppose it. The most articulate and apparently the most effective of the opponents has been Stop ERA and Mrs. Schlafly.

One of the reasons why the fate of ERA is so uncertain is because even well-informed people do not know for sure what all of the implications of enactment would be. Proponents argue that the effects on the family would be minimal, while some opponents argue that the family would be destroyed. The most informed analyses available have been published in the *Yale Law Journal* and the *Harvard Civil Rights-Civil Liberties Law Review*.[17]

Family Relationships. As opponents of the amendment fear, men no longer will automatically be liable for their wives' financial support; the obligation to support will fall upon whichever spouse is able to provide. Fathers and mothers will become equally vulnerable to requests for alimony in the event of divorce. Women will not be required to take their husband's names at marriage; nor will they be required to accept the husband's domicile. Husbands, as well as wives, could be divorced for failure to move with the spouse in order to take a new job.

Special laws protecting females from seduction, statutory rape, and obscene language would become unconstitutional. Forcible rape by men probably will remain a crime because it is based upon the unique physical characteristics of men, but women will become vulnerable to charges of assault should they engage in intercourse with underage boys.

Employment. All forms of discrimination in favor of, or against women, will be eliminated. Only jobs where sex clearly is a requirement for successful performance, such as wet nurses, sperm donors, and locker room attendants, will be the prerogative of one sex. Women will be eligible to engage in hazardous occupations such as mining, police work, and fire protection. Limitations on the weight that can be lifted and upon the number of hours that can be worked will be eliminated or made uniform for the two sexes. Equal pay will be required for equal work.

Military Service. There is little question that women will be eligible

17. *The New York Times,* June 25, 1973.

for military service on the same basis as men, and will be eligible for the draft should conscription be resumed. Height-weight correlations, and I.Q. scores required for induction will have to be made uniform for the sexes. Women with dependent children will be eligible for enlistment, just as men are. If men are granted deferment because of dependent children, women will have the same right. If the sole surviving son in a family where one child has already died in the service is eligible for deferment, then the sole surviving daughter will receive deferment as well. The Women's Army Corps, and similar female units, will have to be abolished. Women will be eligible for combat duties unless it can be shown that they have specific physical disqualifications for them.

Undoubtedly, there are still other implications of the Equal Rights Amendment. Whether this generation will have to face up to them is unknown. Even if the amendment fails, the trend of legislation is in the directions indicated. The struggle for women's rights has been long; and it is not yet over.

SUMMARY

Nuclear families are combined into composite families through plural marriage or through extension of the parent-child relationship. Polygamous marriage, which involves common residence, economic cooperation, and the sexual relationship, is divided into polygyny and polyandry. Polygyny is widespread, polyandry is rare, and group marriage is nowhere the societal norm. Polygamous marriages may involve the taking of siblings as spouses, or the multiple spouses may be unrelated. The terms *levirate* and *sororate* refer to preferential marriage with the sibling of a deceased spouse. Though polygyny usually is accorded higher status than monogamy, most persons in any society are monogamous. The sex ratio and the cost of polygynous marriages are influential here.

Extended families may be compounded either of monogamous or polygamous families. Nuclear families become dependent units in extended family systems. Extended families emphasize blood ties over marital ties and are labeled consanguine. Nuclear families emphasizing marital ties are called conjugal. Consanguine families provide for continuity over the generations, hold property intact, and prescribe the roles of family members in detail. Conjugal families are short-lived, split up the family property, and emphasize flexibility in role performance.

About one-fourth of all societies have the nuclear family only, another fourth have polygamous but not extended families, and about half have some form of extended family. The independent nuclear family is found at both the bottom and top of the economic scale. The extended family predominates in agricultural and pastoral economies.

Since one spouse must move at marriage, rules of residence are necessary. Patrilocal residence is most common, followed by matrilocal residence. Neolocal residence is less common. Some form of bride price is associated with removal of the bride from the community of her parents and is a guarantee of her good treatment. Women seldom are purchased outright.

Authority patterns in the family may be patriarchal, matriarchal, or equalitarian. Even in alleged matriarchies, power is wielded by males of the female lineage.

All societies regulate sex behavior. Only about 5 percent of societies prohibit all sex behavior outside of marriage, however. About 70 percent of societies permit premarital intercourse, sometimes with preferred marriage partners. Intercourse between a married man and an unrelated woman generally is forbidden, but men, in most societies, are granted sexual access to one or more female relatives. The rules of endogamy and exogamy require marriage either within or outside the group.

Universal incest taboos within the nuclear family have striking effects upon family structure. The constant overlapping of nuclear families requires social definitions of kinship. This is accomplished through rules of descent. The significant rules are patrilineal, matrilineal, and bilateral. Rules of inheritance may also be patrilineal or matrilineal, with primogeniture—preference given to the eldest son—often being found.

Incest taboos are always extended beyond the nuclear family, but not universally to any specified relative. The key to these extensions is the family as a social group rather than a biological group. Societies enforce incest taboos primarily through internalization of the taboos during socialization and secondarily through avoidance relationships.

Among explanations proposed for universal incest taboos are the alleged ill effects of inbreeding, alleged instincts against inbreeding, the sexual disinterest which allegedly accompanies intimate familiarity, and the frustrations encountered in the Oedipal situation. All of these explanations are found wanting. An eclectic explanation finds the roots of the taboos in the suppression of sexual rivalries within the nuclear family and the necessity to preserve the family as a cooperative unit.

Family systems over a wide area of the world are tending toward some variant of the conjugal family. Urbanization and industrialization are involved in this trend, but it is too simple to say that they are the cause. For one thing, conjugal families are found in preindustrial societies. Moreover, ideological changes play a partly independent causal role.

The women's rights movement in the United States is over a century old. After universal suffrage was achieved in 1920, the movement split into conservative and radical factions, with the conservative faction being dominant until the 1960s. A revolutionary phase was entered in the 1960s as women's groups and government efforts combined to give women more political and economic power. An Equal Rights Amendment to the Constitution was approved by Congress in 1972, but may or may not be ratified by the states. Either through constitutional amendment or through legislation, further changes in the status of women and in the nature of family relationships may be expected.

SUGGESTED READINGS

Carden, Maren Lockwood, *New Feminist Movement*, New York: Russell Sage, 1974. A carefully researched account of the women's movement by a woman who became a participant in it.

Dreitzel, Hans P., *ed.*, *Family, Marriage, and the Struggle of the Sexes*, New York: Macmillan, 1972. A collection of articles generally addressed to the question of whether new trends in sex role differentiation and the new climate in the struggle between the sexes have made the family obsolete.

Epstein, Cynthia F., and Goode, William J., *eds.*, *The Other Half: Roads to Women's Equality*. Englewood Cliffs, New Jersey: Prentice-Hall, 1971. A representative collection of articles dealing with the Women's Liberation Movement. Includes programs and proposals.

Freeman, Jo, *The Politics of Women's Liberation*, New York: McKay, 1975. A penetrating analysis of women's liberation as a social movement. Written by a member of the younger branch of the movement.

Perrucci, Carolyn C., and Targ, Dena B., *Marriage and the Family: A Critical Analysis and Proposals for Change*, New York: David McKay, 1974. Critiques of various aspects of marriage and the family from feminist viewpoints.

FILMS

Four Families (National Film Board of Canada, Mackenzie Building, Toronto, Ontario), 61 minutes. Comparison of family life in India, France, Japan, and Canada. Margaret Mead discusses how the upbringing of a child contributes to a distinctive national character.

Growing Up Female (New Day Films, 267 West 25th Street, New York, N.Y. 10001), 60 minutes. A documentary about the experience of being a woman in America, through encounters with six females. Good for introducing the issues involved in women's liberation.

How To Make a Woman (Polymorph Films, 331 Newbury Street, Boston, Mass. 02115), 58 minutes. Illuminates the relationship between men and women. Presents the sexual and personal conflicts motivating women today.

Married Life (Time-Life Films, 43 West 16th Street, New York, N.Y. 10011), 45 minutes. Married life in five different settings: a wife with three husbands in the Himalayas; a couple in a prosperous English community; a man with three wives in New Guinea; another with two wives in Botswana; and a young couple in Lancashire.

QUESTIONS AND PROJECTS

1. Describe two ways in which nuclear families may be combined into composite forms. What terms refer to the two types of composite families?
2. Differentiate among polygamy, polygyny, and polyandry. Why are most people monogamous even in societies which value polygyny highly?
3. What economic conditions in a society favor monogamy? Polygyny? Polyandry? How widespread is each over the world?
4. What are the levirate and the sororate? Does either custom exist in our own society? Why or why not?
5. Distinguish between dependent and independent nuclear families.
6. What is meant by a consanguine family? A conjugal family? Detail the advantages and problems of consanguine and conjugal systems.
7. What are incest taboos? Differentiate between incest taboos and endogamy and exogamy. Illustrate rules of endogamy and exogamy in the United States.
8. How does the existence of universal incest taboos necessitate the development of complex kinship systems? Evaluate the proposition that kinship systems are social systems.
9. Define and describe the major rules of descent; the rules of inheritance; the rules of residence. Which are more common over the world? What associations exist among rules of descent, inheritance, and residence?

10. What is a patriarchal family system? Are there any true matriarchies? In what persons is power usually vested in so-called matriarchal societies?
11. What explanations have been proposed for the universality of incest taboos? Evaluate the strengths and weaknesses of these explanations. What is the most adequate explanation of incest taboos?
12. Toward what general form are family systems over the world changing? Evaluate, critically, the proposition: that family systems in other parts of the world are coming to be modeled after the American system.
13. Trace the history of the women's rights movement in the United States. What changes in family relationships likely would follow ratification of the Equal Rights Amendment?

4
The Family System of China

"It is very necessary for young people to go to the countryside to be re-educated by the poor and lower-middle peasants." . . . At least eight million young Chinese have left the cities since the end of 1968 when Mao handed down that pronouncement. . . .

Last summer, as he was completing his second year on the harsh frontier, Chai [Chun-tse] received a letter from his father, a Communist party member of 29 years standing, that contained a suggestion that the son knew to be ideologically illicit. The coal mine near home where the father worked, the letter said, was taking on new workers and giving first crack at the jobs to the sons of its employes. If the young man simply did what he was told by the Coal Bureau and his father, he would be hired and released from exile and a life of rural drudgery.

Putting that missive in the young stalwart's hands was putting a match to a fuse. In no time at all he had called a meeting of his local Communist Youth League chapter to invite debate on the "evil wind" embodied in his father's suggestion; then he drafted a reply . . . in which he vowed grandiloquently "to break with old concepts for the sake of spreading Communism throughout the world." . . .

What the ceaseless exhortation and the indomitable revolutionary rhetoric finally tend to highlight is the conservatism, inertia and tenacity of the Chinese family system. . . . Always the issue is posed as family vs. state ("The parents of educated young people should not regard their children as their private property," a Shantung editorial scolds, "but as valuable assets to the party and state.") . . .[1]

1. Joseph Lelyveld, "The Great Leap Farmward," *The New York Times Magazine* July 28, 1974, pp. 6, 56. Copyright © The New York Times, 1974. Reprinted by permission.

The quotation refers to China in the 1970s, and describes an emerging family system, radically different from the traditional one to be described in the first part of this chapter. The traditional family was a strong, stable one, which persisted for 2000 years. The traditional family still exists, but increasingly it is being replaced by the family patterns described in the latter part of this chapter.

ADVANTAGES IN THE STUDY OF THE CHINESE FAMILY

Major Family Tradition Different from Our Own

Most of this book will be devoted to the analysis of Western family organization, and to the family in the United States. Chapters 2 and 3 already have provided some world perspective but, necessarily, that cross-cultural analysis could not provide a comprehensive, integrated portrayal of any one family system very different from our own. Family practices take on meaning only in the total context in which they appear. Lest strange family customs remain merely as curiosities, we need to present some of them in a context in which they will be wholly intelligible and, at the same time, to present another major type of family system with which our own can be systematically compared.

The traditional Chinese family is very different from our own. Just as ours may represent Western family systems, the Chinese can represent Eastern systems. Instead of a preliterate society of a few hundred people and with tenuous ties to any major civilization, we have selected a society of some 900 million people, the largest nation in the world, whose practices are somewhat applicable to additional hundreds of millions of people. The cultural stream from which Chinese family practices derive has as long and distinguished a history as our own.

A Model of Stability and Change

The Western family, and the American family in particular, has been characterized by rapid change. In contrast, the Chinese family remained relatively unchanged for approximately 2000 years. No society is ever completely static, of course, and some of the apparent lack of change in Chinese society is a function of the inability of Western scholars to see the change which has occurred. Nevertheless, by Western standards, Chinese social change has been slow and China has shown great capacity for absorbing potential agents of change from the outside. Neither Christianity nor Judaism, for example, has had the impact upon China which might have been expected. The Jews who settled there centuries ago were absorbed so that few traces of them remain today.[2] Christianity had somewhat more impact, but there is no evidence of basic change in Chinese institutions which can be traced directly to the religious character of this influence. Similarly, both Mongol and Manchu invasions of China resulted ultimately in the conquerors' adoption of Chinese ways. Although change was present, the appearance presented by the Chinese family to the West was one of great strength and stability.

Even as it serves as a model of stability, however, the Chinese family also presents a model of change. About 150 years ago, urbanization and industrialization began to make their influence felt and China embarked upon rapid change which is still in process. The family system, which had seemed impervious to change, underwent drastic alteration.

Unusually Comprehensive Data Available

There is more reliable literature on the Chinese family than on any other non-Western family system. Both Oriental and Western scholars have been studying China's history and social patterns for decades and, in some cases, centuries. This concerted attention has resulted not only in a massive literature but also in literature of unusual trustworthiness. The interaction between Chinese and non-Chinese scholars has produced modification of many early ideas concerning Chinese family patterns. The descriptions which follow are not based upon the work of one or two people with two or three years of field work experience; they represent the combined efforts of a veritable army of scholars.

Significance in the Modern World

Along with the Soviet Union and the United States, China is one of the world's great powers. It has the largest population of any nation, a huge land area, and virtually untapped natural resources. For over two decades, China has presented a formidable ideological, military, and economic challenge to the rest of the world. Whatever the future, it will be profoundly affected by what happens in China.

2. S. M. Perlmann, *The History of the Jews in China*, London, 1913, as discussed in Marion J. Levy, Jr., *The Family Revolution in Modern China*, Cambridge, Mass.: Harvard University Press, 1949, p. 286.

THE TRADITIONAL CHINESE FAMILY

The phrase "traditional Chinese family" requires qualification. In the broadest sense it refers to family patterns up to about 75 to 100 years ago. The extensive social change which produced the "transitional family" first became evident about then. More narrowly, the traditional family was most characteristic of the Ch'ing dynasty which lasted from A.D. 1644 to 1911.[3] Earlier variations of the traditional family did not differ greatly from that of the Ch'ing dynasty. Moreover, it was the Ch'ing dynasty which gave way to the modern Republic of China.[4]

During most of this traditional period China was a land of over 3.5 million square miles (larger than the United States), where dozens of dialects were spoken, and one in which there was great variation from one section to another and from rural to urban areas. Far from there being one family pattern in such a vast land, there were innumerable variations. Some of these variations we will touch upon. For the most part, however, we will concentrate upon the dominant patterns reflected in Confucian teachings, in literature, and in the law.

The Gentry and the Peasantry

A basic distinction for understanding of the traditional family separates the so-called gentry from the vast majority of Chinese peasants. The gentry were defined by several criteria. First, they received income from land they did not cultivate. Abstinence from manual labor was a source of pride, and essential for acceptance into the class. By and large, the gentry were intellectuals for whom mastery of knowledge was the route to social advancement. China developed, very early, a massive examination system, somewhat analogous to our civil service system, which theoretically was open to all Chinese and through which positions in government were awarded. Actually, the system was controlled by the gentry whose opportunities for leisure gave them great advantage in acquiring the knowledge necessary for success. In addition to their income as landlords, the gentry received income from governmental offices and academic positions which they held. As China began to modernize, the gentry also became involved in industry, commerce, and banking. The gentry probably accounted for less than one-fifth of the population.

3. The discussion of the traditional Chinese family will depend heavily upon that of Marion J. Levy, Jr., *ibid.*, pp. 41–269.

4. The Republic of China is represented by the government of Taiwan.

China was basically agricultural, and the term *peasantry* accurately described most of the population. The peasantry, who worked the land, were very poor by modern standards; physical survival was their primary goal. There was little room in their existence for the elaboration of social customs, and their family patterns were similar to those of poverty-ridden people everywhere. Men and women worked together in the fields and children were pressed into work. There was, however, widespread aspiration for the attainment of gentry status, and just enough upward mobility to keep the dream alive. Consequently, even among the peasantry the family ideals were frequently those of the gentry.[5]

The influence of the gentry cannot be overemphasized. Their ways were highly regarded and set standards for the entire country. It was the gentry patterns that were referred to in literature and song and in law and official records. This preoccupation with gentry patterns was so great that little is actually known about the variety of peasantry patterns. The gentry patterns were the ideal patterns[6] and it is with these ideal patterns that we shall mainly deal.

The Gentry Family

The traditional gentry family was patriarchal, patrilineal, patrilocal, and monogamous. It included the patriarch and his wife, their sons and the sons' wives, unmarried daughters, grandsons and their wives, unmarried granddaughters, great-grandsons and their wives, unmarried great-granddaughters, and so on. The ideal was to have six generations living under one roof, and to go nine generations without a division of property. The gentry family ideally was a very large family, all living together, and maintaining themselves intact for as many generations as possible.

Family Size. The real gentry patterns, however, deviated from this ideal. In practice, China appears not to have been a nation of exceptionally large families. Comprehensive data are difficult to come by, but sev-

5. In addition to the gentry and peasantry there were small merchants, artisans, soldiers, servants, and the like. These groups were relatively unimportant and generally followed the social patterns of the peasantry. If their economic status was high enough, they tended to follow the gentry patterns.

6. Care should be taken not to confuse ideal culture patterns with ideal types. Ideal culture patterns are the models of exemplary conduct toward which a society strives. Real cultural patterns, in contrast, refer to the actual behavior patterns prevailing in the society. See Ralph Linton, *The Cultural Background of Personality*, New York: D. Appleton-Century, 1945, pp. 52–54.

eral studies have shown an average household size of around five persons. Ping-ti Ho reports that a respectable census in A.D. 2 yielded an average household of 4.87 persons and that Chinese family size has not changed appreciably over the past 2000 years.[7] He states further that, "the size of the Chinese peasant family was determined primarily by its basic economic needs and by the fiscal burden it bore."[8]

Census figures, of course, would yield averages much closer to the typical size of the peasant family than to that of the gentry family. Yet, there is reason to think that the typical gentry family probably fell far short of the large, six-generation ideal.

If nothing else, longevity patterns would prevent six generations of the same family living together. Even in modern America where longevity is greater, we do not often find living families extending from great-grandparents through great-grandchildren. Three or four generations must have been the usual maximum in traditional China.

Even this three- or four-generation group probably was not the most common gentry family. Although the gentry were relatively wealthy, it appears that such large family units were not economically feasible for most of them. It appears that when a man achieved additional wealth, he was likely to use that wealth to increase the size of his household in accord with the concept of the ideal family. But it also appears that economic necessity forced most of the gentry to live in smaller units.

The typical Chinese family probably was the stem family.[9] Under this arrangement one of the sons brings his bride to live with his parental family while other sons go out of the family to earn their living. Even though large families could not generally be maintained, there were several factors operating to prevent the Chinese family from breaking down into a simple conjugal unit. One factor was ancestor worship. Taoism, Buddhism, and Confucianism were all major religions in China, but, in addition, virtually all Chinese practised ancestor worship. The worship of ancestors was both a major responsibility and a major goal in life. If one worshipped one's ancestors dutifully and raised sons properly, one

7. Ping-ti Ho, "An Historian's View of the Chinese Family System," in Seymour Farber, Piero Mustacchi, and Roger H. L. Wilson, *eds., Man and Civilization: The Family's Search for Survival,* New York: McGraw-Hill, 1965, p. 18.

8. *Ibid.* For arguments that actual variations in family size from one society to another are less than differences of family ideals would indicate, see Ansley J. Coale, Lloyd A. Fallers, Marion J. Levy, Jr., David M. Schneider, and Sylvan S. Tomkins, *Aspects of the Analysis of Family Structure,* Princeton, New Jersey: Princeton University Press, 1965.

9. Frederic Le Play used the term *famille souche*. See his *Les Ouvriers européens,* Vol. 1, Tours, 1879, p. 457.

would eventually be worshipped as an ancestor himself. One son remained with the parental family to maintain the family burial ground and continue the ancestor worship.

Supporting factors were the doctrine of filial piety, which emphasized the subordination of the child to the parents, and the practice of holding family property in common. These forces were strong enough to perpetuate the large family ideal in circumstances where economic factors did not favor it. Many married sons were forced to live in conjugal units for much of their lives. Apparently many sons lived as meagerly as possible, sending much of their earnings back to the family home and paving the way for the day when they would be able to return and take their places in the family as distinguished elders.

Division of Property. Ideally, the family was to go nine generations without a division of property. The inheritance rules provided that all sons should inherit equally, although the eldest son often received a larger share. This informal inequality reflected a "ceremonial primogeniture," in which the eldest son assumed major responsibility for the ancestor worship. The eldest brother also was destined, if a division of property did not occur, to succeed his father as patriarch. The greater prestige of the eldest brother and the expenses he incurred in maintaining the ancestors' graves often were enough to militate against strictly equal inheritance. In peasant families younger sons often turned their inheritances over to the eldest son, in which case he assumed full responsibility for the ancestor worship.

While the family remained intact, property as held in common under the patriarch. Given the norms of filial piety, sons were unlikely to ask for a division during the father's lifetime. The same allegiance was not owed to the elder brother, however, and there were forces operating to encourage younger brothers to ask for a division at the father's death or retirement. Particularly if the family wealth was not increasing, expansion of the family would reduce each brother's potential wealth accordingly. Thus the brothers were encouraged to request their inheritances while there still was something to inherit. Tensions among the brothers, of course, increased the probability that a division of property would be sought, and, especially, dissatisfaction on the part of wives of the brothers led them to urge their husbands to seek a division.

When a division of property occurred, each brother separated his straightline descendants and established a new branch of the family with himself as patriarch. Such a move permitted younger brothers to attain the status of family head which otherwise would be denied them, but the division of property also was regarded as undesirable and it appears that this kind of motivation was not prominent. Few families were wealthy enough and sufficiently well integrated to avoid a division of property for nine generations. In fact, division often occurred at the death of the patriarch. The strength of the family ideals is illustrated by their continuance despite widespread deviation from them.

The Tsu. The traditional family was more important in the institutional structure of China than almost any family system is in any contemporary nation. This was before the development of modern nation-states in Europe, and there was no strong central government in China. The family performed most of the enforcement, judicial, and welfare functions that we associate with government.

Moreover, the Chinese concept of obligation to others was quite different from the Western concept. Whereas Western culture assumes a generalized obligation to other people, resulting in strangers being able to interact according to universal norms of fair play, no such notion existed in China. Instead the Chinese obligation to others extended more radically to family members than our own but did not extend to people outside the family.[10] This resulted in considerable isolation of gentry families, who could afford and manage it, from contacts with persons outside the family. Virtually all contacts with outsiders were made through the patriarch and even he avoided such contacts whenever possible.

Beyond the family, the chief group in traditional China was the clan or *tsu.* The *tsu* included all persons with a common surname tracing descent from a common ancestor. With the care given to tracing ancestry, the *tsu* might number thousands of persons, and gentry, peasants, servants, and soldiers might be members of a single *tsu.* The importance of the *tsu* varied from one section of the country to another, but in some areas there were whole villages where everyone belonged to the same *tsu.*

The *tsu* operated through a council of elders and intervened in mat-

10. Many students make ethnocentric evaluations of this difference between Western and Eastern norms, deploring the apparent insensitivity of Orientals to the distressed persons who are not members of their own families. The American's reaction is that aid should be provided to any human being in trouble and that anyone who does not provide it is morally deficient and despicable. Conversely, the Chinese is likely to be horrified at American treatment of older family members. No self-respecting Chinese would think of incarcerating aged parents in an institution, but would accord them the place of greatest honor in the home.

American notions of obligation to others also appear to be changing. Witness the publicity given to situations where citizens, obviously aware of what was happening, have refused to aid in cases of rape, drowning, accidents, illness, and even murder.

ters which could not be handled by individual families. Its will was implemented through the patriarch and, in rare instances, against the patriarch himself. A major function of the *tsu* was to aid in the maintenance of the ancestral graves. Its resources were thus used to ensure the continuation of the group when that continuance might be in jeopardy.

The *tsu* also exercised broad welfare functions, paid for by the income from property held for this purpose. It paid for the education of an occasional bright son from a poorer branch of the *tsu* and thus supported some upward mobility. It loaned money to *tsu* members. It also helped families to organize and to pay for lavish weddings and funerals.

Certain enforcement and judicial functions were handled by the *tsu*. It arbitrated disputes between branches of the *tsu* and enforced its rulings. It served as a tax collection agency for the government. It mediated between family members and government authority, protecting *tsu* members from outside aggression and serving as a parole body for *tsu* members who had committed offenses.

The *tsu* was one of a few sources of power in China outside the individual family. It played a role in helping to maintain the integrity of the family. The *tsu* also came under attack as a competing source of power when the present government came into being.

Age and Sex Roles

The traditional Chinese family is an excellent example of a consanguine system. Consistent with the large family ideal, prescribed roles for members were laid down in detail. Position in the family was all-important; little opportunity was provided for personal idiosyncrasies. What mattered was whether one was an eldest son in a well-to-do family or the newest daughter-in-law—not personality characteristics such as whether one was intelligent, phlegmatic, or what have you. Little ad-libbing on the prescribed roles was permitted. Everyone knew how the eldest son or the newest daughter-in-law was supposed to think, feel, and act in most situations, and most people conformed to expectations.

Traditional China was highly structured by age and sex. The roles for family members can be described according to the age groups to which they belonged. Moreover, not only was absolute age important—not only were 40-year-olds treated differently from 20-year-olds—but relative age was also important. By relative age, we mean the age of one person in relation to that of another person. The Chinese emphasized not only whether people were 20 years or 40 years old but also upon whether they were younger or older than the other people with whom they interacted. Prescribed behavior was also defined by sex. There was marked segregation of sex roles with quite different behavior expected of males and females.

Infancy. The Chinese held old age in deference, and they were kind and affectionate toward small children. Children were highly valued, particularly sons. Sons were the means to continuation of the family and provided for continued worship of the ancestors. A marriage which did not produce sons was unfortunate indeed.

Girls, too, were valued and welcomed into the family when their birth did not present grave financial problems and when daughters were not born to the exclusion of sons. In poor peasant families, the situation was different. Female infanticide occasionally was resorted to by poverty-stricken parents, and girl babies occasionally were sold. If resources were scarce, the sons, as the most important children, had first priority.

The length of the infancy period was not hard and fast. Upon the average it lasted about four years, depending upon the wealth of the parents and whether children were born subsequently. Wealthy parents could afford to indulge their children more and if no other siblings were born, infancy could be prolonged.

The child's first years were easy, pleasant ones. Both boys and girls received affection from both parents, while discipline was held to a minimum. Weaning and toilet training were accomplished gradually, and, during the latter part of the period, training in filial piety was begun. This training took the form of stories that were read or told to the children in which the implicit message was that the child was the property of his parents and ancestors. Children learned to be obedient to their parents and to older brothers and sisters.

Childhood. The term *childhood* is American, not Chinese. The Chinese term for this second age period, *yu-nien*, stressed the immaturity and inexperience of the persons involved.

Early in this period, sex differentiation became marked. Gentry boys moved to the father's section of the house and came under his direct supervision. Schooling began also, and the schoolmaster or tutor wielded authority over boys that closely paralleled that of the father. The mother remained as a refuge for the boy against unduly harsh treatment but her position was essentially without power, enabling her only to comfort him. Girls remained under their mother's care and began preparation for their future roles as wives and mothers.

The severe discipline of Chinese life began during this period. Boys received arduous intellectual and physical training, being expected to study—essentially learning by rote—for long hours under austere conditions. Disobedience, willfulness, and failure to perform were dealt with by beatings by father and schoolmaster. The relationship between father and son ceased to be one of warmth and acceptance and became based, instead, upon awe—a mixture of fear and respect. Complete subservience to the father was instilled, along with the notion that, one day, the son would assume the same role with his own sons.

Rebellion against this severe discipline appears to have been uncommon. Acceptance of the discipline and progress in his studies made life easier for the boy, and, even as he was punished, he was made aware of his importance and of the high status which was his to inherit. Too, gentry boys were granted increasing freedom to make contacts outside the household where their sense of personal importance was increased.

The lives of gentry girls were very different from those of boys. Girls were increasingly segregated from the outside world and even from the males of their own household. They became aware of their roles as temporary members of the family. In some instances, girls were listed in the family genealogical tables only by *nu*, the symbol for female; for at marriage they would cease to be members of their fathers' families and become members of their husbands' families.

This blow to a girl's self-esteem was compensated for by the indulgent relationship with her parents. Her mother, knowing of the difficult times ahead, made the girl's life as easy as possible. The father, too, could lavish upon his daughters the affection that was not appropriate with his sons. As a result, and in spite of her increasing sense of worthlessness, childhood was often the happiest period of the girl's life.

The peasantry patterns for both boys and girls differed markedly from those of the gentry. The extensive schooling and segregation simply were not possible, and both boys and girls were inducted early into the labors of adult life. Boys accompanied their fathers to the fields. The girls did not work in the fields as a rule, but at periods of peak load they did. Peasant women could not be isolated from outsiders as gentry women were, and peasant girls retained much more contact with male members of their households and with outsiders.

Entrance to Adulthood. The second age period lasted from 4 years of age to 16 or 17. For peasant boys and girls, and for gentry girls, this age period as followed by entrance into full adulthood. Not so for gentry males. For them, there was a relatively long and structurally significant period referred to by the term *ch'ing-nien*. This third age period for gentry males lasted until roughly age 30, or until the young man was married.

By contrast with the preceding period, the stage of *ch'ing-nien* was a relatively easy one for gentry males. Discipline was relaxed and was replaced by an almost comradely, consultative relationship in which the father trained his son in the exercise of judgment. The son's academic training had prepared him to take the first examinations, and passing those examinations brought higher status and personal freedom. His continued schooling was likely to take place in the towns and cities, away from direct parental supervision, and he had money to spend.

During this period the gentry male was introduced to the common vices of adult life—drinking, gambling, and extramarital intercourse. His first sex experience was likely to be either with a servant or a prostitute. Most gentry families had servants and there were no emotional barriers to sex relationships with males of the household. The strict separation of female family members and the strong incest taboos reinforced the availability of servant girls. Sexual experimentation also was likely with prostitutes in situations involving drinking and gambling. Sooner or later, the parents became aware of these activities and viewed them as threats to the stability of the family.

Parental reaction to the son's incipient dissolution was to seek for him a wife. The responsibility for so doing fell upon his mother, who acted for her husband. She was the person most upset by the debauchery, and she would have the most significant relationship with the bride. The son was not consulted, for custom provided that he should not meet his bride until the engagement. According to Chinese law, marriage was concluded by the heads of the families, not by the young couple themselves.

Theoretically, there was no emotional involvement between gentry males and young women but such involvements did occur. Gentry girls were carefully chaperoned because sexual intercourse would damage their chances of marrying satisfactorily. In some areas, cross-cousin marriages were preferred and more contact was permitted with these future wives than with unrelated girls. Emotional involvement, even with an eligible marriage partner, was a threat to the family and an indication that another suitable marriage should be arranged immediately. The disruption of these relationships was often traumatic and provides a major theme in Chinese literature. Rebellion against the wishes of parents appears to have been rare, however.

Full Adulthood. The next two age periods covered full maturity from marriage to some time between 30 and 40 years of age, and then from

30–40 years to old age. Entrance into adulthood was determined more by marriage than by the reaching of a particular age, for marriage was of extreme importance. Except for a small minority of religious celibates, virtually everyone married. Marriage provided for children, and children were essential to obligations to ancestors and to oneself.

Gentry families usually tried to marry their daughters to provide useful family connections. At the minimum, this meant that the man's family should have considerable property. Where possible, the gentry also tried to assure themselves that their daughter would be well received and well treated in her new family.

Peasants faced more extreme problems. The marriage of a son required a gift to the girl's parents, which gift the girl ideally brought back to the marriage as part of her trousseau. Thus the parents of both families were supposed to make an economic contribution to the marriage and there was negotiation over these contributions. If the man's parents were very poor, they might be forced to keep the gift made to them by the parents of their daughter's groom in order to arrange for the marriages of their own younger sons. Such a practice was considered undesirable, but it appears to have been widely followed.

The situation was further complicated by a chronic shortage of marriageable girls, produced through female infanticide, prostitution, and concubinage. There are no reliable data on the extent of female infanticide but it is known to have existed. In times of famine, drought, high taxes, and the like, it probably reached large proportions. Goodé emphasizes that outright infanticide may have been accompanied by more widespread neglect of daughters during times of great privation so that their death rate may have been considerably higher.[11]

Prostitution flourished and many peasant girls were sold into prostitution by parents who thus escaped the costs of the girl's rearing and marriage. Concubinage was uncommon among the peasants, who could not afford it, but was common among the gentry who usually secured their concubines from peasant families. The factors of infanticide, prostitution, and concubinage combined to produce a shortage of peasant girls, forcing many peasant males to delay marriage.

Chinese girls, including gentry girls, were married early—as soon as possible after puberty. No accurate figures on age at marriage are available, but the present Chinese government is harshly critical of the old "feudalistic pattern of early marriage." Gentry males married at consid-

11. William J. Goode, *World Revolution and Family Patterns*, New York: The Free Press, 1963, pp. 307–9.

erably older ages. Goode reports data from one clan in Canton which show the average age of the father at the time of the birth of his first living son to have been 33 years from A.D. 1150 to 1500, 31 years from 1630 to 1800, and 23 years from 1800 to 1880.[12] The average age at marriage would be slightly younger, of course, but, given the emphasis on bearing sons, the difference probably would not be great.

Marriage normally was arranged by "go-betweens," for families seldom dealt directly with outsiders. Generally, these were male relatives who were trusted members of the family and yet could negotiate with the families of prospective spouses without committing the family. The procedure called for investigation of each family and several ritual exchanges of gifts and information. The information exchanged included the names and birth dates of the couple, which were presented to the ancestors and were subjected to astrological interpretation. If the interpretation was favorable, the negotiations continued. If unfavorable, the negotiations were dropped. There is some evidence that astrologers took into account more than the stars and that if a marriage did not seem mutually advantageous, an unfavorable interpretation provided a mutually face-saving way of calling it off. Eventually, if all went well, the marriage contract was signed and the wedding ceremony held.

The essence of the marriage ceremony, however elaborately embellished, was the transport of the bride to the home of the groom's parents where she was introduced to the worship of their ancestors. The wife thus became a member of her husband's family and her name was eligible for listing in their genealogical tables. After the ceremony, the couple were permitted to spend the night together, but early the next morning the bride arose and served tea to her mother-in-law in bed. This began a period of service to the husband's family and particularly to the mother-in-law, the function of which was to take the bride, as an outsider, and to make her a docile, member of her new family.

Marriage almost amounted more to the parents taking a daughter-in-law than to the son taking a wife. The priority of the parents' relationship with the bride was emphasized by the fact that the lack of affection between the bride and groom was considered irrelevant. Indeed, should affection develop, display of it before other family members was taboo. Hsu reports that newlyweds were expected to occupy the same bed for only seven days, after which they were supposed to occupy separate beds. When a man's parents died, he was expected to show grief that

12. *Ibid.*, p. 286.

was barely short of suicide. If his wife died, he was "expected to show some grief, but never enough to make him forget his filial duties."[13]

Marriage usually brought about the last major change in the man's status. Not so for the woman. For her, there remained the birth of her first son and the retirement of her mother-in-law. The period from marriage to the birth of her first son often was the hardest period in the woman's life. She was removed from her parents to people who had no reason to consider her feelings. As an outsider she had no right to consideration and was dominated not only by the mother-in-law but by all other family members. The parents, her husband, and the husband's siblings all sided against her in the case of disagreement.

About the only relief the young wife had were occasional visits to her parental family. These may have been used consciously to lessen the pressure. If she became pregnant, the pressure might ease somewhat in anticipation of the birth of a son. Her mother also might come to see her through childbirth. The bearing of sons would improve the wife's position; the bearing of daughters might worsen it. In cases of exceptional mistreatment, the wife's parental family might threaten the use of force, with resulting shame to the husband's family.

Occasionally wives were pushed into suicide. Reliable data on suicide rates are not available, but it is believed that, unlike the situation in the West, suicide in traditional China occurred primarily among women between 17 and 35. Actual suicide by harassed wives appears to have been less common than were unsuccessful attempts at it. If the wife were to commit suicide, the husband's family would be shamed for its harsh treatment of her and they would have difficulty in securing another wife for their son. If she attempted suicide but was not successful, the husband's family might be intimidated into according her better treatment.

The wife's status improved as she bore sons, as she became a smoothly functioning member of the family, and as other younger daughters-in-law were added. Strangely, according to Western thinking, there was little tendency for the daughters-in-law to gang up against the mother-in-law. Instead, each wife consolidated her own position at the expense of the newcomer. Each woman prepared for the day when the mother-in-law should die or retire, and she would assume the responsibility for inducting other younger women into the family.

Life for males was less complicated. Marriage and the birth of sons were important, but they were not accompanied by such drastic changes

13. Francis L. K. Hsu, *Under the Ancestor's Shadow*, Garden City, N.Y.: Doubleday, 1967, p. 59.

as were true for women. The man gradually moved into adult work under the increasingly gentle supervision of his father. The fear and respect for the father lessened, and their relationship often developed considerable warmth. Not uncommonly, the father retired or died fairly early in his sons' adulthood, and the eldest son became the patriarch.

Old Age. The last period began at about age 55, considerably before what we usually regard as old age. Longevity was not so great in traditional China, however, and people of 55 probably were at least as "old" as most Americans of 65 today. This was the most secure and comfortable period for both men and women. By this time the man usually was the head of the family, and his wife, rather than being an outsider, was now partner to her husband in maintaining the family intact. Furthermore, age was venerated. Oldsters, as the closest living contacts with ancestors, received deference from younger family members and they had first claim on the family's resources.

The couple made provision for their old age by having sons and now, as grandchildren came along, the grandparents were free to enjoy them as they had never been to enjoy their own children. Gradually, the father turned over responsibility to his sons, who shouldered the burden but maintained deference to the father. By now, father and son usually saw things alike and there was a minimum of friction.

With widowhood, the mother might come out from under male domination for the only time in her life. The official Confucian prescriptions required that she be subordinate to her sons, but actually she often commanded obedience from them, born of long years of affection and respect and because she was a member of an older generation.

Relative Age Roles. Not only absolute age but also relative age was important. Unlike our society where the relationship between brothers is influenced little, if at all, by their relative ages, the Chinese had separate terms for older and younger siblings. Moreover, it was common to use the terms for older brother and younger brother rather than their given names. The term *older brother* was one of great respect, and about the highest honor bestowed upon a friend was to refer to him as "my older brother." Contrast this with the American situation in which one bestows honor on a kinsman by referring to him in non-kinship terms. Americans hold out the idea of father and son becoming "pals."

Younger siblings were expected to defer to older siblings, and the allegiance of brothers to the eldest son was counted upon to keep the family intact and prevent a division of property at the father's death. Normally, older sons and daughters were married before younger siblings, and the wives' status was dependent upon the relative ages of their husbands. Occasionally, when an older sibling married a much younger girl, this resulted in the older woman married to his brothers being subordinated to the younger woman and created confusion and conflict.

The wives of younger brothers had a particularly difficult situation. They were dominated by all other members of the family, and they remained under the mother-in-law's control longest and most directly. The dissatisfactions of these younger women often led them to press their husbands to seek a division of property so that they might become the highest status women in their own households.

Concubinage and Prostitution

The traditional family was monogamous,[14] but it was a different monogamy from that in the United States. Concubinage was fully sanctioned and, among the gentry, was widely practised. Yang reports that the Chinese family was like a balloon, ready to expand whenever there was wealth to inflate it. As soon as there was opportunity to employ the married sons, they would remain in the father's household. Should wealth increase further, concubines and their children would be added.[15]

There are no detailed data on the extent to which concubines were taken. Hsu reports 150 cases in a rural population of 8000.[16] In Lang's sample of 1700 high-school and college students in the 1930s, 11 percent reported a concubine in the home, while the answers of an additional 6 percent hinted that a concubine was there.[17] Levy believes that concubinage was extremely common among the gentry but was not common among the peasantry.[18] Thus the evidence supports Yang's belief that concubines were taken whenever wealth permitted.

Part of the rationale for concubinage lay in the importance attached to sons. Sons were necessary to meet one's obligations to ancestors and

14. Variation from the basic monogamy has been reported. Goode cites the ancient custom of *chien t'iao,* according to which a man might make his nephew his heir while the boy remained his own father's heir also. In ten provinces custom permitted such boys to take two wives, each of whom took charge of the worship of one of the groups of ancestors. Van der Valk also reports that forms of polyandry were found in three different provinces. M. H. Van der Valk, *Conservatism in Modern Chinese Family Law,* Leiden: E. J. Brill, 1956, pp. 45–47, as cited in Goode, *op. cit.,* pp. 279–83.

15. C. K. Yang, *The Chinese Family in the Communist Revolution,* Cambridge, Mass.: Massachusetts Institute of Technology Press, 1959, p. 9.

16. *Under the Ancestor's Shadow,* p. 106.

17. Olga Lang, *Chinese Family and Society,* New Haven: Yale University Press, 1946, p. 221.

18. *Op. cit.,* p. 98.

to ensure one's own future worship as an ancestor. A man without sons might adopt them, but the practice was disapproved of. Men did not like to give up their sons, sons did not like to change surnames, and adopted sons were looked down upon. Occasionally, peasant families permitted their sons to be adopted into gentry families, but the more common solution was for gentry males to take concubines.

If a marriage did not produce sons, the patriarch might demand that his son take a concubine, and even the unfortunate wife might cooperate. Sometimes the wife urged that her own sister be taken so that her position in the family would not be so threatened, and to ease the adjustment to having another woman in the household. Gentry families might wish to aid such an unfortunate daughter, but they did not relish having their other daughters becoming concubines. The concubines generally were secured from peasant families, often being purchased outright.

Concubinage played another role. It offered males relief from their otherwise carefully ordered lives. From boyhood, the male's structurally important relationship with his father was nearly devoid of affection; spontaneity and emotional freedom were sacrificed on the altar of filial piety. When it was time for him to marry, he took the wife selected by his parents and with whom emotional intimacy was not encouraged. His relationships with his own sons—indeed with almost everyone—were structured in terms of responsibility and the subordination of personal needs to family goals. Concubines were likely to be women of his own choosing with whom the relationship was romantic and erotic. Hsu found that in more than half of his cases concubines were taken where the wife had already borne sons.[19]

Large-scale prostitution in traditional China is explained in similar terms. The tea house, to which men repaired to conduct business and to gain relief from their unending obligations, offered drinking, gambling, opium smoking, feminine companionship, and sexual intercourse. Young men who were introduced to these pastimes before marriage often continued them afterward. Yang reports that "merchants as well as government officials transacted much of their business, and traditional scholars wrote some of their best lines of poetry, in whorehouses." He goes on to say that, "a recent well-known Chinese writer who used to entertain his father in houses of prostitution was praised by friends as a filial son who catered to his father's desires."[20]

19. *Under the Ancestor's Shadow*, pp. 105–6.
20. *Op. cit.*, p. 57.

Thus, concubinage and prostitution provided safety valves which drained off emotions that otherwise might have threatened the stability of the family. Neither concubinage nor prostitution was disapproved of on moral grounds. Only when they threatened the stability of the family were they regarded as harmful. A man might be censured for neglecting his wife and children in favor of his concubine, but his right to take concubines was unassailable. Similarly, visits to prostitutes were matters of concern only if family duties were neglected or if the accompanying drinking and gambling threatened to get out of hand.

The incorporation of concubinage into the family system stressed the dominant position of the wife and the priority of her children's rights. There was no ceremony involved in taking a concubine, she had no recognized share in the family income, and she was assigned menial tasks under the wife's supervision. She was not included among her husband's relatives, she was excluded from mourning deceased family members, and she could never, herself, be worshipped as an ancestor. The concubine's children were legitimate, but had limited rights of inheritance unless the wife bore no sons. The fact that the husband often preferred the concubine led to some jealousy between the women and among the women's children.

Patterns of Authority and Affection

The traditional family was organized around the important relationships between father and son, husband and wife, mother-in-law and daughter-in-law, and between brothers. The more important the relationship the less was affection between the parties permitted to influence it.

Affection was almost irrelevant to the father-son relationship, which was based upon respect and fear. These feelings toward the father were quite strong so that an effective, if ambivalent, bond was created. The father had obligations to his sons because of obligations to his ancestors: only if he continued the family traditions through proper indoctrination of the sons could he, himself, expect eventually to join the revered ancestors.

The husband-wife relationship early in marriage was institutionally weak. The wife was an outsider, affection with whom might threaten the family. With time, proper indoctrination by the mother-in-law, and the birth of sons, however, the wife came to have an interest in the family that nearly equalled that of her husband. And, in spite of the fact that the marriage had been arranged, real affection often developed. By the time the wife became a mother-in-law, the marriage was likely to be second in strength only to the father-son relationship.

The mother-in-law–daughter-in-law relationship was strong, but institutionally troublesome. The mother-in-law's power over the bride was nearly absolute. She could require that her son repudiate the marriage and send the girl back to her family. There was no provision for affection between the women, and the girl was likely to hate her mother-in-law. When the Chinese family finally entered a period of rapid change, the accumulated resentments of young married women played a major role in bringing change about.

The relationship between brothers was less strong than that between father and son but was still strong. Younger brothers were expected to defer to their elder brothers and generally did so. The younger brothers did have the right to ask for a division of property, however, and, with urging from their wives, often did so after the father's death. The relationship between brothers and other brothers' wives was also a problem. Despite the taboo on public displays of affection, there was little sex prudery, and the conditions of living closely together encouraged sexual attractions. The relationship between a brother and his brother's wife was one of institutional avoidance, but trouble did occur. Some insight into the problem may be gained from the fact that the only legitimate cause for filial revolt was father–daughter-in-law incest.

Power and responsibility in the family stood generally in inverse relationship. Power was based upon generation, sex, and relative age, and it was vested principally in males of the older generation. The patriarch was virtually all-powerful, males held power over females, and the older held power over the younger. The young had unlimited responsibility toward their elders. The indoctrination of the young was thorough, and, since each person's position in the family improved with age, there was little occasion for revolt against the system.

About the only person free enough to rebel effectively was the patriarch, and he had most to gain from preserving the system. Occasionally, an older male did become so fond of drinking, gambling, and extramarital intercourse that it was feared he would spend the family into ruin. Such dissolution, however, brought down upon the patriarch the contempt of persons outside his immediate family and might result in forcible action being taken against him by elders of the *tsu*.

All in all, the family was a model of stability. The socialization of children and of daughters-in-law into the system appears to have been quite effective. Moreover, with the whole society organized along kinship lines, there literally was no place for a potential rebel to go to escape.

There were strains within the system too. The effects of harsh treatment of sons by their fathers often were not completely overcome even in adulthood. The equal inheritance provisions tended to destroy the economic base upon which the large family depended. Finally, the extreme subordination of women made them potential allies in any agitation for change.

Divorce and Remarriage

There were three kinds of divorce possible in traditional China: divorce by mutual consent; divorce upon the husband's initiative; and divorce under compulsion by the authorities.

Divorce by mutual consent required the consent of the heads of the families, not of the couple themselves, and the very existence of this form of divorce emphasizes the strength of the family. Divorce was regarded as tragic, and if the patriarchs agreed to a divorce, there could be no question that continuation of the marriage would be harmful to the families involved. In this form of divorce it was the welfare of the family that was involved, not that of the couple.

Wives could be divorced by husbands on any one of seven grounds: (1) disobeying the husband's parents; (2) failing to have children; (3) acquiring a loathsome disease; (4) committing adultery; (5) displaying jealousy; (6) being overly talkative; and (7) stealing. In spite of these liberal grounds, however, women were not often repudiated and the divorce rate was low. The poor could not afford divorce and remarriage, and the wealthy did not welcome it. Besides, more acceptable alternatives were available to men. Most of their recreation was outside the home, and feminine companionship and sexual intercourse were readily available. Men also were expected to meet their needs through concubines, rather than by disrupting the marriage relationship.

Divorce was tragic for women. A divorced woman could only be returned to her family; there was no other place for her to go. And her repudiation, early in marriage essentially by the mother-in-law or her later divorce by her husband for cause, brought shame upon her and her family. Other families would not consider her a suitable marriage prospect, she was not entitled to inherit property, and she was denied the opportunity to achieve honor and respect as wife and mother-in-law.

This double standard of morality also applied to the remarriage of widows. Widowed men could remarry without restraint, and gentry males sometimes elevated a concubine to the status of wife upon the death of the first wife. The remarriage of widows was frowned upon, however, and their husbands' families could actually block a remarriage of which they did not approve. Nor could the widow take property with her into a remarriage. The only way a widow could retain a position of honor was to stay as the elderly mother in the home of her sons. The remarriage of gentry widows apparently was rare. Among the peasantry, however, economic conditions forced many remarriages.

THE TRANSITIONAL FAMILY

It is not possible to specify precisely when the Chinese family began to undergo major change. The system never was completely static, of course, and change proceeded slowly throughout the 2000-odd years of apparent stability. Until 1830, however, there was no political, military, or industrial power that could successfully break China's self-imposed isolation from the rest of the world. Marked change followed upon England's successful opening of trade with the Chinese mainland.

With the development of international trade, the Chinese coastal areas began to industrialize and to develop large-scale commercial enterprises. The impact of these developments upon the society and the family was tremendous. The requirements of an industrial economy and the traditional family system were incompatible at many points.

Universalism and Particularism

Traditional China was structured according to highly particularistic criteria. *Particularism* refers to the distribution of opportunities and rewards according to one's membership in a series of social groups rather than according to any special qualifications or abilities which an individual possesses. In traditional China, family membership was all-important. Directly and indirectly, the family controlled the system of rewards and distributed them. Particularly, a person's opportunities for employment—the kind of work he did—was determined largely by his position in a given family. The division of labor was not highly specialized and almost any adult could be trained fairly quickly to fill almost any occupational position. This rudimentary division of labor, with interchangeability of personnel and most persons sharing common skills, is referred to as *functional diffuseness.*

By contrast, the demands of a modern industrial economy are quite different. Such an economy requires the application of universalistic criteria over large areas of life and that there be a high degree of functional specificity. *Universalism* involves the assignment of opportunities on the basis of special training and skills, irrespective of family and other relationships. *Functional specificity* involves a specialized division of labor in which personnel are not readily transferable from one job to another.[21]

As China began to modernize, the particularistic requirements of the family system ran head on into the increasingly universalistic requirements of the occupational system. The traditional norms demanded that contacts with outsiders be minimized, specified that contractual relations with outsiders were not especially binding, and encouraged widespread nepotism. The term *nepotism* refers to the practice of giving employment to kinsmen regardless of ability, and was literally an obligation upon the gentry family. Western experience has indicated that factories and businesses languish when nepotism flourishes. As China industrialized, the men who ran her developing industries were faced with a dilemma. If they acted in terms of traditional norms, their businesses suffered; if they used universalistic criteria to determine employment, they violated sacred obligations and their families suffered. In the long run, it was the family which yielded to the demands of industrialization.

The Influence of Western Ideals

Trade not only encouraged industrialization; it also brought extensive contact with Western ideals that subverted the traditional order. The Western concept of treating women as near-equals with men, and as full companions, was revolutionary. The concept of individualism which elevates the well-being of individuals to superiority over the welfare of the family was equally striking. Although Western religion did not make great impact, its emphasis upon the sacredness of the individual had far-reaching repercussions. Finally, the idea of political freedom—of individuals exercising collective control over the conditions of their existence—formed part of the base for a new social order.

An Alternative Way of Life

The combination of industrialization and ideals of political freedom, individualism, and social equality provided what no influences on Chinese

21. See Talcott Parsons, *The Social System,* Glencoe, Illinois: The Free Press, 1951, pp. 61–63, 65–66, and *passim.*

life had done for 2000 years—the prospect of an alternative way of living. With the growth of cities and factory employment, single persons, married couples, and nuclear families could live apart from their extended families permanently. The separation of the kinship and occupational structures led to a weakening of parental authority; income and status came to depend more upon one's place in the occupational system than upon family ties; industrialization provided new sources of wealth greater than those of the old agricultural system; and people began to think of their individual interests as taking priority over extended family obligations.

No one set of influences brought about these changes. Nor is it possible to assign priority to one of them. It was a combination of industrialization with its application of universalistic criteria to an ever-widening sphere, ideals of individualism, equality, and freedom, and the possibility of an alternative way of life which produced the transitional family.

Emerging Patterns

The family structure of traditional China was an integrated, stable entity. Not so with the transitional family, for it is not clear that a new, stable form has yet emerged.[22] Change has been under way for over a century and has been complicated recently by the family policies of the communist government. How much effect and what kind of effect such policies will have is a matter of debate. What can be done here is to indicate the direction in which the family has been moving and to indicate possible future developments.

Changing Status of Women. For the first time, women and children have become potential sources of additional income. Legally, today, Chinese women have full inheritance rights with men. That Chinese women often do not yet get their full legal rights only underscores the radical nature of the transformation.[23]

In childhood, less segregation of the sexes occurs and both boys and girls come more under the influence of their mothers. Formal education has been extended to almost the entire society and tends to be coeduca-

22. The changes in Chinese family patterns are most typical of and may, in many cases, be confined to urban and coastal areas which have undergone industrialization. The vastness of China, the numerous dialects, and the limited ability of the government to impose policies in the hinterland probably leave hundreds of millions still living according to traditional ways.

23. Lawrence K. Hong, "The Role of Women in the People's Republic of China: Legacy and Change," *Social Problems* 23 (June 1976), pp. 545–57.

> Peking has frequently declared that Chinese women were "liberated" with the Communist takeover, but recent reports indicate that equality has yet to be achieved.
>
> Women have difficulty in becoming senior officials, in obtaining the same pay as men and even in being employed as factory workers, according to articles in the Chinese press. . . .
>
> . . . When the present Central Committee was elected . . . its 170 full members included only 13 women.
>
> At a women's congress . . . to elect a municipal committee, delegates were urged to struggle against the old ideas of "respecting men and despising women and regarding women as slaves and vassals."
>
> "It is essential to oppose the idea of male superiority and to promote equality of the sexes and have housework done by both men and women, each supporting the other and advancing together," a report broadcast by the Provincial Radio Service stated. . . .
>
> *The New York Times*, May 28, 1973

tional. There is less need to marry girls young, and their average age at marriage has been rising. The mother-in-law–daughter-in-law relationship remains difficult but, with the increasing separation of the nuclear family from the extended family, is becoming less so. Chinese women have not yet gained the near-equality of Western women, but the official ideologies are pushing them in that direction.

Development of a Youth Culture. For 2000 years, Chinese culture venerated age and assigned inferior status to youth. That situation has been changing rapidly and may now be reversed.

Chinese youth and young adults have been cut loose in a drastic sense. As they became involved in industry, they were forced, for the first time, to make decisions on their own. This produced an individualism by default, if not by design. The communist movement in China is largely a youth movement which, because it is articulate, assumes importance beyond the number of people involved.

The freeing of youth from notions of family responsibility has produced a problem in relation to the aged. The old norms called for support of one's own parents but carried no responsibility for the aged in general. Now the number of aged persons is increasing and many are in danger of being left without financial support. The government is thus faced with a dilemma. It wishes to substitute allegiance to the government for allegiance to the family, but its success in destroying the sense of family obligation increases the problem of support for the aged.

Development of Romantic Love. With urban living, freer association between the sexes emerged and romantic love is threatening to replace parental arrangement as the basis for marriage. High-school and college students mingle freely, and the attractions of specific boys and girls to one another demand consideration.[24] There are three forms of deviation from the old pattern of arranged marriage: (1) parents arrange the marriage but ask their children's consent; (2) young people select their own mates but ask their parents' approval; and (3) the young people marry without asking parental consent.[25]

A drastic change which is an accompaniment of romantic love is the appearance of groups of unmarried men and women in the cities. Under traditional norms, the unmarried state for adults was regarded almost as perverted and there were no satisfactory social arrangements for single persons. Now, however, with the emergence of apartment living, hotels, restaurants, laundries, and the like, the old definitions of the single state are breaking down.

Increased Rates of Divorce, Suicide, and Illegitimacy. While trustworthy figures are not available, divorce rates have been increasing. Under the traditional system, divorce rates were low and divorce often involved repudiation of the wife by the husband's family. Revisions of the marriage laws have sought to equalize divorce rights of husbands and wives, and most divorces now result from mutual consent or from insistence by either party. One clue to the increase in divorce is found in recent educational campaigns by the government aimed at lowering divorce rates.

Levy reports that suicide rates apparently have been increasing also.[26] Moreover, the pattern has been changing. Whereas suicide was predominantly an alternative for young women under the traditional system, it is more often found now among middle-aged and older persons. Levy attributes the change to the responsibilities placed upon middle-aged people by urban living and to the difficult position of aged parents.

Illegitimacy, in the Western sense, is almost a new problem in China. Lack of free association between the sexes and marriage at early ages,

24. Lucy J. Huang, "Mate Selection and Marital Happiness in the Mainland Chinese Family," *International Journal of Sociology of the Family* 2 (Sept. 1972), pp. 121–38.

25. For an analysis of kinship structure on contemporary Taiwan, see Solomon S. Chu, "Some Aspects of Extended Kinship in a Chinese Community," *Journal of Marriage and the Family* 36 (Aug. 1974), pp. 628–33. See also Fai-Ming Wong, "Industrialization and Family Structure in Hong Kong," *Journal of Marriage and the Family* 37 (Nov. 1975), pp. 985–1000.

26. *Op. cit.*, p. 337.

especially for girls, kept illegitimacy rates low during the traditional period. Too, the extramarital wanderings of males were institutionalized in the custom of concubinage. Now it is increasingly difficult for a man to maintain a concubine either within his household or outside it. China never had puritanical attitudes toward sex and when young people are free to associate intimately, sexual intercourse often occurs. The government is now urging a puritanical morality in an effort to reduce illegitimacy rates.

THE INFLUENCE OF THE CHINESE COMMUNIST GOVERNMENT

The policies and programs of the government of the People's Republic of China are of importance to the entire world. The government's policy is formulated in reaction to the traditional family system as well as in accordance with political, economic, and military goals.

The basic stance of the government is exemplified by the Marriage Law which became effective in May 1950, less than eight months after the establishment of the new government. The new law, which actually is a code for the regulation of many aspects of family life, establishes the following principles: (1) monogamy without concubinage; (2) free choice of spouse; (3) equal inheritance rights for both sexes; (4) protection of children's rights; and (5) divorce by mutual consent or upon insistence by either spouse. It is a complete departure from the traditional system. Noteworthy in the law are provisions for protection of the rights of women and children. Women are given full legal rights; and it has become high fashion for a married woman to retain her own family name. Children born out of wedlock have equal rights with legitimate offspring.

The government has made a determined effort to eliminate prostitution and points with pride to the disappearance of female infanticide. It has sponsored a birth-control program designed to slow population growth and to raise the level of living. Factories turn out contraceptives and birth-control clinics are in operation.

Much public attention has been given to the reported efforts of the communist government to eliminate the family as a threat to its own hold over the populace. The Marriage Law of 1950 is not consistent with such a position but seems instead to embody the highest ideals of Western societies. Where the government has attacked the family system is in all of those areas formerly controlled by the *tsu*.[27] The government's substitute for the *tsu* is the commune.

The new government required years to consolidate its hold over major areas of China and it broke up *tsu* land holdings wherever possible and redistributed them among the peasants. It then followed land reform by organizing agricultural cooperatives designed to rationalize farm production. The government regulated production of major crops, leaving each farmer free to raise his own garden crops. By the middle of 1955, there were more than 600,000 cooperatives involving 14 percent of the farm population and by the end of 1956, almost all peasant families were members of collectives. These cooperatives were not too satisfactory. Their management was not too competent and farm production failed to meet expectations.

The cooperatives were replaced by communes. The first show-place commune was established in April 1958, and by November of that year, 99 percent of the rural population had been grouped into communes of about 5000 households each. In August 1958, 173 urban communes were formed in Honan and by 1960 urban communes were being organized on a grand scale. Up to 20 million people are said to have been involved.

The new communes were bigger than the old collectives and involved the collectivization of much more of daily living. In addition to agricultural production, they were to have charge of such tasks as banking and the building of dams and steel mills. Common dining rooms were provided, nurseries were established for the care of children, and women were expected to play a full role in the occupational system. Universal primary education was offered to children, inexpensive weddings and funerals were provided, and homes for the aged were established.

Western attitudes toward these communes were quite negative. The communes were widely interpreted as an attack on the family—as an attempt to eliminate the family, as we know it, from Chinese society. Actually, it appears that nothing so drastic was intended. Many Westerners also predicted that the communes were bound to fail; an oversimplified prediction to say the least.

In sober retrospect, the communes appear to have been designed to replace the network of authority and loyalty which was part of the extended family system and the clan organization but not to replace the family itself. The communists complain that the old system was corrupt and that it led to the degradation of all but the gentry families who held power. They point to the fact that the allegedly universalistic examina-

27. See Janet W. Salaff, "The Emerging Conjugal Relationship in the People's Republic of China," *Journal of Marriage and the Family* 35 (Nov. 1973), pp. 705–17.

tion system was actually under the control of the gentry; they point to the rampant nepotism which kept positions of wealth, power, and prestige within the gentry; they point to infanticide, prostitution, and sale of women as degrading. And they present themselves as representing the interests of all of the people against the tyranny of the traditional family system. They have sought to free women and children from that tyranny and to redistribute wealth in the society.

That the communists encountered serious problems also is certain. Chandrasekhar reports that the People's Government estimates that between 3 million and 20 million bandits, landlords, warlords, reactionaries, counter-revolutionaries, and other "enemies of the people" were "liquidated."[28] Some of the communes were badly run, and there was public dissatisfaction with them. There were also problems of providing care for the aged, and upsurges in divorce and illegitimacy caused the government to retreat from its ideal of completely independent womanhood and to support once again the doctrine of filial piety.

China underwent political and economic upheaval during the latter 1960s, referred to as the Cultural Revolution, and confirmed anticommunists in the West were quick to conclude that the collective system was on the point of collapse. By the early 1970s, however, the Cultural Revolution was over, the government was in firm control of the country, and the system showed considerable strength.

Western economists, taking advantage of the new freer access to China, estimate that industrial production, in spite of many ups and downs, has increased at an average of 10 percent per year since 1949. Visitors to China report that the worst poverty, long the condition of the peasantry, has largely been eliminated. Living standards for the gentry have been leveled downward in the process.[29]

The communes still are conspicuous features, but they are not so radical as they appear to be in the Western press. The central units of production are small teams (some 4 million) of the sort established in the old collectives. Individual incomes vary according to work points earned, and families still have private plots which they cultivate more carefully than they do the collectively held land. Western economists estimate that agricultural production is now increasing faster than China's population is growing.

It is too early to say that the transformation of the Chinese family

28. Sripati Chandrasekhar, *China's Population: Census and Vital Statistics*, London: Oxford University Press, 1960, p. 61.

29. A. Doak Barnett, "More Thoughts Out of China," *The New York Times Magazine*, April 8, 1973, pp. 36–37, 100–106.

system is complete. The communist government has now been in power for more than 25 years, however, and it continues to urge the family in the same general direction as it is moving in the West.

SUMMARY

Study of the Chinese family has both theoretical and practical implications. First, it serves as a model of an extended, patriarchal, patrilineal system. Second, after 2000 years of relative stability, it is now undergoing rapid change. Finally, China is the most populous nation in the world and poses a grave political, economic, and military threat to the West.

To understand the Chinese family, one must distinguish between the gentry, whose customs and ideals were universally admired and widely imitated, and the vast peasantry, who lived close to the minimum subsistence level and for whom little elaboration of social patterns was possible.

The traditional family was patriarchal, patrilineal, patrilocal, and monogamous. Ideally, it involved six generations and went nine generations without a division of property. Actually, few families contained more than three or four generations and the modal family may have been the stem family. Ancestor worship and the doctrine of filial piety probably kept the family from changing to a simple conjugal system.

The *tsu*, or clan, was composed of all persons of a given surname tracing descent from a common ancestor. The *tsu* served as a buffer between the extended family and the larger society and performed educational, welfare, religious, and judicial functions.

Traditional Chinese society was rigidly structured according to age and sex. Old age was highly esteemed and males dominated females. Role prescriptions for each family member were laid down in detail.

Gentry boys and girls were segregated early in childhood. Boys were remanded to the strict discipline of fathers and tutors while girls were affectionately indulged by both parents. As they grew in responsibility, boys' lots improved while girls could look forward only to harsh treatment at the hands of their husbands' families.

Marriages were arranged by parents. The man's status changed little at marriage, but the bride began a period of servitude to the husband's family, the function of which was to properly socialize her into her new family. The mother-in-law treated the girl harshly, and the resulting antagonisms between them were a source of strain in the family.

The husband continued to grow in responsibility and personal freedom; the wife's status improved as she bore sons. As they moved into old age the relationship between them became quite strong and they received complete deference from their children.

Escape from the order and responsibility of every day life was provided for males through concubinage and through widespread commercial prostitution. Since concubines usually were chosen by the men involved, there often was rivalry between the concubine and her children and the wife and her children. Concubines sometimes were elevated to the status of wife, and the children of concubines were legitimate.

Divorce was uncommon during the traditional period and was regarded as undesirable. Divorce might occur with the mutual consent of the families involved, or the husband might divorce his wife on any one of seven specified grounds. Remarriage was common among men but very difficult for women. Similarly, widowers generally remarried but the remarriage of widows was strongly disapproved of.

Extensive changes began early in the 1880s. As China began to industrialize, the particularistic and functionally diffuse family system came into conflict with the universalistic and functionally specific requirements of the occupational system. Western ideals of individualism, equality, and political freedom helped to subvert the traditional system. The transition finally was made possible by the development of urban institutions, which made an alternative way of life possible.

The character of the transitional family is not fully established. There is an unmistakable trend toward the conjugal form based upon romantic love and with more equality between the sexes. Divorce and illegitimacy rates have risen. With the rebellion of youth against the traditional system, care of the aged has become a problem.

The government which came into power in 1949 has supported these changes and has attacked the traditional system as feudalistic. It has virtually eliminated female infanticide, has outlawed concubinage, and is attempting to stamp out prostitution. It has sponsored birth-control programs, and it demands full equality for women and protection of the rights of children.

The most controversial of the communist innovations are the communes, which were established on a large scale between 1958 and 1960. Westerners often interpret the communes as an attempt to destroy the family. In reality, the communes are intended as a substitute for the *tsu* and for the extended family, but not for the conjugal unit upon which the government already depends. At this writing, the communes appear to have become firmly entrenched in the Chinese social order.

SUGGESTED READINGS

Cohen, Myron L., *House United, House Divided: The Chinese Family in Taiwan*, New York: Columbia University Press, 1976. A carefully drawn portrait of the modernizing of the traditional family. Based upon extensive field work in a farming village.

Curtin, Katie, *Women in China*, New York: Pathfinder Press, 1975. A brief analysis, by a socialist and feminist, of the changes that have taken place in the status of women since the Chinese Cultural Revolution.

Eberhard, Wolfram, *The Upperclass Family in Traditional China*, in Charles E. Rosenberg, *ed.*, *The Family in History*, Philadelphia: University of Pennsylvania Press, 1975, pp. 59–94. A comprehensive analysis covering the whole 2000 years of traditional family patterns.

Meijer, M. J., *Marriage Law and Policy: In the Chinese People's Republic*, Hong Kong: Hong Kong University Press, 1971. A lawyer and sinologist shows how the marriage law of 1950 has been used to destroy the old feudal institutions and to build a new political morality.

Sidel, Ruth, *Families of Fengsheng: Urban Life in China*, Baltimore: Penguin, 1974. Details the extensive community organization in a Peking neighborhood to provide social services for all.

FILMS

Born Chinese: A Study of the Chinese Character (Time-Life Films, 43 West 16th Street, New York, N.Y. 10011), 57 minutes. Shows the daily life of the Lung family, Hong Kong refugees from Red China. The camera studies their daily routine and analyzes the motives behind their behavior. No Westerners are seen.

China: A Hole in the Bamboo Curtain (Association Films, 833 Third Avenue, New York, N.Y. 10022), 28 minutes, color. A documentary odyssey ranging from Shenyang to Peking, Shanghai, and Canton, showing lifestyles, children in school, and people's thoughts of the present and future.

Introduction to Confucius (Greenwood Press, 51 Riverside Avenue, Westport, Conn. 06880), 12 minutes, color. The main tenets of Confucian thought are clearly presented. Photographed in The Republic of China.

QUESTIONS AND PROJECTS

1. Distinguish between the gentry and the peasantry. Why were the gentry patterns so important in traditional China?
2. Describe the "ideal" gentry family, using the concepts of family structure presented in Chapter 2. How did the "real" gentry patterns differ from the ideal? How did the peasantry patterns differ from the gentry patterns?
3. Explain the inheritance patterns in the traditional family. How was "ceremonial primogeniture" important? How was the division of property provided for? How often did it occur?
4. What was the *tsu* and what was its relationship to the extended family? What specific functions did the *tsu* perform?
5. Describe the infancy and childhood periods in the lives of gentry boys and girls. In what way did the relationship between boys and their fathers become a source of strain in the family?
6. Who were the interested parties in arranging a marriage? What was the essence of the marriage ceremony?
7. Describe the relationship between mother-in-law and daughter-in-law. How do you account for the harsh treatment accorded the daughter-in-law?
8. What was the significance of relative age in the traditional family?
9. What functions were served by concubinage? How was the stability of the family linked to extramarital sexual activity on the part of males?
10. What regulations governed divorce in the traditional family? Explain how the practice of divorce by mutual consent actually reflected the strength of the family. How common was divorce in traditional China?
11. What forces finally led to disruption of the traditional family system? Assess the roles of industrialization, ideals of individualism and equality, and the possibility of an alternative way of life.
12. Describe, as completely and accurately as you can, the family system of transitional China.
13. What has been the influence of the People's Republic of China upon the family? Describe how communes are consistent with the government's family policy. What is likely to be the future of the family in China?

5

Utopian Experiments and Alternative Life Styles

> Wanted: Congenial male roommate to share 3-bedroom, 2-½ bth town house with divorcee and 2 children. You get master bdrm., bath and privacy. Dlrs. 150 a month includes util. . . Refs. required.

Donna Valentine, 28, lives with her nine-year-old daughter and four-year-old son. . . . Her income from child support and her job as a sales coordinator . . . totals less than $500 a month. The town house rents for $300 and she needs someone to share the expense. "I just think this is the logical thing," said Donna about advertising for a male roommate. "Most of the women I know are dependent, jealous, and competitive." "I just prefer to have a man around."

In San Francisco, Jim Cole, 27, a divorced project engineer, interviewed both male and female prospective roommates before selecting Lori Rock, 21. "In the past, men roommates have stepped on my toes," he explained. "The male-female arrangement blends and overlaps. I don't want an involvement, and the primary advantage is the sharing of expenses." . . .[1]

Attempts, large and small, to find better ways of living have been going on for a long time. They have ranged from small communities to whole nations. Recently, in the United States, they have emphasized fairly individualistic searches for alternatives to nuclear family living. Most

1. From *Time,* The Weekly Newsmagazine, April 4, 1975, p. 46; copyright Time, Inc., 1975. Reprinted by permission.

such attempts to create utopian ways of living have been fairly short-lived. The quotation above reflects attempts to preserve some of the advantages of conventional family living in an unconventional context.

Analysis of a representative sample of efforts to do away with the family would require more space than we have available. What we will do is consider the Oneida experiment in nineteenth-century America, the Russian experiment after World War I, and the kibbutzim in Israel as background for assessment of proposals for alternative life styles on the contemporary scene.

THE ONEIDA COMMUNITY

The story of the Oneida Community is inextricably linked with the personality and religious beliefs of John Humphrey Noyes.[2] Noyes graduated from Dartmouth and began the practice of law. He underwent religious conversion at a revival meeting, gave up law, and entered the seminary, where the zealousness that was to characterize his later years became evident. He decided that the doctrine of repentance for sinning was wrong and that people should strive, instead, to live a perfect life here on earth. Noyes narrowly escaped being expelled from the seminary, and soon after he began to preach, his license was revoked.

Noyes continued to preach his doctrine of *perfectionism.* Gradually he gathered a group of believers at his home in Putney, Vermont, and this group became, in 1846, the Putney Community—a group who lived together in the first stages of what came to be called *complex marriage.*

The detailed origins of complex marriage may never be known. It was part of a larger "Bible communism" that involved a sharing of wealth, the elimination of private property, and the principle that every adult male should have sexual privileges with every adult female and vice versa. The Putney Community started when Noyes arranged for his two sisters to marry two men in the group. The actual sexual communism began later, when Noyes became attracted to one of the other women who had joined the group. He began to have sex relations with her after he first consulted with his wife and with the woman's husband.

Noyes was a complicated man. His charismatic leadership made men loyal to him and attracted women, sexually and otherwise. He fathered at least eleven children by various women. At the same time, Noyes was

2. Constance Noyes Robertson, ed., *Oneida Community: An Autobiography, 1851–1876,* Syracuse: Syracuse University Press, 1970.

a deeply religious man who genuinely eschewed lust and personal selfishness. Such men usually are not easily tolerated by those around them, and, in 1848, Noyes and his little band were driven out of Putney.

The group re-established itself in central New York State on the Oneida Creek, where it existed for approximately thirty years. The group grew to about 300 people and, after a difficult start, prospered financially. Unlike most utopian American communities which emphasized farming, Oneida developed a sizable industrial base. One of the members invented a steel trap which was widely used, and shortly before the community broke up they embarked upon the manufacture of silverware. The silverware business was profitable and continued after the break-up of the community as the well-known Oneida, Limited.

Complex Marriage

According to the principle of complex marriage, all men should love all women and all women should love all men. Romantic love and monogamy were seen as both cause and effect of selfishness and jealousy, selfishness and jealousy being barriers to leading the perfect life.

Consistent with these beliefs, the Oneidans practised group marriage in which a man had the right to seek sexual relations with any woman. Women were free either to accept or reject a specific proposal. If a man wished to initiate a relationship he was supposed to convey his request to the woman through a Central Committee. An older woman member of the Committee relayed the proposal to the woman, making it easy for her to respond either way without embarrassment. Women seldom refused. The man then appeared at the woman's room at bedtime and retired to his own room again before going to sleep. Such an elaborate procedure may have been used only when a new relationship was begun and probably, after the first visit, matters were more informally handled by the couples involved.

The absence of any right to demand sex is said to have resulted in Oneida men and women remaining more attentive to one another than is usually true in conventional situations. For couples to develop romantic attachments, however, was regarded as unseemly and sanctions occasionally were applied; the couple might be chided and one member of the couple might be sent out of the community for a time.

The Oneidans distinguished between the right to sex and the right to reproduction. The community agreed that during the first twenty years there should be no child-bearing. After the community was firmly established and child-care facilities provided, a committee was appointed to determine which men and women should reproduce. Although modern eugenics did not yet exist, Noyes had been influenced by Galton and Darwin and called his planned parenthood program *stirpiculture.*

Eventually some 53 women and 38 men were selected to become parents and 58 children were born. For the most part, the parents were the authorized ones but a few unauthorized women were highly desirous of having children and managed to become pregnant.

The birth-control technique used by the Oneidans casts light on their concept of appropriate sex relationships. They practised coitus reservatus, in which intercourse is continued without the male reaching ejaculation. This technique has been used in various areas of the world, particularly India. It calls for a high degree of control on the part of the man, however—enough so that there is doubt of its feasibility for whole populations. Moreover, it alters the character of the sex relationship; replacing the explosive sexual climax with a suffuse lower-key pleasure. The combination of free sexual access with intentional toning down of the erotic seems consistent with the deeply religious nature of the Oneida Community.

Associated with this concept of sex was the "principle of ascendance" according to which men learned the techniques of control by having their early sex experiences only with older, experienced women—often those beyond menopause who could not become pregnant. Similarly, young women were taught the intricacies of sex by older men who were "properly spiritual" and would not be carried away.

Apparently, the birth-control technique was effective. There was, however, grumbling on the part of younger men and this may have been one of the factors leading to the breakup. It may have been responsible, also, for John Humphrey Noyes's leaving and going to Canada, where he died. There are unsubstantiated rumors that some of the younger women were under "the age of consent" and that Noyes believed that he might be prosecuted for statutory rape.

Complex marriage also removed the child-rearing function rather completely from the parents. When children attained the age of 15 months, they were removed from the care of their mothers and housed in the children's wing of the great mansion house which, by that time, had been built. The children had a visiting period with their mothers once each day. All adults were supposed to love all children and all children to love all adults, and so the relationship to children was not impersonal or distant.

Students of the Oneida Community have placed emphasis on the structure of the mansion house in determining the social patterns within the group. While each adult had his or her room and while there was a separate wing for the children, there were common dining, recreation, and living areas. The seeking of privacy was discouraged and communal living was expected. Life in the mansion was pleasant and there was a high degree of sharing of interests and activities.

The Oneidans' communistic practices extended through the economic sphere, were buttressed by an ascetic morality, and were accompanied by a lively interest in the arts. Private property was done away with. Property was jointly held, and even clothing and personal effects were furnished from a central supply. Sexual attractiveness was not emphasized. The women wore their hair short and wore knee-length dresses over loose-fitting trousers that extended to the feet. Even the children held their toys in common. There was one brief period when small children were provided with their own dolls, but this encouraged personal selfishness and the privately owned dolls were ritually destroyed.

Effort was made to reinforce the inherent dignity of all work, and status distinctions among different tasks were played down. Whenever possible, people were rotated from one job to another so that permanent status distinctions would not appear. Yet the Oneidans managed their enterprises well, and the community prospered.

Another paradox appeared in that dancing and card playing, which were defined as healthy social activities, were encouraged while alleged personal vices such as smoking, drinking coffee, and the use of alcohol were prohibited. The community also sponsored musical and other cultural programs which outsiders from the surrounding areas were permitted to attend. Except for these occasions, contact between members of the community and outsiders were kept to a minimum.

The Breakup of the Community

Even as the community prospered, its radical ways led to pressures, from within and without, that proved to be its undoing. What priority should be assigned to the various factors cannot be said for sure. But by 1880, barely thirty years after its beginning, the community had broken up.

As nearly as can be determined, most individual members of the community were well thought of by outsiders. They had the reputation of being sober, hard-working, religious people who bothered no one. But complex marriage was too radical for surrounding communities. Rumors grew of sexual orgies, "free love," and the breeding of human beings "like cattle." Older men having sex relationships with young girls not only outraged public morality but also appeared to be in violation of the laws against statutory rape. The pressure grew greater until, by 1879, the community was forced to give up complex marriage and return to official monogamy.

Some of the pressure came from within the community, which was not entirely successful in indoctrinating its young people with their parents' values. Some of the children were sensitive to the taunts of outsiders, who referred to them as "bastards" and "Christ boys." To their parents' dismay, some of the younger people also assumed the romantic and monogamous attitudes of outsiders.

The fate of the community also was linked to the leadership of John Humphrey Noyes. Like many charismatic leaders, he gave unstintingly of himself for the community's welfare but he failed to provide adequately for his own succession. Power in the community was vested in its elders, with the balance of power often being held by Noyes. The younger generation was not trained to leadership and became a divisive force within the community. In 1877, John Humphrey Noyes resigned as leader and was replaced by one of his sons. In 1879, Noyes left for Canada and soon afterward the community dissolved.

Of the many utopian experiments within the United States, Oneida was the most successful. For thirty years and among some 300 people the family virtually ceased to exist. It is significant, however, that the experiment did not last through the raising of éven one generation.

THE SOVIET FAMILY EXPERIMENT

In turning to the great family experiment in the Soviet Union, we jump from an isolated experiment among 300 people to analysis of a system with some 200 million people and which was composed of several ethnic groups and as many as 175 separate nationalities.

The major cultural division in prerevolutionary Russia was between the Slavs who were concentrated in European Russia and the non-Slavic peoples located in the Caucasus, central Asia, the Steppes, and Siberia.

The Slavs composed four-fifths of the population and had a family pattern which loosely associated the conjugal family with a larger bilateral kindred. This stood in contrast to the Kayakh family which was a patrilineal, extended family attached to a larger clan group and governed by Moslem law. The situation was further complicated by differences between the urban minority (about 30 percent of the population) and the vast peasant masses in the hinterlands.

The dominant, bilateral, conjugal family was large by modern standards, tending toward an extended family system. Particularly among the wealthier segments, there was strict patriarchal control associated with the ownership of large tracts of land. The power of these elite families traced directly from the Czar and was supported by the powerful Eastern Orthodox Church. It was against the concentration of power in these three places that the Bolshevik Revolution of 1917 was directed.

Early Soviet Policy

The new Soviet regime, in its second month, issued decrees regulating marriage and divorce. One decree replaced religious marriage with civil marriage, and another made divorce available at the request of one or both parties. In 1918, a comprehensive code supplemented these decrees with the stipulation that, "birth itself shall be the basis of the family. No differentiation whatsoever shall be made between relationships by birth, whether in or out of wedlock."[3] The code provided, further, that neither parents nor children should have rights to one another's property, and that their obligations to support one another should be conditioned upon "destitution and the inability to work." Thus, the Soviet regime adopted policies which attacked the foundations of the family: the church was forbidden to solemnize marriages; divorce was made easy; penalties attached to illegitimacy were removed; the legal obligations of parents and children to one another were minimized; and the family inheritance of property was attacked.

The most radical policies, however, were still to come. In 1926, the Code on Domestic Relations was enacted by the largest Soviet state and was soon adopted by the other Soviet republics. The new code did not require registration of marriages and declared only that registration offered the best proof that a marriage existed. The courts also recognized

3. Vladimir Gsovski, "Family and Inheritance in Soviet Law," in Alex Inkeles and Kent Geiger, *eds., Soviet Society: A Book of Readings,* Boston: Houghton Mifflin, 1961, p. 531.

marriages where there was "the fact of cohabitation, combined with a common household, evidence of marital relations before third parties or in personal correspondence and other documents, mutual financial support, the raising of children in common if supported by circumstantial evidence, and the like."[4] In brief, none of the rights and obligations of spouses, parents, or children were to depend upon whether a marriage had been registered.

The code of 1926 was equally drastic in its provision for divorce. The couple jointly, or either spouse could request divorce without giving any reasons. There was no trial or other judicial procedure. Divorces simply were registered, as marriages were registered. If the divorce was registered by one party only, the other party was notified to appear at the Registry, not to contest the dissolution but to acknowledge it. If he failed to appear, he was notified of the divorce by mail.

Laws relating to sex were conspicuous, early in the regime, by their absence. One of the few laws legalized abortion in 1920. Other laws dropped adultery, bigamy, and incest as punishable offenses. The prevailing attitude was that there should be no barriers to free sex relationships; no reactionary bourgeois morality. Contraceptive devices were made readily available, and all stigma was removed from illegitimacy.

The conclusion is inescapable that the Soviets sought to destroy the family. Perhaps the most explicit Bolshevik spokesman on marriage and the family was Friedrich Engels, who wrote that "the modern monogamous family is founded on the open or disguised domestic slavery of women."[5] Engels equated marriage with prostitution and foresaw the demise of the family in the socialist state.

The Effects of the Soviet Policies

It did not take long for the effects of the new policies to appear. The traditional family system was greatly altered and the family itself was weakened. Some of the changes were consistent with socialist ideology and were approved by the government; some unanticipated consequences, however, eventually forced reversal of the earlier policies.

The Emancipation of Women. The Soviet leaders sought complete equality between men and women. "Bourgeois marriage" involved the subjugation of women and was forbidden by socialist morality. More-

4. *Ibid.*, p. 532.
5. Friedrich Engels, *The Origin of the Family, Private Property, and the State,* Chicago: Charles H. Kerr and Company, 1902, p. 89.

over, if women could be induced to rebel against marriage, the threat to the new regime posed by the family would be removed. Too, the Soviet Union needed workers. If all women worked outside the home, the work force would be doubled and industrialization would proceed faster.

The marriage laws removed the legal disabilities attaching to woman's status. At marriage, she was permitted to adopt the husband's surname, or he could take her surname, or they were permitted to retain their own surnames. Their place of residence had to be fixed by mutual consent. If the husband moved to another location, the wife was under no obligation to follow him. Neither the husband nor the wife was liable for the other's support unless one of them was incapacitated; then the other partner was liable, irrespective of sex. The husband and wife were equally liable for their children and they had equal rights of divorce.

Discrimination in employment was prohibited, and women streamed into factories. They performed manual labor, worked at clerical tasks and, as their educational levels increased, moved into the professions. By 1935, two-thirds of all able-bodied women of working age were employed, compared with about two-fifths in the United States. By 1940, the percentage of all workers who were women was 38 percent in the Soviet Union, compared with 31 percent in Germany and only 24 percent in the United States. By that time, 75 percent of the medical students, 50 percent of the education students, and 23 percent of the engineering students in Russia were women. The peak was reached during World War II when 53 percent of all workers were women. Since then, the proportion has stabilized at just under 50 percent.[6]

The new regime was successful in raising the status of women. The status of women, relative to men, may be higher in the Soviet Union today than anywhere else in the Western world. Some writers point out that this literal equality may mean a heavier burden on women, since they must carry most of the reproductive burden along with the work function.[7]

Rise in the Divorce Rate. The unavailability of systematic data makes it impossible to specify the rise in the divorce rate precisely, but the increase was enough to alarm the Soviet leadership. Accounts were published of marriages contracted only for convenience—for example, to

6. H. Kent Geiger, *The Family in Soviet Russia,* Cambridge, Mass.: Harvard University Press, 1968, p. 178.

7. See Michael P. Sacks, "Unchanging Times: A Comparison of the Everyday Life of Soviet Working Men and Women Between 1923 and 1966," *Journal of Marriage and the Family* 39 (Nov. 1977), pp. 793–805.

qualify for rooms and apartments in the crowded cities—and immediately followed by divorce. A widely circulated story concerned a maiden schoolteacher unable to find a husband who offered a sizable sum to a woman friend if she would locate a husband for her. The scheming friend, already married, arranged for her own husband to divorce her and marry the schoolteacher. As soon as she received the money, the husband was then supposed to divorce the schoolteacher. In attacking such practices, the Soviet press gleefully pointed out that the husband decided that he preferred the schoolteacher and remained married to her.

It was reported in *Izvestia* that the divorce rate in Moscow in 1934 was 37 divorces per 100 marriages, and that in 1935 the rate climbed to 38.3. These figures are believed to be about 50 percent higher than those during the latter part of the Czarist period. The regime became concerned about the divorce rate, both as a symptom of the decay of socialist morality and as a contributor to the falling birth rate.

Fall in the Birth Rate. The precipitous fall in the birth rate was a function of legalized abortion and the rising divorce rate. Some 154,000 abortions were performed in Moscow in 1934 while only 57,000 children were actually born in the city. In 1935, there were 155,000 abortions to 70,000 live births. About 60 percent of the abortions were done for "social" rather than medical reasons. The alarmed government restricted abortion again in 1936, and the Moscow birth rate for the first half of 1937 doubled over that for the preceding year.

Rise of Hooliganism. In its effort to destroy the family, the government sought to make wives independent of their husbands, and to take much of the socialization of children from parents. Universal primary education was instituted, and the educational level of the population was raised markedly. Part of the schooling consisted of indoctrination in Socialist ideology, and this indoctrination was carried out even more vigorously in the youth organizations such as Komsomol and the Pioneers.

Education during the revolutionary years emphasized complete loyalty to the state and attacked religion and the family as sources of corrupt capitalist beliefs. The authority of parents was undermined and, for a time, children actually were encouraged to report counterrevolutionary sentiments on the part of their parents to the authorities. How much open spying developed within families is difficult to say, but we do know that one effect was a rapid increase in what we call juvenile delinquency, and what in Russia is called hooliganism.

By 1929, hooliganism was a major problem. Adolescent gangs roamed the cities, making vicious unprovoked attacks upon helpless citizens. Vandalism, stealing, robbery, rape, and even murder occurred with increasing frequency.[8]

During the early 1930s the government began to rethink its family policies. Universal primary education and the raising of the status of women had brought some beneficial results. But they had been accompanied by widespread increases in almost every form of pathology associated with family life. To cope with these unanticipated problems, the regime reversed itself drastically.

Revised Family Policy

The second stage in the Russian family revolution began in the middle 1930s and extended into the 1950s. This was a period of reaction against the radicalism of the post-revolutionary phase. A law outlawing homosexuality, for example, was passed in 1934 and, in 1935, another law made parents responsible for the delinquent acts of their children. Major recodifications occurred in 1936 and again in 1944.[9]

After 1944, only officially registered marriages were recognized as legal. Common law marriage was outlawed and illegitimacy was re-established. The fathers of illegitimate children were not liable for their support, and such children had no right to inherit from their fathers.

Requirements for divorce became increasingly strict, until divorce in the Soviet Union became more difficult to get than in the United States. The divorce might be petitioned for by either partner, but both had to be summoned to court and the specific grounds for divorce proved to the court's satisfaction. Even then, the People's Court could not grant the divorce, but sought reconciliation of the couple. If that failed, the suit had to be filed again in a higher court. That court might or might not grant the divorce, depending upon whether it judged the divorce to be in the interest of the state. The whole process was also quite expensive.

Such measures were characteristic of the period through World War II and until after the death of Joseph Stalin. Then, in the 1950s, the pendulum began to swing the other way. Abortion was made legal, again,

8. See Walter D. Connor, "Juvenile Delinquency in the U.S.S.R.: Some Quantitative and Qualitative Indicators," *American Sociological Review* 35 (April 1970), pp. 283–97.

9. See Rudolph Schlesinger, *ed., Changing Attitudes in Soviet Russia: The Family in the U.S.S.R.*, London: Routledge and Kegan Paul, 1949.

in 1955, apparently largely to stamp out the flourishing illegal abortion practices that existed.

The extreme difficulty in securing divorces came under attack for encouraging people to enter informal liaisons without having been divorced from their former partners. Recodification came in 1965 when the People's Courts were authorized to grant divorces. Subsequently, even court hearings were done away with where neither partner objected and where there were no minor children. In recent years, 85 percent of Russian divorces have been granted by filling out a form at the Registry, with the divorce becoming final after three months.

The Russians also are trying to make marriage more attractive. Although only civil marriage is recognized, great effort is made to make the registration a solemn affair. The Registry offices are large, attractive, and well furnished. The date for the registration of a marriage must be set in advance, and parents and friends are invited to witness the ceremony. Attractive certificates of the registration are issued, and even wedding rings may be used.

In addition to revising its regulations concerning marriage and divorce, the Soviet Union has continued to support the practice of mothers working and has sought to encourage large families. Although the bulk of Soviet women still are engaged in heavy, unskilled work, women now comprise 63 percent of specialists with secondary education and 53 percent of professionals with higher education.[10] Women receive two months' paid leave before and after their babies are born. Both factories and collective farms maintain nurseries, and mothers receive time off every three hours to nurse their infants. The state also operates kindergartens for children between the ages of three and eight where the children receive three full meals and medical care. This may work better in theory than in practice, for Bronfenbrenner reports that only 10 percent of children under two are enrolled in preschool institutions, with the comparable percentage for three- to six-year-olds being 18.[11]

Large families are encouraged through monetary subsidies, beginning with the birth of the fourth child and increasing through the eleventh child. Initial grants are paid as well as monthly payments from the time the child is a year old until he or she reaches the age of five. Obviously,

10. Norton D. Dodge, *Women in the Soviet Economy: Their Role in Economic, Scientific, and Technical Development*, Baltimore: The Johns Hopkins Press, 1966.

11. Urie Bronfenbrenner, "The Changing Soviet Family," in Michael Gordon, *ed.*, *The Nuclear Family in Crisis: The Search for an Alternative*, New York: Harper and Row, 1972, p. 133.

since the payments end at age five, couples cannot expect to produce children for a profit, but the payments do provide some incentive.[12]

The modal family in the Soviet Union today appears to be a two-generation conjugal family. The birth rate continues to decline under the impact of urbanization and industrialization. A three-generation unit also appears to be relatively common. It involves one or more grandparents living with the parents and children, with the grandparents assuming many household and child-care duties. This arrangement nicely relieves the state of much responsibility for the care of both children and oldsters. Such extended units also are advantageous in the cities, where housing is allotted on the basis of family size.

Soviet women in industry or on farms work less strenuously than their counterparts in the United States and enjoy better working conditions. . . . Soviet laws today forbid the employment of women in certain occupations considered especially hazardous to health, jobs involving heavy lifting, underground jobs, "hot shops," and some jobs in chemical industries.

Women are entitled to earlier retirement benefits than men, at the age of 55, after 20 years of employment. Women who have five or more children are eligible for pensions at the age of 50, after working only 15 years. . . . Pensioners who wish to continue working—and many do—receive full wages as well as either a partial or (in special cases) full pension. . . .

A pregnant woman in any occupation, regardless of length of service, receives 112 days of paid maternity leave. . . . In addition, her job will be reserved for her one year after the birth of the child, her seniority and all other rights being retained. . . .

AUGUSTA STRONG, "Any Soviet Woman Can Find a Job," *U.S.-U.S.S.R. Report, Bulletin of the National Council of American-Soviet Friendship*, August 1974, pp. 5–6

Final Evaluation of the Soviet Experiment

The Russian attempt to do away with the family is the largest such effort ever made. Unlike the communist Chinese who sought to destroy only the extended family, the Russians tried to do away with the family

12. David M. Heer and Judith G. Bryden, "Family Allowances and Population Policy in the U.S.S.R.," *Journal of Marriage and the Family* 28 (Nov. 1966), pp. 514–19.

altogether. Significantly, again, this radical effort did not last for more than a generation. The revolution occurred in 1917 and by the early 1930s the ground was being laid for strengthening the family again. The Soviet family today appears to be remarkably similar to the family in the United States, having many of the same strengths and problems. The great Soviet effort to eliminate the family has ended and few direct results of the effort remain.

THE KIBBUTZ

The American utopian communities were very small, the Russian experiment was on a grand scale, and the kibbutzim fall in between. There are over 240 kibbutzim in Israel, involving some 95,000 members.[13] These kibbutzim are organized into three major federations, one of which–Marxist in ideology and Soviet in inclination–has been most carefully studied. The kibbutz patterns described in this section represent the most completely collectivized and the most antireligious of the kibbutzim.[14]

The kibbutz is an agricultural collective, in which virtually all property is collectively owned, work and consumption are collectively organized, there are communal living arrangements, and the rearing of children is assumed by the group. The original kibbutz settlers were middle-class European intellectuals who migrated to Israel and made physical labor the highest vocational goal. Rather than aspiring to upward mobility, these pioneers deliberately created a socialist enterprise in which all persons would experience satisfaction from working the soil.

The kibbutzim date back to the 1880s when Russian Jews established the first collectives in what, at that time, was Palestine. Between 1882 and 1903, some 25,000 Jews migrated to Palestine. Forty thousand more went between 1904 and the start of World War I. After World War I, the migration continued. By 1931, 116,000 more immigrants arrived. Persecution of the Jews under Hitler brought 225,000 more between

13. Sol Stern, "The Kibbutz: Not by Ideology Alone," *The New York Times Magazine*, May 6, 1973, p. 37.

14. See Melford E. Spiro, "Is the Family Universal?–The Israeli Case," in Norman W. Bell and Ezra F. Vogel, *eds.*, *A Modern Introduction to the Family*, New York: The Free Press, 1968, pp. 68–79; and Yonina Talmon, "The Family in a Revolutionary Movement–the Case of the Kibbutz in Israel," in Meyer F. Nimkoff, *ed.*, *Comparative Family Systems*, Boston: Houghton Mifflin, 1965, pp. 259–86.

1932 and 1939. And in 1948, the State of Israel came into being.[15] By 1936 there were 47 kibbutzim in Palestine, by 1948 there were 149, and in 1954 the number reached 227.

The kibbutzim range in size from 40 to 50 members to more than 2000 members. The pattern was for a nucleus of original settlers to be joined by other groups who had received some training in kibbutz life and organization. The settlers tended to be young, with men substantially outnumbering women. Each collective was operated as though it were a single large household. A general assembly was the governing body, aided by a secretariat and a series of committees.

Living conditions in the early kibbutzim were austere. One of their goals was the reclamation of increasingly arid and barren land on the frontier, necessitating not only a joint economic effort but a low living standard on the part of members. All income, from whatever sources, was paid into the common treasury which, in turn, provided a small personal allowance to each member. Clothing was provided from the central supply. The members lived in small rooms–sometimes several persons to a room–in which there was a minimum of furniture and no conveniences. Bathrooms and showers were centrally located and jointly used.

There was a playing down of differences between persons and between the sexes. All work was regarded as noble and rewarding, with physical labor in the fields being the most noble of all. To the extent to which status differences existed, administrative and clerical personnel had lower, not higher, status. In the early stages, women wore masculine clothes and there was no makeup or other personal adornment. Women were entitled to work in the fields equally with men, and women did military service. There was no segregation of the sexes, and men and women often shared the same sleeping rooms. Actually, some division of labor by sex emerged quite early. Certain of the heavier agricultural tasks simply could not be handled by women, and women disproportionately became involved in the collective's service enterprises–the nurseries, schools, kitchens, dining rooms, and laundries.

The most distinguishing feature of the kibbutz has been its attitude toward the family and the practices which it evolved to implement that attitude. Talmon hypothesizes that "there is a certain fundamental incompatibility between commitment to a radical revolutionary ideology and intense collective identification on the one hand and family solidar-

15. Raphael Patai, *Israel Between East and West: A Study in Human Relations*, Westport, Conn.: Greenwood Publishing Corp., 1970, pp. 59–72.

ity on the other."[16] The kibbutz considered itself to be an effort to revolutionize society and it considered family ties to be incompatible with that goal. Family and kinship are based upon ties between the generations and upon the passing of tradition from one generation to the next. Revolutionary movements seek to break the ties with the past. Thus, from the beginning, the kibbutz was antifamilistic. It sought to eliminate the family as an institution and as a social group.

Kibbutz Morality

The kibbutz rejected the morality of middle-class European society. That society's values of chastity and life-long sexual fidelity, combined with a double standard for men and women and widespread premarital and extramarital intercourse, were seen as hypocritical. The kibbutz taught that sex relationships should reflect physical needs and the emotional relationship between the persons involved. There were to be no barriers to premarital sexual intercourse, and both sex relationships and marriage should continue only so long as there was a deep emotional relationship. Kibbutz members were seen as free men and women, entitled to form and to dissolve relationships at will.

Some people may view such liberal norms as an invitation to license. On the contrary, kibbutz morality was restrained and almost ascetic. In most kibbutzim, there was a disavowal of the erotic and little promiscuity. Nudity was accepted, men and women often slept in the same room without erotic complications, showers were shared, and there was little overt preoccupation with sex. Part of the explanation appears to lie in the conservative family backgrounds of most kibbutz members; ideologically liberal, they remained behaviorally tied to the standards of their upbringing. Important, too, was the commitment to renunciation of physical comfort and pleasure that characterized the kibbutz.

Sexual relationships among youth of high-school age generally were frowned upon. After that, however, young people were free to become involved without censure. No special notice was taken of these relationships, and no sanction was given to them. After some experimentation, most youth settled down to one partner and became monogamous. At some point in their relationships, they were likely to request that they become a "couple" and have a separate room assigned to them.

16. *Op. cit.*, pp. 260–61.

Marriage

Marriage, since it implied the development of an ominous solidarity within the kibbutz, was given little support. The couple simply applied for a room, and moved into it with no fanfare. In many kibbutzim, there was a shortage of sleeping rooms and the couple might have had to wait months for a room. If the shortage was severe, they might also have had to accept sharing the room occasionally with another person. There were no restrictions upon the right of separation and divorce.

Marriage was accompanied by no discernible shift in status, either for the man or the woman. Wives could keep their maiden names and usually did. Husbands and wives were not allowed to work at the same jobs, and often did not even have the same day off. For some time, radios and electric utensils were not permitted in the rooms, to discourage couples from spending time there. Virtually all free time was supposed to be spent in the public areas, with other members of the collective.

There was avoidance of public acknowledgment of the relationship. The husband and wife often did not eat together, but ate with other members as if to reinforce their primary loyalty to the kibbutz. The word "marriage" was not used. Instead, they "became a couple." The man referred to his wife as "my young woman" or called her by her given name, and vice versa. Public display of affection was considered to be in bad taste and aroused feelings of shame in the participants. Ordinarily, a wedding ceremony was held at the birth of the first child, but only because the state required it for the legitimization of the offspring.

Family and Parental Roles

There was no basis for the husband to dominate the wife. Each remained on the kibbutz rolls as a separate person, and continued to receive a personal allowance. The husband shared equally in the little housework required to keep their room in order, and both parents assumed responsibility for children. Anniversaries and birthdays, which might place unseemly emphasis on family relationships, were not celebrated.

Child-rearing was separated as completely as possible from marriage. New-born infants went directly from the hospital to the nursery. From birth, they lived in special children's houses. This arrangement had at least two advantages. First, it permitted children to have a higher standard of living than their parents. In spite of the antifamilistic ideology, children were the means to perpetuation of the collectivist ideology and were highly valued; regardless of what privations parents might undergo, children received the best of food, clothing, and medical care. Separate child-care arrangements also left mothers free to work in the community, and reduced the number of persons required to care for children.

Children spent some time each day with their parents, usually the afternoon and early evening hours. Parents also went to the nursery to put young children to sleep each night. Saturdays and holidays also brought families together. Emotional relationships between parents and their young children were surprisingly close. The relationship was nonauthoritarian, discipline being the function of the persons who supervised the children's up-bringing rather than that of the parents. The parents provided security and love, and played a crucial role in the psychological development of the child. The relationship between all adults and children was a warm, rewarding one. Children were likely to refer to their parents by their given names instead of by kinship terms, while adults referred to all children as "son" and "daughter."

In the children's houses, each age group had its own section. Nurses and teachers were primary sources of indoctrination with the history, norms, and values of the kibbutz. Several writers have pointed out that the relationship among members of each age group became much like that among brothers and sisters in a family. The psychological character of this bond is reflected in the fact that, as they grow to adulthood, these age groups are voluntarily and almost completely exogamous. There are no barriers to marriage within the group, but the young men and women react to one another as though they truly were brothers and sisters.

Thus, in its unique way, the kibbutz went as far as either Oneida or the Soviet Union in attempting to do away with the family. The experiment is still going on today. Moreover, some of the kibbutzim already have lasted longer than either of the other experiments did. Some kibbutz-born children already are adults and, themselves, full-fledged kibbutz members. But the kibbutzim are changing rapidly. The revolutionary fervor of the 1930s and 1940s is fading. As it fades, the kibbutzim are having to accord a more prominent place to the conjugal family.

Emerging Kibbutz Patterns

The kibbutzim began as agricultural collectives, and they still are heavily involved in agriculture. There are now, however, some 232 kibbutz factories, producing 7 percent of the nation's industrial output.[17] This industrial production has become the chief source of income and is responsible for vastly improved living standards. Private living quarters have become the norm, radios and kitchen facilities are common, and private TV sets are becoming so. Many families have some "good" clothes which are cared for at home and treated as private possessions. Afternoon tea in the family quarters is common, and some families eat part or all their meals "at home." Children spend more time with their parents, even going so far as to sleep in the parents' quarters.

Part of what is happening here is the result of a generalized process of differentiation occurring within the kibbutz. The kibbutzim are no longer peopled just by the original pioneers; groups of varying backgrounds and ages have been added. Relationships between the subgroups become complicated by intellectual, religious, political, and economic differences. Hostility develops and social distance widens. With the appearance of differences within the group, the family comes to be assigned a place among the subgroups.

Differentiation within the family itself plays a major role. As long as the kibbutz was peopled predominantly by young persons and gained its recruits primarily through immigration, it did not have to cope with the whole range of family ties. As the kibbutz birth rate rose, generational ties emerged. As parents grow old and children grow to adulthood, these ties become more numerous and more complex. Such ties are reflected in changes in the living quarters. The typical private living quarters may now be a semi-detached flat instead of a room. Grandparents may be housed in separate buildings or they may have quarters adjoining those of their children. The ties also are reflected in terminological changes. Parents are more likely to address offspring as "my son" and "my daughter," and the terms "my man" and "my woman" are taking on connotations usually associated with the terms "husband" and "wife."

The relationships among the *sabras*,[18] as they grow into adulthood, also are different from those which prevailed among their parents. There is less de-eroticization than formerly. Women are dressing more attractively and there is more public display of affection by couples. The sex

17. Sol Stern, *op. cit.*
18. Persons born in Israel.

norms have become more conservative. While there still is no taboo on premarital intercourse, promiscuity is strongly discouraged, liaisons tend to be short and to precede marriage immediately, and increasingly couples are not having sex until marriage. Marriage ceremonies, before beginning life together, are becoming common, and wives increasingly take their husbands' names. Divorce is becoming rare.[19]

In short, the antifamilism of the kibbutz movement seems largely to have ended. For a while, the kibbutz appeared to have functioned without the family because the community itself functioned as a family.

ALTERNATIVE LIFE STYLES

The late 1960s and the early 1970s in the United States produced an effort quite different from the utopian experiments in Oneida, Russia, and the kibbutzim to promote alternatives to conventional family living. The movement was diffuse, unorganized, and extremely varied; collectively it promoted the development of alternative life styles.

The Social Context

The 1960s was a decade of great social turbulence. Black people, joined later by white people, embarked upon an aggressive struggle for equality. Originally an offshoot of the civil rights movement, the women's liberation movement became a major effort in its own right. Then the Vietnam War divided the country as it had seldom been divided before. College students rioted. Drug use spread into the middle classes and young people not only dropped out of college, they dropped out of the "straight" life. Hippie crash pads sprang up all over the country and bizarre communal settlements clustered both in the cities and in isolated rural areas from California to the Appalachians.

Obviously many factors contributed to the widespread need to reject traditional ways of living and to find new and better ways. Two

19. There are differences among kibbutzim belonging to the three different federations. Ideologically, the Artzi is the most militantly collective, and opposes the trends back toward the nuclear family. Seventy-five of the 240 kibbutzim belong to the Artzi. Even the Artzi, however, are unable to hold out against the forces described above. See Harvey Peskin, Zvi Giora, and Mordecai Kaffman, "Birth Order in Child-Psychiatric Referrals and Kibbutz Family Structure," *Journal of Marriage and the Family* 36 (Aug. 1974), pp. 615–18; and Yaffa Schlesinger, "Sex Roles and Social Change in the Kibbutz," *Journal of Marriage and the Family* 39 (Nov. 1977), pp. 771–79.

such factors were an unprecedented demographic phenomenon and the hesitant movement of the nation toward the postindustrial era.

The Demographic Factor. For approximately a decade after World War II, birth rates were very high. Then, in 1957, they began to drop, and they are still dropping.

The effects of these changes began to be noticed in 1964 when the babies who had been born in 1947 reached the age of seventeen, and seventeen-year-olds became the largest single age group in the nation. Each year from 1964 through 1971 saw more people reaching age seventeen than had the year before. After 1971, the number of people reaching seventeen each year began to drop. It will continue to drop for at least another decade. According to one analyst, this bulge in the teenage segment of the population was far greater than had ever occurred before or is likely to ever happen again.[20]

The impact of this huge number of teenagers and young adults was great. The teen years are years of rebellion against parental authority in particular, and societal authority in general. It is the time when they leave the parental home to seek separate identities for themselves. It is also the period of greatest vigor in life. Young people play hardest and probably even work hardest. They drink more, fight more, love more, and use more drugs than any other age group. Given these facts, the large-scale emphasis during the late 1960s on creating alternative life styles probably was not an accident. It was a predictable outcome of a situation in which young people were so numerous that their values, their standards, and their way of life had major influence upon the whole society.

But if the huge number of teenagers during the 1960s contributed to social upheaval, those same people moved into their twenties during the early 1970s. During their early twenties, people typically graduate from college, marry, and begin earning a living. They give up rebellion in favor of establishing themselves in their jobs, securing and paying for a home, and providing a good environment for their children.

Changed economic conditions have reinforced the growing conservatism among young adults. The 1970s saw spiraling inflation and economic recessions go hand in hand. Shortages of natural resources became acute, and an atmosphere of anxiety pervaded the nation. Unemployment rose drastically and stayed high.[21] If the demographic

20. Daniel P. Moynihan, " 'Peace'—Some Thoughts on the 1960's and 1970's," *The Public Interest* 32 (Summer 1973), pp. 3–12.

21. Brigitte Berger, " 'People Work'—The Youth Culture and the Labor Market," *The Public Interest* 35 (Spring 1974), pp. 55–66.

and economic conditions of the 1960s were favorable for experimentation with unconventional life styles, the 1970s saw, and probably the 1980s will see, more emphasis upon the necessity for earning a living.

Toward the Postindustrial Society. The 1960s not only saw unprecedented numbers of teenagers and young adults, they also brought living conditions that alienated young people from the values of the larger society. Casual analysts blamed marriage, arguing that marriage had become irrelevant to the needs of modern society. This analysis was too facile, and ignored major social-structural changes that had been proceeding from about the end of World War II.

What happened was that there was a change in the family life cycle, involving the prolongation of adolescence. We refer to adolescence as a stage in social life rather than a stage in physical maturation, although viewed within a longer time frame, even biological adolescence has been lengthening through a lowering of the age of menarche. Socially, the introduction of prepubescent and barely pubescent youth to experiences formerly reserved for older persons was startling. Both vicariously through the mass media and directly through experience, many youngsters of the 1960s, were more knowledgeable about sex and drugs than were adults of a generation earlier.

If adolescence began earlier, however, its prolongation into adulthood was even more dramatic. This came about as the result of movement of the nation toward a postindustrial stage in which it does not need and cannot use all of its potentially productive adult labor. That the nation was somewhat aware of the problem was revealed by debates concerning whether the work week should be shortened below 40 hours, and whether the age for retirement should be lowered from 65. These questions still haven't been answered, with the result that other forms of adjustment to the problem continue to operate unrecognized.

Universities during the 1950s and 1960s ceased to be just educational institutions and became, figuratively, storehouses for vast numbers of young people for whom there was no place in the adult labor market. Whereas, earlier, people generally entered the labor market at about age 18, or went to college and entered it around 22, the situation changed drastically. Going to college became almost a way of life, rather than a brief interlude between childhood and adulthood. Most people began college on schedule, but often they dropped out for a year or two on the way to the B.A. degree. After five or six years at that stage, they entered the graduate schools in greatly increased numbers where, again, they prolonged their stays through dropping out for extended periods and through general procrastination.[22]

The connection between this and the demographic and economic conditions described in the preceding section should be obvious. An affluent society, accommodating itself to tremendous numbers of young people, could afford, as never before, to keep a sizable portion of its young adults in a stage of financial dependence. If we can broaden the concept of adolescence to include those who remained in this limbo between the child world of being educated and the adult world of gainful employment, then there were large groups of 20-, 25-, and 30-year-old adolescents, and some even older than that.

Such a situation was bound to produce problems. If there is any group in a population which cannot safely be warehoused because its labor is not needed, it is young adults at the peak of physical power, intellectual vigor, and sexual needs. Throughout history, people in their twenties and early thirties have played a major role in running the world. In another time, the 200-pound specimens smoking pot in a crash pad might have been commanding armies or conquering frontiers. It was probably inevitable that much of the energy denied direct expression in useful work would be turned to other ends.

These conditions were ideal for promoting the youth counterculture which emerged during the early 1960s. The leaders of this movement generally were the articulate, idealistic progeny of prosperous parents, whose ambiguous relationship to the adult world made them especially sensitive to hypocrisy, and who joined forces with black and other ethnic groups, and with opponents of the Vietnam War. Being essentially free of the necessity of earning a living, they had time to devote to moral causes. Being basically anti-academic and anti-intellectual, they were unfettered by the lessons of history in their enthusiasm for the development of new social forms. For approximately a decade, they experimented conspicuously with alternative life styles that included group marriage, communal living, and open marriage.

Group Marriage

Group marriages, by definition, involved three or more people in any distribution by sex that functioned as a family, sharing both interper-

22. This section follows, closely, Bennett M. Berger, "The New Stage of American Man—Almost Endless Adolescence," *The New York Times Magazine*, Nov. 2, 1969, pp. 32–33, 131–36.

sonal and sexual intimacy. The most common pattern was four adults, usually the members of two former couples. Occasionally, as many as six adults were involved.[23] The average age of the participants was about thirty, and they varied widely in income level. Because of public disapproval, most group marriages were at least semi-secret, and it is difficult to know how many people actually tried them. There may have been a few thousand of them, but the proportion of the total population was exceedingly small.[24]

Many group marriages combined flexibility in the performance of masculine and feminine roles within the marriage with a fairly conventional adaptation to the outside world. The men typically went to their jobs each morning as other husbands did. One or more of the women often held outside employment, too, and sometimes one of them remained at home in the primary housewife and mother role. Whatever the occupational arrangements, the members of group marriages often were committed to equality between the sexes and to the sharing of roles in the home. Men and women often shared meal preparation, cleaning, and childcare. One of the explicit goals was to provide extra attention to children who were believed to thrive on the security provided to them by multiple, more relaxed, less harried parents, and who were encouraged to avoid the sexual stereotyping believed inherent in more conventional marriages.[25]

Sharing was intended to characterize all aspects of group marriages. Self-disclosure to other members of the group was emphasized, with intimacy with others and personal growth being the goals. Sex was shared also, with the couples typically pairing off informally or on a regular rotation basis. Group sex appears to have been the exception rather than the rule and, where it existed, to have occurred in marriages that had existed for some time.[26]

The reported advantages of group marriages were several. Men and women could share roles flexibly. There were multiple opportunities for intimacy and personal growth. There was sexual variety. Children could grow up in a nonsexist environment. And it was cheaper to maintain one household than two or three. Nevertheless, after a few years of

23. Larry L. Constantine, and Joan M. Constantine, "Where Is Marriage Going?" *The Futurist* (April 1970), p. 44.

24. Albert Ellis, "Group Marriage: A Possible Alternative?" in Gorden F. Streib, *ed.*, *The Changing Family: Adaptation and Diversity*, Reading, Mass.: Addison-Wesley, 1973, p. 86.

25. Larry L. Constantine, and Joan M. Constantine, *op. cit.*, p. 45.

26. Larry L. Constantine, and Joan M. Constantine, "Sexual Aspects of Multilateral Relations," *The Journal of Sex Research* 7 (Aug. 1971), p. 214.

experimentation, even sympathetic analysts concluded that group marriages had many serious disadvantages.[27]

Secrecy was difficult to maintain and many group marriages were subjected to pressure from neighbors and the community. As children of the couples approached adolescence, they often were shamed by or morbidly preoccupied with their parents' sleeping arrangements. Although jealousy among the adults was disapproved, it developed anyway. Some of the jealousy was sexual, and some of it was over leadership in the group. As a consequence of all of these things, many group marriages broke up after a while, their members sometimes returning to conventional married living, sometimes divorcing their legal spouses, and sometimes going on to try other alternative life styles.

Group marriages, or something approximating them, probably have been tried by occasional sets of couples in many times and places. The late 1960s and early 1970s in the United States undoubtedly saw them tried on a larger scale and publicized more than ever before. By the mid-1970s, however, one expert reported, "The majority of them don't work, or they work only for a limited time—a year, two years, four years. They fall apart because of the tremendous complexities . . . the sexual interaction is the least important confusion; they can handle that. It's the other interpersonal relationships—dominance, money, child care, for example—that aren't so simple to contend with."[28]

Group marriages still exist and, undoubtedly, they will continue to do so. Their numbers were never large, however, and are much smaller today than they were a few years ago. They may continue to provide an alternative life style for a small minority, but the challenge they provided to more conventional family living has passed.

Communal Living

Experiments with communal living have a longer and much more explicit history than does group marriage, as evidenced by the discussions of the Chinese family, Oneida, the Russian family experiment, and the kibbutzim. There are also, currently in the United States, a variety of religious communes, many of which are intensely familistic and fiercely monogamous.[29] Our discussion here will be limited to the groups that

27. Larry L. Constantine, and Joan M. Constantine, "Where Is Marriage Going?" *op. cit.*; and Albert Ellis, *op. cit.*, p. 82.
28. Wardell Pomeroy, "Playboy Panel: New Sexual Life Styles," *Playboy*, Sept. 1973, p. 86.
29. Benjamin Zablocki, *The Joyful Community*, Baltimore: Penguin Books, 1971.

emerged during the 1960s and which sought to eliminate conventional family living.

Communal living groups differ from group marriages in several important respects. First, they are larger, ranging from half a dozen to two hundred people, or even more. Second, communes often seek to provide a total way of life, minimizing contacts with the surrounding community. Third, the distinctions between men's and women's work may almost be obliterated. Fourth, many communes strive for economic self-sufficiency. And, fifth, private property, including possessiveness of people, usually is disavowed.

As with group marriages, no one knows precisely how many communes sprang up in the United States during the late 1960s and early 1970s. A *New York Times* survey in 1971 turned up some 2000 communes in 34 different states.[30] At about the same time, an estimate from the National Institute of Mental Health put the number at approximately 3000.[31] Whichever the correct figure, a moment's computation will demonstrate that not more than a few hundredths of one percent of the U.S. population was involved.

The advantages claimed for commune living were essentially those claimed by group marriages, only more so: the complete sharing of relationships and possessions, personal growth and development, and freedom from the "hang-ups" of conventional society. For a while, at least, some members of some communes appeared to achieve these goals. By the mid-1970s, however, the number of such communes had shrunk drastically, and many of the remaining ones, particularly around college campuses, had come to emphasize their cost-sharing arrangements more than their ideologies.

Many communes were unstable. People moved into them and moved out again, without staying long. Many members came from broken marriages, while other marriages broke under the pressures of commune living. Where stable, monogamous marriages persisted, there were often tensions between them and other commune members. Many of the communes, themselves, survived for only a few months or a few years.

The communal ideal of economic self-sufficiency was not often achieved. Leather goods shops, farms, health food stores and restaurants, candle-making operations, and others were established, but a sustained

30. Bill Kovach, "Communal Living Becomes A Factor in the U.S.," *The New York Times*, Jan. 3, 1971.

31. Herbert A. Otto, "Communes: The Alternative Life-Style," *Saturday Review*, April 24, 1971.

work ethic was not part of the communal value system. The work often did not get done, and most communes depended heavily upon outside support. Members applied for unemployment compensation, surplus commodities, and food stamps. They went on welfare. And they welcomed divorcees with alimony checks and child support payments. For a while, such precarious circumstances lent excitement to the venture, but eventually they threatened the stability of the group.

The highly valued sexual freedom and sharing also created problems. Sometimes, sex became an unofficial arena of competition, with some members of each sex becoming defined as more desirable than others. Some had their self-concepts enhanced by being sought after, while others suffered the pain of not being wanted, and the deprivation that results from not being entitled to claim the sexual favors of some other person.

Most communes also had difficulty with, or did not confront, the generational problem. Childbirth was an important ceremonial event in which the whole commune participated, but, after the first few months, the care of babies and small children was usually left to their often disillusioned mothers. Few communes lasted long enough to have to face the problem of educating older children. Finally, there were few older people in these communes. The emphasis was on youth, and there was no place for grandparents and other elders.

Open Marriage

Group marriage and communal living attracted a great deal of public attention, but they afforded possible life styles for only a relatively few. There was also, however, a larger radical following that sought to transform traditional marriage; who sought relief from what they perceived to be marital monotony, in the concept of open marriage.

"Open" marriage was contrasted with the "closed" nature of conventional marriage. Closed marriages were believed to offer few opportunities for growth or change. Open marriage, in contrast, was intended to combine intimacy in a one-to-one relationship with facilitating the personal growth of both partners. Ideally, the growth should occur at the same time and the same pace for both partners, but, if it did not, each partner was supposed to provide supportive assistance for the other's unilateral growth.[32]

32. Nena O'Neill and George O'Neill, *Open Marriage: A New Life Style for Couples*, New York: M. Evans and Co., 1972; and Nena O'Neill and George O'Neill, "Open Marriage: A Synergic Model," *The Family Coordinator* 21 (Oct. 1972), pp. 404–408.

Open marriages were believed to be difficult to achieve because the partners lack the skill to communicate openly and completely, and because they need to be emotionally dependent upon and possessive of their partners. To overcome these handicaps, the creators of the concept of open marriage offer specific guidelines. They are: living for now, realistic expectations, privacy, role flexibility, open and honest communication, open companionship, equality, identity, and trust. In "living for now," they emphasized the emotional and intellectual aspects of the marriage relationship rather than the making of long range plans and the accumulation of material goods. "Privacy" was believed necessary for self-examination and psychic regeneration. "Role flexibility" included the possibility of exchanging some parts, or all, of the traditional roles played by husbands and wives. "Communication skills" had to be worked at constantly because effective and open communication is the key to the whole process. "Open companionship" included the right to each partner to meaningful relationships, including heterosexual ones, outside the marriage relationship. "Equality" permitted no assignment of prerogatives to either partner on the basis of sex. "Identity" emphasized the growing autonomy of each spouse, in the context of the pair relationship. Finally, "trust" was both a precondition for and a consequence of the observance of all of the other guidelines.

Proponents of the concept acknowledged that only "a limited few" couples might be able to achieve completely open marriages, but they believed that many more could use some of the guidelines to good effect. They anticipated that the most troublesome area would be that of striving for flexibility in masculine and feminine roles. Problems of jealousy relating to extramarital liaisons, they believed, would be symptomatic rather than central. Finally, they acknowledged that open marriage would not solve all marital problems. Instead, they believed, it would substitute problems that promote growth and learning for the less constructive problems of conventional marriage.

Problems of sexual jealousy, however, proved more troublesome than anticipated. Some couples found that the idea of a sexually open marriage was little more than a rationalization for extramarital affairs. In other cases, where the commitment to the ideology of open marriage was deep and genuine, one of the spouses reacted with fear and hostility to an outside involvement of the other partner. Severe marital conflict and divorce were common enough results that, by the mid-1970s, proponents of open marriage were emphasizing, somewhat ambiguously, that they advocated change and growth—not swinging marriages.

The social upheaval that began in the 1960s was all but over by the mid-1970s.[33] The Vietnam War was ended, and the population center of gravity had moved up from the teen years into the early twenties. We are still too close to that period to assess how much permanent change in American family patterns resulted. The concept of alternative life styles is still with us. But the total rejection of the family's relevance to modern society has ended, at least for the time being.

SUMMARY

The Oneida Community was founded in 1848 by John Humphrey Noyes, with whose life and teachings the community is inseparably linked. Noyes preached "perfectionism" and saw monogamous marriage and private property as barriers to the unselfishness required by the perfectionist doctrine. "Complex marriage" was based on the assumption that all men should love all women and vice versa. Young men were initiated into sex by older women, and young women by older men, according to the principle of ascendance. Only persons approved by a committee were entitled to become parents. Children were reared apart from their parents. The community prospered financially, but encountered resistance from the surrounding society. Children of the community were ridiculed by outsiders, and there were rumors of legal prosecution of adults. Some of the children failed to accept the teachings of the community. In 1877, Noyes resigned as leader, and by 1880 the community had broken up.

The Soviet family experiment followed the Bolshevik Revolution, and lasted into the 1930s. The Soviets sought to do away with the family as a corrupt bourgeois institution. Marriage and divorce became simple matters of registration. Abortion was made legal, birth control was encouraged, and children were urged to break ties with parents who evidenced counterrevolutionary tendencies. By the middle 1930s a reverse trend had set in. Rising divorce rates, falling birth rates, and rampant juvenile delinquency were by-products the Soviets had not counted on. Laws from 1936 to 1944 re-emphasized the solemnity and permanence of marriage and made divorce very difficult. The equality of women was upheld, and allowances were provided to parents of large families. The Soviet Union now sees a stable family as a bulwark of socialism.

The kibbutzim are agricultural collectives in Israel. Communistic in

33. James L. Spates, "Counterculture and Dominant Culture Values: A Cross-National Analysis of the Underground Press and Dominant Culture Magazines," *American Sociological Review* 41 (Oct. 1976), pp. 868–83.

ideology, they sought to eliminate the family as a competing source of identification. All production and consumption were collectivized and all kinship ties were discouraged. Marriage virtually was done away with, couples simply applying for a room when they wished to make their relationships permanent. Relationships also could be dissolved at will. Children were reared in groups apart, visiting their parents at prescribed times. Time has seen changes in the kibbutzim. Marriage has become somewhat regularized, more adequate quarters have been provided for families, and more functions are being transferred to the home. Extended family relationships are being formed, and contact with kin outside of the kibbutz is increasing.

The 1960s saw a major effort to promote alternatives to family living in the United States. Changing birth rates had produced, relatively, the largest group of teenagers the nation had ever seen, and the teen years are years of rebellion and physical and intellectual vigor. The nation was also moving toward a postindustrial stage in which the labor of many young people was not needed. Social adolescence was prolonged, with resulting chaos.

Group marriages constituted one alternative life style. They were intended to promote unselfishness and sharing, variety in sexual experience, and interpersonal intimacy. They also had financial advantages. Such marriages encountered major problems, however. There was harassment from neighbors and the community. Young children often thrived on the attention they received from multiple parents, but teenage children often were upset by their parents' arrangements. Sexual and interpersonal jealousy also developed. The complexity of group marriage proved almost overwhelming, and few of them lasted for more than a year or two.

Communal living attracted other people. These communes generally abolished private property and sought financial self-sufficiency. They also believed in the open sharing of persons and relationships. In addition to serious financial problems, many of them were also plagued by high membership turnover. As in group marriages, sexual and personal rivalries developed. Children posed special problems, and there were few older people in communes.

Open marriage sought to utilize the strengths of group marriages and communes, without their disadvantages. It promoted personal growth and development, and the elimination of dependence upon and possessiveness of the marital partner. To grow one's self, and to promote growth in one's partner, people were urged to commit themselves to:

living for now, realistic expectations of marriage and of one another, privacy, role flexibility, open and honest communication, open companionship, equality, identity, and trust. When the reality of extramarital involvements thrust itself upon the couples, however, many discovered that they were not as emancipated as they had believed themselves to be.

SUGGESTED READINGS

Kephart, William M., *Extraordinary Groups: The Sociology of Unconventional Life Styles,* New York: St. Martin's Press, 1976. A fascinating account of several experimental communities and life styles: Oneida, the Old-Order Amish, the Father Divine Movement, the Shakers, the Mormons, the Hutterites, and contemporary communes.

Mandel, William M., *Soviet Women,* Garden City, New York: Doubleday, 1975. A comprehensive account of the status of Russian women by an observer who has visited the country six times and who speaks the language.

Melville, Keith, *Communes in the Counter Culture: Origins, Theories, Styles of Life,* New York: William Morow and Co., 1972. Careful analysis of the ideological and historical origins of the communal living movement as a form of rebellion against middle-class culture.

Robertson, Constance Noyes, *Oneida Community: The Breakup, 1876–1881,* Syracuse: Syracuse University Press, 1972. A sequel to the volume cited in the chapter, covering the final years of the experiment.

Tiger, Lionel, and Shepher, Joseph, *Women in the Kibbutz,* New York: Harcourt, Brace Jovanovich, 1975. One of the authors spent most of his adult life in a kibbutz, and, in addition, survey data are employed. Emphasizes the return of kibbutzniks to traditional sex roles.

FILMS

Blackjack's Family (G. V. Hood Films, P.O. Box 22213, Milwaukee, Ore. 97222), 53 minutes. A documentary about a former communal couple's efforts to find its own solutions to universal family problems.

A Great Family on a Collective Farm (National Council of American-Soviet Friendship, Inc., 156 Fifth Avenue, New York, N.Y. 10010), 20 minutes. The daily life of a family with 6 children and 30 grandchildren on a prosperous collective farm. Methods of payment to farmers, and collective social services are discussed.

Serafima Kotova (National Council of American-Soviet Friendship, Inc., 156

Fifth Avenue, New York, N.Y. 10010), 20 minutes. Pictorial story of a Soviet woman, made an orphan in World War II. Mrs. Kotova works in a textile mill, where she is now a forelady. She is also a Deputy of the Supreme Soviet of the Soviet Federation. Film shows her relationships with her husband and her young son.

The Year of the Communes (Association-Sterling Films, 5797 New Peachtree Road, Atlanta, Ga. 30340), 52 minutes. A survey of communes ranging from the ascetic to the hedonistic. Honest, beautifully filmed, and informative.

QUESTIONS AND PROJECTS

1. Describe the role of John Humphrey Noyes in the development of the Oneida Community. What is meant by "Noyes was a charismatic leader"?
2. What factors led to the breakup of the Oneida Community? What are the implications of the Oneida experience for family sociology?
3. Why was the Soviet regime opposed to the family? What steps did it take to eliminate the family?
4. What were the effects of the Soviet family legislation of the 1920s on divorce rates and birth rates? Upon the status of women? Upon juvenile delinquency?
5. Sketch briefly the history of the kibbutzim. Describe the economic organization, the level of living, and the ideology of the traditional kibbutz.
6. What has been the long-term kibbutz experience in attempting to do away with the family? What trends appear likely in the kibbutz in the future?
7. How was the decade of the 1960s, in the United States, demographically unique? What impact did that uniqueness have upon the nation?
8. Trace the ways in which social adolescence was prolonged over the past two or three decades. How is this a function of movement toward a post-industrial society?
9. Differentiate between group marriages and communes in terms of: (a) size, (b) clarity of boundaries, (c) sex roles, (d) attitude toward property, and (e) stability.
10. What special problems did communes encounter in the areas of: (a) finances, (b) operationalizing the communal value system, (c) sex and jealousy, and (d) children?
11. Define the concept of open marriage. What guidelines were offered for the development of open marriages? What do you think the impact will be of the concept of open mariage upon the future of American marriage?

II
Historical and Theoretical Perspectives

MORNING STAR.
Thomas York. Aged 30. March 29 1837.
Harriet York. Aged 26 August 23 1837

6
History of the Western Family

. . . Nowhere is this more evident than in the change in the nature of the family. In the traditional world, work and home life were one, and the family was both an economic and a social unit. Not only that, but it was the setting for almost all the other social functions as well—welfare, recreation, education, and religious instruction.

The modern world has witnessed the separation of the family, as an institution, from most of these functions. There is, more radically, a separation of family from occupation, whether it be the breakup of the family farm, the family business, the family enterprise or the family tradition, such as medicine, law, carpentry, fishing. Education has been taken over almost entirely by the schools, recreation primarily by commercial enterprises, welfare by the government or by social institutions. The family is now focused largely on fulfilling psychological and emotional needs. . . .

The change in the nature of the family—historically the most crucial of all human institutions—has had a contradictory effect on a person's sense of individualism. In a psychological sense, as the ties with a family have weakened or been cut altogether, the feeling of individualism has been enhanced. To the classic question of identity—"Who are you?"—a traditional person would answer: "I am the son of my father." But today a person says, "I am I. I come out of myself, and in choice and action I make myself." The great thrust of the American character—the urge, the compulsion to strike out on one's own, to cut away from the father and even to surpass him—has been one of the richest of the sources of dynamism in American life. . . .[1]

Change in the Western family has been rapid and continuous. We can trace our family system back 3000 years or so, and learn a great deal

1. Daniel Bell, "Toward A Communal Society," *Life Magazine* 62 (May 12, 1967), p. 114.

about how the American family functions today. During that 3000 years, the focus shifts many times and the family changes from a strongly patriarchal, patrilineal, patrilocal, polygynous one to a nearly equalitarian, monogamous, bilateral, conjugal one.

THE ANCIENT HEBREW FAMILY SYSTEM

The family system of the ancient Hebrews is the earliest direct antecedent of our own system, about which there is comprehensive knowledge. The earliest Hebrew records go back approximately 4000 years. Not surprisingly the earliest records are fragmentary and difficult to interpret. By the dawn of history, the Hebrews were a nomadic desert people with a pastoral economy. They roamed the countryside seeking pasture for their herds and maintaining an elaborate kinship organization. Beyond the family, there was a *sib*, a group of kinsmen related through males (a patrilineal descent group), and a *clan*, which included the wives as well. Several related clans made up a *tribe*, and twelve tribes constituted the nation of Israel.[2]

By about the twelfth century before Christ, the Hebrews began to develop agriculture and to settle in towns. The old tribal organization was gradually replaced by a more centralized organization around a king.

During the nomadic period, the Hebrew family was patriarchal, patrilineal, patrilocal, polygynous, and extended. There is evidence of a quite different form of organization before recorded history,[3] and the patriarchy was considerably modified as settled agriculture developed.

Patriarchy

The Hebrew family was a strong patriarchy, the authority of the father being nearly absolute. All women were under the control of one or

2. Stuart A. Queen and Robert W. Habenstein, *The Family in Various Cultures*, Philadelphia: J. B. Lippincott Company, 1974, pp. 153–59.

3. Some scholars believe that the Hebrew family once was both matrilineal and matrilocal. The generations of Esau are traced, in Genesis, through his wives rather than through himself, and Leah and Rachel are referred to as the women who did "build the house of Israel." The incest taboos permitted the marriage of half brothers and sisters where the common parent was the father but not where the common parent was the mother. Certain of the patriarchs and their wives are also known to have lived with their wives' fathers over long periods of time. See Queen and Habenstein, *ibid.*, p. 157; and Panos D. Bardis, "Family Forms and Variations Historically Considered," in Harold T. Christensen, *ed.*, *Handbook of Marriage and the Family*, Chicago: Rand McNally, 1964, p. 416.

more males, the only exception being a widowed mother. Sons were trained in obedience to their mother, whereas other women were considered to be their property.[4] The husband could put his wife to death for adultery, but not for any other reason. All of this implies a low status for women, and their status was low. Yet, there is little evidence that women were abused. On the contrary, wives were highly regarded and often wielded great power. Marriages often were made to cement ties between two extended families, and the wife's family retained an interest in her welfare.

The father had even greater power over his children. The familiar story of Abraham's near-sacrifice of Isaac indicates that he held the power of life and death. Hebrew children were expected to be obedient and respectful, and the Mosaic law provided that persistently disobedient children should be put to death. That there was some limitation on the father's power is indicated by the fact that a stubborn or gluttonous son was to be stoned by his fellow Israelites after the father had testified against him; but he was not to be killed by the father himself.[5]

The father could marry off his children and could sell their labor. Theoretically, the young persons' consent to marriage was required, but they seldom refused. The father's power again was restricted in that he was forbidden to make his daughter a prostitute,[6] and could not sell his children to foreigners (non-Hebrews). The offense of Joseph's brothers in selling him was twofold: first, they usurped the prerogative of the patriarch; and, second, they sold him to foreigners.

Polygyny

The Hebrews practised polygyny and concubinage. Several wives were common among patriarchs and kings, additional concubines being taken from among servant and slave girls. One rationalization for concubinage was the high value placed upon sons. Barren wives might give their female servants to their husbands as concubines, claiming the children as their own. Concubines were treated well, and sometimes were raised to the status of wife after a wife died. Children of concubines could inherit, although not so much as children of wives.

Polygyny was not without problems, although it did not yield completely to monogamy until the Middle Ages. Some jealousy developed

4. Willystine Goodsell, *A History of Marriage and the Family*, New York: The Macmillan Company, 1939, p. 54.
5. Deuteronomy 21:18–21.
6. Leviticus 19:29.

among wives and concubines and it was common for each wife and her children to have a separate dwelling.[7] Sororal polygyny helped to keep antagonisms in check. The vast majority of Hebrews must have been monogamous, of course. Beyond the biological facts of the sex ratio, the custom of bride price restricted polygyny to the well-to-do.

Betrothal and Marriage

According to Talmudic law, the minimum ages for marriage were thirteen for boys and twelve for girls. Fathers could betroth children at younger ages, but the nuptials could not take place until they became of age. In earliest times, betrothal was regarded as the beginning of marriage, even though the marriage was not consummated until later,[8] and sometimes nuptials were not even held.

Gradually, betrothal became distinct from marriage and, when the parties were of age, one year commonly elapsed between betrothal and marriage. Betrothal took two forms: the transfer of money or the preparation of a written instrument. *Kaseph* involved the man giving a coin to the woman and saying, "Be thou consecrated to me." Kaseph is believed to be a symbol of earlier explicit wife purchase. The other ceremony, *kiddushin,* involved the man's giving the woman a document which probably read, "I do hereby betroth thee according to the law of Moses and Israel." Two witnesses were required in both cases, and a benediction was given by the bride's father or by a rabbi.

The marriage ceremony was a private family affair in which the bride was transported to the groom's house to receive the benediction. A rabbi was not required, but ten witnesses were necessary. By the first century B.C., the *ketubah,* or marriage contract, came to be separate from the betrothal agreement. In addition to the vows, the ketubah stated the bride price, or *mohar,* it enumerated the property the bride brought to the marriage (the dowry); it defined the mode of inheritance in case no children were born; and it specified the wife's right to support from her husband and his obligation to have sexual intercourse regularly with her.[9]

7. Genesis 31:33.

8. Sexual intercourse with a person other than the betrothed was regarded as adultery and was punished as such.

9. The husband's obligation to have regular sexual intercourse with each of his wives placed a practical limitation upon the number of wives a man could take. Both husband and wife could be fined if they failed in their marital duties. More important than the right to sexual satisfaction was the importance attached to having children. If sexual intercourse were not had regularly, the production of children would be threatened.

Marriage was highly valued, and to remain celibate was a religious crime. There are many reasons for the high value upon marriage. First, it was designed to produce sons so that a man's house "should not die out of Israel." Second, marriage was a more acceptable alternative than illicit sexual activity.[10] Third, the Hebrews were keepers of herds and flocks, and children, especially sons, were economic assets.

The importance of sons was institutionalized in the levirate. If a man died without sons, the widow was expected to marry the deceased husband's brother. The first son born was then regarded as the offspring of the deceased brother. Since the Hebrews were polygynous, the levirate was possible even if the brother was already married. The only way that the brother could escape the duty of the levirate was to humiliate himself through the custom of *chalitza*, according to which the widow loosened the brother's shoe, spat in his face, and accused him of failing to do his duty to his brother—all in a public ceremony. The levirate prevailed among the Hebrews well into the Middle Ages.[11]

Descent and Inheritance

By the time of the patriarchs, patrilineal descent and inheritance were well established. During the earliest period, there was something very close to complete primogeniture. The eldest son received the father's blessing and inherited almost all of the property. Students will remember the story of Rebekah's and Jacob's treachery in inducing the nearly blind Isaac to give the blessing to Jacob instead of to his older brother, Esau. During this period, daughters did not inherit.

Later, as agriculture developed, the eldest son received a double portion, with the other sons inheriting equally.[12] If there was no son, property passed to the daughters, and if there were no children it passed to brothers or uncles.[13] Sometimes, if there were no sons, the patriarch

10. Sexual attitudes among the Hebrews were characterized by prudery and by preoccupation with avoiding prostitution and perversion. Nudity was regarded as shameful; only foreign women were acceptable as prostitutes; and sodomy was considered repulsive, yet may have been widely practised. Students will recall the story of Lot and the destruction of the cities of Sodom and Gomorrah.

11. The crime of Onan (onanism), which is widely regarded today as masturbation, was actually Onan's refusal to impregnate his brother's widow. In his relations with the widow, Onan practised coitus interruptus.

12. Deuteronomy 21:15–18.

13. Numbers 27:1–11.

would marry his daughter to a male slave and make the slave his heir.[14] Property thus passed from patriarch to grandson with the slave as intermediary.

Further clues to the importance of maternal kin among the Hebrews and to a possible earlier matrilineal stage are found in the incest taboos.

Divorce

Until nearly the time of Christ, the Hebrew husband had almost unlimited power to divorce his wife. The Mosaic law provided, simply, that the husband should hand his wife a bill of divorcement stating, "Be thou divorced from me," and send her out of the house.[15]

Over the centuries, resistance developed to the husband's power to repudiate his wife and, by the time of Christ, the authorities would accept divorce only on certain grounds: adultery, indecency, refusal to cohabit, barrenness, change of religion, refusal to observe ritual laws, and insulting the husband. Gradually, the wife also gained rights of divorce. By the Roman period, she could divorce her husband for: impotence, change of religion, refusal to support her, commission of a serious crime, extreme dissolution, and affliction with a loathsome disease (leprosy). Significantly, she could not divorce him for adultery. Later, the rabbis secured power to separate couples either for adultery or barrenness.

Women who were unjustly divorced did not suffer greatly. They became free agents. They were no longer under the power of their fathers or their husbands. They were also entitled to return of their dowries, which provided them with a livelihood. If they were divorced for cause, however—and the causes were, by modern standards, trivial—then they lost their dowries and suffered loss of status as well.

The Gradual Development of Public Control

The traditional Hebrew family was an organization of great strength and unity. It existed in a social context where there were no other elaborately developed institutions. Political power was held largely by patri-

14. The extended family often was quite large. In addition to the patriarch, his wives and concubines, their unmarried children, married sons and their wives and children, there often were servants and slaves, and sometimes even nonrelatives who had placed themselves under the authority of the patriarch. Servants and slaves were well treated—almost as family members. Consequently, taking a slave as a son-in-law and heir did not seem too unusual.

15. Deuteronomy 24:1–2.

archs; the economy was rudimentary; even religion was primarily a family matter. The patriarch served as priest at worship and presided over ceremonial activities.[16] There was not yet a separate class of rabbis. Under these conditions, the family performed many functions and was a strong and stable unit.

Gradually, with the development of agriculture, other sources of power developed. In the eighth century B.C., Israel was conquered by the Assyrians. Then, in the sixth century B.C., came the Babylonian conquest, and eventually Israel fell under the power of Rome. The public authorities, as they expanded control over the society, undertook increasing regulation of marriage and family matters.

Gradually, too, a class of religious functionaries—the rabbis—emerged. At first, the rabbis did not challenge the power of the patriarchs. But gradually they interpreted the scriptures to limit the power of husbands over wives and of fathers over children. A body of rabbinical law became the foundation for marriage and family life.

The changes brought about by public authorities and rabbis are illustrated by the transformation of the custom of wife purchase and the accompanying changes in the status of women. In earliest times, husbands apparently purchased wives outright—almost as they would cattle. Gradually, bride price became compensation to the girl's father for loss of her services and a guarantee of her good treatment. The bride price was paid either in service or in money. Jacob, it will be remembered, worked for Laban fourteen years to marry Leah and Rachel. During this period women were regarded as chattels.

The rabbis sought to protect women through the marriage contract. The ketubah spelled out the economic interests and rights of both families. As the rabbis took control of marriages, the parties became less the two families and more the particular man and woman. The ketubah listed the bride price, which was gradually transformed into a dower right—money or property to be held for the wife in the event of the husband's death or her unjust divorce. The dowry too—essentially the wife's family's economic contribution to the marriage—was listed. The husband was given life use (usufruct) of the dowry but, again, the wife retained interest in it and might have it returned if she was divorced by her husband. Women came to be legal persons with rights as well as responsibilities.

16. There is a possibility that, in prehistory, the Hebrews were ancestor worshippers. The graven images of the Old Testament are thought to be symbols of ancestors. Moreover, the family burial ground was a sacred place.

THE ANCIENT GREEK FAMILY SYSTEM

The origins of Greek culture, like those of the Hebrews, are lost in antiquity. It is believed that the mainland of Greece was settled by voyagers from Crete, around 1600 B.C. These settlers were invaded successively by the Ionians, by the nomadic Achaeans, and by the also nomadic Dorians. By the seventh century B.C., these three groups had become self-governing city-states, bearing a largely common culture. During the fifth century B.C., the Greek city-states went to war with and defeated the Persian Empire to the east, and Greece reached its zenith. A series of civil wars between the city-states finally weakened the empire, and by 146 B.C. Greece had become just a Roman province.

Description of the family system of ancient Greece is complicated both by continuous social change and by differences between Athens and Sparta. During the earliest (Homeric) period, Greece's economy was mainly agricultural and its family system reflected that economic base. The family was a strong patriarchy in which divorce was uncommon. Beyond the extended family there was the *gens*, a clan consisting of all the extended families which traced descent from a common ancestor. The *gens* established the legitimacy of children, prevented the alienation of land, and saw to it that legitimate heirs were provided. The dominant family patterns became those of the cities of Athens and Sparta. During the "golden age" of Greece, its family system was an urban one, evolved from its patriarchal land-oriented precursor.

Athens was an aristocratic state in which the cultivation of knowledge was highly regarded. Most of the Greek contributions to philosophy, literature, architecture, and engineering originated here. The Athenians also emphasized athletic skills, but Sparta made virtually a fetish of these. The Spartans were militaristic, emphasizing the production of warriors. Spartan boys at the age of seven generally left their parental homes to live in military-style barracks, where they underwent arduous physical training and where they continued to live during most of their adult lives. The separation of husbands and wives entailed by this existence produced different relationships between the sexes than in Athens. Spartan women were freer, more aggressive, and more nearly equal with their husbands.

Patriarchy

The Greek father, like his Hebrew counterpart, was exceedingly powerful. Unlike the Hebrew, however, the Greek father did not hold power in his own right. His power derived from his position as trustee of the family estates and from his role as priest in the worship of ancestors. Membership in the family was based upon being eligible to worship the ancestors and coming under control of the family head.

During the early agricultural period, women had relatively high status—they were virtually the equals of their husbands. However, their status worsened very early and, by the golden age, women were little better off than slaves.

Athenian men dominated women almost completely. Women were defined as biologically, intellectually, and emotionally inferior. They were minors having no legal status, were poorly educated, and were inadequate companions to their learned husbands. Mature men of about thirty often were married to adolescent girls. Once married, a woman was confined to the women's apartments and unable to leave the house without permission. On the streets, she had to be veiled and accompanied by a slave chaperone. When her husband had guests, she was not permitted to eat with them. The husband held power of life and death over his wife only for adultery. If he discovered his wife and her lover in the act, the husband could kill them. If he did not kill his wife immediately, he could only beat her and confine her to the house.

Spartan wives also occupied a very inferior position and were treated without sentiment. There was almost no wedding ceremonial. The bride was taken forcibly to the groom's house,[17] where a servant cut her hair in ragged boyish style, dressed her in men's clothing and shoes, and left her in the dark to await her husband. The husband visited her for sexual purposes and little else. Even in their sex relationship, the emphasis was upon the production of heirs and not upon physical and emotional satisfaction. For companionship and pleasure, the husband turned to a special class of women who were provided for the purpose.

The father's power over children was even more extreme. In the early period he could expose (desert) infants, sell their labor, and bestow them in marriage. The father may have had authority to determine whether any child lived or died. Probably, the right to expose an infant was linked to the emphasis on healthy children who could inherit property and carry on the family line. Exposure seems to have been limited

17. There are references in Greek literature to "wife capture" and there has been speculation whether this was the prevailing means of mate selection in the prehistoric era. The Spartan ceremonial, and the Athenian custom of carrying a bride, who feigned resistance, over the threshold, are sometimes interpreted as symbolic of earlier wife capture. There is no way to tell whether a general practice of wife capture ever existed.

mainly to illegitimate and deformed or sickly children. Girls were more likely to be exposed than boys. Girls could not serve in the military, and their marriage carried heavy dowry obligations.

During the early period, the father could sell both sons and daughters. Although there is no proof, probably he could not sell them into genuine slavery but could sell them into indentured servitude while they were growing up. Even this power was restricted as Greek civilization developed.

In the early period, too, sons remained under the father's control as long as the father lived. The father could "emancipate" the son through a ceremony which excluded the son from worship of the family ancestors and released him from paternal authority. Sons were highly valued, however, and emancipation was rare. Later on, it became common to emancipate the son at maturity.

Inheritance and Descent

Patrilineal descent was tied to ancestor worship.[18] Only men could carry on worship of the ancestors, so descent was traced through males only. This extreme form of patrilineal descent in which relationship is traced only through males is known as *agnation*. Primogeniture existed with landed property, all of the family estates being inherited by the eldest son. The younger sons left home with the movable property; daughters did not inherit.

Great emphasis was placed upon the provision of legitimate heirs. If a man produced daughters but no sons, his daughter was required to marry the father's brother. Since the Greeks were monogamous, this sometimes meant that the brother had to divorce his wife to marry his niece. Or the father might give the daughter in marriage to some other man on condition that the first son be given to him as his own.[19]

Spartan inheritance laws were more liberal. Women could inherit land as well as movable property, and one of the effects of Greece's wars was to concentrate property in the hands of women.

Marriage

Marriage was a sacred obligation. It was the means to continued worship of the ancestors and it provided for inheritance of the family prop-

18. The Greeks may have practised matrilineal descent in prehistoric times.
19. In the more liberal Sparta, older men who were childless sometimes encouraged their younger wives to have intercourse with younger men so that they might become pregnant.

erty. Celibacy was a legal offense; both Athens and Sparta passed laws punishing those who remained single.

During the Homeric period marriage was simple. The groom made "gifts" to the bride's father—a not very subtle form of bride price—and the girl was handed over to her husband. At this stage, the wife ordinarily brought no property to the marriage. As Greece developed, the arrangements became elaborate. Betrothal and marriage were separated. Betrothal was a business contract between the parents, setting forth the bride price and the dowry. The husband was permitted to administer the dowry but it was returned to the wife at the husband's death or in the event of her unjust divorce.

The Athenian wedding ceremony was an extravagant religious affair. The principal ceremonies occurred either in the bride's home or in a temple. There was a ritual eating of sesame-seed cakes to ensure fertility, the bride's father offered sacrifices to the gods, and handed his daughter over to her husband by releasing her from his own power and from the worship of his ancestors. Then there was an elaborate parade to the groom's home, more ritual eating, and the commending of the bride to the husband's ancestors. No special religious functionaries participated. The fathers acted as priests; marriage was a private family affair.

Concubinage and Prostitution

The Greeks were monogamous,[20] but supplemented monogamy with concubinage and prostitution. Concubines were taken by wealthy men generally from among slaves or women who had been captured in war. Concubines had lower status even than wives and were not permitted to worship family ancestors. Their children were not true family members and could not inherit property.

The best known women of ancient Greece are the *hetaerae*. The hetaerae—trained from childhood in knowledge, the arts, and social graces—were captured women of noble birth or were Greek girls who had survived exposure and who were reared to be the social and sexual companions of wealthy men. These women were remarkably free in their daily activities, were highly regarded, and often wielded power and influence. For poorer Greeks, there were ordinary prostitutes. Again, they were exposed girls from poor families or captured women. The city-states licensed houses of prostitution and heavily taxed prosti-

20. Bardis reports that both polygyny and polyandry may have existed in prehistoric times. *Op. cit.*, pp. 423–24.

tutes' income. The taxing was less a matter of morality than of financing the state.

Divorce

If divorce existed during the earliest period, it was rare. Even during Homeric times, the indissolubility of marriage was emphasized. Gradually, however, the husband's right to repudiate his wife emerged. He had only to state his displeasure with her in the presence of witnesses. On either of two grounds—adultery or barrenness—the husband was regarded as justified in divorcing his wife. Gradually, the law came to demand annulment for flagrant adultery on the part of the wife.

At least during the period of urbanization, the wife also had limited rights of divorce. She could not, however, divorce her husband for adultery no matter how flagrant. Only if he was physically cruel or neglected his family was she entitled to divorce. Even then, she had to seek permission from the public authorities, which she could not do unless her husband permitted her to leave the house to do so.

THE ROMAN FAMILY SYSTEM

According to legend, Rome was founded in 753 B.C. Little is known of this period, except that Rome was a village occupied by Latin-speaking tribes. Gradually, these tribes increased in military power and conquered the whole of what today is Italy. The development of the Roman family system is even more progressive than that of the Hebrews and Greeks. For convenience, we divide Roman history into two main periods from 753 B.C. until the close of the Punic Wars in 202 B.C. and from 202 B.C. until the fall of the Empire in the third century A.D.

Before the Punic Wars

The early Roman family was the strongest patriarchy of which we have knowledge. Descent was patrilineal. Marriage was monogamous, and a three-generation extended family was common.

Patriarchy. The family was a large, strong, stable unit. It performed many functions and those functions were concentrated in the patriarch, the *pater familias*. The father was priest of the ancestor worship, he was the only "legal" person in the family, and he held ownership of all property. His power over his children was called *potestas* and extended throughout his lifetime; some famous Roman generals were still under *potestas* and were unable to control their own property or earnings. Newborn infants were brought to their fathers to determine whether they should live or die. If the father decided to expose them, they were left in the countryside to die or to be taken as slaves to some other family. The father also could sell children into slavery, banish them from the country, or kill them. Before he could kill them, he had to consult with the adult males of his *gens*, but, after doing so, no matter what their recommendations, he was free to do as he wished. The father could both marry off and divorce his children even against their will. Even married sons and their sons remained under the patriarch's power. Before the father's death the only escape from *potestas* was emancipation, a mock sale which freed the son to become a *pater familias* himself. Sons were highly valued, however, and emancipation was rare.

Daughters also fell under *potestas* and, at marriage, were transferred to the *manus* (hand) of their husbands. Theoretically, no Roman woman was ever a free agent. The husband could name a guardian for his wife after his own death. Since women were not legal persons, the husband was responsible for crimes his wife committed and he could punish her accordingly. If she caused him financial loss, he could sell her labor to pay it. After consulting with the adult males of both his *gens* and his wife's, he could kill her. If she committed adultery, he could kill her immediately. Paradoxically, Roman women had generally high status. They were respected mistresses of their households, were free to come and go, and were social and intellectual companions of their husbands. Their status is symbolized by the phrase which they uttered upon being carried over the threshold by their new husbands: "Where thou art lord, I am lady." In the home, the Roman woman was located not in women's apartments but in the atrium, the central room of the house.

Descent and Inheritance. The *familia* was a unit of the *gens*, a patrilineal descent group. Like the Greeks, the Romans practised *agnation*, tracing descent through males only. The *gens* was composed of all *familia* which traced descent from a common ancestor. In earliest times, the *gens* held property, provided guardians for dependent or defective members, conducted religious services, maintained burial grounds, and passed resolutions which were binding upon its members.

There was no place for unattached persons. Everyone belonged to a household and came under the control of the family head. At the death of the *pater familias*, each adult son inherited an equal share of the estate and set up his own *familia*. Later on, the widow and daughters who lived at home and were under *potestas* came to receive equal shares. Such daughters had to have the consent of the *gens* to marry, and they were not permitted to dispose of their shares of the estate.

Marriage. The emphasis upon ancestor worship and continuing the family line made marriage both a patriotic and a religious duty. Single persons were heavily taxed, and widowed and divorced persons were urged to remarry. Girls were married young. Often men of twenty-five were married to girls of fifteen. Marriage forms and ceremonies varied according to the social status of the participants. The highest status group were the patricians, or Roman citizens. Then came the plebeians and, finally, the slaves.

Betrothal was common among the patricians. Breaking of an engagement, while disapproved, could be done by either family without penalty. It was not unusual to betroth girls of ten or twelve, and if a betrothed girl were subsequently to engage in sexual intercourse with another man she was guilty of adultery. The major function of betrothal was the setting of a girl's dowry, which tended to become increasingly large. The dowry was controlled by the husband, who received income from it but was not permitted actually to own or dispose of it. At his death, or upon divorce, the dowry was returned to the girl's family.

There were two basic forms of marriage: *matrimonium justum* and *matrimonium nonjustum*. Until 445 B.C., *matrimonium justum* could be entered into only by Roman citizens; after that it could be arranged between a citizen and a noncitizen. *Matrimonium justum* established both *potestas* and *manus* and the children were Roman citizens. *Matrimonium nonjustum* carried neither *potestas* nor *manus* and the children could not become citizens.

There were three ways of celebrating marriage with *manus*. The first, *confarreatio*, was an elaborate religious ceremony presided over by priests and ten witnesses. The bride was carried in elaborate procession to the groom's house, where a sheep was slain, and there was a ritual eating of sacred cake. This ceremony was most common among the patricians or citizens. A second type of ceremony, *coemptio*, rested solely on the consent of the parties (the parents of the bride and groom), and consisted of a mock sale of the bride. The passing of a coin symbolized the woman's being brought under *manus*. The least highly regarded custom was that of *usus* (use), where the marriage grew out of cohabitation. If the man and woman lived together for a year without the woman being gone from the man's home for three consecutive days, she was automatically brought under *manus*. This form was most common among the plebeians.

Although the Romans were monogamous, *matrimonium nonjustum* was a form of concubinage. It was a socially sanctioned relationship between two people who could not legally marry according to *matrimonium justum*, in which the woman had low status and the offspring were not recognized as members of the man's family.

Divorce. The Roman husband always could divorce his wife for adultery, preparation of poisons, or wine-drinking.[21] Divorce was discouraged during the early centuries, however, and was uncommon. Before a man could repudiate his wife, even when she had committed the specified acts, he had to consult with the adult males of both *gentes*. The breaking of a marriage entered into by *confarreatio* was even more difficult. The couple had to endure a *diffarreatio* ceremony to which all of those who had attended the wedding were invited.

Divorce was not interfered with by public authorities. As the centuries progressed, divorce became more common and a distinction between just and unjust divorce emerged. The case of Spurius Carvilius Ruga about 230 B.C. is cited as the first instance of a man divorcing his wife for other than the three specified causes. He was compelled to forfeit half of his property and to turn over the other half to his divorced wife. A man who divorced his wife without cause was required to return her dowry.

After the Punic Wars

There was not, of course, a sharp change in Roman family patterns in 202 B.C. Change had been occurring for centuries and was aggravated by Rome's long wars with Carthage. The immediate effect was to take men off to war and to leave their wives, by default, with increasing power. The wives were no longer under *potestas* and their husbands were away. Women were forced to take over the management of family estates and, in many cases, managed them well. Inevitably, a shift in the power relations between the sexes occurred. Men, when and if they returned, found many wives unwilling to submit to *manus*.

21. This is the first instance of a man being unable to divorce his wife for barrenness. Although child-bearing was highly regarded, a man suffered economic penalties for divorcing his wife because she was childless.

These changes were associated with vastly increased family wealth. Rome emerged victorious over Carthage and went on to subjugate the entire Mediterranean region. The wealth of the provinces was siphoned away to Rome and a vast number of servants and slaves was accumulated. As wealth increased, the size of dowries increased proportionately, and daughters came to inherit property from their fathers. Fathers became more reluctant to see this property going to the husbands, and, after the second Punic War, marriage without *manus* became common. Theoretically, this left the wife under *potestas* but, practically, it worked to free women from direct male control. Many women became quite wealthy. Moreover, some women became learned and active in public affairs. As they did, changes in marriage and family practices took place.

Potestas declined. Civil authorities gradually freed the property of adult sons from the control of their fathers. Caesar gave sons the right to dispose of property acquired in their military careers. The power of the father over children was restricted also. Infant exposure, never common, still was permitted, but the power of life and death over children was taken away. Only very poor parents were permitted to sell their children's labor, and public officials assumed jurisdiction over children who committed legal offenses. Daughters indirectly escaped from *potestas* through marriage without *manus*.

Change in the marriage ideals was not striking. Marriage still was highly regarded, and marriages on the whole remained stable. There was, however, a steady erosion of the foundations of marriage which led to conspicuous increase in various forms of pathology. Marriage had always been a private family matter, resting on the consent of the two families involved. It remained so, but the consent of the husband and wife became more prominent. The customs of *confarreatio*, *coemptio*, and *usus* all but disappeared. The formal trappings of the wedding, in the form of an elaborate torchlight parade and banquet, remained, but much of the substance withered away.

Erosion of marriage ideals took place most conspicuously at the top of the socio-economic order. Within the leisure class, marriage ceased to be a sacred obligation and became primarily a matter of personal satisfaction and convenience. Both men and women married for financial gain, or they married not at all. *Matrimonium nonjustum* degenerated into men taking mistresses much as in modern society. Prostitution increased markedly. The drop in the marriage rate became a matter of concern, and, by the time of Christ, legislation was passed penalizing the unmarried. Single adults were disqualified from receiving inheritances unless they married.

The birth rate also fell. Abortion was widely practised, and the exposure of infants reached scandalous proportions. To correct this situation, laws were passed taxing inheritances of childless couples at 50 percent. The laws exempted children by adoption, however, and it became fashionable to adopt adult children for the purpose of receiving inheritances. Both the couples doing the adopting and the adopted entered such relationships according to calculated advantage. The state grew more concerned, and the birth rate continued to fall.

Divorce, too, became common. Divorce, like marriage, was a private matter, and divorce by mutual consent became possible simply by transferring a bill of divorcement in the presence of seven witnesses. There are no rates of divorce available, of course, so we can judge their increase only by the public concern. This concern is reflected in the following statements by famous men:

Tertullian: "The fruit of marriage is divorce."
Juvenal: "Some women divorce their husbands before the marriage garlands have faded."
Seneca: "Women no longer measure time in terms of the administrations of Roman consuls, but by the number of their husbands."

The famous Julian Law, in 17 B.C., provided that a woman guilty of adultery should be deprived of half her dowry, one-third of her property, and be banished to a desert island. Ironically, one of the women punished was Julia, daughter of Emperor Augustus who had the law passed. The same law deprived an adulterous husband of half of his property and of all his wife's dowry, and banished him from Rome.

THE INFLUENCE OF CHRISTIANITY

The Christians did not have a family system as such. They were not a nation, nor even an ethnic group. They began as a small sect within Judaism and gradually made converts from among Romans, Greeks, traditional Hebrews, and others. Rome remained as the center of political power, and the Christians, as they gained in strength and numbers, contested with the Roman government for control of marriage and family matters.

The new religion spread slowly, for it challenged, both directly and indirectly, the power of the state. The Christians taught that the power of the church was superior to that of the state. They refused to celebrate the emperor's birthday, they would not offer sacrifices to the spirits of departed emperors, and they discouraged their members from serving in the Roman armies. Whereas the emperors were passing laws to penalize celibacy, the Christians taught that the virgin state was an exalted one. As a result of such teachings, the Christians were persecuted by the authorities and by much of the general populace.

The teachings of the Christian church must be seen both in the context of religious history and in terms of the prevailing morality in Rome. In some ways, the Christians sought to resurrect the stern morality of earlier Hebrew, Greek, and Roman periods. For their concept of the relationship between the mind and the body, the spirit and the flesh, they went back to the Persian philosophy of dualism which was some 2000 years old. They saw the demands of the spirit and the flesh as being mutually opposed and believed in suppressing the demands of the flesh. Rome appeared to be catering to the flesh. Divorce, celibacy, infanticide, prostitution, childlessness, and worldliness were common. Christian policies were formed both from tradition and in reaction against the prevailing conditions in Rome.

The church did not immediately take positions on marriage and divorce. It did not develop its own wedding ceremonies. It continued to accept the Roman ideas of marriage and divorce as private matters, and sought to express its ideals within the framework of Roman law and customs. Until the fourth century A.D., the state was clearly dominant. By A.D. 311, the Christians had grown too numerous and too powerful to be suppressed. Finally in 313, Christianity became an officially tolerated religion of Rome.

Attitudes and Policies Concerning Marriage

It is ironic that the Christians should have drastically lowered the status of marriage. Yet, under Christian influence, marriage and the family were more lowly regarded than ever before, or since. The Christians began by attacking adultery, abortion, infanticide, and child exposure. But, in so doing, they became victims of a conception of marriage as a purely sexual union—as a slightly more desirable alternative than fornication. The development and the implications of this concept have ever since been a matter of debate among theologians. Some early church fathers held lofty views of marriage. But over the centuries, the dominant view became that represented by some of the writings of St. Paul. Paul's statement that "it is better to marry than to burn" is widely quoted.[22] The Christians did not actually condemn marriage, for Christ had given approval to it. What they did was to regard the highest state as that of virginity; next came celibacy after marriage; then marriage; and, finally, fornication.

Sexual intercourse in marriage was considered a necessary evil rather than a source of pleasure. It was necessary for producing children and the virgins idealized by the church. At the fourth Council of Carthage in A.D. 398, it was declared that bride and groom should abstain from intercourse on their wedding night out of respect for the benediction. Later, the period was extended to three nights. The couple could avoid the obligation by paying a moderate fee to the church.

Marriage gradually was denied to priests and nuns. For a while, the church also encouraged married couples who had borne children to reassume the celibate state in marriage. The resulting friction was so great, however, that the policy was modified to include only marriages where the husband and wife agreed on celibacy. Second marriages also were condemned. An early Christian manual stated that "a second marriage is wicked, a third one indicative of unbridled lust, and one after the third, synonymous with fornication."[23]

The church disapproved of the Roman practice of permitting first cousins to marry, and gradually created "prohibited relationships" within which people might not marry. Relatives by blood (consanguinity) were taboo within seven degrees of kinship. Relatives by affinity (marriage) likewise were prohibited within seven degrees. Even persons who presided as godfathers and godmothers at baptisms and confirmations were considered to be related (spiritual affinity), and were forbidden to marry. Within a few generations almost everyone in the villages and towns of the day was related within prohibited degrees. For a thousand years, however, efforts were made to check upon such relationships, and, in the thirteenth century, the obligatory publishing of banns in the churches was designed to give those who knew of impediments a chance to speak. By their nature, these prohibitions were not enforceable, and they gave rise to problems.

22. This statement is widely misinterpreted. Some have concluded that Paul offered marriage as an alternative to the fires of hell. Actually the phrase "to burn" referred to the fires of passion, and Paul's statement should be interpreted to say that those who cannot abstain from illicit sexual intercourse should marry.

23. Quoted in Bardis, *op. cit.*, p. 442.

Christianity had no marriage ceremonies of its own for centuries. It accepted the Roman customs, and, later on, it accepted the customs of the Teutonic invaders from the north. What the church did was to urge the couple to seek the blessing of a priest after the nuptials. Not until the ninth century was marriage within the church firmly established. The reaction against marriage was harshest in the early centuries of the Christian era and gradually softened over the years. The sacred nature of marriage was emphasized increasingly as the church gained control, and, by the twelfth century, marriage was defined as one of the seven sacraments.

The Status of Women

The early Christian attitude toward women was paradoxical. On the one hand, men and women were equal in the sight of God, both being possessed of divine souls. Virgins were highly regarded. As "brides of Christ," they were assigned duties of caring for the sick and for needy widows and orphans, of visiting prisoners and administering relief programs. Widows, too, who forsook remarriage had high status and were employed in charitable activities.

On the other hand, the idea of the inferiority of women was pronounced. Women were assumed to represent the evils of sex and to be the unwholesome tempters of men.

> You are the devil's gateway: You are the unsealer of that forbidden tree: You are the first deserter of the divine law: You are she who persuaded him whom the devil was not valiant enough to attack. You destroyed so easily God's image, man. On account of your desert—that is, death—even the Son of God had to die.[24]

It is ironic, in view of the aggressive sexuality of men, that Christianity should have placed responsibility for carnal desires upon women, but women were considered to be tainted with the sin of Eve. They were admonished to confine themselves to housework and prayer. Women were not permitted to teach religion or to perform baptisms.

Divorce

The Christian attitude toward divorce required many centuries to crystallize. As in other areas, there was a split within the church. Christ had

24. Tertullian, *On the Apparel of Women,* Book I, Chapter I, Ante-Nicene Fathers, Vol. 4, p. 14, as quoted in Queen and Habenstein, *op. cit.,* p. 203.

seemed to sanction divorce where adultery had been committed. In general, however, the sentiment was against divorce: "What therefore God hath joined together, let not man put asunder."[25]

By A.D. 140, the church permitted divorce only on grounds of idolatry, apostasy, covetousness, and fornication. Over the next century or two, the policy wavered but tended toward increasingly strict regulation of divorce. In A.D. 314, the Council of Arles affirmed the principle of the indissolubility of marriage but did not make it mandatory. Finally, at the Council of Carthage in A.D. 407, the church took an irreversible stand against divorce. Finally, in the twelfth century, civil law was brought into complete conformity with canon law and absolute divorce almost disappeared from Europe.

THE GERMAN-ENGLISH FAMILY SYSTEM OF THE MIDDLE AGES

The Roman Empire finally succumbed to conquest at the end of the fourth century. For about two hundred years, various portions of the empire were overrun by loosely federated tribes ranging from the Vandals, Visigoths, Lombards, East Goths, Alemanni, and Burgundians in the south to the Angles, Saxons, Frisians, and Jutes in the north. Eventually Great Britain was invaded by the Angles, Saxons, and Jutes, carrying the cultural stream which was to be transported to America. Our knowledge of this period is not complete or reliable. The word *barbarian,* which is customarily attached to the Teutonic tribes connotes, among other things, a disrespect for learning that produced few written records.

Inheritance and Descent

The kinship system of the Germanic and English peoples was a considerable departure from the earlier patri-lineages of the Hebrews, Greeks, and Romans. Both peoples (the Anglo-Saxons in England and the Saxons and Frisians on the Continent) practised double descent. Relationship was traced both through the father's line and the mother's line, with each person being a member of two separate kin groups. These extended kin groups were called the *maegth* in Britain and the *sippe* on the Continent. In each case, membership in the kin group was traced from the grandchildren of a common set of ancestors.

25. Matthew 19:6.

The *sippe* occupied a position between the household and the state, comparable to the position of the *tsu* in China. The state depended upon the *sippe* to enforce the law among its members, and the *sippe* wielded power over the households and individuals. Membership in the *sippe* was by blood or adoption. Illegitimate children had no rights of inheritance; wives remained members of their own *sippes* after marriage. The father admitted each child to the *sippe*. The child was brought to him before it had tasted food, to be accepted or to be condemned to exposure. Although the father could not kill children who had tasted food, infanticide and exposure were permissible at least until the eleventh century.

Among these warlike peoples, membership in a kin group was the primary individual protection. If an individual was killed, his kin avenged the death or extracted payment (*wergild*) from the slayer's kin. If he killed someone else, then the paternal kin paid two-thirds of the *wergild* and the maternal kin paid one-third. A major function of the *sippe* was to restrain its landless male members from aggressive behavior.

In spite of the system of double descent, property passed from father to son in the male line. Wives and daughters were not prohibited from inheriting, however, and sometimes did so. In later centuries, the wife's interitance rights became increasingly fixed through the dower.

Patriarchy

The father's power over children was not so great as among the ancients. Fathers could punish children vigorously, but the laws of the Jutes, for example, provided that he should not break their bones. Anglo-Saxon children could be sold into slavery until they became seven years old, and among the Germanic peoples both wives and children could be sold in time of famine. The power of the *sippe* always was available to protect wives and children from abuse beyond permissible limits.

Anglo-Saxon fathers could give their daughters in marriage without the girls' consent until the eleventh century. They could also commit children to monasteries and nunneries. Girls, whose entrance into a convent often was accompanied by a substantial gift to the church, were not entitled to seek release from the convent even at adulthood.

The rights of sons exceeded those of daughters. While fathers generally had the usufruct of their children's property, the Anglo-Saxon father could not claim his son's earnings. Moreover, the father's power over his sons was drastically restricted when the sons reached majority, most commonly at twelve years of age.

The husband's power over his wife was limited by her membership in her own *sippe*. Her *sippe* remained responsible for crimes she committed and the *sippe* collected *wergild* in the event that harm was done to her. Short of doing severe bodily injury, however, the husband was expected to chastise her for misdeeds. A man who failed to punish an unruly wife might himself be punished by neighbors.

Betrothal and Marriage

By the late Middle Ages, betrothal and the nuptials had become quite distinct among the Germanic peoples. The betrothal, called *beweddung*, originated in an agreement between the groom and the bride's father for a bride price of cattle, money, or arms. Gradually, however, the interval between *beweddung* and *gifta* (marriage) lengthened, until it became common to betroth children and even infants.[26] With child betrothal, only a token sum was paid to the father as a kind of deposit on the full bride price. Eventually, it became common to pay the money to the bride herself and, still later, the payment took the form of a ring —the precursor of the modern engagement ring. The bride price also was transformed from an actual payment to the bride's father into a dower right in the husband's property in the event that the husband should die before she did. This dower right often amounted to half of the husband's property. *Beweddung* was the first step in marriage, and subsequent sexual intercourse on the part of the girl was severely punished.

Gifta, the marriage ceremony, was a private family matter, involving the bride's being turned over to her husband by her father. In some cases, the father also handed over a hat, sword, and mantle, which were the husband's symbols of authority over the wife. In some tribes, the groom then stepped on the bride's foot as a means of reinforcing the symbols. No religious officials were involved. After the tenth century, the girl sometimes selected another male relative to give her away or she gave herself in marriage. This giving of oneself in marriage, *self-gifta*, later evolved into common-law marriage.

These customs were little influenced by the spreading Christian church. As it had among the Romans, the church accepted the native cus-

26. George E. Howard, *A History of Matrimonial Institutions*, Chicago: University of Chicago Press, 1904, Vol. I, pp. 258–72.

toms for centuries. The church emphasized the sacred character of marriage and urged the couple to seek the blessing of a priest following *gifta*. Attending mass on the day following *gifta* became common, and, by the tenth century, *gifta* was often performed just outside the church entrance and in the presence of the priest. The presence of a priest was not necessary, however; marriage remained a private matter, based upon the consent of the parties.

Divorce

The Germanic peoples, like the ancients, had permitted the repudiation of wives. As this power became restricted, the influence of Rome was felt in the appearance of divorce by mutual consent—mutual consent, with the advantages lying with the husband. Adultery by the woman not only was cause for divorce but produced such moral outrage that she might be driven through the village and beaten to death. Men ordinarily could not be divorced for adultery. A man caught in adultery might be killed, not on moral grounds, but for violating the property rights of another man!

The church, it will be recalled, had established the indissolubility of marriage by the fifth century. For another 500 years, however, it continued to compromise with secular customs. Divorce by mutual consent was recognized, and even remarriage was permitted. Often, the bishops demanded that their consent be secured before remarriage. The church even gave slight encouragement to divorce in cases where one of the partners had converted to Christianity, but the other had not.

During these 500 years, the church consolidated its power and steadily assumed control over divorce until, by the tenth century, it had wrested control from the civil authorities. The bishops' courts came to hear all divorce cases and canon law replaced civil law. Canon law permitted two remedies to discontented couples: *divortium a vinculo matrimonii;* and *divortium a mensa et thoro.*

Divortium a vinculo matrimonii, which means "divorce from the bonds of matrimony" was not divorce as we know it, but annulment—an ecclesiastical declaration that a valid marriage never existed in the first place. There were ample grounds upon which annulment might be sought, for the church prohibited marriage within seven degrees for both consanguinity and affinity, and between those who had been religious sponsors for a child. Annulment also was permitted where either the husband or wife had entered into a previous verbal contract of marriage in words of the present tense. By the nature of such a contract, no records were available and the procedure was subject to abuse.

Divortium a mensa et thoro, literally divorce from bed and board, was not absolute divorce either. It was separation, permitted and enforced by the church. The parties remained legally married and escaped none of the obligations of marriage other than cohabitation. *Divortium a mensa et thoro* was permitted on three grounds: adultery, cruelty, and apostasy (heresy).

With *divortium a vinculo matrimonii*, the church had opened Pandora's box. Most couples, if they were determined, could find grounds for annulment. Moreover, the church often was a not too reluctant partner in fraud. Annulments were granted to wealthy persons upon the payment of sums of money, and dispensations permitting marriage within the prohibited degrees were available for the proper consideration.[27]

To understand this situation, one must be aware that the church was not only a religious institution but also an increasingly powerful political one. In contest with civil authorities over morals, the church wielded economic power with good effect. It missed few opportunities to increase its wealth, or its holdings in land. Be that as it may, the church established definitions that were to create problems for centuries.

THE IMPACT OF FEUDALISM

Feudalism developed on the Continent, where the countryside was divided into estates accumulated and held through military power. Kings bestowed vast portions of land upon nobles, who constituted a landed aristocracy paying tribute to the king and contributing armies to his service. In turn, the nobles farmed their holdings with the labor of serfs who were bound to the soil, and who served in the nobles' armies. In addition, there were free men, or yeomen, who owned their farms and who occasionally became prosperous. Finally, there was a growing class of artisans and tradesmen who lived in the towns. It was a more rigidly stratified society than had existed since the Roman Empire. This feudal economy was transferred to England with the Norman invasion, where it was dominant until the time of the Reformation.

Feudalism had major impact upon inheritance, marriage, and the status of women. These changes all stemmed from the necessity to hold

27. Howard, *op. cit.*, Vol. II, pp. 56–59.

estates intact and to keep them under the control of male heirs who could protect them against plunder.

Unogeniture and *entail* became firmly established. Unogeniture means that the estate is transmitted intact to one of the sons. Primogeniture was most common, but ultimogeniture also was found. Entail involved lands being inalienably settled upon a man and his straight-line descendants. Thus, great emphasis was placed upon "heirs of the body," and if a man had sons, no other relatives could inherit his land. Occasionally, younger sons inherited recently acquired lands which were not considered part of the traditional estate, but, by the fourteenth century, even that practice had given way to providing younger sons with life interests in the income from rents and trusts. Wives had only their dower interests, and this was defined as not to include the man's house, which must go instead to his heir.

Feudalism deprived women again of much of the status they had begun to recoup during the early Middle Ages. That the husband became the only legal person is illustrated by Glanvill's statement the "husband and wife were one person and that person was the husband." The husband owned the wife's dowry as long as the marriage survived, and had a life interest in it after her death. If he died first, she might have difficulty in acquiring control of her dower. For a woman to hold land outright, if just for her lifetime, threatened the lord's interest in it: she might marry a man who would alienate the land, or the land might be wrested from her by force. Consequently, when a man died the lord acquired control of the widow almost as he did of the land. She had to secure his consent to a proposed remarriage, or the lord might actually marry the widow off to a knight of his choice to protect his interest in the land.

The plight of children under feudalism was more difficult than that of women. Discipline was harsh, with beatings the approved way of securing obedience and respect. Children often were sent away from home to be trained by other families who would instill discipline and virtue without sentiment. If the father died, his children came under the power of the lord, who could arrange their marriages or sell that right to someone, if he did not wish to avail himself of it.

Arranging marriages became a matter of calculating bargaining, in which children were used as pawns in building estates. Although marriages could not be consummated until the boy reached 14 and the girl 12, much younger children were involved in marriage agreements. Queen and Habenstein quote Coke as writing that a 9-year-old widow should have her dower, "of what age soever her husband be, albeit he were but four years old."[28] Children of 7 could legally contract marriage.

The Influence of Chivalry

As feudalism matured, standards of living of the upper classes improved. The castle served as home, fortress, and social center. Boys and men were trained in warfare while girls learned spinning, sewing, and weaving. There was even some cultivation of knowledge–sometimes directly, and sometimes through the stories and songs of wandering troubadours.

All of this was accompanied by changes in the relations between men and women. Medieval ladies acquired power when their husbands went to war, just as Roman matrons before them had done. Left in charge of the castles and servants, many women developed competence and assurance in the management of their affairs. Too, women could inherit property. If a man died without heirs of the body, his widow might become wealthy and powerful. Ladies, isolated in their castles, gradually became preoccupied with manners and etiquette. How much sheer boredom had to do with it, we cannot say. Then there was the fact that women could not act directly in their own behalf; a woman wronged could only seek recourse through some man who might champion her cause. A man might champion his own wife's cause, but not out of sentiment. Marriage had been arranged on economic grounds, and its purpose was to provide heirs to keep the estates intact. Since emotional needs were not met in marriage, both sexes sought to satisfy those needs outside of marriage in extramarital intrigue, which has since come to be called *chivalry*.

Chivalry appears to have been two-sided. On the one hand, it was lusty and sensual. There was much overt sex-seeking, with little regard for the feelings or reputations of the persons involved, or their families. On the other hand, chivalry fostered an idealization of love and the partner, which had no counterpart in the ancient world. In short, chivalry produced the concept of romantic love. Romantic love and marriage were widely regarded as incompatible with one another, but the ideal of seeking continued, intense satisfaction in a member of the opposite sex was created as a legacy to be passed on to future generations.

How widespread chivalry became in the later Middle Ages is un-

28. Queen and Habenstein, *op. cit.*, p. 255.

known. Probably, it was confined to the upper classes, serving only as an ideal for the great mass of men and women who worked their modest holdings or at trades in the towns. Much less is known of the actual family behavior of people in the Middle Ages than of the ideal standards which the age set for them.

CHURCH POLICY THROUGH THE REFORMATION

After the tenth century, the church vigorously contested the concept of marriage as a private matter, not requiring the participation of clergy. As long as the father gave the bride in marriage, the clergy did not complain openly; but when it became common for other laymen to do it, the clergy demanded that only a priest should give a woman in marriage. Laymen who bestowed a bride in marriage were threatened with excommunication. Much of the Continent, however, and most of England was not prepared to surrender the concept of marriage as a private affair. One result of the church's stand was the spread of "clandestine" marriage.

The old custom of *self-gifta* had evolved into the right of a man and woman to marry simply by stating their vows "in words of the present tense." As the church opposed this custom, it became common for the vows to be said in secret and often without witnesses.

The church was caught in a dilemma. If it refused to recognize such marriages, it would drive the participants from the church and condemn their children to illegitimacy. If it recognized the marriages, it would abdicate its power to regulate family life. During the twelfth century, Peter the Lombard attempted to find a way out by declaring that vows in words of the present tense (I take thee) produced a marriage, but that vows spoken in words of the future tense (I will take thee) did not. The result was chaos. Clandestine marriages were held to be binding. Moreover, in neither English nor German is there any clear distinction between the present and future tenses. If a man says "I will" to a woman, does it mean that he will right now or at some time in the future?[29]

The church's logic was supported by a distinction it created between "legal" and "valid" marriages. Legal marriages were those which met the formal requirements of the church. Marriages which occurred with-

29. A common form of marriage ceremony in use at the present time uses the phrase "I will" rather than the phrase "I do."

out church sanction, although illegal, were still recognized as valid. The church discouraged marriage in words of the present tense by requiring penance of those who were so married, but to no avail. Clandestine marriages increased rapidly, and there were abuses. Some children were held to be validly married, while other couples who had lived together for years were declared not to be married. Unscrupulous men escaped from marriages where there were no witnesses.

In 1215, Pope Innocent III decreed that banns must be read in the church three times before a marriage ceremony could be performed, but the decree was not rigidly enforced. Finally, at the Council of Trent in A.D. 1563, it was declared that, in the future, valid marriages must be celebrated in the presence of a priest and two or three witnesses. The Council also decreed that publishing of the banns should be enforced. Even then, however, the church failed to make publication of the banns a condition of valid marriage, and high-status persons continued to secure their licenses without the banns having been read.

In at least two other areas, the church was plagued by scandal. First, there were continuing abuses centering on *divortium a vinculo matrimonii.* It had proved impossible to enforce kinship restrictions within seven degrees, and Innocent III, in 1215, specified that the prohibited relationships extend only to the fourth degree. Still, the prohibitions were erratically applied. In some instances, spiritual affinity was held to impose restrictions within four or seven degrees, while in other cases, persons consanguineally related within three degrees were given dispensation to marry. Even more irksome, persons of wealth and influence continued to secure annulments when less fortunate persons could not.

Another scandal revolved around the requirement for a celibate priesthood. Enforcement was lax and there were continuous rumors of licentious behavior by priests. On the Continent, some priests took women, had children by them, and then married them just before they died in order that the children might inherit their property.[30] The church even taxed clergy for the privilege of keeping concubines.

The Reformation

A crisis was reached at the end of the fifteenth century, in revolt against the abuses with which the church was plagued. Martin Luther was a symbol of the revolt, and he was influential in reintroducing the con-

30. O. E. Feucht, *ed., Sex and the Church,* St. Louis: Concordia, 1961, p. 63, as quoted in Panos D. Bardis, *op. cit.,* p. 451.

cept of civil marriage. Luther held marriage in high regard and objected to clandestine marriage, to the abuses associated with clerical celibacy, and to fraud in the granting of special dispensation to marry and annulments. Consequently, he held that marriage was not a sacrament, but a civil contract blessed by God. It followed from this that marriage and divorce should be regulated by the state, not by the church. Luther himself, in 1525, married a nun who had fled from a convent.

The church fragmented into Catholic and Prostestant factions, and civil authorities gradually assumed control of family matters. Performance of the marriage ceremony was left to the church for another generation. Nor was there immediate change in the prohibition of divorce; with the restriction on fraudulent annulments, marriage actually became more binding than before.

One early effect of the Reformation was the removal of most of the impediments to marriage. Prohibitions for spiritual affinity were done away with and barriers due to consanguinity were removed beyond the third degree. Interestingly, for modern-day America, the Protestant churches continued to forbid marriages between Christians and non-Christians—so-called "mixed marriages."

Ironically, the Reformation helped preserve one of the evils against which it was directed. The Church of England continued to recognize marriage in words of the present tense until the eighteenth century. Canon law and civil law were in conflict, for while canon law declared the children of such marriages to be legitimate, civil law held that they could not be legitimated even by the subsequent religious marriage of their parents. The church gained power to force a subsequent religious marriage and could jail persons who refused to do so. Be that as it may, the stage was set for the transport of common law marriage to America.

THE ENGLISH FAMILY: THE SIXTEENTH CENTURY TO THE EIGHTEENTH CENTURY

After the feudal era, the class structure changed due to the diversification of occupations, increasing settlement in cities and towns, and the development of trade. Ties to the land were not so universal as before: the top three classes—nobles, freeholders, and yeomen—constituted only about one-fifth of the population. Four-fifths of the population was composed of professionals, tradesmen, craftsmen, and laborers—people who sold their labor for a living.

The English family remained patriarchal, although not so rigidly as before. As late as 1663, a man was legally entitled to beat his wife. Wealthy men remained as the heads of large households, holding authority over kin and non-kin alike who resided within them. On a smaller scale, the same thing applied to craftsmen, tradesmen, and farmers. Marriages still were arranged by parents, but there were the beginnings of free choice based upon romantic love. Children began to go to school in greater numbers, but the majority were still placed in apprenticeship or loaned out to other families to learn discipline and the social graces.

Marriage

Probably the majority practice was that of child betrothal and marriage. Queen and Habenstein report the marriage of a boy three years old,[31] and Goodsell refers to a widow of nine.[32] These child brides and grooms continued to live with their own parents until they reached twelve and fourteen years old. Their marriages were arranged frankly on the basis of financial considerations, to ensure the welfare of parents and to provide for the inheritance of property.

Clandestine marriages increased during the seventeenth and eighteenth centuries. Certain rectors of the Church of England discovered that marrying people without licenses could be profitable, and did it on a large scale. Even more notorious were the "fleet marriages," performed by clergymen who had been imprisoned for debt. These enterprising gentlemen sometimes even arranged to have offices outside the prison, where they performed illegal marriages. After several unsuccessful attempts to do away with such marriages, the Hardwicke Act, in 1573, required that all marriages should be performed before two witnesses by an Anglican clergyman after the publication of banns or the securing of a license. Registers of marriages were kept, and destroying or falsifying a register was punishable by death.

Descent and Inheritance

Inheritance laws changed little from medieval times. Primogeniture and entail were followed with landed property, younger brothers leaving the family home to make their own way. Daughters inherited only in the absence of sons. Wives had a dower right in their husband's prop-

31. *Op. cit.*, p. 278.
32. *Op. cit.*, p. 329.

erty, which amounted to life use of one-third of his property if there were children and one-half of his property if there were not.

One sign of the times was the increased number of men and women who lived apart from kin. During the Middle Ages, the church had maintained monasteries, nunneries, hospitals, and the like, to which unattached persons repaired as the *sippe* or *maegth* declined. Now, with the role of the church restricted, laws were passed making families financially responsible for their indigent members. Where families were not able to provide support, the obligation was now defined as a public responsibility. The Poor Laws of 1597 saw government entrance into a field which formerly had been exclusively the prerogative of the family.[33]

Divorce

There was little change in regard to separation and divorce. Divorce became legally possible, although the Roman church still insisted on the indissolubility of marriage. Divorce cases were heard in the bishops' courts on grounds of adultery, impotence, refusal to cohabit, and cruelty. Apparently, few divorces were granted. Somewhat later, powerful and wealthy people sometimes were granted divorces by special act of Parliament. Stigma, however, was attached to divorce, and few persons endured the ordeal. The groundwork was being laid, however, for more liberal divorce practice in the future.

Transition to the Nuclear Family

Some time after the year 1500, the decline of the *sippe* and the *maegth*, which supported the ideal of extended family living, began to give way to positive sentiments toward nuclear family living. How much of this occurred by default and how much by design is impossible to say. On the one hand, legal changes came to hold individuals, rather than clan groups, responsible for misdeeds. On the other hand, increased geographical mobility both reduced ties to the land and resulted in more people working for wages. Positively, the church began to promote the ideal of family living based upon conjugal affection.

Whatever the precise combination of causes, nuclear families had be-

33. Kenneth W. Eckhardt, "Family Responsibility and Legal Norms," *Journal of Marriage and the Family* 32 (Feb. 1970), pp. 105–9.

come the bases for most households by the mid-1600s. Recent research has shown the average household size to have been about five persons. This is smaller than was previously believed and has led some scholars to conclude that extended families and stem families were not only uncommon in the seventeenth century, but also may not have been common earlier. Since data are not available for earlier periods, the latter point can neither be substantiated nor refuted. The former point requires very careful evaluation.

First, we must again distinguish between ideal and real cultural patterns. That the ancient Hebrews, Greeks, and Romans valued extended families is indisputable. It is also possible, even probable, that economic and other circumstances forced many of them to live in nuclear family circumstances for extended periods of time. We saw, in Chapter 4, that the Chinese ideal of extended family living was not achieved by most of the populace.

This leads to the second point which is that, regardless of the ideal family norms and even if extended family living is systematically achieved, cross-sectional studies will always show most families to be nuclear and household size to be relatively small. Take the stem family pattern as an example. Even if every eldest son brings his bride to live in the parental home, surveys will show them to be living as extended families only for the relatively brief period between the son's marriage and the parents' deaths. Moreover, all of the other sons will leave the parental home at marriage and set up nuclear families. Thus, even in societies where the stem family ideal is carefully adhered to, the majority of households, at any one time, will be organized around nuclear families.

THE FAMILY IN THE AMERICAN COLONIES

No clan organization was transported to America. The immigrants came, not in extended families but in nuclear families and as single persons. Particularly in the southern colonies, there were large numbers of unattached men. Consequently, the basic social units of the New World were two: the nuclear family and the household.

There are fragmentary data on the size and composition of families and households in areas of the New England colonies. Several studies report an average of eight or nine children born to families, although at any one time, nuclear families averaged only about six persons.[34] There often were, in addition, single persons, indentured servants, and unrelated children living with the family. As sons married, the laws of inheritance favored the eldest son bringing his bride to the home of his parents. Adopting the English precedent, the New England colonies followed the modified primogeniture in which the eldest son received a double portion. Settlement in the southern colonies was more often on farms and plantations, the self-sufficiency of which encouraged the development of large households. At the center were the plantation owners and operators who accumulated a large number of indentured servants and Negro slaves; and beyond this elite were an undetermined number of ordinary farmers and "poor whites."

In all colonies, the household size was increased by the emphasis upon marriage and large families. From England, came the tradition of transmitting property intact to one's heirs; the frontier and farming made economic assets of children; and marriage was protection against immorality. New England colonies, in particular, discouraged adults from remaining single, and imposed restrictions upon those who did. In Pennsylvania, single men paid double taxes, and in Hartford "the selfish luxury of solitary living" was taxed twenty shillings per week.[35] In some areas, single persons were required to live with families who were licensed and who would be responsible for their morals.[36]

Colonial families performed almost every service for their members. With help, the men and boys built the house they lived in. Farm buildings, tools, implements, and furniture similarly were provided. Most families provided some of their own food, with the women processing and storing it. Thread was spun, cloth was woven, clothing was sewn, candles were poured, soap was made, and so on. The family was nearly an independent economic unit. It was an educational agency, with the skills of farming or trade and those of housewifery taught at home. Even where there were schools, some education in the three R's often was given at home. The family was both an educational unit and a religious unit. In the north, the orientation was Puritan and in the south it was Anglican, but in both cases the family was a religious unit organized

34. John Demos, *A Little Commonwealth: Family Life in Plymouth Colony*, New York: Oxford University Press, 1970, p. 68; and Philip J. Greven, Jr., "Family Structure in Seventeenth Century Andover, Massachusetts," in Michael Gordon, *ed.*, *op. cit.*, p. 81.

35. Trumbull, *Blue Laws True and False*, 1876, p. 258, as cited in Goodsell, p. 368.

36. In other areas, single men were permitted to set up their own households. John Demos, *op. cit.*, pp. 77–78.

around the father, who directed reading of scriptures, family prayers, and hymn singing.

Patriarchy

English common law was brought to the colonies. Over the centuries, the settling of disputes without clear precedent or explicit legislation had given way to the accumulation of court decisions and a body of parliamentary law. According to these precedents, women and children were held under the power of the husband.

Women held no property unless it was specifically given them by their husbands for personal use; even the wife's personal property and clothing belonged to the husband. On the other hand, husbands were legally responsible for their wives, were obligated for their support, and were even responsible for her debts incurred both before and after marriage.[37] A wife also had a dower interest in the husband's real property which could not be disposed of without her concurrence.[38] If the husband died first, the wife gained control of her own property. If the wife died first, the husband was granted a "courtesy interest" in her property for the rest of his life. The question of whether unmarried women could own land early arose. In New England, the practice was discouraged. In the middle and southern colonies, however, women often held land in their own names.

The status of women varied from north to south. In New England, early Christian notions of the inferiority of women were prominent. In the south women were scarce during the early decades and had high status. The plantation economy also encouraged a high status for upper-class women by providing slaves to do the menial labor and freeing women to develop social graces. The feudal practice of elevating women to high status resulted in an American form of chivalry.

American men were not permitted to beat their wives, and could not even tongue-lash them too freely. "Cruelty" as grounds for legal action against the spouse emerged early and protected both husband and wife

37. The fact that the husband was responsible for his wife's debts incurred before marriage led, in scattered locations, to the custom of "smock marriages," in which the couple would be married in the open countryside, with the bride clad only in a slip. This ceremony symbolized the wife's coming to her husband unencumbered and to free him from the obligation to pay debts which she might owe.

38. This right is recognized today in the requirement that signatures of both the husband and wife appear on any transfer of real estate. Otherwise, if the husband died, the wife might reclaim her dower interest.

from too great abuse by the other. The power of the father over his children was great, but not so great as in the past. He was their legal guardian and could make many decisions concerning them. Laws in Massachusetts and Connecticut even provided that persistently disobedient youth might be put to death. There is no indication of youth actually having been slain under these laws, but the influence of the old Hebrew traditions is clearly there.

Parents sometimes arranged marriages for their children, and, under the common law, boys could be married at fourteen and girls at twelve. Furthermore, a young man could not call upon a young woman without her father's consent. With all this, child marriages appear to have been uncommon, young people were granted considerable freedom and girls could refuse to marry the young men their fathers had selected.[39]

Courtship, Betrothal, and Marriage

The contradictory conditions of rigid control and considerable premarital freedom applied to young people. On the one hand, a young man had to secure the consent of a girl's father to call on her. But on the other hand, young men and women traveled to and from dances unescorted, and even traveled from town to town together. Towns often were far apart and the journey often took more than one day. There is evidence, too, of young couples frequenting taverns together.

The word "courtship" had definite meaning. Young men were not supposed to pay attention to a girl unless they had marriage in mind. If considerable freedom was granted the young couple, it was also expected that they should not delay marriage for long.

An intriguing custom was that of bundling. This practice, imported from Europe, took place in New Amsterdam and the New England colonies. It permitted the couple to retire to bed together fully clothed,

39. For recent analyses, summarizing data which cast doubt on many myths concerning colonial families, see Herman R. Lantz, Margaret Britton, Raymond Schmitt, and Eloise C. Snyder, "Pre-Industrial Patterns in the Colonial Family in America: A Content Analysis of Colonial Magazines," *American Sociological Review* 33 (June 1968), pp. 413–26; Herman R. Lantz, Raymond L. Schmitt, and Richard Herman, "The Preindustrial Family in America: A Further Examination of Early Magazines," *American Journal of Sociology* 79 (Nov. 1973), pp. 566–88; Herman R. Lantz, Jane Keyes, and Martin Schultz, "The American Family in the Preindustrial Period: From Base Lines in History to Change," *American Sociological Review* 40 (Feb. 1975), pp. 21–36; and Rudy R. Seward, "The Colonial Family in America: Toward a Socio-Historical Restoration of its Structure," *Journal of Marriage and the Family* 35 (May 1973), pp. 58–70.

or almost so, to carry on the courtship under the covers.[40] The custom was more remarkable when one considers that the northern attitude toward sex was harsh, and that persons guilty of fornication might be compelled to marry, or be fined, whipped, or forced to stand in the stocks. When a child was born within seven months of marriage, the couple also were forced to make public confession of premarital intercourse.

Defenders of bundling claim that it was quite innocent: the couple were fully clothed; there often was a bundling board between them; and the girl's parents often were asleep in the same room. More cynical persons agree with the observation of Washington Irving that, "To this sagacious custom, therefore, do I chiefly attribute the unparalleled increase of the . . . Yankee tribe; for it is a certain fact, well authenticated by court records and parish registers, that wherever the practice of bundling prevailed, there was an amazing number of sturdy brats annually born unto the state, without the license of the law, or the benefit of clergy." Assuming that the endocrinological makeup of men and women then was comparable to what it is now, we might conclude that the custom was more compatible with short courtships than longer ones.

Bundling was more common among lower economic groups and was an adjustment to frontier conditions. Bundling permitted the couple to carry on their "conversations" after the family retired, without wasting fuel and light. The custom faded as living conditions improved.

Again in New England, formal betrothal, called *precontract*, and analogous to *beweddung*, existed. Precontract required parental consent and was solemnized before two witnesses. It was a promise to marry and was often followed by the preaching of a sermon. Precontract changed the legal and the social status of the couple. Since they were "almost married," they were likely to begin sexual intercourse, and the laws punishing fornication were softened, the penalties prescribed generally being half those imposed upon other couples.

In all the colonies, the arrangement of marriage often hinged upon economic considerations. Single living was discouraged, and both men and women found it socially and economically advantageous to marry. Financial bargaining appeared most unabashedly among widows and widowers. Widows with children were somewhat preferred marriage partners. The children provided a labor force and the widows often

40. For a light-hearted account of the practice of bundling, see Henry R. Stiles, *Bundling: Its Origin and Decline in America*, New York: Book Collector's Association, 1934.

owned property or had a life interest in the property left to them by their first husbands.

Although early writers believed that the colonists married young, more recently tabulated data indicate that the average ages at marriage were higher then than now. Men appear to have been 24 or 25 years old, and women 22 or 23 years old.[41]

The colonies hedged marriage with legal restrictions. In general, they required that (1) parental consent be secured, (2) notice of intention to marry be given, (3) the marriage ceremony be performed by an authorized officiant, and (4) the marriage be officially registered.

Since each colony had its own laws, there was no uniformity from one colony to another. Before long, however, virtually all colonies provided either for the publication of banns or the securing of a license. The banns were either posted or read on three successive Sundays at the church or meeting-house. As an alternative, most colonies permitted the securing of a license from the governor or from the court. Then, as now, exceptions were made for certain religious groups, such as the Quakers, who were permitted to post notice of marriage according to their traditional customs.

In only one colony, New York, did failure to post banns or secure a license render a marriage void. All of the other colonies provided punishment for disobeying the law, but they did not invalidate illegal marriages. In New York, too, failure to have a licensed officiant rendered the marriage invalid; in other colonies lesser penalties were provided. Distrust, in New England, of the established church resulted in ministers being prohibited from performing marriages. All ceremonies had to be performed by justices of the peace or magistrates. In the south, where the Church of England was established, the opposite situation prevailed; only religious ceremonies were permitted. The middle colonies followed a middle course, accepting both religious and civil marriages.

The registration of marriages was carefully controlled. In more closely settled areas of the north, the town clerk registered marriages, births, and deaths. Failure to register a marriage resulted in a heavy fine. Parish ministers often were responsible for registration of marriages in the south, gradually being replaced by elected officials. In the middle colonies, intermediate arrangements prevailed.

Almost from the beginning, and in spite of careful regulation, self-

41. John Demos, *op. cit.*, p. 275; Philip J. Greven, *op. cit.*, p. 83; and Rudy R. Seward, *op. cit.*, pp. 63–64.

marriage crept into the colonies. As we have seen, self-marriage in words of the present tense was firmly established in Europe. In America, the practice emerged mostly in the rural South and on the frontier. In those areas, ministers and civil officials were scarce. Ministers often were circuit riders who visited isolated communities infrequently. In the interim, when a couple wished to marry, they might simply say their vows at a gathering of friends and live together until a preacher appeared to formalize the relationship. In some cases, the couple were so habituated to the marital state that a religious ceremony seemed unnecessary. In isolated sections, even the saying of marriage vows before witnesses was omitted. Colonial laws generally did not declare such marriages invalid, and subsequent court decisions upheld them. Thus, common-law marriage was established in the United States.

The colonies also regulated mate selection. Minimum ages for marriage and the necessity for parental consent already have been discussed. Prohibitions for relationships within specified degrees of consanguinity and affinity were established. Queen and Habenstein report that in some instances there were 30 classes of kinsmen who were forbidden as mates.[42] In some states in the United States today, first cousins are permitted to marry; in others they are forbidden to do so. Persons in New England who married within the prohibited degrees sometimes were punished by being required to wear a large "I" (for incest) sewn prominently on their clothing.

Prohibitions on interracial marriages appeared before 1700. Bardis reports that Chester County, Pennsylvania, prohibited Negro-white marriages in 1698, and that Massachusetts forbade Negro-white and mulatto-white marriages in 1705.[43] White-Indian marriages also were widely forbidden. The southern colonies forbade all interracial marriages.

Divorce

The Puritan rebellion against the Church of England included recognition of absolute divorce. Practices varied from one colony to another. Massachusetts first granted jurisdiction over divorces to the Court of Assistants, but transferred it to the governor and Council before 1700. In many cases, suits were heard by colonial legislatures, each divorce requiring a separate act of the legislature. Only Connecticut administered divorce proceedings solely through the courts.

42. *Op. cit.*, p. 321.
43. Bardis, *op. cit.*, p. 452.

Grounds for divorce also varied. In general in New England, however, the grounds were fairly liberal and discriminated in favor of men. Men could divorce wives for adultery, desertion, and cruelty. Women, on the other hand, were not entitled to divorce on grounds of adultery alone; only if it was accompanied by desertion or failure to provide. Some colonies provided that the woman might be granted alimony if she was unjustly divorced by her husband.

There are few data on the incidence of divorce in these early days, but Calhoun presents some illustrative figures.[44] Between 1639 and 1692, in Massachusetts, 25 divorces were granted. From 1692 to 1739, there are no pertinent records. During the next 20 years, from 1739 to 1760, there were only 3 divorces, two separations from bed and board, and 5 annulments were granted.

Interestingly, more suits for divorce were brought by women than by men. Our history of the Western family showed that divorce rules almost always favored men. Yet, the first time that figures became available more divorces were granted to women. Would this also have been true among the ancient and medieval periods, one might wonder, or was this an American innovation? There are at least two plausible explanations. One is that, although there is male domination, the family is everywhere more central to the lives of women, and, in spite of legal disabilities, women more often seek relief from intolerable circumstances. Another possibility, tracing from the chivalric period, is that men more often permit wives the face-saving alternative of being the seeker of the divorce, even when they themselves wish the marriage to be terminated.

The middle and southern colonies were not so liberal in their attitudes toward divorce. The Church did not recognize absolute divorce; it permitted only separation from bed and board for adultery and cruelty. The southern colonies became even more conservative because, although they accepted the church, they refused to establish church courts. The result was that no organization could hear divorce suits and neither absolute divorce nor legal separation were granted. Some couples separated anyway, of course, and some southern courts heard requests for alimony from persons thus separated.

The middle colonies followed divorce policies closer to those of the southern colonies than to those of the New England colonies. Few absolute divorces were granted in New York or Pennsylvania. The middle colonies generally failed to grant jurisdiction over divorce to the courts, and what few suits there were, were heard by the legislatures.

44. *Op. cit.*, Vol. II, pp. 332–66.

The Colonial Attitudes Toward Sex

New England took its attitudes toward sex from the Hebrew-Christian tradition. Sex was inherently evil, and all sex other than for procreation was sinful. The colonies went to great lengths to discourage premarital and extramarital sexual activity. Yet, there were overtones of interest which belied the official norms. Premarital sex relationships were punishable by fines, whipping, and/or being forced to marry. The offenders might also be forced to stand in the stocks and to be branded on the cheek. The woman who bore a child out of wedlock might be imprisoned. Even couples who bore a child within seven months of marriage were punished. After the birth of the infant, the couple was required to make public confession of their sin before the entire congregation of the church. Church attendance increased substantially for such events and the sensationalism may actually have promoted sexual immorality.

Most New England colonies actually permitted adulterers to be put to death, and some death sentences were meted out. More commonly, the punishment was whipping, branding, and being required to wear the scarlet letter A, for "adulterer." Women were more strictly punished than men, but one unfortunately eager sea captain was forced to stand in the stocks for the "crime" of kissing his wife in public and on Sunday after returning home from a three-year voyage. Queen and Habenstein present data indicating that between 1726 and 1780, in one Massachusetts county, 160 married couples, 31 wives, and 523 single women were punished for sex offenses.[45] In one Groton church, approximately one-third of the parents of first-born children confessed to having had premarital intercourse.

The situation in the South was different. A landed aristocracy combined with a shortage of women and an abundance of women slaves to produce one standard for men and another for women. Legal provisions in the south were less strict than those in the north. The laws did prohibit fornication and adultery, and punishments including fines and whipping sometimes were provided. No stocks were used, however; there were no scarlet letters; and physical punishment was carefully restricted. More important, the laws were not systematically enforced.

Upper-class women occupied a special position. A chivalry not unlike that of medieval England was shown toward them. Unlike medieval

45. *Op. cit.*, pp. 285–86. See also Emil Oberholzer, Jr., *Delinquent Saints: Disciplinary Action in the Early Congregational Churches of Massachusetts*, New York: Columbia University Press, 1956.

ladies, however, upper-class southern women were carefully guarded against sexual involvement before marriage, and against extramarital affairs. The fiction was maintained, and it often may have become a self-fulfilling prophecy,[46] that genteel women generally viewed sex in terms of duty rather than personal fulfillment. Upper-class men, by contrast, enjoyed great freedom, both before marriage and after. If they were victims of their own expectations concerning upper-class women, it was also expected that they would meet their sexual needs wherever they could. With a dependent population of black women available, there was widespread violation of the miscegenation statutes. Many white men used black and mulatto women at their convenience, but there also were numerous liaisons in which men acknowledged their illegitimate offspring and accorded special status to their mistresses. The double standard operated between men and women and also between blacks and whites. The keeping of mistresses by wealthy white men was so open that two state governors saw no need to conceal their extramarital relationships. Censure actually fell upon the wife if she failed to accept the situation graciously. And at the same time that white men openly exploited black women, any hint of sexual interest in a white woman by a black man was cause for him to be put to death.

THE TRANSITION TO THE PRESENT

It is a far cry from colonial days to twentieth-century America. From the original thirteen colonies, we have become a nation of fifty states and over 215 million people. Whereas, at the time of the first United States Census in 1790, the population was 95 percent rural, in 1970 it was 75 percent urban. A volume could be written on the changes in family patterns which have accompanied the development of this country. To some extent, the remainder of this book contrasts the family structure of today with that of colonial times. It remains, in the closing section of this chapter, to indicate a few of the major forces operating to transform the colonial family into that of the 1970s.

46. The phrase "self-fulfilling prophecy" refers to a "false definition of the situation evoking a new behavior which makes the originally false conception come true. The specious validity of the self-fulfilling prophecy perpetuates a reign of error, for the prophet will cite the actual course of events as proof that he was right from the beginning." See Robert K. Merton, *Social Theory and Social Structure*, Glencoe, Illinois: The Free Press, 1957, p. 423.

The Influence of the Frontier

Even in colonial days, there was little elaboration of kinship structure. The household had replaced the clan and the extended family, as the basic unit of society. Households were large. Ties to the land and a tendency toward primogeniture encouraged the formation of stem families; and unmarried kin often had no choice but to attach themselves to existing households. Even then, however, nuclear families often were entire household units. The frontier operated to sever ties from both kin and land and to increase the isolation of the nuclear family.

Following the Revolution, the growing population spread westward, across the Appalachians, the Mississippi, and to the Pacific Ocean. Young men took their nuclear families with them, or they sought wives and built families after they had left the settled communities of the east. The grandparental generation most often was left behind; it had its ties, and the settlement of the frontier was arduous work.

The effects of this migration upon family structure hardly could have been imagined. First, it caused the further decline of patriarchal control. Throughout history, strong patriarchies have been associated with extended families. Children on the frontier never knew the direct authority of their grandfathers and consequently never learned to expect to control their own future grandchildren. True, their father was the final authority in the family, and it was to be many years before women gained legal equality with men. But the isolation and rigor of life on their frontier produced a hardy breed of women who had a *de facto* equality with men. The future could bring only an increasing democratization of relationships within the family.

Equally drastic were the effects upon inheritance. As extended families broke up and spread over the countryside, parents disposed of their property by will. Instead of being held intact for future generations, property was broken up and sold. As the colonies became the United States, the democratic ideology upon which they were founded refused to sanction inherited inequality among siblings, and the various state constitutions outlawed the practice of entail. The tradition developed that all children, girls included, should inherit equally. The immortality of the extended family system was waning. In its place, emerged a conjugal family system without much family tradition and without economic or sentimental ties to a wide array of kin.

The Effects of Large-Scale Immigration

The United States population grew through natural increase and immigration. Up to now, we have dealt only with the dominant English tradition. But the number of migrants from other areas far exceeded those from England for most of two centuries. The United States became a heterogeneous nation, with heterogeneous family patterns.

Little attention is paid, ordinarily, to the fact that the largest migration to America, before 1800, was of Negro slaves. The number probably falls between 10 and 20 million people. By contrast, the migrants from all of Europe during the same period was not over 5 million. The conditions of slavery before the Civil War, and the varied conditions since, have produced family patterns which are both like and unlike their white counterparts. At the present time, there are approximately 22 million people in the United States who are defined as black. The distinctive family patterns of this largest American minority will be treated in detail in a later chapter.

After 1800, mass migration from Europe got under way. During the nineteenth century, approximately 19 million people came, chiefly from northwestern Europe—Great Britain, Ireland, Germany, and France. Beginning about 1890, the countries of origin shifted from northwest Europe to southern and eastern Europe. Between 1890 and 1930, an additional 22 million people came, mostly from Italy, Austria-Hungary, and Russia. In 1930, there were more than 14 million foreign-born persons living in the United States. Since then, a restrictive immigration policy has drastically limited the number of migrants, and the number and proportion of foreign-born in the population have been declining.

The peak migration between 1890 and 1920 differed from earlier ones in several ways. First, the migrants were not so often farmers. Second, they found the country largely settled and, rather than spreading out over the countryside, they created ethnic enclaves in the larger eastern cities. Third, a large proportion of the immigrants was Roman Catholic.

These new migrants were not altogether hospitably received. They reacted to prejudice and discrimination by turning inward, preserving their traditional languages and customs. Their family patterns varied by nationality, religion, and economic status. For generations, they resisted assimilation. They became sources of the preservation of old world family patterns in the new world. In the 1970s they are not nearly so conspicuous as they were a generation earlier. But, even today, they provide significant variations on the major American family theme.

Urbanization and Industrialization

Industrialization got under way shortly after 1800. Cities grew up around the new factories, and there were several effects on family organization. First, the family ceased to be a principal unit of production, becoming transformed into basically a consumption unit. Instead of father, mother, and children working together in an integrated economic enterprise, the father now went out of the home to earn the family's living. Business and industry became structured according to increasingly universalistic standards, while the family remained a haven of particularism.

Second, factory employment freed young adults from direct dependence upon their families. As their wages made them financially independent, the authority of the head of the household weakened further. Urbanization brought the development of hotels and rooming houses, restaurants, bakeries, grocery stores, and laundries, making it possible for people to live apart from families. This situation had special significance for women who no longer had to marry to have a place to live and who no longer had to stay married simply because there was no alternative. The divorce rate began to rise.

Finally, children ceased to be economic assets and became liabilities. Although there was a period of the use and abuse of child labor, legal regulation gradually removed children from the job market. At the same time, educational requirements increased, lengthening dependence upon parental support. Living space in the cities was crowded and expensive; child care was demanding. The birth rate began to fall.

So we come to the contemporary American family. To compress 3000 years of history into one chapter obviously produces oversimplification. We have not presented a detailed history of the Western family, but have traced threads which are relevant to understanding the family system of today. Some "meaning" has been implicit and explicit in this discussion. A few sociologists have confronted this problem of meaning more directly and have formulated comprehensive theories of family structure and family change. Before turning to the modern American family, we will examine three of these theoretical analyses.

SUMMARY

The pastoral Hebrew family was patriarchal, patrilineal, patrilocal, polygynous, and extended. Larger kin groups included the sib, the clan, and the tribe. The patriarch could marry off his children at will, sell them into slavery, or even kill them. Only widowed mothers were free of male control, and wives could be killed for adultery.

Minimum ages for marriage were 13 for boys and 12 for girls. Betrothal took two forms: *kaseph*, involving the transfer of money, and *kiddushin*, which required a written instrument. Marriage was a private matter involving the signing of the *ketubah*, or marriage deed. Marriage was highly valued for producing sons, and included the practice of the levirate. Primogeniture was practised.

Patriarchs could divorce their wives through handing them a bill of divorcement. Wives had no divorce rights. As the rabbis gained power, husbands' rights of divorce were restricted and wives gained the right to divorce for certain specified causes.

The ancient Greek family also was patriarchal, patrilineal, patrilocal, and extended. The patriarch was trustee of the family estates, and priest in the practice of ancestor worship. Athenian women had low status, being defined as inherently inferior to men. The father could expose infants, sell children's labor, and could bestow them in marriage. *Agnation*, or tracing descent only through males, and primogeniture were practised.

Betrothal was essentially a business contract, and marriage was a private family matter. Marriage was a sacred obligation. Monogamy with concubines was the norm. Husbands early gained the right to repudiate their wives. Only later, did wives gain limited divorce rights.

The pre-Punic War Roman family was the most complete patriarchy ever known. The power of a father over his children was called *potestas*, and that of a husband over his wife, *manus*. Nevertheless, women had high status. There were two principal marriage forms, *matrimonium justum* and *matrimonium nonjustum*. Husbands could repudiate wives, with divorce for specified causes emerging gradually.

The family system began to disintegrate after the Punic Wars. Women became powerful and marriage without *manus* became common. *Potestas* declined. Government efforts to limit celibacy, childlessness, divorce, and abortion failed.

The Christians gradually assumed control of family matters. Reaction to Roman excesses resulted in lowering the status of marriage, lowering the status of women, and defining sex as evil. Remarriages were discouraged, and the indissolubility of marriage proclaimed. Broad prohibitions to marriage were established.

The Christians accepted Teutonic family customs, just as they had the Roman ones. The Germanic and English peoples practised double descent, and had extended kin groups called the *sippe* and the *maegth*. Patriarchy continued, but the power of fathers and husbands was limited. *Beweddung* was betrothal, and private marriage, *gifta*, was deeply entrenched. A double standard of morality existed. Gradually, the church eliminated absolute divorce, permitting only *divortium a vinculo matrimonii* (annulment), and *divortium a mensa et thoro* (separation).

Feudalism emphasized warfare, and lowered the status of women again. Primogeniture and entail emerged to hold estates intact; marriages were arranged to build estates. With the absence of husbands, upper-class women became powerful and the romantic tradition of chivalry developed. Romantic love was regarded to be incompatible with marriage.

In wresting control of marriage from laymen, the church unwittingly encouraged clandestine marriage in words of the present tense. The attempt to distinguish valid from legal marriage failed. Other scandals emerged around the celibate priesthood, and the granting of annulments. The Reformation defined marriage as a civil contract and recreated absolute divorce. Most impediments to marriage were removed. The *maegth* declined, but otherwise the English family changed little from the sixteenth to the eighteenth century.

The colonial American family was organized around the nuclear unit and the household. It was a stable system in which the family performed many functions. Patriarchy continued, with the wife's property belonging to the husband, and women not being the legal guardians of their children. The common-law minimum ages for marriage were 14 for boys and 12 for girls. Marriage often was based upon economic considerations, haggling over dower and dowry. Parental consent, notice of intention to marry, performance by an authorized officiant, and the registration of marriages all were required. The northern colonies favored civil marriages and permitted divorce, while the southern colonies favored religious marriages and prohibited divorce.

With time, the influence of the frontier and geographical mobility further weakened the patriarchal tradition and broke up the family estates. Equal inheritance by all children was encouraged. Heterogeneous family patterns were encouraged by large-scale immigration, with black and ethnic family patterns appearing. Industrialization and urbanization transformed the family into a consumption unit. Work and home became separated, and alternatives to family living became feasible.

SUGGESTED READINGS

Gordon, Michael, *ed., The American Family in Social-Historical Prespective*, New York: St. Martin's Press, 1973. An excellent collection of essays, covering different facets of the history of American family life.

Lantz, Herman R., *Marital Incompatibility and Social Change in Early America*, Beverly Hills, California: Sage, 1976. A monograph reporting research into marital incompatibility in eighteenth-century America.

Laslett, Peter, *ed., Household and Family in Past Time*, London: Cambridge University Press, 1972. The most comprehensive collection of reports on research into family history that has yet appeared in print.

Rosenberg, Charles E. *ed., The Family in History*, Philadelphia: The University of Pennsylvania Press, 1975. Contains new data on the development of the nuclear family in England and on the role of women in European families of the nineteenth century.

Shorter, Edward, *The Making of the Modern Family*, New York: Basic Books, 1975. A historian's provocative interpretation of the transition from the traditional to the modern family.

QUESTIONS AND PROJECTS

1. Describe the ancient Hebrew patriarchy. What restrictions existed on the power of the father over his children? On the husband over his wife?
2. What was the purpose of marriage among the Hebrews? How were polygyny and concubinage consistent with that purpose?
3. How did the Greek patriarchy differ from the Hebrew? Describe the sources of patriarchal power, and the status of women.
4. What is the kinship system known as "agnation"?
5. Detail the progressive character of Roman family patterns. What parallels existed among the Hebrews and Greeks?
6. Define: *matrimonium justum, potestas, manus, confarreatio, coemptio, usus, diffarreatio.*
7. Why did the early Christians take the positions they did on marriage, sex, and the status of women? What were the church attitudes on divorce and remarriage?
8. Describe the kinship system of the Anglo-Saxon and Teutonic peoples during the Middle Ages. What was the role of the *sippe* or *maegth?*
9. What were the influences of feudalism on family life? Of chivalry?
10. What family-related problems plagued the church during the Middle Ages? How did the Reformation deal with these problems?

11. Describe the family system in the American colonies. What variations existed from north to south?
12. How did the frontier encourage emphasis on the nuclear family? How did immigration increase the heterogeneity of family patterns? What were the effects of urbanization and industrialization?

E x H
1847

7
Theories of Family Structure and Family Change

The United States, as well as the other countries of western Christendom, will reach the final phases of a great family crisis between now and the last of this century. By that time the social consequences of this crisis will approach a maximum. This crisis will be identical in nature to the two previous crises in Greece and Rome. The results will be much more drastic in the United States because, being the most extreme and inexperienced of the aggregates of western civilization, it will take its first real "sickness" most violently.

Efforts to meet this situation in the United States will probably be very exaggerated. We will probably try all the "remedies" suggested or tried in Greek and Roman civilization, profiting perhaps but little from the mistakes already made in those periods. The violence and abruptness of the changes will probably be extreme indeed. . . .[1]

. . . Prior to modern times the power and prestige of the family was due to seven functions it performed: . . .

These seven functions—economic, status giving, educational, religious, recreational, protective, and affectional—may be thought of as bonds that tied the members of a family together. If one asks why do the various members of a family stay together instead of each going his way, the answer is that they are tied together by these functions. If they didn't exist, it is not easy to see that there would be any family.

The dilemma of the modern family is caused by the loss of many of these functions in recent times . . . at least six of the seven family functions have

1. Carle C. Zimmerman, *Family and Civilization,* New York: Harper and Brothers, 1947, p. 798. Reprinted by permission of Harper & Row.

been reduced as family activities in recent times, and it may be claimed that only one remains as vigorous and extensive as in prior eras.[2]

> . . . I do not regard differentiation as synonymous with decline. Historically one of the very critical events of the development of modern industry in its early phases was the separation of the productive unit from the household. In traditional agriculture they are fused together as one unit. In the farm family, the household is a producer of agricultural commodities, and also a residential consumer household in urban centers. When we use the word "family" to designate the stage before differentiation has taken place, as in the farm family, and use the same word to designate one of the two outcomes of the process of differentiation, we must say, "Of course, the family has lost its function." There is a certain logical absurdity in this. Anything that lives has certain functions, even though they may have declined. I think that the question of whether or not the family has declined in the functional sense of not doing its job must be judged in the context of its contemporary relation to other things because it is often exceedingly desirable that differentiations of this sort be made. . . .[3]

These three quotations are from well-known sociologists who have developed general theories of family structure and change. Each has taken the raw facts of history and contemporary existence, examined and systematized them, and arranged them into a comprehensive explanation of the nature of our family system. It goes without saying that their interpretations are not completely consistent with one another. Zimmerman sees imminent catastrophe unless present trends are halted; Ogburn perceives a family system stripped of most of the functions it once had; and Parsons believes that the modern family is well adapted to the society in which it functions. Obviously, they cannot all be correct. Our purpose here is not to decide which is right but to examine constructively and critically the arguments which have led them to their respective conclusions. In the end, we shall find that it is impossible to prove the validity of one interpretation over the others. Here, as elsewhere, science provides neither final answers nor an unerring guide to social action. We should find that each of these theories has utility in explaining some of the facts of history and of current existence.

A major theme of this book is that there are complex, pervasive, subtle interrelations between the family system and other institutions. This is hardly a startling notion. It represents a systematic way of organizing and interpreting data.

2. William F. Ogburn, "The Changing Family," *The Family* 19 (July 1938), pp. 139–43.
3. Talcott Parsons, panel discussion on "The Forces of Change," in Seymour M. Farber, Piero Mustacchi, and Roger H. L. Wilson, *eds.*, *Man and Civilization: The Family's Search for Survival,* New York: McGraw-Hill Book Company, 1965, p. 56.

Not many family sociologists have had the temerity to develop sweeping theoretical systems. Perhaps this is because they are too aware of the difficulties involved and are unwilling to produce interpretations which they know beforehand will prove inadequate. Most scholars have been content to point out some of the empirical interrelations between family structure and social structure, as we have done in Chapters 2 and 3, and to explore the general problem of the degree to which the family is an active or a passive agent in social change.[4]

When the family is viewed as an active, causal agent in social change, one reasons that changes in the family precede and help to bring about changes in other aspects of the social structure. Ideally, the determination of whether changes in the family produce changes in the larger society derives from examination of the data. Few people, however, including sociologists, can be completely objective about the family and there is fear that occasionally we assign a causal role to family changes out of ideological and personal commitment to the importance of the family.

The family has often been conceived to be a passive agent in social change—to adapt to changes in other areas of society rather than to cause changes in other areas. The economic and political institutions are widely believed to change more rapidly than the family, and change can be produced only by institutions that are themselves changing. Actually, it is oversimplification to say that most scholars treat the family as an active *or* a passive agent in change. Most sociologists see changes in the family as both cause and effect of changes in other institutions.

There have been a few attempts to formulate comprehensive interpretations of the relation between the family and other social institutions. The three theories selected for analysis in this chapter might be labeled, respectively, a cyclical theory, a progressivist theory, and a structure-function theory.[5]

4. See Meyer F. Nimkoff, *Comparative Family Systems*, Boston: Houghton Mifflin, 1965, Chs. 3 and 4.

5. Recently, sociologists of the family have concentrated on developing consistent conceptual approaches to family data and "theories of the middle range," rather than all-embracing "grand theories." For accounts of efforts to develop conceptual approaches, see Wesley R. Burr, *Theory Construction and the Sociology of the Family*, New York: John Wiley and Sons, 1973; and F. Ivan Nye, and Felix M. Berardo, *eds., Emerging Conceptual Frameworks in Family Analysis* (New York: Macmillan, 1966.)

Many middle range theories are discussed in this book. Included are Robert O. Blood and Donald M. Wolfe's theory of marital decision-making in *Husbands and Wives: The Dynamics of Married Living* (Glencoe, Illinois: The Free Press, 1960); Bernard Farber's theory of orderly replacement in *Family: Organization and Interaction* (San Francisco: Chandler, 1964); and Robert F. Winch's theory of complementary needs in mate selection in *Mate Selection: A Study of Complementary Needs* (New York: Harper and Brothers, 1958).

A CYCLICAL THEORY

The best known advocate of a cyclical theory of family structure and change is Carle C. Zimmerman. Zimmerman developed his theory most fully in *Family and Civilization*,[6] and that book is a major source for the following discussion. *Family and Civilization* is an erudite tome of more than 800 pages, covering nearly 4000 years of history. Inevitably, something is lost in assessing Zimmerman's thesis in a few pages, as we must do.

First of all, Zimmerman regards the study of the family in preliterate societies as largely irrelevant to what he calls the "high civilizations." He states that "primitive" peoples probably come from a different universe of societies, that they are not predecessors of our own society, and that they do not represent an earlier stage of development of civilized society. By contrast, he believes that "the range of principles" which determines our family behavior operates among the great societies of the world. He includes in this universe the Mediterranean and European civilizations including American and Australian, and those of Asia. The major part of his analysis draws upon data from the Western tradition beginning with ancient Greece, progressing through Rome, and then coming forward through the Middle Ages to twentieth-century America.

Zimmerman assumes that there is a close connection between the family organization and the nature of the larger society. He assumes, also, that changes in the one are associated with changes in the other. Family and civilization cause changes in one another, the family being both a major cause of social change and being changed by alterations in the larger society. In addition to the family, the church and government are sources of social change and vie with the family for control over family relations. Throughout Western history, Zimmerman finds that there have been three main family types—the trustee family, the domestic family, and the atomistic family.[7] These three types are defined according to the amount of power vested in the family, the width of its field of action, and the amount of social control it exercises.

The Trustee Family

The trustee family derives its name from the fact that living members of the family are not *the family* but are only living trustees of its name,

6. *Op. cit.* Zimmerman's thesis was anticipated, in Europe, by Frederic LePlay. See Pierre Guillaume Frederic LePlay, *Les Ouvriers européens*, Paris, 1879.

7. Zimmerman explicitly states that these are ideal family types rather than empirical family types (p. 120).

its property, and its blood. The family itself is immortal. An extreme familism exists; there is virtually no concept of individual rights and questions of individual welfare are subordinated to the welfare of the group. The trustee family has great power over its members, often power of life and death. The authority of the husband and father is not absolute authority, however, but is delegated to him in his role as trustee, for carrying out family responsibilities. Families are organized into *gentes*, and these combined families make up the state. There is little organized power outside the family, and what little government there is does not interfere in family matters. Membership in the family is based upon formal action, new members being accepted or rejected by the group. Absolute divorce virtually does not exist. What does exist is the right to repudiate a spouse (wife), who fails to support the integration of the group.

The Domestic Family

The domestic family is an intermediate type which evolves from the trustee family. As the state gains power, the control of the family over its members is weakened. The state does not replace the family but comes to share power with it, restricting the right of the family to punish its members and creating a concept of individual rights to be maintained against family authority. The *gens* tends to disappear. The family remains strong, maintaining a balance between familism and individualism. Conceptions of absolute divorce emerge, but divorce is uncommon. The characteristic device for alleviating marital difficulties is legal separation, *divortium a mensa et thoro*.

The Atomistic Family

The atomistic family represents the other extreme. Familism is replaced by individualism. The power and authority of the family are reduced to a minimum and the state becomes an organization of individuals. If self-sacrifice for group goals is the ethic in the trustee family, unabashed hedonism characterizes the atomistic family. Marriage becomes a civil contract instead of a sacrament, and is often broken by divorce. The sacredness now attached to the individual results in the blurring of distinctions between legitimate and illegitimate children; whereas the trustee family tends to destroy illegitimate children as a threat to itself, the state declares illegitimate children to have full rights in the atomistic family. Other evidences of rampant individualism are to be found in feminist movements, childlessness, youth problems, and so on. The atomistic family loses the capacity to carry out necessary family functions, and cannot satisfy the growing demands of individualism.

The Cycle of Change

Zimmerman traces Western history from approximately 1500 B.C. to the present. Social change, he says, has proceeded according to a deterministic pattern, with the family and the level of civilization in mutual cause-and-effect interaction. Up to the present, change has proceeded blindly, without control or guidance. Unless we come to comprehend the nature of social change and control it, it will continue to operate blindly and the decay of the great civilizations of the past will be repeated in the decay of our society.

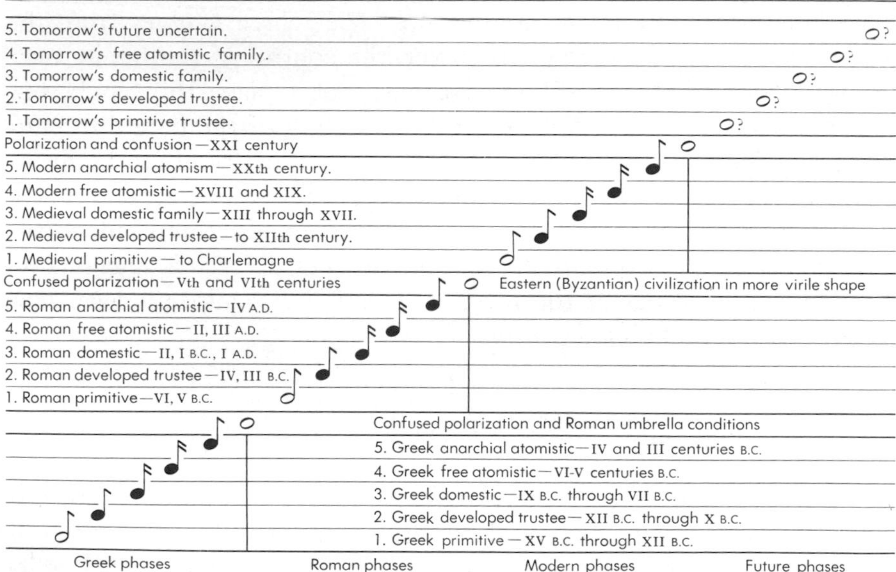

Figure 7.1. The chain reaction pattern in cultural determination for the Western family system since 1500 B.C.

Source: Carle C. Zimmerman, *The Family of Tomorrow: The Cultural Crisis and the Way Out*, New York: Harper and Brothers, 1949, p. 218. Reprinted by permission of Harper & Row.

Change is alleged to occur in giant historical cycles, which are summarized in Figure 7.1. According to Zimmerman, the first of these cycles of which we have adequate record embraced the rise and fall of ancient Greece. Greek civilization grew and declined from the fifteenth through the third century B.C. Roman society then achieved greatness, and declined by the fourth century of the Christian era. During the Dark Ages, there was no great Western civilization. By the twelfth century, the trustee family had emerged again and the greatness of the Renaissance was foreshadowed. The present finds Western society, particularly America, again in a terminal phase. Unless human intelligence is brought to bear—and soon—our society will suffer the fate of Greece and Rome.

The great cycles of change in Greek, Roman, and medieval civilizations followed a common pattern. Each emerged in a relatively primitive state. Order and stability were achieved through the family, which emerged as the trustee type. Under the trustee family, each civilization moved toward greatness. The authoritarian character of the trustee family, however, led to the limitation of its power by state and church. The trustees family gradually evolved into the domestic type which, with its balance between individualism and familism, permitted each civilization to attain greatness. The changes already set in motion, however, led the state to assume greater control until the domestic family was replaced by the atomistic one. In each case, the atomistic family was associated with moral degeneration. Goals of self-sacrifice and creativity in every field gave way to the demands of relentless hedonism.

The cycle gets under way because the trustee family carries within itself the seeds of its own destruction. While its primitive code of justice produces an orderly society, promotes the accumulation of wealth, and emphasizes productive work, its unchecked authority leads to abuses; wives are unjustly repudiated, children are exposed or subjected to despotic control, and the rights of individuals suppressed. There allegedly is a tendency, too, for disputes to break out between families. Religious and governmental powers emerge to mediate between families and to protect individual family members. The autocratic trustee family is thus humanized. As the society develops, the power of the extended kin group diminishes, and the domestic family emerges.

The domestic family is the most common type in civilized societies and offers the most potential for greatness. It becomes the modal type because of forces operating both inside and outside the family. It arises from the desire for more equitable treatment for family members, and from the influences of government and religion. Unlike the trustee family, it does not cause its own destruction; it continues to be acted upon from outside. The state accumulates power and religion takes charge of morality. These institutions further restrict the power of the family and promote the rights of individuals. There is a cultural determinism operative which creates an increasingly antifamilistic attitude.

The atomistic family is both cause and effect of decay. In its later stages, there appear elimination of the real meaning of the marriage ceremony, widespread adultery, acceptance of sexual perversions, easy divorce, childlessness, and delinquency. Concepts of loyalty and self-sacrifice wane; personal selfishness replaces them. Under these conditions, the family cannot carry out its basic functions. Neither can the growing demands for individual freedom and personal satisfactions be met. Nor is there anything in the atomistic family which might produce a swing back toward familism. The decay continues until eventually a new trustee family emerges out of the darkness.

The Lesson of History

Zimmerman's is a voice crying from the wilderness. The United States is destined to experience the last stages of a great family crisis by the end of the twentieth century. By now, however, we can understand the forces which have been operating, and we can alter the course of change. The initiative must be seized by government—the only agency powerful enough to do it—to bring about a resurgence of familism. We must swing back toward the domestic family and toward the personal and national greatness which are associated with it. The morality to be reinstituted is found in the teaching of the church, which has always made virtues of familism and self-sacrifice, but which in recent centuries has lost much of its power and influence. Although he does not say so, we might guess that Zimmerman is pessimistic. He presents us with the blind working of fate and then offers a way out. The very force with which his analysis is developed makes it appear unlikely that our civilization will handle the crisis more effectively than earlier civilizations did.[8]

8. For reaffirmation and extension of this position, see Zimmerman's recent publications: "The Atomistic Family: Fact or Fiction," *Journal of Comparative Family Studies* 1 (Autumn 1970), pp. 5–16; "The Future of the American Family II. The Rise of the Counter-Revolution," *International Journal of Sociology of the Family* 2 (March 1972), pp. 1–9; and "The Future of the Nuclear Family," *International Journal of the Sociology of the Family* 2 (Sept. 1972), pp. 109–20.

Final Critique

When Zimmerman's work was published in 1947, it attracted considerable attention. Even today it is required reading for all students in the field. But although Zimmerman's analysis is provocative, it found few adherents. Social scientists embraced it somewhat less than enthusiastically. Following are some views of the theory which are widely shared.

One must be impressed by the erudition of the analysis. It embraces nearly 4000 years of history and varied civilizations, in detail, and with flourish and assurance. One of the problems with such an erudite analysis, however, is that lesser mortals cannot be certain that Zimmerman's data are adequate and reliable, and that they have the meaning which he attributes to them. While no one questions the integrity of the analysis, many are reluctant to accept it as adequately proven. A second problem derives from the exclusion of data from preliterate societies. Zimmerman takes advantage of our ignorance when he maintains that preliterate societies are inherently different from civilized ones. It cannot be proved that he is wrong, but neither can it be proved that he is correct. Finally, Zimmerman is not alone in his views. Periodically, historians have produced cyclical theories and, in sociology, Zimmerman's mentor and colleague Pitirim Sorokin developed an elaborate parallel analysis which does not focus on the family.[9] Undoubtedly, the prevailing bias of the twentieth century is to view change as unending and without direction. Zimmerman may be wrong. But it is also possible that our preconceived notions of the mutability of everything may be blinding us to some permanence, some regularity in human experience, that actually exists.

A PROGRESSIVIST THEORY

William F. Ogburn's publications spanned more than three decades. The first of his major works was published in 1922,[10] and the last in 1955.[11] It is a mark of the stature of the man that his thinking about social change did not remain constant over his lifetime, but changed in response to professional evaluations of his earlier works and as his own thinking matured. This very intellectual growth, however, makes presentation of his analysis more difficult; for what began as a sweeping theory of social

9. Pitirim A. Sorokin, *Social and Cultural Dynamics*, 4 vols., New York: American Book Company, 1937.
10. *Social Change*, New York: Viking Press, 1922.
11. *Technology and the Changing Family*, Boston: Houghton Mifflin, 1955.

change had become much more tentative and eclectic[12] before his death. In presenting Ogburn's theory, we will present his original formulations first, for in them are to be found his major contributions, and then trace his thinking through his later publications.

Ogburn belonged to what Zimmerman referred to as the "passive school" of family sociologists. He viewed the family, not as an active causal agent in social change but as being acted upon from outside, passively adapting to changes in the larger society. Looking outside the family for the primary source of social change, Ogburn found it in the increasing rate of invention in a technologically oriented society. The range of data used by Ogburn was much narrower than Zimmerman's. He confined his analyses of the family to America, using the preindustrial family as an informal baseline and tracing the changes which occurred during the nineteenth and twentieth centuries. Not surprisingly, his analysis was somewhat culture-bound.

Material and Nonmaterial Culture

A sharp distinction between material culture (factories, machines, means of transportation, engineering achievements, munitions, clothing, and so on) and nonmaterial culture (values, attitudes, customs, institutions, etc.) was central to Ogburn's thinking. He emphasized the different ways in which material and nonmaterial culture change. Change in material culture, he said, tends to be cumulative and directional while change in nonmaterial culture is not characterized by any such regularity.

The difference between material inventions and customs lies in the fact that there are generally agreed-upon standards which are used to evaluate inventions. Thus, an engine may be evaluated in terms of the horsepower it produces, the fuel it consumes, its weight, its cost, and its durability. With the standards agreed upon, a better engine soon is produced, and so on. Change in material culture is rapid and accelerates with time.

In nonmaterial culture, on the other hand, there are few accepted standards of worth. Societies which use the same internal-combustion engines disagree violently over their respective political and economic systems. Or in the arts, who is to determine the merits of Brahms over Mozart or Picasso over Gainsborough? As a consequence of lack of agreement, change in institutions tends to be both slow and without

12. An eclectic theory is one which combines elements from two or more existing theories into a new and presumably more useful one.

continuing direction. And in the uneven rates of change between material and nonmaterial culture are to be found the sources of culture lag.

Culture Lag

The culture-lag hypothesis holds that change in one part of culture requires that corresponding adjustments be made in other related parts. Such adjustments, however, frequently are made only after a time lag of months, years, or decades. The intervening period is one of maladjustment or disorganization. During this period of cultural lag, the attitudes and customs passed down from previous generations seem to have lost their effectiveness and there is widespread personal and group distress.

Ogburn maintained that change may originate in either material or nonmaterial culture and that change in either requires change in the other. Most often, however, he viewed change as originating in material invention, and the necessity for adjustment occurring in the nonmaterial, adaptive culture.

An illustration of cultural lag is found in the family. Before industrialization, the family was adjusted to agricultural conditions. It possessed economic, educational, recreational, religious, and protective functions along with its biological functions. Marriage was a business arrangement, and divorce was serious. With development of the factory system, production was taken out of the home. Women who formerly played an important economic role now found themselves forced either to go out of the home to work or to accept an essentially nonproductive economic role. If they did go to work, problems in the management of household and children arose; if they did not go to work, their estimates of their own worth often suffered. Children, too, encountered problems in the new milieu. They were transformed from economic assets into liabilities. There were not proper places for them to play, and their supervision became onerous for parents and children alike.

Related developments in material culture also played a disorganizing role. The automobile, for example, offered adolescents the opportunity to escape parental supervision and to gain anonymity in minutes. The old norms governing courtship could not operate effectively in the new situation. Parents found it difficult to know the boys and girls with whom their children associated. Dating developed, and neither parents nor young people knew how to cope with its complications. These are examples of what Ogburn called culture lag and social disorganization.

Family Defunctionalization

Empirical documentation that developments in technology stripped the American family of traditional functions is found in a report prepared for President Hoover's Research Committee on Social Trends and published in 1934.[13] In that report, Ogburn discussed seven major functions of the family before modern times and the changes which occurred in them with rapid advances in technology.

The Economic Function. In colonial times, the home was literally a factory, producing virtually all that the family consumed. A man sought in a wife not only a companion but a business partner. Children, too, contributed. Gradually, however, production was assumed by other agencies. The production of tools and furniture was lost early. Gradually, the production of medicines and soaps was lost. By the 1930s, most families had given up baking bread, home canning, and sewing clothing. The transfer of these tasks reduced the wife's economic importance, and increased numbers of women sought outside employment.

The family dwelling changed accordingly. Multifamily dwellings proliferated in the cities. The new dwellings were smaller and much maintenance was assumed by janitors and other employees. Gas and electricity for domestic power simplified the preparation of food. Even so, restaurants and delicatessens increased rapidly, and more meals were taken outside the home. Men increasingly worked outside the home. And, although women continued to put in long hours at "housework," the definition of woman's economic contribution suffered; the phrase "just a housewife," with unflattering connotations, came into use. Children ceased to have much economic value, and home economists began to figure how much it cost to raise each child to adulthood.

The Protective Function. Traditionally, the family protected members from harm and provided them with economic security through childhood, in times of injury, illness, and unemployment, and in old age. In recent decades, much of this protective activity has been assumed by public organizations and by the state. In health care, for example, physicians, hospitals, accident insurance, hospitalization insurance, and workman's compensation have tended to replace family nursing care. Mentally ill and mentally deficient family members also are increasingly cared for in hospitals.

The family shotgun and even the family dog as protection against in-

13. William F. Ogburn and Clark Tibbitts, "The Family and Its Functions," Report of the President's Research Committee on Social Trends, *Recent Social Trends in the United States,* New York: McGraw-Hill Book Company, 1934, pp. 661–708.

truders have been replaced largely by police, sheriffs, detectives, guards, and the like. Protection against fires is provided by public fire departments. Protection against dependency has been transferred largely to the government. Aid to Families with Dependent Children, social security, medicare, unemployment insurance, work-study programs, and the like are more recent versions of government programs already emerging when Ogburn wrote.

The Religious Function. In earlier days, the family was a close-knit religious group. Marriage was a sacrament, and the production of children a divine obligation. The family was primarily responsible for establishment and maintenance of ethical standards. Even the teaching of the scriptures was a family responsibility: family prayers, the saying of grace, the reading of Bible passages, and hymn-singing were common customs. Now, religion has been largely removed from the home. Family prayers have become uncommon, and the saying of grace is disappearing. Marriage has become as much a secular as a sacred matter, and the having of children a matter of rational planning. Parents send their children to church to learn moral and ethical behavior.

The Recreational Function. There has been a tremendous increase in the time devoted to recreational pursuits and in the facilities available for them. The taffy pull, popping popcorn, and group-singing are stereotypes of the old pattern of family-centered recreation. Now even these homely forms of recreation have been removed, for the most part, to church, school, company social program, and to the community at large. More spectacular is the growth of commercialized recreation. Spectator sports of baseball, football, basketball, hockey, horse-racing, tennis, and golf amuse millions of people. Active participant recreation ranging from amusement parks, to swimming pools, night clubs, and so on takes people away from their families more often than it involves the whole family group. A generation ago, some people saw a return to family recreation in the gluing of whole families to the television set in the living room. But as television became widely diffused, the scattering of the family before different sets in different rooms, where each can watch his or her favorite shows, is a common pattern.

The Educational Function. Formal education was not elaborate during colonial days. Academic training was minimal and some of it was done at the family fireside. The past two centuries have seen elaboration of formal academic training, and the transfer of various kinds of education away from the home. Most children are in school by the age of five or six, and some are in kindergartens or nursery schools by the age of three. Paid teachers teach everything from how to tie shoes and button clothes to table manners and social behavior. Not only does the school start earlier today, but it takes up more of the day and lasts longer. A high school education is now the norm, and college and post-graduate work are increasingly common. To some extent, the educational system has become a competitor with the family. Not that there is conscious competition; but the modern school system has its own standards of what children should become, standards that are not always consistent with those of parents.

The Status-Conferring Function. Membership in a family traditionally defined each person's place in the community. In small communities, the fact that a young person was Tim Swenson's son or Tony D'Amato's daughter specified clearly how far they should go in school, what work they would do, whom they would (or could) marry, what part of town they would live in, and so on. In the modern metropolis, this function has been minimized. A family's contact with neighbors may be avoided, with few people even knowing what the parents do for a living. Their statuses as people stem largely from their jobs and may literally be shed when they leave the office or plant. The children compete under the universalistic standards of the school system. Indirectly, the family's way of life is still determined somewhat by the income and by the value system of their occupations, but the direct participation of the family in defining each member's role in the community is much less than it used to be.

Family Disorganization

According to Ogburn, disorganization resulted from the loss of these family functions. One symptom of this disorganization was the rapid increase in broken homes, signifying unhappy men and women whose expectations of harmonious marital life were frustrated in the defunctionalized family. Divorce produces problems, not only for the parents but also for the children, who suffer emotional conflict, loss of a parent, and often financial privation. Frequently associated symptoms of social disorganization include illicit sexual activity, family desertion, and juvenile delinquency. Ogburn did not pursue the analysis of family disorganization beyond this point. He saw the family having its remaining functions strengthened, and he was social scientist enough not to fall victim to the temptation to equate defunctionalization of the family with imminent catastrophe. Ogburn's analysis, however, had great appeal for lay writers who did not share his scientific caution, and the popular press extended his thesis to predict complete family disorganization and even the disappearance of the family as a social institution. Thus, the idea that the family was "breaking down" became firmly implanted in the public mind.

Strengthened Functions

In addition to the functions Ogburn said it has been losing, the family performs certain personality functions for its members. These operate at two levels: between husband and wife, and between parents and children. In the old, multifunctional family, these functions were not conspicuous. The arduous conditions of life, the detailed division of labor within the family, and the emphasis on productivity did not encourage concern with the quality of emotional relationships. The relevant considerations in evaluating a husband were whether he owned property, was hard-working, sober, God-fearing, and just. Women were supposed to be good housekeepers, morally upright, strong, and equipped to bear and rear children. Assuming these qualities, the differences between persons were minimized; one did not expect great and continued emotional satisfaction in marriage. Similarly, children were trained to be industrious, obedient, and well mannered. Whether they were well adjusted and happy was not considered.

As the family ceased to be a productive unit, husbands, wives, and parents were also freed to cultivate relationships. Couples became concerned with happiness, seeking personal growth and fulfillment. Parents sought not only food, clothing, and shelter for their offspring, but increasingly emphasized their social and emotional development. Thus, according to Ogburn, the family has fewer functions today, but may be performing those few functions better than in the past.

Critique

The strength of Ogburn's analysis lay not so much in his theoretical formulations as in his description of the changed relationship between the family and other institutions. He documented the increased participation of government, commercial enterprises, education, in what were once family affairs. The accuracy of Ogburn's facts is unquestioned, and other writers have borrowed heavily from him. Ogburn also alerted a generation to the importance of technology in social change. If he overemphasized the role of material invention in his early writing, his later formulations ascribed causal influence to nonmaterial factors—ideologies, values, birth control, etc.—as well.[14] He never wavered from his belief that technology was a prime mover in social change, but he broadened his scheme to allow more influence from other aspects of culture.

One problem derives from Ogburn's use of the colonial family as the baseline from which to measure change. If we are not careful, we can easily assume that the functions of the colonial family are the *sine qua non* of the family, and that retreat from those basic functions represents breakdown. Actually, we know that the colonial family was simply one historical variant of the Western family, adapted to the agricultural conditions which then prevailed. If Ogburn's description of recent changes is accurate, his implicit conclusions about whether or not the family is doing its job are much more tenuous.[15] Other sociologists also have been critical of the concepts of culture lag and social disorganization. The charge has been made that these are normative concepts, containing hidden value judgments, and that change in nonmaterial culture does not always lag behind material culture. Fashions in clothes, popular music, teen-age jargon, and fads in children's toys are elements of nonmaterial culture which change erratically and rapidly.

Ogburn's analysis is less gloomy than Zimmerman's. Yet one cannot help but sense in it a certain nostalgia for the good old days and a minor foreboding about the future.[16] The small, unstable family of today seems but a pale shadow of the early farm family. To some degree, such conclusions derive inevitably from the mode of analysis used.

A STRUCTURE-FUNCTION THEORY

The structure-function approach to analysis of the family system is less historical than either of the two just discussed. It focuses less on family

14. *Technology and the Changing Family*, *op. cit.*, Chs. 1 and 2.

15. There is a tendency to idealize the colonial family. The stereotype of that family as brimming with satisfaction for its members has been labeled by William J. Goode as "the classical family of Western nostalgia." See his *After Divorce*, Glencoe, Illinois: The Free Press, 1956, p. 3; and *World Revolution and Family Patterns*, New York: The Free Press, 1963, pp. 6–7.

16. Other writers, building upon Ogburn's work, have dropped the more value-laden aspects of his theory and have emphasized the family's role in translating change in the larger society into the socialization process. See William Goode's concept of "the mediating function," in *The Family*, Englewood Cliffs, New Jersey: Prentice-Hall, 1964, pp. 2–3. See also Clark Vincent's concept of "the adaptive function," in "Familia Spongia: The Adaptive Function," *Journal of Marriage and the Family* 28 (Feb. 1966), pp. 29–36.

change and more on the integration between the family and other institutions—particularly the occupational system.

Structure-function analysis is one of the dominant orientations in modern sociology. It is so pervasive that identification of it with one or a few writers is bound to be misleading. The most systematic application of structure-function theory to the family probably has been made by Talcott Parsons, upon whose writings the present discussion is based.[17]

Structural Isolation

The analysis begins with emphasis on the American family system as open, multilineal, and conjugal. The nuclear family is more than ordinarily isolated from larger groups of kin, isolation being built into the family structure. There are, for example, no larger kinship units, recognized by having names given to them and which cut across nuclear families. There is no clan or lineage to which the individual remains attached. Each pair of nuclear families (see Figure 7.2) is linked by only one member whom they share in common. Ego is the common member of the families of orientation and procreation, the spouse shares the same family of procreation but not the same family of orientation, and so on for each other member of the family. At marriage, each person is partially removed from one kinship unit (nuclear family) and creates one new family.

The "poverty" of kinship organization is reflected in an accompanying poverty of kinship terms. We really have only the term "family," which usually refers to the nuclear family, and the term "relatives," which does not refer to a kinship unit, but includes all of the other people to whom a person is regarded as related. The monogamous character of the system is shown by the fact that the terms "mother," "father," "husband," and "wife" apply to only one person at a time. No terminological distinctions are made on the basis of birth order, all brothers and all sisters being called by the same term. Contrast this with the Chinese system in which older and younger brothers are called by separate kinship terms. Furthermore, our terminology ceases to make meaningful

17. Parsons's most comprehensive work on the family is one written with Robert F. Bales, *Family, Socialization and Interaction Process*, Glencoe, Illinois: The Free Press, 1955. The summation of his views, on which the present discussion rests, is found in Talcott Parsons, "The Social Structure of the Family," in Ruth N. Anshen, *ed.*, *The Family: Its Function and Destiny*, New York: Harper and Brothers, 1959, pp. 241–74. See also Talcott Parsons, "Age and Sex in the Social Structure of the United States," *American Sociological Review* 7 (Oct. 1942), pp. 604–16; and Hyman Rodman, "Talcott Parsons' View of the Changing American Family," in Hyman Rodman, *ed.*, *Marriage, Family and Society*, New York: Random House, 1965, pp. 262–86.

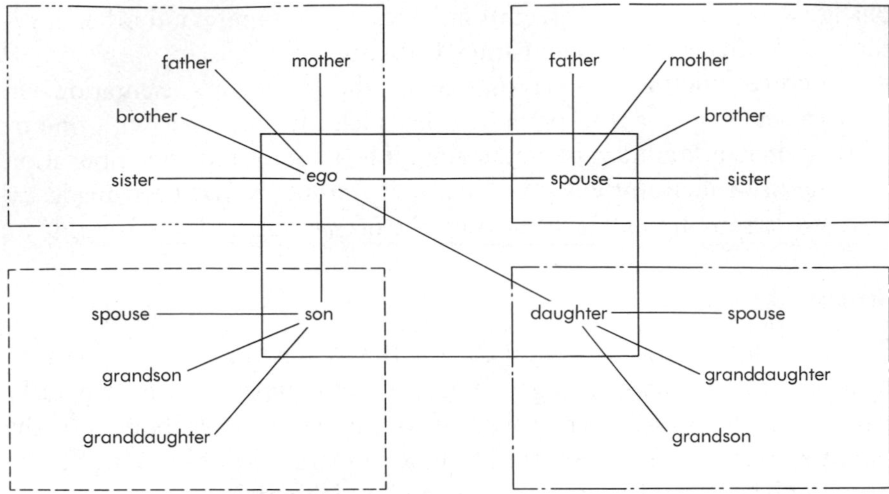

Figure 7.2. Five overlapping nuclear families: each pair of nuclear families shares only one common member

distinctions among relatives beyond the second or third degree.[18] As one traces relationship outward from ego (refer to Figure 2.3), separate kinship terms stop at the levels of cousin, grandparent, and grandchild. From there on, we indicate relationship by using numerical prefixes—first cousin, second cousin, etc.—or by using the prefix "great"—great-grandfather, great-great-grandfather, and so on.

An Open, Multilineal System

The structural isolation of the nuclear family does not end with the endless overlapping of nuclear families and the poverty of kinship units and kinship terms. There is also what Parsons refers to as the "open" and "multilineal" nature of the system. In the terms of Chapter 2, our kinship system is technically bilateral. Parsons prefers the term *multilineal*, however, to emphasize that no kin groups based on lines of descent tend to develop. Each generation selects its mates from outside the circle of relatives, and without consideration for cementing ties with kin of ear-

18. For illustrations of the research use to which kinship terminology and terms of address may be put, see Lionel S. Lewis, "Terms of Address for Parents and Some Clues About Social Relationships in the American Family," *Family Life Coordinator* 14 (April 1965), pp. 43–46; and Jay D. Schvaneveldt, "The Nuclear and Extended Family as Reflected in Autobiographical Dedications: A Comparative Study," *Journal of Marriage and the Family* 28 (Nov. 1966), pp. 495–97.

lier generations. Thus, there are no preferred marriage partners. Any nuclear family, which is the product of the merging of two family lines, is likely to merge with still different family lines at each succeeding generation.

Moreover, there are strict norms which militate against favoritism to either the husband's or the wife's family line. At the marital level, this is shown by the ingenious arrangements worked out by young married couples and their parents to guarantee equal attention on both sides. Thus, if the young couple has dinner with one set of parents on one weekend, they must dine the next weekend with the other parents, or at least work out the equivalent thereto. If Thanksgiving is spent at one parental home, Christmas must be spent at the other, and so on. The norms although not always verbalized, are so clear that all three couples know when the rules are being violated, and corrective action is taken. From the viewpoint of the parents, the same impartiality must be shown to their children. If a gift is made to one offspring and spouse, a corresponding gift must be made to the other.

An unanticipated but significant consequence of these equal-treatment norms is to gradually increase the social distance between the generations and to isolate the separate nuclear families. Eventually, the young married couple begins to form solidarity against the expectations of both parental families. Whereas, in the beginning, each spouse may wish to favor relationships with his or her own parents, finally husband and wife band together to decide that they "want to spend their holidays at home this year," or that they "shouldn't see quite so much of either set of parents." Similarly the parents decide that they won't visit the one son and his wife this weekend because, if they do, they will have to visit each of their other children on succeeding weekends.

The openness of the system is especially evident from the vantage point of the grandchildren, who have no terminological means to distinguish between maternal and paternal grandparents, and who are discouraged from showing favoritism toward either. Grandparents are distinguished only by surname—for example, Grandfather O'Brien from Grandfather Schmidt. With so little basis for making distinctions, grandchildren tend not to grow "too close" to either set of grandparents and, as they grow to adulthood, are likely to lose most contact with both.

The older generation also operates under strictures with regard to inheritance. The wife's interest is protected by her dower right, and minor children are also protected. Beyond these minimums, however, the law presumes in favor of equal inheritance by all children. Parents are expected to leave equal amounts to each of their children, but not to leave too much to any of them. The stereotypes which earlier surrounded the names of John D. Rockefeller and Henry Ford are a case in point. Both men gained the reputation for being stingy and selfish—largely because they amassed extensive property and passed it on to their children. The establishment of the Ford and Rockefeller foundations, which have redistributed some of their wealth in ways our society deems appropriate, has enhanced the reputations of both families.

The equal inheritance norms and the bias against the hereditary transmission of excessive wealth tend to remove the family's ties to the land, and further to isolate successive generations. At the death of parents, their home is likely to be sold and the proceeds distributed among the heirs. Not even the eldest son has reason to locate geographically near his parents, and none of the children has any financial incentive to curry special favor with them or to seek to carry on family traditions.

Emphasis on the Conjugal Unit

Parsons describes marriage as the structural keystone of our kinship system. Unlike the situation in most societies, people in our society have no kinship unit in which they retain membership throughout life. Instead, at marriage, they assume loyalties to spouses and children which outweigh loyalties to parents and siblings. Moreover, residence is neolocal. Young married couples are expected to take up residence apart from the location (and influence) of both parental families.

Consistent with the structural and geographical isolation of the conjugal family unit, parents are not expected to play a significant role in mate selection. In societies having large-family systems, parents do participate in the selection of mates for their offspring because the new spouse will become a member of their kinship unit; parents and other family members have a large stake in the person selected. In our case, however, adjustment between the spouses is paramount, and relationships with other kin are largely irrelevant. Integration of the couple into a larger kin group may even be dysfunctional.[19]

19. In structure-function analysis, society is viewed as a dynamic system of interconnected parts. In analyzing this system, one repeatedly asks, "What are the consequences of each part of the system for every other part and for the system as a whole?" The term *function* is used to refer to such consequences. The term *dysfunction* refers to negative consequences—to situations in which the effect of one part of the system on other parts is harmful to the system.

In the same vein, the structural and geographical isolation of the conjugal unit encourages emphasis on romantic love as the basis for marriage, and as the primary reason for staying married. Large kin groups typically discourage romantic love because attraction between spouses would threaten the priority of their loyalties to parents and to the group. Where the large kin group is absent, however, romantic love serves as a substitute for detailed role prescriptions. When a husband and wife in our society come into conflict, there is no omnipresent group of kin urging them to moderate their differences and solve their disagreements. The emotional attraction between them is the functionally equivalent substitute therefor. The small size of the conjugal unit also permits the married pair to structure their roles in relation to each other in many ways. Romantic love as the basis for marriage provides a strong bond while, at the same time, making a variety of role relationships possible.

Integration with the Occupational System

According to this analysis, the family system cannot be understood without reference to its ties to the occupational system. When the interrelations of these two are analyzed, many alleged symptoms of family disorganization appear not to be that at all. Much of this alleged disorganization represents, instead, an effective adaption to an industrial economy.

The status of the American family is bound up with the husband's occupation through the income, prestige, and style of life which derive from it. If one had to construct a picture of what any family is like from the answer to a single question, the most useful question probably would be, "What does the husband do for a living?" His occupation, and the perquisites that go with it, heavily influence where a family will live, their values and aspirations, how they are regarded by others, their material possessions, the nature of the children's educations, and so on.

In pre-industrial economies, there often is a direct integration between family and occupational system. The father works around the home, and other family members assist him. With the appearance of industry, this is no longer possible. The husband must go outside the home to earn a living. In the universalistic business world, he must not be restricted by the particularistic criteria governing family relationships. Similarly, family relationships cannot be structured according to the universalistic criteria operative in the economy. This dilemma is resolved through the segregation of familial and occupational roles.[20] The world of the family and the world of the job are fairly completely separated.

Normally, only the man plays a fully competitive role in the occupational system. This protects the marriage relationship, which rests solely on continuance of romantic love, against the destructive competition which might result if the wife followed an occupation with the same vigor as her husband. Thus, even though more married women are employed, the proportion of women in the highest-ranking occupations has not increased significantly. Most women work at lower-paid, even temporary, jobs and clearly subordinate their occupational ambitions to their husbands.

The segregation of occupational and familial roles isolates the nuclear family and protects it against destructive internal rivalries. It also permits the social and geographical mobility required by the system. Whereas in an agricultural economy, the son remains on the farm and at the same social level as his father, the requirements of an industrial economy are different. Sons can be successful in the economy only by moving with their jobs, acquiring technical skills, and developing new attitudes and values.

The modern family is adapted to a situation in which scientists, engineers, and managers play more significant roles in the economy than do farmers. University educations, rather than home apprenticeships, prepare people for these new occupations. Moreover, young men, once trained, cannot return to their families. Many parents live in small towns and open areas, while most technical jobs (and the rewarding ones) are found in metropolitan centers from New York to Houston to Seattle. Furthermore, even the boy from New York who is trained as physicist or engineer is likely to find that his occupation requires him to move to distant sections of the country.

Social mobility, too, is involved. The young man who would rise in the world must leave not only the family homestead but also its way of living. Higher education is the means to an occupation which requires that one think, feel, and act differently from one's parents. The isolation of the nuclear family permits the young married pair to follow the de-

20. For accounts of how family and occupational roles impinge upon one another, see Joan Aldous, "Occupational Characteristics and Males' Role Performance in the Family," *Journal of Marriage and the Family* 31 (Nov. 1969), pp. 707–12; and John Scanzoni, "Occupation and Family Differentiation," *The Sociological Quarterly* 8 (Spring 1967), pp. 187–98.

mands of the husband's job and, at the same time, to create a way of life for themselves that is attuned to the job and that is different from the way of life of either set of parents.

In functional terms, our system favors breaking family ties at any point where continuance of those ties would prejudice participation in the occupational system. The major break comes when a young man completes his training and enters the occupational world. At that point, he appropriately "falls in love" with a girl in whom his parents have no special interest, and moves away with her to further his career. The love between them provides a strong bond, and yet permits the continual adaptation of roles to fit the demands of the husband's job.

The subordination of family obligations to occupational ones continues. So long as the segregation of roles remains effective and the marital relationship supports the husband in his job, the couple remain "in love." If, however, the wife competes unduly or if the values, attitudes, social graces, and so on, of husband and wife do not develop apace, the couple "fall out of love." Their rationalizations may be that they are no longer interested in the same things, they have grown apart, or the like. Actually, they are preparing to part, so that each may find another spouse whose interests will be more in harmony with his or her own. Thus, even marital disruption is not seen as pathology but as a means of re-adjusting family roles to meet the requirements of the occupational system. If one presses it far enough, one may make the opposite judgment on divorce from that implicit in the cyclical and progressivist theories. Divorce occasionally becomes useful instead of harmful.

Critique

Alone among the three theories presented, the structure-function theory does not interpret recent changes in family patterns to reflect breakdown or disorganization. On the contrary, Parsons is explicit about the process of differentiation which operates in society to produce increasing specialization of institutions "so that certain functions formerly carried out by one unit are taken over by other specialized units, while the original unit concentrates upon fewer functions. . . ."[21] The freeing of the family from many tasks which it performed previously may enable it to perform its remaining tasks more successfully. As an agency for

21. Hyman Rodman, "Talcott Parsons' View of the Changing American Family," *Merrill-Palmer Quarterly* 11 (July 1965), p. 210.

meeting the affectional and personality needs of adults and children, the modern family is well adapted to the requirements of an industrial society.

Parsons states that the isolated nuclear family is found most extensively among white, urban, middle-class Americans. The isolated nuclear family is presented as the prototypical American Family. It is the family portrayed and admired through TV, the movies, radio, and so on. It is probably the most common family type in America today.

Parsons's emphasis on the apparent isolation of the nuclear family has caused difficulty. The theory assumes, but does not prove, that nuclear families are socially and physically more isolated than they were during the pre-industrial era. Data have been amassed in recent years that cast doubt upon this assumption. However, Parsons maintains, and his point appears valid, that the theory and data are not necessarily contradictory. The explanatory power of the concept of isolation lies principally in the context of anthropological comparisons with other societies and not in the context of the history of our own society. One of our tasks in subsequent chapters is to show how the structural biases of the kinship system are and are not reflected in actual family behavior.

There is much less explicit emphasis on social change in this theory than in either of the others. Change is dealt with only by implication. It is implied that Western family structure was more elaborate before industrialization and that the small, isolated, conjugal family is an adaptation to modern conditions. But the process of change is left unspecified. Some sociologists have been critical of structure-function analysis on this point. They maintain—and structure-function theorists stoutly deny—that emphasis on the interpenetration of parts of the social system and the notion of the system tending toward equilibrium lead to an essentially static conception of society, that by nature structure-function theory is ill adapted to the analysis of social change. The strongest criticism of the theory in recent years has come from women who argue that the emphasis upon role segregation in the family is a thinly veiled rationalization for denying women full occupational opportunities and for perpetuating sexism.

SUMMARY

There are few comprehensive theories of family structure and family change. This chapter summarizes three theories—a cyclical theory, a progressivist theory, and a structure-function theory.

Carle Zimmerman analyzes data from Western civilization, from the ancient Greeks to modern Americans. Throughout history he finds three recurring family types—the trustee family, the domestic family, and the atomistic family. Change, he finds, has occurred in giant historical cycles. As each society emerges out of primordial darkness, its institutions are relatively undifferentiated and the trustee family prevails. The trustee family subordinates individuals, and outside power develops gradually to restrict its abuses. The domestic family, associated with a society's greatest achievements, is intermediate; familism and individualism are in balance. Change, once set in motion, however, continues and the atomistic family form eventuates. The insatiable demands of rampant individualism lead to societal decay and the civilization gives way to another in which the trustee family is likely to be found. Unless we learn the lesson of history, Zimmerman believes that our society faces decay. If we will heed the signs, there still is time to alter our family system back to the idealistic type.

The progressivist theory uses data from colonial times to the present. Ogburn finds technological developments as causes of social change, and has the family as passively adjusting. Changes in nonmaterial culture lag behind changes in material culture, producing temporary social disorganization. Ogburn documents the fact that many functions—economic, protective, religious, recreational, educational, and status—formerly performed by the family, have been removed from the home. He associates rising divorce rates and other pathology with this loss of functions. The two functions remaining to the family—affectional and personality functions—are more important than they used to be.

The structure-function theory focuses on integration of the family with the occupational system. An isolated, nuclear family system is described in which there are no larger kinship groups and in which norms minimize ties with the parental generation. Marriage is the structural keystone of the system, and, because the marital unit is not incorporated into a larger kin group, marriage is based upon romantic love.

The particularism of the family system becomes consistent with the universalism of the occupational system through the segregation of roles, which permits only one family member to be a full participant in the occupational system. The husband's occupational success requires the nuclear family to be geographically and socially mobile.

Provision is made for family ties to give way when they conflict with the requirements of the husband's job. The young man leaves his parental family when he enters the occupational system, and, if his wife ceases to support his occupational advancement, they are likely to divorce and find other partners. This theory interprets our small, relatively unstable family as well adapted to an industrial economy.

SUGGESTED READINGS

Duncan, Otis Dudley, *ed.*, *William Ogburn on Culture and Social Change*, Chicago: University of Chicago Press, 1964. A collection of Ogburn's writings, including selections on the concept of culture lag.

Morgan, D. H. J., *Social Theory and the Family*, London: Routledge and Kegan Paul, 1975. Critique of functionalist theory applied to the family, and a proposal for the substitution of Marxist and existentialist perspectives.

Rodman, Hyman, "Talcott Parsons' View of the Changing American Family," in Hyman Rodman, *ed.*, *Marriage, Family, and Society*, New York: Random House, 1965, pp. 262–86. An excellent interpretive analysis of all Parsons's major views on the American family.

Scanzoni, John H., *Opportunity and the Family*, New York: The Free Press, 1970. Report of a large-scale research project that lends systematic support to the dependence of family cohesion upon the husband's successful participation in the occupational system.

Veroff, Joseph, and Feld, Sheila, *Marriage and Work in America: A Study of Motives and Roles*, New York: Van Nostrand Reinhold Company, 1970. Research in which two psychologists examine motives for affiliation, achievement, and power as these operate in work and family relationships. Emphasizes, again, the interpenetration of work roles and family roles.

FILMS

The Decision (National Film Board of Canada, Mackenzie Building, Toronto, Ontario), 30 minutes. Under the pressures of rising prices, competitive markets, and rising production costs, more and more farmers are being forced to abandon farming as a way of life. A father and son—the father holding to old ways, the son favoring the new—resolve difficulties to enable them to keep abreast of developments in agriculture.

Hazel and David (National Film Board of Canada, Mackenzie Building, Toronto, Ontario), 29 minutes. A husband insulates his family from his job. David feels that what happens at work should not bother his family. Hence, when his job is in doubt, his wife discovers it by accident. In the discussion there is promise of improved communication in the family.

Our Changing Family Life (McGraw-Hill Book Company, Text-Film Division, 1221 Avenue of the Americas, New York, N.Y. 10020), 22 minutes. A farm family in 1880 is an integrated unit. Three generations live under one roof. Religion, recreation, and the sharing of work play roles in holding the family together. Since 1880, industrial expansion, urbanization, and the emancipation of women have changed family life. The farm family has become less important. The roles of husband and wife have changed and companionship has become more important.

QUESTIONS AND PROJECTS

1. What is meant by the family as an "active agent" in social change? A "passive agent"? In which role do sociologists more often see the family?
2. Define: the trustee family; the domestic family; the atomistic family.
3. Describe Zimmerman's theory of social and family change. Make explicit the interaction between family and society at each stage.
4. What, according to Zimmerman, is the significance of this pattern of change for American society? Does Zimmerman propose a solution?
5. Evaluate this cyclical theory of change. To what degree can the theory be verified? To what degree can it be refuted?
6. Distinguish between material and nonmaterial culture. How is this distinction central to Ogburn's analysis of social change?
7. Define the concept of culture lag and give illustrations of its operation. What criticisms of this concept have been offered by other sociologists?
8. What time period and what cultural area does Ogburn's analysis cover? Does this scope influence the direction in which he sees society moving?
9. Describe family functions during colonial days and the subsequent defunctionalization. How has this defunctionalization "disorganized" the family?
10. What structural features of the American kinship system contribute to the isolation of the nuclear family? Include in your answer the nature of kinship units, terminology, and normative pressures operating on each generation.
11. How is marriage "the structural keystone of our family system"? How is marriage based upon romantic love consistent with such a system?
12. How does the segregation of familial and occupational roles help to maintain the system? To which set of roles does our society assign priority?

III
Contemporary American Families

8
Middle-Class Families

Last year, said the executive, our company was involved in the sale of 1,800 homes with a total market value of more than $50 million. . . . TI (Home Transfer Service Corporation), is one of about 14 national companies in the young, growing industry of transferring corporate employees from one area to another. . . .

Transfer service companies usually contract with a company to handle the sale of an employee's home in order to make the transfer more efficient and less of a shock. They may obtain another house for him. They may help finance it. . . .

[The executive], who has moved his own family 14 times in 18 years of marriage . . . estimates that between 300,000 and 500,000 employees will be transferred this year.[1]

The clients of transfer service companies are conjugal families, but they are a far cry from the conjugal families of colonial America. They are but one segment of a huge group of families—probably the largest single family type in the United States—who generally are labeled "middle class." This middle-class family is the one structure-function theorists use as their model family, adapted to the requirements of our urban industrial economy. They believe it, also, to be the family form toward which most non-middle-class groups in America are tending.

The United States is a vast land with over 215 million people, and with conflicting trends toward cultural homogeneity and heterogeneity. Recent years have seen many groups—blacks, Chicanos, Indians, and

1. Associated Press, August 12, 1972.

Jews, to mention a few—rebel against what they perceived to be forced cultural homogenization, and embrace a concept of cultural pluralism emphasizing the perpetuation of their distinctive ways of life. We take no position here on whether middle-class family patterns will, or should, spread further. We will analyze middle-class family patterns, recognizing that some of what we have to say applies also to families who are not explicitly middle class. Relationships between conjugal families and their kin networks, and the operation of the family life cycle provide examples. In subsequent chapters, we will analyze the family patterns of blacks, immigrants, and others whose ways will contribute to understanding American family life.

THE FAMILY'S VALUE SYSTEM

One way to characterize middle-class families is to present the system of moral principles, social norms, or rules and regulations according to which they are structured.

Equality and Democracy

Middle-class people are committed to equality of the sexes. Marriage is defined as a means to personal fulfillment for both parents and involves no subjugation of the woman to the man's interests and needs. Old stereotypes of man's work and woman's work are rejected, in favor of a flexible division of tasks based upon the personal preferences of the couple. As more women work outside the home, husbands participate more fully in housework and child care.

Democracy extends to the relationships between parents and children. Discipline ceases to be an end in itself, with the differential status and power of parents and children being minimized. Parent-child relationships should be characterized by increased participation of children in family decision-making.

Permissive Person-Centered Mate Selection

Improvements in the level of living have freed adolescents from the labor market, increased their leisure, and encouraged casual association between the sexes. Youth use their freedom to meet and evaluate prospective marriage partners. Ultimately, they choose for love and companionship rather than because of family background, religion, and other traditional criteria.

Change in sexual norms has occurred. Both men and women have the right to enjoy sex. Moreover, these rights extend into the premarital period, when participation increases according to the level of emotional involvement. Increasing numbers of parents and offspring alike sanction sexual activity in relationships where a high degree of affection is present.

The Nuclear Family Plus Kin Ties

The traditional functions of child-bearing, socialization, and economic cooperation continue to be performed, but there is more emphasis upon sex and companionship. There also is more attention to articulation of family patterns with other social systems, particularly the occupational system. Family patterns are expected to facilitate participation in the occupational system and to yield whenever the two conflict.

Although emphasis is upon the conjugal unit, ties with extended kin—particularly grandparents and grandchildren—are highly valued. Grandparents, when they are able, are expected to provide financial and moral support to the young families of their offspring, and in a fashion that does not imply financial or emotional dependence. In turn, young parents and children are supposed to encourage participation of the grandparents in the life of the family. Distance often requires interaction by mail and telephone, supplemented by occasional visits. As the grandparents grow older and dependent, younger family members are expected to increase the amounts and types of their support.

Professionalization of Marital and Parental Roles

Greater demands have led to professionalization of parental and marital roles, particularly for the wife. No longer are wives supposed to rely upon folk knowledge. Instead, they are expected to utilize professional help to develop their competence. Classes in preparation for marriage, childbirth, and parenthood are standard fare. In addition, women's magazines and consultations with specialists in medical clinics, schools, and counseling offices are accepted ways of increasing competence in the performance of marital and parental roles.

The permanence of marriage or the stability of family relationships have virtually ceased to be ends in themselves. Marriages are expected to promote the personal growth and wellbeing of the partners. When this does not happen, professional help should be sought. Both partners should work to eliminate the problems but, if they are unable to do so, divorce is preferable to continuation of an unhappy marriage. Similarly, parent-child relations are expected to be rewarding to both generations. When problems are encountered, mutually beneficial solutions, rather than those based upon imposition of authority, should be pursued. Marriage and parenthood are intended for the satisfaction they bring to the participants.

THE FAMILY LIFE CYCLE

The concept of "family life cycle" takes into account changes in family structure, composition, and behavior that accompany the inevitable progression from birth to death. Families, like individuals, have a life cycle which arbitrarily begins with marriage, proceeds through the bearing of children, is hectic and busy as the children grow to adulthood, contracts again with the marriage of the children, and, finally, terminates in the death of the parents.

Figure 8.1 presents the most commonly used eight-stage family life cycle showing the length of each stage.[2] The first stage involves the young married couple who have not yet produced children. Couples remain in this stage for an average of two years. The second stage lasts from the birth of the first child until the child is two and one-half years old. The "families with pre-school children" stage lasts three and one-half years, until the oldest child reaches six years. Stage IV, "families with school children," lasts seven years, as does the "families with teenagers" stage. Thus, the two stages in which children are in school last almost twice as long as the three preceding stages together! The period during which the children marry and leave home lasts an average of eight years.

The length of stages VII and VIII will come as a surprise and perhaps as a shock to many students. The period during which husband and wife remain together after the children are gone and until the husband's

2. Evelyn M. Duvall, *Family Development*, Philadelphia: J. B. Lippincott Company, 1971, Ch. 5. For other provocative analyses of the family life cycle concept, see Sylvia Clavan, "The Family Process: A Sociological Model," *The Family Coordinator* 18 (Oct. 1969), pp. 312–17; Frances A Magrabi and William H. Marshall, "Family Developmental Tasks: A Research Model," *Journal of Marriage and the Family* 27 (Nov. 1965), pp. 454–58; and Roy H. Rodgers, "Toward a Theory of Family Development," *Journal of Marriage and the Family* 26 (Aug. 1964), pp. 262–70.

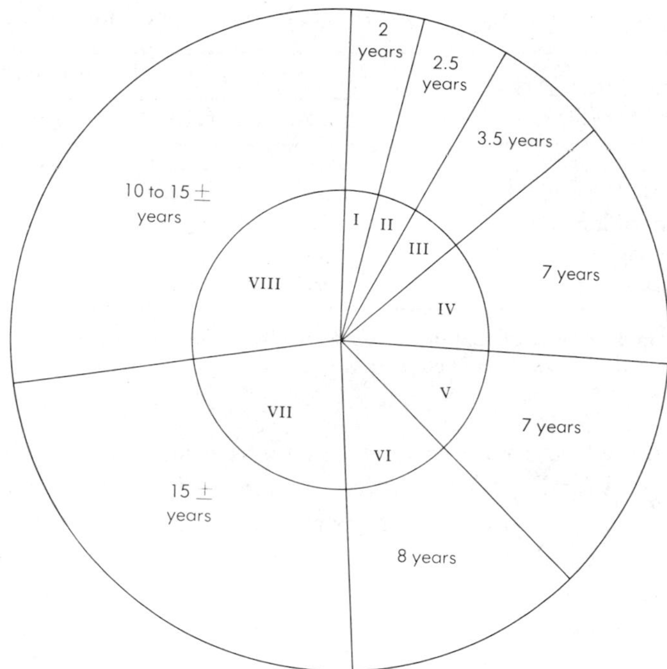

I BEGINNING FAMILIES (married couple without children).
II CHILDBEARING FAMILIES (oldest child birth-30 months).
III FAMILIES WITH PRESCHOOL CHILDREN (oldest child 30 months-6 years).
IV FAMILIES WITH SCHOOL CHILDREN (oldest child 6-13 years).
V FAMILIES WITH TEENAGERS (oldest child 13-20 years).
VI FAMILIES AS LAUNCHING CENTERS (first child gone to last child leaving home).
VII FAMILIES IN THE MIDDLE YEARS (empty nest to retirement).
VIII AGING FAMILIES (retirement to death of both spouses).

Figure 8.1. The family life cycle by length of time in each of eight stages

Source: From *Family Development* by Evelyn Duvall, published by J. B. Lippincott Company. Copyright © 1971, 1962, 1957 by J. B. Lippincott Company. Reprinted by permission.

retirement averages 15 years, seven times as long as they were together before their first child was born. After the husband's retirement, it is from 10 to 15 years until the death of the last partner. The husband who outlives his wife—and most husbands don't outlive their wives—outlives her by an average of about 7.5 years. The wife who outlives her husband survives him by nearly 16 years. Perhaps marital preparation for women should include preparation for prolonged widowhood.

Table 8.1 presents changes in the family life cycle over the past sixty years, as reflected in the median ages of wives at various stages in the

Table 8.1. Median ages of mothers at selected stages of the family life cycle

Stage of the family life cycle	*Approximate period of first marriage*			
	1910s	1930s	1950s	1970s
Age at first marriage	21.2	21.4	20.0	21.2
Age at birth of first child	22.9	23.5	21.4	22.7
Age at birth of last child	32.0	32.0	31.2	29.6
Age at marriage of last child	54.8	53.2	53.6	52.3
Age at death of first spouse	59.6	63.7	65.1	65.2

Source: Adapted from Paul C. Glick, "Updating the Life Cycle of the Family," *Journal of Marriage and the Family* 39 (Feb. 1977), p. 6.

cycle. The age at first marriage has fluctuated, dropping during the Post World War II period, but it is as high today as it was sixty years ago. Two things in the table are particularly striking. First, the age at the birth of the last child has dropped by about two and one-half years and, second, the interval from the marriage of the last child to the death of the first spouse has lengthened from less than five years to almost thirteen years.

The family of today is very different from the family of yesteryear. Just a few generations ago, men married in the middle twenties and often were buried before their last child left home. Women married only slightly earlier and often were worn, tired, and widowed before their children were grown. Now most parents are on their own again by about age 50, and appear younger, healthier, and more active than people of thirty-five to forty did fifty years ago. The increased longevity of the population has increased the overlap of generations tremendously. Grandparents often live to see their grandchildren grown and married. Relationships between parents and their grown children have changed, and family relationships have become more complicated.

GEOGRAPHICAL MOBILITY

Many middle-class families have few geographical roots and move from city to city and region to region as their jobs and personal preferences dictate. The family home is not a particular structure on a given block in a certain town, but is more a set of relationships, goals, and needs among its members. The family's house can be changed almost as readily as its bath towels.

Approximately one family in every five in the United States moves each year. Not that the same families move year after year, of course; some families set up a household at marriage and remain there for the rest of their lives. And some families of migratory workers are on the move constantly. Our thesis is that for a vast intermediate segment of the population, occasional changes of house and community occur as part of the normal demands of many occupations, as an accompaniment of occupational advancement, and as families seek congenial atmospheres in which to fulfill themselves and raise children.

Census data are revealing at this point. Mobility is highest among young adult groups and declines steadily as people get older. Mobility also is highest at middle-income levels, indicating that much of it is a feature of the middle-class style of life. The variety of age groups, social groups, and occupational groups involved is startling, however. Among highly mobile occupational groups are military people, migrant workers, actors and actresses, sales people, bus drivers and truck drivers, construction workers, and airline pilots, stewards, and stewardesses. Ecological forces are shown at work in the migration of blacks to the inner cities, whites to the suburbs, and blacks and whites alike displaced by urban renewal and the construction of highways. Up to 7 million people live in mobile homes. At opposite ends of the age scale, a large proportion of 18–22 year olds lives away from families, and many of those over 65 trek steadily toward Florida or California.[3]

Considerable mobility characterizes young college educated families who form the technical and management base of the nation's large organizations. Historically the moves have been tied to the husband's occupational advancement. One national moving firm reports that of 60 companies responding, 14 move their employees every two years, 16 every three years, and 10 every five years.[4] Such "organization men"

3. See Vance Packard, *A Nation of Strangers*, New York: David McKay, 1972.

4. Several studies have shown that frequent moves are not perceived as too stressful. See Curtis L. Barrett and Helen Noble, "Mothers' Anxieties Versus the Effects of Long Distance Move on Children," *Journal of Marriage and the Family* 35 (May 1973), pp. 181–88; Edgar W. Butler, Ronald J. McAllister, and Edward J. Kaiser, "The Effects of Voluntary and Involuntary Residential Mobility on Females and Males," *Journal of Marriage and the Family* 35 (May 1973), pp. 219–27; Stella B. Jones, "Geographic Mobility as Seen by the Wife and Mother," *Journal of Marriage and the Family* 35 (May 1973), pp. 210–18; Judson R. Landis and Louis Stoetzer, "An Exploratory Study of Middle-Class Migrant Families," *Journal of Marriage and the Family* 28 (Feb. 1966), pp. 51–53; and Ronald J. McAllister, Edgar W. Butler, and Edward J. Kaiser, "The Adaptation of Women to Residential Mobility," *Journal of Marriage and the Family* 35 (May 1973), pp. 197–204.

typically move across the country from suburb to suburb, moving physically but taking the same way of life with them from place to place. As Whyte put it, "With each transfer, the *decor*, the architecture, the faces, and the names may change; the people, the conversation, and the values do not. . . ."[5]

Recently, the pattern has changed somewhat for those middle-class families in which the wife also has some career commitment. Data from the 1970 census show that families in which the wife works are less likely to make long-distance moves than families in which the wife does not work, but are more likely to make short-distance moves. Apparently, the husband's mobility and his occupational advancement are hindered somewhat by the demands of the wife's job. At the same time, the income from her job probably also enables the family to improve its standard of living, including moves to better housing in the same general geographic area. It should also be pointed out that while both partners' occupational advancements are hindered by restrictions on their mobility, the wife's career probably suffers more than the husband's.[6]

ANTICIPATORY SOCIALIZATION

The family life style of the middle class is widely lived and even more widely imitated. We turn now to ways in which the experiences of children and adolescents prepare them to live middle-class family lives even more fully than their parents do. Our thesis is that there is a large and growing segment of the population which has the financial means to afford this life style, and to encourage their children to embrace it.

This group has discretionary income. They are not wealthy in the traditional sense, but they have significant amounts of money left over after the basic necessities of life are provided for. This left-over income may be saved, or it may be used to provide whatever luxuries are consistent with a given family's life style.

By the early 1970s, this discretionary income group could be defined as families with incomes of over $15,000. Twelve million families, about

5. William H. Whyte, Jr., *The Organization Man*, Garden City, New York: Doubleday and Company, 1956, pp. 298–305.
6. Larry H. Long, "Women's Labor Force Participation and the Residential Mobility of Families," *Social Forces* 52 (March 1974), pp. 342–48.

one in four, had reached this level by 1972, and the number is expected to rise to 25 million, or roughly two out of every five families, by 1980. Young corporate executives' families comprise one large segment of this group. Another segment has attained this income level largely through the efforts of wives in gainful employment. Almost 55 percent of American families have more than one working member, with the number of homes with two or more wage earners having doubled since 1950.[7]

Middle-class family life styles vary considerably, but they are almost all characterized by the possession of, or seeking after, a common set of material possessions—automobile or automobiles, furniture, television, radios, refrigerator-freezer, and standard brands of food and clothing. These possessions are called the "standard package"[8] which almost all middle-class families possess and which they can easily transport with them as they move about the country and up the occupational ladder.

There are variations on the package, of course. Differences in region, ethnic group, occupation, and life style are revealed by slight variations within the package. More striking than the variations, however, is the homogenization of taste and style over the country. Sears no longer puts out regional catalogs because essentially the same tastes prevail all over the country. One might cite also the fact that foods such as chow mein, pizza, stroganoff, and shish kabob are served almost everywhere and in communities where nothing is known of their origin. Perhaps the most startling evidence is provided by the emerging popularity of trading houses and possessions over long vacation periods. A family in Cape Cod or New York City arranges by mail, and sight unseen, to trade houses for the summer with a family from San Francisco or Tucson. Moreover, it works. Each wife leaves the linens in the drawers, the china in the cupboards, and even the soap and bathroom tissue. The alternate family moves in and almost within hours is as settled as they were at home. Often the greatest problem lies in finding "where she keeps the bottle opener."

The key to the universality of the standard package is found in the preparation of children and adolescents to want and expect to possess it when they reach adulthood. It begins early in life when, via television

7. Sylvia Porter, "'Supernumerary' Families: New Mass Market," *Your Money's Worth*, syndicated column, Oct. 5, 1972.

8. David Riesman and Howard Roseborough, "Careers and Consumer Behavior," in Lincoln H. Clark, *ed., Consumer Behavior*, Vol. II: *The Life Cycle and Consumer Behavior*, New York: New York University Press, 1955, pp. 1–2. See also John Scanzoni, "The Conjugal Family and Consumption Behavior," Bryn Mawr, Pennsylvania: The McCahan Foundation, Occasional Paper Series #1, n.d.

and the movies, children learn what the components of the package are and witness their parents' desires to own them. The children undergo what sociologists call "anticipatory socialization," a process of role-playing and fantasy which leads them to anticipate the conditions of adulthood and to respond to those conditions in a predetermined way.[9]

The significance of anticipatory socialization lies in the fact that children are thus prepared to live in ways that their parents have not really lived. In fact, they are prepared to live as no one has yet lived; to expect not only the standard package of today but to anticipate the additions that will be made to it from ten to twenty years in the future.

This anticipatory socialization continues through adolescence. The middle-class school often is more modern than the homes from which children come. As they move into college, many students live in fraternity or sorority houses, in modern dormitories, or in apartments that may be even more lavishly appointed than the Greek houses. That their parents may scrimp and save to maintain their offspring in such luxury makes less impression than the fact that this is the way to live. Thus, college living conditions help to prepare young people not only to live better than their parents, but to begin to do so much earlier in life.

Most middle-class parents who have collected the standard package required many years to do so. In their youth they learned to save for years to acquire the amenities. Their children, however, having had most of the package and having had their tastes further upgraded in adolescence, are not so often disposed to wait. They do not wait for marriage, but often marry before they are established in occupations and thus without material possessions. Once married, even though their incomes are adequate by most standards, they use installment buying to spend beyond their incomes and more quickly acquire the complete package. They begin marriage almost at the economic and status level it took their parents twenty years to achieve.

We should emphasize the role of the organization in regulating the family's consumption pattern and in helping to produce tensions between husband and wife. The consumption pattern is regulated indirectly by the need to gauge one's possessions to one's status level, neither understating nor overstating it. Thus the proper automobile for a junior executive may be a new Chevrolet Impala, a Plymouth Fury, or a com-

9. Robert K. Merton and Alice S. Kitt, "Contributions to the Theory of Reference-Group Behavior," in Robert K. Merton and Paul S. Lazarsfeld, *eds., Continuities in Social Research: Studies in the Scope and Method of "The American Soldier,"* Glencoe, Illinois: The Free Press, 1950, pp. 87–89.

parable car. If one's immediate superior drives an Oldsmobile Cutlass, it may be foolhardy to purchase an Oldsmobile 98. At the same time, promising young executives who drive their four-year-old inexpensive cars may find that their superiors question their taste and judgment—in other things as well as automobiles. Nor are such restrictions confined to the husband's possessions. The nonworking wife must be careful to see that her clothing and personal adornment set her apart from the wives of her husband's subordinates, but being careful to see that she does not compete with the wives of her husband's superiors. The house and neighborhood they live in, the schools their children attend, the clubs they belong to, and even vacations they take must be adjusted to what is appropriate to their rank in the organization. As they are promoted, their consumption patterns are adjusted accordingly.

Strains between husband and wife are produced by socialization into the organization way of life, and by upward mobility. The spouse who travels on an expense account, for example, often lives better on the road than the family can afford to live at home. The travel is first class, the accommodations deluxe, the meals expensive, and so on. The spouse, who would like to share the good fortune, is stuck at home caring for the children—one of whom might have a cold or is otherwise difficult to manage—and eating TV dinners or the equivalent. Most often it is the wife who resents her husband's privileges, or at least her inability to share them, and, for his part, the husband must feign dislike for having to travel. At home, the husband cannot help but compare the luxury of his travels with the hectic home existence in a too-crowded house on a too-tight budget with a harassed wife and fussy children.

The necessity to adjust one's standard of living to one's current job status demands a price from both husband and wife. Even where they could afford it out of private income, they must avoid the purchase of a too-lavish home or prematurely putting down roots. The strain of attempting to meet demands that outrun one's income is great. No one who expects to get ahead can forgo golf with the boss, membership in the country club, or expensive but proper entertainment. Moreover, the better the person's prospects, the greater may be the strain. The rising young couple, who feel that they cannot afford the luxuries to which the boss encourages them, know that the boss's judgment that they can afford them is likely to eventuate in a self-fulfilling prophecy. In the meantime, husband and wife, plagued with anxiety over how to make ends meet, unwittingly take out their frustrations the only place they can—on one another.

PARENT-CHILD INTERACTION

Parent-child interaction is bound up intimately with the nature of the interaction between the parents, particularly with the striving pattern in which they are caught up. For, although the incomes of such young families are adequate by most standards, they are usually inadequate to the demands which the parents feel upon themselves. Pregnancy and child-bearing require substantial amounts of money which might otherwise be spent on social and occupational advancement. Nor is the problem one of money alone. Child-bearing and child-rearing consume time and energy. The wife especially finds herself physically tied to the household and unable to join her husband in the pursuit of other goals. Since most activities for middle-class people are engaged in by couples, the husband's freedom is limited too.

Under these circumstances, it would not be surprising if child-bearing was regarded as a burden. Actually the reverse appears to be true. Middle-class people accept, perhaps more than any others, the ideas that child-bearing is to be sought, that children are lovable, and that parent-child relationships are sources of continuous joy. Middle-class people, too, seem to hang on tenaciously to the idea that there is some mysterious parental instinct which results in people having unmixed feelings of love for their children, no matter how troublesome they may be. That such a notion can be adhered to in spite of evidence that some parents (usually not middle class) beat and injure their children, desert them, and even kill them suggests a compulsive quality to middle-class parental love; that it is a protection against hostile impulses lurking below the surface. If this analysis is correct, there should be some complex and ambivalent emotional interaction in middle-class families.

Parsons traces many features of middle-class child-rearing practices to the smallness and relative isolation of the conjugal family. These conditions result in the child becoming dependent upon and vulnerable to the parents. Unlike the situation in a large family, in which the child has protection against the wrath of a parent in the love of grandparents, aunts, cousins, and so on, the middle-class American child has no one else to turn to. From birth, its welfare is overwhelming tied up with the mother. The father, a not-too-active participant during the first year or so, assumes an increasingly important position as the child grows older.

This complete dependence on the parents results in the child's becoming sensitive to any actual or threatened withdrawal of approval by them; its need for the parents' love becomes unconditional. When the child begins to participate in the outside world, however, it finds that playmates and neighbors make judgments, not according to particularistic family standards but according to the universalistic standards of the larger society. It must compete for affection and approval. It quickly learns that its parents are judged by others according to the kind of job the father has, the house they live in, the automobiles they drive, and so on.[10] Moreover, the child is judged by its achievements. If it is a bright, alert youngster who accomplishes more than its fellows, it fares well. If it lags behind, it fares badly.

The child learns not only that it must compete in the outside world for approval, but also that love and approval from its parents are contingent upon performance. For, although the parents are consciously committed to love their child regardless, they too have needs that must be met partly through the child. Put two middle-class mothers of young children together, for example, and some of their interaction can be predicted. They compare the accomplishments of their offspring. If the child of one mother began to talk earlier, then the second mother must find some achievement that her child accomplished first or performs better. The competition between the women (and their children) often is not carefully concealed. If the one mother and child come off badly, we might further predict that the unsuspecting husband and father is in for a bad evening! He is likely to find a quarrelsome wife who may or may not be able to tell him the source of her annoyance.

Chances are that neither spouse will be clearly aware of what is happening. Although most middle-class people are success-striving, other middle-class norms disapprove of too blatant striving, requiring that the competition be carried on in a seeming atmosphere of cooperation and good will. Explicit awareness of disappointment over their child's performance might call forth hostile feelings toward the child which the parents are ill equipped to handle. Middle-class parents have difficulty showing aggression toward children. The widespread preoccupation over whether children should be spanked may reflect fear of hitting the child. Many middle-class parents use more subtle techniques of pun-

10. Students will see that the success-striving middle-class person is illustrated by Sinclair Lewis's *Babbitt* (1922). It should be remembered, however, that "babbittry" is only one form of success-striving. Not all middle-class people have automobiles, boats, houses, and so on. In fact, some people who are especially striving, eschew conspicuous consumption. Striving can just as readily take the form of being knowledgeable about music or art, traveling widely, or giving time and money to charity. College professors, who are often thought to be seeking refuge from the business world and who sometimes glory in their lack of concern with material things, frequently engage in vicious competition for status among their peers. Even ministers compete to outdo one another in efforts at humility!

ishment which are more effective and more devastating. In one way or another, they threaten to withdraw love and approval. If the mother is crude and insensitive, she may say to her child "Mother won't love you if you do that." If she is just slightly sophisticated, she may say "We don't do things like that in our family," implying that the child who misbehaves is a depraved outsider. Middle-class mothers may thus deal a heavier blow with a softly spoken sentence or with a raising of an eyebrow than could be dealt with a strong arm. The effectiveness of withholding love depends upon the child's extreme dependence on the parents. Because it is so dependent, the threat of parental rejection is almost overwhelming. One might expect that many children would respond with anxiety and aggression against the parents. Some children do; but often most of the aggression is repressed and the child becomes conforming instead.

Arnold Green argues that middle-class parents view children with ambivalence and control them through the threat of withdrawal of love and approval. He maintains further that the typical middle-class boy's adjustment, by becoming outwardly submissive and conformist, makes it difficult for him to display the aggression necessary for successful competition among his peers. The boy is thus torn by conflict between the need to be submissive and the need to be aggressive. Whatever he does, he is torn by indecision, anxiety, and guilt. As he grows to adulthood he carries the conflict with him, becoming preoccupied with self-doubt. When he behaves aggressively, he feels guilty; but when he behaves submissively, he feels guilty over not striving to achieve.[11]

Green's analysis implies differences in the socialization of boys and girls, which differences have been systematized by Parsons. Parsons states that middle-class children of both sexes identify, in early childhood, with the mother. For the girl, this identification is functional because the mother serves as a direct role model of what the daughter will be as an adult. Most of the tasks performed by a wife and mother are tangible and easy for the girl to imitate. She role-plays at sweeping, ironing, cooking, and so on. She is not required to change her basic identification anywhere on the road to adulthood, and Parsons believes that this may be one of the factors that accounts for girls appearing to mature emotionally earlier than boys do.[12]

11. Arnold Green, "The Middle-Class Male Child and Neurosis," *American Sociological Review* 11 (Feb. 1946), pp. 31–41.

12. Talcott Parsons, "The Social Structure of the Family," in Ruth N. Anshen, *ed., The Family: Its Function and Destiny,* New York: Harper and Bros, 1959, pp. 256–57.

Not that the road to adulthood is completely uncomplicated for girls. There are at least three potential sources of frustration. First, girls discover, early in life, the prevailing definitions of masculine superiority.[13] The beloved and formerly omnipotent-appearing mother is dependent for livelihood and security upon a man. All women are basically dependent upon men, and the girl must eventually attain security, not through her own initiative, but through her husband. The competitive disadvantages faced by women come as a shock to the girl who has identified with her mother and who believed that the route to security lay in being like her. Parsons believes that considerable hostility may be engendered toward both men and women by this disappointment. That hostility appears later in life and is shown in the beliefs that women are deceptive and not to be trusted and that men are responsible for women's subjection. It may be that some of the ambivalence of women toward sex traces to this situation.

At adolescence, the girl discovers that the domestic attitudes and behaviors that brought approval from her mother and other adults are not similarly valued by her peers. Neither adolescent girls nor boys are especially fond of the "little mother" who cooks, sews, and cleans house. Instead, to be popular, the girl must rebel against parental standards. Rewards now come from conformity to the fads and fashions of the group. Some girls do not make the transition readily, and are left out of most teen-age activity. Others are confused by the conflicting standards, laying the groundwork for continued role confusion later in life.

The third source of frustration appears as the girl moves into adulthood and marriage. Unlike her masculine counterpart, she does not have the opportunity to contend directly for status. Instead, she essentially fixes her status and prospects as she selects her spouse. Moreover, she is required to make this selection at an age when the occupational potentialities of her prospective partner are yet unclear. If he is successful, she will be successful; if he is not, she cannot be. And even the most ardent defender of marriage based upon romantic love is unlikely to claim that it offers the girl any assurance in this respect.

13. The masculine bias in American culture has been revealed by studies on the preference for male children and by the differential evaluations placed on males and females. See Lolagene C. Coombs, "Preferences for Sex of Children Among U.S. Couples," *Family Planning Perspectives* 9 (Nov.–Dec. 1977), pp. 259–65; Gale Largey, "Sex Control and Society: A Critical Assessment of Sociological Speculations," *Social Problems* 20 (Winter 1973), pp. 310–18; Gerald E. Markle, "Sexism and the Sex Ratio," cited in *Family Planning Digest* 3 (March 1974), pp. 14–15; and Nancy E. Williamson, *Sons or Daughters: A Cross-Cultural Survey of Parental Preferences,* Beverly Hills, Cal.: Sage, 1976.

Parsons' formulation of girls' socialization experiences is part of the functionalist model that assumes role segregation within the family and the partial exclusion of women from occupational careers. This situation may still exist for most middle-class families, but a growing group of them are rejecting it in favor of the encouragement of both boys and girls to independence and career commitments. Many parents are trying to teach their daughters to seek security in their own training and efforts and are urging their sons to develop domestic interests as well as occupational ones in preparation for the truly equalitarian relationships in which middle-class people profess to believe.[14]

THE KIN NETWORK

Although the family system in the American colonies was clearly conjugal, without larger kin units such as clans, the evidence points to complex and continuing relationships between generations that suggest an informal kinship structure—the kin network. We will view the kin network in terms of relationships between married couples and their in-laws, visiting with relatives, and mutual aid between related conjugal families.

In-Law Relationships

Relationships between young married couples and their parents on both sides are a source of strain in the American family system. Young people bristle at any intimation of "parental interference," and parents shake their heads sadly, or bristle in turn, at their offspring's seeming obstreperousness. Both generations quote the tired cliche that "no home is big enough for two families"; and then there are all of those mother-in-law jokes.

Evelyn Duvall did a study involving men and women from all over the United States who were married from a few weeks to more than 40 years. Of the 5020 people sampled, 75 percent had one or more in-law problems.[15] John Thomas, studying 7000 broken Roman Catholic mar-

14. See William E. Knox and Harriet J. Kupferer, "A Discontinuity in the Socialization of Males in the United States," *Merrill-Palmer Quarterly* 17 (July 1971), pp. 251–61; and Lenore J. Weitzman, "Sex-Role Socialization," in Jo Freeman, *ed., Women: A Feminist Perspective* (Palo Alto, Cal.: Mayfield, 1975), pp. 105–44.

15. Evelyn M. Duvall, *In-Laws: Pro and Con,* New York: Association Press, 1954, pp. 187–88.

riages, found that in-laws were the most frequent single cause of marital breakup during the first year of marriage.[16] Finally, Judson Landis found that about 10 percent of 409 happily married couples had not achieved satisfactory in-law relationships even after twenty years of marriage.[17]

One study reported that the difficulty couples have with in-laws is related to their age at the time of marriage. Younger couples have more in-law problems; older ones not so much. Of those who married at age 24 or older, 63 percent reported excellent in-law adjustment, while only 45 percent of those who married between the ages of 17 and 19 reported excellent adjustment. This relationship between age and in-law difficulty was confirmed in a study of 909 Michigan families where the percentage of in-law difficulties declined steadily as couples grew older. Fifteen percent reported in-law disagreement during the honeymoon stage, with the percentage decreasing steadily over the rest of the life cycle.[18]

In a study of 544 couples in the early years of marriage,[19] 67 percent of those who reported excellent adjustment to in-laws also reported their marriages to be very happy. Of those who indicated fair or poor adjustment to in-laws, however, only 18 percent reported very happy marriages. This is not to say that good in-law adjustments cause marital happiness. In-law adjustment is one part of total marital adjustment. Where there are excellent adjustments reported it may be that there is a halo effect operating. People whose marriages are happy may tend to overestimate their relationships with in-laws and vice versa. People who report good relationships with in-laws are more likely to report that their marriages are happy than people who report poor in-law relationships.

In a study of 409 couples married for approximately twenty years,[20] the same researcher found that couples who reported satisfactory in-law relationships from the beginning were more likely to report their marriages as very happy. Fifty-two percent of the couples with good in-law relationships from the start of marriage said that their marriages were

16. John L. Thomas, "Marital Failure and Duration," *Social Order* 3 (Jan. 1953), pp. 24–29.

17. Judson T. Landis, "Adjustments After Marriage," *Marriage and Family Living* 9 (May 1947), pp. 32–34.

18. Robert O. Blood, Jr., and Donald M. Wolfe, *Husbands and Wives: The Dynamics of Married Living*, Glencoe, Illinois: The Free Press, 1960, pp. 247–48.

19. Judson T. Landis and Mary G. Landis, *Building a Successful Marriage*, Englewood Cliffs, New Jersey: Prentice-Hall, 1968, pp. 329–43.

20. Judson T. Landis, "Length of Time Required to Achieve Adjustment in Marriage," *American Sociological Review* 11 (Dec. 1946), pp. 666–67.

"very happy," 34 percent described their marriages as "happy," and 14 percent reported their marriages to be of only "average" happiness. The fact that these reports of marital happiness range only from "very happy" to "average" probably is to be accounted for by the nature of the sample. These were couples whose marriages had survived for twenty years and who might overestimate the happiness of their marriages.

Research tends to pinpoint in-law problems in the relationships between wives and their mothers-in-law and sisters-in-law, with husbands, fathers-in-law, and brothers-in-law less frequently and less extremely involved. Duvall found that over one-third of 1337 people said that the mother-in-law relationship was the most difficult. If we exclude 345 people who reported no in-law problems, then about one-half of the sample reported the mother-in-law relationship to be the most difficult. Moreover, 90 percent of the complaints about mothers-in-law came from wives.[21] It is the husband's mother, more than the wife's mother, on whom the difficulty appears to center.

These findings were confirmed in other studies. Landis, reporting on 116 husbands and 160 wives with in-law problems, found that 42 percent of the husbands and 50 percent of the wives reported difficulties with mothers-in-law. Landis found the sister-in-law relationship to be the next most frequent locus of in-law problems. Only 15 percent of the husbands and 11 percent of the wives indicated difficulties with fathers-in-law.[22] Thomas, studying Catholic couples, found the wife's in-laws to be involved in 48 percent of the cases while the husband's in-laws were involved in only 38 percent. He also reported the mother-in-law alone to be involved in 39 percent of his cases.[23] Wallin also reported that more wives than husbands dislike their mothers-in-law.[24]

The structure of the American family system appears to produce a particular range in in-law difficulties. First, parents and their married offspring are primarily concerned about the quality of the interpersonal relationships among them. They guard against "meddling," "interference," and "dependence." Dependence usually is defined more in emo-

21. *Op. cit.*, p. 187.
22. *Building a Successful Marriage*, p. 331.
23. John L. Thomas, *The American Catholic Family*, Englewood Cliffs, New Jersey: Prentice-Hall, 1956, p. 235.
24. Paul Wallin, "Sex Differences in Attitudes to In-Laws—A Test of a Theory," *American Journal of Sociology* 59 (March 1954), pp. 466–69. A study of 58 working-class marriages showed that husbands with less than a high-school education have as much difficulty with their mothers-in-law as their wives do. Mirra Komarovsky, *Blue-Collar Marriage*, New York: Random House, 1964, p. 259.

tional terms than in economic ones. To be sure, young people complain if their parents are either too niggardly or too lavish in their support of the young marriage; but the complaint is against the lack of love shown or the determination to control the young marriage, rather than against financial support as such. What makes financial support acceptable or unacceptable is the conditions under which it is given.

The need of young adults to be "independent" of parents traces back to conditions within the nuclear family and the requirement that people become independent of the family at marriage and at entry into the occupational system. During childhood, physical and emotional dependence upon the parents are relatively complete. During adolescence, the adolescent revolt symbolizes the attempt to free oneself both from parents and from one's own need to remain in a state of child-like dependence. Not all youngsters have remained so dependent that they need to rebel, of course, and not all of those who need to rebel are able to do so. It seems fair to say that a substantial proportion of young people approach adulthood with their needs for emotional dependence less than completely resolved.

The hold of many young married persons on their independence is precarious. They react strongly to any actual or presumed threats to that independence. Parents are likely to have difficulties in this area too. After having had offspring dependent upon them for twenty years—after having organized their lives around their children—they often do not give up those relationships without ambivalence. Parents are reluctant to let go, and their offspring—although they deny it—are often equally reluctant. Often, some time is required for emotional dependence to give way to the emotional give-and-take appropriate to parent-adult offspring relationships. Hence, the associations between age at marriage and in-law difficulty. Although it is a very crude one, age is an index of how far young people have traveled along the road to adult independence. Those who marry before they have traveled too far must complete their striving for independence after they marry; those who marry later are more likely to have this behind them. The association between length of time married and amount of in-law conflict is to be explained similarly. Young age, emotional dependence on parents, and newness of marriage tend to go together. With time, the dependence is resolved and in-law relationships become more harmonious. If the early conflict is bitter, or if someone at either generational level is emotionally incapable of more adult relationships, conflict may become permanent.

That in-law conflicts center in relationships among women probably is to be explained in terms of the distribution of power between the sexes. Ours is yet a somewhat male-dominated society. Women compete for favor with men, and men reinforce their dominance by permitting their favor to be competed for. This can be illustrated by the greater emphasis upon "being a good wife" than upon "being a good husband." Women are more likely to approach marriage fearing that they will not be adequate as wives than men are to fear that they will not be adequate as husbands. The wife is thrown into competition with the husband's mother and is judged in terms of her ability to keep house, cook, and otherwise cater to her husband's needs; moreover, she competes with a woman with years of experience. The husband is judged too—but not so much in terms of performance as a husband. He is judged in terms of success in the occupational world. If he earns a good living, does not run around with other women, and does not drink or gamble the family's livelihood away, not much more is demanded of him as a husband.

In addition, the position of the young husband is one of sufficient power that neither his wife's parents nor his own are likely to risk an open break with him. He does have the power to move his wife (and himself) to another location where there will be no contacts at all; even in the same location he may reject the parents and leave them powerless to do anything about it. This power is illustrated by the idea that a girl marries into her husband's family. The wife's parents' claim that they have gained a son appears feeble in comparison.

The marriage of offspring may also be more threatening to mothers than to fathers. Mothers' lives, more than fathers', are organized around their children. With their offspring's marriage, mothers find themselves rendered essentially functionless; there are too many hours to fill each day and the mere continuance of household duties affords the woman no satisfactory status. The father continues in his occupation, his primary source of status, essentially without interference. His wife, however, is forced to define herself as "getting old." Since high status for women is associated with being young, attractive, and desirable to men, it is not surprising that many mothers strive to retain their favored relationship with their married sons.

Conflict among women may also be more difficult to control because it is relatively covert. Conflict among men is likely to move rapidly to a confrontation in which the issues are resolved or some accommodation achieved. Women, however, to compete effectively, must do it without being obvious about it. If they force a crisis, their husbands are likely to take control and neither can win. Therefore, hostility between mother-in-law and daughter-in-law often remains partly hidden. They compete for favor with the men, using terms of endearment such as "dear" and "honey" to mask the barbs they hurl at one another. This is a part of the feminine culture to which men have only limited access. Men often underestimate conflict among women because, literally, they do not see it. One might also venture the hypothesis that men (un)wittingly ignore this conflict to some extent and thereby reinforce their own positions of dominance.

Visiting with Kin

Many studies show that a large proportion of conjugal families are in regular communication with relatives and that they visit with kin frequently. Studies in Detroit, Los Angeles, and San Francisco all showed about 50 percent of families see relatives at least once a week, and that an additional 25 percent see them as often as once a month.[25] A study of the kin relationships of 161 Boston-area families produced lower figures but still showed 14 percent interacting with kin at least once a week and 31 percent interacting at least once a month.[26] It appears that the Boston sample had fewer kin in the metropolitan area than was true for any other of the samples. Support for this interpretation is provided by a study of 133 migrant black women in Philadelphia, showing that of 56 percent who had relatives living in Philadelphia, 46 percent visited with relatives at least once a week.[27]

A study of 731 married women in Detroit tested relationships between the frequency of interaction with kin and marital adjustment, finding that interaction with kin up to about once a week is associated with good adjustment. Interaction more frequently than that appears to interfere with marital adjustment.[28]

25. Morris Axelrod, "Urban Structure and Social Participation," *American Sociological Review* 21 (Feb. 1956), p. 16; Aida K. Tomeh, "Informal Participation in a Metropolitan Community," *The Sociological Quarterly* 8 (Winter 1967), pp. 85–102; Scott Greer, "Urbanism Reconsidered: A Comparative Study of Local Areas in a Metropolis," *American Sociological Review* 21 (Feb. 1956), p. 22; Wendell Bell and Marion Boat, "Urban Neighborhoods and Informal Social Relations," *American Journal of Sociology* 62 (Jan. 1957), pp. 391–98.

26. Paul J. Reiss, "The Extended Kinship System: Correlates of and Attitudes on Frequency of Interaction," *Marriage and Family Living* 24 (Nov. 1962), pp. 333–39.

27. Leonard Blumberg and Robert R. Bell, "Urban Migration and Kinship Ties," *Social Problems* 6 (Spring 1959), pp. 328–33.

28. Robert O. Blood, "Kinship Interaction and Marital Solidarity," *Merrill-Palmer Quarterly* 15 (April 1969), pp. 171–84.

Finally, there is conflicting evidence over whether ties are closer with the husband's or the wife's kin. Sweetser summarized several studies which show a bias in favor of the wife's family,[29] and a recent study of 800 midwestern adults showed that women report more close kin than men do.[30] A carefully designed study of 530 working-class couples, however, found that these apparent relationships may be illusory. These researchers found that each spouse provides the linkage with his or her family of orientation and that when kin are not seen jointly by the couple, each spouse sees his or her own kindred separately.[31]

Mutual Aid Among Kin

Not only is visiting with kin very common, but there is an elaborate pattern of mutual aid among parental families and those of their married children. An early study of relationships between 97 middle-class, white Protestant, parental couples in Cleveland and their 195 married children living away from home found that the parents wanted to help their married children and wished, in return, to remain a part of their children's lives. For their part, the young married couples wanted the friendly encouragement and assistance of their parents. These wishes were realized in an extensive pattern of financial aid that flowed from parents to children. In 154 of the 195 cases, the parents were giving either direct financial support or help and service. The parents were quite definite that they did not expect their children to support them in turn.[32]

Parental aid to the young couples included financial aid in making larger purchases, such as homes and automobiles, and gifts of kitchen equipment and furniture. The parents provided services, such as repairs to and painting of the home, gardening, landscaping, and baby-sitting. Ordinarily they drew the line at providing a weekly or monthly check. Such support would produce or reflect a dependence that neither the parents nor their children would think appropriate.

Much aid was indirect. Rather than pay the doctor's bill at the birth

29. Dorrian A. Sweetser, "Intergenerational Ties in Finnish Urban Families," *American Sociological Review* 33 (April 1968), pp. 236–46.
30. Alan Booth, "Sex and Social Participation," *American Sociological Review* 37 (April 1972), pp. 183–93.
31. George S. Rosenberg and Donald F. Anspach, *Working Class Kinship*, Lexington, Mass.: D. C. Heath and Co., 1973.
32. Marvin B. Sussman, "The Help Pattern in the Middle Class Family," *American Sociological Review* 18 (Feb. 1953), pp. 22–23.

of a grandchild, for example, the parents provided savings bonds, layettes, or other gifts to the child. Similarly, parents arranged to rent a vacation cottage large enough for children and grandchildren, in addition to themselves. The parents thus bore most of the expense of a vacation their children could not afford, and without having to make a direct gift. The study also found direct mutual aid between parents and married children. In 120 of the cases, parents and children took care of one another during illness, regardless of the distance between their homes. Most frequently this involved mothers' providing services to daughters at childbirth. The mother either provided direct nursing service, or cared for older grandchildren during the confinement.

There was a surprising awareness of the function of parental aid in permitting children to prepare themselves for continued upward mobility. In 118 of the 154 cases where a help pattern existed, the parents recognized the need for their help if the children were not to suffer a drop in socio-economic level after their marriage.

The existence of an elaborate mutual-aid network was confirmed by a study in Detroit, where approximately 70 percent of all couples both gave aid to and received aid from relatives.[33] The most frequent types of help were baby-sitting and help during illness. Next most common was financial aid. Help with housework was given frequently. Other aid such as giving business advice, helping to find a job, and the giving of valuable gifts were found less often. The distinctive contribution of this study was to show the pattern of aid according to the age of the persons involved. It is primarily younger women who receive baby-sitting help. In fact, help received, in each of the four major categories, declines steadily with age. Apparently, younger couples who have just begun their families are more in need of help from kin than are older, more established families. A surprising thing, however, is the relative constancy of aid given over the life cycle. With the exception of aid with housework, which undoubtedly reflects the diminishing physical capacity of the older woman, the aid extended to relatives remains at a high level up to the age of retirement.

Still other studies have confirmed this network of aid from parents to their married children. Christopherson, Vandiver, and Krueger, studying married college students, found financial subsidies ranging from 5

33. Harry Sharp and Morris Axelrod, "Mutual Aid Among Relatives in an Urban Population," in Ronald Freedman, Amos Hawley, Werner Landecker, Gerhard Lenski, and Horace Miner, *eds.*, *Principles of Sociology: A Text with Readings,* New York: Holt, Rinehart, and Winston, 1956, pp. 434–35.

to 80 percent of their total money income being received by 38 percent of the student families.[34] Thus, in many locations and among a variety of samples, the same general finding obtains. Young people, at marriage, generally establish themselves apart from their parents, and both parents and children accept that they should be financially independent as well. Nevertheless, a widespread, intricate pattern of mutual aid exists. Married children and grandchildren continue to be important in the lives of parents, and young people generally welcome the continued interest and support of their parents. Many nuclear families are not so isolated, emotionally or financially, as they appear. Rather, they are embedded in an inconspicuous kin network in which there is considerable continuity from one generation to the next.

The Conditions of Intergenerational Continuity

Not all parents and their married children are close. Some are very close; others maintain a safe distance and regulate their contacts carefully; in still other cases, there is outright alienation. In this section, we examine data on factors which affect the level of intergenerational continuity.

The study of 97 New Haven parents and their 195 married children dealt not only with the extent of mutual aid but also with the conditions under which intergenerational continuity flourishes. Each of the 195 cases was classified according to the degree of intergenerational continuity. Four ratings were used. "High" continuity describes cases in which the parents and the married child's family completely accept one another. "Good" family continuity describes cases where the parents and the offspring completely accept one another, and where the parents and the offspring's spouse partially accept one another. "Fair" continuity exists where the parents and the young married couple partially accept each other. "Poor" continuity is marked by partial or complete mutual acceptance by parents and their offspring, but mutual rejection of parents and the offspring's spouse. Of the 195 cases, 122 were rated as high continuity, 27 cases displayed good continuity, 25 cases had only fair continuity, and 21 cases had poor continuity.[35]

Four different factors were related to intergenerational continuity:

34. Victor A. Christopherson, Joseph S. Vandiver, and Marie N. Krueger, "The Married College Student, 1959," *Marriage and Family Living* 22 (May 1960), pp. 126–27.

35. Marvin B. Sussman, *Family Continuity: Selective Factors Which Affect Relationships Between Families at Generational Levels*, Ph.D. dissertation, Yale University, 1951, p. 113.

(1) similarity of the sociocultural backgrounds of the young married persons; (2) the type of courtship and marriage ceremony; (3) the type of child-rearing they had experienced; and (4) the distance between the residences of the young couples and the parents.

When the young people married persons with ethnic, religious, social class, and educational backgrounds similar to their own, the vast majority had harmonious relationships with their in-laws and almost none had relationships marked by mutual rejection. Where backgrounds were dissimilar, on the other hand, few managed to develop relationships of mutual acceptance, and the majority of relationships were strained and structured in terms of prevailing stereotypes of the out-group into which the young person had married.[36] Sociocultural background was more highly related to intergenerational continuity than any of the other factors tested and seems to indicate that the price attached to marrying someone of radically different background often includes some alienation from one or both sets of *parents*.

The type of courtship and marriage ceremony was measured by whether there was the traditional church wedding and reception, following a courtship in which the parents had ample opportunity to become acquainted with their future son-in-law or daughter-in-law. This traditional courtship and wedding was followed by high continuity in 115 cases and by low continuity in only 7 cases. Where the young people eloped or otherwise violated the expectations of parents, there were only 6 cases of high continuity compared to 16 cases of poor continuity.

The analysis by the type of child-rearing showed that so-called developmental child-rearing, where the young person was encouraged to become independent and self-reliant but to continue affectionate ties with other family members, was associated with high continuity, whereas traditional child-rearing practices—stressing strict control over the children and creation of a dependent relationship between children and parents—was associated with low continuity. Traditionally oriented parents had difficulty severing their emotional ties to their children and were likely to interfere in their offspring's marriages.

36. *Ibid.* A second study indicates that intergenerational continuity is associated with higher incomes and with less marital tension over religious affiliation. See Joan Aldous, "The Consequences of Intergenerational Continuity," *Journal of Marriage and the Family* 27 (Nov. 1965), pp. 462–68. Still another report suggests that integration into a kin network may be associated with lower rates of marital dissolution. See John Scanzoni, "A Reinquiry into Marital Disorganization," *Journal of Marriage and the Family* 27 (Nov. 1965), pp. 483–91.

The analysis of residential location provided different findings. Only in this case was there no significant relationship with intergenerational continuity. About 84 percent of the families living in neighboring communities were characterized by high continuity; but an equally high proportion of those living in distant communities had high continuity.[37] The explanation for this anomaly probably lies in the fact that the location of the couple's residence is determined by their jobs rather than by relationships with other family members. It is important to emphasize that physical nearness is no guarantee of good relationships and that distance is not a great barrier to high intergenerational continuity.

The Modified Extended Family

The American nuclear family is not so isolated as structure-function theory might lead us to believe. Instead, we find a network of visiting, mutual aid, and emotional support which in some ways is reminiscent of the classical extended family. It may be, of course, that a more isolated nuclear family was characteristic of the first stages of industrialization. When the extended family was still strong, young people may have been more constrained to sever ties with it completely than they are today. There may have been no happy medium; to maintain ties at all may have been to accept subordination to parents and kin. Too, both transportation and communication were less efficient than today. A distance of 50 miles between the young couple and their kin may have been nearly insurmountable. It may have taken longer to travel that 50 miles than it takes to travel 300 miles today.

That there may have been more isolation of nuclear families from one to several generations ago seems plausible. By the very nature of the thing, it is impossible to verify that plausibility empirically.

It is also plausible that recent changes should have made the continuance of intergenerational contacts easier. First, as the classical extended family waned, the threat of parental domination of young marriages may also have lessened. Contemporary norms favoring equal status for all adults in the family may make it easier for young people to continue relationships with parents, and yet to retain their independence. Second,

37. *Ibid.*, p. 118. An exception, where kin relationships were somewhat less important and were unrelated to the adjustment of migrants to a new community, has been reported by Berardo. See Felix M. Berardo, "Kinship Interaction and Migrant Adaptation in an Aerospace-Related Community," *Journal of Marriage and the Family* 28 (Aug. 1966), pp. 296–304; and Felix M. Berardo, "Kinship Interaction and Communications Among Space-Age Migrants," *Journal of Marriage and the Family* 29 (Aug. 1967), pp. 541–54.

transportation and communication have improved tremendously. Air mail and inexpensive long distance telephone service have made it easier to stay in close contact. High-speed highway and air travel have effectively lessened distances and lowered barriers to the maintenance of interpersonal relationships.

Third, the development of huge, diversified urban centers may have reduced the need for young people to migrate to put their specialized training to use. When most families lived in small communities, getting a college education and putting it to use almost necessitated migration to an urban center. Now, however, three-fourths of the population is urban. In areas like New York, Philadelphia, Chicago, Los Angeles, and dozens more, almost any technical or professional skill may be put to use right in the area. The young couple can remain in the midst of the kin group and still seek occupational advancement.[38]

Whether there was a stage when the nuclear family was more isolated than it is today or whether there has been a fairly elaborate kin network all along may never be answered. What is clear is that another concept is needed to describe the incorporation of the nuclear family into the kin network. This is the concept of the modified extended family.

The concept of the modified extended family assumes that cohesion of the extended family in the United States is prohibited neither by occupational nor by geographical mobility.[39] Instead, extended family relations can exist in a mature industrial economy and may, for bureaucratic occupations at least, actually promote occupational and geographical mobility.

Litwak describes the modified extended family as follows:

> . . . The modified extended family structure . . . consists of a coalition of nuclear families in a state of partial dependence. Such partial dependence means that nuclear family members exchange significant services with each other, thus differing from the isolated nuclear family, as well as retain con-

38. Marvin B. Sussman and Lee Burchinal, "Kin Family Network: Unheralded Structure in Current Conceptualizations of Family Functioning," *Marriage and Family Living* 24 (Aug. 1962), pp. 231–40. See also Bartolomeo J. Palisi, "Ethnic Generation and Family Structure," *Journal of Marriage and the Family* 28 (Feb. 1966), pp. 49–50.

39. Eugene Litwak, "Occupational Mobility and Extended Family Cohesion," *American Sociological Review* 25 (Feb. 1960), pp. 9–21; Eugene Litwak, "Geographic Mobility and Extended Family Cohesion," *American Sociological Review* 25 (June 1960), pp. 385–94. See also Eugene Litwak and Ivan Szelenyi, "Primary Group Structures and Their Functions: Kin, Neighbors, and Friends," *American Sociological Review* 34 (Aug. 1969), pp. 465–81.

siderable autonomy (that is, not bound economically or geographically), therefore, differing from the classical extended family.[40]

Thus, we have a concept of extended family relationships being consistent with the demands of an industrial economy.[41] Three features of this modified extended family warrant discussion: class differences, implicit norms of noninterference, and the support of upward mobility.

Social Class Differences. Little is known about class differences in the kin network. Conceptualization of the modified extended family emphasizes middle-class patterns and tells little about lower-class patterns.

One study that dealt only with frequency of kinship interaction in a national sample found that social class makes a difference only when distance is not controlled.[42] Lower-class people visit kin more frequently because they live nearer to them, not because they are more familistic. At the same distances, there are no consistent differences in frequency of visiting by social class, rural-urban status, ethnicity, or religion.[43]

Norms of Noninterference. In generations past, in-law relationships were plagued by problems of dependency and control. There was a threat inherent in young couples accepting aid from their parents; if the

40. Eugene Litwak, "Extended Kin Relations in an Industrial Democratic Society," in Ethel Shanas and Gordon F. Streib, *eds., Social Structure and the Family: Generational Relations,* Englewood Cliffs, New Jersey: Prentice-Hall, 1965, p. 291. For additional evidence concerning the character of the modified extended family, see Bartolomeo J. Palisi, "Patterns of Social Participation in a Two-Generation Sample of Italian-Americans," *The Sociological Quarterly* 7 (Spring 1966), pp. 167–78.

41. Although this discussion focuses upon the United States, there is evidence of a modified extended family in other countries. See Everett D. Dyer, "Upward Social Mobility and Nuclear Family Integration as Perceived by the Wife in Swedish Urban Families," *Journal of Marriage and the Family* 32 (Aug. 1970), pp. 341–50; Guenther Leuschen, Robert O. Blood, Michael Lewis, Zachary Staikof, Veronica Stolte-Heiskanen, and Conor Ward, "Family Organization, Interaction and Ritual: A Cross-Cultural Study in Bulgaria, Finland, Germany and Ireland," *Journal of Marriage and the Family* 33 (Feb. 1971), pp. 228–34; James R. Mapstone, "Familistic Determinants of Property Acquisition," *Journal of Marriage and the Family* 32 (Feb. 1970), pp. 143–50; Helgi Osterreich, "Geographical Mobility and Kinship," *International Journal of Comparative Sociology* 6 (March 1965), pp. 131–44; Leonard I. Pearlin, *Class Context and Family Relations: A Cross-National Study,* Boston: Little, Brown and Company, 1971; Ralph Piddington, "The Kinship Network Among French Canadians," *International Journal of Comparative Sociology* 6 (March 1965), pp. 145–65; and Colin Rosser and Christopher Harris, *The Family and Social Change: A Study of Family and Kinship in a South Wales Town,* New York: Humanities Press, 1965.

42. Sheila R. Klatzky, *Patterns of Contact with Relatives,* Washington, D.C.: The American Sociological Association, 1973. See also Michael Gordon and C. Edward Noll, "Social Class and Interaction with Kin and Friends," *Journal of Comparative Family Studies* 6 (Autumn 1975), pp. 239–48.

43. See John Mogey, "Residence, Family, Kinship: Some Recent Research," *Journal of Family History* 1 (Autumn 1976), pp. 95–105.

parents supported they could interfere; and if the parents supported now, they could expect support, in return, in their old age.

Perhaps until this generation—and remnants are to be found today—there existed explicit verbal norms to the effect that young people should become economically self-sufficient at marriage.[44] If they could not be self-sufficient, they had no right to marry. If parents were required to support their children after marriage then the children were, by definition, immature and the parents had the right to say how their money was used. The reverse aspect of this problem was that there was economic dependency in old age. Before Social Security and company retirement plans became widespread, the plight of many aging parents was serious. Unable to save enough money for retirement out of their modest incomes, their security often lay in the possibility of "moving in with" or being supported by their married children. Under these circumstances, giving and accepting help from kin was fraught with hazard. Much of the bad reputation of in-law relationships may have stemmed from this situation.

The economic situation has changed drastically. A large proportion of parents have income for their old age and need no longer fear dependency upon their children. In addition, levels of living have risen to the point where many parents can subsidize offsprings' marriages with no hardship to themselves. Under these new conditions, the norms governing parental aid to married children have changed appreciably.

By and large, today, the norms provide that parents not interfere in their married children's lives. To prevent the implication of dependency of the young people upon the parents, subsidies must not be too obvious. The young husband might reject a check from his father or father-in-law indignantly. But when coming for a weekend, the parents load up the car with luxury foods and furniture "that they don't need any more." Since the parents will help eat (a very small portion of) the food, and since they would just have to get rid of the furniture anyway,

44. This does not necessarily mean that there was any less parental support in times past than today. Particularly in the farming economy, parental support often was elaborate and continuous. At marriage, the son might move his bride into his parents' house or into a house on the parental farm. Or, if the young couple were determined to be "independent," the father might lend them money for a down payment on the adjoining farm and advance money for seed, lend them equipment, and assist with the planting and harvesting the crops.

The norm requiring independence at marriage may have emerged only as the economy became industrialized and lengthy academic preparation was required for success. If so, the independence norm may have been used as a weapon by parents to discourage sons from marrying too early and thereby hurting their chances for occupational success.

there is no reason to reject the gifts, and the parents are not entitled to special consideration on the basis of them. There is an exchange in such cases, but what the parents wish, and their children give, is emotional rather than monetary. The parents seek entrée to the lives of their children and especially to their grandchildren. Since the norms state that it is good for children to know and love their grandparents, the ground is laid for amiable supportive relations between generations.

The Support of Upward Mobility. The model of the isolated nuclear family argued that ties with parents and kin were an obstacle to occupational success. The model called for the son of a father who ate dinner in his undershirt, and of a mother who disapproved of drinking and smoking, to become a sophisticated young executive. He could more easily rid himself of dysfunctional attitudes and behavior and take on new ones if he moved away from his parents.

The modified extended family is not, however, a threat to upward mobility.[45] Indeed, in some ways, the parents aid mobility, reward their offspring for it, and themselves derive prestige from it. The role of parents in aiding children to acquire the standard package regarded as essential to middle-class living has already been described. Suffice it to say here that, without parental support through college training, and without parental subsidization of the young marriage, upward mobility would be slower and less certain. This fact, while not emphasized by many parents, is not lost on most young people, who appear willing to have parents share vicariously, at least, in their successes.

Continued interaction with parents, after upward mobility, may also be rewarding both to parents and offspring. Parents may continue to achieve through their children long after they themselves have climbed as high as they are going to go. Visits from their high-status offspring provide an opportunity to "show off" that vicarious achievement to friends and neighbors. For their part, the young people may be uncomfortable in the lower status environment of their youth but they may enjoy and receive enhanced self-esteem from the homage paid to them by parents and other kin. Implicit in this arrangement is some segregation of the young people's kin relationships from their relationships with

45. J. M. Bruce, "Intragenerational Occupational Mobility and Visiting with Kin and Friend," *Social Forces* 49 (Sept. 1970), pp. 117–27; Mark Hutter, "Transformation of Identity, Social Mobility and Kinship Solidarity," *Journal of Marriage and the Family* 32 (Feb. 1970), pp. 133–37; Harry K. Schwarzweller and John F. Seggar, "Kinship Involvement: A Factor in the Adjustment of Rural Migrants," *Journal of Marriage and the Family* 29 (Nov. 1967), pp. 662–71.

current associates. By making occasional visits "back home," and having parents visit them periodically, the young couple can make sure that their parents are not embarrassed by being thrown in with friends with different attitudes and values and that, similarly, their friends do not have to help entertain their parents. Although neither parents nor offspring verbalize it, both recognize that they can thus avoid being embarrassed or ashamed.

This is becoming less of a problem with the passage of time. The most acute embarrassment over social origins probably occurs among those who have not climbed very far and are of low socio-economic background. The higher people climb, and the more secure they become in their new status, the less need there is to hide parents, like skeletons in the closet. Moreover, with the increasing affluence of parents, the completion of the assimilation of European immigrants, and with the leveling of tastes and styles of life, the gulf between parents and their upwardly mobile children is not so wide as it was. There is even a spreading awareness among young middle-class people on the rise that most of them have similar parental backgrounds and they need not be ashamed of them. To this degree, there may even be some mingling of parents with the young couples' current associates.

SUMMARY

The middle-class family life style is the most widely lived one in America. It is emulated by many who are not explicitly middle class. That life style is built upon values of equality, democracy, person-centered mate selection, emphasis on the conjugal family maintaining extended kin ties, and the professionalization of marital and parental roles.

Life-cycle analysis traces changes in family organization from family formation at marriage to its dissolution through death of the partners. Changes over the past century have compressed child-bearing, and lengthened the couples' life together after their children have married.

Approximately one out of every five families moves each year, mobility being highest among young adults and middle-income groups. Much of this mobility is occupationally related, and helps create a fairly homogeneous middle-class life style. Middle-class children and adolescents undergo lengthy anticipatory socialization—learning from parents, the mass media, and colleges—to begin married life in possession of the standard middle-class package of consumer goods. They begin married life at the level it took their parents twenty years to achieve.

The middle-class way of life closely regulates consumption patterns and produces strains between husband and wife. The couple must live up to the standards expected of them, without infringing upon the perquisites of their superiors. Often this requires them to spend more than they can afford. The husband's extravagant expense-account living contrasts sharply with the budget-saving measures demanded of his wife at home. Children add to the financial pressures, and children are quickly drawn into the competitive struggle. Parents use threats of withdrawal of love to secure conformity.

Girls' maternal identifications provide them with appropriate adult role models. They encounter frustration in the discovery that women are subordinate to men, in the rewards offered to non-domestic qualities during adolescence, and in having to secure their futures through young men whose potentialities are not yet evident. Boys reject their early maternal identifications and assume a compulsive masculinity that plagues their relationships with women. Boys also are handicapped, in adopting male roles, by the intangible nature of middle-class occupations and the lack of clearly defined masculine role models.

Conjugal families typically live apart from parents and in-laws, but maintain a variety of kin ties. Relationships with in-laws vary with age at marriage, younger couples reporting more difficulty than older ones. In-law adjustment also is related to total marital adjustment, those reporting good marital adjustment also tending to report good in-law adjustment. Problems appear more often to revolve around women than around men. Difficulties between the young bride and her mother-in-law are most common; problems with sisters-in-law come next. Husbands, fathers-in-law, and brothers-in-law are less frequently involved.

In-law problems may stem from conditions in the nuclear family which require young adults to rebel against their emotional dependence upon parents. Until independence is secured, "meddling" by parents probably is both more common and more commonly perceived, even where it may not exist. The concentration of in-law problems among women may be related to women's dependent position. Accommodation between a man and his in-laws is likely to be reached, or a break follows. Women, however, are not often in a position to issue ultimatums.

A large proportion of families have kin nearby, and up to half visit with kin at least once a week. Visiting up to that level appears associated with good marital adjustment; beyond that, it implies overdependence. There may be bias shown in favor of the wife's kin, or each spouse may take the lead with his or her own kin. Mutual aid is widespread, with aid flowing from parents to married children. The aid is arranged, carefully, not to interfere with the independence of either family.

Ties between the generations are likely to be closer when the young person's spouse is of similar sociocultural background, when the courtship has been a conventional one, and when the child-bearing pattern has been developmental. The distance between the residences of the parents and their married children is less important.

It is unknown whether Western society went through a stage when the nuclear family was more isolated than it is today. In any event, efficient transportation and communication, high standards of living, and the development of huge urban complexes all facilitate the maintenance of kin ties today. The modified extended family, unhampered by either occupational or geographical mobility, is an important feature of the American family system. This modified extended family operates at different social class levels, includes tacit norms of noninterference, and does not hinder the upward mobility of the younger generation.

SUGGESTED READINGS

Bane, Mary Jo, *Here to Stay: American Families in the Twentieth Century*, New York: Basic Books, 1977. Refutes the contention that the American family is in decline. Cautions against social policies that might inadvertently weaken the family.

Ishwaran, K., *ed.*, *The Canadian Family: A Book of Readings*, Toronto: Holt, Rinehart and Winston, 1971. Emphasizes pervasiveness of the kin network and relations between the family and other groups.

Klatzky, Sheila R., *Patterns of Contact with Relatives*, Washington, D.C.: The American Sociological Association, 1973. This doctoral dissertation is the methodologically most rigorous analysis that has yet been done of the effects of distance upon contacts with relatives outside the family of procreation.

Scanzoni, Letha, and Scanzoni, John, *Men, Women, and Change: A Sociology of Marriage and Family*, New York: McGraw-Hill, 1976. A basic textbook emphasizing stability and change in the family.

Shanas, Ethel, and Streib, Gordon F., *eds.*, *Social Structure and the Family:*

Generational Relations, Englewood Cliffs, New Jersey: Prentice-Hall, 1965. An interdisciplinary symposium on the three generation family. Emphasizes role relationships of older family members.

Wakil, S. Parvez, *ed.*, *Marriage, Family, and Society: Canadian Perspectives*, Toronto: Butterworth and Co., 1975. A comprehensive collection of articles featuring much new data on Canadian families.

FILMS

The Cage (National Film Board of Canada, Mackenzie Building, Toronto, Ontario), 27 minutes. Questions whether getting that important job and keeping up with the Joneses are worth the strains and tensions that go with them. Each person needs to find his or her own way out of the cage that modern living imposes upon us.

Marriage Is a Partnership (Coronet Films, Coronet Building, Chicago, Ill.), 20 minutes. Analyzes adjustments of a young married couple. Illustrates the tendency of each spouse to be overdependent on parents. Shows resolution of the problem to be a function of the young people's attitudes.

Suburban Living—Six Solutions (National Film Board of Canada, Mackenzie Building, Toronto, Ontario), 60 minutes. Surveys six suburbs in England, France, Holland, Sweden, and Canada. All except the Canadian example offer light, airy homes in park-like settings at rentals of about one-sixth of income.

QUESTIONS AND PROJECTS

1. Describe the value system of the middle-class family. To what extent are these values held by most American families?
2. Define the concept of "family life cycle." What changes have occurred in the cycle over the past few generations?
3. Define the concept of "anticipatory socialization." How are middle-class youths conditioned to develop high-success drives? Do they necessarily strive for financial success?
4. What emotional and financial strains plague upwardly mobile young couples? How do these strains affect their relationships with children?
5. Describe how middle-class boys achieve adult masculine identifications. Contrast this pattern with that typically experienced by girls. What frustrations does each encounter?
6. Identify each of the prominent groups on your campus, and relate their behavior to the satisfaction of success needs.

7. How are age at marriage and total marital adjustment related to in-law adjustment? How do you explain these relationships?
8. How frequently do urban families visit with relatives? What patterns of mutual aid exist? How do these vary over the life cycle?
9. What is meant by "intergenerational continuity?" What social variables are related to it? How do you explain the lack of any relationship with distance between family residences?
10. What is the modified extended family? How does it differ from the classical extended family?
11. Might there have been a stage in the development of Western society when the nuclear family was more isolated than it is today? What recent changes have made it easier for families to maintain contact with kin?
12. Explain how the modified extended family may actually promote occupational mobility.

9
Black Families

Laura is the daughter of a lawyer and a magazine writer. When the Calhouns first moved into the wealthy Chicago suburb of Kenilworth, they were greeted by crank calls and a cross burned on their lawn. Since last June, Laura has been wearing her hair Afro. "My God, yes, black is beautiful," says Laura. "The psychological tragedy of this country is that people have not come to grips with blackness. The black woman has got to realize that black is beautiful."

Laura reflects the growing tendency of middle-class blacks to feel self-conscious about their own success and concerned about their brothers and sisters in the ghettos, "I'm not really black," she says, "until I know what's happening on every level of being black. For all that's happened in this country, we are still American citizens. Salvation for the black kids will come through education and then beating the white man at his own thing. . . ."[1]

Black people make up the largest racial or ethnic minority in the United States—over 24 million people. They also have a unique history. Both that history and the heterogeneity of so large a population must be taken into account in our description of black family patterns and the degree to which they conform to and differ from white middle-class family patterns.

FAMILY PATTERNS UNDER SLAVERY

The first blacks arrived in Virginia in 1619. Purchased from a Dutch ship, they had the same status as white indentured servants.[2] After they

1. *Time*, April 6, 1970, p. 46.
2. E. Franklin Frazier, *The Negro in the United States*, New York: The Macmillan Company, 1957, pp. 22–26; Alphonso Pinkney, *Black Americans*, Englewood Cliffs, New Jersey: Prentice-Hall, 1969, p. 1.

had worked to earn their purchase, they were released from servitude. This happened in some cases and free Negroes in the United States existed almost from the beginning. Under demands for a permanent, cheap labor supply, however, slavery was not long in emerging. The slave status of blacks in Virginia became fixed by law in 1670. At the first United States census in 1790, there were about 700,000 slaves; before the Civil War, the number had increased to almost 4 million.

A striking feature of black American family life from the beginning was the almost complete absence of influence from African culture. The English, Poles, Italians, and others transported many of their traditional patterns to the United States. The conditions of slavery, however, effectively prevented blacks from doing this. Before shipment to America, members of various African cultures often were mixed to prevent the development of resistance among them. Then, in the New World, the process continued in the sale and training of slaves. The newcomers had to learn a new language, adopt new habits, and assume, in some form, the customs in their new environment. The children born into this situation never learned much of their African heritage and, almost within a generation, the old ways were lost.[3]

Early sexual, marital, and family practices also were influenced by a grossly disproportionate sex ratio. Although precise data are not available, the early shipments of slaves were heavily male and not until around 1840 did the number of black women approach that of black men. Not surprisingly, many informal sexual liaisons developed first between indentured black men and indentured white women and later on between slaves and indentured white women. Miscegenation may have been proportionately more frequent during those early decades than it has ever been since.

The unbalanced sex ratio contributed also casualness of sexual contact between many black women and men. The primary factors here were the attitudes and policies of white slave-owners. Some owners literally considered their slaves as livestock and sought to breed them in comparable fashion. Strong, healthy males were used as studs and the formalities of marriage often were dispensed with. Too, fathers were sold or traded without their wives and children, and vice versa. Under these circumstances, whatever tendency there was to seek sexual satisfaction without assuming further obligations was greatly intensified.

3. W. E. B. Du Bois, *The Negro American Family*, Atlanta: Atlanta University Press, 1908; and E. Franklin Frazier, *The Negro Family in the United States*, New York: Dryden Press, 1948, pp. 15–17.

Conditions on the plantations were not everywhere alike or even similar for all slaves on a given plantation. Some owners apparently treated their slaves with kindness and consideration, and encouraged the development of stable family life among them. In these instances, the family patterns that emerged were not significantly different from those which existed among whites and free blacks.[4]

On the same plantations, there often were differences between the family patterns of house slaves and field hands. The house servants were exposed intimately to the ideas and manners of their owners; black women assumed much of the care and training of white children, and the family lives of owners and slaves became intertwined. The family patterns of the house slaves often did not differ significantly from their owners'. Often, there was great social distance between house slaves and field hands. The house servants reinforced their superiority by identifying with their owners, while the field hands were cut off from such opportunities and frequently were brutalized in the process.

Field hands typically were under the supervision of an overseer whose only interest was in production, and who was prone to treat them as chattel. The harshest effects of slavery were found in this context, and what has come to be considered the ideal-typical slave family was that of the field hands. It was among field hands that the husband and father sometimes became a shadowy figure in the family. The field hands were most likely to be used as breeding stock, and emphasis was placed on the mother-child unit. Marriages seldom were regularized, and when families were split up there was a tendency to keep small children with their mother. Many owners reinforced the primary position of the mother and sabotaged the father by assigning to the woman the cabin in which she and her children lived and by issuing to her the rations of food. Men were not encouraged to assume responsibility for wives and children, and many did not. Thus, under slavery there emerged a mother-centered family that was to continue in modified form into the post-slavery period.

4. For analyses supporting the thesis that the slave family structure was basically nuclear, see Robert W. Fogel and Stanley L. Engerman, *Time on the Cross: The Economics of American Negro Slavery*, Boston: Little, Brown, 1974; Eugene Genovese, *Roll, Jordan, Roll: The World the Slaves Made*, New York: Pantheon Books, 1974; and Herbert Gutman, *The Black Family in Slavery and Freedom, 1750–1925*, New York Pantheon Books, 1976. A recent analysis of black family patterns in the South after the Civil War presents data indicating that both Du Bois and Frazier, and their recent critics probably were partly correct. See Barbara Finlay Agresti, *Household and Family in the Postbellum South: Walton County, Florida, 1870 and 1885*, Ph.D. Dissertation: University of Florida, 1976.

Black family life was further complicated by miscegenation. In the beginning, miscegenation was two-way, with intercourse between black men and white indentured women sometimes being encouraged by owners who wished to increase their indentured servants. As the "principles" of white domination and racial integrity became fixed, however, laws were enforced against unions between black men and white women. Although there are no precise data, relationships between white men and black women continued to be widespread.

Relationships between white men and black women ranged from the completely casual to those in which the slave was emancipated and made a legal wife. In some instances, slave-mistresses were later sold, and their mulatto children with them. Often, however, the slave-mistress received special consideration and the children were treated with affection. The woman sometimes was brought directly into the household, and sometimes had her own small house near by. The children often were freed and occasionally were sent to college. Nor was miscegenation confined to plantations. There were, in cities like New Orleans, Charleston, and Mobile, large mixed-blood populations, as well as free Negroes. Attractive mulatto, quadroon, and octoroon women were sought after by well-to-do men, with all of the results that characterized such relationships in rural areas. Since the children of such unions were free, they helped to swell the ranks of free Negroes in the United States.

By 1860, there were nearly half a million free Negroes. Frazier reports that more than one-third, as compared to an estimated one-twelfth of the slave population, were probably of mixed blood.[5] Among these free Negroes, another family pattern emerged. These families sometimes were almost patriarchal, with the husband and father wielding more power than in corresponding white families. For one thing, the free black man often purchased his wife from slavery and, where she had children, purchased them too. Thus, we have the anomaly of slave-owning blacks. There is even evidence of husbands selling their wives back into slavery when the marriages did not work out.[6]

On the whole, the families of free Negroes prior to the Civil War appear to have been quite stable. Their members frequently were former house slaves who had adopted the attitudes and customs of upper-class whites. Many free Negroes became landowners and assumed responsible places in their communities. These free Negroes began a pattern, which

5. *The Negro in the United States,* p. 67.
6. Frazier, *The Negro Family in the United States,* p. 139.

continues today, in which social class or economic status is far more closely associated with variations in family life than is race.

EMANCIPATION

The effects of emancipation upon black families were as diverse as the family forms which preceded it. In fact, emancipation seemed mostly to sharpen trends already evident. The families of previously free Negroes and of those who had achieved stability under slavery were not affected greatly. They continued to live much as they had lived, with the father moving into a position of full responsibility for the support of his family and acquiring the authority that goes with it.

Where family ties were less secure, they often broke under the stresses that followed emancipation. Many men who were not formally married to women whose children they had fathered, simply left their homes to test the limits of their newly acquired freedom. They clustered about Union army posts, went to the cities, and roamed aimlessly. Some women, chiefly those without children, did the same thing. Many people struggled to achieve family stability under very difficult societal conditions, sometimes succeeding and sometimes failing. The failure of given marriages seldom produced disillusionment with family living in general, however, and frequent marriages following marital breakups produced something approximating serial monogamy.

The instability of much family life following emancipation further emphasized the mother-child relationship. Men, and women without children, were free to come and go. But the woman with children could not be free of responsibility. She had to pretty much stay in one place, she had to find some means of economic livelihood, and she had to accept men, if at all, on their own terms. To have a man even temporarily was to have some affection and some security.

MIGRATION AND URBANIZATION

Free Negroes, even before the Civil War, were concentrated in urban areas. At the first census in 1790, 10 percent of the populations of New York and Baltimore were black. The majority of blacks, however, lived in the rural South. After the war, a trek toward southern cities, then to northern cities, and finally to the West got under way.

From 1860 to 1870, the black population of 14 southern cities increased by 90 percent and the black population of 8 northern cities increased by 50 percent. After this first postwar surge into urban areas, the migration slowed down somewhat and consisted chiefly of movement into southern cities. By 1910, 70 percent of the urban black population still was in the South.

The large-scale migration of blacks northward got under way during World War I. The southern economy was in serious decline and a major labor shortage developed in northern cities. Labor recruiters toured the south, offering transportation to those who would go, and northern Negro newspapers urged their brethren to escape from southern tyranny. Over one million blacks migrated north during the war.[7] All northern cities except Pittsburgh and Kansas City increased their black populations by over 50 percent. Philadelphia's black population increased by 59 percent; New York's increased by 80 percent; Chicago's by nearly 150 percent; and Detroit's blacks increased by over 600 percent.

The influx of blacks into northern cities changed the pattern of race relations there and created problems that plague whites and blacks today. Before the war, Chicago, for example, was considered a model of black-white relations.[8] Over half the blacks lived on the South Side on amicable terms with their white neighbors.[9] Then thousands of uneducated, unskilled black migrants moved into the area. Homes and apartments were subdivided and then subdivided again. The dilapidated areas where rents were lowest were seized upon first, and then the human tide spilled over into adjacent middle-class areas. A huge and expanding "black belt" was exploited by unscrupulous realtors who frightened whites away with threats of loss of property values, and then increased rents and prices to incoming black people. The resulting tensions culminated in race riots, and a pattern of rigid residential segregation was established.

Migration to the urban North intensified family problems. The extreme overcrowding in residential areas made normal family life difficult. In 1930, over 40 percent of the black families in New York's Harlem had from one to four lodgers living with them. And, in 1939, one single Harlem block had a population of 3871 people, and was reputed

7. E. Franklin Frazier, "Ethnic Family Patterns: The Negro Family in the United States," *American Journal of Sociology* 53 (May 1948), p. 436.

8. St. Clair Drake and Horace Cayton, *Black Metropolis,* New York: Harcourt, Brace, 1945, p. 73.

9. Robert C. Weaver, *The Negro Ghetto,* New York: Harcourt, Brace, 1948, p. 31.

to be the most crowded living area in the world. Much irregularity of black family life, and much social and personal disorganization, traced to inadequate living quarters and the inability to find decent housing.[10]

Studies have also shown that the urbanization of black people has been accompanied by more family disorganization, higher proportions of broken marriages, higher proportions of families with female heads, more quasi-families, and larger numbers of unrelated members in households. While black family life in the rural south was sometimes irregular, it was, at least, governed by a host of personal controls and was accommodated to the environment. Illegitimacy, for example, was not as much of a problem. Illegitimate children and their mothers were accepted with less stigma, often being incorporated into a maternal household. Little money was required to provide the minimum of food and clothing expected, and the group pooled its resources to provide these. With migration north, however, illegitimacy became a major problem. Mothers and children were stigmatized, and the failure of the father to provide produced a crisis. A vast, shifting group of homeless men, women, and children was created, dependent upon public welfare and confused in its attempts to cope with an anonymous, impersonal urban world.

The migration northward continued and, during and after World War II, spread to the West. With few exceptions blacks settled in the central cities while former white residents moved to the suburbs. Between 1940 and 1950, 1,300,000 blacks migrated to the central cities. Between 1940 and 1960, the black populations of Philadelphia and New York doubled, those of Detroit and Chicago tripled, and that of Los Angeles increased by 500 percent. Between 1960 and 1970, black people continued to move north and west at the rate of about 140,000 per year.

CONTEMPORARY FAMILY PATTERNS

There are over 24 million black Americans. It stands to reason that there are no one, two, or even three family patterns among them. Over 70 percent of these people live in urban areas, but "urban areas" include southern as well as northern cities, and cities of 5000 people along with those of five million. More than 6.5 million black people live in nonmetropolitan areas, and a million live on farms. That differences exist

10. Otis D. Duncan and Beverly Duncan, *The Negro Population of Chicago*, Chicago: University of Chicago Press, 1957, p. 84.

from south to north and from rural to urban is certain. Undoubtedly there are still other differences. But there is one dimension which is most relevant of all to the analysis of black family patterns—socio-economic status. Black families vary more according to their position in the occupational structure than according to any other variable.

Variations by Social Class

Black people are not yet fully integrated into the American economy. In 1974, 34 percent of the black population lived in officially defined poverty while only 9 percent of the white population did so.[11] Moreover, the trend during the 1960s for the income levels of black people to rise in relation to those of whites has not been sustained. In 1950, for example, the median income of blacks was 61 percent of that of whites. In 1975, the median family income of blacks was 62 percent of that of whites.

Economic discrimination against black people can be shown in other ways. Although blacks are 11.2 percent of the population, they are less than 7 percent of the members of trade unions. Furthermore, under 2 percent of federal employees earning $16,000 or more are black, only 2 percent of military officers are black, 2 percent of the nation's businesses are owned by blacks, and only 250 of 40,000 state troopers are black. The jobless rate for blacks, as late as 1976, was almost twice that of whites.

If black people as a whole are making few gains toward income equality with whites, some younger, well educated black people are making significant progress. The proportion of nonwhites earning $10,000 or more, to take one illustration, rose from 22 percent in 1966 to 33.7 percent in 1972. Young black families (husband under 35) with both husband and wife working had a median income of $11,800 in 1971, compared with $11,206 for similar white families.[12] If income equality has been reached here, however, it should be remembered that such black families are only 16 percent of all black husband-wife families in the country, and only 10 percent of all black families. The other 90 percent continue to be unequal.[13]

Some of the difficulties in any attempt to adequately characterize con-

11. In 1974, the official poverty level was $5038 for a nonfarm family of four. *Time*, Aug. 11, 1975, p. 6. For other evidence of racism, see Kenneth C. W. Kammeyer, Norman R. Yetman, and McKee J. McClendon, "Family Planning Services and the Distribution of Black Americans," *Social Problems* 21 (June 1974), pp. 674–90.

12. *Ibid.*

13. See Wayne Villemez and Alan R. Rowe, "Black Economic Gains in the Sixties: A Methodological Critique and Reassessment," *Social Forces* 54 (Sept. 1975), pp. 181–93.

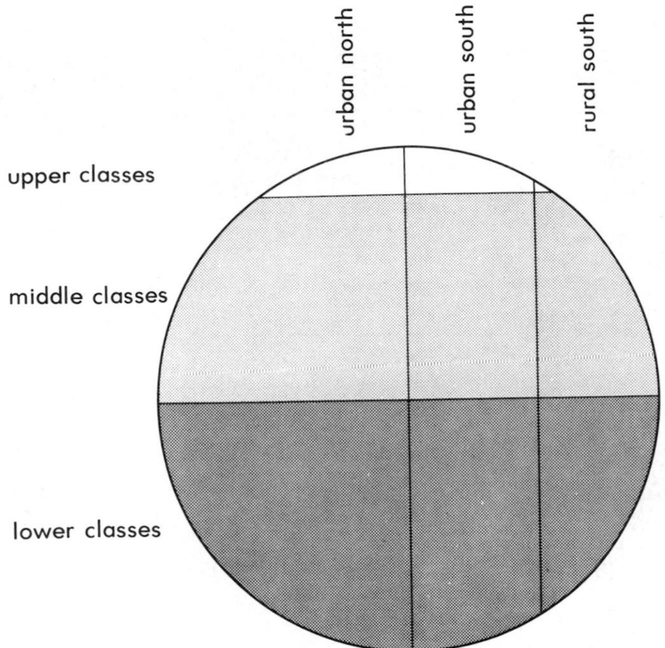

Figure 9.1. The urban and regional distribution of black families in the United States

Source: Andrew Billingsley, *Black Families in White America*, Englewood Cliffs, New Jersey: Prentice-Hall, 1968, p. 7.

temporary black families may be gleaned from Figure 9.1, which is a somewhat impressionistic portrayal of the distribution of black people in the United States by social class and by rural-urban residence. Roughly half of all black people live in the urban north, one-fourth live in the urban south, and one-fourth live in the rural south. Similarly, one-half of all black people are lower class, some 40 percent are middle class, and approximately 10 percent upper class.[14]

14. Furious debate, among both black and white scholars, rages over the most accurate and useful way to classify black people by social class. As indicated in Figure 9.1, Billingsley classifies some 40 percent as middle class. A recent, widely publicized analysis argues that "a slight majority" of black Americans can now be considered as middle class. See Ben J. Wattenberg, and Richard M. Scammon, "Black Progress and Liberal Rhetoric," *Commentary* 55 (April 1973), pp. 35–44. Many black scholars insist, however, that the most appropriate criterion is the income level the government says is needed for an urban family of four to enjoy an intermediate standard of living. By this standard, only about 25 percent of the black population is middle class. See *The Social and Economic Status of the Black Population in the United States, 1972* (Washington, D.C.: U.S. Government Printing Office).

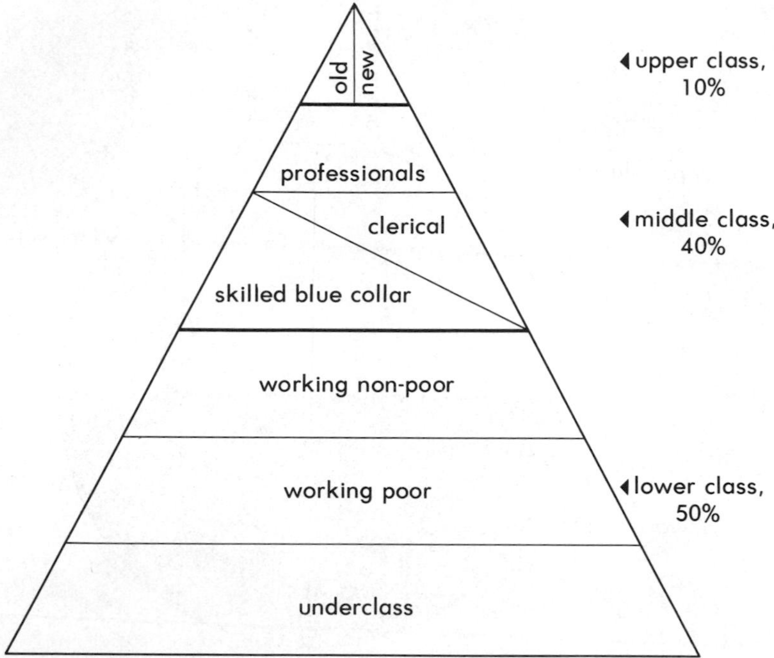

Figure 9.2. The social class distribution of black families

Source: Andrew Billingsley, *Black Families in White America*, Englewood Cliffs, New Jersey: Prentice-Hall, 1968, p. 123.

Andrew Billingsley, who is responsible for this schematic, indicates that it is important to compare black families not only with white families, but also to compare them by social class and to link them to their urban or rural moorings. Of these dimensions, social class is most salient, and the class structure of the black population is complex.[15] Emphasizing that biases in social science have kept it from studying black social structure adequately, and have caused scholars to mis-perceive what they have found, Billingsley classifies black Americans into three broad social classes—upper, middle, and lower—and then subdivides each of these, as shown in Figure 9.2.

The upper class is composed of two fairly distinct groups, according to how long they have enjoyed upper-class status. Adults of the "older" upper class had parents who also were either middle class or upper

15. Andrew Billingsley, *Black Families in White America*, Englewood Cliffs, New Jersey: Prentice-Hall, 1968, p. 8.

class—businessmen, executives, college presidents, judges, physicians, dentists, and so on. In some cases, high status can be traced back to pre-Civil War days when the ancestors were either house slaves or free Negroes. Well-known families in this group would include those of Supreme Court Justice Thurgood Marshall, Senator Edward Brooke, former Secretary of the Department of Housing and Urban Development Robert Weaver, former United Nations official Ralph Bunche, Mayor Maynard Jackson, Congressman Julian Bond, the Reverend Martin Luther King, and many others. There are family histories of college educations, professional occupations, financial success, and family stability.

The "new" upper class is composed of families who have risen from obscurity to great achievement in a single generation. Included would be present or former mayors of six of our major cities: Kenneth Gibson of Newark, Walter Washington of Washington, D.C., Carl Stokes of Cleveland, Coleman Young of Detroit, Richard Hatcher of Gary, Indiana, and Thomas Bradley of Los Angeles. Other examples include the Reverend Ralph Abernathy, Roy Innis, Henry Aaron, and the Reverend Jesse Jackson, to name only a few. All of these families have substantial incomes, can afford comfortable housing, travel, and college educations for their children.

Billingsley divides the black middle class into three sub-groups: professional, clerical, and skilled blue collar. These terms are almost self-explanatory. The professions are those which do not rank as high as those which bring upper-class status—schoolteaching, accounting, social work, nursing—or the heads of the families have still not quite "made it" in the major professions—young attorneys, ministers of small congregations, and so on. The line between upper-class and middle-class professionals is not sharp. The incomes of middle-class clerical workers and of skilled blue-collar workers may be as high, and sometimes higher, than those of the professionals. Skilled blue collar workers may also have job security through union membership. Family life tends to be stable, with equalitarian marital relationships, and achievement aspirations instilled in children from an early age. Compared to their white middle-class counterparts, these families have lower incomes, less job security, and wives are more likely to have to work outside the home.

The lower class again is divided into three subgroups: the working non-poor, the working poor, and the underclass. The highest of the groups, the working non-poor, is composed of the families of men who work at steady jobs in the industrialized sector of the economy—factory workers, truck drivers, and so on. Again, the line between this group and the skilled blue-collar workers of the middle class often is blurred.

The working poor families are headed by men who work hard and steadily at their jobs—janitors, porters, unskilled factory workers, and service workers—but who cannot earn enough money to escape poverty. They lack job security, and are the first to be laid off or fired in times of recession. Billingsley estimates that they compose as much as one-third of all black families. In spite of the problems which they face, most of these families are intact families with father and mother present, and most manage to scrape by without accepting public welfare.

The final lower-class group, the underclass or the nonworking poor, constitutes 15 to 20 percent of black families, the adults in which generally were school dropouts, have few salable skills, and work sporadically, if at all. They live in such poverty that Billingsley maintains that they should be considered as outside and below the formal class structure, rather than as part of it. Dependent largely upon support by relatives and public welfare, this is the group which receives most attention in the press. Here, family disorganization prevails. Most states literally coerce family disorganization by prohibiting welfare payments if there is a man in the home. The specific conditions of life vary from the rural south to the urban south to the urban north, but the consequences probably range from severe malnutrition to outright starvation. Problems of family organization yield to the problem of sheer survival.[16]

Types of Black Families

Black scholars maintain that white social scientists, reflecting the values of the racist society in which they live, have long distorted the nature of black family patterns. In addition to the social class variation described in the preceding section, black family patterns may be classified into three basic types: nuclear, extended, and augmented. These types, in turn, are divisible into subtypes, as shown in Table 9.1.

Nuclear Families. The nuclear family is the familiar unit of husband, wife, and children. Billingsley's division of nuclear families into incipient, simple, and attenuated subtypes acknowledges that there is a prechildbearing period during which the married couple constitute an *incipient* nuclear family. It also acknowledges that separation, divorce, military service, distant employment, imprisonment, hospitalization,

16. *Ibid.*, pp. 137–42. For a devastating analysis of how the public welfare system has failed black children, see Andrew Billingsley and Jeanne M. Giovannoni, *Children of the Storm: Black Children and American Child Welfare*, New York: Harcourt Brace Jovanovich, 1972.

Table 9.1. The structure of black families

Types of Family	*Household Head*		*Other Household Members*		
	Husband and Wife	Single Parent	Children	Other Relatives	Non-relatives
Nuclear Families					
I: Incipient nuclear family	X				
II: Simple nuclear family	X		X		
III: Attenuated nuclear family		X	X		
Extended Families					
IV: Incipient extended family	X			X	
V: Simple extended family	X		X	X	
VI: Attenuated extended family		X	X	X	
Augmented Families					
VII: Incipient augmented family	X				X
VIII: Incipient extended augmented family	X			X	X
IX: Nuclear augmented family	X		X		X
X: Nuclear extended augmented family	X		X	X	X
XI: Attenuated augmented family		X	X		X
XII: Attenuated extended augmented family		X	X	X	X

Source: Andrew Billingsley, *Black Families in White America*, Englewood Cliffs, New Jersey: Prentice-Hall, 1968, p. 17.

death, and other conditions occasionally remove one parent from the home, leaving the other parent and the children as an *attenuated* nuclear family.

The importance of this classification derives from the unconscious assumption that the majority of white families are simple nuclear families and the frequently quoted statistics concerning the large proportion of broken black families. The assumption about white families is wrong, and the alleged facts about black families are misleading. *Simple* nuclear families, with both parents and children living in the home, are a minority among both races and, if there are any differences in the proportions of blacks and whites with such arrangements, they are relatively small. Billingsley indicates that about 36 percent of all black families, more than 1.5 million families, are of the simple nuclear type.[17] Another 20

17. *Black Families in White America, op cit.*, p. 18. This section continues to draw heavily upon Billingsley's work.

percent of black families, about one million families, are incipient nuclear families; either married couples who have not yet produced children, or older couples whose children are grown and gone.

Attenuated families, commonly referred to as broken or one-parent families, contrary to the prevailing stereotype, constitute only 6 percent of black families. Over 90 percent of these families are headed by women, providing much of the factual support for the widespread conception of a contemporary matricentric black family. It should not be overlooked, however, that nationwide values and judicial practice both support children remaining with their mothers in separation or divorce, and regardless of whether the families are black or white. The tendency of welfare regulations to force the fathers of poor families out of the home was also discussed in our analysis of social class variations.

Almost two-thirds of all black families, in summary, are nuclear families of one of these three subtypes. Roughly one-fourth of all black families are extended families, and around 10 percent are augmented families.

Extended Families. In earlier chapters, we have used the term *extended family* in the conventional way to refer to residential units of three or more generations. The usage here to analyze black family structure is somewhat looser and includes all families where other relatives live with a nuclear family. An *incipient extended* family is one in which a husband and wife without children at home have other relatives living with them. The *simple extended* family includes other relatives along with the parents and children. *Attenuated extended* families consist of one parent with his or her children, plus other relatives in the home.

The "other relatives" who live with nuclear families fall into four categories. First, they may be minors, such as grandchildren, nieces, nephews, and cousins. Second, they may be peers of the parents in the home: siblings, cousins, or other adult relatives. Third, they may be grandparents. Fourth, they may be other elderly relatives, such as aunts and uncles. There may, of course, be various combinations of these living with given families.

Billingsley estimates that about 15 percent of black families have minor relatives living with them, and over 25 percent have adult relatives in the home. A majority of female-headed attenuated families care for other relatives. Many families, of course, have both adult relatives and children living with them. In an independent analysis, Robert Hill found that four times as many black incipient nuclear families as of white incipient nuclear families, proportionately, have minor relatives living with them. Among female-headed attenuated nuclear families, the disparity is even greater: 41 percent of the black families, compared to only 7 percent of the white families care for minor relatives.[18]

Augmented Families. The concept of augmented families was developed to include families who take non-relatives—roomers, boarders, lodgers—into the home on a long-term basis. Such non-relatives may be taken in, either by nuclear families or extended families. Consequently, there are six types of augmented families, as shown in Table 9.1. The number of augmented families is unknown, but Billingsley reports almost one-half million black people living with family groups to whom they are not related. Two-thirds of these are men, and one-third are women. Most are adults, and a considerable number are older people.

Thus, the structure of American black families obviously is much more complicated than generally is known.[19] The basic family type is that of the nuclear unit. There are many incipient nuclear families who represent early and late stages in the family life cycle. Many families have relatives or non-relatives or both, living with them. Attenuated, or broken, families are not so common as believed. These facts call into question the old assumptions that black families are "disorganized," "deteriorating," or caught up in a "tangle of pathology."[20]

THE STRENGTHS OF BLACK FAMILIES

The phrase "the strengths of black families" was originated by the Research Director of the National Urban League to title a research report in 1971. In that report, he presented data showing that five characteristics of black families have been functional for their stability and survival in a hostile social environment: strong kinship bonds, strong work orientation, adaptable roles, strong achievement orientation, and strong religious orientation.[21]

18. Robert B. Hill, *The Strengths of Black Families*, New York: Emerson Hall, 1971, p. 5. For additional supporting evidence, see William C. Hays and Charles H. Mindel, "Extended Kinship Relations in Black and White Families," *Journal of Marriage and the Family* 35 (Feb. 1973), pp. 51–57.
19. For evidence that black families are even more complex, see J. Allen Williams, and Robert Stockton, "Black Family Structures and Functions: An Empirical Examination of Some Suggestions Made by Billingsley," *Journal of Marriage and the Family* 35 (Feb. 1973), pp. 39–49.
20. Daniel P. Moynihan, *The Negro Family: The Case for National Action*, Washington, D.C.: U.S. Government Printing Office, 1965.
21. *Op. cit.*

Strong Kinship Bonds

Contrary to the popular stereotype of black families as broken families, over two-thirds of all black families have both parents present. Moreover, the proportion of intact nuclear families increases with income, rising to over 80 percent among those whose annual incomes exceed $8000. Most black families are stable families.[22]

The well-known greater frequency of female-headed families among blacks than among whites is real and is not only being perpetuated, but actually is increasing as more whites escape poverty and as poverty is increasingly associated with blackness. In 1950, for example, some 17 percent of black families were headed by women. In 1960, the figure had climbed to 22 percent, and in 1970 to 27 percent. The figure for whites has hovered around 9 percent over the twenty-year period.

In 1960, when roughly one-fifth of the American population was officially defined as living in poverty, about 60 percent of the nonwhite population was so designated. By 1970, 34 percent of all black families remained in poverty, while the proportion for the country as a whole had dropped to about 12 percent. Since 1970, the situation has worsened. In 1972, 1.6 million more whites climbed above the poverty level, while an additional 300,000 blacks slipped below it. One-third of all blacks remain in poverty, while the proportion among whites is down to 9 percent.[23]

Even among poor black families, however, families headed by women are a minority, and these black families have proved amazingly cohesive, with a remarkable capacity for caring for children. Six times as many black women as white women without husbands present are caring for relatives under 18 years of age. In part, this is due to the fact that black people have been denied access to public adoption agencies and, while white families have placed children for adoption, black families have had to care for their own. Moreover, the burden upon black families has been proportionately greater because of their lower incomes.

Strong Work Orientation

Although white society has long rationalized discrimination against black people by saying that blacks either are too lazy to work or are emotion-

22. Hylan G. Lewis, Elizabeth Herzog, *et al.*, *Agenda Paper No. V: The Family: Resources for Change–Planning Session for the White House Conference.* "To Fulfill These Rights," Nov. 16–18, 1965.
23. *Time*, Sept. 3, 1973, pp. 74–75.

ally alienated from work, systematic data show a strong work orientation among blacks. Hill points out, for example, that poor black people are more likely than poor whites to be employed. In 1969, 59 percent of the heads of poor black families were gainfully employed, while only 53 percent of the heads of poor white families were employed.[24]

This strong commitment to work also is apparent at both ends of the economic scale, and in both intact and attenuated families. Among relatively prosperous young black families whose incomes exceed $10,000, wives are more likely to be employed than in comparable white families. Moreover, almost two-thirds of the women who head black families also work outside the home. Most of them work full time.

The most crucial data on work orientation come from federal studies of the effects of a guaranteed minimum income on work behavior. Not all of these people were black, of course, but many were. Seven hundred twenty-five families in five cities in Pennsylvania and New Jersey and 450 families in rural Iowa and North Carolina were given income supplements. Each family faced a "break even point" at which subsidies were reduced so that it could retain no more income by working than by relying on the income supplement alone. Few recipients withdrew from the labor market, but some quit their unskilled jobs to train for better jobs. In addition, preliminary analyses of the data indicate that black people who received the income supplements earned more money while working than did a control group of black people who did not receive the extra income.[25]

Adaptable Roles

Several studies show that husband-wife relationships in most black families are equalitarian. A comparison of black and white marriages in Detroit indicated that the black husbands had slightly more power than the white husbands, but that both fell within the equalitarian range.[26] Three separate studies of national samples of the population showed both black and white husbands to have slightly more influence than their wives in family decision making, but also implied that most decisions are

24. *Op. cit.*, p. 9.

25. Irene Lurie, *ed., Integrating Income Maintenance Programs,* New York: Academic Press, 1976. See also Robert Staples, "Public Policy and the Changing Status of Black Families," *The Family Coordinator* 22 (July 1973), pp. 345–51.

26. Robert O. Blood, Jr., and Donald M. Wolfe, *Husbands and Wives: The Dynamics of Married Living,* Glencoe, Illinois: The Free Press, 1960, p. 35.

made by the partners jointly.[27] Black husbands also share significantly in the performance of household tasks. In both low-income and middle-income families, the picture which emerges is one of active, involved husbands and strong, but not dominant women.

The situation concerning female-headed families was analyzed earlier, and there is no need to repeat it here. Contrary to the impression that these families are caught up in a tangle of pathology, many of them show impressive stability under difficult circumstances. Moreover, although it is widely assumed that being reared in one-parent homes has a negative impact upon children, it has not been demonstrated by research.[28] The *quality* of relationships with the parent or parents present appears to be more influential than *how many* parents are present.

Strong Achievement Orientation

Social science has shown that middle-class youth have higher educational aspirations than lower-class youth. It is also well known that most black youth have been lower class. From these facts, many writers have jumped to the unwarranted conclusion that black youth are not highly motivated to succeed educationally. The data show, instead, that most lower-class youth have college aspirations. Moreover, since there are so many lower-class black youth, the number of such youths attending college may be greater than the number of middle-class black youth attending college. Finally, research indicates that parental influence to complete college may be greater among lower-class blacks than among lower-class whites. In one study, 80 percent of the black parents exerted such influence, while only 64 percent of the white parents did so.[29]

Strong Religious Orientation

The church probably has been the most conspicuous organization in most black communities. Not only has it been a source of solace for a downtrodden people, and a steady source of moral standards in an almost anarchic social environment, but it also has served as a vehicle for rebellion and social advancement. During slavery, rebellions often were organized with the aid of ministers, and churches aided runaway slaves

27. Reported in Robert B. Hill, *op. cit.*, pp. 18–19.
28. Elizabeth Herzog and Cecelia E. Sudia, *Boys in Fatherless Families,* Washington, D.C.: Office of Child Development, 1970.
29. Reported in Robert B. Hill, *op. cit.*, p. 31.

on their journeys north. More recently, churches and ministers were deeply involved in the development of the civil rights movement of the 1960s. Names such as those of Dr. Martin Luther King, Jr., the Reverend Ralph Abernathy, and the Reverend Jesse Jackson will go down in history. The role of the church in promoting family solidarity among black people is obvious enough, but most of the history of the relationship between the two remains to be written.

SUMMARY

Although the first black people came to America as indentured servants, slavery soon appeared. Under slavery, all traces of African culture were deliberately expunged and a variable family system, reflecting the division of labor among blacks and the policies of the white owners, emerged. Field hands frequently were discouraged from developing stable families. Whether or not there was a deliberate policy of breeding slaves, the primacy of the mother-child unit was emphasized in the assignment of living quarters and the distribution of food supplies. Men were sold or traded without their families; there was little opportunity for the development of masculine responsibility. The family patterns of house slaves often were modeled upon those of the owners. Stability and morality were emphasized; the father played a more prominent role. A father-centered family also appeared among a growing class of free black people, in which miscegenation figured prominently.

Emancipation seemed generally to heighten trends already present in black families. Stable, father-centered families remained stable, and the husband acquired increased responsibility. Families who were disorganized before, disintegrated further. The disorganized mother-centered family became recognizable in both urban and rural areas.

After the Civil War, a large-scale migration of black people, first to the cities, and then northward, began. The northward movement received impetus during World War I and resulted in strict residential segregation, overcrowding in black areas, and the intensification of family problems. Informal norms of casual sex contact and illegitimate births created havoc in the urban situation where black people were deprived of their old primary group supports. The present status of black family patterns reflects the fact that black people are not yet fully incorporated into the occupational system. What differences exist appear to be more closely linked to socioeconomic status than to race.

One classificatory system divides black families into upper, middle, and lower classes, but attaches special meanings to those labels and further subdivides the three classes. The upper class is divided into "old" and new families, depending upon when eminence was achieved. Some "old" upper-class families have histories of achievement and stability that extend back before the Civil War. Others have become prominent more recently, but all have had upper-class status for at least two generations. The "new" upper-class by contrast, has acquired wealth and status within the past generation.

The middle-class is composed of three subclasses: the professional, clerical, and skilled blue collar. These terms are fairly self-explanatory. The middle-class professions are those that do not have enough prestige to warrant upper-class status: school teachers, accountants, nurses, and social workers for example. Some are young attorneys, ministers, and the like, who may eventually acquire upper-class status. Middle-class clerical workers cover the whole range from file clerks and typists to supervisors and office managers. The skilled blue-collar workers may not have as much prestige as some of the clerical workers, but their incomes often are higher.

The line between upper-class and middle-class black families often is not a sharp one. The incomes of middle-class clerical workers and those of blue-collar workers may be as high, and sometimes higher than those of the professionals. The skilled blue-collar workers may also have job security through union membership. Family life tends to be stable, with equalitarian marital relationships, and high aspiration levels instilled in children.

The black lower class again is divided into three subclasses: the working non-poor, the working poor, and the underclass. The working non-poor overlap significantly with the middle-class. Typical occupations include those of truck driver, equipment operator, and factory worker, stable occupations in the industrialized sector of the economy. The working poor are fairly steadily employed, at jobs such as service workers, porters, and janitors, that yield incomes too low to permit their holders ever to rise out of poverty. The underclass, which constitutes only about 15 to 20 percent of the black population is the one around which most popular stereotypes of black families are built.

Black families may be divided into nuclear, extended, and augmented types, and these may be further subdivided. Such a classification shows that most black families are intact nuclear families, and differ little from most white families. Extended black families offer testimony to the adaptability of black families under conditions of adversity. Augmented families show a similar capacity of black people to care for non-relatives in a family situation.

Social scientists have focused far too much upon the problems faced by black families, and have paid too little attention to evidences of strength and resiliency in the system. The strength of kinship bonds is shown in the large proportion of intact nuclear families, and in the apparent stability of low-income, mother-headed families. A strong work orientation among black people is reflected in the high percentage of gainfully employed men, in the high proportion of working wives, and in the results of income maintenance experiments. Role flexibility is shown in the preponderance of equalitarian marital relationships, and in significant participation of husbands and fathers in household duties. The attitudes of both parents and youth, and aspirations for college educations, demonstrate a strong achievement orientation. Finally, a strong religious orientation has a long history, and is related to the church's continuing involvement in the struggle for equality.

SUGGESTED READINGS

Bracey, John H., Jr., Meier, August, and Rudwick, Elliott, *Black Matriarchy: Myth or Reality?*, Belmont, California: Wadsworth Publishing Co., 1971. A symposium beginning with the analyses of E. Franklin Frazier and carrying through that of Daniel P. Moynihan to current questioning of long-held stereotypes.

Heiss, Jerold, *The Case of the Black Family: A Sociological Inquiry*, New York: Columbia University Press, 1975. Report of a major research project into the structure of black families in major metropolitan areas.

Pinkney, Alphonso, *Black Americans*, Englewood Cliffs, New Jersey: Prentice-Hall, 1969. Monograph on history and contemporary status of black Americans. One chapter on family patterns.

Scanzoni, John H., *The Black Family in Modern Society*, Boston: Allyn and Bacon, 1971. A systematic and perceptive monograph based upon information gathered from 400 black households in Indianapolis.

Staples, Robert, *ed.*, *The Black Family: Essays and Studies*, Belmont, California: Wadsworth Publishing Co., 1971. A comprehensive set of readings on many aspects of the family life of black people.

Willie, Charles V., *ed.*, *The Family Life of Black People*, Columbus, Ohio: Charles E. Merrill Publishing Co., 1970. Valuable essays and research reports that put black family patterns in demographic and sociological perspective.

FILMS

The Black Woman (Audio-Visual Center, Indiana University, Bloomington, Ind. 47401), 52 minutes, black and white. Black women discuss the role of black women in modern society and the problems they confront. Includes the relationships of black women with black men and black women in the liberation movement.

Diary of a Harlem Family (Indiana University, Audio-Visual Center, Bloomington, Ind. 47401), 20 minutes. Poignant view of the plight of a Harlem family, through the photographs of Gordon Parks. Shows the impotence of poverty agencies and others to help.

"*Hey Mama*" (Vaughn Obern, 501 Bay Street, Apt. B, Santa Monica, Calif. 90405), 18 minutes. The offspring of one black woman in a stark documentary of lives in a black ghetto that might be anywhere.

Lay My Burden Down (Indiana University, Audio-Visual Center, Bloomington, Ind. 47401), 60 minutes. The plight of black tenant farmers and their families in the South. Their only hope is the recently obtained right to vote.

QUESTIONS AND PROJECTS

1. What is the difference between indentured servitude and slavery? How did indentured servitude influence the development of black family patterns in the United States?
2. Describe black family patterns under slavery. Describe the differences between the patterns of house-servants and field hands.
3. How did emancipation influence black family patterns? How did it increase the prominence of the matricentric family?
4. Describe the urban and northern migration of black people after the Civil War. What was the impact upon family life?
5. What evidence is there that black people are not yet fully integrated into the economy? What gains, if any, have been achieved over the past two decades?
6. How are social class and rural-urban residence important in the analysis of black family patterns? Which of these two factors do you believe to be more important? Why?
7. What is the difference between the "old" and the "new" upper class? Why is it difficult to describe the patterns of the new upper class?

8. What variations exist within the middle class? Within the lower class? Comment upon the effects of widespread emphasis upon the family patterns of the underclass.
9. Define the following concepts as they apply to black families: nuclear families; extended families; augmented families. What subtypes exist within each classification?
10. What is the most common family type among black people? What authority relationship (patriarchal-equalitarian-matriarchal) is most common? What kind of division of labor exists within the home?
11. What evidence is there on the work orientation and the achievement orientation of black people?
12. What do you understand by the phrase "the strengths of black families"? Take several "facts" about black family life and show how they can be interpreted either as indications of strength or weakness in black families.

10
Ethnic Families

When a Mexican immigrant . . . opened the H&H Meat Products Company, Inc., in 1947, the firm had a payroll of three. Now . . . the business is the largest in Mercedes, Texas, grossing 14 million dollars a year and employing 137 persons. . . .

The firm's success reflects the end product of a nationwide drive by an estimated 20 million Spanish-speaking Americans for more political and economic power, reminiscent of recent efforts by the nation's 24 million blacks. . . . Spanish-speaking Americans–mainly of Mexican, Puerto Rican and Cuban origins–expect immigration and their high birth rates to propel them into first place as the nation's largest minority by 1985. . . .

Recently, . . . Latinos have pushed more ardently into the political arena. Their numbers now include five U.S. Representatives in Congress. . . . Both New Mexico and Arizona have Mexican American governors. . . . Senator Antonio Gabaldon . . . says the drive for more political representation is largely the result of better education.

Although Latinos still rank below Anglos and blacks in average years of schooling, they have gained considerably in recent years. . . .

The lawmaker typifies the changes that have swept the Southwest. Born . . . the youngest of 12 children, Gabaldon did not speak English until he started school. He went to work at the age of 12, but managed to finish both high school and college. Later, he became an elementary school principal . . . before being elected to the Senate. . . .[1]

This vignette, and the possibly apocryphal story of President Franklin D. Roosevelt welcoming a convention of the Daughters of the American Revolution during the 1930s with the statement, "Welcome, fellow immigrants!" should remind us, again, that contemporary American

1. *U.S. News and World Report,* Dec. 13, 1976, p. 56.

family patterns have developed at the confluence of a number of cultural streams. The dominant Western European influences were detailed in Chapter 6, and black American family patterns were described in the chapter which precedes this one. We now pursue, further, the idea of variability in American family patterns.

It will be recalled that, beginning about 1890, migration to the United States shifted substantially from northwestern Europe to southern and eastern Europe. Between 1890 and 1920, 22 million people came, mostly from Italy, Austria-Hungary, and Russia. Restrictive immigration policies after 1920 greatly reduced the number of migrants, caused the proportion of foreign-born in the population to decline and encouraged assimilation toward a common American family pattern.

The Immigration Act of 1965 changed the situation drastically again. Under the new law, about 400,000 immigrants have been coming to the United States annually. In 1974, the largest single group, over 70,000, came from Mexico, with over 30,000 coming from the Philippines. Over 15,000 came from Italy, more than 24,000 came from the West Indies, 10,000 came from Greece, and almost 18,000 came from Cuba.[2] Immigration, recently, has been accounting for almost 20 percent of the growth in the population.

The 1960s also saw a new emphasis upon various ethnic groups seeking to preserve their cultural heritages. Whereas, formerly, there had been attempts to rid themselves of traits which set them apart from "native Americans," many groups now endorsed a "cultural pluralism" which emphasized the contributions that their ways of life had made, and could continue to make, to a fuller and richer American culture. Our portrayal of contemporary American family patterns would not be complete without description of these family systems. We cannot describe them all, but we will take a few representative ones. In this chapter, we will analyze Italian American families, Mexican American families, Japanese American families, Cuban American families, and, because of its unique character, an elite family system found among the descendants of some of our very earliest migrants.

ITALIAN AMERICAN FAMILIES

Italians have been selected to represent migrants from southern and eastern Europe around the turn of the century because they were the

2. U.S. Bureau of the Census, *Statistical Abstract of the United States, 1975* (Washington, D.C.), p. 101.

largest of these groups.[3] Their assimilation also was complicated by language differences, Roman Catholic religious affiliation, a low level of occupational skills, and stereotyping by the host population as dirty, ignorant, and generally undesirable.

Most of the migrants were from southern Italy and Sicily, where they lived in small villages and farmed for a living. Life was organized around the family and village, there being suspiciousness and hostility toward outsiders. When they migrated to the United States, they located in northern cities, and clustered in neighborhoods composed primarily of people from their own and neighboring villages. In many cities, these ethnic settlements came to be known as "Little Italy."

Italians in the United States received a less than enthusiastic reception. Set apart by differences in language, religion, and dress—and usually of low economic status—the immigrants were shunned by most residents of the cities into which they moved. They reacted by clustering even more tightly together in residential enclaves. They sought out their own kind and sought to preserve the old ways. They spoke Italian, read Italian newspapers, patronized Italian stores and businesses, preserved traditional foods and styles of clothing, and developed social organizations to provide recreation and reinforce ethnic solidarity.

The family system they brought was more patriarchal than that of the "old Americans." It revolved around the father, who ruled with something ranging from benevolent despotism to outright tyranny. He was the chief provider, but he also controlled incomes earned by other family members. He dominated his wife and controlled his children. When it came time for the children to marry, he helped to select their marriage partners. And, as in the old country, the norms were clearly spelled out. If the system was oppressive, people knew just where they stood.[4]

3. Michael Lalli, "The Italian-American Family: Assimilation and Change, 1900–1965," *The Family Coordinator* 18 (Jan. 1969), pp. 44–48.

4. This section draws upon a number of sources. See Paul J. Campisi, "Ethnic Family Patterns: The Italian Family in the United States," *American Journal of Sociology* 53 (1948), pp. 443–49; Francis X. Femminella, "The Italian-American Family," in Meyer Barash and Alice Scourby, *eds., Marriage and the Family: A Comparative Analysis of Contemporary Problems,* New York: Random House, 1970, pp. 127–39; Herbert J. Gans, *The Urban Villagers: Group and Class in the Life of Italian-Americans,* New York: The Free Press, 1962; Francis A. J. Ianni, "The Italo-American Teen-Ager," *The Annals of the American Academy of Political and Social Science* 338 (Nov. 1961), pp. 70–78; Bartolomeo J. Palisi, "Ethnic Generation and Family Structure," *Journal of Marriage and the Family* 28 (Feb. 1966), pp. 49–50; and Bartolomeo J. Palisi, "Patterns of Social Participation in a Two-Generation Sample of Italian-Americans," *The Sociological Quarterly* (Spring 1966), pp. 167–78.

Assimilation

In America, assimilation tended to proceed by generations. The term *first generation* describes the immigrants themselves—the young husband and wife who spoke a foreign tongue and who were isolated from the mainstream of American culture. It was they who located in an ethnic enclave and began to raise a family.

As a general rule, assimilation proceeded slowly. The father had to accommodate to the society to some degree in order to get and hold a job. His foreign tongue was a handicap, so he began to learn English. In the ethnic settlement at the end of the day, however, he reverted to the old language and the old ways. His wife might not even make this much concession. Bewildered by the strange ways and repelled by indifference or hostility from outsiders, she was likely to seek security in the time-honored ways. Often, she avoided learning English and confined her activities to the ethnic group. As her husband's halting efforts toward assimilation created a gulf between them, she often responded by clinging more desperately to ethnic customs. Primarily, it was she who dressed her children in the traditional way and who taught them to speak the old language.

If the first generation was resistant to change, their children could not often resist it. Even before school, the children were likely to have contacts outside the ethnic group and to learn from their more Americanized peers how funny their clothes were, how shameful it was to speak a foreign language, and how bad it was to be different.

Perhaps the primary agent of assimilation was the school. School teachers were likely to be middle class and often were, themselves, attempting to reject their ethnic origins. The official language was English, and the school taught that to be successful, as everyone should, one must adopt middle-class ways. The schools also taught values of democracy, equalitarianism, and individualism that conflicted with the values of the parents and subverted the old form of family organization.

Children responded by refusing to speak anything but English, by protesting against being different from their peers in any way, and by adopting the attitudes of the larger society toward their parents and their ways. The parents' ways were "old-fashioned" and a barrier to the young person's need to belong.

A crisis often developed in adolescence. Resistance to parental ways approached open defiance. Whereas the parents' lower-class lives were conforming and stable, their children turned to the streets to show their contempt for the adult world. With the street gang as their primary reference group, they frequently sought status in gang warfare, delinquency, and sexual experience. To the adult world, the situation appeared to be one of complete unregulation; but among the youth the governing normative structure was quite clear. William F. Whyte shows this clearly in an analysis of a slum sex code which sanctioned sexual intercourse with sexually experienced girls but which strictly forbade it with virgins.[5]

Conflict developed between parents and their adult children over income and the selection of marriage partners. By parental standards, the income earned by the young people should be turned over to the father, who would dole out an allowance. Some young people accepted such an arrangement only eventually to rebel against it; some rebelled from the first. Parents' hopes that their children would marry within the group often were frustrated as their children found Americanized young people to be more attractive than those who clung to the ethnic traditions.

For all the complications in their lives, many of those young people fared well as they moved into marriage and the occupational world. The school had performed its acculturation function well; except for the family name (and often it was changed—Capobianco became Whitehead, and Campagnia became Bell, for example), few traces of ethnic status remained. While the parents generally worked at unskilled jobs, their offspring frequently were equipped to come into the white-collar and skilled labor worlds. Their rejection of ethnic ways led them to locate their families of procreation in non-ethnic middle-class areas. When they had children, the children were likely to be reared to seek full participation in the mass consumption middle-class world.

Distinctive Italian American Patterns

By the middle of the twentieth century, the assimilation of many of the Italians in the United States was virtually complete. Many of the people living the organization way of life described in chapter 8 are third generation immigrants. Several qualifications must be added, however.

First, the identity as Roman Catholics still separates many Italo-Americans from much of the non-Catholic population. Some of the implications of this will be analyzed in the chapter on mate selection. Here, we should note that the Roman Catholic value system continues to strengthen the authority of the father, and the fact that children

5. William Foote Whyte, "A Slum Sex Code," *American Journal of Sociology* 49 (July 1943), pp. 24–31.

frequently are unplanned alters the relationship of parents to them. There is less emphasis upon meeting the emotional needs of children and "developing" them into rounded adults. Care for the children and their education both are provided within a context of firm parental discipline.

Among many second generation and some third generation families, there also are differences in husband-wife relationships from those of other Americans. Tracing back to the strong patriarchy in Italy and the necessity for wives to control husbands unobtrusively, if at all, role relationships between second generation immigrant husbands and wives tend to be "segregated," with a clear division of labor defining women's work and men's work, and with a minimum of joint decision making and sharing of activities and interests. There is less communication, less conversation, and less emphasis upon gratification of the spouse's emotional needs than in the dominant middle-class family pattern.[6]

Still a third way in which Italian American family patterns remain distinctive derives from pressures to adapt to the Italian community and yet to become full-fledged members of the American community. The conflict thus generated has been heightened as the concept of ethnic pride has spread among Italian Americans and other ethnic groups. Tomasi has described three patterns of reaction to this conflict.

The Rebel Reaction. Rebels seek to solve the nationality problem by rejecting their Italian heritage and becoming fully assimilated. They seek as spouses either people who are not Italian or who, like themselves, are seeking to escape ethnic identification. They rebel against turning over their pay to the father and, after marriage, they limit their contacts with their parents, brothers, and sisters. Further, they advocate equalitarian husband-wife relationships, and democratic relationships between parents and children. Because of the psychological costs to the individuals involved, Tomasi believes this pattern to be uncommon.

The Ingroup Reaction. Those who choose this pattern seek to confirm their identities as Italians while gradually structuring their families in accord with prevailing American norms. They date Italians and non-Italians, but generally marry within the group. Having continued to accept parental authority themselves, they insist upon it with their own children. The acceptance as Americans which they seek is not simply personal acceptance for themselves, but is acceptance for Italians as a group. This appears to be the most common adjustment pattern, and reinforces ethnic solidarity.

The Apathetic Reaction. In this form of adjustment, people seek to

6. Lydio F. Tomasi, *The Italian American Family,* New York: Center for Migration Studies, 1972, p. 32.

escape conflict over assimilation by de-emotionalizing the whole issue, and denying its importance. They show no preferences in the opposite sex either for Italians or non-Italians, perhaps marrying other Italians only because the similarity of background makes them more comfortable. There is considerable intermarriage, and the families of these apathetic persons remain marginal to the cultural worlds of both Italians and other Americans. Tomasi believes this adjustment pattern to be quite rare. The events of the last decade probably have made it even more uncommon than before.

Only time will tell whether the tendency toward complete assimilation has been halted permanently, and whether a distinct family type is emerging. Ethnic bonds are stronger today than they were a few years ago. Still, there is prejudice against those who are different, and the temptation to escape discrimination by conforming is strong.

MEXICAN AMERICAN FAMILIES

The Original Spanish Settlers

The first Mexican Americans became part of the United States through annexation, rather than through immigration; the Mexicans were here when what is now Texas, New Mexico, Arizona, and California were incorporated into the Union. The land they occupied was huge, and the original settlers were scattered, numbering not more than 75,000 in 1860. Quite distinct social patterns existed, however, among them.[7]

Cattle ranching dominated the economy in Texas throughout the nineteenth century, and, as land ownership rather than cattle became the determining factor, the Mexicans became a depressed class, working the land and running cattle for the Anglos. An exception existed along the Rio Grande where middle-class Mexican communities prospered in towns like Brownsville and Laredo. During the last decades of the century, cotton farming invaded the area, creating demand for cheap labor, and new Mexican immigrants joined the old Mexican settlers to fill the need. The suppression of Mexicans became complete, and supporting stereotypes of Mexicans as ignorant, shiftless people solidified.

The situation in New Mexico was very different. There, where there were some 60,000 Mexican settlers by 1850, there were relatively few Anglos, and Spanish-speaking ranchers both dominated the economy

7. This discussion follows closely the treatment in Joan W. Moore with Harry Pachon, *Mexican Americans*, Englewood Cliffs, New Jersey: Prentice-Hall, 1976.

and controlled the legislature. Intermarriage between Mexican and Anglo families occurred frequently, and the two groups lived in relative harmony. Gradually, depletion of the lands through over-grazing, the invasion of the railroads, and the diversion of lands into mining shifted the balance of power toward the Anglos, and much of the Mexican minority concentrated in towns where they worked as laborers.

The few Spanish-speaking residents of what is now Arizona lived mostly in Tucson during the middle of the nineteenth century, where they clustered for protection against the Apache Indians. Soon, the railroads brought an Anglo invasion, and the land was opened for mining. The Anglos gained control, operated the mines, and encouraged the immigration of Mexicans to work them. Discrimination against the Mexican workers was more drastic than in either Texas or New Mexico. Company stores often offered the only shopping, and physical brutality was the likely reward of workers who challenged the system.

Geographical isolation was instrumental in structuring the situation in California, where wealthy and powerful Mexican *rancheros* dominated the southern and central part of the state. The discovery of gold, in the central region, changed the situation drastically, bringing in hordes of Anglo miners and massive migrations of Mexicans. The elite and genteel culture of the native Castilians clashed with the crude and aggressive ways of the miners. The Anglo miners fought the Mexicans, and made no distinctions, in their hatred, between lower-class Mexican miners and wealthy and cultured landowners. As mining withered, agriculture developed, and Anglos simply settled on and appropriated large portions of the old Mexican land grants. The wresting of the land from the Mexicans followed at a slower pace in southern California. But it proceeded inexorably. Los Angeles, settled by a mixture of lower-class Mexicans, Indians, Chinese, and Anglos became a center of racial and ethnic violence.

By the dawn of the twentieth century, only in New Mexico did Spanish-speaking people retain some economic and political power. Elsewhere, the dominant Anglo majority stereotyped all people of Spanish descent as "Mexicans" and forced most of them into manual labor, poverty, and subjection.[8]

Immigration

No reliable figures on the extent of Mexican migration to the United States are available for earlier than 1910, and even after that one must

8. *Ibid.*, pp. 11–20.

distinguish between legal and illegal migrants. Statistics are available to assess legal immigration only. In 1910, nearly 18,000 legal immigrants came, with the figure dropping to a low of 11,000 and rising to 29,000 over the next decade. During the 1920s, the pattern was erratic but higher, averaging almost 50,000 per year. Mexican immigration dropped off to almost nothing during the depression years of the 1930s, remained low during World War II, and then began to climb again during the 1950s. During the 1960s, the rate fluctuated above and below 40,000, the 1970 figure being almost 45,000.

Although accurate estimates are not possible, some authorities believe that, in some years at least, three times as many Mexicans have entered the United States illegally as legally. From early in the twentieth century, agricultural and mining enterprises in the border states required large amounts of cheap labor, and by World War I Mexicans provided about the only supply. Special immigration regulations admitting "temporary" workers were instituted in 1917, with the result that most of the so-called temporary residents admitted remained permanently in the United States.

Migrants, both legal and illegal, came into the country fairly easily during the 1920s, but, with the onset of the depression, the Immigration Service sought the deportation of illegal aliens on a large scale. The Mexican and United States governments cooperated in schemes to expel persons of Mexican descent and were not careful to exclude persons who were United States citizens. The combination of deportation and lessened immigration during the 1930s lowered the number of Mexicans in the United States from 639,000 in 1930 to 377,000 in 1940.

As World War II drained manpower into the armed forces, United States immigration policies changed again, and Mexican laborers (*braceros*) were actively recruited. Farm owners encouraged the illegal immigration of *wetbacks* also, for although unauthorized immigration was illegal, the employment of illegal aliens was not. Illegal immigrants may have outnumbered legal ones by four to one. The Immigration Service continued to expel illegal aliens in large numbers, sometimes promptly readmitting them as *braceros,* and maintaining the fiction that the policies were rational and humane. This disgraceful situation continued through the 1940s and 1950s, generating distrust and hatred of the authorities in many Mexican American communities.

Organized labor in the United States had opposed the large-scale immigration of Mexicans since the end of World War II, with little effect until the early 1960s. In 1963, the Department of Labor established an informal quota by requiring that before a Mexican immigrant could be admitted, it must be certified by a state employment agency that he or she would not take a job that would "adversely affect domestic wages or working conditions," or a job for which there were American applicants. The very next year, the *bracero* program was discontinued. The Immigration Act of 1965 limited the number of immigrants from the whole Western Hemisphere to 120,000 and was expected to curtail Mexican immigration still further. To date, however, the administration of the law has permitted Mexico to furnish the largest number of migrants of any nation in the world, over 40,000 people annually.[9]

Demographic Characteristics

There are over 6 million people of Mexican descent in the United States, most of them in the four states of original settlement plus Colorado. In those five states, they are the largest minority, constituting 12 percent of the population. Mexican Americans are heavily concentrated in Texas and California, each of those states having approximately 1.5 million. The Los Angeles area alone has over two-thirds of a million. There has been some limited dispersal over the country, there now being small communities of Mexican Americans in Illinois, Kansas, Michigan, and Wisconsin.

Within Texas and California, Mexican Americans also are concentrated in certain areas. In Texas, south Texas, along the Rio Grande is the area of greatest concentration. In California, too, the concentration is in and around cities in the southern part of the state.

In many cities, Mexican Americans live in segregated neighborhoods called *barrios*. These are comparable to the "Little Italy's" and other ethnic settlements of the northeast and midwest except that, in this case, the Mexicans were the original settlers, and the Anglos moved in around them. Many *barrios* adjoin the original plaza which has continued as the "Mexican Downtown." In other cities, Mexican Americans are not segregated and, literally, dominate the city. Laredo, Texas, may be the largest such city, but the pattern exists in many small towns in southern Texas and northern New Mexico. Finally, despite rapid migration to the cities, many Mexican Americans still reside in rural areas. No other minority group has such highly varied living conditions.

The nativity patterns of Mexican Americans have varied, as a consequence of vacillating immigration policies. Most Mexican Americans

9. *Ibid.*, pp. 38–44. See also Alejandro Portes, "Return of the Wetback," *Society* 11 (March/April 1974), pp. 40–46.

became U.S. citizens by treaty in 1848. Then, large-scale immigration increased the number and proportion of foreign born. Early in this century, the native-born population became dominant again and, now, immigration is increasing the foreign born again.

First, second, and third generation Mexican American experience may be compared to that of European immigrants. Most of the first generation, of course, have been unskilled laborers of low economic status. Incomes rise among the second generation but, probably as a result of discrimination, do not show significant increase again among the third generation. Third and subsequent generation Mexican Americans generally are better educated, less likely to work at manual occupations, and more likely to intermarry with Anglos. The evidence on divorce rates is somewhat contradictory. Most analyses indicate that third-generation families are more stable and that, following divorce, they are more likely to remarry than are more recent migrants. An analysis of 1960 census data showed Mexican American divorce rates to be higher than those of Anglos and approaching those of blacks.[10] When the 1970 figures for Mexican Americans were compared with those of Anglos and blacks in the same five southwestern states, however, the Mexican American divorce rates were lower than those for either Anglos or blacks.[11]

A high birth rate among Mexican Americans is linked to a low average age. Mexican American families average 4.8 persons, compared to 4.5 persons for black families in the same region, and 3.4 persons in comparable Anglo families. The median age among Mexican Americans is 19.6 years, fully ten years younger than among Anglos. More than 40 percent of all Mexican Americans are under 15 years of age.[12]

Variation in Family Patterns

Mexican American family patterns are not simply a function of rural-urban status and social class; that would imply a uniform pattern of

10. Peter Uhlenberg, "Marital Instability Among Mexican Americans: Following the Patterns of Blacks?" *Social Problems* 20 (Summer 1972), pp. 49–56.

11. Isaac W. Eberstein and W. Parker Frisbie, "Differences in Marital Instability Among Mexican Americans, Blacks, and Anglos: 1960 and 1970," *Social Problems* 23 (June 1976), pp. 609–21. See also, Frank D. Bean, Russell L. Curtis, and John P. Marcum, "Familism and Marital Satisfaction Among Mexican-Americans: The Effects of Family Size, Wife's Labor Force Participation, and Conjugal Power," *Journal of Marriage and the Family* 39 (Nov. 1977), pp. 759–67.

12. Joan W. Moore, *op. cit.*, pp. 52–57.

assimilation, which simply does not exist. There is, for example, great variation from one area to another. Generally, families in California, particularly in the larger cities, are more completely assimilated than are families in Texas. The more rural the Texas environment, the more traditional is the family system. At the other extreme, some old-family Mexican Americans in Colorado and New Mexico show virtually no tendencies toward assimilation. They may speak Spanish exclusively, follow traditional occupations, and appear to have totally resisted the forces of change.

Lower-Class Rural Families. Large numbers of poor people live in the *barrios* of agricultural towns. These segregated enclaves, which appear to continue almost unchanged from generation to generation, maintain that appearance through the outmigration of numbers of young people and elders who have any aspirations toward another way of life. Spanish is the principal language and there are a few professional people, such as doctors and lawyers, and retail business people, such as storekeepers and filling station operators.

In this setting, the extended family is *the* important institution. Relationships are traced outward on both sides of the family, and family rights and responsibilities are clearly defined. The man is the unquestioned head of the family, and his *machismo* (masculinity) is demonstrated through the production of children, through imposing himself sexually upon his wife, and through extramarital liaisons. He is supported in these activities by a peer group of other men.[13]

The wife and mother role in the family is modeled after the Madonna. Women are expected to be paragons of virtue, subordinating themselves completely to their husbands and other male relatives, eschewing sexuality, and devoting themselves to their children. Daughters are raised to continue the pattern. Different branches of the family often have their homes located close to one another, and warm, affectionate relationships among the women are a major source of solidarity.

A special kinship device which promotes continuing close relationships among extended families is that of *compadrazgo* (godparenthood). A man and a woman are chosen to be godparents for each child, committing themselves to see that it is brought up in the church, and im-

13. One study shows more equalitarianism than expected between spouses in farm-labor families. See Glenn R. Hawkes and Minna Taylor, "Power Structure in Mexican and Mexican-American Farm Labor Families," *Journal of Marriage and the Family* 37 (Nov. 1975), pp. 807–11. For further analysis of variability in Mexican-American Families, see Alfredo Mirandé, "The Chicano Family: A Reanalysis of Conflicting Views," *Journal of Marriage and the Family* 39 (Nov. 1977), pp. 747–56.

plicitly obligating themselves to care for it if something should happen to the parents. Special ties develop between a man and his godson, who are referred to as *compadres*. Godparenthood also is a way of establishing ties with higher status families, when the godfather is a boss, or *patrón*.

Middle- and Upper-Class Rural Families. Rural middle-class Mexican Americans, particularly in Texas, live better than their lower-class counterparts; they patronize physicians rather than faith healers, they use attorneys rather than priests for legal counsel, and they may send their children to college. But, like lower-class people, they remain almost isolated from Anglo society and their lives continue to center on a traditional kinship group. Again in comparison with what has often been reported for middle-class black people, they live the middle-class life style even more enthusiastically than most other middle-class people do.

There is also a small Mexican American upper class in some of the towns of the Rio Grande valley. Some of these people have business interests on both sides of the border, and some who are United States citizens live in Mexico and commute to their American places of business. By and large, they have escaped the caste-like isolation of middle-class and lower-class Mexican Americans and associate freely with Anglos. They sometimes belong to Mexican country clubs, and their sons and daughters may intermarry with upper-class Mexican families across the river.[14]

Urban Families. Unlike the situation among most immigrants of European origin, the residential segregation of Mexican Americans in U.S. cities does not decrease regularly by generation. As a general rule, segregation has broken down most rapidly in large California cities such as Los Angeles, which has more residents of Mexican descent than any other city in the U.S. and more than any Mexican city except for Mexico City and Guadalajara. We will discuss here the general impact of urban living upon the traditional Mexican American family patterns.

First of all, extended family relationships become much less prominent. Few people are willing to double up families in the same household, and the existence of welfare services and health services relieve other family members of most obligations to support and care for the poor, the sick, and the disabled. Another symptom of change is the lessened importance and the changed character of *compadrazgo*. While it has by no means disappeared, it is less common, and it has taken on political overtones as it is used to forge ties among unrelated adult males.

14. *Ibid.*, pp. 102–7.

The roles of men in the cities have changed more than those of women. The trend is away from arbitrary male domination and toward an equality in which important decisions are reached jointly by the married pair. As extended family relationships diminish in importance and frequency, marital relationships become more important, with men no longer requiring their wives to be subservient and with men sharing in household duties and child care. Nevertheless, women still function primarily as wives and mothers; fewer Mexican American women attend college, and most men still disapprove of their wives working outside the home.

It is in the cities that Mexican American families come to share most of the value system of other middle-class Americans. They strive to get ahead financially and to climb occupationally. At the same time, they continue to value deference to elders and to emphasize the importance of children. Their birth rates are beginning to drop as they hesitantly experiment with family planning.

The Chicano Movement

A vigorous Mexican American political action movement emerged around 1966 among young, urbanized, Anglicized, middle-class youth, and spread rapidly to include both urban and rural, middle class and lower class, and young people and adults. The movement challenges the stereotyped perceptions of Mexicans that have been held by the Anglo majority and by many Mexican Americans. It uses both conventional political tactics, such as voting, and direct confrontation of established authority to accomplish such goals as changing the public school system to provide more opportunities for Mexican American youth and to increase the numbers of older youth in colleges and universities. It includes the struggles to secure adequate unionization of farm workers. But most of all, it seeks to restore the Mexican American biological and cultural heritage as sources of pride, and emphasizes the contributions of Mexican culture to contemporary American culture.

The Chicano movement has created divisions within the Mexican American population, as the predominantly younger group presses for rapid change and articulates a radical rhetoric. Many older Mexican American leaders have disassociated themselves from the movement and denounced it as irresponsible. The division is clearest over the desirability of assimilation. Young Mexican Americans oppose this, and they are a very large proportion of the Mexican American population. As of this writing, the movement has not yet become articulate about how its values might impinge upon family patterns. Militant young people who demand the right of self-determination for others as well as themselves also demand respect for Mexican values which have included a traditional authoritarian family system.

JAPANESE AMERICAN FAMILIES

Although there were differences, the family system of traditional Japan was a strong, stable, extended one, comparable to that of China.[15] Japan was also rigidly stratified and by the nineteenth century there were four principal classes: the *samurai* (warrior) upper class, an agricultural middle class, a class of artisans and artists, and the lower, merchant class. Unlike other migrations, the Japanese who migrated to the United States were mostly middle-class persons of some formal education, with experience in the ownership and management of land.

Immigration

The first significant migration of Japanese to the United States began around 1890. Most of the early migrants were young men who became farm workers or who worked in or established their own small businesses. The men were soon followed by women of comparable middle-class background who were brought to be their marriage partners.[16]

These early immigrants had the misfortune to come at a time when California was in reaction against the wave of Chinese immigration which had come following the gold rush of 1849. The Chinese were widely hated because of their willingness to work for low wages, because of religious differences, and because they were slow to assimilate.

Some 28,000 Japanese came to the United States between 1890 and 1900, most finding work in the lower-paid areas of railroading, mining, canning, and meat packing. Another 59,000 came between 1900 and 1910, most of whom had agricultural backgrounds and, by 1910, about 30,000 Japanese Americans were working on farms. Thriftiness, hard work, and expertise in the intensive cultivation of crops permitted many of them to either lease land or acquire it outright. The Japanese became

15. For an account of the contemporary family in Japan, see Ezra F. Vogel, *Japan's New Middle Class*, Berkeley: University of California Press, 1963.
16. This discussion follows the treatment in Harry H. L. Kitano, *Japanese Americans: The Evolution of a Subculture*, Englewood Cliffs, New Jersey: Prentice-Hall, 1976.

agricultural competitors to white farmers, and the white-dominated government retaliated through legislation.

The California Alien Land Act, in 1913, prohibited aliens from leasing land for more than three years, and from bequeathing it. The law was never too effective because, by then, many Japanese had children or American friends in whose names they could place their land. The demands of World War I lessened the pressure, and the hold of Japanese people upon agriculture expanded. After the war, a second wave of reaction set in, and a revised alien land law, in 1920, prohibited first generation Japanese from acting as guardians for the land of native-born minors. The amended law was more effective, and Japanese farms in California declined from over 5000 in 1920 to under 4000 by 1930. The denials to Japanese of the right to citizenship and of the right to own land were serious blows, only slightly less devastating than what was to come with World War II.

After the very earliest period, Japanese immigrants faced less serious discrimination in the cities than in agriculture. They established small businesses—restaurants, laundries, barbershops, dry goods stores, and so on—which catered to both Japanese and non-Japanese. The almost assured Japanese clientele aided these establishments, and organized pools of money and credit (*tanomoshi*) provided banking services. Many of these efforts were organized by members of the same *ken* or Japanese state, and some of the ken specialized in certain businesses, such as insurance and barbering. Incipient white boycotts of Japanese businesses were thwarted through threat of counter-boycotts by the well-organized Japanese. Of increasing importance up to, and after, World War II was contract gardening in which skilled Japanese workers assumed the management of urban estates, lawns, and gardens.

That Japanese were ineligible to become citizens has already been mentioned. The Alien Land Acts discriminated against the Japanese further, and other efforts were made to discourage Japanese businesses, and to isolate Japanese residents. In 1921 and 1924, restrictive immigration acts virtually cut off Japanese migration to the United States. The full effects of these policies may never be known, but they may have contributed directly to the Japanese attack on Pearl Harbor in 1941. The restrictive immigration laws of the 1920s involved unilateral repudiation of the "Gentleman's Agreement" between the governments of Japan and the United States in 1908, whereby both nations agreed to restrict migration and both agreed that neither would enact discriminatory legislation against the other.[17]

17. *Ibid.*, pp. 10–29.

By 1940, there were almost 127,000 Japanese residing in the U.S. mainland, and 157,000 more in Hawaii. When war broke out, first the west coast, and then the nation, were engulfed in hysteria fed by long-standing racial prejudice. Mass arrests of Japanese Americans and curfews were followed, early in 1942, by removal of more than 110,000 people from the entire west coast. More than two-thirds of these people were second and third generation and were United States citizens.

The effects of relocation were drastic. Families had their property confiscated or stolen. Many were ruined financially. The humiliation suffered, and the damage done to individual and group self-concepts can scarcely be imagined today. Family structure was profoundly affected. The authority of the first generation immigrants was undermined. Husbands could no longer be effective wage earners. Dormitory living and having meals in mess halls almost removed any family privacy. There was provision for individual security clearances and for leaving the relocation camps to re-settle away from the Western Defense Area.

Some 35,000 younger, predominantly second generation people managed eventually to re-settle in the midwest and east. These young people were freed from family authority as never before. Even in the camps, the absence of dominant non-Japanese residents both permitted and forced Japanese into positions of leadership in all areas of life.

This shameful period came to an end in 1946 when the camps closed down. Many Japanese Americans returned to the west coast where, after initial hostility toward them, the government made token attempts at compensation for confiscated property. The otherwise reactionary McCarran-Walter Immigration Act of 1962 at least permitted first generation Japanese to undergo naturalization and provided them a token immigration quota. Second and third generation Japanese Americans on the west coast and in the midwest and east resumed the climb toward occupational success and, today, have as large a proportion engaged in professional occupations as does the native white population. Income and educational levels have risen correspondingly. A growing influence in recent decades has been the *Kai-sha* Japanese, the American representatives of large Japanese corporations. Most of these corporations are on the east coast and have both oriental and caucasian employees.[18]

Family Patterns

The traditional Japanese family was patriarchal and extended, with the clan providing linkage between the family and the larger society. Age

18. *Ibid.*, pp. 47–51.

was venerated and there were special terms of address for elders. Men dominated women and, because males continued the family line, the father-son relationship was especially important. Filial duty was emphasized and go-betweens aided parents in selecting proper spouses for their offspring. Occasionally, a man married a woman from a family with daughters only, assumed her family's name and continued the family line.

The Issei Family. The term *Issei* refers to first generation immigrants, most of whom came to the United States between 1890 and 1920. Death is taking its toll rapidly of this generation, and those who remain are elderly, mostly in retirement. Many live with, or near, their children where they are accorded prestige and honor, both as symbols of the traditional order and because of the sacrifices which they have made for their children and grandchildren. For their part, they rest comfortably in the security of their families, but reflect somewhat sadly upon the apparent breakdown of time-honored ways.

The original migrants were overwhelmingly young men, many of whom expected, one day, to return to their homeland. Facing hostility in the new environment, being isolated by cultural differences, and being accustomed to arranged marriages, most selected mates who were sent to them from Japan. The mates were from the same *ken*, and most of the Japanese in California lived in rooming houses inhabited by a group of families from the same *ken*. Thus, small communities were created, ethnic enclaves, in which traditional ways were perpetuated and assimilation hindered. These immigrant families followed the traditional patriarchal model, the chief difference being that there was no grandparental generation present to provide direct ties with the ancestors and to serve as models for indoctrinating the young in the traditional ways.

When children came, they acquired the American citizenship which was denied their parents. Too, because of alien land laws, many of the second generation (*Nisei*) became land owners early. While the parents remained tied to the traditional ways, their children adopted the values and norms of mainstream American society. The gap between the two generations also widened because of limited communication among family members, particularly from parents to children. Parents typically "gave orders" which the children were expected to obey unhesitatingly. There was little "discussion" of problems, and no consideration of the well-being of individuals apart from the family group.

Under these circumstances, youthful rebellion against parental controls and against the "funny ways" of the Japanese community would have seemed to be a likely possibility. It did not happen, however. Instead, indoctrination of youth with the idea that discredit upon one Japanese discredited them all was extraordinarily effective. *Nisei* children generally were models of obedience and conformity, a source of pride to their parents, and the envy of most American parents who knew them.

If sacrifice was required of children, they had role models for it in their parents. Most adults viewed their marriages, not as sources of happiness but as networks of obligation and duty, beginning with "contracts" between brides and grooms who did not even know one another, and continuing as combined obligations to ancestors, children, and the Japanese community. Although many *Nisei* were aware of lack of harmony between their parents, separation and divorce were rare. There was also much unacknowledged sacrifice by parents for the welfare and education of the children. Few parents were prosperous when their children were young, and good clothes and shoes for them often meant old and worn clothes for the parents. Many parents deprived themselves severely so that their children might receive university educations.

What *Issei* remain today still are almost completely unassimilated. In fact, they appear in many ways to be more traditionally Japanese than present-day adults living in Japan. Japan has been changing very rapidly, and life in her larger cities is thoroughly modern. *Issei* who return to visit, expecting that they will be returning to the world they left years ago, often hurry back to the United States to their traditional families here.

The Nisei Family. The Nisei, or second generation Japanese Americans, were born for the most part between 1910 and 1940. Unlike their parents, they were citizens and could own property. Much of the property accumulated by the *Issei* in the names of their children was lost in internment, but the *Nisei* recovery from that has been remarkable. Today, Japanese Americans are better educated and have higher incomes than any other minority group in the United States.

The *Nisei* occupy an intermediate position on an assimilation continuum. Habituated to American values and customs, they still confine most of their contacts to other Japanese Americans. Many Japanese consider them to be American, but most Americans still regard them as Japanese. There has been little intermarriage with white Americans, and, although some successful *Nisei* have moved into suburban areas, there is still marked residential segregation, with most *Nisei* living on the fringes of slum areas and in racially mixed neighborhoods.

As a group, the *Nisei* now are middle aged and generally affluent. There appears to be a correlation between Americanization and financial prosperity; Americanization may contribute to success and vice versa. The marriages of the *Nisei*, like those of most other Americans, are judged increasingly in terms of personal happiness and, although the evidence is far from satisfactory, it appears that some rise in divorce is occurring. As when they were children, the *Nisei* appear to be socially and emotionally well-adjusted, but the presence now of a few Japanese psychiatrists in Los Angeles attests to the price to be paid for assimilation to American patterns.

The Sansei Family. It is somewhat premature to write of the third generation Japanese American family because its character is not yet fully evident. Most *Sansei* have been born since World War II and few have yet completed childbearing. The most we can do is to make some inferences from their early life experiences.

To the slight dismay of their parents, the *Sansei* appear virtually to have completed assimilation. If they still are better behaved than most other American children when they are with their parents, they shed their inhibitions at school and in peer group situations. Teachers complain that they have become distressingly like other children. There is still some structural isolation, with the *Sansei* continuing to belong to Japanese groups and organizations. In college, for example, patterns vary from membership in strictly ethnic fraternities and sororities to membership in fully integrated ones. Many *Sansei* reject and resent any reference to themselves as other than American.

Ties to the family still are strong, and most *Sansei* appear to be remaining on the west coast and engaging in predominantly Japanese-run businesses. There has been some Japanese penetration of the higher management echelons of corporations, however, particularly among those who have migrated to the midwest and east. Intermarriage may also be increasing among this group. Residential segregation seems to be breaking down rapidly on the west coast as well as elsewhere.

A logical conclusion to this account would be a statement that assimilation will continue until, soon, the Japanese Americans will no longer exist as an identifiable minority. Perhaps so. Japanese Americans have not displayed much of the ethnic militance which has characterized other groups in recent years. In-marriage, however, is still the rule rather than the exception, and national and group pride has been strong. It remains to be seen whether a plateau in assimilation has been reached.

CUBAN AMERICAN FAMILIES

The Cubans are among the most recent of the many migrant groups in the United States, having come generally since the revolution of 1959. Thus, the majority of Cuban families have been here for less than a single generation, very little time for there to have been marked changes in family patterns. We begin with the family in Cuba, turn to the immigration to the United States, and finally to Cuban families in this country.

The Family in Cuba

The dominant tradition in pre-modern Cuba was that of feudal Spain, a consequence of the settlement of Cuba by sixteenth-century *conquistadores.* Spanish law and institutions, including the Roman Catholic Church, were firmly established, and the native Indian population was virtually exterminated before the year 1600. The importation of slaves from Africa was begun in 1517, and more than a million black people were brought to the island before slavery ended in 1886. As a result of extensive miscegenation, a large mulatto population developed, and accurate racial classification of much of the population became almost impossible. By the early twentieth century, perhaps one-half of the population was white, approximately one-fourth was black, and one-fourth was mixed.[19]

The family system of the Spanish elite was firmly patriarchal, the father dominating his wife and children. Women could not appear in court without their husbands' permission, could not make major financial transactions, and were required to follow the husband to whatever residence he chose. Divorce was forbidden by the church, but civil authorities permitted the divorce of wives for adultery. Men could be divorced for adultery only if it was flagrant, resulting in public scandal or neglect of the wife.[20]

Social changes militated against the perpetuation of this elite colonial family type far into the present century. Feudal estates were never firmly established in Cuba, and legal changes were steadily in the direction of increasing equality for women and children. Too, the black population under slavery suffered ravages of family life comparable to

19. *Problems of the New Cuba: Report of the Commission on Cuban Affairs,* New York: The Foreign Policy Association, 1935, pp. 28–29.
20. Lowry Nelson, *Rural Cuba,* Minneapolis: University of Minnesota Press, 1950, pp. 174–79.

those encountered by black people in the United States. Although most black Cuban families, by the 1930s, were legally sanctioned families, a substantial minority lived in consensual unions, the problems of which were aggravated by poverty. Finally, there were no legal barriers to racial intermarriage, and this blurred differences between the racial groups.

By the middle of the twentieth century, the principal variables influencing Cuban family patterns had become those of social class and rural-urban residence. These two variables operated in combination because most of the rural population also was lower class. For our purposes, three main family patterns may be described: the upper-class family, the urban lower-class family, and the rural farm family.

The Upper-Class Family. This is the immediate descendant of the elite colonial family. The father is a business or professional man, or a wealthy farmer. The household includes servants, wife, and children, and the father is dominant over them all. The wife leads a life of relative ease, secluded from most public contacts, and is submissive. Young children are cared for by nursemaids, and older children are chauffeured about. They attend private schools and have few responsibilities. There may also be grandparents present, and wealthy families are expected to assist siblings who may have fallen upon hard times as well.

In a less prosperous variant of the upper-class family, financial restrictions limit the number of servants to one, there may be no automobile, and there is great emphasis upon keeping up appearances. Children are likely to come more directly under the care of the mother, and to assume regular duties around the home.

The Urban Lower-Class Family. Many families of manual workers live in *solares,* which are alleys in wealthy sections of town, lined with one-room shacks. Father and mother work in a desperate and frequently unsuccessful effort to make ends meet. The wives usually are servants for upper-class families, requiring them to be away for long hours and to leave their children without adequate supervision. Although there are compulsory school attendance laws, many children drop out after a few years because of boredom with school and the need to earn money. They shine shoes, run errands, and take odd jobs. There are never enough jobs and their earnings are meager. The obvious differences in wealth move many of them to panhandle upper-class persons and foreigners and to engage in petty thievery.

Women are likely to marry young, and consensual unions are common. Men may be three or four years older than their wives. Birth rates are relatively high, Cuban families being one-fourth larger than others in the United States. Because the children of consensual unions technically are illegitimate, official counts of illegitimacy are very high.

Relationships between husbands and wives are complicated by *machismo,* a concept of masculinity which ties a man's feelings of self-worth to his ability to father children, to continue to father them, and to his success in extramarital liaisons. Lower-class wives are not so subordinate to their husbands as upper-class wives are, but the tradition of patriarchy still is strong, and wives are caught in a continuing, self-defeating child-bearing. The crowded and unstable conditions of living in the *solares* encourage extramarital liaisons, as too many children make life increasingly difficult, as communication between spouses breaks down, and as men and women need outside support for their sagging egos.

Although the family ideals are those of traditional Catholicism, the everyday influence of the church is not strong. The relatively limited and unsuccessful use of birth control, for example, appears to be more a function of poverty, ignorance, and lack of motivation than of religious taboo.[21] The religious prohibition may play a direct role in keeping the divorce rate down, although, here too, the low rate may be at least as much a function of consensual marriage and the proclivity to terminate marriages as informally as they were established originally.

The Rural Farm Family. Farm families vary in financial status, ranging from wealthy sugar, coffee, and tobacco planters and cattlemen to impoverished peasants. In general, their family patterns correspond to those of the urban social classes whom they parallel. One obvious difference in family structure is the greater preponderance of actual or modified stem families in rural areas. Where finances permit, the eldest son is likely to bring his bride to the parental home where the son is groomed to assume the father's position and possessions at his death or retirement. Even where limited resources do not permit the full development of a stem family, there is more continuity from generation to generation than among comparable urban families. Male dominance exists in this setting also. This is illustrated by the fairly common practice of women serving meals to the men but not sitting down to eat with them. Fathers also dominate their children rather completely, and even grown sons defer to their fathers at least until they are married.

21. For an analysis linking high Latin American birth rates to female unemployment and illiteracy, see Nora S. Kinzer, "Priests, Machos and Babies: Or Latin American Women and the Manichaean Heresy," *Journal of Marriage and the Family* 35 (May 1973), pp. 300–312.

Immigration to the United States

The large-scale Cuban migration to the United States began after Fidel Castro came to power in 1959. That revolution, which was supported initially by significant proportions of virtually all elements of the Cuban population, eventually proved to be more of a revolution than many people expected. As Premier Castro openly espoused economic socialism, and as power was transferred more and more to lower-class and predominantly nonwhite segments of the population, large numbers of prosperous, light complexioned Cubans began to flee the country with Miami, Florida, as their principal destination.

The migrants came in three main waves. The first lasted from January 1959 to October 1962, during which commercial airline flights were available. Then, from October 1962 through December 1965, when there was no regular air transportation, people came any way they could—by small boat, for example, and through third countries such as Mexico. The third stage began in 1965, when the Cuban government authorized twice-daily airline flights. This continued until April 1973.

We do not know exactly how many migrants from Cuba there were. Some came, originally, as tourists, others as residents. Some came through third countries, obscuring their points of origin. Not all registered with the Cuban Refugee Center in Miami, whose figures show almost 448,000 migrants. Another way to get some measure of the migration is to compare 1970 census figures with those for 1960. In 1960, there were listed 79,150 persons of Cuban birth, and 45,266 persons of Cuban parentage, for a total of 124,416. By 1970, the figures had climbed to 439,048 persons of Cuban birth, and 121,580 persons of Cuban parentage, for a total of 560,628. Recent careful research has indicated systematic underenumeration by the census, and puts the figures for 1970 at 479,789 persons of Cuban birth, 132,859 persons of Cuban parentage—612,648 in all.[22]

As already indicated, upper economic groups are overrepresented among the migrants. Persons of professional and semiprofessional backgrounds are overrepresented by a factor of five, while people from agriculture and fishing are underrepresented by a factor of sixteen. Educationally, 4 percent of the Cuban population in 1953 had completed the twelfth grade; in 1963, 36 percent of the refugees had at least that much education. Adults and older age groups are overrepresented too. Non-

22. Rafael J. Prohías and Lourdes Casal, *The Cuban Minority in the U.S.: Preliminary Report on Need Identification and Program Evaluation, Final Report for Fiscal Year 1973*, Boca Raton: Florida Atlantic University, 1973, p. 25.

whites are underrepresented. The distribution of the sexes is approximately equal.

The assimilation of the migrants has been complicated by the expectations of many that they would, one day, return to their homeland and by their legal statuses. There are three legal groups. First, "immigrants" are those who were admitted as permanent residents, having acquired that status before leaving Cuba, or in other countries. Second, are the "non-immigrants" which includes all others (students, tourists, etc.), who were granted indefinite voluntary departure dates upon the expiration of their entry permits. Finally, there are the "parolees." The parolees include all refugees who sought asylum in the United States without having secured entry visas. They are ineligible for permanent alien registration until they have been in the United States for two years, and are barred from categories of employment requiring at least resident alien status.

In a time period ranging from a few months to less than 15 years, there are outward signs of substantial assimilation. While the largest number of Cubans still reside in Florida (206,000 Cubans by birth in 1970), there are substantial numbers in approximately 20 other states. Most of the Cubans reside in metropolitan areas, with large concentrations in New York, New Jersey, California, and Illinois. Between 1951 and 1970, almost 69,000 persons of Cuban origin became naturalized citizens.

A study of the assimilation of 48 Cuban families in Milwaukee in 1969 produced several indicators of fairly rapid integration and assimilation. Fifty-eight percent of the husbands, for example, declared themselves to be quite satisfied with their present lives in the United States, and an additional 31 percent were somewhat satisfied. Thirty-five percent stated that they would not return to Cuba even if the Castro government should fall, and 19 percent more were undecided. Forty-two percent preferred that their children too assume American identities and follow American customs, while only 35 percent preferred their children to retain a Cuban identity and to preserve the Cuban customs.[23]

Finally, the Cuban migrants have already reached income levels close to the United States averages. Almost 22 percent have incomes of $15,000 or over, while another 22 percent average under $5000. Family incomes are significantly affected by whether wives work outside the home, another indirect measure of assimilation. As might be expected, fewer of the wives of families who have remained in the Miami area than

23. Alejandro Portes, "Dilemmas of a Golden Exile: Integration of Cuban Families in Milwaukee," *American Sociological Review* 34 (Aug. 1969), pp. 505–18.

those who live elsewhere work. By March 1972, 54 percent of all women of Cuban origin were in the work force, and high rates of participation were maintained even among women with children.[24]

Cuban Families in Miami

Since the vast majority of Cuban families have been in the United States for less than one generation, there has not been much time for major changes in family structure. Nor has there yet been much research on this matter. One study, however, of 120 Cuban wives in Miami, and 30 of their husbands, has shown that changes are occurring.[25]

The families were young, the mean age of the husbands being 35 years and that of the wives being 32 years. The modal number of children was 2, with 10 percent having only 1 child, and another 10 percent having 5 children. Sixty percent of the children were preadolescent. The husbands were relatively well educated, over 45 percent having either university or professional degrees. Fewer wives had received higher educations, but over three-fourths had completed secondary school. Over two-thirds of the husbands, and almost half of the wives had at least a conversational knowledge of English. Reflecting their recent arrival in this country, and the difficulties associated therewith, the husbands' occupational and income levels were below those appropriate to their educational backgrounds. Almost three-fourths were skilled blue-collar, clerical, or sales workers, earning $550 per month or less. Fifty-five percent of the wives also worked outside the home.[26]

The study measured assimilation in terms of the degree of departure from ideals of male dominance and the amount of independence granted to children. Both variables showed substantial assimilation, the amount of assimilation depending upon other social factors.

Of the factors studied, the amount of contact with native Americans seemed most important; those who had frequent and regular contact were most assimilated, and those who remained within the Cuban community were least assimilated. Other factors associated with assimilation were the length of residence in the United States, knowledge of English,

24. Rafael Prohías and Lourdes Casal, *op. cit.*, pp. 58–63.
25. Marie L. Richmond, "Immigrant Adaptation and Family Structure Among Cubans in Miami, Florida," Ph.D. dissertation, Florida State University, 1973.
26. *Ibid.*, pp. 54–55, 166–69. In 1970, the median income of Cuban families in the U.S. was $8091. See Susan Jacoby, "An Immigrant Success Story," *The New York Times*, Sept. 29, 1974.

higher education, the possession of job skills, and the wife's working. As had been found in studies of earlier immigrant groups, wives were somewhat less assimilated than husbands, being more likely to accept traditional ideas of male dominance.

One finding which surprised the researcher, but which is consistent with the experience of other ethnic groups, was that the younger males held more tenaciously to the ideology of male dominance than did the older men. While this could be the result of the younger men being more recent migrants, it could also be the effect of a consciousness of ethnic pride and a determination not to lose their ethnic identity.

UPPER-UPPER CLASS FAMILIES

Although most people are not accustomed to thinking of upper-class, old American family patterns in ethnic terms, the elite upper-class, like all of the other peoples discussed in this chapter, are set apart by cultural differences; they are, in that sense, an ethnic group. They are the possessors of a distinct way of life, at the opposite end of the economic scale from many other immigrant groups, which they seek to protect against the inroads of the spreading middle-class life style.

This upper class is the one labeled as upper-upper by W. Lloyd Warner, and reported to include only about 1 percent of the population in those communities where it exists at all.[27] It is most discernible in the old cities of the urban Northeast and the deep south. In less bold relief it is found in some cities of the midwest and far west.

A distinguished American ancestry, income from inherited wealth, and residence in the community for several generations are criteria for membership in this class. In the east, emphasis is placed upon establishment of the family in America during the colonial period and the accumulation of the family fortune prior to the Civil War. Careers in government, business, and the professions are followed by the men, after educations at Ivy League schools. The families are of old English stock and few Catholics or Jews are to be found among them. In the south, the background is either English or French. The family history is traced to pre-Civil War days and to gracious plantation living.

Upper-class families in eastern cities generally have established them-

27. W. Lloyd Warner and Paul S. Lunt, *Social Life of a Modern Community*, New Haven: Yale University Press, 1941, p. 203.

selves in the community for eight or nine generations. In the midwest only four or five generations in the community are sufficient to confer upper-class status, while in the far west the time may be shorter still. The longer the family history, the greater the emphasis placed upon illustrious forebears; the shorter the history, the more essential is significant accomplishment by recent generations.

The structure of the upper-class family suggests the trustee family of ancient times. The present members of the family are not *the family*, but only its current representatives. They guard the status and wealth created by earlier generations and they are obligated to pass it on intact or enhanced to their successors. This timelessness of the family is emphasized in its material possessions, its style of life, and even in the selection of family names.

Upper-class families are not conspicuous consumers. They do not often live in spreading ranch houses, drive new Cadillacs, or indulge in fads. Instead they live in ancestral family homes, furnished with heirlooms handed down over the generations. The automobiles are expensive but sedate—and, for the older members, often chauffeur-driven. Their wealth supports, not extravagant purchases, but indulgences in charity, the sponsoring of favorite projects, and, perhaps, travel abroad.

Both given names and surnames have a significance unmatched at other class levels. The surnames of earlier branches of the family frequently are used as given names to emphasize family continuity. Henry Cabot Lodge, for example, exemplifies the ties between two of Boston's upper-class families. Similarly, Franklin Delano Roosevelt represented ties to both the Franklins and the Delanos. The names Nathaniel, Richard, and Leverett appear recurrently in the Saltonstall family, and there were Josiahs in four generations of the Quincy family.[28]

The integration and continuity of upper-class families also are illustrated by widespread intermarriage among them and by a large group of kin with whom close ties are maintained. Cavan describes them as nuclear families closely connected by blood, marriage, history, and the current joint ownership of property.[29] The marriage of cousins once or twice removed is common enough so that kin ties pervade the whole

28. Cleveland Amory, *The Proper Bostonians*, New York: Dutton, 1947, p. 19, as cited in Ruth S. Cavan, *The American Family*, New York: Thomas Y. Crowell, 1963, p. 92. Contrast this situation with that described by Rossi for middle-class families. See Alice S. Rossi, "Naming Children in Middle-Class Families," *American Sociological Review* 30 (Aug. 1965), pp. 499–513.
29. *Op. cit.*

upper-class community. Aunts, uncles, and cousins are members of the family, and the ties among them are reinforced by living on adjacent estates and by common interests in both real and industrial property.

Although upper-class families are not true extended families, there is more prominence given to generational ties and the larger kin group than among middle-class families. The prominence of extended family relationships traces to the position of elders, as holders of family income and property and as bearers of family traditions. Older members often control the income of younger family members, sometimes making provision, through trusts, for the distribution of wealth two or three generations in the future. Consequently, middle-aged couples with half-grown children may remain financially dependent upon their parents. Ceremonially, the position of the elders is analogous to that in the Chinese gentry family; as the closest living connections with the ancestors, they derive special status as bearers of the family traditions.

Technically, descent is bilateral, but there is a pervasive bias in favor of the husband's family. Wealth and power tend to be passed through the male line, sons tend to follow in the occupations of fathers and grandfathers, and boys are more often named for the father's relatives than for the mother's. Ironically, the person around whom family activities revolve frequently is a woman. Women usually outlive their husbands, with the result that the oldest person in the family is a grandmother. Again as among the Chinese, by the time a woman reaches this position, she is so thoroughly socialized that she represents her husband's family almost as he would do.

Mate selection and marriage operate differently among the upper class. First, there is an attempt to raise young people in relative isolation from the children of other classes. After being under the care of nurses or governesses, they are sent to private schools where they associate only with upper-class children and where upper-class attitudes and behavior are carefully cultivated. In both school and college, sex-segregated schools often are preferred to coeducational ones. Carefully arranged relationships among small groups of men's colleges and women's colleges protect young people against "unfortunate involvement" with unsuitable persons. When the time for marriage approaches, "coming out" parties introduce eligible young men and women to each other.

Upper-class men and women marry relatively late. Although national data are not available, Warner's research in Yankee City showed an average age at marriage three to four years older than for the general population.[30] The careful restriction of marriage partners to other members of the upper class provides for the smooth incorporation of the couple into the larger kinship group. The young wife is required to take her place as a family member as well as a wife. In those rare instances when a man does marry outside the class, the couple—particularly the wife—may face ostracism and there may be ill-concealed hope that the marriage may break up in favor of a more appropriate one.

It cannot be emphasized too much that the primary reference group for this upper class is the class itself. It does not accept the mass-consumption, mobility-oriented, middle-class model as an ideal; indeed it perpetuates its status partly through deliberate rejection of that ideal. Marriage is subordinated to perpetuation of the family traditions. Married love must compromise with the suitability of the relationship. Children are born to benefit the family; the family does not exist for the children. Conventionality in both marital and nonmarital roles is less important than in the middle class. A certain amount of deviation in sex, in drinking, and so on is not so threatening as at middle-class levels, providing, of course, that this deviant behavior does not threaten the position of the family in the community.

These upper-class patterns, significant beyond the number of people involved, represent a hold-out against the middle-class model.[31] Whether this group will be able to maintain its aloof position in the future is uncertain. There are signs of incipient breakdown. The segregation of younger members of the group is a special problem. As education becomes increasingly coeducational and as young people of varied backgrounds are thrown together, the landed aristocracy may be yielding to a "jet set" which mirrors the middle-class model in exaggerated form.

SUMMARY

The Italian Americans, Mexican Americans, Japanese Americans, and Cuban Americans are some of the prominent ethnic groups who have brought distinctive family patterns to this country. Each group has accommodated itself to the dominant middle-class family life style in its own way. The general trend is toward assimilation and the minimization

30. W. Lloyd Warner and Paul S. Lunt, *op. cit.*, p. 423.

31. Paul M. Blumberg and P. W. Paul, "Continuities and Discontinuities in Upper-Class Marriages," *Journal of Marriage and the Family* 37 (Feb. 1975), pp. 63–77.

of cultural differences. In recent years, however, there has been a resurgence of ethnic pride, and many younger adults are seeking to preserve and strengthen their cultural heritages.

Italian Americans have had assimilation complicated by language, religious differences, and lack of occupational skills. Mainly farm people from southern Italian villages, they settled in northern cities in ethnic enclaves widely known as Little Italys. Hostility from older Americans reinforced their cultural isolation and hindered assimilation.

The patriarchal family system came under strain as the migrants' children emulated their American peers and adopted the standards of their middle-class teachers. Assimilation proceeded, generally, by generations, becoming virtually complete among many of the third generation. Some third generation Italian Americans, however, have sought to reconfirm their ethnic identities.

Spanish settlers were living in much of the southwestern United States before the Anglos. Many were cattle ranchers. Some were wealthy, and held vast tracts of land. With the exception of small groups in New Mexico and California, virtually all were dominated by invading Anglos, and were reduced to manual laborers in the fields, mines, and industries.

Immigration from Mexico was erratic from 1910 through the 1950s, reflecting U.S. policies and economic conditions. The fiction was maintained that many people were admitted as temporary workers, and still more came illegally. During periods of slack demand for labor, the government shamelessly rounded up Spanish-speaking people and shipped them back to Mexico. Today, there are over 5 million people with Spanish surnames in the United States, the largest minority in the southwest.

The assimilation of Mexican Americans has proceeded unevenly and there is considerable variation in family patterns. Lower-class, rural families are nominally extended and traditional. *Machismo* thwarts effective husband-wife communication. Women are subservient, organizing their lives around home and family. *Compadrazgo* (god-parenthood) cements ties between families. Middle-class rural families live better than lower-class families, but still remain generally isolated from Anglo society. A small rural upper class intermingles freely with Anglos and often have businesses and ties on both sides of the border.

Assimilation is most complete in the cities, particularly in California. Extended families are uncommon, welfare agencies have assumed many former family functions, and many marriages are rather equalitarian.

Birth rates are dropping, divorce rates are increasing. The family style approximates that of other urban Americans. The Chicano movement is concentrated in the cities, but includes attempts to improve the economic situation for farm laborers also. It opposes assimilation apparently without being prepared to resurrect the traditional family system.

Most Japanese migrants to the United States were middle-class people, with some formal education and experience with land ownership. Substantial migration began around 1890, the first migrants being young unattached men. By about 1910, they were perceived as a major threat to other American farmers, and discriminatory legislation covering the ownership and leasing of land was initiated. The resourceful Japanese coped with the problem by putting land in the names of their American-born children. Small Japanese businesses in the cities prospered, as the group provided financing and a guaranteed clientele.

Harshly restrictive immigration policies initiated during the 1920s were one of the factors leading to World War II, and war led to further discrimination against Japanese Americans and eventually to their forced relocation. The camp life during the war helped to break down the authority of the first generation (*Issei*). Some of the younger, second generation people (*Nisei*) secured individual security clearances, and migrated to the midwest and to the east. After the war, most Japanese Americans returned to the west coast.

The last of the *Issei* remain traditional in their beliefs about proper family life, often more so than people of the same age still in Japan. They raised their children to be obedient and respectful and regard changes in family life as symptoms of breakdown. Most of the *Nisei* generation today is adult, middle aged, and reasonably prosperous. Although most have accepted American values and are not distinguishable behaviorally from other Americans, they remain residentially segregated and confine most of their contacts to other Japanese Americans. Their children, the *Sansei* (third generation), have moved further toward complete assimilation. Generally, however, they are still too young for the character of their family patterns to have become fully evident.

The major Cuban migration to the United States began in 1959. Colonial Cuba was dominated by the Spanish who intermingled with more than a million black slaves, creating a considerably mixed population. The family system of the Spanish elite was a traditional patriarchy, subordinating women and children, and forbidding divorce. By the present century, however, families varied chiefly by rural-urban residence and social class. Upper-class families remained rather traditional, while lower-class families struggled for survival. *Machismo* complicated relationships at all levels. Modified stem families were common in rural areas.

There now are more than 600,000 persons of Cuban parentage in the United States, most having been here for less than a decade. Already, however, the old pattern of male dominance is lessening, and children are being granted more independence. Some younger people are beginning to oppose these trends, and to value their ethnic identity.

Although not often thought of in this way, the upper-upper class particularly in the northeast and the south may also be analyzed in ethnic terms. Its family system resembles the trustee system of ancient Greece, preserving names, heirlooms, and estates as symbols of the family's status. Authority is often wielded by the oldest living generation in an extended family context. Mate selection is regulated carefully, and there is emphasis upon socializing new spouses. It is becoming increasingly difficult for this class to preserve the social isolation in which it has flourished, and there is evidence of change in the younger generation.

SUGGESTED READINGS

Baltzell, E. Digby, *Philadelphia Gentlemen: The Making of a National Upper Class*, Glencoe, Ill.: The Free Press, 1958. A study of the American upper class in Philadelphia, Boston, and New York.

Gallo, Patrick J., *Ethnic Alienation: The Italian Americans*, Teaneck, N.J.: Fairleigh Dickinson University Press, 1974. A report of research based on forty-five in-depth interviews with Italian Americans and a control group.

Mindel, Charles H., and Habenstein, Robert W., eds., *Ethnic Families in America: Patterns and Variations*, New York: Elsevier, 1976. Contains descriptions of fifteen different ethnic family systems in the United States.

Murguia, Edward, *Assimilation, Colonialism and the Mexican American People*, Austin: Univ. of Texas Press, 1975. Examines the past, present, and future of Mexican Americans in terms of assimilation and cultural pluralism.

Richmond, Marie L., "Immigrant Adaptation and Family Structure Among Cubans in Miami, Florida," Ph.D. dissertation, Florida State University, 1973. Study showing less male domination and more child independence among Cuban immigrant families than in traditional Latin American families. A principal source used in the writing of this chapter.

FILMS

Mama (Soho Cinema, Ltd., 225 Lafayette Street, New York, N.Y. 10012), 30 minutes, color. A Sicilian woman's journey to New York that lasts sixty-nine years. Shows her experiences as one of the first Italian-Americans, her marriage and family.

A Mexican-American Family (Atlantis Productions, Inc., 1252 La Granada Drive, Thousand Oaks, Calif. 91360), 16 minutes. Provides insight into the life of a Mexican American family: their traditions, their warmth and closeness, and their difficulties.

North From Mexico (Greenwood Press, 51 Riverside Avenue, Westport, Conn. 06880), 20 minutes, color. Follows the route of Coronado along the Rio Grande and into New Mexico. Brings Anglo-Hispanic relations into historical perspective and examines the basis for the current Chicano movement.

QUESTIONS AND PROJECTS

1. What factors hindered the assimilation of Italian immigrants to the United States? What kinds of family problems were thus created?
2. Describe the adjustment patterns of Italian Americans that have been labeled, "rebel," "ingroup," and "apathetic."
3. Explain and qualify the statement that, "Mexican Americans are a conquered rather than an immigrant group." Trace the subjugation of the Spanish minority in each of the southwestern states.
4. Trace the policies of the United States government in relation to the immigration of Mexicans. How have these policies influenced assimilation?
5. Describe the varied family patterns of Mexican Americans today, using the concepts of *machismo* and *compadrazgo*.
6. Contrast the Mexican and Japanese migrations to the United States. How were they similar? How were they different?
7. What was the effect of "relocation" during World War II upon Japanese American family patterns?
8. Describe the family patterns of the *Issei*, the *Nisei*, and the *Sansei*. What changes would you predict during the next generation? Why?
9. Detail the influences of the Spanish and of the black population upon the family system in Cuba. What changes appear to be occurring in Cuban American family patterns?
10. Explain the rationale for analyzing American upper-upper class families in ethnic terms.

11. Is it accurate to describe the upper-upper class family as a trustee family? Why or why not? How is that family changing?
12. Search among your classmates for people who are not more than third generation Americans. Get as many different backgrounds as possible, and arrange a panel discussion focusing upon the changes in their families from their grandparental generation to their own.

WOMEN
ON THE MOVE

II
The Status of Women

The International Labor Organization . . . has lent its imprimatur to a concept that most women have already absorbed and many men are coming to accept: that working wives are overburdened and their husbands should share household work.

Studies have shown . . . that working mothers generally have less than two-thirds the free time enjoyed by their husbands. They frequently work between 70 and 80 hours a week on household chores and in outside jobs. . . . Household responsibilities [also] tend to restrict their employment opportunities.

The labor organization reports a steady increase in female workers in most countries. It cites a more equitable sharing of household chores as one prerequisite of sexual equality in employment. "The key issue for working women is still how to reconcile their home with their new occupational status," the report said.[1]

The intercultural and historical analyses in earlier chapters, to say nothing of the functionalist interpretations of the contemporary American family system, have shown persistent and systematic discrimination against women. There is little reason for us simply to take satisfaction in the apparent progress toward equality which women have made, either over the centuries or during just the past few years. Discrimination against women still is a fact of American life. No analysis of family patterns which did not take this discrimination into account could pretend to be complete. We think that the topic is important enough to de-

1. *The New York Times*, Jan. 12, 1975, p. E7.

vote a separate chapter to it here. The marital and family roles of women will be analyzed in subsequent chapters.

OCCUPATIONAL STATUS

Although it might seem simple to ascertain the status of women in the world of work and how much that status has improved, close inspection shows the matter to be quite complicated. Our analysis requires two sets of data: data showing what proportions of various job categories are filled by women; and information on what proportions of women workers are found in the various occupational categories. Moreover, to see how much change is occurring, both sets of facts need to be traced historically.

Information for 1950 through 1976 on the proportions of women workers at various occupational levels is shown in Table 11.1. To trace the changes in this dimension, we read across the table, row by row. Thus, the proportion of professional and technical workers who were women was just under 40 percent in 1950, dropped slightly over the next two decades, and rose almost four percentage points by the mid-1970s. If a finer breakdown of these data was available, it would show that men have clustered in the professional segment of the category and in the higher-status professions, while women have clustered in the technical and lower-status professions.

Table 11.1. Percentage of employed persons who were women, by occupational category, 1950, 1960, 1970, and 1976

Occupational Category	1950	1960	1970	1976
Professional, technical	39.5	38.1	38.5	42.0
Managers, proprietors	13.5	14.4	15.9	20.5
Clerical workers	62.3	67.6	74.6	79.2
Sales workers	33.9	35.8	43.1	42.2
Craft and kindred workers	3.0	2.9	3.3	4.8
Operatives	27.1	27.4	30.9	31.2
Laborers, except farm	3.7	5.4	3.6	9.5
Service workers	44.6	52.3	66.2	60.9

Source: Dean D. Knudsen, "The Declining Status of Women: Popular Myths and the Failure of Functionalist Thought," *Social Forces* 48 (Dec. 1969), p. 186; and U.S. Bureau of the Census, *Statistical Abstract of the United States: 1976* (Washington, D.C.), p. 372.

Women comprised only 13.5 percent of all managers and proprietors in 1950, with the proportion climbing slowly during the 1950s and 1960s. A more substantial improvement occurred between 1970 and 1976, with a rise of over 4.5 percentage points. Since these are generally higher-status and better paid positions, the trend suggests a lessening job discrimination against women. As we work down the table toward the lower-status occupations, we see that the proportions of women workers are high in all categories except craftsmen and laborers. Skilled blue-collar work and much heavy unskilled labor have traditionally been defined as masculine. Skilled blue-collar work is relatively well paid, so the virtual exclusion of women from these occupations exacts a heavy economic cost. Unskilled manual labor is neither highly regarded nor well paid. The exclusion of women here provides a somewhat hidden benefit of sexist discrimination. If women are denied their share of high-status jobs, they also escape their share of some low-status ones.

The largest proportion of women workers are clerical workers, followed by service workers. Neither of these categories is particularly well paid, which is probably both cause and effect of their being defined, substantially, as women's work. Moreover, the proportions of all workers in these two categories who are women have increased considerably over the past two decades or so. Women were just over three-fifths of the clerical workers in 1950, but were about four-fifths in 1976. Similarly, women climbed from under 45 percent of the service workers in 1950 to over 60 percent in 1976.

In summary, the profile painted by the data in Table 11.1 is ambiguous. Women, as they have entered the labor market in larger numbers, have become larger proportions in most occupational categories. In one sense, that is progress. Women have become a slightly higher proportion of managers and proprietors and professional and technical people. The biggest increases, however, have come in the traditionally feminine clerical and service occupations.

A true portrayal of the status of women—in occupation, income, education, or anything else—requires more than just historical comparisons. The status of women is always relative to the status of men, and sex comparisons must be made to show whether the status of women has been improving more, about the same as, or less than that of men. As Knudsen puts it, the fact that nearly 2.75 million women are in professional, technical, or kindred positions, up 41 percent in one decade, is impressive until one also considers the fact that almost 4.50 million men hold such positions and that their increase during the same decade was 51 percent.[2]

Between-sex comparisons of the distributions of men and women workers among occupational categories for 1950 through 1976 are shown in Table 11.2. The figures in this table should be read downward, comparing the male and female columns for each year. Within sex comparisons can also be made. Thus, the table shows that, in 1976, 16.1 percent of all women workers were professional and technical, 5.5 percent were managers and proprietors, and so on.

Table 11.2. Percent of employed women and men, by occupational category, 1950, 1960, 1970, and 1976

Occupational Category	*Female*				*Male*			
	1950	1960	1970	1976	1950	1960	1970	1976
Professional, technical	12.4	13.0	14.7	16.1	7.3	10.3	14.8	15.4
Managers, proprietors	4.3	3.7	4.5	5.5	10.7	10.7	15.1	14.9
Clerical workers	27.3	29.7	35.1	35.7	6.5	6.9	6.0	6.5
Sales workers	8.5	7.8	7.2	6.7	6.3	6.9	7.5	6.4
Craft and kindred workers	1.5	1.2	1.1	1.5	18.6	19.5	21.2	21.2
Operatives	19.2	15.4	14.8	12.1	20.1	19.9	20.7	18.5
Laborers, except farm	0.7	0.5	0.5	1.2	8.1	6.9	7.7	7.7
Service workers	12.2	13.4	22.0	21.1	5.8	6.0	7.1	9.4

Source: Dean D. Knudsen, "The Declining Status of Women: Popular Myths and the Failure of Functionalist Thought," *Social Forces* 48 (Dec. 1969), p. 185; and U.S. Bureau of the Census, *Statistical Abstract of the United States: 1976* (Washington, D.C.), p. 372.

If we concentrate, first, on the left side of the table, showing the distribution of women among the occupational categories, we see that the proportion of women in professional and technical occupations has ranged from 12.4 percent to 16.1 percent, having shown a modest increase since 1950. Few changes have occurred in the occupational distribution of women over the last three decades except that the proportion of women in clerical jobs has increased substantially, and the proportion of women in service jobs has almost doubled.

2. Dean D. Knudsen, "The Declining Status of Women: Popular Myths and the Failure of Functionalist Thought," *Social Forces* 48 (Dec. 1969), p. 184. For other evidence of occupational discrimination, see James W. Grimm and Robert N. Stern, "Sex Roles and Internal Labor Market Structures: The 'Female' Semi-Professions," *Social Problems* 21 (June 1974), pp. 690–705.

When we shift to the right side of the table and compare changes in the distribution of men in the various categories with that for women, we see dramatic differences. The proportion of men in professional and technical occupations has more than doubled, while women in these high-status, rewarding occupations have increased by only less than four percentage points. The proportion of male managers and proprietors increased by nearly 50 percent while, for women, it was only about one-fourth. Men's participation in clerical jobs, on the other hand, increased virtually not at all, while that of women increased by one-third.

Thus the data comparing male occupations with female occupations show that men have made more progress than women have toward higher-status, better paid occupations. While women have made absolute gains in acquiring paid employment over the past three decades and have made slight and uneven gains toward more employment in more prestigious jobs, they have lost status in relation to men.

INCOME

It will come as no surprise to anyone that discrimination against women in employment is accompanied by lower salaries and wages for women who work. Sex differences in earnings, uncomplicated by comparisons within specific occupational categories, are shown in Table 11.3. Since the figures are for full-time workers only, the argument that women receive lower earnings because many are part-time workers does not apply. During the 20 years from 1955 through 1974, men's earnings almost tripled and women's earnings more than doubled. The dollar differences

Table 11.3. Median earnings of fulltime men and women workers, 1955–1974

Year	*Men*	*Women*	*Dollar Difference*	*Percent Women's Earnings of Men's Earnings*
1955	$4250	$2700	$1550	64%
1960	5400	3300	2100	61
1965	6400	3800	2600	60
1970	9000	5300	3700	59
1974	11900	6800	5100	57

Source: U.S. Department of Labor, "The Earnings Gap Between Men and Women," 1976, p. 6.

between men's and women's earnings more than tripled. The crucial figures, the percentages that women's earnings were of men's earnings, show that women lost ground steadily. The gap was smallest in 1955, when the median earnings of women were 64 percent those of men, and increased until, in 1974, women were earning only 57 percent as much as men. Again the data show that the apparent progress achieved by women in recent decades is largely illusory.

Earnings figures by occupational category, for 1974, are shown in Table 11.4. These data confirm the fact that women disproportionately

Table 11.4. Earnings of men and women full-time workers, by occupational category, 1974

Occupational Category	*Women*	*Men*	*Dollar Gap*	*Percent Women's Earnings of Men's Earnings*
Professional, technical	$9570	$14,873	$5303	64.3
Managers, administrators	8603	15,425	6822	55.8
Clerical workers	6827	11,514	4687	59.3
Sales workers	5168	12,523	7355	41.3
Craft and kindred workers	6492	12,028	5536	54.0
Operatives	5766	10,176	4410	56.7
Laborers, except farm	5891	8,145	2254	72.3
Service workers	5046	8,638	3592	58.4

Source: U.S. Department of Labor, "The Earnings Gap Between Women and Men," 1976, p. 8.

occupy the lower-status positions within occupational categories.[3] The largest wage gap, for example, is to be found among sales workers where men more often have the higher-paid non-retail jobs while women work primarily in retail trade. The smallest wage gap both in dollars and in percentages is found among laborers, the lowest paid wage group for men.

3. See also McKee J. McClendon, "The Occupational Status Attainment Processes of Males and Females," *American Sociological Review* 41 (Feb. 1976), pp. 52–64; and Donald J. Treiman and Kermit Terrell, "Sex and the Process of Status Attainment: A Comparison of Working Women and Men," *American Sociological Review* 40 (April 1975), pp. 174–200.

THE DAY-CARE CONTROVERSY

Nearly 12 million mothers in the United States, more than 6 million with children under six years, work outside the home.[4] Added to the burdens of sexual segregation within the occupational system and pay scales which make their take home pay less than that of men, these women must make arrangements for the care of their children while they work. The problem is most acute where there are children of preschool age. Such children may be cared for at home by grandmothers or other relatives, in the homes of relatives or friends, in the homes of women who keep a few children for pay, in nursery schools, or in day-care centers that are either publicly or privately operated.

Until fairly recently, relatively little public attention was devoted to providing child-care facilities for working mothers, but with the combination of increased numbers of working mothers and the forces of women's liberation, it has now become a major public issue. Women are demanding that day-care centers be provided as the *right* of parents and children, and the *obligation* of society.

The History of the Movement

The first day-care centers were established in the United States during the 1850s. They were founded by wealthy women who provided housing and care for poor or unwed pregnant women during their confinements and the postpartum period. After that, the recipients of the care were offered employment as domestic servants while their children were cared for in the center. The system provided help for expectant mothers, a labor supply for the wealthy, and indoctrination in middle-class values and standards for young children.[5]

Early in the twentieth century, social reformers popularized the settlement house, and young social workers took over the task of day-care from the wealthy women of earlier generations. They combined the provision of social casework services with comprehensive child-care that included medical and dental care, along with enlightened preschool instruction. Many of these centers were well run, and some 695 of them were licensed by 1916. Unfortunately, the high standards were not long

4. B. Bruce Biggs, " 'Child Care': The Fiscal Time Bomb," *The Public Interest* 49 (Fall 1977), pp. 87–102.

5. Sheila M. Rothman, "Other People's Children: The Day Care Experience in America," *The Public Interest* 30 (Winter 1973), pp. 11–27. The following paragraphs follow this analysis closely.

maintained. Financial and personnel problems combined to reduce the care which most of them offered to a minimum custodial level.

Other changes contributed to the deterioration of the movement. An emerging ideology held that respectable women should not work, but rather should remain at home with their children. Legislation permitted them to receive relief payments at home, and, soon, women who worked in factories came to be stigmatized as mostly unwed mothers who could not qualify for relief payments. The children who needed day-care shared their mothers' stigma, with the consequence that mothers were reluctant to use the facilities that were available.

During the 1920s, social workers adapted to the new circumstances and sought out, for service, the hard-core poverty groups they formerly disdained. Their new model was that of the child guidance clinic where poor children and parents could receive counseling and services intended to uproot personal and social pathologies. The new jargon was Freudian, but the approach and the goals of the movement were still to indoctrinate client families with proper middle-class standards.

Then the depression of the 1930s almost destroyed private charity organizations, virtually eliminated the labor market for women, and pressed most social workers into government relief agencies. One form of relief was WPA day nurseries which employed out-of-work teachers and provided free meals for poor children. This was a temporary expedient that did not outlive the worst years of the depression.

World War II brought another crisis. Millions of men entered the armed forces and millions of women took their places in factories, offices, and elsewhere. Their patriotism, however, did not prevent a high rate of absenteeism from the job or high rates of turnover. Women workers changed jobs twice as often as men, and were absent twice as often. The most important cause of this was the double burden of job plus home and family duties carried by these women, three-fourths of whom were married. Women who worked all day found that many stores, banks, ration boards, and so on were closed before they could get there. After shopping and running other errands, there still was dinner to fix, cleaning to be done, and children to be cared for. Absenteeism from work rose because women needed time off to catch up on their domestic duties, or they were exhausted and needed to rest.[6]

Child-care became an evident social problem by 1943 when the War Manpower Commission estimated that 2 million children were in need of outside assistance, and absenteeism from work statistics were trans-

6. William H. Chafe, *The American Woman: Her Changing Social, Economic, and Political Roles, 1920–1970*, New York: Oxford University Press, 1972, pp. 159–60.

lated into the numbers of airplanes and tanks that were not built. Newspapers carried stories of babies and small children, left by their mothers in locked automobiles in factory parking lots. A very few industries and scattered communities built and managed child-care centers, but most looked to the federal government for assistance. Government policy vacillated, and finally was stabilized around administration of the Lanham Act which snarled in bureaucratic red tape most efforts to build day-care centers. To compound the difficulties, the Federal Works Administration and the Federal Security Agency feuded over which was to control the program. The FWA saw its mission to construct the largest number of facilities in the shortest time, regardless of quality. The FSA represented the professional social workers who advocated the long-term development of quality programs. Some centers were built but, even by 1945, only about 100,000 children were cared for in them.

The Lanham Act expired after World War II, ending federal support for day-care centers. New York State, for a while, reluctantly appropriated funds for centers in New York City, but the rationale was to combat juvenile delinquency in slum areas. Moreover, mothers who wished to use the centers were required to submit to a "means test" to establish eligibility for public assistance. Even then, the program was attacked by officials and the press who labeled it as communistic and as social welfare abused by prosperous women workers who brought their children to the centers in taxicabs. In 1948, the state discontinued support of the program.[7]

After World War II and up to the 1960s, there were significant changes in the composition of the female labor force. Middle-class women began to work in much larger numbers, and many more of them had children. In 1948, 20 percent of working women had children under 18 years of age, while a decade later, the proportion had risen to 30 percent. The day-care movement changed very little. Only 2 percent of the more than 5 million children under 12, whose mothers worked, received day care, and only 4 percent of the children under 6 years of age were so cared for.[8]

The Current Controversy

From the end of World War II until the mid-1960s, the day-care issue was not very conspicuous. Mothers from poor families worked in large numbers, of course, and few were able to make adequate provision for

7. *Ibid.*, pp. 186–87.
8. Sheila M. Rothman, *op. cit.*, p. 21.

their children. The poor were mostly an "invisible minority," and what few public utterances there were on the matter reinforced the idea that day-care was subversive of traditional values, and threatened the mother-child relationship and the mental-emotional health of children.

By the mid-1960s, poverty once again had become a conspicuous social problem, and part of the federal government's "war on poverty" included the establishment of Head Start centers for preschool-age poor children. The intent was to provide culturally deprived children with a stimulating environment, adequate nutrition, medical care, and compensatory education to prepare them to do well in school and, eventually, to escape from poverty. Unfortunately, evaluation studies generally failed to support the claims made for the program. What gains the children made during the preschool period were quickly lost during the early school years.[9] Undaunted, the advocates of day-care for poor children simply argued that compensatory education programs should start earlier in life and be made more comprehensive.

The major thrust for resurrection and expansion of the day-care movement has come, however, not from poor families or their advocates, but from the middle-class and upper-middle-class activists of women's liberation.[10] These women view day-care primarily as a means of facilitating their own occupational careers and only secondarily in terms of the welfare of children. If they do not see day-care as particularly good for children, at least they do not view it as harmful.

By 1972, day-care had become an explosive political issue. The immediate catalyst was President Nixon's veto of the Comprehensive Child Development Act of 1971 which would have ranked, in financial cost and social implications, with Medicare or federal aid to education.[11] In longer-range perspective, the increasing numbers of working women who are clamoring for assistance and the perceptions of senators and congressmen that this is an issue which they may ride to higher political office almost guarantees the passage of other bills and furious public debate over the costs, benefits, and liabilities involved. Without entering the political debate, the principal issues appear to be (1) the need for day-care centers; (2) custodial versus developmental programs; (3) the costs; (4) and the different needs of middle-class and poor families.

9. Sara Stein and Carter Smith, "Return to Mom," *Saturday Review of Education* (April 1973), p. 37.

10. Louise Gross and Phyllis MacEwan, "On Day Care," in Writings from the Women's Liberation Movement, *Liberation Now,* New York: Dell Publishing Company, 1971, pp. 123–26.

11. William V. Shannon, "A Radical, Direct, Simple, Utopian Alternative to Day-Care Centers," *The New York Times Magazine,* April 30, 1972, p. 13.

The Need. There are approximately 12 million working mothers in the United States, 6 million of whom have children under 6 years of age. To meet their need, there are only 17,500 licensed day-care centers, providing space for some 575,000 children. Over one-third of these centers are privately operated. The number of centers and the number of spaces available are lower than those achieved during World War II.

Nearly half of the children of working mothers are cared for in their own homes by fathers, grandmothers, older siblings, or nonrelatives. Other arrangements include care in the homes of other people, care by the mothers who work only during school hours, and no care at all, with the children being left to fend for themselves. In at least 70 percent of the cases, there is no direct monetary payment for the child-care, any exchange being of goods or services. Where money payments are made, 27 percent pay less than $10 per week, over 50 percent pay between $10 and $19, and only about 20 percent pay $20 or more.

Most mothers, when asked, state that they are dissatisfied with their child-care arrangements. Almost half indicate that they would take advantage of day-care facilities if they were available under public or private sponsorship. More black than white women and more poor women than middle-class women favor community-sponsored centers.[12]

Custodial versus Developmental Programs. Almost from the beginning, progressive advocates of day-care have argued that centers should do more than provide mothers with a place to "park" their children while they work. On the one hand, society has an interest in seeing to it that children grow up to become informed citizens and productive workers who will help the economy grow and not drain it by becoming welfare recipients. On the other hand, they believe that child development experts are better qualified to facilitate the growth and physical and emotional health of children than are most families.

The Comprehensive Child Development Act would have located child development centers in each community. Two meals per day would have been provided, along with comprehensive medical, dental, and psychiatric care. Educational programs during the standard school year would have been supplemented by weekend and summer "vacation" programs. Although this act was vetoed, similarly comprehensive bills already are in preparation for submission to future congresses.[13]

The Costs. The opponents of day-care programs have concealed their objections to the costs of expanded programs by focusing upon the al-

12. Shirley S. Angrist and Judith R. Lave, "Issues Surrounding Day Care," *The Family Coordinator* 22 (Oct. 1973), pp. 458–59.
13. William V. Shannon, *op. cit.*, p. 71.

leged importance of keeping children with their mothers, but the issue of costs is very real. The U.S. Office of Child Development has estimated that centers providing only custodial care, but otherwise meeting minimum standards, incur costs of approximately $1400 per child per year. Those which are operated as development centers have costs of almost $2400 per child per year.[14]

Some efforts have been made to translate these individual costs into national costs. The Comprehensive Child Development Act, for example, originally proposed spending of $2 billion during its first year of operation, $4 billion during the second year, and $7 billion during the third. It was soon discovered, however, that the costs quickly would jump to $20–30 billion per year. The highest estimate yet made public has reached $39 billion. Not surprisingly, some people, even those generally sympathetic to day-care, have suggested that the money might be better spent in direct grants to families, enabling many women to forego working for pay in order to stay home and care for their children.[15]

Programs for the Poor and the Middle Class. Since the mid-1960s, the most articulate advocates of federally financed day-care have been the spokeswomen of women's liberation; the National Organization for Women, for example, demands free 24-hour day-care. Although these partisans are explicit about the rights of women to pursue careers as unhampered by child-rearing as men are, they also purport to speak for poor women who must work out of financial necessity. They view themselves as working to alleviate the problems of the poor. Ironically, they have become, in some ways, the unwitting allies of groups and programs that would further oppress the poor.

Over the past several years, political pressures at city, state, and federal levels to reduce the costs of public welfare have become great. Efforts have been to try to rid welfare rolls of so-called "cheaters" and "shirkers" and to force mothers receiving welfare payments to accept paid employment rather than to remain home with their children. Thus, for them, day-care would not be an option to be chosen voluntarily or rejected, but would be forced upon them by the government.

Such coercion got under way in 1967 through the federal Work Incentive Program, designed to provide welfare recipients with job training. Most of the men on welfare who were the original target group proved to have physical or mental handicaps which made them unemployable, so attention shifted to welfare mothers. Poor mothers were

14. Figures cited in B. Bruce Biggs, *op. cit.*, p. 94.
15. William V. Shannon, *op. cit.*, p. 76.

forced to accept job training and, to do that, they had to put their children in day-care centers. Although it was publicized that quality day-care centers were available, this seldom was the case. Most mothers had to make arrangements for their children on their own, and most of these arrangements were unsatisfactory. The Work Incentive Program also failed to make many women employable. It did succeed in its basic political purpose, to intimidate many women into dropping off the welfare rolls.[16]

Up to now, day-care simply has not lived up to its promise. A study by the National Council of Jewish Women, in 1972, of 500 day-care centers all over the country found that 62 percent of the public non-profit centers and 85 percent of the privately operated ones provided only custodial care. In another study in New York City, 52 of 240 licensed centers failed to meet minimum standards of health, sanitation, and safety.[17]

The conclusion seems inescapable that the kind of day-care facilities sought by middle-class women by and large do not exist and would be terribly expensive to provide. Even if fees were scaled according to income they would be most uneconomical for poor women, and most of the benefits would accrue to the middle classes. Middle-class women, educated as teachers, physicians, social workers, and psychologists, would staff the centers and would be paid something like $8–$10 per hour for caring for poor children. Most poor mothers would be little better off financially, if at all, than they were on welfare when they stayed home and cared for their children at a cost of $1–$2 per hour.[18]

EDUCATIONAL STATUS

One barrier to occupational advancement and higher incomes for women operates in the educational system which prepares people to be employed in higher-status, more rewarding positions. Many of these positions require a college education and graduate training. We focus, here, upon two problems facing women in education: first, the effect marriage has upon women's careers in graduate education; and, second, upon discrimination against women in employment on university faculties.

16. Sheila M. Rothman, *op. cit.*, pp. 22–23.
17. *Ibid.*, p. 25.
18. *Ibid.*, p. 24.

Marriage and Graduate Education

In 1969, researchers, under the sponsorship of the Carnegie Commission on Higher Education, studied 33,000 graduate and professional students attending 158 U.S. colleges and universities to determine, among other things, the effect of marriage upon graduate education. They found that more men graduate students are married (69 percent) than women graduate students (56 percent), and that women graduate students are more likely to be divorced (6 percent to 2 percent).[19]

As shown in Table 11.5, they also discovered that married women

Table 11.5. Percentages of married graduate students whose spouses attended graduate school, by age and sex

Age	*Males*	*Females*
22 or younger	14	63
23	20	54
24	22	69
25	33	63
26–27	27	64
28–29	29	70
30–34	22	58
35–39	20	64
40+	24	41

Source: Martin A. Trow, *et al., Technical Report: National Surveys of Higher Education,* Berkeley, Calif.: Carnegie Commission on Higher Education, 1971.

graduate students are much more likely to be married to spouses who have also had graduate training than is true for married men graduate students. Moreover, the differences are substantial for all age groups. When the age groups are combined, over half the women are married to men who have some graduate education, while fewer than 25 percent of the men have wives with graduate education. These differences reflect societal norms which favor husbands having equal or higher educational status than their wives, and mean that many women find that marriage effectively denies them the opportunity to continue their educations.

Not only does marriage keep some women out of graduate education

19. This section follows closely Saul D. Feldman, "Impediment or Stimulant? Marital Status and Graduate Education," in Joan Huber, *ed., Changing Women in a Changing Society,* Chicago: The University of Chicago Press, 1973, pp. 220–32.

but, apparently, it also interferes with the academic progress of women who do become enrolled. Table 11.6 shows the percentages of men and women graduate students who attend school full time and part time, by marital status. In every marital status category, there are more men than women full-time students. The difference is much greater, however for married students (51 percent vs. 29 percent) than either for single students or for those who are separated or divorced.

Table 11.6. Percentages of graduate students enrolled full time and part time, by sex and marital status

Sex and marital status	*Full-time*	*Part-time*
Single men	76	24
Single women	62	38
Married men	51	49
Married women	29	71
Divorced-separated men	64	36
Divorce-separated women	52	48

Source: Martin A. Trow, *et al.*, *Technical Report: National Surveys of Higher Education,* Berkeley, California: Carnegie Commission on Higher Education, 1971.

Still other data demonstrating the interference of marriage with women's graduate education are the age distributions of married men and women students. Only 9 percent of men graduate students, compared with 28 percent of women, are 35 years or older. Men are likely to begin graduate school shortly after receiving their baccalaureate degrees and to continue directly to graduate degrees. Women, on the other hand, more often cannot begin graduate school until their husbands have completed their educations and are established in the occupational world, or, perhaps, until their children are in school.

This same survey showed that large proportions of men and women graduate students plan careers in college teaching. Readily available data, however, show that relatively few women are employed on college and university faculties, and that those who are so employed tend to be clustered in the lower academic ranks and at lower salary levels. A report in the *New York Times*, for example, states that The University of Chicago has less than 8 percent women faculty members, Harvard less than 9 percent, the University of California at Berkeley, 11 percent, and Columbia University slightly over 13 percent.[20]

20. *The New York Times,* April 2, 1972.

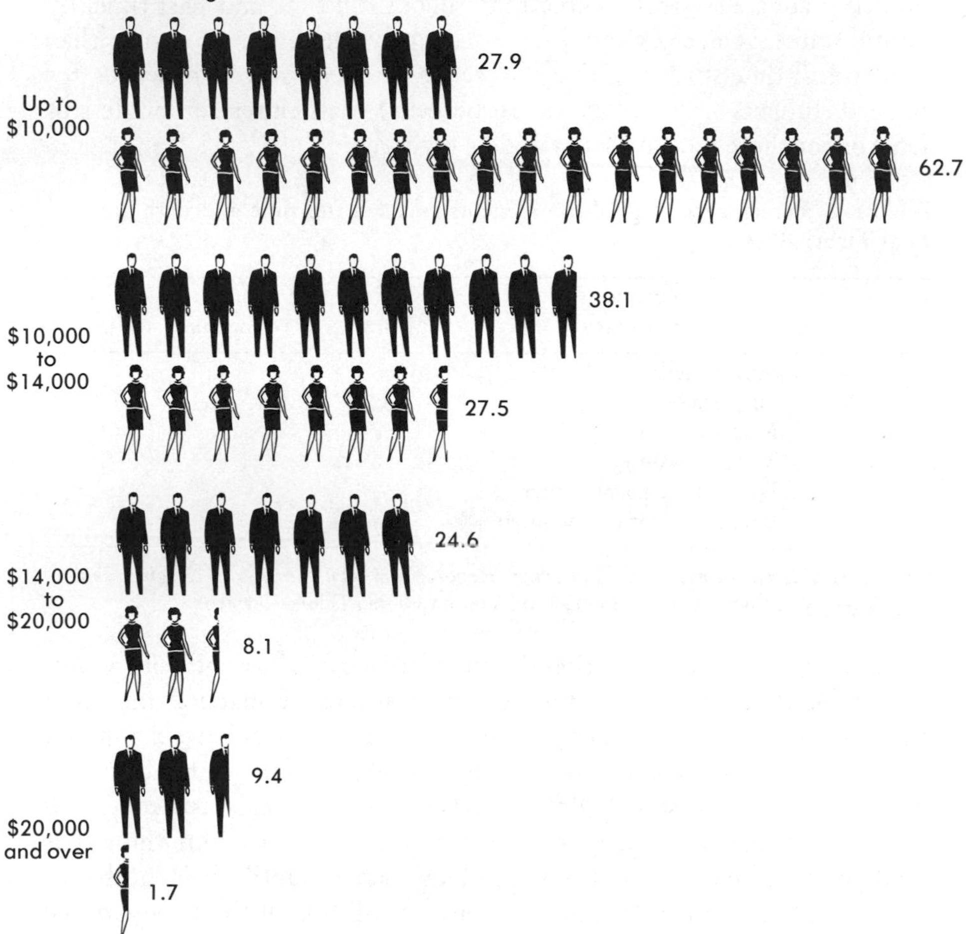

Figure 11.1. Salary ranges of men and women faculty members of U.S. colleges and universities

Source: American Council on Education.

More evidence appears in Figure 11.1, which shows the percentages of male and female faculty members at various salary levels. Over three-fifths of women earn $10,000 or less, while only about one-fourth of men are at this level. At the other extreme, almost 10 percent of men, but less than 2 percent of women, earn $20,000 or more. Relatively few women get faculty positions, and they are not rewarded as their male colleagues are.

More concerted effort to eliminate job and pay discrimination against women is being made, under some duress, in colleges and universities than anywhere else in the economy. Over a decade ago, President Lyndon Johnson signed an executive order requiring federal contractors having more than 50 employees to file "affirmative action" plans setting specific goals and timetables for hiring more women and other minorities. The Office of Civil Rights monitors the program closely, and, for a while, held up federal funds to some 40 universities until it determined them to have complied with the executive order.

Progress in the employment of women by universities is being made, but there is also controversy over the program. Many administrators and faculty members believe that the government is using the thinly disguised concept of "quotas" to force them to hire less qualified women. The Office of Civil Rights denies that its "goals" and "timetables" are euphemisms for quotas, but acknowledges that it is difficult to determine what a reasonable affirmative action plan should contain and how much evidence universities should provide of their attempts to meet their goals. Until these problems are worked out, the combination of marital impingement upon graduate study opportunities for women will combine with direct job discrimination to reinforce discrimination in other areas of life.

MENTAL HEALTH STATUS

Evidence has been accumulating for almost four decades showing, consistently, that women have higher rates of mental illness than men do. This is true for the so-called "functional" types of mental illness where there is no apparent physiological causation, ruling out the possibility that the differences are a function of physiological susceptibility. The findings also hold regardless of the criteria of mental illness: community surveys, admissions to mental hospitals, psychiatric treatment in general hospitals, treatment in psychiatric outpatient clinics, or treatment for psychiatric symptoms by general physicians.

The studies also have shown that single people, the divorced, and the widowed have higher mental illness rates than married people, leading to the suspicion that the higher mental illness rates for women could be accounted for by very high rates among unmarried women. This accorded with prevailing stereotypes of unmarried women as maladjusted and was reflected in epithets such as "spinster" and "old maid." Recently, however, more systematic analyses have shown that this is not the case. In fact, the contrary situation prevails. The highest mental illness rates seem to occur among married women and among single men.[21]

The findings of 16 separate studies on mental illness rates among married women and men are summarized in Table 11.7, which gives the number of men and women in each study and the ratios of the mental illness rates of the women to those of the men. Every one of the ratios exceeds 1.00, and in two cases the women's mental illness rates were more than two and one-half times those of the men. Mental illness rates for married women are substantially higher than those for married men.[22]

Studies of mental illness rates among single men and women and among previously married men and women show a different pattern. In 15 separate studies of single persons, 4 showed women having higher mental illness rates, but 11 showed single men having higher rates. In 11 studies of divorced persons, 3 showed women having higher rates, while 8 showed men having higher rates. Similarly, in 9 studies of widowed persons, only 2 showed higher mental illness rates for women, while 7 showed higher rates for men. Thus mental illness rates are higher for unmarried men than they are for unmarried women.

If married women have high rates of mental illness, there must be something in the social role of married women which is especially stressful. Walter Gove has indicated five ways in which marriage is hazardous for the adjustment of women in modern industrial societies. First, he points out that while men generally have two major roles to afford them status and satisfaction, head of the family and bread-winner, women typically have only the role of housewife. If a man's family life is unsatisfactory, he can find solace in his work, and vice versa. If a woman's family life is unsatisfactory, however, she has no major alternative role to which she can readily turn.

A related problem is that the role of housewife is not technically demanding, carries little prestige, and is not highly rewarded. This is frustrating for women who have had considerable formal education, and who have internalized values of equality and been led, by teachers, par-

21. This discussion draws heavily upon the work of Walter R. Gove. See his "The Relationship Between Sex Roles, Marital Status, and Mental Illness," *Social Forces* 51 (Sept. 1972), pp. 34–44; and Walter R. Gove and Jeannette F. Tudor, "Adult Sex Roles and Mental Illness," *American Journal of Sociology* 78 (Jan. 1973), pp. 50–73.

22. For a challenge to the view that marriage is harmful to the mental health of women, see Norval D. Glenn, "The Contribution of Marriage to the Psychological Well-Being of Males and Females," *Journal of Marriage and the Family* 37 (Aug. 1975), pp. 594–600.

Table 11.7. Studies showing comparative rates of mental disorder among married men and women (persons per 100,000)

*Researchers**	*Men*	*Women*	*Ratio: Women/Men*
1. Tauss	18,000	35,100	1.95
2. Srole *et al.*	19,300	19,900	1.03
3. Hagnell	900	2,500	2.78
4. Cooper	17,400	29,000	1.67
5. Shepherd *et al.*	8,934	16,154	1.81
6. Miles *et al.*	788	926	1.18
7. Susser	465	706	1.52
8. Hollingshead and Redlich	504	566	1.12
9. Innes and Sharp	495	651	1.32
10. Kramer (n.d.)	83	96	1.16
11. Jaco	62	92	1.48
12. Thomas and Locke (New York)	68	92	1.35
13. Thomas and Locke (Ohio)	65	66	1.02
14. Gregory	45	59	1.31
15. Kramer (1967)	16	29	1.81
16. Frumkin	4.2	10.7	2.55

* B. Cooper, "Psychiatric Disorder in Hospitals and General Practice," *Social Psychiatry* 1 (1966), pp. 7–10; R. Frumkin, "Social Factors in Schizophrenia," *Sociology and Social Research* 38 (July-Aug. 1954), pp. 383–86; J. Gregory, "Factors Influencing First Admission Rates to Canadian Mental Hospitals III: An Analysis by Education, Marital Status, Country of Birth, Religion and Rural-Urban Residence," *Canadian Psychiatric Association Journal* 4 (April 1959), pp. 133–51; Olle Hagnell, *A Prospective Study of the Incidence of Mental Disorder,* Sweden: Barlingska Boktryckeriet, 1966; A. Hollingshead and F. Redlich, *Social Class and Mental Illness,* New York: Wiley, 1958; G. Innes and G. Sharp, "A Study of Psychiatric Patients in North-East Scotland," *Journal of Mental Science* 108 (July 1962), pp. 447–56; E. G. Jaco, *The Social Epidemiology of Mental Disorders,* New York: Russell Sage Foundation, 1960; M. Kramer, "Epidemiology, Biostatistics, and Mental Health Planning," in R. Monroe *et al., eds., Psychiatric Epidemiology and Mental Health Planning,* Washington, D.C.: American Psychiatric Association, 1967; M. Kramer, *Some Implications of Trends in the Usage of Psychiatric Facilities for Community Mental Health Programs and Related Research,* Public Health Service Publication No. 1434, Washington, D.C.: U.S. Government Printing Office, n.d.; H. E. Miles *et al.,* "Accumulative Survey of All Psychiatric Experiences in Monroe County, N.Y.," *Psychiatric Quarterly* 38 (July 1964), pp. 458–87; M. Shepherd *et al., Psychiatric Illness in General Practice,* London: Oxford University Press, 1966; L. Srole *et al., Mental Health in the Metropolis,* New York: McGraw-Hill, 1962; M. Susser, *Community Psychiatry,* New York: Random House, 1968; W. Tauss, "A Note on the Prevalence of Mental Disturbance," *Australian Journal of Psychology* 19 (Aug. 1967), pp. 121–23; and D. Thomas and B. Locke, "Marital Status, Education and Occupational Differentials in Mental Hospitals," *Milbank Memorial Fund Quarterly* 41 (April 1963), pp. 145–60.

Source: Adapted from Walter R. Gove, "The Relationship Between Sex Roles, Marital Status, and Mental Illness," *Social Forces* 51 (Sept. 1972), p. 38.

ents, and others, to expect that they will be achieving productive adults. A third difficulty lies in the fact that enactment of the housewife role is relatively private and hidden from direct monitoring by others. If a woman, displeased with her lot, begins to perform household tasks in a slipshod manner, or to procrastinate unduly, there is no automatic corrective such as operates in the direct supervision of most men on the job. The woman, home alone, may brood over her problems to the point where symptoms of mental illness appear before her husband or anyone else has opportunity to intervene. Even then, the woman remains essentially isolated and thrown on her own resources during a good part of her waking hours.

Even when married women work outside the home, they are likely to be denied most of the satisfactions employment ofen affords to men. Educated women are likely to be sought for jobs which do not permit them to put their professional training and skills to use, and which pay less than comparable jobs filled by men. Moreover, their employment is likely to be defined, both by themselves and by others, as supplementary to the husband's employment, and not to compete with it. Still further, the working wife's husband may help with housekeeping duties, but most of the after-work burden of meal preparation, housekeeping, child-care, and so on, fall upon her.[23] Paid employment, then, may do as much to compound her problems as to relieve them.

Finally, Gove points out, role expectations for women are considerably more diffuse, and less clear, than those for men. While men explicitly weigh alternatives in terms of what is best for them and for advancement in their careers, women's choices usually are presented in the context of contingencies; they can do only what their husbands' choices will permit them to do. The uncertainty and the lack of autonomy for women in this situation is perceived to be a major source of frustration.

SUMMARY

Discrimination against women is a fact of life. In the world of work, women are overrepresented in traditionally female occupations such as household work, clerical work, and other service work. Moreover, the concentration of women in these occupations has increased over the past 25 years. Women have made slight gains in becoming managers, pro-

23. Walter R. Gove and Michael R. Geerken, "The Effect of Children and Employment on the Mental Health of Men and Women," *Social Forces* 56 (Sept. 1977), pp. 66–76.

prietors, and professionals. Improvement in the status of women must also be compared to improvement in the status of men. Systematic data show that men have made more progress toward higher-status occupations over the past few decades than women have.

Discrimination against women in employment is accompanied by lower salaries and wages. Between 1955 and 1974 the percentage which full-time women workers' earnings were of men's earnings dropped from 64 percent to 57 percent. When the figures are broken down by broad occupational categories, the trends are uneven. The relatively few women who are in professional and technical occupations made some gains, while the far more numerous women in clerical, sales, and service work incurred substantial losses.

Some 12 million mothers in the United States, one-half of them with children under 6 years of age, now work outside the home, and public clamor has developed for the government to provide day-care facilities for them. Actually, the day-care movement is quite old, going back to the 1850s. By the early 1900s, there was a fairly large and well run day-care effort under the auspices of social workers who fought to keep it from being defined as charity, and as basically a program for unwed mothers. The depression of the 1930s virtually eliminated private welfare efforts, and during World War II day-care re-emerged as a means of reducing absenteeism from the job by working mothers. Unfortunately, federal agencies competed for control of the program, with the result being to limit what was accomplished. After World War II, day-care languished, again, until the current controversy emerged during the 1960s.

As part of the so-called federal "war on poverty," Head Start pre-school centers to provide compensatory education, adequate nutrition, and medical care for poor children were established. The major push, however, came from middle-class working mothers who demanded that the government relieve them of child-care responsibilities so that they could pursue occupational goals. By the 1970s, day-care had become a major political issue that was being argued in terms of need, philosophy, costs, and the special problems of the poor.

Advocates of day-care point out that there are fewer facilities today than there were during World War II, and that most working mothers are dissatisfied with their child-care arrangements. Most of those who favor day-care also argue that centers should be true child development centers and not merely offer custodial care. A major obstacle to this goal is that of cost. Official estimates indicate costs running as high as $2400 per child per year. Finally, it has become apparent that the needs of middle-class mothers and poor mothers are not synonymous. Politicians have used the well-intentioned efforts of middle-class women to force poor women off the welfare rolls, both to their disadvantage and to that of their children.

One area in which there is currently a great deal of agitation for improvement in the status of women has to do with opportunities for graduate education and for employment and equal opportunities on college and university faculties. The special problems faced by women in graduate schools become apparent when it is realized that over half of the women students are married to men who have some graduate education. Married women, it appears, have limited access to graduate training unless their husbands are, or have been, in graduate school. In addition, women graduate students are more likely to be part-time students than men are, and women graduate students are older than men. These differentials reflect both attitudes that women's needs should be subordinated to those of men and that women should delay pursuit of occupational goals at least until their children reach school age.

Graduate education, for large proportions of both men and women, is preparation for academic careers. Yet both the number of women on university faculties and the salaries paid them are very low. Affirmative action programs required by the federal government are beginning to correct these situations, but there are many knotty issues involved, and progress is slow.

One final area, in which no apparent progress has been made and where it is difficult to construct specific remedial programs apart from general revamping of our economic, educational, and familial institutions is the apparently greater social-emotional burden which married life places upon women. Studies show higher rates of mental illness among married women, which appear to be linked to the low prestige, the lack of visibility of, and the ambiguity of the role of housewife.

SUGGESTED READINGS

Arafat, Ibtihaj, and Yorburg, Betty, *The New Women: Attitudes, Behavior, and Self-Image*, Columbus, Ohio: Charles E. Merrill, 1976. Traces the changing status of women, and presents data on various aspects of their new life styles.

Freeman, Jo, *The Politics of Women's Liberation*, New York: David Mc-

Kay, 1975. Traces the development of women's liberation as a social movement.

Huber, Joan, *ed.*, *Changing Women in a Changing Society*, Chicago and London: The University of Chicago Press, 1973. Reprint of a special issue of the *American Journal of Sociology* devoted to reporting the results of research about women.

Safilios-Rothschild, Constantina, *Women and Social Policy*, Englewood Cliffs, New Jersey: Prentice-Hall, 1974. Synthesizes the relevant research as a basis for comprehensive policy recommendations for American society.

Sweet, James A., *Women in the Labor Force*, New York: Seminar Press, 1973. Uses U.S. census data to examine the employment status of married women. For the serious student.

FILMS

Day Care Today (Polymorph Films, 331 Newbury Street, Boston, Mass. 02115), 27 minutes. Shows three day-care centers, one community-oriented, one factory-related, and one university-connected, illustrating the potential for meeting the needs of preschool children and their families.

How To Make a Woman (Polymorph Films, 331 Newbury Street, Boston, Mass. 02115), 58 minutes. Film adaptation of an award-winning play. A strong, dramatic statement of what women's liberation is all about.

Modern Women: The Uneasy Life (Audio-Visual Center, Indiana University, Bloomington, Ind. 47401), 60 minutes, black and white. Explores the feelings of college-educated women about their various roles. Interviews with housewives and career women are included. The attitudes of men toward educated women also are explored.

QUESTIONS AND PROJECTS

1. Trace the changes which have occurred since 1950 in the proportions of workers in various occupational categories who are women. What do the data indicate about progress toward occupational equality?
2. Why is it necessary to compare the progress made by women to that made by men? What does such a comparison show, as far as employment in higher-status occupations is concerned?
3. How much do full-time women workers earn in comparison to men? Are there any trends evident here?

4. How many working mothers are there in the United States? How many of them have children under six years old?
5. Trace the day-care movement in America. What changes have there been in philosophy, groups served, and government participation?
6. What forces caused a resurgence of interest in the day-care movement during the 1960s? How well do the needs of middle-class mothers and poor mothers for day-care coincide?
7. What is the nature of the debate over whether day-care centers should be developmental or custodial? How is this related to costs?
8. How have politicians taken advantage of the drive for more adequate day-care facilities to suppress the poor further? Do you see any possibilities for future class conflict here?
9. Describe the handicaps faced by women in securing graduate education.
10. How are women discriminated against by universities? What is "affirmative action"? How does it work? What difficulties does it entail?
11. How do mental illness rates compare among married women and married men? Single women and single men? What factors in the role of housewife appear related to these differences?
12. Read George F. Gilder's *Sexual Suicide* (Quadrangle/The New York Times Book Co., 1973), and contrast thc arguments contained therein with the viewpoint of this chapter. Which do you think has the better of the disagreement? Why?

IV
The Family Life Cycle

12
Premarital Involvement

The phone call on Monday for a date on Saturday is going the same route as the party dress and the prom—out. In fact, the whole practice of dating seems to be disappearing.

That funny old way mom and dad did things—the nervous inital conversations on the phone, the old anticipation of the "big night," the worry over whether "he" would call is "sort of quaint," says Gil Speilberg, an Adelphi College student. And his friends shake their heads. Such things are unheard of.

The whole way of "dating" has changed. Instead of emphasizing couples, they emphasize themselves, with men taking less and less of the responsibility for planning and paying.

"It's just hanging around together," says blonde Kim Lovett, 15. "You don't need to make a deal of it." She and her high school friends—boys and girls—often travel in groups, and often end up at her house on a Saturday night just talking, being together. "I don't call it a party," she says quickly, "I call it company." . . .

[Howard Brody] says most of his friends do go out on "dates," as well as groups, that the main change is just that "you don't go through that formalized thing." The relationships are more depressurized, "more a mutual thing." "You know, inside—there's more understanding. They just don't want to play a game."

"Going steady," however, is still popular and some counselors, psychologists, and parents feel that young people either go in groups or go steady, with no inbetween. "I think that the young people who go steady are more likely to have one particular boyfriend or girlfriend. There's such a tremendous feeling of loneliness, such alienation," says Dr. George Goldman, a New York psychologist. "They get much more of a sense of fulfillment from one person they know they understand and who understands them."

But the way to find that person is no longer by "dating." It is more likely to begin in a casual group at someone's house, in a casual group that goes to the movies together, to get a pizza, or even to hang around a shopping center. "In school you don't get to know anybody," says Brody . . . "so you meet at someone's house or something and that's how a lot of relationships get started."[1]

Dating in the United States, at least among middle-class youth, has been changing rapidly. The changes are so recent and, as yet, are of such undetermined scope that it is difficult to say just where we stand. The quotation above reflects the "cutting edge," the newest teenage patterns. The quotation that follows reflects where American society has been and where many American youth probably still are.

. . . The "date" starts as an invitation from a young man to a girl for an evening's public entertainment, typically at his expense. . . . The entertainment offered depends upon the young man's means and aspirations, and the locality; . . . The male (the "escort") should call for the girl in a car (unless he be particularly young or poor) and should take her back in the car. . . .

"Showing the girl a good time" is the essential background for a "date," but it is not its object, as far as the man is concerned; its object is to get the girl to prove that he is worthy of love, and therefore a success. In some cases superior efficiency in dancing will elicit the necessary signs of approval; but typically, and not unexpectedly, they are elicited by talk. . . .

Since, on first "dates" the pair are normally comparative strangers to one another, a certain amount of autobiography is necessary in the hopes of establishing some common interest or experience, at the least to prove that one is worthy of the other's attention. These autobiographies, however, differ at most in emphasis, in tone of voice, from those which should accompany any American meeting between strangers. What distinguishes the "date" from other conversation is a mixture of persiflage, flattery, wit and love-making which was formerly called a "line" but which each generation dubs with a new name.

The "line" is an individual variation of a commonly accepted pattern which is considered to be representative of a facet of a man's personality. Most men are articulately self-conscious about their "lines" and can describe them with ease; they are constantly practiced and improved with ever differing partners. The object of the "line" is to entertain, amuse, and captivate the girl, but there is no deep emotional involvement; it is a game of skill.

The girl's skill consists in parrying the "line" without discouraging her partner or becoming emotionally involved herself. To the extent that she falls

1. Penelope McMullan, "Is the Date Becoming Extinct on the Teen Scene?" *Newsday*, March 7, 1971; copyright 1971, Newsday, Inc. Reprinted by permission.

for the "line" she is a loser in this intricate game; but if she discourages her partner so much that he does not request a subsequent "date" in the near future she is equally a loser. To remain the winner, she must make the nicest discriminations between yielding and rigidity.

The man scores to the extent that he is able to get more favors from the girl than his rivals, real or supposed, would be able to do.[2]

These two quotations reflect the paradoxical situation in the United States today. On the one hand, they acknowledge profound changes that have occurred over the past decade or so in the ways in which young men and women relate to one another. They are changes that are still in process, which are spreading, but which have not spread to the whole population yet. Swept in on the youth counterculture of the late 1960s and early 1970s, the new patterns may eventually replace the older ones. As of now, however, they exist side by side with the more traditional dating and sexual patterns. Ironically, the traditional patterns themselves were considered revolutionary when they emerged during the 1930s and 1940s.

THE TRADITIONAL DATING SYSTEM

As far back as the 1940s, young children had boy friends and girl friends, and "dated" in imitation of the somewhat more sophisticated patterns of adolescents. Several studies showed, for example, that the more adventurous youngsters of both sexes began dating by the ages of 10 to 12.[3] Arbitrarily, we shall refer to the activities of these youngsters and those through high school as early dating.

Norms Governing Early Dating

Many students may be surprised to learn that parents a generation ago had as many misgivings concerning the dating of their children as to-

2. Geoffrey Gorer, *The American People: A Study in National Character,* New York: W. W. Norton and Company, 1948, pp. 114–17.

3. Alan E. Bayer, "Early Dating and Early Marriage," *Journal of Marriage and the Family* 30 (Nov. 1968), pp. 628–32; Carlfred B. Broderick and Stanley E. Fowler, "New Patterns of Relationships Between the Sexes Among Preadolescents," *Marriage and Family Living* 23 (Feb. 1961), p. 29; William J. Cameron and William F. Kenkel, "High School Dating: A Study in Variation," *Marriage and Family Living* 22 (Feb. 1960), pp. 74–76; and S. Parvez Wakil, "Campus Dating: An Exploratory Study of Cross-National Relevance," *Journal of Comparative Family Studies* 4 (Autumn 1973), pp. 286–94.

day's parents have about coeducational dorms and living together. Parents saw the less desirable aspects of dating and viewed it both as risky and as poor preparation for marriage. Young people themselves often acted in terms of two conflicting sets of norms, one set explicit and the other set implicit.

Insight into how the system worked may be facilitated by pointing out that most boys and girls faced dating with some trepidation. Studies demonstrated that up to two-thirds of the members of both sexes were shy, self-conscious, ill at ease, and felt inadequate as dating partners.[4]

Consciously, most young people sought to use dating to become widely acquainted with members of the opposite sex and to develop standards for what they would desire eventually in marriage partners. Studies showed, for example, that the traits desired in dating partners were essentially the same ones that their parents believed to be important and included such things as being dependable, trustworthy, considerate, and pleasant; and taking pride in his/her appearance, desiring a normal family life, acting his/her own age, and being clean in speech and action.[5] Thus, the formal norms reflected a conscious awareness of the relationship between early dating, later pairing-off, and marriage.

Alongside these explicit norms, however, was another implicit set, the function of which was to facilitate competition for status within each sex and between the sexes. Young people competed not only for grades and possessions; they also competed for success with the opposite sex. Even then, long before the youth counterculture, the values of youth deviated substantially from those of their parents. Boys could acquire status by dating the prettiest, most popular, most wholesome girls in the class, but they might acquire even more status by dating the girls who liked to "neck" and with whom they might "score." Similarly, girls competed with other girls to date the outstanding boys in the class, but they also gained status by showing that they could date "dangerous" boys and handle them without giving in.[6]

4. Warren Breed, "Sex, Class and Socialization in Dating," *Marriage and Family Living* 18 (May 1956), p. 144; Carlfred B. Broderick, and Jean Weaver, "The Perceptual Context of Boy-Girl Communication," *Journal of Marriage and the Family* 30 (Nov. 1968), pp. 618–27; and John R. Crist, "High School Dating as a Behavior System," *Marriage and Family Living* 15 (Feb. 1953), p. 25.

5. Harold T. Christensen and Kathryn P. Johnsen, *Marriage and the Family*, New York: Ronald Press, 1971, pp. 160–63; and Lester E. Hewitt, "Student Perceptions of Traits Desired in Themselves as Dating and Marriage Partners," *Marriage and Family Living* 20 (Nov. 1958), pp. 344–49.

6. See Jerold S. Heiss, "Variations in Courtship Progress Among High School Students," *Marriage and Family Living* 22 (May 1960), pp. 165–70; Robert D. Herman, "The 'Go-

College Dating

The most perceptive analyst of traditional dating patterns among young adults, particularly college students, was Willard Waller, who observed them at Pennsylvania State University. First of all, Waller distinguished between dating and courtship.[7] Dating, he said, allowed a period of dalliance and experimentation between the sexes. Couples were encouraged to associate under all of the conditions which, in other times and places, had led directly into marriage. The norms governing dating, however, defined it as an end in itself. Fun, rather than marriage, was the intended outcome.

Prominent in dating was the seeking of what Waller called "thrills," physiological stimulation and the release of tension. Settings and activities conductive to thrill-seeking included dancing, petting, necking, the automobile, the amusement park, and drinking and attending the movies. The thrills sought were alleged to vary somewhat between the sexes. Beyond the general excitement widely sought by the young, men were inclined to seek thrills in sex. Women at this age were less often interested in sex for its own sake. They had been taught that they must resist involvement in it. Women often were intensely interested in dating itself and in other rewards which dating brought them.

What frequently developed was a more or less explicit bargaining relationship. The man provided the woman with satisfactions she wanted from dating, in the expectation that she would reward him with equivalent necking and petting on the way home.

What women wanted from dating was to advance themselves in the competition for status with other girls and to form relationships with more desirable men. The achievement of these aims required the man to spend money. He needed an automobile if he was to take the woman to the fashionable dating places and if he was to take her there in a fashion that would attract the desired attention. Both the car and the dating cost money; and the most desirable dating activities usually cost the most

---

ing Steady' Complex: A Re-Examination," *Marriage and Family Living* 17 (Feb. 1955), pp. 36–40; Charles W. Hobart, "Emancipation From Parents and Courtship in Adolescents," *Pacific Sociological Review* 1 (Spring 1958), pp. 25–29; and E. A. Smith, *American Youth Culture: Group Life in Teenage Society*, New York: The Free Press, 1962; and James S. Wittman, Jr., "Dating Patterns of Rural and Urban Kentucky Teenagers," *The Family Coordinator* 20 (Jan. 1971), pp. 63–66.

7. Willard Waller, "The Rating and Dating Complex," *American Sociological Review* 2 (Oct. 1937), pp. 727–34.

money. Although to make it explicit would have called forth a stout denial from both parties, the implicit assumption was that the more money the man spent (the better time he showed the girl) the more disposed the girl should be to show him affection later on.

Implicit in this bargaining relationship was a certain latent antagonism between the dating partners. Each sought the best bargain possible and—to a degree—each distrusted the other. This antagonism was illustrated by some of the stereotypes each sex held of the other. Thus, women often likened men to the octopus—all arms and hands seeking to intrude and overwhelm. In turn, men stereotyped women as gold-diggers—selfish, grasping creatures interested only in the money that they could induce their dates to spend on them. These stereotypes lurked below the surface and threatened to come out whenever either partner got the worst of it.

According to Waller, the bragaining worked out equitably in many cases and became the basis for a series of commitments that transformed dating into courtship and eventually led to marriage. Often, however, the bargaining was not equal and led to exploitation of one partner.

If the man had more bargaining power than his date he was in a position to exploit her sexually. He demanded necking and petting; the woman could either acquiesce or give up the relationship. Similarly, if the woman had superior bargaining power she could induce her date to take her where she wanted to go, when she wanted to go, and to spend money. Moreover, she was relatively free to concentrate on attracting men who were more desirable than her present dating partner.

Waller formalized this competitive-exploitative dating into what he called the "rating and dating complex." The rating and dating complex described the classification of students according to their desirability as dating partners, the pairing-off among them, and the resulting interaction on dates. The desirability of men was determined by such things as fraternity membership, a car, spending money, being a good dancer, dressing well, and being smooth in manners and appearance. Fraternity men ranked higher than nonfraternity men, and the fraternities themselves carried different status, with some fraternities ranking higher than others. Similarly, having an automobile was better than not having access to one. A new car was better than an old one, and a new sports car was better yet. The more the man approximated the campus ideal, the higher his status; and the more money at his disposal, the more successfully he could compete.

The traits establishing the desirability of women were similar. Sorority membership helped, and a top sorority was better than a lower one. Appearance and physical beauty were more important for women; the prettier and more shapely the woman, the more desirable she was as a date. She, too, should be a good dresser and able to dance well. Perhaps most important of all for women was their popularity. Men competed to date the girls whom other men wanted to date.

One further important characteristic for both sexes was the possession of a good "line," a pattern of verbal banter used to flatter, tease, and heighten the interest of the other. While the man might have been more aggressive, the woman, too, used compliments, flattery, sarcasm, and so on to keep her partner off balance—to prevent him from knowing her true feelings toward him and whether she wished to continue the relationship. Each partner worked to induce the other to become emotionally involved without him- or herself becoming involved in any way. The better one's line, the higher he or she ranked on the dating desirability scale.

"Rating" in dating was not altogether an individual matter. Rather, there existed an informal hierarchy on the campus, analogous to the class system in the larger society. Some people ranked at the very top of the dating desirability scale. Waller placed such men and women in a hypothetical Class A. Somewhat farther down the scale, there was a Class B, and then a Class C, Class D, and so on. At the bottom of the scale were people who were socially and physically unattractive.[8]

Persons at each level tended to date members of the opposite sex whose dating desirability was comparable to their own. Thus members of certain fraternities confined most of their dating to certain sororities; the highest-ranked fraternity and sorority members sought one another's company, the middle-ranked Greeks associated together, and the lowest-ranked groups interacted by default, if not by design. Similarly, people

8. See Mark Krain, Drew Cannon, and Jeffery Bagford, "Rating-Dating or Simply Prestige Homogamy? Data on Dating in the Greek System on a Midwestern Campus," *Journal of Marriage and the Family* 39 (Nov. 1977), pp. 663–74; Richard F. Larson and Gerald R. Leslie, "Prestige Influences in Serious Dating Relationships," *Social Forces* 47 (Dec. 1968), pp. 195–202; Gene N. Levine and Leila A. Sussman, "Social Class and Sociability," *American Journal of Sociology* 64 (Jan. 1960), pp. 391–99; Everett M. Rogers and A. Eugene Havens, "Prestige Rating and Mate Selection on a College Campus," *Marriage and Family Living* 22 (Feb. 1960), pp. 55–59; and Eldon E. Snyder, "Socioeconomic Variations, Values, and Social Participation Among High School Students," *Journal of Marriage and the Family* 28 (May 1966), pp. 174–76.

who lived in residence halls tended to date other residence-hall residents, town boys tended to date town girls, and so on.[9]

The rating and dating system functioned most smoothly, according to Waller, when people did date at their own levels. In this instance, the dating partners were likely to have approximately equal bargaining power, reducing the probability that either partner would be in a position to exploit the other. Since they had equal bargaining power, each commitment to the relationship made by one partner was contingent upon a compensating commitment made by the other partner, and the relationship progressed relatively rapidly toward marriage.

There were dysfunctional aspects of the system even when people dated at the same level. This was felt most by people who ranked low in the rating and dating complex. Aware of their low status, some men and women preferred not to date at all rather than to have to date at levels where they could compete successfully. There were many men and women who sat at home night after night because they were unwilling to accept their places in the system.

Not all dating, of course, took place within levels of the hierarchy; occasionally people dated up or down. When they did, the results were either functional, dysfunctional, or both. People who dated downward suffered loss of prestige for so doing but they also placed themselves in a better competitive position vis-à-vis the dating partner. Thus, the high-status male who dated a lower-ranking woman could demand more sexual favors from her. If she wished to continue the relationship, she had to accede to his demands. In the same way, a high-status woman who dated a lower-status man was relieved of some of the obligation for necking and petting that she might otherwise feel. She could use her escort manipulatively to take her places, while she established a relationship with a higher-status man.

In brief, dating outside one's own level was conducive to exploitation

9. Waller's theses provoked many attempts at empirical testing. See Robert O. Blood, Jr., "Uniformities and Diversities in Campus Dating Preferences," *Marriage and Family Living* 18 (Feb. 1956), pp. 37–45; Reuben Hill, "Campus Norms in Mate Selection," *Journal of Home Economics* 37 (Nov. 1945), pp. 554–58; John W. Hudson, and Lura F. Henze, "Campus Values in Mate Selection: A Replication," *Journal of Marriage and the Family* 31 (Nov. 1969), pp. 772–75; Marvin R. Koller, "Some Changes in Courtship Behavior in Three Generations of Ohio Women," *American Sociological Review* 16 (June 1951), pp. 366–70; Eleanor Smith and J. H. G. Monane, "Courtship Values in a Youth Sample," *American Sociological Review* 18 (Dec. 1953), pp. 635–40; William M. Smith, Jr., "Rating and Dating: A Restudy," *Marriage and Family Living* 14 (Nov. 1952), pp. 312–17; and S. Parvez Wakil, "Campus Mate Selection Preferences: A Cross-National Comparison," *Social Forces* 51 (June 1973), pp. 471–76.

of the lower-status partner. Waller formalized this idea as the "principle of least interest."[10] The principle of least interest holds that control in a relationship redounds to the one who has the least interest in continuing the relationship. Since this person has less to lose by discontinuing the relationship, demands can be made upon the other partner. The partner who has more to lose by discontinuing the relationship often has no choice but to yield.

Lower-status partners who were exploited in a relationship might suffer personality damage as a result. Sooner or later they had to face up to the fact that they were being exploited and revised their self-concepts downward. Even if they chose to break the relationship rather than to continue to submit to exploitation, they could not escape the definition that they were used by the other partner.[11] Some of the "man-haters" or "woman-haters" on any campus probably were people who had reacted to earlier exploitation by being defensive and thus protecting themselves against exploitation in the future. Their defensiveness testified to a low self-concept and also operated effectively to deny them the positive rewards of dating.

In one respect dating outside of one's own level proved quite functional for the individual and for the society at large. Such cross-class dating opened an avenue of upward social mobility to lower-status women. Men dated lower-status women—more often than women dated lower-status men—for the sexual advantages in such relationships. That college men dated town girls for this purpose was well known around many campuses.

At first, it appears that the advantages were all on the side of the male; and it is true that a great deal of sexual exploitation took place. How-

10. See also Kenneth N. Eslinger, Alfred C. Clarke, and Russell R. Dynes, "The Principle of Least Interest, Dating Behavior, and Family Integration Settings," *Journal of Marriage and the Family* 34 (May 1972), pp. 269–72; and James K. Skipper, Jr., and Gilbert Nass, "Dating Behavior: A Framework for Analysis and an Illustration," *Journal of Marriage and the Family* 28 (Nov. 1966), pp. 412–20.

11. The patterns used by the sexes, in confronting exploitation, differed and reflected the different operation of the masculine and feminine subcultures. The man who had to face the fact that his date had been using him was likely to go to his peer group and share his anguish with them. His friends were likely to identify with his plight, to sympathize, and to afford him catharsis. He felt better for having gotten it off his chest, in finding that his buddies had similar experiences, and in having reestablished solidarity with them. His buddies, in addition to sharing his contempt for the girl, might decide that it was their collective obligation to revenge themselves upon her.

In contrast, the girl who was sexually exploited was less free to seek the support of girl friends. The feminine subculture did not blame the boy who did the exploiting, but the girl who permitted it. Thus, the girl was denied the group support the boy had.

ever, some lower-status women more or less consciously risked exploitation in the hope that the men would become emotionally involved and that the relationships might lead to marriage. Since the social class of the couple was determined largely through the man, the woman had a great deal to gain in such relationships. It was not entirely unknown for women deliberately to become pregnant to make sure that the relationship led to marriage.

In the society at large, such cross-class dating helped to preserve the fluidity of the social class system. If the rating and dating complex served perfectly to restrict dating to persons of the same class level, it would have worked to make class lines more rigid and to restrict opportunities for upward mobility. As it was, the risk of exploitation sometimes was weighed against the chance of marrying into a higher class.

Waller's analysis of dating and his analysis of emotional involvement were not separable. Courtship, he said, grows out of dating as one or both partners become emotionally involved. The dating game, it will be recalled, called for each partner to titillate the other's emotions, but for both partners to resist involvement. Many relationships remained at this level for some time. Each partner, however, to some degree, pretended greater involvement than he or she actually felt. Especially the man attempted to convince the woman that he had fallen in love with her and, by this pretense, invited her to reciprocate. Under these circumstances, either partner might actually become involved and, when they did, a different pattern of interaction ensued.

Emotional involvement tended to lead the other partner, whether deliberately or not, into being exploitative. This is consistent with the principle of least interest—whoever is least interested in the relation tends to control it. In the ideal situation, the same process was going on in both partners at the same time; only neither knew it. The artificiality of the "line" resulted in both partners' being kept unsure of the other's true feelings. They continued in this fashion for a while, with each fearing being exploited and hoping that they were not. Tension built until suddenly it came out in a "lovers' quarrel," the essence of which was the open accusation of exploitation, and the function of which was to redefine the relationship at a new level.

We should point out here that the young men and women who were caught up in this intrigue consciously sought trustworthiness, consideration, and dependability in their marriage partners. When either the young man or woman was confronted with accusations of exploitation, they were likely to deny—to themselves as well as to the partners—that such was the case. In lovers' quarrels, the cards probably were stacked in favor of both partners' making further avowals of love and serious intent.[12]

With the resolution of this crisis, each partner gained security in the relationship, and the intimacy between them increased. The relationship moved along on a fairly even keel for a while, until one or both partners again became fearful of the extent of the other's involvement. Another quarrel then ensued, the relationship was redefined at a deeper level of involvement, and so on and on until it reached marriage. Either partner might arrive at marriage without knowing quite how he or she got there or whether, indeed, he or she intended this outcome.

Waller was not clear whether he believed that courtship was different in kind from the dalliance relationships of dating, or whether the latter tended to be transformed into the former. Probably, he conceived of dating as tending to become transformed into courtship with the development of emotional involvement. He indicated that while courtship had a directional trend, it could be arrested on any level or the relationship might be broken. Ordinarily, however, once involvement and commitment were under way, the couple could not return to an earlier level of involvement. The process was irreversible.

Central to Waller's analysis of courtship was the concept of "idealization." He believed that each partner tended to idealize the other; that under the influence of the "line," the partners created idealized images of others as they would have liked them to be. The man presented to the woman only that portion of his personality which was consistent with his idealized image of her. She, in turn, idealized him and behaved toward him selectively. Each reinforced the other's lack of objectivity, and they created a private world. Here emerges whatever truth there is

12. An interesting question is the degree to which the involvement led to the quarrel which then only made the involvement a matter of record and the degree to which the involvement actually grew out of the quarrel and the subsequent avowal of love. It is not difficult to imagine, for example, that the man actually had been exploiting the woman sexually. In accord with the masculine subculture, he might have been somewhat aware of what he was doing. In accord with the norms of family and community, however, he might avoid being too conscious of this exploitation. When the woman confronted him, in a lovers' quarrel, with her suspicions that he was using her, what she really did was to reinforce the family and community norms. The surprised young man could hardly do other than to deny exploitation and to profess love. Later on, he might think to himself, "You know, until tonight, I never realized that I loved her." Or, if he was a bit more sophisticated, he might think, "I wonder if I really do love her." If this analysis is correct, it may help explain the lingering feelings of doubt that many young men and women had as they approached marriage.

in the cliché that "love is blind." Waller described love as sentiment formation overcoming objectivity. The couple's absorption in one another becomes an *egosime à deux* that border upon *folie à deux*. Outsiders may see more clearly than the couple involved but, assuming that the relationship is a socially acceptable one, they ordinarily throw their support behind the relationship by treating them as a couple and helping to move them toward marriage.

Love Relationships

Waller's conception of love was inseparable from his analysis of courtship. He viewed love as deriving from the efforts of partners to involve the other, without becoming involved themselves. Love, he said, emerges when sentiment formation overcomes objectivity. Inherent in the development of love, he said further, was idealization. Without being aware of it, partners strive to be like the dating partners' idealized images of them. Thus, each assumes, during courtship, a stature and nobility that otherwise are not characteristic of them. What they are not able to achieve in actual behavior, the partners complete in their imaginations.

This conception of love views it as nonrational, or even irrational. The partners are caught up in a powerful flow of emotion and are swept along toward marriage. The further they travel, the less able they are to exercise critical judgment. By the time they reach marriage, they are hoplelessly caught up in their fantasies and, as a consequence, the early stages of marital adjustment involve the necessity to reorient the relationship to reality. Love, in this view, is a powerful force pushing people toward marriage. The unreality of it also poses later adjustment difficulties for them. Other views of love have been proposed.[13] Kolb took issue with those who would de-romanticize dating and courtship by arguing that love provides protection against the development of completely endogamous norms of mate selection.[14] If people did simply marry in accordance with the norms handed down by their parents, he said, the result would be an extreme conventionality and would stifle further personality growth or creativity in interpersonal relationships.

Biegel also rose to the defense of romantic love, claiming that it is an

13. Margaret E. Donnelly, "Toward a Theory of Courtship," *Marriage and Family Living* 25 (Aug. 1963), pp. 290–93; and Glenn M. Vernon and Robert L. Stewart, "Empathy as a Process in the Dating Situation," *American Sociological Review* 22 (Feb. 1957), pp. 48–52.

14. William H. L. Kolb, "Family Sociology, Marriage Education, and the Romantic Complex," *Social Forces* 29 (Oct. 1950), pp. 65–72.

expression "of a socio-psychological process that aims at the reconciliation of basic human needs with frustrating social conditions."[15] He pointed out, further, that romantic love is not only not harmful but that it has done much to raise the status of women and promote equality between the sexes. Love, in a society where there are few institutional supports for the permanency of marriage, aids and assists couples to adjust to the inevitable frustrations encountered in their relationships.

A different approach to the nature of love was taken by Foote, who views it as that relationship between two people which is most conducive to the optimum development of both. He sees the family as affording each person the opportunity to develop increasing competency in interpersonal relationships.[16] He argues against the idea of romantic love as an unstable emotion, and contends that people commit themselves to one another on the basis of real possibilities which can emerge in marriage with proper trust and cultivation.

The most impressive conceptualization of the sociological significance of love has been made by Goode.[17] He notes that definitions of love are notoriously open to attack because value judgments are implicit in them. Most of us, however, have had the experience of love just as we have experienced other emotions, such as disgust, melancholy, and hate.

Societies vary, says Goode, according to the degree to which they institutionalize love. In some societies love is treated as an aberration, while in other societies it is given such approval that it is almost shameful to marry without it. Traditional China illustrates the first approach, while middle-class America illustrates the second.

In all societies, according to Goode, love is potentially disruptive. Unless it is controlled in some way, it may lead to unions that would weaken the stratification and lineage patterns. To be effective the control must be exercised before love appears, and societies impose such control through child betrothal and marriage, rigid definition of eligible spouses, the isolation of young people from ineligibles, institutionalized chaperonage, and even through formally free courtship practices.

Our own society is an example of this last pattern. We encourage love play among youngsters and depend upon the influence of parents and the peer group to narrow gradually the individual's choice to a "socially

15. Hugo G. Biegel, "Romantic Love," *American Sociological Review* 16 (June 1951), p. 326.

16. Nelson N. Foote and Leonard S. Cottrell, Jr., *Identity and Interpersonal Competence: A New Direction in Family Research,* Chicago: University of Chicago Press, 1955.

17. William J. Goode, "The Theoretical Importance of Love," *American Sociological Review* 24 (Feb. 1959), pp. 38–47.

acceptable" member of the opposite sex. Parents "seek to control love relationships by influencing the informal social contacts of their children: moving to appropriate neighborhoods and schools, giving parties and helping to make out invitation lists, by making their children aware that certain individuals have ineligibility traits (race, religion, manners, tastes, clothing, and so on). Since youngsters fall in love with those with whom they associate, control over informal relationships also controls substantially the focus of affection."[18] Research has been done on the development of love relationships among college students. Hobart used a romanticism scale with students at a west coast, sectarian, coeducational college. He found that male romanticism increased as the men moved from no favorite date, to favorite date, to going steady, and to becoming engaged. Among women, however, no such trend appeared.[19] This was interpreted to mean that, in late adolescence, women were still less emancipated from their families than were men.

Other analyses of the data showed some tendency for both men and women to experience disillusionment as they move from courtship into marriage. The tendency was more pronounced among men than among women. Hobart was not able to establish a definite relationship between romanticism and subsequent disillusionment, but he did find indications that such a relationship may exist.[20] Thus, Hobart did find tendencies toward romanticism among men and he did find both men and women experiencing some disillusionment early in marriage.

Dean attempted to cast further light on the development of romanticism in courtship by relating it to emotional maturity or immaturity among college women. He found no relationship between romanticism and emotional maturity, but he did find that women of lower social status show more romanticism than women of higher social status.[21]

One final bit of evidence on love involvement is provided by a study

18. *Ibid.*, p. 45.

19. Charles W. Hobart, "The Incidence of Romanticism During Courtship," *Social Forces* 36 (May 1958), pp. 362–67. See also Eugene J. Kanin and Karen R. Davidson, "Some Evidence Bearing on the Aim-Inhibition Hypothesis of Love," *The Sociological Quarterly* 13 (Spring 1972), pp. 210–17; Eugene J. Kanin, Karen R. Davidson, and Sonia R. Scheck, "A Research Note on Male-Female Differentials in the Experience of Heterosexual Love," *The Journal of Sex Research* 6 (Feb. 1970), pp. 64–72; and David H. Knox, Jr., and Michael J. Sporakowski, "Attitudes of College Students Toward Love," *Journal of Marriage and the Family* 30 (Nov. 1968), pp. 638–42.

20. Charles W. Hobart, "Disillusionment in Marriage, and Romanticism," *Marriage and Family Living* 20 (May 1958), pp. 156–62.

21. Dwight G. Dean, "Romanticism and Emotional Maturity: A Preliminary Study," *Marriage and Family Living* 23 (Feb. 1961), pp. 44–45.

of 1000 engaged couples by Burgess and Wallin.[22] These authors believe there is some idealization in love affairs but that it is not universal and that, where it exists, it is not usually extreme. They present data on how much in love couples say they are at marriage and on whether they have ever had doubts about whether they wanted to marry their fiancé(e)s. Fewer than one-fourth of the men and women described themselves as head over heels in love, the answer that should reflect extreme idealization. Approximately 70 percent said that they were "very much" in love. Forty-one percent of the men and 48 percent of the women also indicated that, at some time, they had felt hesitation about marrying their fiancé(e)s.

Research has not yet provided final answers on the nature of love involvement before marriage. Neither has it indicated how functional or dysfunctional love is for subsequent marriage adjustment. In all likelihood, love involvement is variable, ranging from being completely overwhelmed to those cases in which the existence of love is rationalized only because of the public expectation that it should exist. The effects of love on marriage probably are no less variable.

TRADITIONAL PREMARITAL SEX PATTERNS

Most sexual involvements before marriage have occurred in the context of their broader associations in dating and courtship. These processes began, for many people, early in childhood and proceeded in fairly regular stages toward adult relationships and marriage.

Pre-adolescent Sex Play

That some boys and girls display signs of sexual arousal almost from birth and engage in sexual behavior before puberty are now widely accepted. Three decades ago, Kinsey reported that approximately 10 percent of boys were engaging in sex play by age 5, and more than 35 percent by age 10. Fifty-seven percent of older boys and men recalled sex play before adolescence.[23] Among girls, he found that 4 percent were

22. Ernest W. Burgess and Paul Wallin, *Engagement and Marriage*, Philadelphia: J. B. Lippincott Company, 1953. For a recent report, see Marion L. Schuman, "Idealization in Engaged Couples," *Journal of Marriage and the Family* 36 (Feb. 1974), pp. 139–47.
23. Alfred C. Kinsey, Wardell B. Pomeroy, and Clyde E. Martin, *Sexual Behavior in the Human Male*, Philadelphia: W. B. Saunders Company, 1948, pp. 162–65.

responding sexually by 5 years of age, 16 percent by age 10, and 27 percent before adolescence. Fully 14 percent of the girls had reached orgasm by age 13.[24]

Pre-adolescent sex play can be solitary, homosexual, or heterosexual. Kinsey reported that about 20 percent of boys began to masturbate by age 12 and that during adolescence the figure rose to over 90 percent. Masturbation was the most common source of first ejaculation and remained the commonest source of sexual outlet during early adolescence.[25] Some 12 percent of Kinsey's female sample had masturbated to orgasm by age 12, and by age 15 the figure had climbed to 20 percent.

An interesting comparison, although it goes beyond pre-adolescence, is that the total incidence of female masturbation reached only 62 percent, compared to over 90 percent among males. Moreover, the proportion of males who masturbated was highest during the late teens and declined thereafter, while the proportion of females who masturbated increased up to middle age.[26] Masturbation was also the technique through which the highest proportion of women were able to reach orgasm. Of the 62 percent of women who ultimately masturbated, 58 percent also reached orgasm. No other technique, including marital coitus, produced such a high proportion of orgasmic response.[27]

Among pre-adolescent boys, homosexual play was actually more common than heterosexual play. Kinsey attributed this to the greater accessibility of boys to other boys than to girls, to young boys' disdain for girls, and to the greater curiosity of boys about their genitalia. The incidence of girls who experienced homosexual play before adolescence, 33 percent,[28] actually exceeded the proportion who reported sexual arousal before adolescence, and reflects a fundamental fact about female sexual behavior: it need not reflect, or even be accompanied by, sexual arousal. At these early ages, the motivations often were those of simple nonerotic curiosity. Only a minority of boys or girls carried their homosexual experimentation into adolescence or adulthood.

24. Alfred C. Kinsey, Wardell B. Pomeroy, Clyde E. Martin, and Paul H. Gebhard, *Sexual Behavior in the Human Female*, Philadelphia: W. B. Saunders Company, 1953, pp. 103–5. See also Carlfred B. Broderick and George P. Rowe, "A Scale of Preadolescent Heterosexual Development," *Journal of Marriage and the Family* 30 (Feb. 1968), pp. 97–101.

25. *Sexual Behavior in the Human Female,* p. 173.

26. *Ibid.* For more recent data, see Ibtihaj Arafat and Wayne L. Cotton, "Masturbation Practices of Males and Females," *The Journal of Sex Research* 10 (Nov. 1974), pp. 293–307.

27. *Sexual Behavior in the Human Male,* p. 168.

28. *Sexual Behavior in the Human Female,* p. 114.

Altogether, Kinsey found preadolescent heterosexual play in about 40 percent of his male histories and in about 30 percent of his female histories. Much of this play, however, was not clearly separable from other forms of play in which children imitate adult behavior, and much of it was not overtly erotic. The "doctor" games, and "mother and father" games that were typical often were carried through without sexual arousal on the part of any of the participants. Such nonerotic play shaded off into frankly sexual play and attempts at intercourse.

Heterosexual Petting

In adolescence, male sex play became pointed to sexual arousal and satisfaction. The incidence and nature of petting were found to be closely related to educational level, with 84 percent of grade-school-level males and 92 percent of high-school and college-level males involved before marriage. Among the males with grade-school educations, petting tended to be a brief prelude to coitus, while among the better educated it often was prolonged without ever resulting in intercourse. Orgasm from petting occurred among 16 percent of the grade school-level males, 32 percent of the high-school-level males, and 61 percent of the college-level males who were not married by the age of 30.[29]

The statistics on petting among females are not strictly comparable to those among males, but show the proportion of women who became involved to be related to age, and to the behavior of the men involved. Approximately 40 percent of Kinsey's female sample had petting experience by 15 years of age, between 69 and 95 percent had experience by age 18, and almost 100 percent of the women petted before marriage. That women sometimes participated to please their male companions was shown by the fact that only 80 percent of the sample reported that they had been erotically aroused in petting. Thirty-nine percent of the women had responded to orgasm at least once.[30]

Petting by women was not related to educational level as among men, but was related to age at marriage. The higher-educated women who had more petting experience also married later. Finally, although there was no relationship between petting experience and religious faith (Catholic, Protestant, Jewish), religiosity did make a difference. Devout Catholics and Protestants were less likely to become involved in petting than were inactive members of either faith.[31]

29. *Sexual Behavior in the Human Male,* p. 537.
30. *Sexual Behavior in the Human Female,* p. 233.
31. *Ibid.,* p. 278.

Premarital Intercourse

Although the date is arbitrary, we will use the year 1965 as the dividing line between traditional and contemporary patterns of premarital sexual intercourse. A score of major studies provide estimates of the incidence of premarital intercourse for males and females from the 1920s to the 1960s. The Kinsey statistics, again, are the most comprehensive available and are generally consistent with those provided by other investigators.

As with petting, premarital intercourse among males was related to educational level. Among men who went to college, only 67 percent had intercourse before marriage; among those who did not go beyond high school, the figure was 84 percent; and among those who stopped with grade school, the proportion climbed to 98 percent. It appears that, at lower social levels, coitus was considered to be the "normal" way to pursue sexual interests, and most males became involved during their teens. At the upper levels, however, where greater value was placed upon virginity, petting often served as a substitute for coitus.[32]

Although the proportions of males having premarital intercourse did not change significantly over the 40 years under discussion, the proportion of women involved changed markedly, with the major change having occurred among women who reached adulthood at or shortly after World War I. Between 1915 and 1930, the percentage of women who had intercourse before marriage increased from approximately 15 percent to 30–35 percent. In Kinsey's total sample approximately 50 percent had intercourse before marriage. Most was confined to the year or two just before marriage, and a good proportion was had with the fiancé only. Forty-six percent had intercourse with the fiancé only, 41 percent had it with the fiancé and other men, while 13 percent had it with some other man but not with the fiancé.[33]

Again we find a relationship with religious background. Religiously inactive women were more likely to become involved than were the devout. Among those who had not married by age 35, over 60 percent of inactive Protestants and Jews, and 55 percent of inactive Catholics were involved. The corresponding figures for the devout were about 30 percent for Protestants and 24 percent for Catholics.[34]

32. *Sexual Behavior in the Human Male,* p. 552.

33. *Sexual Behavior in the Human Female,* pp. 292–98.

34. *Ibid.,* p. 304. These general findings have been confirmed in other studies. See Richard R. Clayton, "Religious Orthodoxy and Premarital Sex," *Social Forces* 47 (June 1969), pp. 469–74; Jerry D. Cardwell, "The Relationship Between Religious Commitment and Premarital Sexual Permissiveness: A Five Dimensional Analysis," *Sociological Analysis*

Beyond providing statistics on premarital intercourse, other studies related sex experience to dating patterns and love involvement. One study of 1157 students at the University of Florida, for example, found that while most men and women tended to date persons from their own social class and to have their most intimate sexual experience with those persons, of those who did date outside their own class, more of the men had their most intimate experiences with women of a lower social class while most of the women had theirs with men of the same or a higher class.[35] These general findings were confirmed in another study at a midwestern university where the incidence of premarital intercourse was highest among couples where the husband came from a higher social class than his wife, was intermediate where they were of the same social class, and was lowest where the wife was from the higher social class.[36]

The Florida research also classified dating relationships into those with acquaintances, friends, and lovers, classified respondents according to the most intimate sex behavior that they had experienced, and classified them according to "personal code," or the most intimate behavior they considered permissible with an acquaintance, friend, or lover. Far more men had had intercourse with friends and acquaintances (56 and 60 percent) than had done so with women they loved. Moreover, far more men considered coitus acceptable with friends and acquaintances than with lovers. Among women, the pattern was reversed. Very few women had intercourse with friends or acquaintances (6 percent and 2 percent), while more (17 percent) had done so with men whom they loved. The women believed that intimacy is more acceptable in love relationships and their behavior closely paralleled their standards.

---

30 (Summer 1969), pp. 72–81; Jean Dedman, "The Relationship Between Religious Attitude and Attitude Toward Premarital Sex Relations," *Marriage and Family Living* 21 (May 1959), pp. 171–76; Eugene J. Kanin and David H. Howard, "Postmarital Consequences of Premarital Sex Adjustments," *American Sociological Review* 23 (Oct. 1958), pp. 556–62; Frank Lindenfield, "A Note on Social Mobility, Religiosity, and Students' Attitudes Toward Premarital Sexual Relations," *American Sociological Review* 25 (Feb. 1960), pp. 81–84; Howard J. Ruppel, Jr., "Religiosity and Premarital Sexual Permissiveness: A Response to the Reiss-Heltsley Debate," *Journal of Marriage and the Family* 32 (Nov. 1970), pp. 647–55; Alfred J. Prince and Gordon Shipman, "Attitudes of College Students Toward Premarital Sex Experience," *Family Life Coordinator* 6 (June 1958), pp. 57–60; and Gordon Shipman, "The Psychodynamics of Sex Education," *The Family Coordinator* 17 (Jan. 1968), pp. 3–12.

35. Winston W. Ehrmann, *Premarital Dating Behavior*, New York: Holt, Rinehart and Winston, 1959, pp. 144–45.

36. Eugene J. Kanin and David H. Howard, *op. cit.*, p. 558.

Both dating and sex relationships in the traditional system were complicated by these attitudinal differences between men and women and by their elaboration into a distinctive masculine subculture. This masculine subculture exercised an imperious force in most boys' lives, which most girls—because there was no truly feminine equivalent of it—seldom understood. The most prominent symbol of the masculine subculture among boys and young men probably was the bull session.

Although other things were discussed and other functions were served, the primary functions of young male bull sessions were three. First, they provided opportunity to participate vicariously in, and to receive erotic arousal from, one another's sex lives. A typical procedure was for each boy to tell of a sexual exploit, embellishing it with exciting detail. As the session progressed, each narrator tried to top his predecessor, making himself appear more experienced than the others. This, then, was the second function; to permit each boy to enhance his conception of himself as a male, at the expense of the others.[37]

It might be appropriate here to point out that the primary ingredient in most bull sessions really was "bull." Honesty was not one of the virtues of a bull session. Honesty would have seriously hampered the first function of providing erotic stimulation, for most of the boys had neither as many nor as exciting experiences as they reported. With frequent, intense participation in bull sessions, however, the experiences which were fabricated took on reality for the teller until, after a while, he was not sure himself where experience left off and fantasy began. Each boy was likely to be somewhat aware that he was not wholly honest but, unfortunately, his insight did not enable him to be equally critical of his fellows' accounts. One result was that even while he was enhancing his ego by exaggerating his experiences, he was acquiring an uncomfortable sense of inadequacy by listening to and believing the wilder tales of his companions.

Thus the bull session's third function was brought into being. On the fringe of the session were likely to be one or more wide-eyed innocents. These honest boys' inability to get into the swing of things made them the logical scapegoats for the accumulating fears of inadequacy in other members of the group. One of the ringleaders might turn and say something like, "Hey, look at Joe. I'll bet he has never had any." Everyone

37. For current data bearing upon these phenomena, see David G. Berger and Morton G. Wenger, "The Ideology of Virginity," *Journal of Marriage and the Family* 35 (Nov. 1973), pp. 666–76; and Donald E. Carns, "Talking About Sex: Notes on First Coitus and the Double Sexual Standard," *Journal of Marriage and the Family* 35 (Nov. 1973), pp. 677–88.

then jumped on Joe and, by making him feel terribly inexperienced, they relieved somewhat their own feelings of inadequacy. The end result was to leave each boy with the idea that everybody else was making out better than he was and that not only should he get his share but he was not much of a man if he didn't.

Remember that these were not especially depraved young men. Many were middle-class boys who still had difficulty believing that their mothers enjoyed going to bed with their fathers and who would defend their sisters against any male who tried to make it with them. But the pressure on these young men was great. While they were dating women and trying to get to know them as people, they had to cope with more than their own natural sex urges and those of their dates. In addition, they were haunted by the need to acquire trophies to have for their own satisfaction and to be able to share in future bull sessions.

One byproduct of the masculine subculture apparently was some sexual aggression in dating. In one midwestern study the researchers distinguished five different degrees of erotic aggressiveness: attempts at necking; petting above the waist; petting below the waist; sexual intercourse; and attempts at sexual intercourse with violence or threats of violence. A total of 56 percent of the women reported that they had been offended by forceful attempts at intercourse and 6 percent by aggressively forceful attempts at intercourse that involved threats or the infliction of pain.[38]

Another finding was a significant association between offensiveness at a mild level of intimacy in casual dating relationships, and offensiveness at more intimate levels in engaged relationships. Apparently, an emotional relationship between the man and woman is no protection against sexual aggression. Offenses at the petting levels tended on the average to be repeated twice and, in half of the cases, attempts at intercourse were repeated. Only when attempted intercourse was accompanied by threats or violence were the relationships likely to be broken off.

Less than 6 percent of the offenses were reported to parents or academic authorities. The women were more inclined to reason with and rebuke the offender, and were more likely to keep secret the offenses at advanced intimacy levels. In a study of offenses at the high-school level, Kanin found that female proneness to sex aggression was related to the

38. Clifford Kirkpatrick and Eugene Kanin, "Male Sex Aggression on a University Campus," *American Sociological Review* 22 (Feb. 1957), pp. 52–58. See also Eugene J. Kanin, "Male Sex Aggression and Three Psychiatric Hypotheses," *The Journal of Sex Research* 1 (Nov. 1965), pp. 221–31.

absence of older male siblings.[39] Presumably, girls with older brothers are more likely to have some insight into the masculine subculture and are more able to prevent aggression from occurring.

EMERGING SEXUAL NORMS

In distinguishing between traditional and emerging premarital sex norms, we arbitrarily selected the year 1965 as the dividing point. Prior to 1965, the gradual increases in the number of young people having intercourse were largely the result of couples becoming involved soon before marriage. The dramatic increases that began to show up after 1965, however, reflected significant changes in public attitudes toward premarital sex. A Gallup Poll in August 1973, for example, compared attitudes at that time with those reported four years earlier. In 1969, two out of three adults said that premarital sex relations were wrong. By 1973, 48 percent said they were wrong, but 43 percent gave approval. Age and marital status were related to the opinions given. Only 29 percent of young people aged 18–29 said that premarital sex was wrong, and only 27 percent of single persons, compared to 51 percent of married persons, thought so.[40]

A Gallup Poll in 1972 found that most adults believe that teenagers should have access to birth control. More than 70 percent favored nationwide programs of birth control education in the high schools, and 54 percent approved of health programs to give free birth control to teenage girls who request it. Interestingly, Roman Catholics reported attitudes as favorable as those of non-Catholics.[41]

Teenage Sex Patterns

A study of 4220 Michigan high school students from the eighth grade through the twelfth grade found that 25 percent of the boys and 14 percent of the girls had already had coitus. Among the students who were 17 years old, 33 percent of the boys and 26 percent of the girls

39. Eugene J. Kanin, "Male Aggression in Dating-Courtship Relations," *American Journal of Sociology* 63 (Sept. 1957), pp. 197–204. See also Eugene J. Kanin, "Selected Dyadic Aspects of Male Sex Aggression," *The Journal of Sex Research* 5 (Feb. 1969), pp. 12–28.
40. Gallup Poll, syndicated column, Aug. 12, 1973. See also Danny E. Harrison, Walter H. Bennett, Gerald Globetti, and Majeed Alsikafi, "Premarital Sexual Standards of Rural Youth," *The Journal of Sex Research* 10 (Nov. 1974), pp. 266–77.
41. Gallup Poll, reported in *Family Planning Digest* 2 (Sept. 1973), pp. 4–5.

had had intercourse. This incidence is lower than Kinsey reported for 17-year-old boys, but more than twice as high as he reported for 17-year-old girls.[42]

Until recently, estimates of the incidence of intercourse among teenagers were suspect of possible biases in the samples studied. In 1971 and again in 1976, however, a team of researchers studied national probability samples of never-married girls, age 15–19. These samples provided the first reliable national estimates.

The percentages reporting having had intercourse in 1976, by race, are shown in Table 12.1. Eighteen percent of the 15-year-olds were sexually experienced and, by age 19, the figure rose to 55 percent. Sharp differences at every age level appeared between the races, with black girls being more experienced. At age 15, almost two-fifths of black girls, compared to one-eighth of white girls, had had intercourse. By age 19, over four-fifths of the black girls and almost half of the white girls had had coitus.[43]

Table 12.1. Percentages of unmarried women, 15–19 years of age, who have had coitus, by age and race, 1976

Age	(N = 654) *Black*	*White* (N = 1232)	*Total*
15	38.4	13.8	18.0
16	52.6	22.6	25.4
17	68.4	36.1	40.9
18	74.1	43.6	45.2
19	83.6	48.7	55.2
Total Sample	62.7	30.8	34.9

Source: Melvin Zelnik and John F. Kantner, "Sexual and Contraceptive Experience of Young Unmarried Women in the United States, 1976 and 1971," *Family Planning Perspectives* 9 (March-April 1977), p. 56.

42. Arthur M. Vener, Cyrus S. Stewart, and David L. Hager, "The Sexual Behavior of Adolescents in Middle America: Generational and American-British Comparisons," *Journal of Marriage and the Family* 34 (Nov. 1972), pp. 696–705; and Arthur M. Vener and Cyrus S. Stewart, "Adolescent Sexual Behavior in Middle America Revisited: 1970–1973," *Journal of Marriage and the Family* 36 (Nov. 1974), pp. 728–35. See also Patricia Y. Miller and William Simon, "Adolescent Sexual Behavior: Context and Change," *Social Problems* 22 (Oct. 1974), pp. 58–76.

43. It should be pointed out that these percentages do not tell us what proportion of all teenage girls have coitus before marriage. Since this sample is of never-married girls, it excludes girls already married, some of whom had premarital intercourse. Total figures for premarital intercourse, if they were available, would be higher than those reported here.

Although, at first glance, these percentages seem high and suggest possible teenage promiscuity, this is not the case. Almost half of the experienced girls, for example, had not had intercourse during the month prior to the interview, and another 25 percent had intercourse only once or twice. There were no appreciable differences in frequency between black girls and white girls. Moreover, half of the girls had had only one sex partner during their entire lives. This information was not available in 1976, but in 1971, about half of the girls of both races said that they had intercourse only with the man whom they expected to marry.[44]

The evidence, then, shows an increasing incidence of sexual intercourse among teenagers. It does not, however, support the stereotype of promiscuous, irresponsible behavior. Instead, the image conveyed is of young girls becoming involved in serious heterosexual relationships for which they are generally unprepared. This impression is strengthened by the fact that most of the girls were quite ignorant of reproduction and made ineffective use of contraception. Some 76 percent of the black girls and 56 percent of the white girls, in 1976, were unable to answer multiple choice questions about the time of greatest pregnancy risk. Almost three-fourths either never used contraceptives or used them only occasionally.[45]

College Sex Patterns

While the younger girls in the national study were high school girls, many of the 18- and 19-year-olds were college students. Hence, our distinction between teenage and college sex patterns is blurred. Nevertheless, we should note that the shifts in attitudes toward, and participation in, premarital intercourse already demonstrated for the general population are especially pronounced among college students.

One study gave an attitude scale to college students in 1968 and then gave it to comparable groups of students again in 1972, finding that both sexes showed considerably more liberal attitudes toward premarital

44. John F. Kantner and Melvin Zelnik, "Sexual Experience of Young Unmarried Women in the United States," *Family Planning Perspectives* 4 (Oct. 1972), pp. 9–10.

45. One interesting study suggests that pregnancy often is a function of the unavailability of contraceptives and that well-meaning mothers who oppose premarital sex hoping to protect their daughters against pregnancy may actually be making them more vulnerable to it. See Frank F. Furstenberg, Jr., "Birth Control Experience Among Pregnant Adolescents: The Process of Unplanned Parenthood," *Social Problems* 19 (Fall 1971), pp. 192–203.

coitus in 1972.[46] Other studies showed behavioral changes got under way about 1965. One study compared students at a southern university in 1975 with students at the same university in 1970 and 1965. The three waves of the study showed that the increases in heavy petting and sexual intercourse that were evident between 1965 and 1970 continued through 1975. The increases were larger among women than among men. The percentages engaging in heavy petting, for example, were 71 percent for men in 1965 and 80 percent in 1975. Among women there was an increase from 34 percent to 73 percent. The proportions of men with coital experience increased from 65 percent in 1965 to 74 percent in 1975. Among women, there was an increase from 29 percent to 57 percent.[47]

Most premarital intercourse for women before 1965 appears to have been the result of relationships between soon-to-be-married couples, and much premarital sex today still is of that variety. The dramatic increase since 1965, however, appears to be more the result of intercourse in relationships of affection and intimacy, but where there is no formal or informal commitment to marriage. This was the conclusion of investigators who found that the proportion of nonvirgins at one western university increased from 48 percent to over 60 percent between 1965 and 1970.[48]

46. James W. Croake and Barbara James, "A Four Year Comparison of Premarital Sexual Attitudes," *The Journal of Sex Research* 9 (May 1973), pp. 91–96. For other supporting data, see Robert R. Bell and Jay B. Chaskes, "Premarital Sexual Experience Among Coeds, 1958 and 1968," *Journal of Marriage and the Family* 32 (Feb. 1970), pp. 81–84; Frank W. Finger, "Changes in Sex Practices and Beliefs of Male College Students Over 30 Years," *The Journal of Sex Research* 11 (Nov. 1975), pp. 304–17; Robert A. Lewis, "Parents and Peers: Socialization Agents in the Coital Behavior of Young Adults," *The Journal of Sex Research* 9 (May 1973), pp. 156–70; William F. Eastman, "First Intercourse," *Sexual Behavior* (March 1972), pp. 22–27; Eleanore B. Luckey and Gilbert D. Nass, "A Comparison of Sexual Attitudes and Behavior in an International Sample," *Journal of Marriage and the Family* 31 (May 1969), pp. 364–79; Peter O. Peretti, "Premarital Sexual Behavior Between Females and Males of Two Middle-Sized Midwestern Cities," *The Journal of Sex Research* 5 (Aug. 1969), pp. 218–25; and Ira E. Robinson, Karl King, Charles J. Dudley, and Francis J. Clune, "Change in Sexual Behavior and Attitudes of College Students," *The Family Coordinator* 17 (April 1968), pp. 119–23.

47. Karl King, Jack O. Balswick, and Ira E. Robinson, "The Continuing Premarital Sexual Revolution Among College Females," *Journal of Marriage and the Family* 39 (Aug. 1977), pp. 455–59. For evidence of comparable changes among Canadian students, see Charles W. Hobart, "Sexual Permissiveness in Young English and French Canadian Students," *Journal of Marriage and the Family* 34 (May 1977), pp. 292–303.

48. Mervin B. Freedman and Marjorie Lozoff, "Some Statistical Background," *Sexual Behavior* (Nov. 1972), pp. 30–32.

The most dramatic and comprehensive findings come from a survey of 2026 people in 24 urban areas, conducted for the Playboy Foundation in 1973. They found that premarital intercourse is beginning earlier in life and is occurring more frequently. For men, the chief differences were in age of initiation. More than half of the men with some college education had experienced coitus by age 17, twice as many as Kinsey reported a generation earlier. For single women under 25, about 75 percent had had coitus compared to only 33 percent in Kinsey's day. Among the youngest married women (ages 18–24), fully 80 percent had had intercourse before marriage.[49]

EMERGING RELATIONSHIP NORMS

Changes in the specifically sexual behavior of young people have been accompanied by changes in the larger context in which that behavior occurs. We will discuss three general areas of change: college dating, coed dorm living, and living together.

College Dating

To some degree, spontaneous group activity has replaced the formal dating patterns of earlier generations. Pairing off still occurs, however, and as people move into adulthood there is more activity by pairs and more of what still is recognizable as dating. Insight into the changes that have been taking place among college students is provided by a study of the Harvard University classes of 1964 and 1974.

Students were asked to rank six reasons for dating: recreation; having an understanding listener; sex; finding a wife; being seen with girls who would enhance one's reputation; and finding a female friend. They were also asked to rate qualities of a good date, such as being uninhibited, artistic, altruistic, and being intelligent and showing it. Finally, they rated dating activities as to importance. Activities rated included sitting

49. *Time*, Oct. 1, 1973, pp. 63–64. For similar findings at a major southern university, see Karl E. Bauman and Robert R. Wilson, "Sexual Behavior of Unmarried University Students in 1968 and 1972," *The Journal of Sex Research* 10 (Nov. 1974), pp. 327–33; and J. Richard Udry, Karl E. Bauman, and Naomi M. Morris, "Changes in Premarital Coital Experience of Recent Decade-of-Birth Cohorts of Urban American Women," *Journal of Marriage and the Family* 37 (Nov. 1975), pp. 783–87.

around talking, watching TV, going to nightclubs, attending lectures, engaging in sports, taking walks, and making love.[50]

Based upon responses of the class of 1964, four dating patterns were identified. In the *companion* pattern, emphasis was upon informal pair activities and finding a friend and sympathetic listener. These were friendships in which the activities were private and intimate. *Instrumental* relationships approximated the traditional dating relationship, with emphasis upon sexual conquest and the enhancement of one's reputation. The girls were taken to dances, nightclubs, football games, and so on, where they could be seen and appreciated. In what researchers labeled the *traditional* pattern, the most important goal was to find a wife. Girls of good reputation, sexual inhibition, and comparable social status were sought. Finally, the *intellectual* dating pattern may be most common at elite colleges. In it, emphasis was upon finding a girl who was the man's intellectual equal and sharing intellectual discussions with her.

The results from the class of 1974 showed that changes had occurred over the decade. The companion pattern still emphasized finding a friend, but the variety of activities had broadened; recreational activities of many sorts were now engaged in together. The intellectual dating pattern had not changed much except that it now seemed to be less of a defensive mechanism for brilliant, but socially inadequate men.

The instrumental dating pattern had changed substantially. There was less emphasis upon showing off conquests and more emphasis upon political activities, taking drugs, and making love. The "bad girl" syndrome was still there, but the emphasis was now upon being "swingers," rather than "studs." The traditional dating pattern had changed most of all, with men generally no longer being interested in socially acceptable women, but being attracted to women who are liberated and unconventional. They now wanted women who would support their own opposition to traditional social patterns.

These changes in the four dating patterns do not tell us what proportions of the men follow the various patterns and, indeed, the study does not provide us with hard data on that score. We are told that the instrumental and intellectual patterns have not changed much in popularity, while the popularity of the companion pattern has increased greatly, as that of the traditional pattern has declined almost to zero.[51]

50. Rebecca S. Vreeland, "Sex at Harvard," *Sexual Behavior* (Feb. 1972), pp. 3–10.
51. *Ibid.*, p. 7.

Coed Dorm Living

In the late 1960s, some colleges and universities began to move toward eliminating the segregation of men and women students in separate dormitories. Locating men and women in adjacent wings of the same dormitory was followed by placing them on alternate floors and, in some instances, by assigning rooms randomly by sex. In some cases, live-in faculty counselors were provided, graduate students sometimes served in that capacity, and in other cases there were no special counselors at all. The trend was consistent with what was happening in heterosexual relationships generally; a trend toward informality, spontaneity, and intimacy outside the framework of traditional dating.

Coed living proved to be a rewarding experience to many participants, and a quite unsatisfactory one to a few. Since coed living almost always is voluntary, the overwhelmingly favorable response may be partially a result of the selection of who lives in coed dorms; those who are ready for such intimacy, choose it. In any event, the dynamics of coed living are quite complex.

Men and women agree that settling into coed living occurs rather easily and naturally. Women who are used to living with fathers and brothers, and men who are accustomed to mothers and sisters, don't react that strongly to having the opposite sex in the next room, or on the next floor. If anything, women may adjust more quickly than men, as when men ogle or snicker the first few times a girl walks down the hall in her bathrobe or nightgown. Men don't automatically escape the effects of the masculine subculture just by moving into a coed dorm.[52]

Generally, however, coed living fosters cross-sex friendships that are, at the same time, casual and deep. Men soon think nothing of walking into women's rooms, and vice versa, and talking seriously about whatever happens to be on their minds—something that seldom happens in traditional living situations. Similarly, there are no barriers to a woman or a group of women inviting one or more men to join them on almost any kind of outing. Spontaneous, group activity tends to replace many formal dating activities. Most coed dorm men express relief at not having to call women for dates and having to be on display when they call for them and return them at the end of the evening.

Women residents often report satisfaction at being known to their male co-residents as whole persons and not being treated primarily as

52. Harold I. Lief and Michael B. Guthrie, "What It's Like To Live in a Coed Dorm," *Sexual Behavior* (Dec. 1972), p. 21.

sexual objects as so often happens in more segregated contexts. On the other hand, some women report, wistfully, that they get tired of being treated "as one of the guys," and that they miss being sought out by specific men who think that they are something special. In more formal terms, they fear that the coed living situation encourages them to lose their identities as women.

Both sexes also report paradoxical experiences with sex. On the one hand, the physical and social situations encourage sexual involvement and make it acceptable. Both men and women tend to view sex in the context of their total relationships and are relieved of pressures either "to score" or to feign reluctance when they actually want to become involved. Curiously, however, they often find that friendship gets in the way of development of the relationship into a sexual one. Each partner tends to hold back for fear of being rejected, or out of fear of jeopardizing the friendship. Some groups report the emergence of informal exogamous tendencies, the development of sexual relationships outside the socially intimate residential group.

Some persons also show distress over pressures to accept more sex, or become involved in more sex, than they are ready for. At the least involved level, men and women are annoyed when their roommates "move in" their boyfriends or girlfriends and intrude upon their privacy and convenience. Because they don't have other places to go, they simply have to sit there, uncomfortably, while the couple engage in love play. The norms of the coed living situation almost forbid them from expressing disapproval. If they do object, most of the other residents are likely to believe that the situation reflects the objector's hang-ups more than lack of consideration by the involved couple.

At a deeper level, feelings of inadequacy as a man or as a woman may be generated in persons who do not become involved. The pressures are akin to those of the male in the traditional situation who does not score, or the woman who is not sought after for dates. Ironically, the changed sexual attitudes over the past generation have reversed the situations of sexually inexperienced and experienced persons. Formerly, it was those who had had intercourse, particularly women, who were defensive and guilty about it. Now it may be those, particularly men, who have not had coitus who suffer self doubts and anxiety.[53]

53. See Richard H. Driscoll and Keith E. Davis, "Sexual Restraints: A Comparison of Perceived and Self-Reported Reasons for College Students," *The Journal of Sex Research* 7 (Nov. 1971), pp. 253–62; and Mary W. Hicks and Donald Taylor, "Sex on Campus: The Student's Dilemma," *Sexual Behavior* (Mar. 1973), pp. 43–47.

The most surprising thing about coed dorm living, perhaps, is not that some men and women have casual sex relationships or experiment with their new found sexual freedom, but that so many are so conventional and monogamous. Attitudes of exclusiveness and fidelity operate at several different levels.

First, some men and women find themselves caught between the pressures toward sexual involvement in their day-to-day situations and their loyalties to boyfriends and girlfriends who are at other colleges, back home, or where have you. In some cases, they reject sexual overtures from dorm mates whom they like and to whom they are attracted, without telling the other person why, thus unintentionally creating anxieties and otherwise complicating the relationships.[54] Knowing of their own temptation to become involved with others, the loyal person may also wonder whether the absent boyfriend or girlfriend is being equally faithful.

In other cases, the coed dorm resident becomes sexually involved and then suffers anxiety and guilt, both at the inability to become deeply involved with the sexual partner and at the disloyalty to the absent friend. The situation is complicated further when the friend comes for a visit and learns of the other relationship. Several outcomes are possible. All three persons, intellectually committed to ideals of openness and nonexclusiveness in relationships, may simply find themselves without clear guidelines concerning how to behave, and have doubts about themselves and about the relationship heightened. Apparently more often, at least one of the three participants is deeply involved in the relationship and finds himself or herself hurt and bewildered.

Both men and women express fear about the possibility of "using" their dorm mates sexually, holding ideals of freedom and spontaneity but still feeling that sexual involvement implies emotional involvement and some responsibility for the welfare of the other person. A surprising number of persons of both sexes, when it comes right down to it, find it very difficult to accept casual sex.

Finally, many persons of both sexes report that their primary search is for love and affection, rather than for sex alone. They seek exclusive relationships of the sort that embody the highest ideals of married love.

54. Disdain by today's students for the old rating and dating complex has not eliminated the fact that some people are more desirable than others and that some men and women will be rejected as sexual partners even in the intimacy of coed living. In segregated living, these unfortunates at least are spared the pain of being direct witnesses to others' successes.

Not all relationships turn out that way, of course, and when intimate relationships break, it often is traumatic for one or both partners. There may be serious feelings of loss and damaged self-esteem, all complicated by the fact that one's dorm mates know what has happened and by having to continue to live in the same group situation.

Living Together

Even the most casual observer can scarcely avoid knowing that many unmarried couples around college and university campuses these days are living together. The openness with which they do so and the degree to which university officials, landlords, and others ignore the matter stands in marked contrast to the situation just a few years ago. There are no comprehensive statistics available on how many couples live together, but scattered evidence indicates that the number is sizable and growing.

On the national level, the U.S. Census Bureau reports that the number of single adults living with a member of the opposite sex approximately doubled between 1970 and 1976. In 1976, there were 660,000 such households involving 1.3 million persons. Almost half of these people had never been married, and 72 percent of the males were under 45 years old. Lest the proportion of people living together appear greater than it is, it should be pointed out that these households constitute only about one percent of all households. It should be emphasized, too, that some of these people are not lovers, but are roomers, employees, and others.[55]

Careful study has been done of the incidence of dynamics of couples living together around university campuses. One study of 762 students at a large, urban, northeastern university, in 1971, found that approximately one-fifth of them were living with a member of the opposite sex. More surprising is the fact that almost four-fifths would enter such an arrangement if they had the opportunity. Men and women expressed equally favorable attitudes, while older students and those with strong religious backgrounds were less favorable.[56]

At the other end of the country, 29 percent of the men and 18 percent

55. "Marital Status and Living Arrangements: March 1976," *Current Population Reports,* Series P-20, no. 306, Jan. 1977, pp. 4–5. See also Judith L. Lyness, Milton E. Lipetz, and Keith E. Davis, "Living Together: An Alternative to Marriage," *Journal of Marriage and the Family* 34 (May 1972), pp. 305–11.

56. Ibtihaj Arafat and Betty Yorburg, "On Living Together Without Marriage," *The Journal of Sex Research* 9 (May 1973), pp. 97–106.

of the women in a random sample of 300 southwestern university students had cohabited. Moreover, almost 60 percent of the men and 35 percent of the women answered "yes" to the question, "would you want to?"[57] Back northeast again, data from two samples of Cornell University students showed 28 percent and 34 percent already having lived together and that 40 percent or more would do so before completing college.[58] Finally, a survey of 1191 students at state universities in seven different geographical regions showed that about 25 percent, 34 percent of the males and 23 percent of the females, had lived with someone. Few regional differences were evident.[59]

Reasons for Living Together. At the most general and idealistic level, young people are disenchanted with the superficiality of traditional dating and the exploitation of sex. They strive for realism in their relationships, without the complications of marriage.[60] Part of it simply is a matter of expediency; the couple already are having intercourse, and it is too much trouble for one of them to get up late at night and return home. Other practical reasons include the fact that it is less expensive, one partner has no place to go because someone else is living with his or her roommate, there is curiosity about what it would be like, and there is a desire to test the relationship.[61]

Two studies found motivations to vary by sex. In one, 36 percent of the men said that their primary motivation was sex,[62] and the other study reported that women are more faithful in living together arrangements and are more satisfied with them.[63] Thirty percent of the women at the northeastern university reported their primary motivation was marriage; if they didn't live with him, someone else would. Overall, 80 percent of the men and over 67 percent of the women said that eventual

57. John W. Hudson and Lura F. Henze, "A Note on Cohabitation," *The Family Coordinator* 22 (Oct. 1973), p. 495; and Lura F. Henze, and John W. Hudson, "Personal and Family Characteristics of Cohabiting and Noncohabiting College Students," *Journal of Marriage and the Family* 36 (Nov. 1974), pp. 722–27.
58. Eleanor D. Macklin, "Heterosexual Cohabitation Among Unmarried College Students," *The Family Coordinator* 21 (Oct. 1972), pp. 463–72.
59. Donald W. Bower and Victor A. Christopherson, "University Student Cohabitation: A Regional Comparison of Selected Attitudes and Behavior," *Journal of Marriage and the Family* 39 (Aug. 1977), pp. 447–53.
60. David H. Olson, "Marriage of the Future: Revolutionary or Evolutionary Change?" *The Family Coordinator* 21 (Oct. 1972), pp. 383–93.
61. Eleanor D. Macklin, *op. cit.*, p. 466.
62. Ibtihaj Arafat and Betty Yorburg, *op. cit.*, p. 101.
63. John W. Hudson and Lura F. Henze, *op. cit.*

marriage was not their goal. What few men did give marriage as a reason were cynical about it: "You wouldn't buy a new car without trying it out first!" About two-thirds of both sexes said that they were not sure of their original motives, and slightly over half did not know whether they would eventually marry one another.[64]

Circumstances of Living Together. Living together is less the result of deliberate planning than of gradually drifting into it. Among the Cornell couples, staying together one night at a time was followed by spending weekends together and then by adding one or more nights in between. The researcher classified couples as living together when they spent four or more nights a week together for three consecutive months.[65]

Most often, the girl partially moves in with her boyfriend in an apartment or house he shares with others. Usually, she keeps her own quarters, keeps some of her clothes there, receives her mail, and eats some meals there. This helps conceal the relationship from her parents, helps her maintain relationships with other women, and provides a refuge when the relationship with the boyfriend is not going well. Among Cornell couples, about half spent seven nights a week together and in the other half, the woman spent occasional nights at her own residence.

When asked about their relationships with the men with whom they were living, about half the Cornell women said that theirs was a strong and exclusive affectionate relationship. They resisted the idea that they were going steady. About one-third of the women said that they were also interested in other dating relationships. About 10 percent were tentatively or formally engaged. Most women intended to continue the relationships as long as they were mutually rewarding, many thought of marriage as an ultimate possibility, but most resisted the idea of a definite commitment to marriage.[66]

Few couples fully share finances. The man generally keeps his income, and the woman hers, sharing some expenses of food and entertainment. This arrangement symbolizes and ensures the woman's independence. Some household chores, such as doing the laundry and

64. Ibtihaj Arafat and Betty Yorburg, *op. cit.*, pp. 101–2.
65. Eleanor D. Macklin, *op. cit.* For a study using a more flexible definition of living together, see Dan J. Peterman, Carl A. Ridley, and Scott M. Anderson, "A Comparison of Cohabiting and Noncohabiting College Students," *Journal of Marriage and the Family* 36 (May 1974), pp. 344–54.
66. *Ibid.*, pp. 466–67.

shopping, are shared, but women still do most of the cleaning and cooking and some of them resent it.[67]

Advantages and Problems. Most participants in these relationships believe them to be successful, maturing, and pleasant. Even couples especially conscious of problems in their relationships emphasize how much emotional growth they have produced. Most also state that they would not consider marriage without having lived together first.

Many couples also are frank about their problems. Among the Cornell couples, the major emotional problem was the tendency for one or both partners to become overinvolved, overdependent upon the relationship, and isolated from other friends. Some people felt "trapped," and others believed that they were being "used" by their partners. Over two-thirds of the couples reported no such problems, however, and no guilt. Where guilt was found, it most often stemmed from having to conceal the relationship from parents.

About two-thirds of the women encountered some sexual problems. Differing degrees of or periods of sexual interest were reported most frequently, followed closely by lack of orgasm. Fear of pregnancy, in spite of almost universal contraception, was reported in over two-fifths of the cases. In spite of the sexual problems, however, more than three-fourths of the women described their relationships as sexually satisfying.

In virtually all studies, relationships with parents are a major problem. Fear of discovery, guilt over deceiving the parents, and ultimatums from parents who learn of the situation, all are common. Over two-thirds of the Cornell women had tried to conceal their relationships from parents by not telling them everything, distorting the truth, or by using elaborate schemes to prevent discovery. About half of the women believed that they had been successful in concealing cohabitation, about one-fourth were sure their parents knew, and the other one-fourth were unsure whether their parents knew. The mens' parents were much more likely to know and were less likely to cause problems over it.

SUMMARY

The traditional dating system in the United States emerged from the 1920s into the 1940s. Early dating was governed by explicit norms that

67. See Rebecca Stafford, Elaine Backman, and Pamela Dibona, "The Division of Labor Among Cohabiting and Married Couples," *Journal of Marriage and the Family* 39 (Feb. 1977), pp. 43–57.

emphasized its use for becoming acquainted with members of the opposite sex in eventual preparation for the selection of marital partners and by implicit norms that focused upon competition for success and the enhancement of self-esteem.

College dating patterns were analyzed by Waller, who distinguished between dating, a dalliance relationship, and serious courtship. Dating was characterized by a quest for thrills, men bargaining for sexual favors while women sought to be sought after. When bargaining power was unequal, exploitation of the less successful partner often resulted. This status system was conceptualized as the "rating and dating complex," in which such characteristics as fraternity or sorority membership, dressing well, having smooth manners and a car were important. Physical attractiveness was also important for women. For both sexes, the possession of a good "line"—verbal banter designed to titillate the other—was important.

When people did not date at their own level in the hierarchy, the lower-status person was likely to be exploited, sometimes with unfavorable personality consequences. Cross-class dating, however, also opened the possibility of upward mobility to lower-class girls, if they could secure marriage.

Courtship developed when the partners began to succumb to one another's blandishments. If uneven, the involvement might be accompanied by exploitation of the more involved partner, according to the "principle of least interest." The balance between the partners tended to be restored through lovers' quarrels which produced increasing commitment to the relationship and led toward marriage. Involvement was accompanied by idealization of each partner by the other.

Theories of romantic love show how it is both functional and dysfunctional for the larger social system. It threatens the society's endogamous norms and follows idealization with disillusionment. At the same time, it prevents the mate selection system from becoming overly rigid.

Research verified the existence of romanticism during courtship, finding more of it among men than among women. It also showed some disillusionment with movement into marriage. Most couples, however, profess not to be unrealistically in love at the time of marriage. People approach marriage by different routes and with different degrees of involvement.

Data a generation or more ago showed that some boys and girls display sexual interest from an early age and that numbers of both sexes engage in sex play before puberty. Most preadolescent sex play is masturbation, some of which is motivated as much out of curiosity as out of definite erotic interest. Beginning in adolescence, petting became prominent, and the goals were explicitly sexual arousal and satisfaction. Among men, the incidence of petting was positively associated with educational level, and among women it was inversely related to church attendance.

Data on premarital intercourse also showed relationships with educational level and religiosity. The incidence of premarital coitus among men has not changed much over the past few generations, but more women have become involved. Most intercourse is confined to the year or two before marriage, and a good proportion is with the fiancé only. Other studies have shown premarital intercourse is more likely when the man is of higher class than the woman, and that men accept it more in casual relationships, while women accept it more readily in serious ones.

Drastic changes in premarital sex began to appear around 1965, with more intercourse occurring and there being less public condemnation of it. Among young teenagers, the portrait emerges of young girls in serious heterosexual relationships, usually rather monogamous, often without adequate knowledge of reproduction or contraception.

Comparable increases in intercourse have occurred among college students, whose dating includes less emphasis on conquest and more emphasis on sharing and making love. These patterns are reflected in and encouraged by coed dorm living, which is approved by most participants. Coed living is complicated, however, by ambivalence about combining friendship with sex, and by pressure, to become involved, upon people who are not yet ready for it. One surprising thing about coed dorm living is not that some people experiment with casual sex, but that so many people still seek deep interpersonal relationships and accept sex mostly in that context.

The trend of unmarried students openly living together, on campus or off, also is an emerging pattern. Several studies show sizable proportions of men and women having this experience before graduation. Participants consider it less artificial than traditional dating and do not see it culminating, automatically, in marriage. Men are motivated more by sex and women are motivated more by the possibility of further development of the relationship. Most describe their relationships as very satisfactory and report problems not too different from those of young married couples. A special problem is to conceal the relationship from the woman's parents.

SUGGESTED READINGS

Bell, Robert R., and Gordon, Michael, *eds., The Social Dimension of Human Sexuality*, Boston: Little, Brown and Company, 1972. The first section of this judiciously selected collection is devoted to exploring the area of premarital sexual behavior.

Edwards, John N., *ed., Sex and Society*, Chicago: Markham, 1972. An excellent collection of essays on the social context of human sexuality. Includes one section on premarital behavior.

Hill, Reuben, and Aldous, Joan, "Socialization for Marriage and Parenthood," in David A. Goslin, *ed., Handbook of Socialization Theory and Research,* Chicago: Rand McNally, 1969, pp. 885–950. An excellent summary of the state of theory and research. Contains sections on dating, going steady, and engagement.

Lantz, Herman R., and Snyder, Eloise C., *Marriage: An Examination of the Man-Woman Relationship,* New York: John Wiley and Sons, 1969, Chs. 6, 7, 9, 10. These chapters on the nature of heterosexual love and dating and courtship in middle-class America are perceptive and constructive.

Mann, W. E., *Canadian Trends in Premarital Behaviour: Some Preliminary Studies of Youth in High School and University*, Toronto: Bulletin No. 198, The Council for Social Service, The Anglican Church of Canada, December 1967. A comprehensive and careful report of the dating and sexual behavior of Canadian high school and university students.

Morrison, Eleanor S., and Borosage, Vera, *eds., Human Sexuality: Contemporary Perspectives*, Palo Alto, California: National Press Books, 1973. Various articles deal with the development of human sexuality, masculinity and feminity, and adult heterosexual behavior.

Readings in Marriage and Family, 77–78, Guilford, Conn.: Dushkin Publishing Group, 1977. The section on formation of interpersonal relationships contains selections on the self in relationships and on love and partner selection.

Williamson, Robert C., *Marriage and Family Relations*, New York: John Wiley and Sons, 1972. An outstanding textbook on preparation for marriage and family life.

FILMS

Achieving Sexual Maturity (John Wiley and Sons, 605 Third Avenue, New York, N.Y. 10016), 21 minutes. Deals with the sexual anatomy, physiology, and behavior of both sexes from conception through adulthood. Uses explicit live photography to explain anatomy.

How Do I Love Thee? (Educational Media Services, Brigham Young University, Provo, Utah 84601), 29 minutes. The new morality is explained to Keith by his roommate, and Keith is convinced to try it. Film shows how his conflict is resolved.

Joe and Roxy (National Film Board of Canada, Mackenzie Building, Toronto, Ontario), 30 minutes. Analyzes going steady, planning for a secure future, and seeing education in proper perspective. Shows how the inadequate home lives of Joe and Roxy fail them during adolescent adjustment.

Lucy (Pictura Films, 43 West 16th Street, New York, N.Y. 10011), 13 minutes, color. A pregnant teenager tells her story; her relationship with the boy; her conflicts when she discovers she is pregnant. She evaluates the alternatives and decides to have her baby.

Teenage Pregnancy (Sterling Educational Films, 241 East 34th Street, New York, N.Y. 10016), 14 minutes. The discovery that a teenage daughter is pregnant causes upheaval in a family. The frantic mother tries to restore unity.

QUESTIONS AND PROJECTS

1. Describe the explicit norms that governed early dating in the traditional dating system. Then describe the parallel set of implicit norms, and comment on the functions served by both sets of norms.
2. Outline Waller's theory of rating and dating in the college context. Specify the relationship between bargaining and exploitation. Are there any positive effects of cross-class dating and exploitation?
3. Describe Goode's arguments on the significance of love for the social structure. What functions does love serve? What problems of control does it pose?
4. According to Waller, how does idealization develop in courtship? What does research evidence show about idealization in courtship? What proportion of couples appear to be madly in love at the time of marriage?
5. What does research show about the involvement of preadolescents in sex play? What generalizations can be made? What variation exists?
6. How is comparative social class related to premarital sexual involvement? Reconcile this with findings concerning dating interaction in general.
7. How does the masculine subculture condition boys toward the pursuit of nonmarital sex? What proportion of girls can accept nonmarital sex?
8. What proportion of U.S. teenagers have sexual intercourse? How promiscuous are these relationships?
9. What changes have occurred in college dating patterns over the past dec-

ade or so? Speculate about the impact of these changes upon marital relationships.

10. How widespread is male sex aggression in dating relationships? Is it confined to casual relationships? How do women handle such aggression?
11. Describe the impact of coed dorm living upon friendships and sexual involvement. How do coed dorm residents evaluate their situations?
12. How common is living together around college campuses? Why do couples say they live together? What advantages do they find in such arrangements? What problems?

13
Mate Selection

The family is the oldest institution of the human race. Other institutions have always depended on it and I think people will go right on doing this. But if we would take a look at the modern world we would realize that people today are taking extraordinary risks. Young people are marrying across wide expanses of the world, choosing partners of other classes, other religions, other races. And people who are taking these risks ought to realize that they are doing something different but that they take the risk because they feel it is worth it—because they care about differences, because they care about contrast, because they care about intensity. If you are not going to marry the boy next door—and if you do you may die of boredom—then you have got to work much harder.[1]

All societies have mechanisms for controlling who gets married to whom. In this chapter, we will look systematically at the ways in which mates are sorted in American society.

HOMOGAMY

Marriage based on romantic love is the norm in America and is spreading rapidly over the world. No society, however, leaves falling in love solely to the whims of the young. The general regulation of mate selection is subsumed under the concepts of endogamy and exogamy; people

1. Margaret Mead, "We Must Learn To See What's Really New," *Life Magazine* (Aug. 1968), p. 34.

are required to select spouses from within certain groups and are forbidden to choose them from certain groups. These norms may be formalized into law or they may be largely implicit, and, thus, studied only through analysis of who actually marries whom.

Comparatively, America has few exogamous norms. The incest taboos extend outward roughly to first cousins, but there are no clans or other kinship structures within which mate selection is prohibited. Endogamous norms are more pervasive. It will be recalled that Christianity has a long history of forbidding marriage with outsiders. Early in colonial days, interracial marriage also was forbidden. In few other respects are there laws requiring people to marry within their own groups. There is, however, evidence of a widespread tendency for people to marry others who are like themselves in ways that are not subject to formal regulation. This tendency for like to marry like is called *homogamy*.

Hundreds of studies have been done of homogamy. They embrace homogamy by age and marital status, social status, religion, ethnic affiliation, race, and a host of other social and personal characteristics. Only a small portion of this research can be presented here.

Age and Marital Status

Laws concerning age at marriage are intended to assure reasonable maturity in the contracting parties and to make certain that they are old enough to give valid consent. Under the old English common law, the minimum ages were 14 for boys and 12 for girls, with parental consent. Virtually all of the states in the United States subsequently passed laws setting minimum ages for marriage with and without parental consent.[2] The most common provision permits men of 21 and women of 18 to marry without parental consent.[3] With parental consent, the most common ages are 18 for men and 16 for women. In some states, both men and women must be 21 to marry without parental consent, and, in a few others, 12-year-olds may marry with parental consent. In many states, courts may grant special permission for underage couples to marry when the girl is pregnant.

2. The Constitution reserves the area of domestic relations laws to the states, so each of the 50 states and the District of Columbia has its own laws, and the laws vary widely from one jurisdiction to another.

3. A Utah district court, in 1975, ruled that such laws are unconstitutional because they discriminate against men: Associated Press, October 11, 1975. Until and unless the Supreme Court rules on the matter, most states probably will continue to enforce existing statutes.

From the last part of the nineteenth century until 1960, the average ages at marriage, for both men and women, moved downward. In 1890, for example, the median ages at marriage were 26.1 for men and 22.0 for women. By 1960, these averages had dropped to 22.8 and 20.3. Then they began to rise again. They climbed to 23.2 and 20.8 in 1970 and rose further to 23.8 for men and 21.3 for women in 1976.

Obviously, most Americans marry young. What is just as impressive, however, is the narrow age range within which most people marry. Sixty percent of all first marriages occur within a four- or five-year period and 75 percent occur within three or four years on either side of age 21.[4] Apparently, the mechanisms that get people married work with remarkable efficiency around graduation from high school and college.

Homogamy in age at marriage is indicated by the relative ages of brides and grooms. On the average, brides are 2.5 years younger than their grooms and in 10 percent of all cases they are the same age. In three-fourths of all cases, brides are younger, and in one case out of seven the bride is older than the groom.

Homogamy, by age, holds for all groups in the population that have been studied. Hollingshead compared the ages of black and white couples in first marriages and remarriages.[5] In all four types and within both races, the correlations were high. Glick verified age homogamy at different occupational levels ranging from professionals to laborers.[6]

The age-homogamy norms are themselves a function of age; they operate most strongly at youthful ages and become less effective as people grow older. At age 20, men marry women of median age 19—only one year's difference. By age 25 there is three years' difference, by age 30 there is nearly five years' difference, and by age 60, there is almost ten years' difference. Women, of course, typically choose husbands who are older, but the pattern fluctuates widely with the age of the woman. Girls who marry at age 15 choose men almost five years their seniors. By age 20 the difference has dropped to less than three years, and by age 30 there is less than one year's difference. Beyond age 30 the difference begins to increase again. After age 30, women tend to marry men who are from two to four years older than they are.

4. John Mogey, "Age at First Marriage," in Alvin W. Gouldner and S. M. Miller, *eds.*, *Applied Sociology: Opportunities and Problems*, New York: The Free Press, 1965, pp. 248–59.

5. August B. Hollingshead, "Age Relationships and Marriage," *American Sociological Review* 16 (Aug. 1951), pp. 492–99.

6. Paul C. Glick and Emmanuel Landau, "Age as a Factor in Marriage," *American Sociological Review* 15 (Aug. 1950), pp. 517–29.

Age is related to whether people are marrying for the first time. Bowerman studied these relationships in Seattle and reached the following conclusions. First, single persons as marriage partners are younger, on the average, than persons who have been married; among the previously married, widows are older than divorcées. These generalizations hold regardless of the age, sex, and previous marital status of the person. Second, as men get older they marry increasingly younger women. The age differences are least when men marry widows. As women get older, on the other hand, they marry men more nearly their own age, the age differences being greatest when they marry widowers. Finally, those who are remarrying do not differ significantly in the age difference from their mates who are marrying for the first time.[7]

In summary, these data show homogamy by age, but that the effectiveness of the norms varies by age and the previous marital status. There are several possible explanations. First, age differences seem greater to the young; at age 20, a difference of two years may loom larger than a difference of five years at age 40. Second, the range of association with persons of different ages probably becomes greater as one grows older. Third, the opportunities for selecting a mate at one's own age level become more restricted with increasing age; most of one's age mates already are married. If one wishes to marry, one may have to be more flexible in one's age requirements. The competitive situations of men and women differ here. Although this can be overemphasized, the initiative in mate-seeking tends to rest with men, and men seek physical attractiveness in women. As men get older, frequently their economic status improves and they are able to attract younger women. As women get older, however, they face a declining market and have to accept marriage with older men or with men their own ages who have been married before.

Age Relationships and Marital Success. A number of early studies showed that age at marriage is related to marital happiness,[8] with marriages under the age of 20 being most hazardous. The same pattern was

7. Charles E. Bowerman, "Age Relationships at Marriage, by Marital Status and Age at Marriage," *Marriage and Family Living* 18 (Aug. 1956), pp. 231–33.

8. Ernest W. Burgess and Leonard S. Cottrell, Jr., *Predicting Success or Failure in Marriage,* New York: Prentice-Hall, 1939; Judson T. Landis and Mary G. Landis, *Building a Successful Marriage,* Englewood Cliffs, N.J.: Prentice-Hall, 1973, pp. 106–7; and Lewis M. Terman, *Psychological Factors in Marital Happiness,* New York: McGraw-Hill Book Company, 1938.

discovered when divorce rates were related to age at marriage; young marriages had the highest divorce rates.[9]

The most recent study in this area was of the marital experience of 5442 white, ever-married women under age 45, in the 1970 National Fertility Study. Fifteen percent of these women were separated from or had divorced their first husbands. Again, women who married before age 20 had considerably higher rates of marital disruption than those who married at older ages. Moreover, these higher rates were found not to be due to interrupted educations or to premarital pregnancy. Heterogamous marriages by age had higher marital disruption rates when the age differences were large (wives 14–17 married to husbands 25 and older), and when wives were older than their husbands.[10]

The logic underlying these findings, of course, is that age is related to emotional and social maturity;[11] persons who marry after age 20 are less likely to be rebelling against authority, are less likely to be forced into marriage by pregnancy,[12] are less likely to be broken up by parents, and encounter fewer financial hardships than those who are

9. Judson T. Landis and Mary G. Landis, *op. cit.*, pp. 108–9; Harvey J. Locke, *Predicting Adjustment in Marriage: A Comparison of a Divorced and a Happily Married Group,* New York: Henry Holt and Co., 1951, pp. 101–2; and Thomas P. Monahan, "Does Age at Marriage Matter in Divorce?" *Social Forces* 32 (Oct. 1953), pp. 81–87.

10. Larry L. Bumpass and James A. Sweet, "Differentials in Marital Stability: 1970," *American Sociological Review* 37 (Dec. 1972), pp. 754–66. See also Gary R. Lee, "Age at Marriage and Marital Satisfaction: A Multivariate Analysis with Implications for Marital Stability," *Journal of Marriage and the Family* 39 (Aug. 1977), pp. 493–504.

11. Lee G. Burchinal, "Adolescent Role Deprivation and High School Age Marriage," *Marriage and Family Living* 21 (Nov. 1959), pp. 378–84; J. Ross Eshleman, "Mental Health and Marital Integration in Young Marriages," *Journal of Marriage and the Family* 27 (May 1965), pp. 255–62; Floyd M. Martinson, "Ego Deficiency as a Factor in Marriage," *American Sociological Review* 20 (April 1955), pp. 161–64; Floyd M. Martinson, "Ego Deficiency as a Factor in Marriage–A Male Sample," *Marriage and Family Living* 21 (Feb. 1959), pp. 48–52; and J. Joel Moss and Ruby Gingles, "The Relationship of Personality to the Incidence of Early Marriage," *Marriage and Family Living* 21 (Nov. 1959), pp. 373–77.

12. Of all girls who marry while still in high school, from one-third to one-half are pregnant. Half to three-fourths of the high-school-age boys who marry are involved in premarital pregnancies. See Lloyd Bacon, "Early Motherhood, Accelerated Role Transition, and Social Pathologies," *Social Forces* 52 (March 1974), pp. 333–41; Lee G. Burchinal, "Comparison of Factors Related to Adjustment in Pregnancy-Provoked and Non-Pregnancy-Provoked Youthful Marriages," *Midwest Sociologist* 21 (July 1959), pp. 92–96; Rachel M. Inselberg, "Marital Problems and Satisfaction in High School Marriages," *Marriage and Family Living* 24 (Feb. 1962), pp. 74–77; and Martin L. Norris, "Teenage Marriages: Facts and Figures," paper presented at Indiana Council on Family Relations, March 24, 1962.

younger. That many marriages of high-school age youth do encounter these special problems seems inescapable.

The trend toward youthful marriages has been assessed by Burchinal, who found that the number and proportion of marriages in which at least one partner was 18 years of age or younger increased steadily from 1910 to 1950. The increases occurred among both males and females and among blacks and whites. Among nonwhite girls, the greatest increases occurred between 1910 and 1930, while among white girls the largest increase occurred between 1940 and 1950. Emphasis is placed upon the marriage of young girls because roughly five times as many girls as boys are married by age 18.[13]

Contrary to widely held belief, however, youthful marriage rates have not increased since 1950. The rates have remained stable or may even have declined slightly.

Part of the public attention given to young marriages today may be accounted for by the fact that the public schools are changing their policies in dealing with such marriages. Before World War II, young people who married while still in high school were dropped from school almost automatically. Many schools, either formally or informally, still have such policies. An increasing number, however, are attempting to keep such youngsters in school.[14]

The divorce rate among high-school-age marriages is estimated at two to four times that among marriages of persons after the age of 20, part of which is accounted for by the fact that young marriages are con-

13. Lee G. Burchinal, "Trends and Prospects for Young Marriages in the United States," *Journal of Marriage and the Family* 27 (May 1965), pp. 243–44. See also Karl E. Bauman, "The Relationship Between Age at First Marriage, School Dropout, and Marital Instability: An Analysis of the Glick Effect," *Journal of Marriage and the Family* 29 (Nov. 1967), pp. 672–80; and Lolagene Coombs, R. Freedman, J. Friedman, and W. F. Pratt, "Premarital Pregnancy and Status Before and After Marriage," *American Journal of Sociology* 75 (March 1970), pp. 800–820.

14. See Wayne J. Anderson and Sander M. Latts, "High School Marriages and School Policies in Minnesota," *Journal of Marriage and the Family* 27 (May 1965), pp. 266–70; Glenn C. Atkyns, "School Administrative Policy Related to Motherhood, Pregnancy, and Marriage," *The Family Coordinator* 17 (April 1968), pp. 69–73; B. B. Brown, "Married Students in Public High Schools: A Texas Study," *The Family Coordinator* 21 (July 1972), pp. 321–24; Vladimir de Lissovoy, "High School Marriages: A Longitudinal Study," *Journal of Marriage and the Family* 35 (May 1973), pp. 245–55; Vladimir de Lissovoy and Mary Ellen Hitchcock, "High School Marriages in Pennsylvania," *Journal of Marriage and the Family* 27 (May 1965), pp. 263–65; June M. Henton, "The Effects of Married High School Students on Their Unmarried Class-Mates," *Journal of Marriage and the Family* 26 (Feb. 1964), pp. 87–88; Wilson Ivins, "Student Marriages in New Mexico Secondary Schools: Practices and Policies," *Marriage and Family Living* 22 (Feb. 1960), pp. 71–74.

centrated among high divorce-rate groups: those of low educational levels, low socio-economic levels, and those who are premaritally pregnant.[15] Even when the influence of these factors is partialed out, however, the disadvantage remains. Those who marry very young appear more likely to marry out of dysfunctional emotional needs and to encounter a disproportionate set of "outside" problems.

One writer has criticized the condemnation of young marriages. Doress argues that such criticism ignores the large number of apparently successful young marriages and questions whether couples who marry in their late twenties and early thirties may not have developed individual patterns of living that are scarcely affected by marriage. The stability of these later marriages, he says, may be largely due to the fact that they do not involve the deep commitments of young marriages. There may be less welding, less joining together, less *egoisme à deux*.[16]

Unquestionably, disapproval of young marriages has much to do with their high failure rate. If society were to support young marriages with enthusiasm, the present negative effects of emotional immaturity might be largely overcome. This does not change things, however. There are few signs that society will become more accepting of youthful marriages in the near future. Society is more tolerant of marriages occurring later than of those occurring earlier.

Social Status

Data in the last chapter showed both that people tend to date at their own status levels and that dating outside one's level is associated with sexual involvement, exploitation, and the hope of marriage on the part of the lower-status partner. These data should lead us to expect both status homogamy and status heterogamy in marriage; and, indeed, this is what we find.

Early studies found mixed evidence. Burgess and Wallin found that 1000 engaged couples tended to select persons of similar family back-

15. While early studies showed a relationship between premarital pregnancy and subsequent divorce, these studies did not control for related factors such as low economic status, youthful ages, low educational achievement, and so on. Recent controlled studies have cast doubt on the long-term effects of premarital pregnancy. See Larry L. Bumpass and James A. Sweet, *op. cit.*, p. 758; and Phillips Cutright, "Timing the First Birth: Does It Matter?" *Journal of Marriage and the Family* 35 (Nov. 1973), pp. 585–95.

16. Irving Doress, "The Problem of Early Marriage," *The Bulletin on Family Development* 2 (Spring 1961), pp. 20–23.

ground.[17] Centers, using a national sample, found that men and women marry persons from their same occupational level more often than they marry persons from any other one occupational stratum. He also found, however, that fewer than 50 percent marry within their own occupational level and that, despite the endogamous tendency, more men of each occupational level are married to women of strata other than their own than are married to women of it.[18] In Connecticut, Hollingshead discovered that men and women tend to marry persons from the same class of residential area and from the same educational level.[19] Hunt, using data on marriages occurring in Massachusetts, however, failed to find much evidence for status endogamy.[20] Only women from the lowest status levels made mostly endogamous marriages. At all other status levels, there was no uniform tendency for the selection of partners from any status level.

Leslie and Richardson studied students who married while they were in college. These researchers reasoned that, while status endogamy may operate in the larger society, it might not be effective in a group virtually all of whom were middle class. They reasoned further that, if parents tend to pressure their offspring toward endogamous marriages, such pressure might be less effective when students marry while they are away at college and subject to the democratic norms found on most campuses. They discovered only a slight tendency toward homogamy among students who married someone whom they had known at home before attending college, and none at all among couples who met and married while on campus.[21] They concluded that the campus situation, by encouraging the association of persons of diverse backgrounds and through its formal democratic norms, favors heterogamous pairings. Direct group pressures operating at the time of marriage appear to be at least as influential as homogamy-oriented norms internalized earlier in life.

17. Ernest W. Burgess and Paul Wallin, "Homogamy in Social Characteristics," *American Journal of Sociology* 49 (Sept. 1943), pp. 117–24.
18. Richard Centers, "Marital Selection and Occupational Strata," *American Journal of Sociology* 54 (May 1949), pp. 530–35.
19. August B. Hollingshead, "Cultural Factors in the Selection of Marriage Mates," *American Sociological Review* 15 (Oct. 1950), pp. 619–27.
20. T. C. Hunt, "Occupational Status and Marriage Selection," *American Sociological Review* 5 (Aug. 1940), pp. 495–504.
21. Gerald R. Leslie and Arthur H. Richardson, "Family Versus Campus Influences in Relation to Mate Selection," *Social Problems* 4 (Oct. 1956), pp. 117–21. At least one study indicates that some apparent homogamy may develop as a function of interaction between the couple. See Eloise C. Snyder, "Attitudes: A Study of Homogamy and Marital Selectivity," *Journal of Marriage and the Family* 26 (Aug. 1964), pp. 332–36.

Coombs, studying married couples at the University of Utah, supported the idea that campus norms favor status heterogamy, while community norms favor status endogamy. He found that status homogamy was much higher when both parties to the couple lived at home during courtship than when neither lived at home.[22]

These data suggest that status homogamy might be declining with the passage of time, at least in some segments of the population. This interpretation is supported by the data on 5442 women from the 1970 National Fertility Study. Using education as the measure of social status, this study found that marital disruption rates did not differ significantly between homogamous and heterogamous marriages unless the differences in background were large. Disruption rates were highest for college women who had married high school dropouts.[23]

The Mating Gradient. Just as patterns of dating and premarital sex involvement led us to expect both status homogamy and status heterogamy in marriage, they should also lead us to expect certain patterns in heterogamous marriages. The data showed that men more often date below their social levels while women often date above theirs. In fact, there seems to be a tendency for men to wish to marry at their own levels or below on a wide range of characteristics. That men tend to marry down in terms of age was shown in the preceding section. Early studies also demonstrated that men tend to marry down in education and I.Q. This tendency for men to marry downward has been labeled the mating gradient.

Most studies on status homogamy have shown the operation of the mating gradient. The data suggest further that, except at the very top and bottom, men have wider mate choice than women do.[24]

An interesting implication of the mating gradient is that it works to keep some of the highest status women and the lowest status men from

22. Robert H. Coombs, "Reinforcement of Values in the Parental Home as a Factor in Mate Selection," *Marriage and Family Living* 24 (May 1962), pp. 155–57.

23. Larry L. Bumpass and James A. Sweet, *op. cit.*, p. 762. See also Leonard I. Pearlin, "Status Inequality and Stress in Marriage," *American Sociological Review* 40 (June 1975), pp. 344–57.

24. Some methodological difficulties in getting a definitive test of the mating gradient are analyzed in the following articles: Zick Rubin "Do American Women Marry Up?" *American Sociological Review* 33 (Oct. 1968), pp. 750–60; John F. Scott, "A Comment on 'Do American Women Marry Up?' " *American Sociological Review* 34 (Oct. 1969), pp. 725–28; J. David Martin, "A Comment on Whether American Women Do Marry Up," *American Sociological Review* 35 (April 1970), pp. 327–28; Norval D. Glenn, Adreain A. Ross, and Judy Corder Tully, "Patterns of Intergenerational Mobility of Females Through Marriage," *American Sociological Review* 39 (Oct. 1974), pp. 683–99; and Richard C. Rockwell, "Historical Trends and Variations in Educational Homogamy," *Journal of Marriage and the Family* 38 (Feb. 1976), pp. 83–95.

marrying. Women at the highest levels have a smaller pool of potential mates to begin with, because it is not generally acceptable for them to marry downward. In addition, these high-status women must compete both against one another and against women from other status levels for high-status men. To the extent that high-status men marry downward, they leave high-status women without partners. Among men, the reverse obtains. The lowest-status men generally are not eligible to marry higher-status women; yet higher-status men may select lower-status spouses. Thus, unmarried women may be, disproportionately, high-status women, and unmarried men may be, disproportionately, low-status men.

Racial Background

Nowhere are homogamy norms more widely held to than in the area of race. Over twenty years, the courts have tended to strike down laws forbidding miscegenation and intermarriage and, in 1967, the Supreme Court declared Virginia's law unconstitutional, thereby nullifying similar prohibitions in the 16 other states that still had them.

Although persons of different races may now legally marry, the intermarriage rate is still so low as virtually to defy reliable measurement. Studies of intermarriage rates in various states and cities up to 1960 showed rates of one-half to one and one-half percent. The first census reporting of data on the races of married persons in the United States occurred in 1960, with the result that 0.44 percent of the over 40 million couples reported themselves interracially married.

By 1970, the percentage had increased to 0.70 percent. This represents a 63 percent increase over the decade, but since the base in 1960 was so small, the number of intermarriages increased only from 163,800 couples to 266,994. During the decade, the number of white men married to black women dropped from 25,913 to 23,556 while the number of black men married to white women increased from 25,496 to 41,223.[25]

Intermarriage rates were reported for several minority groups. Among American Indians, 33 percent of the men had white wives; 24 percent of the Filipino men, 8 percent of the Japanese men, 8 percent of the Chinese men, and 2 percent of black men had white wives. There

25. See David M. Heer, "The Prevalence of Black-White Marriage in the United States, 1960 and 1970," *Journal of Marriage and the Family* 36 (May 1974), pp. 246–58; and Thomas P. Monahan, "An Overview of Statistics on Interracial Marriage in the United States, with Data on Its Extent from 1963 to 1970," *Journal of Marriage and the Family* 38 (May 1976), pp. 223–31.

were also increases over the decade of white men with American Indian wives and white men with Japanese wives.[26]

In spite of the small number of people involved—or, perhaps, because of it—there is an almost morbid curiosity about the kinds of people who intermarry. Several studies have sought to specify some of the social and emotional characteristics of the racially intermarried.

Several studies have shown that interracial marriages more often involve nonwhite men and white women.[27] Golden found that 58.5 percent of black-white marriages in Philadelphia were of this combination, and Pavela found the corresponding percentage among Indiana interracial marriages to be 72.6. These figures probably do not mean that white men do not form sexual associations with nonwhite women, but only that such relationships do not tend to lead to marriage. White women have more bargaining power when they enter interracial relationships and are more able to get the men to marry them.

The same studies found that persons in interracial marriages are older at marriage than are those who enter racially homogamous marriages. There is some evidence that these higher ages at marriage are associated with the persons having previously been married. More than one-third of the black grooms interviewed in Philadelphia, and almost one-fourth of the brides, had been previously divorced. In Indiana, Pavela found that 29 percent of black brides and 25 percent of black grooms had been divorced; the corresponding percentages among the white brides and grooms were 18 percent and 21 percent.

The personal and emotional characteristics of those who intermarry are more difficult to get at. It is widely believed that interracial marriages must be highly selective in terms of personal characteristics. Both Golden and Pavela demonstrated that families and friends of both races exert strong pressures against such marriages.[28]

26. *The New York Times,* Feb. 15, 1973. See also Delores P. Aldridge, "The Changing Nature of Interracial Marriage in Georgia: A Research Note," *Journal of Marriage and the Family* 35 (Nov. 1973), p. 641; and Robert C. Schmitt, "Recent Trends in Hawaiian Interracial Marriage Rates by Occupation," *Journal of Marriage and the Family* 33 (May 1971), pp. 373–74.

27. John H. Burma, "Research Note on the Measurement of Interracial Marriage," *American Journal of Sociology* 57 (May 1952), pp. 587–89; Joseph Golden, "Characteristics of the Negro-White Intermarried in Philadelphia," *American Sociological Review* 18 (April 1953), p. 178; and Todd H. Pavela, "An Exploratory Study of Negro-White Intermarriage in Indiana," *Journal of Marriage and the Family* 26 (May 1964), pp. 209–11.

28. Joseph Golden, "Patterns of Negro-White Intermarriage," *American Sociological Review* 19 (April 1954), pp. 144–47; and Todd H. Pavela, *op. cit.*, p. 210.

The study going into the greatest depth may be that of Freeman, who studied interracial couples in Hawaii.[29] All of his respondents described early feelings of rejection, frequently tracing back to parent-child relationships. All respondents also reported poor social adjustment in grade school and high school. The backgrounds of rejection produced frustration and hostility toward the individuals' ethnic groups. They desired to escape identification with the ethnic group and turned toward deviant behavior to do so. Exposure to other ethnic groups led to idealization of opposite-sex members of those groups, dating, and, often, marriage. Many of the interethnic dating relationships were short-lived and, when marriage occurred, adjustment was a long, difficult process in which the rebelliousness abated.

Although Freeman's conclusions are widely shared, Burchinal argues that interracial marriages may occur disproportionately among a very different class of youth.[30] In cities, especially among students and professional people, he says, racial equalitarianism and integration are widely supported. Interracial dating occurs with increasing frequency and interracial marriage becomes increasingly likely.

In support of this argument, Blood and Nicholson found that acquaintances with students from other nations were almost universal on campus and that almost half of the women had dated foreign students. Of those who had not dated, most said that they would if they were asked.[31] Moreover, international dating was not related to rebellion or to any crusade against prejudice. The women reported satisfaction with their experiences, their women friends were sympathetic, and their parents and American boy friends typically were neutral.[32]

29. Linton Freeman, "Homogamy in Interethnic Mate Selection," *Sociology and Social Research* 39 (July-Aug. 1955), pp. 369–77. The unique situation in Hawaii has been studied extensively. See, for example, Paul H. Besanceney, "On Reporting Rates of Intermarriage," *American Journal of Sociology* 70 (May 1965), pp. 717–21; Andrew W. Lind, "Interracial Marriage as Affecting Divorce in Hawaii," *Sociology and Social Research* 49 (Oct. 1964), pp. 17–26; Thomas P. Monahan, "Interracial Marriage and Divorce in the State of Hawaii," *Eugenics Quarterly* 13 (March 1966), pp. 40–47; Margaret A. Parkman and Jack Sawyer, "Dimensions of Ethnic Intermarriage in Hawaii," *American Sociological Review* 32 (Aug. 1967), pp. 593–607; and Robert C. Schmitt, "Demographic Correlates of Interracial Marriage in Hawaii," *Population Index* 30 (July 1964), pp. 312–13.

30. Lee G. Burchinal, "The Premarital Dyad and Love Involvement," in Harold T. Christensen, *ed., Handbook of Marriage and the Family*, Chicago: Rand McNally, 1964, p. 648.

31. Robert O. Blood, Jr. and Samuel O. Nicholson, "The Attitudes of American Men and Women Students Toward International Dating," *Marriage and Family Living* 24 (Feb. 1962), pp. 35–41.

32. Robert O. Blood, Jr., and Samuel O. Nicholson, "International Dating Experiences of

Racial Heterogamy and Marital Success. Many people believe that interracial marriages are fraught with hazard and doomed to failure. Research, however, shows the situation to be anything but simple.

One perceptive study was made of marriages between American service men and Japanese women in the 1950s. The couples were living in the Chicago area. The study challenged the assumption that Oriental-Caucasian marriages are subject to greater strains than the ordinary marriage, contending that, as in other marriages, the strains that occur in mixed marriages are patterned and predictable. Some Japanese-American marriages, the researcher says, are likely to be quite stable and to involve fewer strains than many American marriages.[33]

These husbands were mostly semiskilled or skilled laborers, professional soldiers, or white-collar workers; not upwardly mobile. Some had married without their parents' knowledge, but most had received either enthusiastic or grudging approval. Their wives had married at an average age of 22, they were usually urban working girls, and their marriages to Americans frequently were opposed by their parents. The couples faced the usual adjustment problems with food, sex, play, work, finances, and so on. In addition, they faced problems of learning how to communicate, of handling the women's parents, and of becoming parents. By the time of interview several years later, however, differences of age, class, religion, and education did not cause strain. There were strains in these marriages still, however. Some were more serious and some of them less so than in most marriages.

The strains involved in leaving the parental family were different from typical in-law problems, but not automatically more or less severe. Few women had much stress over having left their parents or Japan. There was some nostalgia to see their parents and country again, and a few wives were attempting to get their husbands to return to Japan.

Few couples experienced strong institutional pressures. They had few organizational affiliations and were not usually deeply religious. A few brides had become Catholic, thus avoiding sharp differences between themselves and their husbands. Much of their recreation took place in

---

American Women Students," *Marriage and Family Living* 24 (May 1962), pp. 129–36. See also Ann Baker Cottrell, "Cross-National Marriage as an Extension of an International Life Style: A Study of Indian-Western Couples," *Journal of Marriage and the Family* 35 (Nov. 1973), pp. 739–41; Harrop A. Freeman and Ruth Freeman, "Dating Between American and Foreign College Students," *Journal of Sex Research* 2 (Nov. 1966), pp. 207–14.

33. Anselm L. Strauss, "Strain and Harmony in American-Japanese War-Bride Marriages," *Marriage and Family Living* 16 (May 1954), pp. 99–106.

their own homes or those of friends. Their problems in this area seemed to be fewer than in many American marriages.

There was a fairly complete separation of home and work. The women were satisfied with their husbands' incomes and did not pressure them; similarly, the husbands did not expect their wives to have careers, although some of them worked. These couples seemed satisfied on steady, modest incomes.

Relationships with the husbands' families generally were good, and the in-laws often helped the bride learn American ways. When in-law conflict did develop, there was severe strain as in comparable American marriages. Relationships with friends also appeared good, but selective; much interaction was with other interracially married couples. It would be interesting to speculate whether this pairing-off of interracially married couples reflected common interests or from rejection by other couples.

Presumably, the strains involved in Oriental-Caucasian marriages may be less than those in black-white marriages. Data on black-white marriages also reveal the situation to be complicated.

At least three in-depth studies of black-white marriages have been completed: in New York, in Philadelphia, and in Indianapolis.[34] The number of couples was small: 22, 50, and 9, respectively. All couples were carefully interviewed. Although there were differences of location and time span, the three studies present a rather consistent picture of what such marriages are like.

The evidence suggests that many people who enter intermarriages are relatively isolated from their families to begin with. Often, the family of the white partner, at least, does not know of the courtship, which tends to be carried on with some secrecy. In some cases, the secrecy is continued after the marriage. Golden found that some white spouses avoided contacts with their parents and former white friends. On the other hand, not all white parents oppose the marriages. Pavela found both some opposition and some support among white parents. Both Golden and Pavela found much less opposition from black parents; acceptance or rejection of the white partner was more likely to be based upon his or her personal characteristics than upon the mere fact of race.

No couple was completely ostracized by both races. They tended to live in borderline residential areas, with more couples living in all-black areas than in all-white areas. Relations with neighbors usually were ami-

34. Joseph Golden, "Patterns of Negro-White Intermarriage," *op. cit.;* Todd H. Pavela, *op. cit.;* and Charles E. Smith, "Negro-White Intermarriage—Forbidden Sexual Union," *The Journal of Sex Research* 2 (Nov. 1966), pp. 169–78.

cable but not intimate. Friends were more often black than white; relatively few had extensive contacts with other interracial couples. Some of Smith's New York couples even reported that they probably had more social contacts than similar white or black couples.

Many couples did report special difficulties. Being stared at in public places was emphasized by New York and Philadelphia couples. Some white spouses had lost jobs when their employers learned of their marriages; others concealed the fact from employers and fellow employees. Some couples were discriminated against in housing, a problem sometimes solved by sending the white partner to inspect the property and sign the lease. In general, the problems encountered by interracial couples were those typically met by black couples.

Over half the Philadelphia and Indianapolis couples had children, and none of the New York couples had decided against having children. If they had fewer children than average, this may be related to their older age at marriage. Relatively little discrimination against the children was experienced at the hands of blacks, but virtually all parents acknowledged that their children would be raised as blacks. Many couples longed for the day when prejudice would not be a problem.

Golden reported that 34 couples out of 50 had been married five years or longer. He concluded that these marriages have a good chance of survival. Pavela's conclusion is consistent with Burchinal's analysis of the changing nature of interracial marriage. He says: "In many respects, the Negro-white marriages studied contradict the picture of such marriages in the public mind or even in much sociological literature. It would appear that such intermarriage now occurs between persons who are, by and large, economically, educationally, and culturally equal and who have a strong emotional attachment, be it rationalization or real. The external pressures faced by interracial couples are often great, but certainly do not appear to be overwhelming."[35]

Religious Affiliation

The norms supporting religious homogamy in the United States have long been strong—only slightly less strong than those supporting racial homogamy. In 1950 in New Haven, Connecticut, for example, Hollingshead reported that 97 percent of Jewish marriages, 94 percent of

35. See Thomas P. Monahan, "Are Interracial Marriages Really Less Stable?" *Social Forces* 48 (June 1970), pp. 461–73; Thomas P. Monahan, "Interracial Marriage and Divorce in Kansas and the Question of Instability of Mixed Marriages," *Journal of Comparative Family Studies* 2 (Spring 1971), pp. 107–20; and Robert C. Schmitt, "Age and Race Differences in Divorce in Hawaii," *Journal of Marriage and the Family* 31 (Feb. 1969), pp. 48–50.

Catholic marriages, and 74 percent of Protestant marriages were religiously homogamous.[36] Other studies have challenged the existence of extreme religious endogamy, however, and have shown that even the computation of rates of religious homogamy is very complicated.

Thomas, for example, gathered data for Catholic dioceses in different sections of the country and reported mixed-marriage rates ranging from 10 percent in El Paso to 70 percent in Raleigh and Charleston.[37] The mixed marriage rate for one-half of the Catholic dioceses in the United States was about 30 percent. For Connecticut, Thomas estimates that the rate probably is about 50 percent.

If taken at face value, the figures reported by Hollingshead for New Haven and by Thomas for all of Connecticut appear to be in serious conflict. Part of the discrepancy is to be accounted for by the fact that these are not comparable rates. The rate reported by Hollingshead is a mixed-marriage rate for individuals while Thomas's rate is a rate for marriages. A *mixed marriage rate for individuals* refers to the percentage of married persons (in any category) who enter mixed marriages; a *mixed marriage rate for marriages,* in contrast, refers to the percentage of marriages (in any category) that are mixed.[38] Making Thomas's figures comparable to Hollingshead's, his rate for Connecticut turns out to be 33.3 percent.

Even after the data are rendered comparable, Thomas's point that the New Haven data are not representative appears well taken. Burchinal and Chancellor found individual mixed-marriage rates in Iowa to range from 9 to 24 percent.[39] In New York City, Heiss found 18 percent of Jews, 21 percent of Catholics, and 34 percent of Protestants to be inter-

36. *Op. cit.*

37. John L. Thomas, "The Factor of Religion in the Selection of Marriage Mates," *American Sociological Review* 16 (Aug. 1951), pp. 487–91.

38. The importance of distinguishing between mixed marriage rates for individuals and for marriages has been pointed out by Rodman, who also provided the following illustration. If there are six homogamous Catholic marriages and four mixed marriages, the mixed marriage rate can be either 40 percent or 25 percent. Four of the ten marriages are mixed, but only one out of four of the Catholics is involved in a mixed marriage. Hyman Rodman, "Technical Note on Two Rates of Mixed Marriage," *American Sociological Review* 30 (Oct. 1965), pp. 776–78.

39. Lee G. Burchinal and Loren E. Chancellor, "Ages at Marriage, Occupations of Grooms, and Interreligious Marriage Rates," *Social Forces* 40 (May 1962), pp. 348–54. There have been numerous other studies of the incidence of interfaith marriages in various groups. See, for example, Donald H. Bouma, "Religiously Mixed Marriages: Denominational Consequences in the Christian Reformed Church," *Marriage and Family Living* 25 (Nov. 1963), pp. 428–32; and David M. Heer, "The Trend of Interfaith Marriages in Canada: 1922–1957," *American Sociological Review* 27 (April 1962), pp. 245–50; and Thomas P. Monahan, "Some Dimensions of Interreligious Marriages in Indiana, 1962–67," *Social Forces* 52 (Dec. 1973), pp. 195–203.

Table 13.1. Sample transformations of the two rates of mixed marriage

Mixed marriage rate for marriages	*Mixed marriage rate for individuals*
0.0	0.0
10.0	5.3
20.0	11.1
33.3	20.0
40.0	25.0
50.0	33.3
57.1	40.0
60.0	42.9
66.7	50.0
75.0	60.0
80.0	66.7
88.9	80.0
94.7	90.0
100.0	100.0

Source: Hyman Rodman, "Technical Note on Two Rates of Mixed Marriage," *American Sociological Review* 30 (Oct. 1965), p. 778.

married.[40] Finally, Rodman's computations yield individual mixed-marriage rates of 3.7 percent for Jews, 4.5 percent for Protestants, and 12.1 percent for Catholics.[41]

If prohibitions against religious intermarriage were effective through the 1950s, intermarriage rates increased during the 1960s and 1970s. With several studies showing the individual mixed marriage rate for Catholics to be about 30 percent, Pope Paul VI, in 1970, dropped the requirement that the non-Catholic partner to a mixed marriage promise to raise the children as Catholics, and ruled that local bishops may grant dispensation, "for serious reasons," from the requirement that the marriage ceremony be performed by a priest. Even more drastic change has occurred in Jewish-Gentile marriages. A study by the Council of Jewish Federations and Welfare Funds reported that one-third of the American Jews who married between 1966 and 1972 had non-Jewish spouses, more than double the rate of the preceding five years, and more than four times the pre-1960 rate. The same study showed that one-fifth of Reform rabbis would perform mixed marriages without conditions, and

40. Jerold S. Heiss, "Premarital Characteristics of the Religiously Intermarried in an Urban Area," *American Sociological Review* 25 (Feb. 1960), pp. 47–55.

41. *Current Population Reports,* "Religion Reported by the Civilian Population of the United States: March, 1957," Series P-20, No. 79, Washington, D.C.: U.S. Bureau of the Census, 1958, as reported in Hyman Rodman, *op. cit.,* p. 777.

that an additional one-fifth would do so when the couple pledged to raise the children as Jews.[42]

One factor closely associated with variation in intermarriage rates is the proportion that the religious group is of the community; the larger the proportion which the group is of the total community, the lower the intermarriage rate. In Iowa, a correlation of .66 was found between the proportion of Catholics in county populations and the proportion of homogamous Catholic marriages.[43] This general finding has been borne out by studies using data from the *Official Catholic Directory*,[44] and from the Dominion Bureau of Statistics in Canada.[45]

Interreligious marriages also vary inversely with the cohesiveness of the ethnic group; the more integrated the group, the lower the intermarriage rate. Research shows that ethnic bonds weaken first, marriages occurring across nationality lines but still within the major religious groups.[46] One study of Polish and Italian residents of Buffalo showed in-group marriages among the Poles falling from 79 percent to 35 percent between 1930 and 1960, and in-group Italian marriages falling from 71 percent to 27 percent. The decreases were particularly great after 1940.[47]

A study of religiously intermarried New York City residents casts light on the influence of early family experiences. Heiss found that intermarried Catholics were more likely to have nonreligious parents, expressed greater dissatisfaction with their parents when young, reported greater early strife with their parents, and were more emancipated from parents at the time of marriage. The relationships for the Protestant intermarried were smaller, but in the same direction. None of the relationships held for Jews except for the strength of their family ties while young and at the time of marriage.[48]

Religious Heterogamy and Marital Success. As with racial intermar-

42. *The New York Times*, Feb. 11, 1973, p. E8.
43. Lee G. Burchinal and Loren E. Chancellor, "Proportions of Catholics, Urbanism, and Mixed-Catholic Marriage Rates Among Iowa Counties," *Social Problems* 9 (Spring 1962), pp. 359–65.
44. Harvey J. Locke, Georges Sabagh, and Mary Margaret Thomes, "Interfaith Marriages," *Social Problems* 4 (April 1957), pp. 329–33.
45. David M. Heer, *op. cit.*
46. Ruby Jo Reeves Kennedy, "Single or Triple Melting Pot? Intermarriage Trends in New Haven, 1870–1940," *American Journal of Sociology* 49 (Jan. 1944), pp. 331–39. See also Brent A. Barlow, "Notes on Mormon Interfaith Marriages," *The Family Coordinator* 26 (April 1977), pp. 143–50; Simon Marcson, "Predicting Intermarriage," *Sociology and Social Research* 37 (Jan.-Feb. 1953), pp. 151–56.
47. B. R. Bugelski, "Assimilation Through Intermarriage," *Social Forces* 40 (Dec. 1961), pp. 148–53.
48. *Op. cit.*

riages, religious intermarriages are widely believed to be associated with marital failure. A number of studies of the divorce rates of mixed and nonmixed religious marriages bear this out.

Studies show divorce rates to be lowest among Catholics and Jews, somewhat higher among Protestants, higher still in mixed marriages, and highest of all where there is no religious affiliation.[49]

One of the more definitive studies of divorce rates in interfaith marriages was done for the state of Iowa, using data for a seven-year period. This study, which imposed controls for age and social status, partly confirmed the results of earlier studies and partly called their findings into question. It did show the divorce rate in homogamous Catholic marriages to be lower than in marriages where Catholics were married to denominationally affiliated Protestants. The differences, however, were considerably reduced, and there were no differences according to whether the Catholic spouse in the mixed marriages was husband or wife. The researchers concluded that the smaller differences did not justify generalizations of considerably greater marital difficulties facing Catholics who marry outside their faith, providing the person they marry is identified with a Protestant denomination.[50]

A special contribution of this study was the computation of marital survival rates for many types of religiously homogamous and heterogamous marriages. Several factors stand out in the data in Table 13.2. First, the survival rates almost form a continuum without sharp breaks until the last two categories are reached. Second, while homogamous Catholic marriages had the highest survival rate, a number of other homogamous and mixed marriage types had survival rates nearly as high. Third, many of the rates ranged within a single percentage point of one another. Fourth, the lower-middle segment of the table includes homogamous Protestant marriages, marriages of Catholics with Methodists or Baptists, and the total for all interreligious marriages.

Of particular interest is the fact that Presbyterians, Methodists, and Baptists married to other Protestants had higher marital survival rates than members of those same denominations who were homogamously married. Moreover, the data indicated that the marital survival rates were influenced more by age at marriage and social status than by the fact of religious differences. Marital survival rates were consistently

49. Judson T. Landis, "Marriages of Mixed and Non-mixed Religious Faith," *American Sociological Review* 14 (June 1949), pp. 401–7; and Larry L. Bumpass and James A. Sweet, *op. cit.*, pp. 758–65.

50. Lee G. Burchinal and Loren E. Chancellor, "Survival Rates Among Religiously Homogamous and Interreligious Marriages," *Social Forces* 41 (May 1963), pp. 353–62.

Table 13.2. Rank order of marital survival rates, by religious affiliation types

Religious affiliation types	*Marital survival rates*
Homogamous Catholic	96.2
Mixed Presbyterian	94.6
Homogamous Lutheran	94.1
Residual specified Protestant	94.0
Mixed Lutheran	93.0
Mixed Methodist	92.9
Homogamous Methodist	91.4
Homogamous Presbyterian	91.0
Catholic-Lutheran	90.5
Mixed Baptist	90.0
Catholic-Presbyterian	89.8
Homogamous Baptist	89.8
Catholic-residual specified Protestant	89.1
Homogamous Protestant	86.2
Catholic-Methodist	83.8
Mixed unspecified Protestant	82.7
Catholic-Baptist	81.6
Catholic-interreligious	77.6
Homogamous unspecified Protestant	35.0
Catholic-unspecified Protestant	28.7
Total Population	87.6

Source: Lee Burchinal and Loren Chancellor, "Survival Rates Among Religiously Homogamous and Interreligious Marriages," *Social Forces* 41 (May 1963), p. 360.

higher among marriages involving older brides and couples marrying at higher status levels.

In summary, we conclude that, in spite of the apparently higher divorce rates among some types of mixed marriages, the data are somewhat equivocal. Some authors have gone further, and argued that the frequent admonitions concerning the hazards of mixed marriages reflect a widespread bias against such marriages as much as they reflect data on divorce rates. Vernon, for example, states that family-life educators should be taken to task for presenting only one side of the question. The statistics on the proportion of each type of each marriage which endure are ignored, he says, in the usual presentation of data.[51] Vincent makes a similar point and claims that data on divorce rates could as easily

51. Glenn M. Vernon, "Bias in Professional Publications Concerning Interfaith Marriages," *Religious Education* 55 (July-Aug. 1960), pp. 261–64.

be used to indicate that the problem is not so much one of intermarriage as it is the persistence of religious differences.[52]

At best, divorce rates are a crude index of marital success or failure. We cannot even assume that all of the marriages which result in divorce are unhappy marriages. Among some groups, divorce may be sought whenever the advantages appear to outweigh those involved in remaining married. At the other extreme, divorce may not be acceptable to some no matter how great the unhappiness. No one knows what proportion of religiously homogamous marriages may survive simply because the church condemns divorce.

A number of studies of religiously heterogamous marriages have been made and, again, the evidence is far from one-sided. One part of Heiss's study in New York City, for example, included comparisons between matched samples of intermarried and intramarried couples. The findings showed intermarried Catholics to be more dissatisfied, to worry more about marriage, to be in poorer mental health, to have fewer children, and to have more problems with their children. Differences between intermarried and intramarried Jews were smaller and less consistent, but Heiss concluded that intermarried Catholics and Jews may carry something of an additional burden. The pressures on intermarried Protestants were not quite so great.[53]

Two other studies present the other side of the picture. In a study of 194 interfaith marriages, Prince found that nearly half of the spouses were the offspring of interfaith marriages. Moreover, more than half reported themselves either very much satisfied or entirely satisfied with their marriages. Fewer than 10 percent reported any dissatisfaction.[54]

Dyer and Luckey made carefully controlled comparisons among the marriages of 522 former University of Minnesota students and concluded that there was no relation between religious affiliation and marital happiness. This was true in both denominationally homogamous and heterogamous marriages. In testing the relationship of personality variables and marital happiness, no differences were found. The researchers

52. Clark E. Vincent, "Interfaith Marriages: Problem or Symptom?," in Marvin B. Sussman, *ed.*, *Sourcebook in Marriage and the Family*, Boston: Houghton Mifflin, 1963, pp. 349–59.

53. Jerold S. Heiss, "Interfaith Marriage and Martial Outcome," *Marriage and Family Living* 23 (Aug. 1961), pp. 228–33.

54. Alfred J. Prince, "A Study of 194 Cross-Religion Marriages," *Family Life Coordinator* 11 (Jan. 1962), pp. 3–7. For evidence that intermarriage does not change things very much, see Rudolf K. Haerle, Jr., "Church Attendance Patterns Among Intermarried Catholics: A Panel Study," *Sociological Analysis* 30 (Winter 1969), pp. 204–16.

pointed out that these were young couples who had hardly embarked upon parenthood and who might encounter difficulties later. On the other hand, they believe that their results may reflect a trend to accept and deal with heterogamous marriages more adequately.[55]

RESIDENTIAL PROPINQUITY

Years ago, sociologists discovered that many people select their marriage partners from among those who live near them geographically. This tendency to select partners from those near at hand is called *residential propinquity*.

The first study of propinquity, in Philadelphia, showed that one-sixth of 5000 pairs applying for marriage licenses lived within one city block of each other. One-third lived within five blocks, and half lived within 20 blocks.[56] Bossard concluded that the proportion of marriages decreases markedly as the distance between the parties increases.

Several other studies verified the fact that people select marriage partners disproportionately from those who live nearby, but they did not substantiate the *steady* decrease with increasing distance that Bossard had hypothesized.[57] Rather than concentrate on couples selecting mates from within one-block, five-block, and ten-block distances, these researchers focused on whether the general findings would hold up in increasingly controlled studies and upon developing theoretical explanations for residential propinquity.

The propinquity studies have assumed that distance is related to mate selection through the opportunities that people have to become acquainted. Clarke tested this assumption in Columbus, Ohio, by securing

55. Dorothy T. Dyer and Eleanore B. Luckey, "Religious Affiliation and Selected Personality Scores as They Relate to Marital Happiness of a Minnesota College Sample," *Marriage and Family Living* 23 (Feb. 1961), pp. 46–47.

56. James H. S. Bossard, "Residential Propinquity as a Factor in Marriage Selection," *American Journal of Sociology* 38 (Sept. 1932), pp. 219–24.

57. Ray H. Abrams, "Residential Propinquity as a Factor in Marriage Selection: Fifty Year Trends in Philadelphia," *American Sociological Review* 8 (June 1943), pp. 288–94; Alfred C. Clarke, "An Examination of the Operation of Residential Propinquity as a Factor in Mate Selection," *American Sociological Review* 17 (Feb. 1952), pp. 17–22; Alan C. Kerckhoff, "Notes and Comments on the Meaning of Residential Propinquity as a Factor in Mate Selection," *Social Forces* 34 (March 1956), pp. 207–13; Marvin R. Koller, "Residential Propinquity of White Mates at Marriage in Relation to Age and Occupation of Males. Columbus, Ohio, 1938 and 1946," *American Sociological Review* 13 (Oct. 1948), pp. 613–16; Joseph R. Marches and Gus Turbeville, "The Effect of Residential Propinquity on Marriage Selection," *American Journal of Sociology* 58 (May 1953), pp. 592–95.

the addresses of the partners at the time of their first date as well as at marriage. He found that nearly half of the sample had changed addresses between the time of the first date and the application for a marriage license. Some couples moved closer and some moved farther away, with the result that the proportion residing within 16 city blocks remained approximately the same.[58] He did find that the proportions reporting the same address or living within four city blocks increased by the time of applying for the license.

Having established that propinquity does not emerge simply from courtship interaction, we turn to two major theoretical interpretations. Katz and Hill propound a norm-interaction theory. Briefly, that theory holds that (1) mate selection is normatively regulated; (2) within eligible groups of potential spouses, the probability of marriage varies directly with the probability of interaction; and (3) the probability of interaction is governed by distance and by the segregation of racial, religious, economic, and other groups in the community.[59] According to this theory, groups that are most segregated residentially will be the most propinquitous; and where the homogamy norms are strong there will be more propinquity.

This norm-interaction theory is useful in explaining the variations in propinquity that have been found. Catton and Smircich, using data from Seattle, however, find that the most useful model is one which interprets distance gradients as reflecting economy of time and energy rather than competition between near and remote courtship opportunities or the operation of norms.[60] They suggest that the number of "meaningful" mate-selection opportunities that most people have are rather few; most people simply do not become intimately acquainted with many eligible persons of opposite sex. The probability that any one person of opposite sex will be included among that small number probably depends upon the time and energy costs in traveling.

The Catton and Smircich theory has not been adequately tested as yet. It is important, however, because it implies that norms in mate selection may not be as important as we think. It holds, instead, that propinquity may lead to homogamous marriages and that the familiarity of homogamous marriages leads to the development of homogamy norms.

58. *Op. cit.*

59. See Alvin M. Katz and Reuben Hill, "Residential Propinquity and Marital Selection: A Review of Theory, Method, and Fact," *Marriage and Family Living* 20 (Feb. 1958), pp. 27–35.

60. William R. Catton, Jr. and R. J. Smircich, "A Comparison of Mathematical Models for the Effect of Residential Propinquity on Mate Selection," *American Sociological Review* 29 (Aug. 1964), pp. 522–29.

THE THEORY OF COMPLEMENTARY NEEDS

The discussion of homogamous norms in mate selection was confined to homogamy in *social* characteristics. This does not mean that there are no homogamous tendencies in the area of *personal* characteristics, for there are. Early studies showed similarity between husbands and wives in physical traits, attractiveness, intellectual ability, attitudes, and temperament. More recently, Schellenberg studied the similarity in values among engaged and married couples and found more similarity than in a group of artificially paired couples.[61] Kerckhoff and Davis, studying consensus on family values, found it to increase as dating couples moved toward more permanent relationships.[62]

The evidence in favor of homogamy in personal characteristics is not so convincing, however, as that on homogamy in social characteristics. There were, even among the early studies, some which suggested that people may choose marriage partners who have traits opposite from their own. Kretschmer found such a pairing of opposites among 170 married couples, and Gray found the mating of complementary types rather than the mating of homogamous personality types.[63]

Formulation of a theory of mate selection in terms of complementary personality needs and the partial testing of that theory were accomplished by Winch and associates.[64] This theory holds, first, that human behavior is oriented toward the gratification of needs. Important needs

61. James A. Schellenberg, "Homogamy in Personal Values and the Field of Eligibles," *Social Forces* 39 (Dec. 1960), pp. 157–62. For similar findings with regard to empathy, see Norman Goodman, and Richard Ofshe, "Empathy, Communication Efficiency, and Marital Status," *Journal of Marriage and the Family* 30 (Nov. 1968), pp. 597–603.

62. Alan C. Kerckhoff and Keith E. Davis, "Value Consensus and Need Complementarity in Mate Selection," *American Sociological Review* 27 (June 1962), pp. 295–303. Snyder found, however, that homogamy in self, social, and total adjustment, and in I.Q. existed among 20 couples prior to their selection of one another as marital partners. See Eloise C. Snyder, "Marital Selectivity in Self-Adjustment, and I.Q.," *Journal of Marriage and the Family* 28 (May 1966), pp. 188–89.

63. This literature is summarized in Clifford Kirkpatrick, *The Family: As Process and Institution,* New York: The Ronald Press Company, 1963, pp. 335–36.

64. The research appeared in a series of articles. See Thomas Ktsanes, "Mate Selection on the Basis of Personality Type: A Study Utilizing an Empirical Typology of Personality," *American Sociological Review* 20 (Oct. 1955), pp. 547–51; Robert F. Winch, "The Theory of Complementary Needs in Mate Selection: A Test of One Kind of Complementariness," *American Sociological Review* 20 (Feb. 1955), pp. 52–56; Robert F. Winch, "The Theory of Complementary Needs in Mate Selection: Final Results on the Test of the General Hypothesis," *American Sociological Review* 20 (Oct. 1955), pp. 552–55; Robert F. Winch, Thomas Ktsanes, and Virginia Ktsanes, "Empirical Elaboration of the Theory of Complementary Needs in Mate Selection," *Journal of Abnormal and Social Psychology* 51 (Nov. 1955), pp. 508–13.

become organized in the personality and give pattern to behavior. Not all of these needs are always conscious, so people are aware of some of their needs, partly aware of others, and completely unaware of some.

Needs are learned in personality development and, so, become subject to normative regulation. They must be expressed within the general endogamous and exogamous norms of the group. The endogamous and exogamous norms define, for people, the "field of eligibles"—those persons from among whom they are permitted to select mates.

Building upon these assumptions, Winch describes how love and mate selection operate. Love, he defines, as the positive emotion expressed by one person in a relationship in which the second person meets certain important needs of the first, or manifests or appears to manifest personal qualities highly valued by the first. In mate selection, then, each person selects, from within the field of eligibles, that person who gives greatest promise of providing the maximum need gratification. The partners' need patterns, consequently, will be complementary rather than similar. The complementariness, further, was hypothesized to be of either of two kinds. First, the needs of the one spouse may be different in kind from the needs of the second spouse. Or, second, the needs of the one spouse may differ in degree or intensity from those of the other.

The research which sought to verify these hypotheses was very complex and used a very limited sample. Lengthy "need" interviews and case history interviews were supplemented through the use of projective testing. Ratings of personality needs were then based upon content analysis of the need interview and case history materials, summarized and evaluated at conferences of the investigators.

The sample from whom these data were secured were only 25 undergraduate, childless couples at Northwestern University. The data were subjected to elaborate statistical analysis. The analyses were too technical to be reported here. Suffice it to say that the results generally supported the hypotheses. An early test, for example, supported the notion that the assertive-receptive dimension is important in mate selection; high assertives tended to marry high receptives. Similarly, it was found that when the same traits in husband and wife were correlated (abasement with abasement, hostility with hostility, dominance with dominance, and so on), the relationships were generally negative. They found little evidence of personality homogamy. When the husbands' hostility scores were correlated with the wives' abasement scores, by contrast, the relationship was positive; their needs were complementary.

The results required careful qualification. Winch acknowledged that they were not as compelling as they might have been. He concluded, however, that the bulk of the data supported the theory of complementary needs. Moreover, that portion of the results which did not clearly support the theory of complementary needs did not support the idea of homogamy in personal needs either; they simply showed little relationship among the variables.

The theory of complementary needs attracted considerable attention. If subsequent research should establish its validity, it would contribute greatly to our knowledge of mate selection. It is not surprising that there have been several attempts to test the theory.

At least five studies attempted to test Winch's findings directly, using the Edwards Personal Preference Schedule to measure personality needs and to get at complementariness. One study used 60 college couples who either were regular dating partners or were engaged,[65] one used 36 unmarried couples and 64 married couples,[66] one used an accidental sample of 50 relatively well-adjusted married couples,[67] one used 62 couples who were either dating, going steady, or engaged,[68] and the fifth used 258 Swedish couples who had published the banns.[69] In all five studies, the results were essentially negative; no real support was found for the theory of complementary needs.

It should be pointed out that these studies were not strictly comparable to Winch's study. The instruments and procedures differed. Moreover, the samples were small and selective. The theory of complementary needs cannot be said to have been either adequately established or adequately refuted. Perhaps the most valuable contribution so far has been to lead to attempts to improve the theory itself.

Rosow pointed out that the theory of complementary needs is oversimplified. He maintains that there are at least four kinds of complementarity that affect marital cohesion: (1) the relations strictly between the couple, as studied by Winch; (2) the relations which involve either partner acting for the couple with outsiders; (3) relations between the couple, as a couple, with outsiders; (4) relations in which each partner

65. Charles E. Bowerman and Barbara R. Day, "A Test of the Theory of Complementary Needs as Applied to Couples During Courtship," *American Sociological Review* 21 (Oct. 1956), pp. 602–5.

66. James A. Schellenberg and Lawrence S. Bee, "A Re-examination of the Theory of Complementary Needs in Mate Selection," *Marriage and Family Living* 22 (Aug. 1960), pp. 227–32.

67. John A. Blazer, "Complementary Needs and Marital Happiness," *Marriage and Family Living* 25 (Feb. 1963), pp. 89–95.

68. Jerold S. Heiss and Michael Gordon, "Need Patterns and the Mutual Satisfaction of Dating and Engaged Couples," *Journal of Marriage and the Family* 26 (Aug. 1964), pp. 337–39.

69. Jan Trost, "Some Data on Mate Selection: Complementarity," *Journal of Marriage and the Family* 29 (Nov. 1967), pp. 730–38.

separately seeks, within the marriage, to balance satisfactions or frustrations encountered outside the family. He points out, too, that needs exist, as organized patterns and that the importance of these patterns in an individual life may change over time.[70]

Udry suggested, further, that we react to others on the basis of our perceptions of them, and that perception may or may not coincide with measured personality traits. He found that mates' perceptions of one another exaggerate personality differences and involve projection of their own traits. One implication is that an adequate theory of complementary needs will need to be more complex than the existing theory.[71]

Finally, Bolton introduced balance into theories of mate selection by arguing that, while both homogamy and complementary theories have utility, mate selection must be studied not only in terms of variables brought by the partners to the courtship situation, but also in terms of the process by which their relationship moves toward marriage. There are many turning points and commitments.

A DEVELOPMENTAL APPROACH TO MATE SELECTION

The development of a courtship is not mechanically predetermined by either social or personality variables. Instead, the outcome is the product of a long series of advances and retreats, changing definitions of the situation, and the resolution of tensions. Bolton describes five different types of developmental processes:[72]

Type I: *Personality meshing developmental processes.* The predominant characteristic of this type is the mutual perception of personality "fit," bringing into meshing the existing personality orientations of the two parties and providing the qualities of experience which serve as indexes of a marriageable relation. Couples tend to be homogamous in background and values, but complementary in personality needs and organization. Attraction is felt early, the developmental tempos of the pair are in close rhythm, and interactions increase in frequency with

70. Irving Rosow, "Issues in the Concept of Need-Complementarity," *Sociometry* 20 (Sept. 1957), pp. 216–33. See also Jan Trost, "Some Data on Mate Selection: Homogamy and Perceived Homogamy," *Journal of Marriage and the Family* 29 (Nov. 1967), pp. 739–55; and Ellen S. Karp, Julie H. Jackson, and David Lester, "Ideal-Self Fulfillment in Mate Selection: A Corollary to the Complementary Need Theory of Mate Selection," *Journal of Marriage and the Family* 32 (May 1970), pp. 269–72.

71. J. Richard Udry, "Complementarity in Mate Selection: A Perceptual Approach," *Marriage and Family Living* 25 (Aug. 1963), pp. 281–89.

72. Charles D. Bolton, "Mate Selection as the Development of a Relationship," *Marriage and Family Living* 23 (Aug. 1961), pp. 234–40. See also Robert G. Ryder, John S. Kafka, and David H. Olson, "Separating and Joining Influences in Courtship and Early Marriage," *American Journal of Orthopsychiatry* 41 (April 1971), pp. 450–64.

erotic interaction, empathy, and idealization important. These relations correspond fairly closely to romantic expectations.

Type II: *Identity clarification developmental processes.* The central theme is the clarification or change of one or both individuals' identities. Though the two individuals may differ initially about values, interaction brings about increasing agreements along with a role pattern tending to be equalitarian. The assumption of compatibility either is made early or emerges out of interaction about identity problems. . . . Identity problems are precipitated by interaction, such as through conflict with parents or threat to defenses against intimate involvement. The relation cannot progress to marriage until the identity problems are resolved. The importance of interpersonal strategies is great; turning points are frequent; and shared understandings of considerable depth are built up. There is a withdrawal into the relationship and away from outside influences.

Type III: *Relation-centered developmental processes.* The central theme is the building up of images of the other, amorous identifications and bonds which lead the couple to marriage. Personalities do not spontaneously mesh; their "fit" remains in doubt throughout the premarital period. Adjustments, shared understandings, and commitments are consciously built up, though they may not have much depth. There is initial superficial commitment, and then one or both parties begin having questions, and the theme becomes the viability of the relation. There are more ups and downs, breaks, rivals, and outside pressures to maintain the relation than in any other type.

Type IV: *Pressure- and intrapersonal-centered developmental procesess.* The two parties are similar and traditional in background, and dislike conflict. But their personalities decidedly do not mesh. One party uses direct, frontal pressure, while the other depends upon subtle manipulation, with one being relatively free of blocks while the other has personality barriers to intimate involvements. Several themes emerge: (1) one member, being under pressure to marry, falls in love quickly and pressures the other for marriage, but the resisting member blocks; (2) a concentration directly upon marriageability and upon securing commitments; (3) a dependence of one or both members more upon the relationship per se than upon one another; and (4) importance of fantasy for one or both members. Identity problems are avoided except at crises—and then interaction halts short of efforts at resolution—and even amorous identifications are built up primarily in intrapersonal processes. The lack of congruity of definitions is met by fantasy and tactical maneuvering. There is an emphasis upon formality, romanticism, and role playing, with avoidance of the directly erotic. Often crucial developments come by correspondence, where the inhibited member feels freer and ambiguity is harder to maintain.

Type V: *Expediency-centered developmental processes.* The relation centers on a strongly felt pressure to marry on the part of one or both members, in the context of a basic personality problem or identity crisis. Where this pressure characterizes only one partner, the other is inexperienced in heterosexual relationships, highly suggestible, or apathetic. If expediency exists at the outset, the process is short; if it emerges after a casual relation is in progress, there are sharp turning points and tactical maneuvers through which the relationship quickly moves toward marriage. Personality "fit" and mutuality of values are only superficially considered, though some fantasy is important.

Whether or not these five types cover all of the processes whereby future spouses are selected, their construction displays a broad, perceptive knowledge of personality and courtship. They indicate the importance of personal, interpersonal, and situational variables within the general context imposed by social homogamy.

A STIMULUS-VALUE-ROLE THEORY

One final theory of mate selection has been developed by Murstein who holds that most couples pass through three stages before they marry: the stimulus stage, the value stage, and the role stage.[73]

The theory holds that people are first attracted to one another by their perceptions of their attractive qualities. This is the stimulus stage. The attractive qualities are both physical and social: good looks, strong, tall, petite, jovial, considerate, aggressive, and so on. Without being wholly aware of it, each partner prepares a mental balance sheet, comparing the other's attractive and unattractive features, and then comparing them with his or her own. If the one partner is substantially more or less attractive than the other, the relationship is likely to be broken off by the more attractive partner.

If the couple are fairly evenly matched, the relationship may develop on into the value stage. Now the partners talk. They discuss their attitudes toward men's and women's roles, and toward marriage. They discuss such abstract subjects as politics and religion, and such intimate ones as practicing birth control and having children. The more similar the discovered values, the stronger their attraction to one another becomes, and the more time they spend together. They are falling in love.

73. Bernard I. Murstein, "A Theory of Marital Choice and Its Applicability to Marriage Adjustment," in Bernard I. Murstein, *ed., Theories of Attraction and Love,* New York: Springer, 1971, pp. 100–151.

Some couples marry at this point, but most move on into the role stage. Now the pair's association is so continuous that they not only hear one another's expressed values, but they see how those values are expressed in real life situations. They see whether the other partner is cheerful or moody, dependable or erratic, generous or selfish, punitive or forgiving, and so on. The more they interact, the more they perceive what it would be like to be married to one another. Again the concept of the hypothetical balance sheet applies. If the bargain continues to be favorable and fairly equal, marriage is likely to be the outcome.

The stimulus-value-role theory, along with developmental theory, and complementary needs theory, all help us to understand how couples sorted originally by homogamy and propinquity move on toward marriage.

Finally, it should at least be questioned whether we do not over-rationalize the process of mate selection. Our emphasis upon free marital choice seems to imply that one chooses a mate as rationally as one buys a garden tool or a tube of toothpaste. At the same time, it seems apparent that, at about a certain age, strong cultural pressures are generated for people to find mates and they do just that—telling themselves, all the while, how carefully their choices are being made. Some writers have suggested that, while the percentage of marriages that are purely of the "supply and demand" variety may be small, possibly most marriages embody some element of chance.

SUMMARY

Homogamy, the tendency for like to marry like, reflects endogamous norms. Homogamy has been verified for age, marital status, social status, race, religion, and ethnic background.

Most Americans marry young, and marry persons of nearly their own age. Age-homogamy norms become less effective in remarriages. Studies show that age at marriage is related to marital success, with those marrying very young having poorer chances of achieving marital happiness. The proportion of marriages of high-school-age youth increased from 1910 to 1950, but the rate has not increased since then. The divorce rate among such young marriages is estimated at from two to four times that among persons who marry after 20 years of age. The high divorce rate is related to low educational levels, low economic levels, premarital pregnancies, and possibly to personality difficulties. Whether young marriages that remain intact are of higher or lower quality than other marriages is unknown.

Status homogamy operates by occupational level, educational level, and class of residential area. When status homogamy does not hold, however, the general pattern is for men to marry downward. This "mating gradient" may leave high-status women and low-status men among the unmarried. Status homogamy may be declining with time.

Traditionally, the norms requiring racial endogamy have been strong. Perhaps no more than 1 percent of all marriages are interracial, although the intermarriage rate is increasing. There is great interest in that small proportion of the population which does intermarry.

Studies show that spouses in interracial marriages tend to be older than those entering homogamous marriages, that they may have been married before, and that they may have histories of rejection by parents and their own racial group. On the other hand, equalitarian norms may be leading groups to contemplate interracial dating and marriage without the historically associated conditions of rebellion and nonconformity.

Interracial marriages are widely believed to be doomed to failure. Studies of war-bride marriages and black-white marriages do not bear out the belief, however. Instead, studies show that strains are patterned and predictable, just as they are in racially homogamous marriages. The strains in black-white marriages include isolation from parental families, particularly the white family, and having to raise children as black. Discrimination may be encountered in housing, employment, and in public. Most of the marriages studied, however, appear to be as stable as other marriages.

Studies of religious homogamy have shown wide variation in intermarriage rates. In general, the larger the proportion a religious group is of the community, the lower its intermarriage rate and vice versa. Intermarriage also varies inversely with the cohesion of the ethnic group. Religious intermarriage rates are increasing.

Research shows divorce rates to be higher in marriages where Catholics marry non-Catholics than in Catholic marriages. The differences are smaller than generally believed, however, and do not cover all types of religious mixed marriages. Marital survival rates are influenced more by age and social status than by religious differences. Studies of adjustment in interfaith marriages have produced conflicting findings. Some studies show special problems of adjustment, and some do not. Society may be becoming increasingly accepting of interfaith marriages.

Residential propinquity refers to the tendency of persons to select marriage partners who live near to them. Propinquity operates at the first date and at marriage. Theories explaining propinquity have emphasized residential segregation, homogamous norms, the relation between distance and the likelihood of interaction, and the sheer time and energy costs involved in traveling.

The evidence for homogamy in personal characteristics is not so strong as that in social characteristics. In fact, there is some evidence that people seek marital partners who complement themselves in personality. A theory of complementary needs has received some empirical support; subsequent testing failed to confirm the original findings, however. Efforts to develop the theory continue. Full understanding of mate selection requires that relationships be viewed developmentally, in addition to the perspective provided by homogamy, propinquity, and complementary needs. The development of courtship is not completely predetermined but involves a series of advances and retreats, changing definitions of the situation, and commitments.

Finally, mate selection is not yet fully explained. There may be fortuitous factors operating. Few instances of mate selection can be ascribed wholly to chance, but some chance elements may enter into most relationships.

SUGGESTED READINGS

Barron, Milton L., *ed.*, *The Blending American*, Chicago: Quadrangle Books, 1972. An anthology containing articles on religious, nationality, and racial intermarriage. One section deals with the consequences of intermarriage.

Carter, Hugh, and Glick, Paul C., *Marriage and Divorce: A Social and Economic Study*, Cambridge, Mass.: Harvard University Press, 1976. A rich compilation of data, from federal sources, on marriage patterns in the United States.

Gordon, Milton M., *Assimilation in American Life: The Role of Race, Religion and National Origins*, New York: Oxford University Press, 1964. Brilliant theoretical analysis of the assimilation of racial, ethnic, and religious groups. Deals with problems and processes of intermarriage.

Lenski, Gerhard, *The Religious Factor: A Sociological Study of Religion's Impact on Politics, Economics, and Family Life*, Garden City, N.J.: Doubleday and Company, 1961. Comprehensive report of research which, among other things, indicates that subculture differences among the major religious groups may be increasing rather than declining.

Vernon, Glenn M., *The Sociology of Religion*, New York: The McGraw-Hill Book Company, 1962. Good introductory treatment of the sociological analysis of religious phenomena. One section deals with the interrelation between religion and other social institutions, including the family.

FILMS

Are You the One? (Educational Media Services, Brigham Young University, Provo, Utah 84601), 24 minutes. Through analysis of one couple, pinpoints some of the issues to be considered in selecting a mate.

Marriage: What Kind for You? (Educational Media Services, Brigham Young University, Provo, Utah 84601), 25 minutes. An engaged couple view different couples at an office party. Makes sharp contrasts between healthy and deteriorating relationships.

Never a Bride: Preparing for Marriage (Educational Media Services, Brigham Young University, Provo, Utah 84601), 22 minutes. A self-seeking girl discovers that it is more important to be the right person than to find the right person for marriage.

QUESTIONS AND PROJECTS

1. What is meant by homogamy? How are homogamous norms related to endogamy and exogamy?
2. What is the pattern of homogamy by age? How is it related to marital status?
3. What trends have been evident in very youthful marriages? What factors are related to success or failure of such marriages? Can you see any elements of a self-fulfilling prophecy operating?
4. Does homogamy operate by status levels in the society? What is the evidence? Is there any evidence that status homogamy may be weakening?
5. What is meant by "the mating gradient"? What influence does it have on determining what groups are likely to remain among the unmarried?
6. How much interracial marriage is there in the United States? How rapidly is the rate increasing?
7. What are the consequences of interracial marriages? Are these in accord with traditional stereotypes? What do we know about the personality needs of those who intermarry? What change may be occurring?
8. How much religious homogamy is there in the United States? What factors are related to intermarriage rates? Is intermarriage increasing? What do studies show of attitudes toward intermarriage?
9. What is the relation between religious heterogamy and divorce rates? Is the relationship a simple one? What does research show about the relationship between marital happiness and interfaith marriage?
10. Define residential propinquity. How does it operate? What explanations have been proposed for it?
11. Explain the theory of complementary needs. What does research show? Is further development of the theory needed?
12. How may mate selection be conceived of as a developmental process? Relate this concept to Waller's theory of dating and courtship.

MIRÓ

14
Marital Adjustment

. . . Now marriage is, in actual fact, just a way of living. We don't expect life to be all sunshine and roses, or even beer and skittles. But somehow we do expect marriage to be that way. People who are accustomed to bickering with everyone else are shocked when they find that they bicker with their wives. Women who have found everything somewhat disappointing are surprised and pained when marriage proves itself no exception. Most of the complaints about the institution of holy matrimony arise not because it is worse than the rest of life, but because it is not incomparably better.

There are reasons for this almost universal feeling of disillusionment about marriage. One is that we are taught to expect too much from it. . . . But even if we have become profoundly cynical about marriage in general we are apt to be disillusioned about our own, because most of us marry while we are in love. . . . The sexual excitement, the uncertainties and novelties of the new relationship actually lift us out of ourselves for a time. With the best will in the world we cannot during the falling-in-love stage show ourselves to our beloved as we really are, nor see her in her everyday personality. We are quite genuinely not our everyday selves at this period. We are more intense, more vital than usual. Moreover we see ourselves through the eyes of our beloved. Unconsciously we match our feeling about ourselves with the glorified impression she has formed of us.

This excited state of mind cannot endure the protracted association of marriage. The thrilling sexual tension which normally keeps engaged couples in a state of fervid and delighted expectation abates with frequent, satisfying intercourse. The element of uncertainty is dissipated—and there is no doubt that a goal we have not yet won is more intriguing than one which is wholly ours. . . . Sooner or later, when flamboyant anticipations of betrothal give way to the sober satisfactions of marriage, we lapse back into our ordinary selves. Fortunately, we can surpass ourselves during emotional crises without seriously depleting our reserves. We can run from a bear very fast indeed, but if we made that speed habitual we would soon collapse entirely. Walking is the most practicable gait for common use, and marriage too must be paced at the rate of our usual temperament. This inevitable change of pace is what we call disillusionment. Our disillusionment does not proceed wholly, or perhaps even primarily, from the unromantic facts we learn about our partner in the course of daily observation. It comes largely from our bored recognition of the same old self within our own breast. Our own newfound charm and prowess and glamour evaporate when we can no longer read them in a worshipping gaze, when we are no longer stimulated by the desire for conquest. . . .[1]

The last two chapters have shown that the routes whereby couples approach marriage are multiple and varied. It seems likely that some persons exercise rationality in their selection of spouses and approach marriage with realistic expectations. At the other extreme are couples caught up in overwhelming attraction for one another. Some of these relationships develop essentially without exploitation and involve intense idealization of each partner by the other. In others, one partner is clearly dominant, with the disadvantaged partner more or less successfully concealing the already present pain the relationship produces. Some couples are trapped into marriage by pregnancy. Some appear to result primarily from the pressures exerted by partners and friends, and the lack of a better alternative. Some defy explanation.

We cannot even list all of the qualities of relationships and all of the courtship processes that lead to marriage. It is obvious, however, that the adjustments required in marriage are related to the relationships upon which marriages are based; the adjustment of 22-year-old college graduates with parental approval and adequate finances will differ from that of high-school students trapped by pregnancy. Moreover, the adjustment of an aggressive, unattractive 25-year-old bride and a divorced man will differ from both. Processes of marital adjustment are unlikely to be fewer or simpler than those of courtship.

No one has yet succeeded in developing a fully adequate theory of marital adjustment. In fact there is scarcely a satisfactory definition of marital adjustment. In this chapter, we will look first at some common patterns of interaction in early marriage and then subject the concept of marital adjustment to critical scrutiny.

1. John Levy and Ruth Munroe, *The Happy Family*, New York: Alfred A. Knopf, 1948, pp. 65–67.

THE DYNAMICS OF MARITAL ADJUSTMENT

Marriage may or may not involve a drastic change in living arrangements. Clarke, for example, found that 10 percent of the couples he studied reported the same address on the marriage-license application form.[2] Some of this might be accounted for by couples reporting the address to which they were moving rather than where they had previously been living. Some of these couples, however, already were living together.

Other evidence indicates that whether the couple already are having intercourse influences their early marital adjustments. Kanin and Howard found that couples who were having premarital intercourse were less likely to take wedding trips, were less likely to practice contraception early in marriage, and were more likely to report both sexual satisfaction and aspiration toward better sexual adjustment in marriage.[3]

Honeymoon Interaction

For most couples, marriage represents a sharp break with conditions of prior living. The marriage ceremony endorses whatever relationship already exists and, often, propels them into a twenty-four-hour-a-day physical and emotional intimacy for which they are not wholly prepared. Marriages seldom are scheduled to coincide with readiness for full intimacy but are arranged, instead, in terms of less relevant criteria such as graduation from college, attaining the minimum legal age, having the harvest in, and so on. It should not be surprising if the sudden transition occasioned by the wedding ceremony were accompanied by both bliss and strain for most young couples.

A perceptive analysis of early marital adjustment has come from Willard Waller. It cannot be said that he described the adjustment processes in all young marriages, but something approaching some of the conditions he describes may appear in most of them.[4]

Waller describes the early weeks of marriage as suffused with erotically tinged euphoria. To the degree idealization has developed during courtship, each partner carries into marriage a romanticized conception

2. Alfred C. Clarke, "An Examination of the Operation of Residential Propinquity as a Factor in Mate Selection," *American Sociological Review* 17 (Feb. 1952), pp. 17–22.

3. Eugene J. Kanin and David H. Howard, "Postmarital Consequences of Premarital Sex Adjustments," *American Sociological Review* 23 (Oct. 1958), pp. 556–62.

4. The following discussion draws heavily on Willard Waller and Reuben Hill, *The Family: A Dynamic Interpretation*, New York: Dryden Press, 1951, pp. 253–321.

of what the other is like. Each has been living somewhat beyond himself—on cloud nine as it were. It seems wonderful to be marrying such an extraordinary person as the partner appears to be and, if the partner is so exceptional, then one must also be special to merit such a partner.

Many forces operate in the premarital period to enhance the egos and general well-being of the couple. To have found a partner at all represents success in the competition for mates. To have found such an ideal partner produces something akin to a mild, continuing intoxication. Then as the sex relationship progresses, there is the overwhelming desire for complete fulfillment. As with other forms of fulfillment, the anticipation, the fantasy, and the accompanying feelings probably are as important as the achievement itself. Finally, the approval and vicarious participation of family and friends in the relationship brings psychic rewards. One's position has shifted a little closer to the center of the universe, and one experiences emotions that surely are denied most ordinary people.

This heady euphoria continues into the early weeks of marriage. Moreover, it is reinforced by the excitement of the new married status, acquiring new possessions, moving into new quarters, and establishing new routines. According to Waller, this anesthetizes each partner against the too early and too violent intrusion upon pre-existing habit patterns of the nonmeshing habits of the partner. Thus, a man, fussy about food can eat the undercooked eggs without the gastrointestinal spasms they would otherwise produce. Similarly, the young wife who finds that her husband wears his underwear for three days and then throws it under the bed is not immediately overcome with revulsion. Locked in one another's arms, in their fantasies, in their new status, and in the interest and approval of others, most couples experience—whether or not they take a wedding trip—an initial blissful adjustment which merits the sentimental term *honeymoon*.

Even during this early period, however, the couple move toward a *modus vivendi*. Our system does not provide rigidly structured roles into which husband and wife must fit, but depends upon the attraction between them to see them through the development of roles appropriate to their situation and which will enhance their social and economic status. There are large areas of behavior which must be defined in a short time.

Paradoxically, the so-called honeymoon period also is characterized by unusual sensitivity of each spouse to the behavior of the other. The euphoria alternates with, periods of excessive hurt and shock at actual or alleged slights. If idealization frequently accompanies courtship, so does doubt—of self, of partner, and of the relationship. To the degree to which love serves as a rationalization of the movement toward marriage, the partner who has these feelings may react violently to their confirmation in the marriage. The first time, for example, that the husband comes home too tired to go out with his wife may constitute irrefutable proof that he does not love her. The first time that the wife crawls into bed and goes promptly to sleep may signal to the husband that he should have heeded his doubts about getting married in the first place.

The opportunities for rebuffs and slights in early marriage are legion. Moreover, marriage forces upon people an intimacy which is not all erotic. Husbands cannot escape confrontation with the paraphernalia attending menstruation or with hair curlers and the washing of lingerie. Many wives must handle dirty socks and underwear and clean up the bathroom which has been turned into a swamp during their husbands' showers. Both sexes must contend with messy toothpaste tubes and catsup bottles—rendered that way by inconsiderate partners.

Waller defined the honeymoon as that period in the psychic adjustment of the couple while illusion lasts. Eventually, he thought, the opposition between idealization on the one hand and the intrusion of humdrum reality on the other yields to reality. Inherent in this is some disillusionment, both with the partner and with oneself. If the partner is not so different from others, then the special desirability that was imputed to oneself must be illusory also. The shattering of dreams is painful and the onset of disillusionment sets the stage for conflict.

There is some empirical support for the idea of generalized disillusionment early in marriage. Hobart reports a study of 258 couples ranging from "favorite date" to "married" at a West Coast college. He found strong evidence of disillusionment in the transition from engagement to marriage. The data indicated more disillusionment among men than among women and more tendency among men for disillusionment to be associated with prior romanticism.[5] What is particularly striking is the implication that disillusionment may occur early in marriage even where there has not been excessive unreality in courtship.

Indirect evidence of disillusionment in early marriage also is provided by separation and divorce rates. Landis, studying 544 college couples who had been married about two years, found that one-fifth of them had

5. Charles W. Hobart, "Disillusionment in Marriage, and Romanticism," *Marrige and Family Living* 20 (May 1958), pp. 156–62; Peter C. Pineo, "Development Patterns in Marriage," *The Family Coordinator* 18 (April 1969), pp. 135–40.

considered separation.[6] In Oregon, Johannis found that one-third of 54 college couples married three years had considered separation. For the country as a whole, there are more divorces during the first year of marriage than in any year after the fourth year. Moreover, the highest divorce rates occur during the second and third years of marriage.[7] Many of these couples have separated after only a few months of living together. While these rates do not automatically testify to disillusionment, they indicate that many couples undergo severe stress in the early months and years of marriage.

When disillusionment occurs, conflict develops. No one enjoys being hurt and the marriage partner is not only the most available target but is also, by a perverse sort of logic, responsible for one's plight. What is more natural than to attack?

The Emergence of Conflict

The incidents that set off conflict more often than not are trivial. The same undercooked eggs that one gamely ate before now become intolerable. The messy catsup bottle, the messy bathroom, lack of enthusiasm for going to the movies or making love—all produce rage. Often, of course, one's partner is undergoing comparable frustrations and meets rage with rage. Even when a spouse is not disposed to quarrel, he or she seldom is prepared to withstand hostile attacks from the partner. Whatever doubts and anxieties surround oneself and the relationship become the focus of attention. Without intending to, and without wanting to, many young couples test their relationships severely.

Waller and Hill emphasize the potential destructiveness of quarreling. They point out that ordinarily people in general, and spouses in particular, handle carefully the little fictions, rationalizations, and half-truths according to which people order their lives and protect their self-concepts.[8] A woman may know, and her husband may know, that she is not very attractive. Usually, however, she emphasizes her good points,

6. Judson T. Landis, "On the Campus," *Survey Midmonthly* 84 (Jan. 1948), pp. 17–19.
7. Theodore B. Johannis, Jr., "The Marital Adjustment of a Sample of Married College Students," *Family Life Coordinator* 4 (June 1956), p. 29.
8. Willard Waller and Reuben Hill, *op. cit.*, p. 301. See also Wells Goodrich, Robert G. Ryder, and Harold L. Raush, "Patterns of Newlywed Marriage," *Journal of Marriage and the Family* 30 (Aug. 1968), pp. 383–91; Robert G. Ryder, John S. Kafka, and David H. Olson, "Separating and Joining Influences in Courtship and Early Marriage," *American Journal of Orthopsychiatry* 41 (April 1971), pp. 450–64; and Jetse Sprey, "The Family as a System in Conflict," *Journal of Marriage and the Family* 31 (Nov. 1969), pp. 699–706.

such as wavy hair or well-shaped legs. Her husband, too, emphasizes her good features. There is a tacit conspiracy in which each protects the other and both protect the relationship. As long as they get along well, it works just fine. Even in marriage, each partner preserves some of the adoration so carefully cultivated in courtship.

When conflict develops, this breaks down. Each partner is hurt and wishes to inflict hurt in turn. How better to do it than to attack where the other is vulnerable? The husband's occupational success is important. The degree to which he is a success depends upon many factors, not the least of which is his wife's ability to play the hostess and companion. Even if she is extraordinarily adroit at furthering her husband's career, usually she plays it down and basks in his success. When he tells her how astutely he put over a program, she tells him what a wonderful executive he is. Not until they come into serious conflict will she point out that much of his success depends upon the friendship that she has cultivated with the boss and the boss's wife. Only then will she tell him that most people think of him as only an average boy who was fortunate to marry a talented woman.

The example could be multiplied hundreds of times and turned against the husband and wife equally. The point is that, under provocation, each partner sets out to destroy the little fictions that are so important to maintaining the self-concept. And in these bitter attacks upon one another, they may soon destroy the basis upon which their relationship is built. In the illustration, the husband who has been confronted by his wife will find it difficult to share his successes with her in full enthusiasm again. Once it has been said, neither of them can assume the full pretense that operated before. If he is to adjust benignly, the husband may seek approval more from his coworkers. In that case, his marriage suffers only by attrition. In more destructive forms, the husband may cherish the adoration bestowed upon him by a secretary, a girl he picked up in a bar, or even the attentive ear of a bartender.

Overt Conflict

There are many ways to conceptualize conflict. One way is to describe it in terms of acute, progressive, or habituated forms.

Acute conflict is most characteristic of early marriage, and stems from the many undefined situations which exist then. Its function is to permit the couple to work out a joint pattern of life in which the frustrations that accompany early disillusionment have been worked through.

The question, of course, is whether accommodation will be achieved before quarreling has destroyed the foundation upon which it must rest. As the particular problems that a couple face are resolved, acute conflict tends to disappear from the marriage. It may reappear, however, whenever any basic change in conditions produces a new undefined situation. Acute conflict, for example, may reappear when the first child is born and continue until techniques for handling the accompanying changes are worked out. Similarly, a promotion, a move to another city, the marriage of one's children, and having to care for one's aged parents all may provoke new outbursts of acute conflict.

Acute conflict involves intense explosions of hostility with great emotional involvement by both spouses. It is the kind of conflict in which each party sets out to inflict maximum damage upon the other. Its potential for disruption of the relationship is great. Apparently most couples resolve most basic issues before too much damage is done. And having eliminated most acute conflict from a marriage apparently improves the chances that subsequent outbursts will also be handled successfully. Some marriages do break down, however, after 10, 20, or 30 years of marriage. Some of these probably have proved to be ultimate victims of the inability to resolve acute conflict.

Unless couples learn rather quickly to resolve conflict, the probability is great that the conflict will take a directional form; it will become progressive. When acute conflict is not resolved, each quarrel leaves a residue of hard feeling and an area in which the couple cannot communicate effectively. Then each time a quarrel develops, there is not only the new issue to solve, but the hard feelings and unresolved issues from earlier quarrels too. The conflict spirals, with the disagreement becoming wider and the feelings more bitter. Very much of this may produce estrangement—a condition in which the partners are permanently alienated. Unless the couple is irrevocably committed to the permanence of marriage, movement toward separation and/or divorce may follow.

The tendency for acute conflict to become progressive may help explain the large number of marriages which result in separation during the first year. What is not known is whether marriages that remain intact involve less conflict. At present, it appears that most intact marriages that survive do show less conflict; it also appears that some intact marriages continue in spite of marked estrangement between the spouses.

In the "best" of marriages, there may be little apparent conflict after the initial adjustments are worked out. In the "worst" of marriages, husband-wife interaction, except for conflict, virtually may not exist. Most marriages probably fall in between. In most areas they have worked out a reasonably satisfactory adjustment, but there also remain areas where they have reached only tentative compromises or where they cannot agree. This may happen in the areas of in-law relationships and money management. In spite of our equal treatment norms, either spouse may be unable to accept the in-laws completely. They may avoid contact with them and may lash out at the spouse whenever he or she is tactless enough to force the issue. Similarly, after the budget, insurance payments, and all of the rest have been worked out, one spouse may consistently overspend or underspend as compared to the partner's expectations. The situation may generally be kept under control, with open conflict emerging only at the time the bank statement is received, say, or when the couple run out of money before the end of the month.

Such areas of conflict which crop up again and again, with a stable accommodation never quite being achieved, may be labeled habituated. Habituated conflict differs from acute conflict in that there is not the same emotional investment in it; it is less explosive. In early marriage, when a husband sleeps on the living room sofa it may throw his wife into an unreasoning rage. After a stable adjustment has been reached, he may continue to nap on the sofa and his wife may mutter with some disgust that he is a lazy slob, but neither she nor he is greatly upset. Habituated conflict also differs from progressive conflict in that it does not become worse. The wife may even reach the point where she refers to her husband as a lazy slob, with some overtones of affection.

Marriages vary widely in the amount of habituated conflict in them and in the amount of such conflict that they can tolerate. In some there may be very little, while in others there may be little else. The dynamics of marital accommodation may be as variable as the personality structures of husbands and wives, as the interests which they do and do not share, and as the patterns of interaction which led them into marriage.

Physical Violence

Although most marital conflicts occur as quarrels, researchers have learned in recent years that couples engage in a surprising amount of physical fighting. One survey of 385 college students, for example, reported that 16 percent of them were aware of recent episodes of violence between their parents.[9] And these were couples who had been

9. Murray Straus, "Leveling, Civility, and Violence in the Family," *Journal of Marriage and the Family* 36 (Feb. 1974), pp. 13–29.

married for many years. A second study of 80 married couples reported 55 percent of them had had at least one incident of physical violence.[10] The National Commission on the Causes and Prevention of Crime and Violence estimated that between one-fourth and one-fifth of all adult Americans believe that it is acceptable for spouses to hit one another under certain circumstances.

In one of the most revealing studies to date, Steinmetz secured 78 questionnaires from college students and their older friends. Thirty percent of these families had used physical aggression to resolve marital conflicts. Among them, Steinmetz classified four basic types of problem solvers. The first type, labeled "screaming sluggers" were couples who made both verbal and physical attacks upon one another. The second type, the "silent attackers" avoided quarreling, but eventually released their frustrations through physical assault. "Threateners" attacked verbally and threatened the use of violence, but did not resort to it. Finally, the last type, who were called "pacifists," were able to resolve issues without either verbal or physical attack.[11]

Probably most of the married couples who fight physically do so only occasionally, and then with restraint. There is some pushing or shoving, a slap, or pushing the other down on a bed or chair. There are no data adequate to tell us what the effects of such violence are upon marriages. If the violence is frequent and severe, it becomes spouse abuse, and usually leads to separation or divorce.[12] Steinmetz reports, however, that some people who are prone to attack physically may also be more likely to engage in a great deal of kissing, hugging, and embracing as well. Further research is badly needed to help us unravel this very complex situation.

Covert Conflict

So far, we have dealt with marital conflict as though it were synonymous with open fighting. We have assumed that quarreling is normal in marriage as it is in the rest of life and that most couples learn to handle quarreling in marriage as they do elsewhere. To conceive of marital

10. Richard J. Gelles, *The Violent Home: A Study of Physical Aggression Between Husbands and Wives*, Beverly Hills, Cal.: Sage Publications, 1972.
11. Suzanne K. Steinmetz, "The Use of Force for Resolving Family Conflict: The Training Ground for Abuse," *The Family Coordinator* 26 (Jan. 1977), pp. 19–26.
12. Richard J. Gelles, "Abused Wives: Why Do They Stay?" *Journal of Marriage and the Family* 38 (Nov. 1976), pp. 659–68.

conflict in such limited terms, however, is to miss some of the most significant and devastating ways in which people struggle against one another.

Throughout this book we have assumed that behavior occurs at varying levels of awareness. Some behavior may best be understood as fully conscious and rational. In other instances, people act in ways that do not make sense unless one is willing to assume that certain functions of the behavior are different from the apparent ones. We saw how this operates in dating and mate selection. Now we observe it in marriage.

The pervasiveness of covert conflict in marriage is difficult to estimate. By definition it is hidden and cannot be observed directly. Only through psychotherapeutic evaluation can it often be definitely established. Yet there is widespread agreement that there is a whole series of "emotional withholdings" in many relationships that reveal under-cover hostility. Some would say that some conflict is inherent in all relationships and that, if a couple do not at least occasionally disagree openly, one is sure to find evidences of unknowing sabotage in the relationship.

Perhaps the most widely recognized forms of emotional withholding in marriage are in the sexual area. Lack of sexual responsiveness in wives and impotence in husbands are examples. This is not to say that there may not be occasional instances where there are organic problems or that there may not be deep-seated psychological factors operating in other cases. The incidence of apparent frigidity and impotence is far greater than can be accounted for in these terms, however. What better way for a spouse, who cannot show hostility openly, to hurt his or her partner than to fail to respond sexually?

Short of actual frigidity or impotence, husbands and wives even more commonly contest with one another by being "too tired" for sex. The seriousness of such conflict is difficult to estimate because often there are legitimate reasons for being too tired. All fatigue cannot be interpreted as covert conflict. However, whenever the fatigue is recurrent and cannot be accounted for medically, there is a strong presumption of problems in a relationship. On the basis of impressionistic evidence and the testimony of psychotherapists, such conflict is widespread.

There are other forms of withholding—ways of making one's partner suffer without appearing to do so. The spouse who is hypochondriacal often unwittingly uses illness to control the partner and to deny the partner the full joy of living; the ill one must be cared for and catered to, but cannot be expected to be a satisfying sex partner and companion. At less extreme levels, the whole range of psychosomatic symptoms—

rashes, allergies, headaches, ulcers, obesity, almost any unexplained symptom—may represent marital conflict. In very minor form, such problems may plague all marriages.

One problem is that one cannot always be certain that psychosomatic symptoms trace to marital problems. The underlying problems may derive more from conditions at work than at home. They may stem from frustrations encountered outside the home; and they may be tied to problems with parents or children. Given the central role that marriage plays in the life of American adults and the interpenetration of family with the occupational and community spheres, however, many such conditions may either reflect or cause problems in the marriage.

Mental hygienists affirm that covert conflict is potentially more damaging than is open fighting. When people quarrel, they are at least aware of a problem. The chances are good that they will find some sort of solution. When the problem is masked as something else, however, it may take its toll without the difficulty ever being discovered. The loss of efficiency and personal satisfaction stemming from covert conflict may be greater, in some ways, than open conflict which leads to marital dissolution.

On the other hand, some marriages may become stabilized around covert conflict. There is the possibility that the personal and social costs of organizing some marriages around an ulcer or migraine headaches may be less than the costs of confronting those couples with the neurotic character of their interaction. Few reasonable people would deny that many ulcerous parents have had outwardly successful marriages and raised apparently healthy, successful children.

The Role of Insight

This brings up the whole question of what factors are linked with the successful resolution of marital conflict. And, in all candor, it must be acknowledged that, even though we can describe typical processes of conflict, we know little about the ways in which conflicts are limited or eliminated, or why some couples apparently do it better than others.

One important factor—but which, unfortunately, operates in very complex fashion—is the kind and amount of insight each partner develops into his own behavior and that of his or her spouse. Some people appear totally incapable of comprehending underlying motivations for either their own or others' behavior, while other people shrewdly anticipate one another and quickly recognize the long-term consequences of given courses of action. This capacity for insight is not an all-or-none matter. Probably people can be ranged along a continuum according to how insightful they are. Differences among them are of degree rather than differences in kind.

In general, insight probably increases harmony in marriage. Many attacks which marital partners make upon one another are motivated out of hurt or fear. When one realizes that one's partner is only retaliating for injury or is afraid that he or she will be rejected, it becomes easier to react in ways that will lessen the hurt and fear rather than to leap to the attack oneself. Once the process of understanding instead of hurting becomes established, the interaction takes on spiral form. Here, we have the reverse of progressive conflict. An insightful, constructive response from one partner calls forth a constructive response from the other partner, and so on. There may be critical points early in most marriages where the interaction takes on spiral form. If it spirals negatively, estrangement soon results. If it spirals as a function of insight development, the areas of sharing may rapidly be enlarged.

This assumes, of course, that both partners show some insight development. In some cases undoubtedly they do. Many couples are unequal in their capacities for insight, however, just as they are unequal in other regards. What happens when they are unequal in insight is less certain and leads to less optimistic conclusions.

If both partners are somewhat insightful, the more insightful partner is in a position to control the relationship. By anticipating more quickly and more accurately, he or she may be able to influence the partner. That power may be exercised either in the interests of both partners and the relationship or it may be used to profit the one partner at the expense of the other.[13] Some exploitation of the less insightful partner may be a frequent occurrence.

In some instances the partners' capacities for insight may differ markedly, leading to the domination of the more insightful spouse by the less insightful one. Particularly if the less insightful spouse is rigid to begin with, he or she may continue the conflict regardless of the ultimate harm done. The more insightful spouse, foreseeing the outcome, may yield rather than destroy the relationship or the partner.[14] This is not a very

13. For evidence that altruism is not always associated with good marital adjustment, see Jack V. Buerkle, Theodore R. Anderson, and Robin F. Badgley, "Altruism, Role Conflict and Marital Adjustment: A Factor Analysis of Marital Interaction," *Marriage and Family Living* 23 (Feb. 1961), pp. 20–26.

14. Darwin L. Thomas, David D. Franks, and James M. Calonico, "Role-Taking and Power in Social Psychology," *American Sociological Review* 37 (Oct. 1972), pp. 605–14.

comforting thought to those who believe that the possession of insight is accompanied by power.

There has also been speculation on the quality of marriages in which the more insightful partner is dominated by the less insightful one. It stems from doubt that perceptive persons can endure continued domination and continue to invest themselves fully in the marriage. What appears plausible is that the insightful partner may gradually withdraw emotionally from the relationship. Outwardly the marriage may be quite stable, but emotionally it may be hollow.

There is relatively little research bearing directly upon these problems. One project did show that satisfaction in marriage is related to the wife's accurate perception of her husband's self-concept, but that satisfaction was not related to the accuracy of the husband's perception of his wife's self-concept. This difference between the sexes may reflect the fact that wives are required to make the greater adjustments in marriage.[15] The findings are in accord with the widely accepted generalization that subordinate persons and groups tend to be more insightful than those who are able to control through the open use of power.

At least two studies failed to establish any relation between insight and marital adjustment. Corsini, studying 20 volunteer couples, concluded that there is no evidence that happiness in marriage is a function of understanding the mate.[16] Udry, Nelson, and Nelson studied 34 couples married from one to ten years and found that agreement between husband and wife was not associated with frequency of interaction or length of time married. In addition, there was no relationship between "understanding" and either the frequency of interaction or the length of time married. The couples with the least "togetherness" could predict the responses of their spouses as well as those who spent the most time together, and those married for only a short time could predict their spouses' reactions as well as those who had been married for years.[17]

15. Eleanore B. Luckey, "Marital Satisfaction and Congruent Self-Spouse Concepts," *Social Forces* 39 (Dec. 1960), pp. 153–57.
16. Raymond Corsini, "Understanding and Similarity in Marriage," *Journal of Abnormal and Social Psychology* 52 (May 1956), pp. 327–32.
17. J. Richard Udry, Harold A. Nelson, and Ruth Nelson, "An Empirical Investigation of Some Widely Held Beliefs About Marital Interaction," *Marriage and Family Living* 23 (Nov. 1961), pp. 388–90.

ESTIMATES OF MARITAL HAPPINESS

Noting that some conflict normally develops in early marriage, may lead uncritical people to the interpretation that marital adjustment is seldom very satisfactory. It would be surprising, however, if this were the case, for the American ethos places great emphasis upon the achievement of success in various aspects of life. If the majority of people did not define their marriages as successful, serious strain would be placed upon the system and would be felt by the spouses.

Several studies have sought to determine the proportions of various samples who define themselves as being happily married. The results of some of these studies are summarized in Table 14.1.

Table 14.1. Marriage happiness ratings reported in selected studies (in percents)

	Marriage happiness rating		
Slected study	*Very happy*	*Pretty happy*	*Not too happy*
1738 Respondents from ten metropolitan areas	60	36	3
360 Illinois Men	76	23	1
1865 Married U.S. Respondents	68	29	3
792 California Couples	85	9	5
526 Illinois Couples	63	14	22

Source: Susan R. Orden and Norman M. Bradburn, "Dimensions of Marriage Happiness," *American Journal of Sociology* 73 (May 1968), p. 717.

These studies took place over approximately 30 years from the mid-1930s to the mid-1960s, and were remarkably consistent over that time. Burgess and Cottrell's 526 Illinois couples had been married an average of just over three years. Over 60 percent described their marriages as happy, while only one couple out of five would admit to being unhappy.[18] Terman's study of 792 middle-class California couples reported even higher percentages of happy marriages.[19]

The most recent of these studies done in 1965, collected information from 781 husbands and 957 wives. Table 14.1 shows its findings, along

18. Ernest W. Burgess and Leonard S. Cottrell, Jr., *Predicting Success or Failure in Marriage*, New York: Prentice-Hall, 1939, p. 32.

19. Lewis M. Terman, *Psychological Factors in Marital Happiness*, New York: McGraw-Hill Book Company, 1938, p. 78.

with those of the other four studies. Orden and Bradburn found 60 percent of their respondents saying they were very happy and only 3 percent admitting to being not too happy.[20] Even allowing for people to report more happiness than they actually experience, these figures are impressive. They strongly suggest that, early in marriage at least, the majority of couples find their marriages to be pretty satisfactory.

THE MEASUREMENT OF MARITAL ADJUSTMENT

Sociologists have not been content with simple estimates of marital happiness and have long sought to develop measures of marital adjustment. In the process, the value problems inherent in various concepts of marital adjustment have emerged strongly.

The earliest comprehensive study of marital adjustment was that of Burgess and Cottrell. These authors, who developed a scale to predict marital success, distributed lengthy questionnaires to nearly 7000 couples and received 526 completed questionnaires from Illinois couples who had been married from one to six years.

The questionnaires contained items on the premarital backgrounds of the husband and wife and items on their postmarital attitudes and experiences. Each couple was asked to rate the happiness of its marriage. Then an index of marital adjustment was constructed from the answers to 27 items on the questionnaire. In constructing this scale of marital adjustment, Burgess and Cottrell assumed that a well-adjusted marriage is one in which (1) the husband and wife agree on critical issues in their relationship; (2) share common interests and joint activities; (3) share demonstrations of affection and mutual confidences; (4) have few complaints about the marriage; and (5) are not bothered with feelings of loneliness, irritability, and miserableness. Scores on the marital adjustment scale correlated satisfactorily with the marital happiness ratings. From then on in the research, individual items were tested to determine how well they correlated with total marital adjustment scores.

A large number of social background factors proved to be associated with marital adjustment. Some of the more significant include:

1. The greater the similarity in family backgrounds, the larger was the proportion of couples in the very high adjustment class.

20. Susan R. Orden and Norman M. Bradburn, "Dimensions of Marriage Happiness," *American Journal of Sociology* 73 (May 1968), pp. 715–31.

a. The husband's family background appeared more closely related to adjustment than did the wife's family background.
b. The economic and social status of the parents seemed less important for marital success than did other factors.
c. Rural backgrounds for persons who migrated to the city were more favorable than a childhood spent in either town or city.
d. Differences in educational background or religious affiliation showed no relation to marital adjustment. Church attendance, however, was associated with marital success.

2. The domestic happiness of the parents was correlated with the marital adjustment of their children.
   a. Closeness of attachment and absence of conflict between parents and son showed a small positive relationship to marital adjustment.
   b. Size of family also was more important for the adjustment of the husband than for that of the wife. Two- to five-child families were more favorable than only-child families.
3. Several factors relating to the couple's social type were found to be related to marital adjustment.
   a. Marriage between 28 and 30 years of age for men was found to be favorable. Very early marriages were unfavorable.
   b. Marriage success scores were positively associated with increased educational achievement for both spouses.
   c. Going to Sunday School until age 19 was associated with marital success. Marriage in a church also was favorable.
   d. Having several friends of both sexes and belonging to organizations was associated with good adjustment.
   e. Residence in a suburb was more favorable than residence in an apartment or rooming-house area.
   f. The longer the period of intimate association before marriage, the greater were the chances for marital success.
   g. Security and stability of occupation were more important than income level.
   h. The desire for children was associated with good adjustment.

Burgess and Cottrell emphasized that the correlations between single items and marital success scores were very low. To be used for prediction, a large number of items had to be combined in a scale. They developed a scale, which has been used in further research and in clinical work.

Probably the greatest significance of the Burgess and Cottrell research is the general concept of marital adjustment that emerged from it. Good adjustment—defined in terms of husband-wife agreement, common interests and activities, sharing of affection and confidences, few complaints, and absence of loneliness—was found to be associated with similarity of the couple's background, happiness in the parental family, and a fairly conventional adjustment in other areas of life.

At the time the Burgess and Cottrell research was under way, Lewis Terman was searching for personality factors associated with marital adjustment. He had questionnaires filled out by 792 middle- and upper-middle-class urban California couples who had been married, on the average, about 11 years. Precautions were taken to see that there was no collaboration between husbands and wives in filling out the questionnaires.

Terman derived total marital happiness scores from questions on common interests, agreements and disagreements, method of handling disagreements, frequency of regretting marriage, whether one would marry the same person again, contemplation of divorce or separation, rating of marital happiness, length of unhappiness, and number of complaints about the marriage. Then 300 happily married couples and 150 unhappily married couples were equated for age, years married, schooling, and occupation. These groups were used to test the general idea that a large proportion of incompatible marriages are so because of a predisposition to unhappiness in one or both of the spouses.

In all, 132 items discriminated between happily married and unhappily married persons. Following is a portrait of the husbands and wives.

Husbands

Happy: emotionally stable, cooperative, equalitarian in ideals, extroverted, responsible, methodical, and conservative.

Unhappy: moody, neurotic, feel inferior and insecure, domineering and radical.

Wives

Happy: kindly, cooperative, methodical, meticulous, conservative, conventional, self-assured, and optimistic.

Unhappy: emotionally unstable, feel inferior, rivalrous, overactive, radical, and egoistic.

Terman does not claim that all unhappy marriages can be explained in terms of basic personality problems, but he does believe that such factors play a large causal role.

Terman also used a number of social background factor items from the Burgess and Cottrell research and included items on premarital sex experience. Some of the general findings in these areas were:

1. For men to marry under age 22 and for women to marry under 20 was slightly unfavorable. Relationships where the husband was ten or more years older or younger than his wife were slightly favorable.
2. Wives of husbands of inferior mental ability tended to be unhappy while their husbands were happy. Markedly superior husbands tended to be unhappy, but their wives were happy. Both spouses had the best chances for marital happiness where husband and wife were equal in ability or the husband was slightly superior.
3. There was an association between length of acquaintance and length of engagement and marital success.
4. Marital happiness was correlated with happiness of the parents' marriages.
5. Happiness was associated with attachment to and lack of conflict with parents.
6. Childhood happiness and firm but not harsh discipline were favorable.
7. A number of items relating to sex education, attitudes, and premarital experience were favorable for marital happiness.
   a. Frank parental responses to sex curiosity, without evasion.
   b. Indifference to or pleasant anticipation of the sex relationship on the part of the male. Both passionate longing and aversion were unfavorable.
   c. "No petting" before marriage, for the wife, appeared favorable.
   d. Wife's admission of present or past desire to be of the opposite sex was unfavorable.
   e. For husbands, premarital intercourse with wife was not unfavorable. Wives who had premarital intercourse with men other than the husband had low happiness scores.
8. Some items relating to marital sex experience also were associated with marital happiness.
   a. Happiness ratings of wives who found their first sex experiences disgusting were lower than those of wives who found them enjoyable.
   b. Husbands above average in sexual desire had lower happiness ratings while wives above average in desire had higher ratings.
   c. Where the spouses were equal or the wife was slightly less passionate, the happiness ratings of both spouses were highest.

d. Wife's orgasm capacity was highly correlated with happiness scores of both spouses.

In spite of the relationships found, Terman concluded that happiness could be predicted almost as well from personality and background factors as from those factors and the sex factors combined. Most sexual maladjustment was seen as stemming from personality and background factors, with little unhappiness resulting from biological sexual incompatibility.

The Burgess and Cottrell and Terman studies were done in different parts of the country and used different samples and techniques of data collection. One emphasized background factors and one emphasized personality and sexual factors. Their results, however, were surprisingly consistent. Where items were similar, their findings were similar. They found that mature, stable, conventional, conforming people from untroubled family backgrounds scored high on marital success and happiness.

Several investigators sought to test these findings and to improve the prediction of marital success. Kelley used Terman's background and personality items with 300 unmarried couples whom he checked for adjustment after two years of marriage.[21] King used the Burgess and Cottrell items with a southern black sample,[22] and Stroup used them with a random sample in Akron, Ohio.[23] Locke used items from both early studies in comparing happily married with divorced couples in Indiana,[24] and Karlsson did a similar study in Sweden.[25] Although these studies

21. E. Lowell Kelley, "Concerning the Validity of Terman's Weights for Predicting Marital Happiness," *Psychological Bulletin* 36 (1939), pp. 202–3.

22. Charles E. King, "The Burgess-Cottrell Method of Measuring Marital Adjustment Applied to a Non-white Southern Urban Population," *Marriage and Family Living* 14 (Nov. 1952), pp. 280–85.

23. Atlee L. Stroup, "Predicting Marital Success or Failure in an Urban Population," *American Sociological Review* 18 (Oct. 1953), pp. 558–62. King's and Stroup's interest in the utility of the Burgess and Cottrell scale with persons of different social class backgrounds was extended in Julius Roth and Robert F. Peck, "Social Class and Social Mobility Factors Related to Marital Adjustment," *American Sociological Review* 16 (Aug. 1951), pp. 478–87.

24. Harvey J. Locke, *Predicting Adjustment in Marriage: A Comparison of a Divorced and a Happily Married Group*, New York: Henry Holt and Company, 1951. See also James L. Hawkins, "The Locke Marital Adjustment Test and Social Desirability," *Journal of Marriage and the Family* 28 (May 1966), pp. 193–95.

25. Georg Karlsson, *Adaptability and Communication in Marriage: A Swedish Predictive Study of Marital Satisfaction*, Uppsala: Almqvist and Wiksells, 1951.

used different samples and varied their techniques, the general findings were highly confirmatory.

The most comprehensive study of marital prediction was made by Burgess and Wallin as a follow-up to the study of Burgess and Cottrell and in response to recognized limitations in the early studies. Those studies were not truly predictive because the adjustment and prediction scales were built upon couples who were already married.

Burgess and Wallin secured questionnaires from 1000 engaged couples in the Chicago area; almost one-fourth of the couples also were interviewed. Data were then collected from those couples after they had been married for at least three years. Some couples had not married, some already were divorced, and some could not be located, but marital adjustment questionnaires were secured from 666 of the original couples.

For predicting marital success, three groups of premarital items were used: (1) social background items similar to those used by Burgess and Cottrell, (2) personality items similar to Terman's, and (3) items about the couple's engagement history. A group of "contingency" items also was used, in which husband and wife were asked to anticipate such conditions of their marriage as whether the wife would work, the number of children they expected to have, and where they would live. The general findings were quite consistent with those of Burgess and Cottrell and Terman.

An index of engagement success proved to be the best single predictor of subsequent marital adjustment scores. Apparently a better guess about marital adjustment can be made on the basis of how a couple gets along during engagement than on the basis of any combination of background or personality factors.[26]

26. Ernest W. Burgess and Paul Wallin, *Engagement and Marriage*, Philadelphia: J. B. Lippincott Company, 1953. Several investigators have done follow-up work to this study. See Purnell Benson, "Familism and Marital Success," *Social Forces* 33 (March 1955), pp. 277–80; and Purnell Benson, "The Common Interest Myth in Marriage," *Social Problems* 3 (July 1955), pp. 27–34; Charles E. Bowerman, "Adjustment in Marriage: Overall and In Specific Areas," *Sociology and Social Research* 41 (March-April 1957), pp. 257–63; Raymond J. Corsini, "Multiple Predictors of Marital Happiness," *Marriage and Family Living* 18 (Aug. 1956), pp. 240–42; Benjamin J. Keeley, "Value Convergence and Marital Relations," *Marriage and Family Living* 17 (Nov. 1955), pp. 342–45; Eugene Litwak, Gloria Count, and Edward M. Haydon, "Group Structure and Interpersonal Creativity as Factors which Reduce Errors in the Prediction of Marital Adjustment," *Social Forces* 38 (May 1960), pp. 308–15; Nathan Hurvitz, "The Significance of Discrepancies Between the Scores of Spouses on a Marital Adjustment Scale," *Alpha Kappa Deltan* 29 (Spring 1959), pp. 251–55; and Harvey J. Locke and Robert C. Willamson, "Marriage Adjustment: A Factor Analysis Study," *American Sociological Review* 23 (Oct. 1958), pp. 562–69.

A variety of studies extend our measurement of marital adjustment.[27] Buerkle and Badgley, for example, constructed items to get at role-taking in marital interaction, which measured new dimensions of adjustment and indicated need for further conceptual analysis.[28] Work on indirect measures of marital adjustment that would eliminate the tendency for persons to overstate their marital happiness has been reported by Kirkpatrick, Taves, and Frumkin.[29] Finally, a different approach to the measurement of marital adjustment has been tried by Farber, who used a consensus index and a role-tension index.[30]

Other studies related marital satisfaction to the ways in which spouses perceive themselves, one another, and their parents. Luckey reported that better adjusted persons agree on (1) perception in regard to self and the perception of self by spouse, (2) perception of self and the parent of the same sex, (3) perception of spouse and parent of the opposite sex, and (4) perception of one's ideal mate and of one's spouse.[31] Other findings which generally support these findings have been reported by Stuckert and by Katz and associates.[32]

The effort to measure marital adjustment and to predict marital suc-

27. Millard J. Bienvenu, Sr., "Measurement of Marital Communication," *The Family Coordinator* 19 (Jan. 1970), pp. 26–31; James L. Hawkins, "The Locke Marital Adjustment Test and Social Desirability," *Journal of Marriage and the Family* 28 (May 1966), pp. 193–95; and Michael J. Sporakowski, "Marital Preparedness, Predictions and Adjustment," *The Family Coordinator* 17 (July 1968), pp. 155–61.

28. Jack V. Buerkle and Robin F. Badgley, "Couple Role-Taking: The Yale Marital Interaction Battery," *Marriage and Family Living* 21 (Feb. 1959), pp. 53–58. See also Jack V. Buerkle, "Self-Attitudes and Marital Adjustment," *Merrill-Palmer Quarterly* 6 (Jan. 1960), pp. 114–24.

29. Robert M. Frumkin, "The Kirkpatrick Scale of Family Interests as an Instrument for the Indirect Assessment of Marital Adjustment," *Marriage and Family Living* 15 (Feb. 1953), pp. 35–37; Clifford Kirkpatrick, "Community of Interest and the Measurement of Marriage Adjustment," *Family* 18 (1937), pp. 133–37; Marvin J. Taves, "A Direct vs. an Indirect Approach in Measuring Marital Adjustment," *American Sociological Review* 13 (Oct. 1948), pp. 538–41.

30. Bernard Farber, "An Index of Marital Integration," *Sociometry* 20 (June 1957), pp. 117–18.

31. Eleanore B. Luckey, "Marital Satisfaction and Its Association with Congruence of Perception," *Marriage and Family Living* 22 (Feb. 1960), pp. 49–54; Eleanore B. Luckey, "Perceptional Congruence of Self and Family Concepts as Related to Marital Interaction," *Sociometry* 3 (Sept. 1961), pp. 234–40.

32. Irwin Katz, Judith Goldston, Melvin Cohen, and Solomon Stuckers, "Need Satisfaction, Perception, and Cooperative Interactions in Married Couples," *Marriage and Family Living* 25 (May 1963), pp. 209–13; and Robert P. Stuckert, "Role Perception and Marital Satisfaction—A Configurational Approach," *Marriage and Family Living* 25 (Nov. 1963), pp. 415–19.

cess goes on.[33] In recent studies there is an attempt not only to improve the measurement but also to arrive at a more adequate concept of marital adjustment. Scholars are becoming more sensitive to ethical implications of a general concept of marriage adjustment unwittingly carried forward from the early studies. That concept of marital adjustment emphasizes the prosaic nature of ordinary human beings who are tacitly urged toward making conventional, conforming, stable marriages by selecting their partners from within their own race, nationality, religion, and social class. Thus, the very existence of norms governing mate selection, it is suggested, have come to be used to reinforce an anti-individualistic, anti-personal-freedom bias in American society.

CRITIQUE OF THE CONCEPT OF MARITAL ADJUSTMENT

The most effective critic of the concept of marital success implicit in the marital adjustment studies has been Kolb. In two provocative papers,[34] he developed the thesis that there are implicit value judgments in the criteria used to define successful marriage. These value judgments lend support to a family structure which is in basic conflict with democratic values and with ideals of personal growth and freedom. Moreover, the family structure which results from the use of these criteria is

33. Graham B. Spanier, "Measuring Dyadic Adjustment: New Scales for Assessing the Quality of Marriage and Similar Dyads," *Journal of Marriage and the Family* 38 (Feb. 1976), pp. 15–28.

34. William L. Kolb, "Sociologically Established Family Norms and Democratic Values," *Social Forces* 26 (May 1948), pp. 451–56; and William L. Kolb, "Family Sociology, Marriage Education, and the Romantic Complex: A Critique," *Social Forces* 29 (Oct. 1950), pp. 65–72. See also Vernon H. Edmonds, "Marital Conventionalization: Definition and Measurement," *Journal of Marriage and the Family* 29 (Nov. 1967), pp. 681–88; James L. Hawkins and Kathryn Johnsen, "Perception of Behavioral Conformity, Imputation of Consensus, and Marital Satisfaction," *Journal of Marriage and the Family* 31 (Aug. 1969), pp. 507–11; Mary W. Hicks and Marilyn Platt, "Marital Happiness and Stability: A Review of the Research in the Sixties," *Journal of Marriage and the Family* 32 (Nov. 1970), pp. 553–74; Edwin L. Lively, "Toward Concept Clarification: The Case of Marital Interaction," *Journal of Marriage and the Family* 31 (Feb. 1969), pp. 108–14; Graham B. Spanier, "Further Evidence on Methodological Weaknesses in the Locke-Wallace Marital Adjustment Scale and Other Measures of Adjustment," *Journal of Marriage and the Family* 34 (Aug. 1972), pp. 403–4; Alexander B. Taylor, "Role Perception, Empathy, and Marriage Adjustment," *Sociology and Social Research* 52 (Oct. 1967), pp. 22–34; and Robert N. Whitehurst, "Premarital Reference Group Orientations and Marriage Adjustment," *Journal of Marriage and the Family* 30 (Aug. 1968), pp. 397–401.

one which is unsatisfactory even in terms of ensuring conventionality and stability.

Kolb presents a composite picture of the "successful" marriages emerging from the marital adjustment studies. First, he says, the spouses in such marriages describe themselves as happy. Second, they agree on what decisions need to be made. Third, the couple agree on leisure-time preferences and engage in outside interests together. Fourth, there is affection and confidence. Finally, they are satisfied with their marriage. In addition, they expect the marriage to be permanent, that it will conform to community expectations, and that it will involve interdependence between husband and wife.

A major problem with this concept of marital adjustment is that it does not specify what the people are happy about, what they are adjusted to, what goals are at the center of family stability, and what value content is at the center of family integration. In some cases, Kolb says, these factors will be associated with other goals that we value and in some cases they will not.

A dual image of the "happy," "adjusted" family emerges from the literature. Which of the two images fits a given family may depend upon the vantage point from which it is viewed. In Kolb's words:

> One [image] is that of a family characterized by absence of conflict, the prevalence of accommodative habits, mutual affection, the middle-class paraphernalia of status, i.e., an owned home, radios, bathtubs, and automobiles, social conservatism and conformity, discreet and cautious extramarital adventures, and the unending struggle for success. . . . The other image contains the above characteristics, . . . but emphasizes the structure of this family as the breeding ground of neurosis and conflict. It pictures the role of the . . . wife as empty, stultifying, and confused; the role of the husband as that of the individual subjected to all the pressures of the struggle for success; and the role of the child as determined by the ambivalent attitudes of his parents toward one another and toward him.[35]

Remember that this grim portrayal is of couples who do well on marriage adjustment scales; it does not describe unhappy relationships. It criticizes the concept of marital adjustment as being negative—as defining marriage in terms of absence of conflict and accommodation to the status quo, rather than in terms of the achievement of positive goals. No matter how much "adjustment," "happiness," and "integration," such marriages are seen as stunting the personal growth and development

35. "Sociologically Established Family Norms and Democratic Values," *op. cit.*, p. 454.

of the partners. Without defining personality growth—which is an extremely difficult idea to define adequately—it is argued that personality growth "cannot mean the extreme concentration upon status and economic struggle which is characteristic of the middle-class family."

Kolb does not argue that the concept of marital adjustment should be discarded. He knows the role which the normative regulation of mate selection and marital interaction play in maintaining order and stability in the society. He does propose that goals of new experience and personality development should be part of the test of a "happy" marriage. He also concludes that major changes in the social, political, and economic structure of American society may be necessary before such marriages will become a reality.

TWO PROVOCATIVE ANALYSES OF MARITAL ADJUSTMENT

Most sociologists share Kolb's dissatisfaction with the conventional concept of marital adjustment. Most of them know that the image of couples existing in a state of cow-like contentment is too simple. It fails to encompass the richness of love and hate, exultation and sorrow, boredom and excitement that are part of the lives of even outwardly drab persons. Yet, efforts to develop a more vital concept of marital adjustment are few and far between. Few among us show any flair for conceiving of marriage in any but conventional terms. Let us look briefly at two analyses of marital adjustment, unconventional enough to be somewhat frightening in their implications, but which also have been based upon perceptive study of real people.

Presented here are typologies of marital adjustment that have stemmed from research. Neither of the two projects was methodologically very rigorous. Neither of the authors would argue that he or she was dealing with a representative sample, that the methods were foolproof, or that the findings can be generalized to all couples. Each did, however, gather data systematically, and then exercise a fertile mind in developing a composite picture of what the marriages studied were like. To say the least, the findings provide food for thought.

Carolyn (Levy) Cline and her students at the University of Kansas City conducted 112 interviews with people married from 1 to 46 years. All were at least high-school graduates, most were white, and they were estimated to vary from upper-lower to upper-middle class. The respondents were classified according to basic themes observed running through the interviews. The themes are not mutually exclusive, and more than one theme sometimes was apparent in a given marriage. Five themes around which these 112 marriages appeared to be organized were labeled (1) mass-produced marriages; (2) inside-out romantic complex marriages; (3) I've grown accustomed to my fate marriages; (4) marriage makes estranged bedfellows marriages; and (5) she and empathy marriages.

We can do no better than to describe these five types of marriages in Cline's words:

Mass-produced Marriages. The "mass-produced marriage" refers to the marriage of those who seem to marry because that is what is done and seem likely to stay married because that is what is done. They refer to their spouses more nearly as room-mates of the other sex rather than partners in the intimacy of marriage. They seem to view unhappy marriages with little more than a mild curiosity and explain happiness or unhappiness in terms such as, "If people would just do what they're supposed to do, everything would be all right." They use themselves as the yardstick and, being conformists themselves—often without being aware of conforming—almost by definition are apt to have fewer problems of which they are aware. They seem not to verbalize or recognize problem areas.

Perhaps it will more clearly state the case if we designate this theme of mass-produced marriage as mass-producing marriage, for such may be the products, members of masses, not individuals. We might call them "omni-directed." For the omni-directed there are many alternatives, but all of them seem so similar. All the mass media, offering so many variations of choices seem still to offer, all of them essentially the same thing. And more than that, the whole society seems to the omni-directed to be in agreement on that same thing. The omni-directed, then, do not have, like Riesman's other-directed, a sensitive radar mechanism to follow a varying lead of others. Instead, they see themselves as following "all"—since the mass media say to them, "Everybody's doing whatever you're doing."

These omni-directed (or automatons of the mass-mesmerizing media) often may appear to be the well integrated, upright citizens who "get things done" and are always "Johnny on the spot." But omni-directed action must be differentiated from autonomous action. Living in a world where there are many alternatives does not mean that the individual, even when aware of them, is able to implement alternatives in his own decision-making process.

Inside-out Romantic Complex Marriages. Although the "inside-out romantic complex" theme was not as prevalent as the "mass produced" in these interviews, it might account for many of the marriages in that group. It differs from the "mass-producing" marriages in that the individuals are aware of and are, at least verbally, attempting to deal with the stereotypes of marriage as conveyed by the mass-mesmerizing media. Many respondents, and most poignantly, the teenagers said, "We want to prove we can make it work." They not only did not mention "love" or any of its grammatical relatives as a reason for getting married, but also they attempted to show a picture of themselves as being "not romantic" adolescents. This stance can be summed up by the statement, "What Hollywood, we won't." This is tantamount to the partners in the marriage saying, "We are not going to ask that our marriage be the all and end all of being; we are not going to be led down that primrose path to divorce. We, on the other hand, are going to imitate the going version of adult (middle-age and routinized) marriage behavior and ask, and settle for, a marriage of accommodation along the competitive lives of a push-pull arrangement . . . and thereby show that we are responsible individuals and have our feet on the ground."

I've Grown Accustomed to My Fate Marriages. [This] theme is typified by the woman who after twenty years of wondering why her husband wished to remain married to her and finally ended up divorcing him said, "I think he wanted a Mother, and that was not the kind of love I had to offer. I don't know what it is, but things happen to me that don't seem to happen to other people. I've had an awful lot of trouble; I guess some people are just born luckier than others. I'm one of the unlucky ones." Another wife said, "At first I kept saying, 'Well, it'll be different after we get more used to one another.' But it didn't. I kept hoping he'd change, or I would, but we didn't. Now it doesn't seem to matter much."

These are people who distrust themselves as choosers. Perhaps they even "will to lose." They feel themselves to be pawns in a completely deterministic life. Everyone else is a pawn too and even the knights and kings and queens move in their directed ways.

Marriage Makes Estranged Bedfellows. [This] theme is illustrated in the following quotations:

A wife reported, "During the first years we had sex so often I would have been ashamed for anyone to know how often. We still do more than other people who are 'old married couples.' The only time we don't argue is in bed."

Another wife said, "I cried a lot during the first year. Nothing was the way I expected. In bed it was just matter-of-fact. Still is. But I don't cry anymore."

And a husband stated estrangement directly. "Sometimes it's like living with a stranger—without the excitement. But she never did really enjoy it—and I can get my kicks elsewhere, if you know what I mean."

While in these interviews no effort was made to probe sexual compatibility and incompatibility, the theme of estrangement either assuaged or reinforced in sexual relations appears not to be uncommon.

She and Empathy Marriages. [This] category . . . is most nearly opposite to that of the "mass-produced" marriage theme. And, just as the mass-produced theme seems to be most frequently found in these interviews, this romantic emphasis upon understanding and insight is rarely found. People in this category seem (1) acutely aware of the state of their marriage (especially the women, and even more poignantly so, the teen-aged women), and (2) ready to act to do something about the marriage. More women than men fall into this category and, also, more romanticists. One wife said:

"The best thing about our marriage is that we can talk. We always could—and get through to each other."

Her husband said, "It's relaxing with her—sometimes I think about other women—prettier, smarter, maybe—and think, wouldn't it be fun—but then I think, fun okay but what else? Of course I feel guilty too."

Another wife said, "I was very much in love with him when we were married, couldn't get enough of him. Loved him more than he did me. But I could see he felt kind of smothered. It hurt me, but I learned to handle it."[36]

The emphasis in this research was on the development of types, so no figures are given on how many couples fell into each category. It is clear that the mass-produced and inside-out romantic complex marriages were the most common and that the she and empathy marriages—those that most closely fit the American ideal of what marriage should be like—were the least numerous.

The author points out that the validity of these themes has not been established. She maintains, however, that the results are highly suggestive. The outcome of mass-produced marriages, she says, may be predictable after the first few months of marriage. The inside-out romantic complex operating early in a marriage may indicate a mass-producing marriage in the future. Unsatisfactory relationships at the beginning of marriage may suggest a future phrased in terms of "I've become accustomed to my fate." Estrangement may develop either early in marriage or later. Among the most significant of the author's suggestions is the possibility that romanticism early in a marriage may be predictive of a warm empathic relationship later on. Romanticism may not be simply a sign of emotional immaturity, but may be associated with achievement of the finest that marriage has to offer.

A second classification of marriages derives from a study of 437 persons, 35 to 55 years of age. Although single, divorced, and widowed persons were interviewed also, the analysis reported here is based upon couples who had been married at least 10 years and who had never seriously considered separation or divorce. They were upper-middle

36. Carolyn (Levy) Cline, "Five Variations on the Marriage Theme: Types of Marriage Formation," *The Bulletin on Family Development* 3 (Spring 1962), pp. 10–13.

class, highly educated, widely traveled, articulate, financially successful people who had been exposed to a variety of emancipating experiences. None displayed signs of gross emotional maladjustment.

Cuber and Harroff presented descriptions of five general themes pervading marriage relationships:

Conflict-Habituated Relationships. In this husband-wife configuration there is much tension and conflict—although largely "controlled." At worst, there is some private quarreling, nagging, and "throwing up the past" of which members of the immediate family, and more rarely even close friends and relatives, have some awareness. At best, the couple is discreet and polite, "genteel about it" when in the company of others, but rarely succeeds completely in concealing it from the children—although the illusion is common among them that they do. The essence, however, is that there is awareness by both husband and wife that incompatibility is pervasive, conflict is ever-potential, and an atmosphere of equilibrated tension permeates their lives together. These relationships are sometimes said to be "dead" or "gone" but there is a more subtle valence here—a very active one. So central is the necessity for channeling conflict and bridling hostility that these imperatives structure the togetherness. Some psychiatrists have gone so far as to suggest that it is precisely the conflict and the habituated need to do psychological battle with one another which constitutes the cohesive factor which ensures continuity of the marriage. Possibly so, but from a less psychiatric point of view, the overt and manifest fact of habituated attention to handling tension, keeping it chained, and concealing it, becomes the overriding life force. And it can, and does for some, last for a lifetime.

Devitalized Relationships. Here the relationship is essentially devoid of zest. There is typically no serious tension or conflict and there may be aspects of the marriage which are actively satisfying, such as mutual interest in children, property, or family tradition. But the interplay between the pair is apathetic, lifeless. There is no serious threat to the marriage. It will likely continue indefinitely, despite its numbness. It continues, and conflict does not occur in part because of the inertia of "the habit cage." Continuity is further ensured by the absence of any engaging alternatives, "all things considered." Perpetuation is also reinforced, sometimes rather decisively, by legal and ecclesiastical requirements and expectations. These people quickly explain that "there are other things in life," which are worthy of sustained human effort. But the relationship *between the pair* is essentially devoid of vital meaning, essentially empty, by comparison to what it was when the mating began and what was then considered to be its *raison d'être.*

This kind of relationship is exceedingly common. Many persons in this circumstance do not accurately appraise their position because they frequently make comparisons with other pairs, many of whom are similar to themselves. This fosters the illusion that "marriage is like this—except for a few odd balls or pretenders who claim otherwise."

While these relationships lack vitality, there is "*something* there." There are occasional periods of sharing at least of something, if only memory. Formalities can have meanings. Anniversaries can be celebrated, even if a little grimly, for what they once commemorated. As one said, "Tomorrow we are celebrating the anniversary of our anniversary." Even clearly substandard sexual expression is said by some to be better than nothing, or better than a clandestine substitute. A "good man" or "good mother for the kids" may "with a little affection and occasional companionship now and then, get you by."

Passive-Congenial Relationships. This configuration seems roughly about as prevalent as the preceding one. There is little suggestion of disillusionment or compulsion to make believe to anyone. Existing modes of association are comfortably adequate—no stronger words fit the facts. There is little conflict. They tip-toe rather gingerly over and around a residue of subtle resentments and frustrations. In their better moods they remind us that "there are many common interests" which they both enjoy. When they get specific about these common interests it typically comes out that the interests are neither very vital things nor do they involve participation and sharings which could not almost as well be carried out in one-sex associations or with comparative strangers. "We both like classical music"; "We agree completely on religious and political matters"; "We both love the country and our quaint exurban neighbors"; "We are both lawyers."

We get the strong feeling when talking with these people that they would have said the same things when they were first married—or even before. When discussing their decisions to marry, some of them gave the same rationales for that decision that they do now for their present relationship, some twenty or thirty years later. This is why we have said that they seem to be passively content, not disillusioned even though, as compared to the next type, they show so little vitality and so little evidence that the spouse is important—much less indispensable—to the satisfactions which they say they enjoy.

Vital Relationships. It is hard to escape the word, vitality, here—vibrant and exciting sharing of some important life experience. Sex immediately comes to mind, but the vitality need not surround the sexual focus or any aspect of it. It may emanate from work, association in some creative enterprise, child rearing, or even hobby participation. The clue that the *relationship is vital* and significant derives from the *feelings of importance about it* and *that that importance is shared.* Other things are readily sacrificed to it. It is apparent, even sometimes to the superficial observer, that these people are living for something which is exciting; it consumes their interest and effort, and the particular man or woman who shares it is the indispensable ingredient in the meaning which it has.

Total Relationships. The total relationship is like the vital relationship with the important addition that it is *multi-faceted.* This kind of man-woman relationship is rare in marriage or out, but it does exist and undoubtedly could exist more often than it does were men and women free of various impediments. One will occasionally find relationships in which all important aspects of life are mutually shared and enthusiastically participated in. It is as if neither partner had a truly private existence. Cynics and the disillusioned scoff at this, calling it "romance" and usually offering an anecdote or two concerning some such "idyllic" relationship which later lost its totality, if not its vitality too. This should not be taken to mean, however, even if accurately interpreted and reported, that the relationship had not been total at the prior time. Or it may simply be evidence of the failure of the observer to be more discriminating in the first place.

Relationships are not *made* vital, much less total, by asserting them to be so, by striving to make them so, or by deceiving the neighbors that they are so. This is not to deny, however, that the total relationship is particularly precarious; precisely because it is multi-faceted, it is multi-vulnerable as circumstances change.[37]

Cuber and Harroff do not indicate how many relationships fell into each type, but it is clear that the majority ranged from conflict-habituated to passive-congenial. Total relationships are rare; vital relationships presumably are more common. Like Cline, these authors make no claim for the validity of their types. In fact, they state that their findings should not be generalized beyond the upper-middle-class segment of the society from which the couples came.

The findings of these two studies are sobering; they suggest that the majority of marriages may be routinized and unexciting. They also suggest that the marriages which rank high on marital adjustment scales may include many mass-produced, passive-congenial relationships. If Cline, Cuber, and Harroff are guilty of presenting a pessimistic picture of marital adjustment, perhaps it is because they set their aspirations high.

SUMMARY

The early weeks of marriage often are suffused with an erotically tinged euphoria that provides protection for each partner while the initial adjustments are being made. This is the *honeymoon period.* Under the

37. John F. Cuber and Peggy B. Harroff, "The More Total View: Relationships Among Men and Women of the Upper Middle Class," *Marriage and Family Living* 25 (May 1963), pp. 140–45.

pressure of 24-hour-a-day living, however, idealization breaks down. Extraordinary sensitivity to the moods of the partner brings the honeymoon to an end and brings conflict into the relationship.

Middle-class couples fight with words, which they use with devastating effect. Instead of protecting the partner as in the past, each spouse becomes hurt and sets out to inflict pain in return. Overt conflict may be classified into three types. First there is acute conflict, the function of which is to enable the couple to work out a *modus vivendi.* If acute conflicts are not resolved, they cumulate in a worsening spiral; the conflict becomes progressive. Even after most of the basic issues have been solved, some touchy areas remain and become the source of intermittent, habituated conflict. Recent research shows physical fighting to occur among married couples much more commonly than was formerly recognized. Most such violence is infrequent and limited.

Conflict may also be covert. In this case, couples who are not fully aware of their resentments resort to emotional withholdings such as frigidity, impotence, and physical illness, or they develop other unexplained symptoms, one result of which is to sabotage the relationship with the spouse. Mental hygienists emphasize that covert conflict is dangerous because its true nature is disguised.

Insightful understanding of the spouse should be an aid in adjustment. Whether insight will be used for the benefit of the relationship or to control it, however, is not predetermined. Where the spouses are greatly unequal in insight, the relationship may be controlled by the less insightful partner whose insensitivity makes him or her a formidable antagonist.

Most couples, when asked about the happiness of their marriages, report them to be relatively happy. One-fifth or less report their marriages to be unhappy. Even when measuring devices are used, the pattern holds. Most middle-class people report satisfactory marriages.

A general concept of marital adjustment has emerged out of research designed to predict and measure adjustment. In general, well-adjusted marriages are described as relatively free of conflict, the husband and wife are in relative agreement on major issues, they enjoy the same leisure interests, and they show affection for one another. Well-adjusted spouses are mature, stable, conventional, conforming people who come from untroubled family backgrounds.

This concept of marital adjustment has been criticized for implicit value judgments. It is maintained that these value judgments support a family structure which is in conflict with basic democratic values of personal growth and freedom. What traditionally have been defined as successful marriages may emphasize stability and conventionality at the expense of vitality in the husband-wife relationship and may stunt the emotional growth of children.

A satisfactory alternative concept of marital adjustment has yet to be developed. Two provocative studies have produced typologies of marriages which suggest that the average "successful" marriage may be devoid of zest. While these studies are less optimistic than the early marital adjustment studies, they also find evidence of the existence of a minority of marriages that are deeply satisfying to the people involved and which contribute to the full joy of living.

SUGGESTED READINGS

Christensen, Harold T., and Johnsen, Kathryn P., *Marriage and the Family*, New York: The Ronald Press, 1971. Part IV of this sophisticated textbook presents an insightful and scholarly analysis of marital interaction.

Eshleman, J. Ross, *ed.*, *Perspectives in Marriage and the Family: Text and Readings*, Boston: Allyn and Bacon, 1969. Chapter 8 offers a judicious selection of readings on husband-wife interaction in the early years of marriage.

Lantz, Herman R., and Snyder, Eloise C., *Marriage: An Examination of the Man-Woman Relationship*, New York: John Wiley and Sons, 1969. Chapters 13–18 offer an unusually readable and penetrating analysis of the factors involved in adjustment in young marriages.

Leslie, Gerald R., and Leslie, Elizabeth McLaughlin, *Marriage in a Changing World*, New York: Wiley, 1977. A functional textbook in preparation for marriage. Four chapters analyze various aspects of early marriage adjustments.

Steinmetz, Suzanne K., and Straus, Murray A., *Violence in the Family*, New York, Dodd, Mead and Company, 1974. A collection of essays that includes sections on violence between spouses and approaches to controlling violence.

FILMS

Being in Love (NET Film Service, Indiana University, Bloomington, Ind.). Film opens with two brothers meeting in a restaurant. One brother plans to divorce his wife to marry a woman he has met in business.

Psychotherapist discusses the possibilities of success for such a second marriage and questions whether the man is mature in his attitude.

Jealousy (McGraw-Hill Book Company, Text-Film Division, 1221 Avenue of the Americas, New York, N.Y. 10020, 16 minutes. Incidents from the life of a young couple demonstrate the unfortunate results of a treacherous imagination and lack of faith and understanding in a marriage relationship. Stresses the importance of continuous self-appraisal and indicates that a change of attitude often is necessary to combat jealousy.

Marriage Problems (NET Film Service, Indiana University, Bloomington, Ind.). Conversation between two sisters, one recently married and the other about to have her second child. Neither is happily married. Psychotherapist points out that young couples often are the victims of their own unrealistic expectations.

QUESTIONS AND PROJECTS

1. How can the honeymoon, as distinguished from the wedding trip, be defined in terms of emotional dynamics?
2. What factors during the honeymoon bring about disillusionment with self and partner? What evidence is there for such disillusionment?
3. Describe three major types of overt conflict in marriage. What is the significance of each? Contrast overt with covert conflict. Give examples of, and estimate the significance of, covert conflict.
4. How may insight into self and spouse influence marital adjustment? May the possession of insight be related to the power structure that develops? How may the less insightful partner dominate a marriage?
5. How do most middle-class people rate the happiness of their marriages? What proportions acknowledge that their marriages are unhappy?
6. Describe the early Burgess and Cottrell study of marital adjustment. What concept of marital adjustment was used? Summarize the findings relating social background factors to marital adjustment.
7. Compare Terman's study of happiness with the Burgess and Cottrell study of marital adjustment. How did the studies compare?
8. How did the Burgess and Wallin study differ from the two earlier ones? What was the best single predictor of marital success?
9. What criticism has been offered of the concept of marital adjustment deriving from prediction studies? How valid is this criticism? Why?
10. Recall the typologies of marital adjustment developed in the two studies reported in this chapter. Do these give cause for optimism? Why?
11. Suppose you wanted to reconcile some of the apparent contradictions in

research findings on marital adjustment. What methods or techniques could you devise to get at what marriages are really like?

12. Arrange a panel discussion among married students in the class. Draw out various concepts of marital adjustment. Have the panel react to the concepts of adjustment developed in this chapter. See whether a typology of marital adjustment makes sense for these students.

15

Sex Adjustment, Child-bearing, and Child-rearing

Shepard and Linnette Erhart got married in a field near the old mill where they had been living for 18 months. . . . A small group of close friends and relatives gathered in the field for the wedding. . . . Everyone spent the night in the mill and the next morning the newlyweds set off in a Volkswagen loaded with camping equipment. . . . "Sure," said Shepard, . . . "we took a honeymoon but it wasn't some archaic kind of thing where we travelled to an isolated island to sleep together for the first time. . . . That would be absurd. . . ."

Christine and Henry Greene were quite another story. Twenty-year-old Christine was so flustered she forgot to wear her corsage. . . . "I had never even been out of New York," she remarked as she sipped a rum punch in the lounge at Cove Haven, a resort exclusively devoted to honeymoon couples . . . in the Poconos. She wore a name tag on her collar, a plastic party hat on her head, and leis around her neck. . . . "The whole thing," she continued . . . , "was really frightening. I guess it really was terrible. . . . I was so embarrassed. . . . But, on the other hand," she went on . . . , "it was so beautiful and all. Your honeymoon is supposed to be the most perfect time of your life."[1]

I have a daughter who was born in 1949, a son born in 1951, and then in 1953 we had another daughter and finally we had our youngest, a boy, in 1955. [Do you want more?] Heavens, no! I am 34 and my husband is getting close to 40. I like to be young with my children and enjoy them, and since we got

1. Lacey Fosburgh, "New Fashions in Honeymoons: Hip, Super Hip, and Super Square," *The New York Times,* June 13, 1971; © 1971 by The New York Times Company. Reprinted by permission.

married so darned young I want time alone later. My husband's in complete agreement with me. With the high cost of education and the necessity of having a child go to college we would be foolish to have more. I used a diaphragm before and after our children were born until I started using the pill (about three years ago). I hated the diaphragm and so did my husband—it was messy and miserable. I'm so glad we have the pill. We both have complete faith in it. It is such a convenient thing to pop a pill in your mouth every morning. I'm completely sold on it.[2]

More than four out of ten couples in the United States produce a child during the first year of marriage. Ultimately, about 90 percent of married couples have children. The average age of the wife at the birth of her first child is about 22.7 years; she produces two children on the average; and is finished with childbearing by about age 30. During about the first ten years, the facts of sex, contraception, and reproduction are very prominent in marriage. After that, attention frequently has shifted to the children that have been produced.

SEXUAL ADJUSTMENT

As was shown in the chapter on premarital involvement, most couples have begun sexual adjustment before marriage. Their interest in and readiness for sex relationships in marriage, however, usually are not equal. The pattern which develops tends to be a compromise with varying satisfactions and frustrations for each partner.

Frequency of Intercourse and Sexual Adjustment

According to the Kinsey research, the 1965 National Fertility Study, and a national survey in 1972, married couples in their teens have intercourse nearly three times per week on the average.[3] This drops to about twice a week at age 30, and one and one-half times per week at age 40, once a week by age 50, and to once about every 12 days by age 60. These figures, of course, conceal wide variation among couples. Fourteen percent of the teen-aged wives had intercourse as often as once a day, and 5 percent of the 30-year-old married women did so.

2. Lee Rainwater, *Family Design: Marital Sexuality, Family Size, and Contraception*, Chicago: Aldine Publishing Company, 1965, p. 17.

3. The median is used because it is less affected by extreme cases near the ends of the distribution. If arithmetic mean figures were used, they would be slightly higher than those reported here.

As significant as the figures on frequency of coitus are the discrepancies between the figures reported by men and by women (see Table 15.1). The median figures reported by men are slightly lower than those reported by women, suggesting the possibility of relative satiation of the women and deprivation of men. Women, who would prefer less sexual intercourse, may overestimate the actual frequency while men, who would prefer more, underestimate the actual frequency.[4] From the beginning of marriage, differential interest in sex is a problem for many couples.

Table 15.1. Reports of frequency of marital intercourse at various ages

<table>
<tr><th></th><th colspan="2">Median frequencies per week (Kinsey)</th><th colspan="2">per month Mean frequencies</th></tr>
<tr><th>Age group</th><th>Men</th><th>Women</th><th>1965 Study</th><th>1972 Study</th></tr>
<tr><td>16–20</td><td>2.6</td><td>2.8</td><td>10.3</td><td></td></tr>
<tr><td>21–25</td><td>2.3</td><td>2.5</td><td>8.1</td><td></td></tr>
<tr><td>26–30</td><td>2.0</td><td>2.1</td><td>7.3</td><td>9.4</td></tr>
<tr><td>31–35</td><td>1.8</td><td>1.9</td><td>6.7</td><td rowspan="2">7.4</td></tr>
<tr><td>36–40</td><td>1.6</td><td>1.5</td><td>5.9</td></tr>
<tr><td>41–45</td><td>1.3</td><td>1.2</td><td>5.1</td><td rowspan="2">6.1</td></tr>
<tr><td>46–50</td><td>0.9</td><td>0.9</td><td></td></tr>
<tr><td>51–55</td><td>0.7</td><td>0.8</td><td></td><td>4.1</td></tr>
<tr><td>56–60</td><td>0.6</td><td>0.4</td><td></td><td></td></tr>
</table>

Source: Alfred C. Kinsey, Wardell B. Pomeroy, Clyde E. Martin, and Paul H. Gebhard, *Sexual Behavior in the Human Female*, Philadelphia: W. B. Saunders Company, 1953, p. 77; Leslie A. Westoff and Charles F. Westoff, *From Now to Zero: Fertility, Contraception and Abortion in America*, Boston: Little, Brown and Co., 1971, p. 24; and Robert R. Bell and Phyllis L. Bell, "Sexual Satisfaction Among Married Women," *Medical Aspects of Human Sexuality*, Dec. 1972, p. 141.

The existence of wide differences in sexual desire between husbands and wives was verified by Nye in a study of 210 couples in the state of Washington (see Table 15.2). About four-fifths of both husbands and wives report that the husbands desire sex more frequently. Thirteen percent of the husbands and 20 percent of the wives report that their desires are equal. The percentages stating that the wives desire sex more

4. Research shows that husband and wife agree more closely in their estimates of sexual aspects of their relationship than of other aspects. See Bruce Thomason, "Extent of Spousal Agreement on Certain Non-Sexual and Sexual Aspects of Marital Adjustment," *Marriage and Family Living* 17 (Nov. 1955), pp. 322–24.

Table 15.2. Spouse who desires sex more frequently (in percents)

Desire	*Husband's report* (N = 207)	*Wife's report* (N = 205)
Husband much more frequently	37.2	34.6
Husband somewhat more frequently	41.6	38.1
Husband and wife the same	13.0	20.0
Wife somewhat more frequently	6.8	6.3
Wife much more frequently	1.5	1.0
Totals	100.1	100.0

Source: Adapted from F. Ivan Nye, *et. al., Role Structure and Analysis of the Family*, Beverly Hills, Cal.: Sage, 1976, p. 108.

frequently are small and approximately equal, 8.3 percent as reported by the husbands and 7.3 percent as reported by the wives.[5]

One might hypothesize a relationship between mutual high sex desire of husband and wife and good marital adjustment. Research shows, however, that it is not that simple. Wallin and Clark found that maritally satisfied husbands perceived their wives to be similar to themselves in preferred frequency of coitus more often that did maritally dissatisfied husbands. The relationship did not hold equally well for wives, however.[6] Further light was thrown on this situation by Adams in a study of 150 women who had been married for an average of eight years. He found that wives' sexual adjustment was related to their marital happiness but that the relationship between the wives' sexual responsiveness and marital happiness was low.[7] Thus, the relationship between frequency of desire for coitus, sex adjustment, and marital adjustment is more complicated among women than among men.

Although most men desire intercourse more frequently than their wives do, there are cases where the reverse is true. Moreover, with the

5. F. Ivan Nye, *et al., Role Structure and Analysis of the Family*, Beverly Hills, Cal.: Sage, 1976, pp. 27, 107–8.
6. Paul Wallin and Alexander Clark, "Marital Satisfaction and Husbands' and Wives' Perception of Similarity in their Preferred Frequency of Coitus," *Journal of Abnormal and Social Psychology* 57 (Nov. 1958), pp. 370–73. See also George Levinger, "Systematic Distortion in Spouses' Reports of Preferred and Actual Sexual Behavior," *Sociometry* 29 (Sept. 1966), pp. 291–99.
7. Clifford R. Adams, *An Informal Preliminary Report on Some Factors Relating to Sexual Responsiveness of Certain College Wives*, Mimeo., 1953. See also John N. Edwards and Alan Booth, "Sexual Behavior In and Out of Marriage: An Assessment of Correlates," *Journal of Marriage and the Family* 38 (Feb. 1976), pp. 73–81.

trend toward equality between the sexes, the number of women who are highly responsive probably is increasing. Wallin and Clark studied 604 couples to determine the relative acceptability of marriages in which the husband's sex drive was stronger, the drives of the partners were equal, and in which the wives' sex drives were stronger. They found that equality of sex drive in husband and wife, or a stronger drive in the husband are acceptable, but a stronger drive on the part of the wife is not.[8] Apparently, husbands want their wives to be responsive, but not have more drive than they do.

Perhaps the most objective measure of the satisfaction of women in intercourse is the regularity with which they achieve orgasm. Table 15.3 presents Kinsey statistics showing the proportions of marital coitus leading to orgasm during the first, fifth, tenth, fifteenth, and twentieth years of marriage. The table shows that, during the first year, one-quarter of the women failed to achieve orgasm at all and approximately half achieved it less than 60 percent of the time. Approximately four women out of ten almost always achieved orgasm. In subsequent years, the proportion never experiencing coital orgasm declined but, even during the twentieth year, 11 percent of women were still found in this category. At the other extreme, the proportion of women almost always having

Table 15.3. Percentage of marital coitus leading to female orgasm, by length of marriage

Percent of coitus with orgasm	*Year of marriage*				
	1st	5th	10th	15th	20th
None	25	17	14	12	11
1–29	11	13	14	16	13
30–59	13	15	13	11	12
60–89	12	15	17	16	17
90–100	39	40	42	45	47
Number of cases	2244	1448	858	505	261

Source: Alfred C. Kinsey, Wardell B. Pomeroy, Clyde E. Martin, and Paul H. Gebhard, *Sexual Behavior in the Human Female,* Philadelphia: W. B. Saunders Company, 1953, p. 408.

8. Paul Wallin and Alexander Clark, "Cultural Norms and Husbands' and Wives' Reports of their Marital Partners' Preferred Frequency of Coitus Relative to Their Own," *Sociometry* 21 (Sept. 1958), pp. 247–54.

orgasm rose with length of time married. At the maximum, however, Kinsey found fewer than half of all women in this category.[9]

Kinsey found certain correlates of the frequency of marital coitus and of the frequency of the wife's experiencing orgasm. Interestingly, the data indicate that the frequency of marital coitus declined over several decades. In the age group 16–20, for example, the median frequency dropped from 3.2 per week among women born before 1900 to 2.6 per week among the group born from 1900 to 1909.[10] Similar trends were found among other age groups. The rates stabilized among women born after 1909 and further declines were not evident.

Evidence of change in the other direction appeared in the 1970 National Fertility Study which reported an increase in the frequency of marital intercourse of from 17 to 21 percent just in the five years since 1965. Acknowledging that some of the apparent increase could be due to greater willingness to talk about sex, the researchers nevertheless believe most of the increase to be real and to be due to the liberating affects of the widespread use of effective contraceptives.[11]

The only other variable which is related to the frequency of intercourse is that of religious devoutness. Interestingly the association is with the husband's religiosity and not with the wife's. Since the husband is usually the more aggressive partner in sexual activity, perhaps this should not be surprising. Data comparing religiously active and religiously inactive Protestants show that, at each age level, inactive men report higher frequencies of intercourse. Between the ages of 21 and 25, inactive Protestants report a median frequency of 2.5 per week and the active group reports only 2.2 per week. What effect differences in frequency of intercourse among different religious groups have on marital or sexual adjustment has not been adequately studied. In general, the data do not show that the proportion of marital coitus producing female orgasm is lower among the more devout.

9. A study of marital adjustment among blacks yielded similar findings. King found that 131 out of 418 black wives reported that they always had orgasm in marital intercourse; 160 said that they usually did, 107 said they sometimes did, and 20 reported that they never experienced orgasm. See Charles E. King, "The Sex Factor in Marital Adjustment," *Marriage and Family Living* 16 (Aug. 1954), pp. 237–40.

10. *Op. cit.*, pp. 358–59, 397. Some recent statistics indicate that the proportion of women who almost always reach orgasm is rising somewhat, and may now be between 50 and 60 percent. See Robert R. Bell and Phyllis L. Bell, "Sexual Satisfaction Among Married Women," *Medical Aspects of Human Sexuality*, Dec. 1972, p. 142; and *Time*, Oct. 1, 1973, p. 63.

11. Charles F. Westoff, "Coital Frequency and Contraception," *Family Planning Perspectives* 6 (Summer 1974), pp. 136–41.

As might be expected from Table 15.3, Kinsey found that the proportion of marital coitus that produces female orgasm increases steadily with age, at least up to age 50. Adequate data on the responsiveness of older women are not available. This *proportionate* increase in orgasm experience must be seen, of course, in the context of a steadily decreasing frequency of sexual intercourse with age, and an absolute decline in the frequency of marital orgasm.

The data also show that orgasm in marital coitus is related to the decade of the woman's birth, her father's occupational class, and her educational level. The likelihood of achieving orgasm at all, the likelihood of achieving orgasm within any five-year period, and the proportion of marital intercourse producing orgasm all are higher among women born in more recent decades, among those whose fathers followed upper-white-collar or professional occupations, and among those with more formal education.[12] The widely held stereotype that regards lower-class women as being sexually more responsive appears simply to be wrong.

A retabulation of the Kinsey data on 1026 women in intact marriages, and a national study of 2372 women married an average of 13 years showed a correlation between the regularity with which the wives achieved orgasm and their marital happiness.[13] Approximately 60 percent of the Kinsey wives who reported achieving orgasm from 90 to 100 percent of the time also reported their marriages to be very happy. At the other extreme, only 4 percent of the wives who never reach orgasm reported very happy marriages, and 19 percent of the no-orgasm group said that their marriages were very unhappy. Gebhard concludes that the strong correlation between female orgasm and marital happiness probably is causal in both directions; more responsive women are happier and regular orgasm brings happiness.

Lack of Responsiveness in Women

Lack of sexual responsiveness in women is associated with problems in marriage. Rainwater, summarizing findings from studies of four different lower-class groups in the United States, England, Puerto Rico, and Mexico, states that women use a variety of techniques to cut down on intercourse. They feign sleep, menstruation, and illness; they raise the

12. See Marilyn Peddicord Whitley and Susan B. Poulson, "Assertiveness and Sexual Satisfaction in Employed Professional Women," *Journal of Marriage and the Family* 37 (Aug. 1975), pp. 573–81.

13. Robert R. Bell and Phyllis L. Bell, *op. cit.;* and Paul H. Gebhard, "Factors in Marital Orgasm," *Journal of Social Issues* 22 (April 1966), pp. 88–95.

possibility of pregnancy; and they prolong the abstinence before and after the birth of children. Some also provoke arguments with the husband that give them an excuse for not being affectionate.[14] Middle-class women may be more subtle in their attempts to regulate the frequency of intercourse, but the testimony of many husbands indicates that some of the same techniques are employed.

When the wife's lack of responsiveness is either extreme or consistent, the term *frigidity* often is applied. Vincent points out that although some frigidity may be due to personality disturbances or physiological impairments, many cases can be explained in interactional terms. In marriages across social class lines, for example, a wife who is not aloof to sex, as such, may be repulsed by her husband's sexual values and attitudes. If she has married a lower-status man, she may find him crude and vulgar. If she has married into a higher class, on the other hand, she may come to suppress her own sexuality if it is out of harmony with the considerate and gentle attentions of her husband.[15]

Vincent refers to the lack of sexual responsiveness in situations such as this as symptomatic frigidity. The difficulty is not sexual alone but is symptomatic of wider and more basic differences in life.

In some cases, couples may define the wife as frigid simply because her interest in sex is not at the arbitrary level they believe is normal and desirable. A husband and wife, for example, who have been relatively satisfied with their sex life may suddenly experience a problem upon discovering that most couples their age have intercourse more frequently. Vincent refers to this as the "tyranny of the majority norm." If the couple had not become aware of the idealized standard, they might never have thought of themselves as having a problem.

Closely related is the problem of overemphasis upon technique in love-making and the glorification of mutual orgasm. Many marriage manuals, in seeking to educate people to the basic facts of anatomy and physiology, have encouraged a mechanical approach to sexual arousal of the partner that robs the relationship of love, spontaneity, and fun.[16] Some wives complain bitterly of being able to tell when their husbands

14. Lee Rainwater, "Marital Sexuality in Four Cultures of Poverty," *Journal of Marriage and the Family* 26 (Nov. 1964), pp. 457–66.

15. Clark E. Vincent, "Social and Interpersonal Sources of Symptomatic Frigidity," *Marriage and Family Living* 18 (Nov. 1956), pp. 355–60.

16. See Dennis Brissett and Lionel S. Lewis, "Guidelines for Marital Sex: An Analysis of Fifteen Popular Marriage Manuals," *The Family Coordinator* 19 (Jan. 1970), pp. 41–48; and Nelson N. Foote, "Sex as Play," *Social Problems* 1 (April 1954), pp. 159–63.

are turning from page 37 to page 38! Rather than being more fully aroused by such techniques, some wives reject sex altogether.

Sexual responsiveness in women appears to be more situationally determined than among men. Women who are harassed with child care, who feel unloved, who are worried, who doubt their own worth—all are likely to be temporarily unresponsive. If such conditions persist, it may become almost irreversible. Men, who would not respond to the same pressures in the same way, often cannot understand their wives' reactions and apply the label "frigid" to them in both anger and dismay.

Finally, a misunderstanding by wives of their husbands sometimes leads them to stereotype their needs and to withdraw from meeting them. There is an impression that men use sex only for physical satisfaction and not for the expression of love. This impression is likely to be vivid in a wife whose husband wants to make up a quarrel by going to bed with her. Her own desire having been eliminated by the upset of the quarrel, she cannot imagine that her husband's proposal for sex is his means of showing that he loves her and reassuring himself of her love in return. Instead, she feels "used" and withdraws from sex even more.

This does not exhaust the interpersonal factors that maintain the difference in sex desires between husband and wife. The sex pattern that is established often represents a compromise between the greater sexual interest of the husband and the lesser interest of the wife. The wife is likely to regard her husband as oversexed and the husband often finds his wife disappointing.

Substitute Outlets

The frequency of intercourse is highest at younger ages and declines steadily. For husbands, this has manifold significance. To some degree the decreasing frequency reflects physiological aging and decreased frequency of sexual activity of any sort. Kinsey found that male sexual activity reaches its peak in adolescence and then drops steadily with increasing age. Psychological causation operates too. Fatigue develops due to the wife's lack of responsiveness and the husband's being discouraged by her. In addition, there is loss of interest in endlessly repeating the same sexual experience. The opportunities for trying new techniques, new positions, and new situations must eventually end.

The decrease in frequency of marital intercourse often represents more than physiological and psychological fatigue, however. Many males whose sexual urges are quite strong find substitute outlets. The commonest is masturbation. At lower educational levels, 30 to 40 percent of married men masturbate at some time, while among those who have attended college almost 70 percent do so. These college-educated married men may masturbate as often as once or twice per week.

Almost as widespread as masturbation is extramarital intercourse. Kinsey estimated the proportion of men who become involved at about 50 percent. Again, differences are found by educational level. The highest incidences for those with less formal education appear at younger ages and decrease steadily with age. Among college-educated men, on the other hand, not more than 15 to 20 percent are involved at younger ages. The proportion who are involved increases steadily until approximately 27 percent are having extramarital intercourse by age 50. Among these same college-educated men, the frequencies of extramarital intercourse are not more than once every two or three weeks between 16 and 30 years of age, but climb to almost once a week at age 50.[17]

Obviously, marital intercourse accounts for only part of the sexual activity of married men. Among college-educated men, it supplies about 85 percent of the outlet during the early years of marriage but, by age 55, it is accounting for only 62 percent. Apparently, college-educated men as they grow older may conclude that the restraints on their early sexual involvements were not justified and frequently deal with their wives' lack of responsiveness by finding other partners.

The situations of wives are different. Their initial lack of responsiveness, much of which is due to repressive early training, gives way to increasing sexual interest as they become more experienced. Kinsey estimated that women reach a peak of responsiveness at about 30 years of age and that this higher level of sexual interest is then maintained until the fifties or sixties. At some point, the desires of the wife surpass in frequency those of the husband. Some wives find alternate sources of sexual satisfaction.

The proportion of women who are active in masturbation at given ages is much higher at higher educational levels. The active incidence of masturbation to orgasm by married women between the ages of 21 and 25 is close to 30 percent for women with college and postgraduate educations. By age 31–35, it has climbed to 34 percent among college-educated women and to 40 percent among those with some graduate education. The percentages continue to climb at least through age 36–40, with

17. Alfred C. Kinsey, Wardell B. Pomeroy, and Clyde E. Martin, *Sexual Behavior in the Human Male*, Philadelphia: W. B. Saunders Co., 1948, p. 587.

a high of 48 percent of graduate-school-educated women masturbating in the period from 41 to 45 years.[18] One can only conclude that many of these women are now being forced to seek sexual satisfaction which they cannot get from their husbands.

Many women also have extramarital intercourse. Relatively few are involved during their teens and early twenties, and the majority who do become involved early are women from lower educational levels. The proportion of women who have extramarital coitus rises from 7 percent in the teens to 16 percent by age 30, 23 percent by age 35, and to a maximum of 26 percent by age 40. The proportion who are having such relationships during any one age period is, of course, somewhat lower. Between 16 and 20 years of age, only 6 percent are actively involved; the percentage climbs to 9 percent between 21 and 25 years, to 14 percent between 26 and 30, and to 17 percent between 31 and 35. It then remains relatively constant to about age 45.[19]

There are differences by educational level (see Table 15.4). Not until age 25 have college-educated women become involved in as large numbers as women of less formal education. By age 35, more college-educated women have become involved and the gap continues to widen through age 45. The percentage of college-level women who have had

Table 15.4. Percentage of women with experience in extramarital intercourse, by educational level and age

Age	*Total sample*	*Educational level*		
		9–12	13–16	17+
18	8	6	6	
19	7	8	4	
20	6	7	6	6
25	9	10	10	7
30	16	16	16	17
35	23	21	26	25
40	26	24	31	27
45	26	22	29	27

Source: Alfred C. Kinsey, Wardell B. Pomeroy, Clyde E. Martin, and Paul H. Gebhard, *Sexual Behavior in the Human Female*, Philadelphia: W. B. Saunders Company, 1953, p. 440.

18. *Sexual Behavior in the Human Female, op. cit.*, p. 181.

19. A poll funded by *Playboy* magazine indicates that more young married women are having affairs (24 percent by age 25). How representative this sample may be is open to question. See *Time, op. cit.*

extramarital coitus reaches a high of 31 percent at age 40.[20] Thus, both men and women at higher educational levels are more likely to become involved in extramarital relationships after several years of marriage. It is ironic that, among the couples who should be most able to communicate with one another, noncommunication in the sexual area should be so pervasive.

In spite of widespread interest in the topic, relatively little research has assessed the impact of extramarital affairs upon marriages. Kinsey reported that the extramarital activities not infrequently led to emotional involvements that interfered with their relationships with their husbands. Difficulty was least likely when the husbands did not know of the relationships, and crises often developed when the spouses learned of the affairs.[21]

The situation with regard to sexual adjustment may be likened to that involving total marital adjustment. Most couples report their sexual adjustment to be good. In the Burgess and Wallin study 75 percent of the husbands and 61 percent of the wives reported receiving complete relief from sexual desire through marital coitus.[22] Yet, along with these reassuring reports must be considered the steadily decreasing frequency of intercourse as marriages continue, orgasm incapacity in women, and the resort of spouses to other sources of sexual satisfaction. The communication between many husbands and wives about sexual matters leaves something to be desired and that, if anything, the communication becomes poorer as marriages continue.

Swinging

The above discussion of extramarital intercourse focuses upon the solitary, generally secretive adventures either of the husband or the wife. Whether "one night stands" or "affairs" are involved, the participating spouse usually conceals the activity from the partner; in this context, the joint participation of husband and wife is not even considered.

Yet, joint extramarital sexual participation is not new, nor has it been

20. *Ibid.*, pp. 439–40.

21. See also Robert R. Bell, Stanley Turner, and Lawrence Rosen, "A Multivariate Analysis of Female Extramarital Coitus," *Journal of Marriage and the Family* 37 (May 1975), pp. 375–84; John N. Edwards, "Extramarital Involvement: Fact and Theory," *The Journal of Sex Research* 9 (Aug. 1973), pp. 210–24; and Minako K. Maykovich, "Attitudes versus Behavior in Extramarital Sexual Relations," *Journal of Marriage and the Family* 38 (Nov. 1976), pp. 693–99.

22. Ernest W. Burgess and Paul Wallin, *Engagement and Marriage*, Philadelphia: J. B. Lippincott Company, 1953, p. 669.

particularly rare. During the 1940s and 1950s, for example, there existed organized extramarital activities that were referred to as "wife swapping," and there were persistent rumors, in most communities of the existence of "key clubs."

Key clubs were the predecessors of today's swinging. Although the techniques of pairing off varied, the term *key club* stemmed from the technique of having all of the women place their keys in a hat. The men then drew keys, spending the night with the woman whose keys they had drawn. The number of key clubs was unknown because they were highly secretive. Apparently, they were also very unstable. The initiative usually was taken by a few of the husbands, and some wives participated reluctantly. Public censure would follow discovery, jealousies developed, and many participants believed that there must be something seriously wrong with them or their marriages, or else their spouses would not want to participate in such behavior.

Wife swapping differed from key clubbing as much in attitude as in technique. In wife swapping, there often were only two couples, and the switch of partners might continue irregularly for a time. The very term *wife swapping*, however, has sexist connotations, implying that wives are property whose favors might be traded. Wife swapping was less equalitarian than key clubbing, and the potential for conflict was greater. Public knowledge of the arrangements often emerged when one of the partners sought separation or divorce.

Swinging as a distinct phenomenon appeared on the American scene in the early 1960s. Approximately 50 magazines having substantial circulation sprang up, carrying advertisements inviting contacts for sexual purposes.[23]

The essence of swinging is the joint participation of husband and wife in sexual activity with at least one other person, usually with other married couples. The sexual activity is an end in itself and both partners are willing to accept sexual intercourse with strangers.

There are no reliable estimates of how many couples swing. The most extravagant estimate comes from a sample of 407 swinging couples, only 4 percent of whom placed or replied to ads in swingers' magazines.

23. See Duane Denfeld and Michael Gordon, "The Sociology of Mate Swapping: Or the Family that Swings Together Clings Together," *The Journal of Sex Research* 6 (May 1971), pp. 85–100; Richard M. Stephenson, "Involvement in Deviance: An Example and Some Theoretical Implications," *Social Problems* 21 (Fall 1973), pp. 173–90; Carolyn Symonds, "A Vocabulary of Sexual Enticement and Proposition," *The Journal of Sex Research* 8 (May 1972), pp. 136–39; and Mary L. Walshok, "The Emergence of Middle-Class Deviant Subcultures: The Case of Swingers," *Social Problems* 18 (Spring 1971), pp. 488–95.

Since almost 70,000 couples did use the magazines, the investigators estimated the total number of swinging couples at 8 million.[24] From another study of 350 Chicago couples, another researcher estimated that there are 8000 swinging couples within a 200 mile radius of that city.[25] The most trustworthy generalization comes from Robert Bell, who concluded that "there are more swingers than non-swingers believe, but not as many as swingers think."

Since we do not even know how many swingers there are, we cannot know their social characteristics. The groups who have been studied are primarily middle class, many having some college education. Many follow white-collar or professional occupations. Most appear to be relatively young. Interestingly, except in the sexual area, they seem to be conventional and conservative people. They conceal their swinging from their children and friends, and they are committed to swinging as a means of improving their marital adjustment.

An explicit set of social norms governs the behavior of swingers. First, there is no double standard. What is right for the husband also is right for the wife. No jealousy or private restrictions on the spouse's behavior are accepted. Second, sex among swingers must be kept strictly physical and impersonal. No "dates" outside the swinging sessions are permitted. Third, no one may be pressured into sexual activity. Women are free to reject overtures. Fourth, no moral judgments are permitted; one may choose not to participate in oral intercourse or homosexual intercourse, for example, but one may not disapprove of them in others.

Swingers maintain that swinging actually improves their marriages. They argue that most non-swingers are "hung-up" on the idea of sexual possessiveness and that they have poor marriages as a result. By keeping sex with their spouses based upon emotional as well as physical desire, and by satisfying their physical needs in shared, non-hypocritical fashion, they believe that their marriages are happier and stronger than most.

Few objective studies of swinging have yet been done. One of the best studies involved questionnaires filled out by 965 marriage counselors, of whom 473 had counseled couples who had tried swinging, but who had given it up. Among the 1175 couples reported on, 109 stated that they had problems of jealousy resulting from swinging. The men tended to be jealous of their wives' popularity or sexual performance. The

24. William Breedlove and Jerrye Breedlove, *Swap Clubs*, Los Angeles: Sherbourne Press, 1964.

25. Gilbert D. Bartell, *Group Sex: A Scientist's Eyewitness Report on the American Way of Swinging*, New York: Peter H. Wyden, 1971.

women feared they would lose their husbands. Sixty-eight couples reported fights and hostilities developed between them, and, as a result, their marriages were threatened. In 53 cases, emotional attachments to swinging partners developed, and 29 couples actually separated or divorced. Other problems reported were disappointment and boredom with swinging, fear of discovery, and the wife's "inability to take it."[26]

A Canadian study, in which 25 women swingers were interviewed by a woman researcher, focused upon how couples reached the decision to swing and reported that the man made most of the decisions and that swinging is not the non-sexist, equalitarian arrangement it is reputed to be.[27] Dodson also reports that she found the same problems at orgies that occur in marital bedrooms, like women not having orgasms and the operation of the double standard.[28]

FAMILY PLANNING AND CHILD-BEARING

Nearly one out of every two couples produces a child during the first year of marriage, and at least 90 percent of all couples produce at least one child eventually. Curiously, the proportion of couples who remain childless has been dropping during the period when improvement in contraceptive methods logically would have made the choice to remain childless easier and more likely. As recently as 1950, 17 percent of native-born, white wives aged 45–49 had not produced a child. Among native-born white wives reaching 45–49 years in 1965, however, more than 90 percent had produced at least one child.

Recent Trends in Family Size

Data on family size are available for about the last 100 years. They show that from 1860 to 1930 birth rates and the size of families steadily declined. The number of persons per household declined from 5.1 to 4.1. Birth rates stayed at low levels until the end of World War II, when a

26. Duane Denfeld, "Dropouts from Swinging," *The Family Coordinator* 23 (Jan. 1974), pp. 45–49. For an analysis reporting lack of harmful results from swinging, see Charles L. Cole and Graham B. Spanier, "Comarital Mate-Sharing and Family Stability," *The Journal of Sex Research* 10 (Feb. 1974), pp. 21–31.

27. Anne-Marie Henshel, "Swinging: A Study of Decision Making in Marriage," in Joan Huber, *ed., Changing Women in a Changing Society*, Chicago and London: The University of Chicago Press, 1973, pp. 123–29.

28. Betty Dodson, "Playboy Panel: New Sexual Life Styles," *Playboy, op. cit.*, p. 85.

rush of marriages deferred during the depression of the 1930s and the war began to produce rapidly increasing numbers of births. The crude birth rate climbed to 25 in 1946. A better indication than the crude birth rate of what happened is changing preferences in family size.

During the 1940s, a national sample of women was asked how many children they considered to be ideal. Again in 1955 and 1960, national samples of married women were asked the same thing. In all three periods, about 90 percent stated that they wanted, two, three, or four children. The proportions wanting two children steadily declined, however, while the proportions wanting four children steadily increased. In 1960, the proportion wanting four children was higher than the proportion wanting any other number.[29]

By 1960, however, birth rates had started down, and expected family size changed drastically. By 1976, young women expected to have an average of only 2.4 children each.[30]

Number of Children and Marital Adjustment

Early studies sought out the relationship between marital adjustment and number of children. Most studies failed to find any consistent relationships. Two pre-World War II studies found that couples with either one or two children were happier than couples with more children, reflecting the congruence between child-bearing patterns and the prevailing child-bearing values.[31] Just after World War II, two additional studies yielded findings that corroborated the inverse relationship between family size and marital adjustment.[32]

A study of 731 urban and 178 farm wives in Detroit in 1955 showed that mothers of three children were better satisfied with their marriages than mothers with either more or fewer children. The mothers of more than three or four often reported they wished they had not had so

29. Pascal K. Whelpton, Arthur A. Campbell, and John E. Patterson, *Fertility and Family Planning in the United States*, Princeton, N.J.: Princeton University Press, 1966.
30. *The New York Times*, Feb. 6, 1977, pp. 1, 42.
31. Ernest W. Burgess and Leonard S. Cottrell, Jr., *Predicting Success or Failure in Marriage*, New York: Prentice-Hall, 1939. R. O. Lang, "The Rating of Happiness in Marriage," unpublished M.A. thesis, University of Chicago, 1932.
32. Robert B. Reed, "Social and Psychological Factors Affecting Fertility: The Interrelationship of Marital Adjustment, Fertility Control, and Size of Family," *The Milbank Memorial Fund Quarterly* 25 (Oct. 1947), pp. 383–425; and Harold T. Christensen and Robert E. Philbrick, "Family Size as a Factor in the Marital Adjustments of College Couples," *American Sociological Review* 17 (June 1952), 306–12.

many.[33] Again, there is an association between marital adjustment and correspondence between preferred and actual child-bearing. Several more studies confirmed these relationships.[34]

Planned Childlessness

During the late 1960s and early 1970s, scattered groups of married couples received support from some sociologists for rejecting the ideal of parenthood altogether. Bernard, for example, while acknowledging that childless marriages have higher divorce rates than those with children, pointed out that *surviving* childless marriages report higher marital happiness ratings than marriages with children.[35] A study of over 5000 people in California confirmed that couples currently raising children make lower marital happiness scores.[36]

In 1971, a national organization, the National Organization for Non-Parents, was formed to promote childlessness as a superior way of life and to support couples who do not wish to have children. It is too early to tell whether the organization will grow, significantly, or whether the ideal of childlessness will spread. Of the about 600 people who joined NON during its first year or so, about one-fourth were couples with children.

Little study of deliberately childlessness marriages has been done as yet. Veevers reported on 52 voluntarily childless wives in Canada, and found that they divided into two groups: those who decided on childlessness before marriage, and those who decided later. The latter group

33. Robert O. Blood, Jr. and Donald M. Wolfe, *Husbands and Wives: The Dynamics of Married Living,* Glencoe, Illinois: The Free Press, 1960, pp. 262–63.
34. Charles R. Figley, "Child Density and the Marital Relationship," *Journal of Marriage and the Family* 35 (May 1973), pp. 272–82; Gerry E. Hendershot, "Familial Satisfaction, Birth Order, and Fertility Values," *Journal of Marriage and the Family* 31 (Feb. 1969), pp. 27–33; Eleanore B. Luckey and Joyce K. Bain, "Children: A Factor in Marital Satisfaction," *Journal of Marriage and the Family* 32 (Feb. 1970), pp. 43–44; Brent C. Miller, "Child Density, Marital Satisfaction, and Conventionalization: A Resarch Note," *Journal of Marriage and the Family* 37 (May 1975), pp. 345–47; F. Ivan Nye, John Carlson, and Gerald Garrett, "Family Size, Interaction, Affect, and Stress," *Journal of Marriage and the Family* 32 (May 1970), pp. 216–26; Robert G. Ryder, "Longitudinal Data Relating Marriage Satisfaction and Having a Child," *Journal of Marriage and the Family* 35 (Nov. 1973), pp. 605–6; and Arland Thornton, "Children and Marital Stability," *Journal of Marriage and the Family* 39 (Aug. 1977), pp. 531–40.
35. Jessie Bernard, *The Future of Marriage,* New York: World, 1972.
36. Karen Renne, "Correlates of Dissatisfaction in Marriage," *Journal of Marriage and the Family* 32 (Feb. 1970), pp. 54–67.

decided first to "postpone" child-bearing and gradually drifted into making the decision permanent. All of the wives are reported to feel some social pressure to have children, and many have given some thought to the possibility of adoption if they decide, later on, that they want children after all.[37]

FAMILY PLANNING

The National Fertility Study, begun in 1965, now surveys the contraceptive and child-bearing practices of married women in the United States every five years. These surveys of national probability samples yield a remarkably comprehensive and accurate account of both current practices and past and future trends.

The 1975 survey was based upon interviews with 3329 once-married white women who married before the age of 25 and who had not yet passed the age of 44. The results showed that contraceptive use has been spreading rapidly and that almost all couples now use contraception at some time during their married lives; of couples married from 5 through 9 years, for example, only 2.1 percent have not yet used it.

Table 15.5 presents the percentages of the women studied who were currently using or not using contraception, and the types of practices employed. The figures show that the percentage practicing contraception at any one time is about 80 percent. Of the non-users, the majority are anticipating a pregnancy, in a pregnancy, or have just had a pregnancy. Some do not need contraception because their marriages are sterile, and only a small percentage are ignoring the risk of pregnancy.

Overall, the pill is the most popular method of birth control, but sterilization is right behind. Moreover, when age is taken into consideration, the pill is the most widely used method only among women who have been married fewer than ten years, many of whom anticipate having more children. Among women married ten years or more, sterilization is the most popular method; among couples who have had all of the children they want, 43.5 percent have resorted to sterilization and only 24.1 percent are using the pill.

37. J. E. Veevers, "Voluntarily Childless Wives: An Exploratory Study," *Sociology and Social Research* (April 1973), pp. 356–65; and J. E. Veevers, "The Moral Careers of Voluntarily Childless Wives: Notes on the Defense of a Variant World View," *The Family Coordinator* 24 (Oct. 1975), pp. 473–86. See also Sharon K. Houseknecht, "Reference Group Support for Voluntary Childlessness: Evidence for Conformity," *Journal of Marriage and the Family* 39 (May 1977), pp. 285–92.

Table 15.5. Current exposure to the risk of conception among continuously married white women 1975 (N = 3329)

Type of Exposure	*Percents*			
Percent total		100.0		
Using contraception			79.0	
Not using contraception			21.0	
Pregnant, postpartum, or trying to get pregnant				12.0
Sterile and other non-use				9.0
Contraceptive users				
Pill	34.3			
Wife Sterilized	16.3			
Husband Sterilized	15.0			
Condom	10.9			
IUD	8.7			
Diaphragm	3.9			
Foam	3.6			
Rhythm	2.8			
Withdrawal	2.0			
Douche	0.4			
Other	2.2			
Total users	100.1			

Source: Adapted from Charles F. Westoff and Elise F. Jones, "Contraception and Sterilization in the United States, 1965–1975," *Family Planning Perspectives* 9 (July-August 1977), p. 154.

The only other method to become significantly more popular over the last decade is the IUD. Fewer than 1 percent were using it in 1965, while almost 9 percent were using it in 1975. Most of this increase occurred before 1973. There is some evidence that the increase stopped, following widespread publicity given to the dangers of the Dalkon Shield which was withdrawn from the market in 1974.

All of the other methods continue to decline in use. Condoms, used by about 11 percent of the couples, dropped from 14 percent in 1965. The diaphragm, used by 6.3 percent of the couples in 1965, was used by only 3.9 percent in 1975. Although data are not yet available to show it, there is some suspicion that these two methods may be increasing slightly in popularity again as the result of complications people are encountering in the use of the pill and the IUD.

Because of the opposition of the Roman Catholic Church to all methods of contraception other than rhythm, trends in the use of this method are especially interesting. Almost 7 percent of married women were using the rhythm method in 1965; by 1975, the percentage had dropped to 2.8. Over two-thirds of Catholic women use prohibited methods, and researchers predict that their birth control practices will become indistinguishable from those of non-Catholics in just a few years.[38]

Table 15.6. Percentages of unintended pregnancies over a one-year period, by method of contraception used

Method	*Percent having pregnancies*
Pill	6
IUD	12
Condom	18
Diaphragm	23
Foam	31
Rhythm	33
Douche	39

Source: "Contraceptive Failure Linked to Age, Intent, Although Pill, IUD Most Effective Methods," *Family Planning Digest* 3 (Jan. 1974), p. 6.

Although the adoption of more efficient means of contraception has reduced the number of unwanted pregnancies, the problem has not been eliminated. Table 15.6 shows the percentage of contraceptive users in the 1970 National Fertility Study who had an unintended pregnancy in a one-year period, by the contraceptive method employed. Over-all, 14 percent of the couples wanting no more children had an unwanted pregnancy, and 24 percent of those wishing to delay further pregnancies had an unexpected one. These figures are only half what they were 10 and 15 years ago, respectively.

In the context of these data for the total United States, let us now examine a less quantitative study that throws light on the relationship between family planning and the roles that men and women play in marriage. Rainwater interviewed 409 men and women from 257 marriages. The respondents were mostly from Chicago, Cincinnati, and Oklahoma

38. "Two-thirds of Catholic Women Use Contraceptives Other Than Rhythm: More than Twice as Many as 15 Years Before," *Family Planning Digest* 2 (March 1973), pp. 7–8. See also Leon F. Bouvier, "Catholics and Contraception," *Journal of Marriage and the Family* 34 (Aug. 1972), pp. 514–22.

City and provided approximately equal numbers of upper-middle-, lower-middle-, upper-lower-, and lower-lower-class persons. Quotas of Catholics were included within each class group.[39]

First, marital roles varied by social class. Upper-middle-class couples tended to have joint conjugal role relationships in which they shared many activities.[40] Although there may be a division of labor between them, each spouse is actively interested in the duties of the other. Most leisure time is spent together. The lower-middle-class couples were about equally divided between joint role relationships and an intermediate type in which there is some sharing of tasks and activities and also some segregation of roles. The trend toward role segregation continues as we move down in social class until the majority of lower-lower-class couples followed segregated roles. Such segregated roles involve the husband and wife coordinating their daily activities, but with each largely going his own way. There is no special value seen in sharing.

The joint or segregated marital roles were reflected in means of solving problems, in sex relationships, and in family planning. Joint role relationships involved solving problems through discussion, compromise, and mutual accommodation. These techniques, associated with a high level of marital satisfaction, stood in contrast to the lack of effective communication in segregated role relationships. Segregated roles often were accompanied by dissatisfaction with the marriage.

Sexual gratification varied by class and by role organization. Lower-class women were more likely to report dissatisfaction with sex than were middle-class women, and lower-class women whose marriages were role segregated were the most dissatisfied of all. Such women tended to define sex as being primarily for the satisfaction of men and often considered their husbands to be inconsiderate of the wife's feelings.

Although it dealt with lower-class couples only, an earlier report described patterns of sex relationships and of family planning which may have relevance for middle-class people also. Of the 96 women interviewed in this part of the study, about half were Protestant, one-third were Catholic, 5 percent were Jewish, and a few had no religious affil-

39. Lee Rainwater, *Family Design: Marital Sexuality, Family Size, and Contraception*, Chicago: Aldine Publishing Company, 1965.

40. The idea of marital roles ranging from "joint" to "segregated" was developed in Elizabeth Bott, *Family and Social Network*, London: Tavistock Publications, 1957, pp. 53-55.

iation. Rainwater classified them into four types according to patterns of family planning: the early planners, the "do nothing" group, the sporadic users, and the late "desperate" planners.

The early planners often do not begin using contraception until after one or two pregnancies, but they act before they have achieved their ideal family size and they are reasonably effective in their contraceptive efforts. Although specific figures are not given, this apparently is a rather small group. The "do nothing" group probably is self-explanatory. It represents the opposite end of the continuum from the early planners and includes couples who have had several children and still make no use of contraception. Like the early planners, it is a small group. Many are Roman Catholics who value having large families.

The largest single group were the sporadic or careless contraceptive users. Most had used several different contraceptives, but had not used any of them effectively. They want to limit their children but they are not able to follow a consistent program of action. Communication between the husband and wife is poor and wives often feel victimized by their husbands. They also tend to blame their failures upon the contraceptives, rather than upon themselves.

The last category of late "desperate" planners often had been sporadic users earlier. Having had all of the children they want, or more, they have now become effective contraception users out of sheer desperation. Significantly, the device or technique that they now use effectively often is one of the ones that they failed with earlier.[41]

These categories "make sense" in terms of the findings of the National Fertility Study. Not only do they make sense, however, but Rainwater has also effectively linked these patterns to psychosexual factors in the style of life of these couples. Specifically, he further classifies the couples into three groups: (1) those in which both husband and wife derive considerable gratification from sex relations; (2) those in which the wife's pleasure is subject to interference from other concerns; (3) and those in which the wife receives little gratification and intercourse is performed for the husband's satisfaction.

The first pattern is one of mutuality. Both husband and wife enjoy sex and it is important to them. Over two-thirds of this group—which constituted just under half of the total sample—had intercourse three or

41. Lee Rainwater and Karol K. Weinstein, *And the Poor Get Children: Sex, Contraception, and Family Planning in the Working Class*, Chicago: Quadrangle Books, 1960, pp. 29–42.

mores times per week. There was openness in their discussions of family planning, they cooperated in contraception, and their family planning was effective. The women had little difficulty using feminine methods of contraception and assumed much responsibility for it.

The second group constituted less than one-third of the couples and were labeled "repressive compromisers." Three-fourths reported having intercourse fewer than three times per week, with variable results. When things are going well in the marriage and in a woman's daily life, she may be a willing, responsive participant in sex. But when there are problems with children or money or conflict with her husband, she is not responsive. The women tend not to have very positive images of their husbands but concentrate, instead, upon their negative virtues—"he doesn't drink"; "he doesn't gamble"; "he's good to the kids." Fewer of such couples were effective users of contraception, tending in that respect to be like the third category.[42]

The most negative conceptions of sex and of their husbands were held by the "active rejectors." Constituting nearly one-third of the sample, 18 out of 19 wives reported intercourse fewer than three times per week. Women in this category react to sex with disgust, fear, or anxiety, regarding it as an unpleasant duty. Many wives complain of their husbands' drinking, bad tempers, sloppiness, low moral standards, and lack of consideration for their wives. An interesting question is whether these husbands really are different from the husbands of other women. Whatever the causation, communication in these marriages is poor and few are effective in family planning. Most of the women are repulsed by the idea of handling their genitals for the use of contraception and insist that the responsibility is the husband's.

What these findings indicate is that the effectiveness of contraception and family planning do not depend simply upon the technical efficiency of the methods. Instead, sexual interaction and family planning vary with the kind and amount of communication between husband and wife. This communication is a function of the larger roles the spouses

42. For a somewhat different, but supportive, conceptualization of this situation, see Nicholas Babchuk and Angelo La Cognata, "Crises and the Effective Utilization of Contraception," *Marriage and Family Living* 22 (Aug. 1960), pp. 254–58. See also Charles H. Hawkins, "What's Good in a Contraceptive Method?" *The Family Coordinator* 19 (Jan. 1970), pp. 45–56; and Linda L. Heath, Brent S. Roper, and Charles D. King, "A Research Note on Children Viewed as Contributors to Marital Stability: The Relationship to Birth Control Use, Ideal and Expected Family Size," *Journal of Marriage and the Family* 36 (May 1974), pp. 304–6.

play. In general, communication, sexual satisfaction, and success in family planning all are better at middle-class levels than at lower-class levels. At least one study suggests that these social class differences may be diminishing and that couples at all levels are becoming more oriented to open communication between husband and wife. Hawkins and his colleagues studied 171 couples who had been married for at least three years and who had at least one child, classifying their communication styles into contactful, speculative, conventional, and controlling types. While there was a relationship between the husband's educational level and preference for contactful and speculative communication, all educational groups ranked these two open, intimate communication styles first and second.[43]

PREGNANCY AND CHILD-BEARING

At least 75 percent of all pregnancies are welcomed by the prospective parents. Under these circumstances, the pregnancy experience should be rewarding. Conversely, unplanned and unwanted pregnancies should be accompanied by problems. If this is true, however, it is later pregnancies, rather than the first one, that create problems.

The first pregnancies of 212 university students' wives were classified into those where the wives had not wanted the conception, those where they had not tried to achieve or avoid conception, and those where conception was sought. During the first trimester of pregnancy, there were more feelings of unhappiness and more emotional upset among those who had not wanted to conceive. But by the second trimester these differences had virtually disappeared, indicating that most couples quickly make their peace with the first pregnancy, whether planned or not. The nausea experienced by the wives during pregnancy was not related to whether the child was planned, and there were no relationships between planning status and the ease or difficulty of delivery.[44] Brodsky, studying other student wives, found that the self-acceptance of pregnant women did not differ significantly from that of wives who were not pregnant.[45]

43. James L. Hawkins, Carol Weisberg, and Dixie L. Ray, "Marital Communication Style and Social Class," *Journal of Marriage and the Family* 39 (Aug. 1977), pp. 479–90.

44. Shirley Poffenberger, Thomas Poffenberger, and Judson T. Landis, "Intent Toward Conception and the Pregnancy Experience," *American Sociological Review* 17 (Oct. 1952), pp. 616–20.

45. Stanley L. Brodsky, "Self-Acceptance in Pregnant Women," *Marriage and Family Living* 25 (Nov. 1963), pp. 483–84. See also William R. Rosengren, "Social Sources of

The first study showed that pregnancy often has some effect upon sex adjustment. Fifty-eight percent of the couples indicated that their sex adjustment had not been affected, but 24 percent believed their adjustment to have been adversely affected, while 18 percent stated that their adjustment had improved. In general, those who had good sex adjustment before the pregnancy continued to have good adjustment. Where previously poor adjustment improved, the improvement might have occurred without the pregnancy or it might have been linked to the pregnancy. Some husbands and wives described themselves as more considerate of one another during the pregnancy. Where poorer adjustment developed, it was frequently explained in terms of the added responsibilities that child-bearing entailed; the wife sometimes became too busy and too tired to be interested in sex. There also was a tendency for the frequency of sex desire of both husband and wife to decrease during pregnancy and to remain lower after the birth of the child. Fear of another pregnancy hindered sex adjustment after the birth, and sex adjustment was better where the wife had confidence in the contraceptive subsequently used.[46]

Studies of family planning and general knowledge would lead us to expect that the effects of subsequent pregnancies, particularly unwanted pregnancies, would be different. That this is true is verified by data collected by Kinsey. He found that some pregnancies at each birth order are terminated by induced abortion. Only about 10 percent of second pregnancies were so terminated, 16 percent of third pregnancies, 19 percent of fifth pregnancies, and 34 percent of sixth pregnancies ended in induced abortion.[47]

The abortion situation in the United States changed rapidly in the late 1960s and early 1970s, as 17 states liberalized their abortion laws. Then, in January 1973, the Supreme Court issued a landmark ruling that virtually wiped out both the old laws and most of the new ones. The court held that, during the first trimester of pregnancy, the decision to have an abortion must be left solely to the woman and her physician. The only restriction permitted is that the abortion must be performed

---

Pregnancy as Illness or Normality," *Social Forces* 29 (March 1961), pp. 260–67; and William R. Rosengren, "Social Instability and Attitudes Toward Pregnancy as a Social Role," *Social Problems* 9 (Spring 1962), pp. 371–78.

46. Judson T. Landis, Thomas Poffenberger, and Shirley Poffenberger, "The Effects of First Pregnancy upon the Sexual Adjustment of 212 Couples," *American Sociological Review* 15 (Dec. 1950), pp. 766–68.

47. Paul H. Gebhard, Wardell B. Pomeroy, Clyde E. Martin, and Cornelia V. Christenson, *Pregnancy, Birth and Abortion*, New York: Harper and Brothers, 1958, p. 136.

by a physician licensed by the state. During the second trimester, the state may impose regulations "reasonably related to maternal health," still not limiting the grounds for abortion but stating the qualifications of persons permitted to perform the procedure and specifying the nature of the facility, such as a clinic or hospital. After the fetus becomes viable (24–28 weeks), laws prohibiting abortion for the purpose of promoting the state's "interest in the potentiality of human life" are permitted, unless abortion is necessary for the preservation of the life or health of the mother, including her mental health.[48]

The number of legal abortions performed has risen spectacularly since about 1969. From 18,000 in 1968, the number climbed to 50,000 in 1969, 230,000 in 1970, 600,000 in 1971, 700,000 in 1972, and about one million in 1975.

Tentative findings suggest that these increases in legal abortions have been accompanied by lower birth rates, particularly of illegitimate births, falling morbidity and mortality rates, and diminished emotional consequences for the women involved. This is particularly significant in view of the fact that, even at the time of the Kinsey studies, 82 percent of the married women who had been aborted reported no unfavorable consequences.[49]

Obviously, reactions to pregnancy vary with the number of pregnancies and whether the pregnancy is desired. Most early pregnancies appear to be wanted and produce only minor effect on the marriage. Later pregnancies, after the couple have had all the children they want, are more likely to have negative repercussions and to end in abortion.

If there is justification for conceiving of pregnancy as possibly crisis-producing, there also is justification for reasoning that child-birth may sometimes produce a marital crisis. Le Masters studied 46 middle-class couples who were having their first child. He found that 38 of the 46 couples (83 percent) reported an "extensive" or "severe" crisis in adjusting to the birth of the child. Since 35 of these 38 children were "desired" or "planned," the crisis could not be attributed to unwanted pregnancy. Neither could the crises be attributed to poor marital adjustment or psychiatric problems. Instead, Le Masters concluded that these par-

48. The political struggle over abortion is far from ended. Thirty-one states passed abortion laws in 1973 and 1974, specifying some combination of conditions under which abortion may be performed, who may perform them, at what stage of pregnancy, and in what facilities. As of now, most of these laws probably are unconstitutional, but there will be organized efforts to reverse the Supreme Court's January 1973 decision.

49. *Op. cit.*, pp. 203–11.

ents had romanticized parenthood and were unprepared for the reality of having a baby in the home. The mothers often complained of feeling tired, of being confined to their homes, and of having to give up social activities and employment. The fathers also complained of financial pressures, of worry about another pregnancy, and of lessened sexual interest on the part of their wives.[50]

Four other studies have attempted to confirm or refute Le Masters' findings. Dyer studied 32 middle-class couples in Houston, Texas, and reached conclusions similar to Le Masters's. Fifty-three percent of his couples experienced extensive or severe crisis after the birth of their first child. The crises often lasted for several months. Both Le Masters and Dyer found that the large majority of couples eventually made satisfactory recovery from the crises.[51]

Hobbs studied a broader sample of couples whose babies averaged only about ten weeks of age, and found that 87 percent experienced only a slight crisis, and only 13 percent experienced even a moderate one.[52] This study was replicated a decade later, in 1975, with essentially the same findings.[53] A final study of 300 Minneapolis couples whose babies ranged from 6 to 56 weeks of age produced similar findings.[54] Hobbs quotes Feldman as saying that the low proportion of couples experiencing crisis at this early period may be due to a "baby honeymoon." Feldman believes that couples experience early elation over parenthood but that after four to six weeks crisis begins to set in.[55] All investigators agree that whatever trauma is involved in early parenthood is successfully resolved by most couples within a few years.

50. Ersel E. Le Masters, "Parenthood as Crisis," *Marriage and Family Living* 19 (Nov. 1957), pp. 352–55.
51. Everett D. Dyer, "Parenthood as Crisis: A Re-Study," *Marriage and Family Living* 25 (May 1963), pp. 196–201.
52. Daniel F. Hobbs, Jr., "Parenthood as Crisis: A Third Study," *Journal of Marriage and the Family* 27 (Aug. 1965), pp. 367–72. See also Arthur P. Jacoby, "Transition to Parenthood: A Reassessment," *Journal of Marriage and the Family* 31 (Nov. 1969), pp. 720–27.
53. Daniel F. Hobbs, Jr. and Sue Peck Cole, "Transition to Parenthood: A Decade Replication," *Journal of Marriage and the Family* 38 (Nov. 1976), pp. 723–31; and Daniel F. Hobbs, Jr. and Jane Maynard Wimbish, "Transition to Parenthood by Black Couples," *Journal of Marriage and the Family* 39 (Nov. 1977), pp. 677–89.
54. Candyce Smith Russell, "Transition to Parenthood: Problems and Gratifications," *Journal of Marriage and the Family* 36 (May 1974), pp. 294–302.
55. Feldman also found that the advent of the first child begins a critical period in the marital relationship. See Harold Feldman, *Development of the Husband-Wife Relationship: A Research Report*, Cornell University, mimeo., n.d.

PATTERNS OF CHILD-REARING

The sociological study of child-rearing covers too vast an area for full treatment here.[56] We shall summarize research from just one of the many areas of sociological interest—that having to do with the values that middle-class parents instill in their children, with a brief look at differences between middle-class and lower-class patterns.

One of the first studies, after World War II, was done in Chicago of the child-rearing practices of 48 middle-class and 52 lower-class mothers. This study found that middle-class parents were more rigid in infant-care practices than were lower-class parents; they were more likely to schedule feed, to wean early, and to toilet-train early. Differences were more pronounced by social class than by race, with middle-class white and black practices being more similar than were the practices of either middle-class group to either lower-class group. The researchers concluded that middle-class parents were generally stricter than lower-class parents, and that ". . . middle-class children are subjected earlier and more consistently to the influences which make a child an orderly, conscientious, responsible and tame person." Middle-class children were seen as suffering more frustration of their impulses than were lower-class children.[57]

At about the same time, Duvall studied 433 Chicago members of mothers' groups, finding that middle-class mothers defined a "good" child as one who is happy and contented, loves and confides in its parents, shares and cooperates with others, and is eager to learn. Working-class mothers placed less emphasis upon these traits and emphasized, instead, that the child should be neat and clean, that it should respect and obey adults, and that it be honest, polite, and fair.[58]

Over the next decade or so, a whole series of studies were done, some of which yielded findings consistent with those of the two earlier studies

56. For an excellent summary and synthesis of much of this literature, see Edward Z. Dager, "Socialization and Personality Development in the Child," in Harold T. Christensen, *ed.*, *Handbook of Marriage and the Family*, Chicago: Rand McNally, 1964, pp. 740–81; and Ersel E. Le Masters, *Parents in Modern America*, Homewood, Illinois: The Dorsey Press, 1977.

57. Allison Davis and Robert J. Havighurst, "Social Class and Color Differences in Child-rearing," *American Sociological Review* 11 (Dec. 1946), pp. 698–710.

58. Evelyn M. Duvall, "Conceptions of Parenthood," *American Journal of Sociology* 52 (Nov. 1946), pp. 190–92. See also Rachel A. Elder, "Traditional and Developmental Conceptions of Fatherhood," *Marriage and Family Living* 11 (Summer 1949), pp. 98–100, 106; and Ruth Connor, Helen F. Greene, and James Walters, "Agreement of Family Member Conceptions of 'Good' Parent and Child Roles," *Social Forces* 36 (May 1958), pp. 353–58.

and some of which showed flatly contradictory findings.[59] One study of 375 Boston-area mothers found middle-class mothers were not more rigid, but were more lenient than lower-class mothers. The middle-class mothers were more permissive in toilet training, dependency, sex training, and the expression of aggression. Middle-class mothers also were less punitive, less restrictive in activity permitted in the home, and more permissive of free-ranging activity outside the home.[60]

The conflict over whether middle-class parents are more permissive or more strict than lower-class parents was resolved by Bronfenbrenner, who reanalyzed data from earlier studies. He made the social class groupings more consistent from study to study and estimated the approximate dates at which the findings had been secured. In so doing, he found that there had been a gradual shift in child-care practices. Before World War II, it did appear that middle-class mothers were more rigid. By the end of World War II, however, the situation had reversed, and middle-class mothers were more permissive.[61]

The shift in middle-class and lower-class child-rearing practices occurred within the context of a general shift toward permissiveness at all social levels. It will be recalled that Western society has a long history of children being under the domination of their parents, particularly of their fathers. Even in the immediate premodern era, parents were supposed to be strict disciplinarians whose duty it was to break the will of the child, to make it submissive, and to train it in the denial of its innate evil impulses. Early in the present century, there began to appear a massive child-guidance literature which, by the 1930s, was advocating more permissive child-rearing. Parents were urged to assume friendly, loving

59. Ethelyn H. Klatskin, "Shifts in Child Care Practices in Three Social Classes Under an Infant Care Program of Flexible Methodology," *American Journal of Orthopsychiatry* 22 (Jan. 1952), pp. 52–61; Martha S. White, "Social Class, Child-Rearing Practices, and Child Behavior," *American Sociological Review,* 22 (Dec. 1957), pp. 704–12; Richard A. Littman, Robert A. Moore, and John Pierce-Jones, "Social Class Differences in Child-rearing: A Third Community for Comparison with Chicago and Newton," *American Sociological Review* 22 (Dec. 1957), pp. 694–704; and Walter E. Boek, Marvin B. Sussman, and Alfred Yankhauer, "Social Class and Child Care Practices," *Marriage and Family Living* 20 (Nov. 1958), pp. 326–33.

60. Robert R. Sears, Eleanor E. Maccoby, and Harry Levin, *Patterns of Child-Rearing,* Evanston, Illinois: Row, Peterson and Company, 1957.

61. Urie Bronfenbrenner, "Socialization and Social Class Through Time and Space," in Eleanor E. Maccoby, Theodore M. Newcomb, and Eugene L. Hartley, *eds., Readings in Social Psychology,* New York: Henry Holt, 1958, pp. 400–424. See also Donald G. McKinley, *Social Class and Family Life,* New York: The Free Press, 1964; and William H. Sewell, "Social Class and Childhood Personality," *Sociometry* 24 (Dec. 1961), pp. 340–46, 358–61.

roles and to allow their children to develop "naturally" and at their own pace. Bronfenbrenner's analysis showed a close correspondence between the trend toward permissiveness and child-rearing and the practices recommended in the child-care literature.[62]

Differences between the middle and lower classes in the characteristics believed desirable in children have persisted throughout the general trend toward permissiveness. In recent studies, Kohn found that middle-class mothers valued happiness, considerateness, and self-control in their children, while lower-class mothers were more likely to value neatness, cleanliness, and obedience.[63]

The most provocative thesis yet developed to explain recent changes in child-rearing patterns assumes an increasingly dominant middle-class way of life and that the way in which the family is integrated into the economic structure is a major influence on the family's child-rearing philosophy.[64] Particularly, the values and way of life of the parents are molded by their experiences in that part of the economic structure within which the father works. The characteristics or traits that are rewarded in this setting are emphasized in child-rearing. The parents treat their children the same way they treat themselves and others, in line with their values and expectations.

Miller and Swanson defined two types of middle-class "integrational settings": an *individuated-entrepreneurial*, and a *welfare-bureaucratic* setting. The concept of the individuated entrepreneur is based on a rural-urban dichotomy in which it is proposed that urbanites meet one another in segmented roles, relate to one another in a superficial competitive way, lack close and continuing contacts, and become isolated and lonely. When these experiences are linked with an occupation that involves risk-taking, is subject to the fluctuations of the market place, and is dependent upon personal judgment and manipulative skill to stay

62. *Ibid.* See also Gerald R. Leslie and Kathryn P. Johnsen, "Changed Perceptions of the Maternal Role," *American Sociological Review* 28 (Dec. 1963), pp. 919–28; and Martha Wolfenstein, "The Emergence of Fun Morality," *Journal of Social Issues* 7 (1951), pp. 15–25.

63. Melvin L. Kohn, "Social Class and Parental Values," *American Journal of Sociology* 64 (Jan. 1959), pp. 337–52; Melvin L. Kohn, "Social Class and Parent-Child Relationships: An Interpretation," *American Journal of Sociology* 68 (Jan. 1963), pp. 471–80; and Viktor Gecas and F. Ivan Nye, "Sex and Class Differences in Parent-Child Interaction: A Test of Kohn's Hypothesis," *Journal of Marriage and the Family* 36 (Nov. 1974), pp. 742–49. For needed cautions in the conduct of research in this area, see Kathryn P. Johnsen and Gerald R. Leslie, "Methodological Notes on Research in Child-rearing and Social Class," *Merrill-Palmer Quarterly* 11 (Oct. 1965), pp. 345–58.

64. Daniel R. Miller and Guy E. Swanson, *The Changing American Parent*, New York: John Wiley and Sons, 1958.

in business, the concept of the individuated entrepreneur emerges. This orientation the authors attribute to the older middle classes who put a premium on self-control, rational behavior, denial of present gratifications for future gains, and an active manipulative approach to the environment.[65]

For research purposes, families were classified as entrepreneurial if they met any of the following five criteria: (1) if the husband was self-employed; (2) if he received at least half of his income from profits, fees, or commissions; (3) if he worked in an organization having only two levels of supervision; (4) if either the husband or wife was born on a farm; or (5) if either was born outside the United States.

The concept of welfare bureaucracy was based on an emerging pattern in large-scale organizations which the authors believe is modifying the older individually oriented society. Bureaucracy implies specialization and supervision governed by a set of rules, and "welfare" implies that the organization offers security to its members. The authors see the values of persons, so integrated, as stemming from the demands made upon the personnel of such organizations. These include the steady, faithful performance of duty, without rewards for imagination or initiative, these traits being desirable only if they are under the control of the organization. Excessive drive and competition are discouraged. Employees must not be too aggressive or ambitious. In the organization, people are supposed to find each other's presence so mutually rewarding and so lacking in threat that they feel comfortable and seek to preserve their happy, productive state. To fit into this secure world, children should be warm, friendly, and supportive. As adults they will have less need for strict consciences or internal controls, since as members of large organizations they will be supervised and guided carefully.

Miller and Swanson see American society moving gradually toward the bureaucratic integrational setting, in which a more relaxed approach to parenthood is spreading; where methods of discipline are physical or external because internal controls are neither necessary nor wanted in the bureaucratic system. Thus the family becomes the means of supplying the economic system with the kind of personalities it needs.

To test this thesis, the authors classified as bureaucratic those families where (1) both husband and wife were urban-born; (2) the husband worked for an organization with three or more supervisory levels; and

65. For this summary and critique of *The Changing American Parent* the author is indebted to Kathryn P. Johnsen, "Trends in Child-Rearing Advice Compared with Actual Parental Practices," paper prepared for research seminar on the family.

(3) their income was primarily wages or salary. Four hundred seventy-nine white, middle-class Detroit mothers constituted the sample, with comparisons between the two middle-class groups being based upon 99 mothers in the entrepreneurial category and 86 in the bureaucratic category.

Several predictions were made. First it was predicted that entrepreneurial mothers would emphasize development of internal controls in their children through earlier bowel training, scheduled feeding, not immediately tending to a crying baby, and the use of symbolic rather than physical punishment. It was also predicted that bureaucratic mothers would permit more thumb-sucking and sexual exploration, would place less emphasis on the achievement of independence, and would not emphasize differences between male and female occupations.

The findings generally bore out the predictions and the over-all thesis. The entrepreneurial mothers were more likely to begin bowel training by the time the baby was ten months old, were more likely to feed the baby on schedule, were more likely to delay giving attention to a crying baby, and were more likely to use symbolic punishment. The entrepreneurial mothers also were more likely to use harsh means to stop thumb-sucking, to feel it necessary to do something when the child touched its sex organs, to believe it good to leave the child with a competent person because the mother benefits, to agree that the child should be on its own as soon as possible, and to feel that only boys should perform activities traditionally associated with their sex among adolescents. The authors stated, ". . . We consider it correct and conservative to conclude that our prediction is upheld. Entrepreneurial middle-class mothers are more likely than those in a bureaucratic integration to use practices which emphasize self-control in training children."[66]

The Miller and Swanson research is open to a number of criticisms. The classification of families as entrepreneurial was based too heavily upon rural or foreign birth, with the result that a portion of the results may be due to rural-born differences.[67] The assumption that competition and ambition are no longer values as such is unproven. The com-

66. *Op. cit.*, p. 98. A recent study challenges this conclusion. See Jack L. Franklin and Joseph E. Scott, "Parental Values: An Inquiry Into Occupational Setting," *Journal of Marriage and the Family* 32 (Aug. 1970), pp. 406–9.

67. Urie Bronfenbrenner, *op. cit.* For recent findings on the development of internal-external controls, see Dennis C. Scheck, Robert Emerick, and Mohamed M. El-Assal, "Adolescents' Perceptions of Parent-Child Relations and the Development of Internal-External Control Orientation," *Journal of Marriage and the Family* 35 (Nov. 1973), pp. 643–54.

parisons often were based upon small numbers, the mothers had children of different ages, the integration setting used was the current one rather than the one applying when the child was an infant, the items used to test the thesis may not have been the best ones, and so on.

At this stage, the Miller and Swanson thesis has not been adequately tested. Neither, of course, has it been disproved. It has been shown that there has been a pervasive trend toward more permissive child-rearing at both middle-class and lower-class levels.

SUMMARY

At marriage, husbands typically desire sexual intercourse more frequently than their wives do and the adjustment reached generally represents a compromise. Husbands often evaluate their marriages in terms of the sex adjustment, while wives are more likely to evaluate sex adjustment in terms of other areas of marital interaction.

One problem is illustrated by some orgasm incapacity in a substantial proportion of women. The proportion of women regularly experiencing orgasm increases with age, even though the frequency of intercourse is declining. Orgasm performance also is related to decade of birth and to economic and educational level. The relative lack of sexual responsiveness in wives may be due to a variety of factors and tends both to cause and to accompany breakdown in marital communication.

Both men and women find substitute outlets for marital intercourse. Among men, masturbation and extramarital intercourse are common. At lower educational levels, extramarital intercourse is most common during the early years of marriage, while at higher educational levels the proportion involved increases up to age 50. The involvement of women in masturbation and extramarital coitus follows the development of sexual responsiveness. Particularly at higher educational levels, the peak participation comes during the thirties and forties.

Swinging appeared in the early 1960s, with unknown numbers of couples participating. Participants appear to be predominantly middle class and otherwise conventional. Most swingers believe that swinging improves their marriages, but no longitudinal studies have been done yet. Some evidence indicates that swinging produces its own problems and that it is not the non-sexist phenomenon it is reputed to be.

Most couples move quickly into child-bearing. After an upsurge in desired family size from 1940 to 1960, the long-term downward trend in birth rates resumed. Studies of the relationship between number of children and marital success have shown an inverse relationship. In part, this apparent relationship is due to the deleterious effect of excess child-bearing. Children, up to the preferred number, may contribute to marital happiness, while children beyond the preferred number cause strife and problems.

Virtually all couples try family planning. The pill is the most popular contraceptive, followed by surgical sterilization after the couple have had the children they want. Use of the IUD has increased significantly in recent years. Differences between Catholics and non-Catholics in contraception are declining and appear destined to disappear. Contraceptive failure rates are diminishing but are still a problem.

A study of middle- and lower-class couples throws light on the relationships between marital roles, sex adjustment, and family planning. Joint marital roles involving adequate communication between husband and wife are associated with good sex adjustment and with effective family planning. Segregated marital roles are associated with lack of sexual responsiveness in the wife, depreciation of the husband, and ineffective family planning.

The impact of pregnancy and child-bearing upon the marital relationship also has been studied. Most first pregnancies either are desired, or quickly accepted. Few differences exist in the adjustment to pregnancy between couples who had planned the pregnancy and those who had not. Variable effects of pregnancy upon sex adjustment are reported; slightly over half of all couples report no effect, while some report improvement and some report deterioration. There is a tendency for the frequency of sexual intercourse to decrease during the latter part of pregnancy and to remain lower after the birth of the child.

Subsequent pregnancies are less often welcomed, and the proportion of couples resorting to abortion increases with succeeding pregnancies. Abortion laws began to liberalize in the late 1960s, and, in 1973, the Supreme Court barred virtually any interference with it during the first trimester of pregnancy. The number of legal abortions has increased spectacularly, with depressed birth rates, falling mortality and morbidity rates, and diminished emotional consequences for women being results.

Studies show that the birth of the first child often produces a crisis in the home. The new arrival forces the restructuring of marital roles and some time often is required to do this. Most couples do achieve such readjustment with time.

Research on child-rearing indicates a trend toward permissiveness over the last 30 to 40 years. During that period, the relative positions of the middle and lower classes have reversed; whereas, formerly, middle-class parents were stricter parents, the reverse has been true since World War II. One recent study postulated a shift in middle-class conditions of life that encourages permissive child-rearing. It is argued that the old middle-class emphasized ambition, competitiveness, risk-taking, and the development of internal controls in the individual. By contrast, the new middle class is oriented toward participation in large-scale organizations and emphasizes getting along with other people. Child-rearing patterns, it is argued, are changing accordingly.

SUGGESTED READINGS

Benson, Leonard, *Fatherhood: A Sociological Perspective,* New York: Random House, 1968. A well-documented analysis of parental interaction with one another and with their children. Unique analysis of the father's role in the family.

Dager, Edward Z., "Socialization and Personality Development in the Child," in Harold T. Christensen, *ed., Handbook of Marriage and the Family*, Chicago: Rand McNally and Co., 1964, pp. 740–81. One of the best summaries and interpretations of the available data on child-rearing.

Edwards, John N., *ed., Sex and Society*, Chicago: Markham Publishing Company, 1972. A comprehensive set of essays covering marital sex, extramarital sex, and sex among widows and divorcees.

Le Masters, Ersel E., *Parents in Modern America*, Homewood, Illinois: The Dorsey Press, 1977. The first systematic, comprehensive sociological analysis of parenthood in the United States. Contains chapters on minority group parents and parents without partners.

Neubeck, Gerhard, *ed., Extramarital Relations*, Englewood Cliffs, New Jersey: Prentice-Hall, 1969. A varied collection of essays on a formerly taboo topic. Contains a section on causes and effects of extramarital relations.

FILMS

Adapting to Parenthood (Polymorph Films, 331 Newbury Street, Boston, Mass. 02115), 20 minutes, color. The stress that results from the birth of a first baby, and the effect upon a marriage.

Birth (Filmaker's Library, 290 West End Avenue, New York, N.Y. 10023),

40 minutes, black and white. A *cinéma vérité* study of a young expectant couple, their hopes and expectations, and the actual birth of the baby in which the husband takes an active role.

Each Child Loved (Planned Parenthood-World Population, 267 West 25th Street, New York, N.Y. 10011), 37 minutes, color. Scenes in a licensed clinic give viewers a view emphasizing the safety and simplicity of abortion when an unwanted pregnancy is terminated early. Shows the vacuum aspiration method.

It Happens to Us (New Day Films, 267 West 25th Street, New York, N.Y. 10011), 30 minutes, color. Women of different ages, marital statuses, and races speak candidly of their abortion experiences. Explores the problem of illegal versus legal, medically safe abortions.

QUESTIONS AND PROJECTS

1. What is the relationship between age and marital intercourse? What interpretation would you place upon the discrepancies between husbands and wives in reported frequencies of intercourse?
2. How widespread is lack of sexual responsiveness among women? What are some of the origins of this lack of responsiveness?
3. What is the commonest sex-adjustment problem confronted by young married couples? Does this problem change with time? If so, how?
4. What associations are there between sexual frustration in marriage and extramarital intercourse? Are these purely biological frustrations? Use data by social class to show that they are not.
5. Describe the normative structure that regulates swinging. Evaluate the available evidence on the effects of swinging upon marriage.
6. What does research show about the relationship between number of children and marital adjustment? What factor, other than simply the number of children, needs to be taken into account?
7. Describe racial, religious, and age differences in the use of contraception. What has happened to rates of contraceptive failure in recent years? Describe the problem that remains.
8. How is success in family planning related to communication between husband and wife? How does sex adjustment fit into the picture?
9. What does research show about the adjustment of couples to the first pregnancy? How do statistics on abortion indicate a different pattern of reaction to subsequent pregnancies?
10. What evidence is there for assuming that the birth of the first child is likely to produce a crisis in the marital relationship? What time sequence appears to be involved? Are most such crises successfully resolved?
11. What trends have been occurring in American child-rearing patterns

over the past three or four decades? What social-class differences existed in the past? At present?

12. Describe the thesis developed by Miller and Swanson to explain recent changes in child-rearing patterns. Has it been adequately proven?

16
Marriage in the Middle Years

> A growing number of American families are getting accustomed to living on two paychecks instead of one. Within a few years, in fact, the family with two income earners will be the rule, not the exception. Since 1960, the number of two-breadwinner families . . . has zoomed from 29 percent of all husband-wife households to 42 percent.
>
> Behind this phenomenon are several factors. Sheer necessity—to help pay rent, buy food and clothing—has always kept many wives on the job. In other instances, rising expectations of American families have collided with living costs which have gone up even faster. . . .
>
> In other cases, women are entering the work force when their children grow up. Many wives and mothers in all age brackets are working today because they seek an active life in a society that they feel measures people by what they do or how much they earn. . . .
>
> Many women, of course, have chosen not to enter or re-enter the work force. Many working women would rather be housewives. Some seek to blend the two life styles. . . .[1]

Couples average only two years together before their first child is born, a half-dozen years in child-bearing, about 20 years in child-rearing, and almost 20 years more before retirement. The middle years of marriage, as we use the phrase here, refers not so much to one specific part of that time period as to the whole series of changes that occur over the middle part of the family life cycle. These include changes in marital adjustment, in the distribution of power between husband and wife, and in

1. *U.S. News and World Report,* Feb. 7, 1977, p. 54.

roles. We will pay special attention to the changing roles of women and the rising popularity of dual-career families.

MARRIAGE AS A DEVELOPMENTAL PROCESS

One analyst conceives of mate selection in terms of matching husband and wife in phases of development, rather than in terms of particular traits brought by the partners to the marriage.[2] He assumes that the matching of personalities is a continual process, and that personalities change throughout adult life. He questions whether it is possible to determine, at marriage, whether a given match will prove to be a good or bad one. Changes that occur in the partners during the marriage itself may be just as important.

Foote cites several kinds of evidence to support this view. Studies of the stresses faced by couples undergoing enforced separation are a case in point. The separation of couples by military service strains their relationship and requires complex readjustments upon reunion.[3] Other kinds of separation, such as those required by migration, employment, and confinement in institutions, have similar effects. In less drastic circumstances, the involvement of husband and wife in different groups in the community may provide them with experiences that they cannot satisfactorily share with one another in the few evening hours they have together.

The implication that there are forces encouraging couples to grow apart finds support in popular interpretations of causes for divorce. One frequently hears it said that one of the spouses outgrew the other. Their occupations frequently force them into new experiences and into extensive contact with members of the opposite sex who, in time, may come to share more aspects of their daily lives than does the spouse. This is one of the major challenges facing people in contemporary marriages, and one of which they are becoming more aware.

Although we emphasize the fact that more separations occur during

2. Nelson N. Foote, "Matching of Husband and Wife in Phases of Development," *Transactions of the Third World Congress of Sociology, International Sociological Association* 4 (1956), pp. 24–34.

3. Reuben Hill, *et al., Families Under Stress: Adjustment to the Crisis of War Separation and Reunion,* New York: Harper and Brothers, 1949; and Hamilton I. McCubbin, Barbara D. Dahl, Gary R. Lester, Dorothy Benson, and Marilyn L. Robertson, "Coping Repertoires of Families Adapting to Prolonged War-Induced Separations," *Journal of Marriage and the Family* 38 (Aug. 1976), pp. 461–71.

the first year of marriage than any other, other averages suggest that marriages deteriorate over time.[4] The median length of marriages ending in divorce is about three years, while the mean length may be as long as ten years. Some divorces occur even after 20 or 30 years. Such figures indicate that simple mismatching does not account for all divorces. "A better hypothesis would be that those who were sufficiently matched to marry became sufficiently unmatched to unmarry."[5]

An analogy may also be made between marriage and friendship. Friendship is one component in marriage and marriage may improve or worsen as friendship between the partners prospers or withers. Significantly, there are, for most people, few lifelong friendships outside of marriage. Instead, friendships develop, change, and decline. Little is known about the development and decline of friendships, and no more is known about friendship in marriage. It is plausible that friendship, both in and out of marriage, depends upon shared interests; and since interests change, the continuance of friendships rests in part upon the development of new common interests. The more marriage comes to center on companionship and friendship, the more crucial it becomes that spouses share new common interests. This probably is little related to conventional social homogamy, but may be related instead to some sequence of developmental stages in the individual.

The notion of developmental stages in marriage has been conceptualized by Farber, who describes the family as a set of mutually contingent careers. That people pass through a progression of statuses in their occupations is well recognized. It is also recognized that changes in occupational careers impinge directly upon people's relationships with the family. Farber extends the notion of career to all members of the family and he sees careers as being not only occupational but also familial, recreational, and so on. Significant changes, then, in any aspect of any career of any family member impinge upon the careers of other family members. In this sense, the family is not only a set of careers but a set of intercontingent careers.[6]

Marriage as mutually contingent careers does not require that husband and wife both pursue careers outside the home, nor does it assume any other kind of invariant relationship between them. It regards personal happiness as an unsatisfactory criterion of marital success both because

4. Thomas P. Monahan, "Is Childlessness Related to Family Stability?" *American Sociological Review* 20 (Aug. 1955), pp. 446–56.
5. Nelson N. Foote, *op. cit.*, p. 17.
6. Bernard Farber, *Family: Organization and Interaction*, San Francisco: Chandler Publishing Company, 1964, pp. 334–35.

it is unstable and because happiness is affected by too many variables apart from the marital relationship. It hypothesizes that the spouses' judgments of their marriages may depend as much upon prospects for the future as upon the present relationship. If there is a single variable that predicts the future of a marriage, Foote believes that it is communication—the degree to which husband and wife are truly able to communicate when they are together.

Foote acknowledges that his conception of modern marriage is a demanding one. It is not necessarily discouraging, however. He points out that the segment of the population which makes the most stable marriages—the professional class—is also the one in which the concept of marriage as a set of mutually contingent careers emerges most clearly. He implies that the number and proportion of stable, rewarding marriages may increase as the professionalization of the society continues.

THE TREND OF MARITAL ADJUSTMENT

Research has begun to assess the changes in marital adjustment that occur after the early years of marriage. Studies have appeared, based upon a variety of populations, that trace the trend in adjustment over 5, 10, and 20 or more years of marriage. Without exception, they show that the high levels of commitment characteristic of early marriage are not commonly maintained. The data indicate that marriage as a set of mutually contingent careers may be more of an ideal than an accomplished fact. However marital adjustment is conceived, the long-term trend is apparently downward.

Longitudinal Studies of Marital Adjustment

The first longitudinal study of marital adjustment was Burgess and Wallin's study of 1000 engaged couples whom they attempted to follow through early marital adjustment and into middle life. As reported earlier, only 666 of the couples married and were available after 4 to 6 years of marriage. Further losses occurred up to the point when 400 couples were restudied after they had been married up to 20 years.[7]

The results of the comparison of 400 couples after about 5 years of marriage and again after nearly 20 years of marriage showed a large and pervasive drop in marital adjustment.

7. Ernest W. Burgess and Paul Wallin, *Engagement and Marriage*, Philadelphia: J. B. Lippincott Co., 1953.

The greatest losses are in the category labeled marital satisfaction. Pineo, who did the analysis, believes that this is a phenomenon of such magnitude that the phrase "loss of satisfaction" "is insufficient to express the fact that this . . . appears to be generally an inescapable consequence of the passage of time in a marriage."[8] He conceptualizes decreasing marital satisfaction as being "disenchantment." This disenchantment appears inevitable and need not have its roots in idealization of the partner prior to marriage. That it is a general process rather than a series of independent changes is indicated by two things. First, there is an association between the losses experienced by husbands and those experienced by wives. Second, changes on one score are associated with changes on other scores.

Pineo theorizes that disenchantment sets in after the early years of marriage, stating explicitly that personality changes in the partner and changes in the context in which marriage will operate cannot be determined before the wedding. What happens is that people marry on the basis of a "good fit" between them at the time. When they are already well matched, the changes that inevitably occur after marriage are more likely to worsen that fit than to improve it. As Pineo puts it, "The deviant characteristics which provided the grounds upon which the marriage was contracted begin to be lost, as later changes tend toward the population mean and the couples become more and more like ones who married at random rather than by choice."[9]

One possibility, of course, is that the drop in marital adjustment might be a function of a drop in personal adjustment over the same period—a function of aging. The data, however, contradict this hypothesis. Some changes in personal adjustment were detected, but personal adjustment was as likely to improve as to worsen and there was no association between a drop in personal adjustment and a drop in marital adjustment.[10]

It should be pointed out that the drop in general marital adjustment does not mean that *all* couples suffered a drop in adjustment. Some couples actually improved their adjustment, many appeared not to have changed significantly, and some, of course, declined. Unfortunately,

8. Peter C. Pineo, "Disenchantment in the Later Years of Marriage," *Marriage and Family Living* 23 (Feb. 1961), p. 6. For a comprehensive final report on the results of the third wave of interviews, see Jan Dizard, *Social Change in the Family*, University of Chicago, Community and Family Study Center, 1968.

9. Pineo, "Disenchantment," *op. cit.*, p. 7.

10. *Ibid.*, p. 8; and Robert A. Dentler and Peter Pineo, "Sexual Adjustment, Marital Adjustment and Personal Growth of Husbands: A Panel Analysis," *Marriage and Family Living* 22 (Feb. 1960), pp. 45–48.

the researchers do not give us detailed figures on this point. They do indicate that 75 percent of the husbands maintained their early levels of adjustment, with only 25 percent changing significantly. Among those who changed, two-thirds changed from high to low adjustment.

In addition to the drop in marital satisfaction, some other conclusions may be drawn from the data. For one thing, the greatest drop outside that in general marital adjustment occurs in the sharing of interests and activities. Since these couples had already been married a few years at the time of measurement, this drop cannot be attributed to marriage alone. It seems to be associated with child-rearing and the many duties which child-rearing imposes upon parents.

A decrease occurs also in the frequency of sexual intercourse, with the results of this decrease being different for husbands than for wives. Among wives, the decrease may occur without an accompanying drop in general satisfaction. About a fourth of all husbands, however, experience a drop in sexual adjustment and in marital adjustment.

Two other items, on "traditionalism" and "dominance," indicate paradoxical shifts. There is a general decrease in the traditionalism of husbands and wives over time. Yet, husbands also tend to become more dominant and wives more submissive. Couples give lip service to the ideal of equalitarian relationships, but, as they grow older, relationships between them actually become more authoritarian. Both Pineo and Goode have analyzed this situation in terms of the power which accrues to middle-class husbands as a function of high incomes and occupational prestige.[11] Irony exists in the fact that lower-class couples who are more likely to endorse verbal norms of dominance and submission are actually more equalitarian because of the relatively greater economic power of the wife, while equalitarian-oriented middle-class couples actually have relationships based more on dominance and submission.

Finally, there were differences in several areas between couples who experienced a drop in marital adjustment and those who did not. Those who had dropped in adjustment were more likely to regret their marriages and to state they would not marry the same person again. They were also more likely to report decreases in kissing and confiding and to indicate less reciprocity in settling disagreements. The couples who did not suffer disenchantment showed no drops in these areas. Ninety-nine percent would marry the same person again and also reported no

11. Peter C. Pineo, *op. cit.*, p. 8; and William J. Goode, *World Revolution and Family Patterns*, New York: The Free Press, 1963, pp. 20–22.

decrease in kissing. Ninety-nine percent continued to confide in their spouses, and 96 percent settled disagreements by give and take.

The couples studied by Burgess and Wallin were married in the late 1930s and early 1940s, and it could be that the drop in adjustment was characteristic of that particular generation Changes in circumstances might not produce the same pattern in succeeding generations. To check that possibility, let us examine another study—done on a much smaller scale—that was completed in 1965.

Luckey studied two groups of 40 married couples each, who were classified as satisfactorily or unsatisfactorily married on the basis of marital-adjustment scale scores.[12] The couples had been married for a mean average of 7.7 years. Six years later, they were studied again. Responses were received from 36 wives in the Satisfied group, 34 wives in the Unsatisfied group, and 31 husbands from each of the two groups.[13] Changes in adjustment between the seventh and thirteenth years of marriage were measured by changes in adjustment scale scores. When the two groups were analyzed together, both husbands and wives made lower scores in 1963 than they did in 1957. Thus the results are consistent with those of the earlier, larger study.

The findings are presented separately for the originally Satisfied and Unsatisfied groups. The scores of the Satisfied couples were more likely to decline over the six-year period, while for the originally Unsatisfied couples the reverse was true; the scores of poorly adjusted couples increased. There are at least two possible explanations. First, the Satisfied couples, by virtue of higher aspiration levels for their marriages, may be less likely to discover that their experience lives up to expectations. Second, the scores of the Satisfied group are so high in the first place that they have only one direction to go. By the same token, the low scores of the Unsatisfied group may have to increase if divorce is to be avoided. This interpretation is strengthened by the fact that three of the original Unsatisfied couples had divorced during the six-year period.

Other Comparative Studies of Marital Adjustment

Other studies that involved studying couples married different lengths of time—rather than following the same couples through time—have

12. Eleanore B. Luckey, "Perceptional Congruence of Self and Family Concepts as Related to Marital Interaction," *Sociometry* 24 (Sept. 1961), pp. 234–50.

13. Bethel L. Paris and Eleanore B. Luckey, "A Longitudinal Study in Marital Satisfaction," *Sociology and Social Research* 50 (Jan. 1966), pp. 212–23.

yielded data that inferentially support the longitudinal studies. These studies include data from lower socio-economic groups and middle-class couples.

A study of 731 city families and 178 farm families in the Detroit area provides a variety of relevant data. These data were derived from interviewing wives who ranged from 21 to more than 60 years of age and who had been married from less than 1 to more than 40 years. The samples were representative of the Detroit area and covered virtually the whole range of socio-economic and occupational statuses.[14]

The authors describe time as a corrosive influence, wearing away the strength of marriages. Of women married for two years or less, 52 percent described themselves as being very satisfied with their marriages and none said that they were notably dissatisfied. Among those married 20 years or longer, however, only 6 percent remained fully satisfied and 21 percent were conspicuously dissatisfied. Much dissatisfaction, according to the authors, reflects decreases in the things that spouses do for and with each other. Many husbands and wives permit their marriages to go to seed. Middle-aged people find satisfaction in children, in jobs, in friends, and elsewhere, but they seldom find as much satisfaction in one another.

More wives chose doing things with their husbands as the most valuable aspect of marriage than chose love, understanding, standard of living, or the opportunity to have children. For women, companionship apparently is the most important thing in marriage. Companionship too, however, tends to decline at least through the middle years of marriage. The mean satisfaction scores of wives with companionship with their husbands declined steadily during the honeymoon, the preschool stage, the pre-adolescent stage, the period when they had adolescent children, and the period when there were adult, but still unmarried children in the home.

That wives tend, with time, to turn away from their husbands is illustrated by their responses to questions concerning how they handle small emotional crises. Blood and Wolfe asked, "After you've had a bad day, what do you do to get it out of your system?" Most often the wives coped with their problems by sitting down and relaxing, going to bed early, reading, watching television, or going for a walk. Only 8 percent of the city wives and 3 percent of the farm wives mentioned their husbands in their response to this question. And of the 8 percent of city

14. Robert O. Blood, Jr. and Donald M. Wolfe, *Husbands and Wives: The Dynamics of Married Living,* Glencoe, Illinois: The Free Press, 1960, pp. 5–7, 263–73.

wives, almost half attacked their husbands rather than turned to them for comfort. Some consolation may be gained from the fact that the wives who took out their frustrations on someone were also more likely to choose persons other than the husband for that purpose. The picture is softened, too, by the fact that one-fifth of the wives reported that they almost always tell their husbands of their problems and an additional one-fourth or more usually do so.

A study of 58 marriages in which the husbands followed blue-collar occupations, had gone only through high school, and were under 40 years of age bears out some of Blood and Wolfe's findings. Komarovsky found that about one-third of the husbands and wives could hardly be called friends since they did not share hurts, worries, and dreams with one another. When the wives were asked, "What helps you when you feel bad, unhappy or worried about something, or generally low?" they mentioned a total of 278 different aids but mentioned the husband only 22 percent of the time. Forty-four percent did not mention their mates at all. High-school graduates were more likely to share feelings with their spouses than were those with less formal education, and communication between mates declined with number of years married.[15] Komarovsky also found that two-thirds of the wives had at least one person other than the husband in whom they confided. In 35 percent of the cases these other confidants, most often kinswomen, shared some aspect of the wives' lives more fully than did the husbands.

Another study secured questionnaires from two samples of 120 couples each. These couples were well educated and middle or upper class. Most were in their first marriages, and most of the wives were not working outside the home. The findings on the trend of marital adjustment were as follows. Marital discussions are most frequent early in marriage, and decline with time. Couples, as they move into the middle years, may not need to communicate verbally because they understand one another without the necessity for talk, or they may find each other less interesting, or they may simply have less to talk about.[16]

15. Mirra Komarovsky, *Blue-Collar Marriage,* New York: Random House, 1964, pp. 140–86.

16. Harold Feldman, *Development of the Husband-Wife Relationship: A Research Report,* Cornell University, n.d., p. 119. See also Wesley R. Burr, "Satisfaction with Various Aspects of Marriage Over the Life Cycle: A Random Middle Class Sample," *Journal of Marriage and the Family* 32 (Feb. 1970), pp. 29–37. For somewhat contrary views, see Boyd C. Rollins and Kenneth L. Cannon, "Marital Satisfaction Over the Family Life Cycle: A Re-evaluation," *Journal of Marriage and the Family* 36 (May 1974), pp. 271–82; and Boyd C. Rollins and Harold Feldman, "Marital Satisfaction Over the Family Life Cycle," *Journal of Marriage and the Family* 32 (Feb. 1970), pp. 20–28.

A final report of the trend of marital adjustment comes from a study of 80 couples who had been married from 2 to 21 years. It found that marital adjustment scores were negatively correlated with the number of years married and that the longer couples were married the less favorable personality qualities each partner saw in his or her mate. As Luckey phrased it, "subjects in happy marriages tended to see their spouses less admirably, while those in unhappy marriages tended to see their spouses as being more undesirable," with the passage of time.[17]

All of this evidence is impressive. Studies have yielded a remarkably consistent pattern, showing a tendency for marital adjustment to decline steadily from almost the beginning of marriage at least to the point where children are grown and leave home. The conclusion seems inescapable that romance is closely linked to novelty in most relationships. On the other hand, it should not be overlooked that, in almost all of the studies, a sizable proportion of marriages continued to be characterized by closeness, affection, and effective communication. Some marriages even improve in communication and empathy as the years go by. A major task for future research is to determine what factors account for some marriages' being able to withstand the corrosive effects of time.

Marriage, of course, does not typically end with the middle years, and there are data available on the trend of adjustment during the postparental years. These data on the latter stages of the family life cycle will be presented in a later chapter.

MARITAL POWER

For approximately two decades, researchers have sought to relate marital adjustment to the distribution of power between husband and wife, and to trace changes in marital power over the family life cycle. The Blood and Wolfe study of Detroit-area families provided some of the earliest data. They reported that the power of the husband over the wife is greater among white-collar families than among blue-collar families, and that the husband's power increases directly with his income.[18] They also found that the husband's power varies by stage of the family life cycle and by whether the couple has children.

17. Eleanore B. Luckey, "Number of Years Married as Related to Personality Perception and Marital Satisfaction," *Journal of Marriage and the Family* 28 (Feb. 1966), pp. 44–48.
18. *Op. cit.*, p. 31.

Interestingly, childless wives had more power, for at least the first 22 years of marriage, than did those with children. This was hypothesized to be linked to the fact that childless wives are more likely to continue working and to have more economic resources than do women with children. Among couples with children, becoming a mother appeared to increase the wife's dependence upon her husband. As the children grew older, her dependence upon her husband lessened somewhat and the husband's power declined slightly. For reasons that are not wholly understood, the husband's power increased slightly again after the children were grown. Perhaps the prospect of the husband's demise before his wife led the wife to defer more to the husband. The husband's retirement and associated loss of income led to a decline in his power again in the final stage of life.

The Blood and Wolfe research led to the formulation of what has been called the "resource theory" of marital power. In brief, the theory holds that the more resources a spouse possesses, the greater his or her power over the other spouse. Since more husbands than wives work, and since the husbands usually have more income, they commonly dominate their wives to some degree.[19]

This resource theory of marital power has been challenged as being an oversimplification. Heer, for example, pointed out that, in addition to their usually having more resources, widespread social norms hold that husbands should have greater power than their wives.[20] The major challenge to the resource theory comes from the work of Rodman who compared the correlates of marital power in the United States, France, Greece, and Yugoslavia. In France and the U.S., the husband's power increased with higher occupational, educational, and income statuses; in Greece and Yugoslavia, however, men of higher occupation, income, and education exercised less power over their wives. Rodman concluded

19. Stephen J. Bahr, Charles E. Bowerman, and Viktor Gecas, "Adolescent Perceptions of Conjugal Power," *Social Forces* 52 (March 1974), pp. 356–67; Denise B. Kandel and Gerald S. Lesser, "Marital Decision-Making in American and Danish Urban Families: A Research Note," *Journal of Marriage and the Family* 34 (Feb. 1972), pp. 134–38; Sharon Price-Bonham, "A Comparison of Weighted and Unweighted Decision-Making Scores," *Journal of Marriage and the Family* 38 (Nov. 1976), pp. 629–40; and Darwin L. Thomas, David D. Franks, and James M. Calonico, "Role-Taking and Power in Social Psychology," *American Sociological Review* 33 (Oct. 1972), pp. 605–14.

20. David M. Heer, "Dominance and the Working Wife," in F. Ivan Nye and Lois W. Hoffman, *eds., The Employed Mother in America,* Chicago: Rand McNally, 1963, pp. 251–62. See also, Maximiliane E. Szinovacz, "Role Allocation, Family Structure and Female Employment," *Journal of Marriage and the Family* 39 (Nov. 1977), pp. 781–91.

that, in such developing countries, higher-status men are more likely to have been exposed to developing cultural norms favoring equality for women. They grant their wives more authority in spite of a traditional patriarchal culture.

This led Rodman to formulate a theory of "resources in cultural context" to explain marital power. He postulated that the balance of marital power is determined by the interaction of the comparative resources of the husband and wife, and by the cultural or subcultural expectations about the distribution of marital power.[21] Theorizing continues. The more the concept of marital power is analyzed and the more research is conducted upon it, the more complex the matter becomes. In addition to resources and cultural norms, the perceptions of husbands and wives and the nature of their attempts to control the relationship need to be taken into account.[22]

Several early studies asked whether husbands or wives exercise more power in family decision making, and generally showed the husbands to have more influence. Then, in 1971, a group of researchers studied a sample of 776 husbands and wives in California, classifying them into four types (see Table 16.1). The greatest number of marriages, accord-

21. Hyman Rodman, "Marital Power and the Theory of Resources in Cultural Context," *Journal of Comparative Family Studies* 3 (Spring 1972), pp. 50–69. See also Marilyn H. Buehler, Andrew J. Weigert, and Darwin L. Thomas, "Correlates of Conjugal Power: A Five Culture Analysis of Adolescent Perceptions," *Journal of Comparative Family Studies* 5 (Spring 1974), pp. 5–16; Wesley R. Burr, Louise Ahern, and Elmer W. Knowles, "An Empirical Test of Rodman's Theory of Resources in Cultural Context," *Journal of Marriage and the Family* 39 (Aug. 1977), pp. 505–14; Ronald E. Cromwell, Ramon Corrales, and Peter M. Torsiello, "Normative Patterns of Decision Making Power and Influence in Mexico and the United States: A Partial Test of Resource and Ideology Theory," *Journal of Comparative Family Studies* 4 (Autumn 1973), pp. 177–96; Ronald E. Cromwell and Stephen G. Wieting, "Multidimensionality of Conjugal Decision Making Indices: Comparative Analysis of Five Samples," *Journal of Comparative Family Studies* 6 (Autumn 1975), pp. 139–52; Greer Litton Fox, "Another Look at the Comparative Resources Model: Assessing the Balance of Power in Turkish Marriages," *Journal of Marriage and the Family* 35 (Nov. 1973), pp. 718–30; and Marie La Liberte Richmond, "Beyond Resource Theory: Another Look at Factors Enabling Women to Affect Family Interaction," *Journal of Marriage and the Family* 38 (May 1976), pp. 257–66.

22. See David H. Olson and Carolyn Rabunsky, "Validity of Four Measures of Family Power," *Journal of Marriage and the Family* 34 (May 1972), pp. 224–34; Boyd C. Rollins and Stephen J. Bahr, "A Theory of Power Relationships in Marriage," *Journal of Marriage and the Family* 38 (Nov. 1976), pp. 619–27; Constantina Safilios-Rotschild, "A Macro- and Micro-Examination of Family Power and Love: An Exchange Model," *Journal of Marriage and the Family* 38 (May 1976), pp. 355–62; and James L. Turk and Norman W. Bell, "Measuring Power in Families," *Journal of Marriage and the Family* 34 (May 1972), pp. 215–22.

Table 16.1. The distribution of power in 776 marriages, as reported by husbands and wives

Power type	*Husbands' reports*	*Wives' reports*
Autonomic	70%	67%
Syncratic	16%	20%
Husband-dominant	10%	9%
Wife-dominant	4%	4%
Totals	100%	100%

Source: Adapted from Richard Centers, Bertram H. Raven, and Aroldo Rodrigues, "Conjugal Power Structure: A Re-Examination," *American Sociological Review* 36 (April 1971), p. 271.

ing to both men and women are *autonomic* ones in which the husbands and wives have equal but independent decision-making power. The second most common type was the *syncratic* one in which decisions are made equally and jointly by the spouses. Approximately 10 percent of the marriages were reported to be husband dominant, and only 4 percent were said to be wife dominant.

The study also classified the four types of marriages according to the percentage of respondents reporting them to be "very satisfactory." Those data appear in Table 16.2. The autonomic type provided the highest percentage of very satisfactory marriages, followed rather closely by the husband-dominant type, and then by the syncratic type. The vast majority of all three of these types were described as very satisfactory.

Table 16.2. Percentages of marriages rated as very satisfactory, by conjugal power type

Conjugal power type	*Percent very satisfactory*
Autonomic	79
Husband-dominant	73
Syncratic	70
Wife-dominant	20

Source: Adapted from Richard Centers, Bertram H. Raven, and Aroldo Rodrigues, "Conjugal Power Structure: A Re-Examination," *American Sociological Review* 36 (April 1971), p. 274.

Of the 4 percent of the marriages that were classified as wife dominant, only one-fifth were rated as very satisfactory.[23]

THE ENACTMENT OF MARITAL ROLES

Just as marital adjustment does not end with the middle years, so marital roles do not begin in the middle years. The roots of marital adjustment and marital roles are formed in childhood, develop in early marriage, and change through the middle years right on into old age. There are at least two kinds of justification, however, for analyzing marital roles in connection with the middle years. First, the years of child-rearing and the postparental years so greatly outnumber those in all other stages of the life cycle. Second, people become acutely conscious of the roles they play during this period. Adolescents anticipate marital roles, and young marrieds play them, but middle-aged people wrestle with role problems in an especially self-conscious way.

Marital Role Expectations

Perhaps no other area of family relationships has been more widely researched in recent years than that of the marital role expectations of men and women. Attention has concentrated on the changing expectations of women.

Although women's expectations have changed markedly, marriage still plays a central role in the plans of the overwhelming majority. A study of 1063 freshmen women at the City University of New York, for example, reported that 76 percent had definite expectations for marriage, with only 2 percent wanting to be unmarried career women (see Table 16.1). The 19 percent who were classified as uncertain may contain a few more women who will reject marriage for occupational careers, but an estimate that at least 95 percent of the women desire marriage does not seem at all unreasonable.[24]

23. See also Stephen J. Bahr and Boyd C. Rollins, "Crisis and Conjugal Power," *Journal of Marriage and the Family* 33 (May 1971), pp. 360–67; Lois Pratt, "Conjugal Organization and Health," *Journal of Marriage and the Family* 34 (Feb. 1972), pp. 85–95; and Trudy M. Kolb and Murray A. Straus, "Marital Power and Marital Happiness in Relation to Problem-Solving Ability," *Journal of Marriage and the Family* 36 (Nov. 1974), pp. 756–66.

24. See also Marie S. Dunn, "Marriage Role Expectations of Adolescents," *Marriage and Family Living* 22 (May 1960), pp. 99–104; Charles W. Hobart, "Orientations to Marriage

Table 16.3. College freshmen women's desired roles fifteen years in the future (N = 1063)

Preferred role	*Percent*
Married career woman with children	48
Housewife with children	28
Uncertain	19
Unmarried career woman	2
Married career woman without children	2
Housewife without children	0
Total	99

Source: Gilda F. Epstein and Arline L. Bronzaft, "Female Freshmen View Their Roles as Women," *Journal of Marriage and the Family* 34 (Nov. 1972), p. 672.

Almost half of the women in Table 16.3 want occupational careers, along with marriage and children. Other studies have shown that young women whose mothers have worked outside the home and whose perceptions of themselves have been influenced by college professors and other professional people are more likely to expect to work outside the home themselves.[25]

Several studies have shown that women's role expectations have

Among Young Canadians," *Journal of Comparative Family Studies* 3 (Autumn 1972), pp. 171–93; Albin J. Moser, "Marriage Role Expectations of High School Students," *Marriage and Family Living* 23 (Feb. 1961), pp. 42–43; William G. Dyer and Dick Urban, "The Institutionalization of Equalitarian Family Norms," *Marriage and Family Living* 20 (Feb. 1958), pp. 53–58; Alver H. Jacobson, "Conflict of Attitudes Toward the Roles of the Husband and Wife in Marriage," *American Sociological Review* 17 (April 1952), pp. 146–50; Theodore Johannis, Jr., "Roles of Family Members," in Iowa State University Center for Agricultural and Economic Development, *Family Mobility in Our Dynamic Society*, Ames, Iowa: Iowa State University Press, 1965, pp. 69–79; William F. Kenkel and Dean K. Hoffman, "Real and Conceived Roles in Family Decision Making," *Marriage and Family Living* 18 (Nov. 1956), pp. 311–16; Debi D. Lovejoy, "College Student Conceptions of the Roles of the Husband and Wife in Family Decision Making," *Family Life Coordinator* 9 (Mar.-June 1961), pp. 43–46; and Genevieve M. Wise and Don C. Carter, "A Definition of the Role of Homemaker by Two Generations of Women," *Journal of Marriage and the Family* 27 (Nov. 1965), pp. 531–32.

25. Elizabeth M. Almquist and Shirley S. Angrist, "Career Salience and Atypicality of Occupational Choice Among College Women," *Journal of Marriage and the Family* 32 (May 1970), pp. 242–49; and Elizabeth M. Almquist and Shirley S. Angrist, "Role Model Influences on College Women's Career Aspirations," *Merrill-Palmer Quarterly* 17 (July 1971), pp. 263–79. See also Harold C. Meier, "Mother-Centeredness and College Youths' Attitudes Toward Social Equality for Women: Some Empirical Findings," *Journal of Marriage and the Family* 34 (Feb. 1972), pp. 115–21; and Charles W. Mueller and Blair G. Campbell, "Female Occupational Achievement and Marital Status: A Research Note," *Journal of Marriage and the Family* 39 (Aug. 1977), pp. 587–93.

changed substantially over the past decade and that there has been much less change in men's role expectations. A study at Rutgers University, for example, showed a marked shift toward feminist attitudes among women, but little change in the women's perception of men's attitudes.[26] A much larger study, employing data from five surveys, then reported substantial changes in women's sex-role attitudes between 1964 and 1974. This study also found that the changes had occurred equally among high-status and low-status women.[27]

A study of particular interest, of a random sample of junior and senior students at Florida State University, compared men's and women's attitudes directly, reporting that men gave more traditional responses to 25 items on a 32-item scale. Interestingly, both men and women approved a fairly sharp division of labor within the family with the woman continuing to have primary responsibility for the home and child care. Men were most supportive of change on "outside" issues such as equal jobs, equal pay, child care and the ERA. They were least supportive of changes that would place women in supervisory, decision-making, and leadership roles outside the family. The researchers conclude that, overall, their study shows that little sex-role change has occurred and that little is likely to occur in the near future.[28]

Differential change in the attitudes of men and women suggest the possibility of increasing role strains in marriage, with women demanding concessions that men are unwilling to concede. This is suggested directly in Table 16.4, which compares typologies of college women's and men's role types deriving from two separate studies. While the women's and men's types are not strictly comparable, they have been placed in the table roughly from most traditional to most modern. The noncareerist women were those who, throughout their college careers, remained

26. Ann P. Parelius, "Emerging Sex-Role Attitudes, Expectations, and Strains Among College Women," *Journal of Marriage and the Family* 37 (Feb. 1975), pp. 146–53.
27. Karen Oppenheim Mason, John L. Czajka, and Sara Arber, "Change in U.S. Women's Sex-Role Attitudes, 1964–1974," *American Sociological Review* 41 (Aug. 1976), pp. 573–96. See also Donna Brogan and Nancy G. Kutner, "Measuring Sex-Role Orientation: A Normative Approach," *Journal of Marriage and the Family* 38 (Feb. 1976), pp. 31–40; and Ruth C. Cronkite, "The Determinants of Spouses' Normative Preferences for Family Roles," *Journal of Marriage and the Family* 39 (Aug. 1977), pp. 575–85.
28. Marie Withers Osmond and Patricia Yancey Martin, "Sex and Sexism: A Comparison of Male and Female Sex-Role Attitudes," *Journal of Marriage and the Family* 37 (Nov. 1975), pp. 744–58. See also Brent S. Roper and Emily Labeff, "Sex Roles and Feminism Revisited: An Intergenerational Attitude Comparison," *Journal of Marriage and the Family* 39 (Feb. 1977), pp. 113–19.

Table 16.4. A comparison of college men's and women's role types

Women (N = 87)		*Men* (N = 62)	
Noncareerists	33%	Traditionalists	24%
Defectors	13%	Modified traditionalists	48%
Shifters	14%	Views not crystallized	5%
Converts	22%	Pseudo-feminists	16%
Careerists	18%	Feminists	7%
Total	100%	*Total*	100%

Source: Shirley S. Angrist, "Variation in Women's Adult Aspirations During College," *Journal of Marriage and the Family* 34 (Aug. 1972), pp. 465–68; and Mirra Komarovsky, "Cultural Contradictions and Sex Roles: The Masculine Case," *American Journal of Sociology* 78 (Jan. 1973), p. 117.

committed to the traditional wife-mother role; the defectors entered college planning to have careers, but changed their minds and became home and family oriented. Together, these two traditional types comprised almost half of the women. Among the men, the traditionalists were those who expected their wives to play the wife-mother role, and the modified traditionalists conceded that their wives might work only before children were born and again after they were grown. These men might hire housekeepers, but they had no intention of modifying their own roles so that their wives might work. Inspection of the table shows that almost three-fourths of the men fell into these two traditional categories.

At the other extreme, 40 percent of the women were either committed to careers throughout their college years, or became converted to working after marriage while they were in college. The proportion of men who would actively support their wives' careers was only 7 percent and those who gave some "lip service" to the idea were only an additional 16 percent. Overall, 40 percent of the women, compared to perhaps no more than 15 percent of the men, expressed modern attitudes favoring the equal participation of husbands and wives in the occupational sphere.

Working Wives and Mothers

The percentage of married women living with their husbands and working outside the home has been increasing irregularly for the last 30 years.

In 1940, the percentage was only 15 percent. By the end of World War II, it was approximately 20 percent, and, by 1960, it had climbed to 31 percent. Since 1960, the percentage has fluctuated upward, reaching a high of 43 percent in the early 1970s.

The percentage of married women who work is related to their ages. It drops off in the early child-rearing years, and then climbs to its highest level as the children grow older and leave home.

Effects of Wife's Employment upon Marital Adjustment. Several studies have sought the effects of the wife's employment on marital adjustment. Blood, reanalyzing data from the Detroit study, concluded that employment of the wife decreases her housekeeping duties and increases the husband's sharing in those duties. In some families, this produces conflict over marital roles. Working wives from low-income families reported more marital satisfaction than did nonworking wives. Where the husband's income was $5000 or more, however, the reverse was true; working wives reported less marital satisfaction.[29] Blood was not able to study the husband's reaction to his wife's employment.

Nye collected data from 1993 mothers and found more conflict in marriages where mothers were employed. Not only did mothers report more conflict with their husbands, but adolescent children verified their mother's reports. Whether the criterion of conflict was the frequency of quarreling, having separated one or more times, or having considered divorce, the working mothers showed up poorest in every case.

Nye's findings contradict Blood's concerning variations in marital adjustment by socio-economic status. Nye found that any adverse effect of maternal employment on adjustment is less among higher economic groups than among lower economic groups. The difference almost disappeared among the higher income and educational groups. Nye also found that dissatisfaction with the wife's employment by either spouse was associated with poor adjustment. He cautions that a husband's dissatisfaction may be either a cause of poor adjustment or a result of the poorer marital adjustment produced by the wife's working.[30]

Feld, analyzing data from 438 wives as part of a national sample, con-

29. Robert O. Blood, "The Husband-Wife Relationship," in F. Ivan Nye and Lois W. Hoffman, *eds., op. cit.,* pp. 282–305. See also Robert N. Whitehurst and Edward Z. Dager, "The Lower-Class Working Mother: Some Findings from a Small Sample Comparison Study," paper presented to National Council on Family Relations, Toronto, October 1965.

30. F. Ivan Nye, "Marital Interaction," in F. Ivan Nye and Lois W. Hoffman, *eds., op. cit.,* pp. 263–81.

firmed Nye's findings. She discovered that, with educational level and family income controlled, working mothers show more marital unhappiness than do their housewife counterparts. She, too, points out that it is impossible to determine the direction of cause and effect from these data.

Two recent studies have provided contradictory data concerning the effects of the wife's employment upon the husband's adjustment. Burke and Weir, studying 189 couples, found that the husbands of employed women were in poorer health and were less contented with their marriages than were husbands whose wives were not in the labor force. Subsequently, Booth, studying a probability sample of Toronto families, reported that the husbands of employed women evidenced no more signs of marital discord and stress than did the husbands of housewives.[31]

Effects of Working Mothers upon Children. The connection between maternal employment and problems of adjustment has contributed to widespread awareness of working mothers as a social problem. There is also a series of alleged connections between maternal employment and undesirable effects upon the children. It has been claimed that children of working mothers are likely to become delinquent, that they are more anxious, more antisocial, more likely to make a poor adjustment in school, and so on. Fortunately, a growing body of research permits us to put such generalizations to empirical test.

The research on the effects of maternal employment upon children has been summarized by Hoffman, who points out that research does not show meaningful differences between the children of working and nonworking mothers. Scattered research has reported differences, but these probably are due to chance because they are so few among the many tests made and because they have not been verified in repeat studies.[32]

31. Alan Booth, "Wife's Employment and Husband's Stress: A Replication and Refutation," *Journal of Marriage and the Family* 39 (Nov. 1977), pp. 645–50; and Ronald J. Burke and Tamara Weir, "Relationship of Wives' Employment Status to Husband, Wife, and Pair Satisfaction and Performance," *Journal of Marriage and the Family* 38 (May 1976), pp. 279–87. See also Leland J. Axelson, "The Marital Adjustment and Marital Role Definitions of Husbands of Working and Nonworking Wives," *Marriage and Family Living* 25 (May 1963), pp. 189–95; and David A. Gover, "Socio-Economic Differential in the Relationship Between Marital Adjustment and Wife's Employment Status," *Marriage and Family Living* 25 (Nov. 1963), pp. 452–58.

32. Lois W. Hoffman, "Effects on Children: Summary and Discussion," in F. Ivan Nye and Lois W. Hoffman, *eds., op. cit.*, pp. 190–212. See also Claire Etaugh, "Effects of Maternal Employment on Children: A Review of Recent Research," *Merrill-Palmer Quarterly* 20 (April 1974), pp. 71–98.

Hoffman cautions against interpreting this to mean that maternal employment has no effects at all, however. She argues, instead, that only research that imposes careful controls will reveal what relationships actually exist. She summarizes studies that have imposed controls by social class, by full-time versus part-time employment, by age and sex of child, and by the mother's attitude toward her employment.

Three studies find a relationship between maternal employment and juvenile delinquency among middle-class, but not among lower-class youth. Nye found that children of working mothers were more likely to be delinquent than children of nonworking mothers. Nye's sample was mostly middle-class, however, and the findings were found to hold only for the middle-class respondents.[33] Glueck and Glueck, using contact with the police as the criterion of delinquency and studying lower-class youth, found no relationship between full-time employment of the mother and delinquency.[34] In a third study, Gold compared the children of blue-collar and white-collar families and found a relationship only within the white-collar group.[35]

These statistical correlations do not answer, of course, the question of why maternal employment is related to delinquency in the middle class and not in the lower class. Perhaps the nature and conditions of maternal employment are different in the two classes. Perhaps the effects upon family structure are different. It remains for future research to tell.

Research supports the position that part-time employment has a favorable effect upon adolescent children. Four separate studies have found such an association.[36] It appears likely that the factors leading mothers of adolescents into part-time employment are quite different from those leading mothers of younger children into full-time employment. Whereas the latter group are likely to be of lower economic status and under pressure to work to help support their families, the former

33. F. Ivan Nye, "The Adjustment of Adolescent Children," in F. Ivan Nye and Lois W. Hoffman, *eds.*, *op. cit.*, pp. 133–41.

34. Sheldon Glueck and Eleanor Glueck, "Working Mothers and Delinquency," *Mental Hygiene* 41 (July 1957), pp. 327–52.

35. M. Gold, *A Social-Psychology of Delinquent Boys*, Ann Arbor, Mich.: Institute for Social Research, 1961.

36. Elizabeth Douvan, "Employment and the Adolescent," in F. Ivan Nye and Lois W. Hoffman, *eds.*, *op. cit.*, pp. 142–64; F. Ivan Nye, "Adolescent-Parent Adjustment: Age, Sex, Sibling Number, Broken Homes, and Employed Mothers as Variables," *Marriage and Family Living* 14 (Nov. 1952), pp. 327–32; F. Ivan Nye, "The Adjustment of Adolescent Children," *op. cit.;* and Alice M. Propper, "The Relationship of Maternal Employment to Adolescent Roles, Activities, and Parental Relationships," *Journal of Marriage and the Family* 34 (Aug. 1972), pp. 417–21.

are more likely to work by choice. Women who work by choice, who still have time for their household duties, and who are not under financial pressure may be likely both to derive satisfaction from their work to compensate for working by presenting a positive role model to their children. The part-time employment presents less of a threat to the husband than full-time employment would and, yet, the status of the wife is raised. Such women, since they have outside interests, may be more likely to grant adolescents the increasing freedom they need.

Long-established belief has it that it is especially detrimental for mothers to work while their children are young. There is also evidence that the lot of working mothers of young children is harder; they are under financial pressure, and their children require a good deal of care and supervision. By and large, however, research has failed to support the idea of adverse effects of maternal employment upon young children.[37] Few significant differences have been found. Maternal employment during the child's preschool years has no observable effects at later ages, and the mother's work history makes little difference; no effects have been found whether the mother works continuously or intermittently. Whether the expectations concerning the effects of maternal employment upon young children are wrong, or whether research simply has not uncovered such effects cannot be said for sure.

The effects of maternal employment might be different for boys than for girls, and evidence indicates that this is so. A series of studies has shown that girls' concepts of themselves and their concepts of female roles differ when their mothers work. The daughters of working mothers make fewer differentiations between household tasks deemed appropriate for men and women to perform, see women as less restricted to their homes, and are more favorable to the employment of women. Such girls are also more likely to wish to work themselves when they have children.[38] Hoffman concludes that working mothers provide role models which their daughters admire and emulate.

37. Lee G. Burchinal, "Personality Characteristics of Children," in F. Ivan Nye and Lois W. Hoffman, *eds., op. cit.,* pp. 106–21; and from the same source: F. Ivan Nye, Joseph B. Perry, Jr., and Richard H. Ogles, "Anxiety and Anti-Social Behavior in Preschool Children," pp. 82–94; Kathryn S. Powell, "Personalities of Children and Child-Rearing Attitudes of Mothers," pp. 125–32; and Alberta E. Siegel, Lois M. Stolz, Ethel A. Hitchcock, and Jean Adamson, "Dependence and Independence in Children," pp. 67–81.

38. Elizabeth M. Almquist and Shirley S. Angrist, "Role Model Influences on College Women's Career Aspirations," *Merrill-Palmer Quarterly* 17 (July 1971), pp. 263–79. For analysis of effects upon maternal participation in mate selection, see John A. Bruce, "The Role of Mothers in the Social Placement of Daughters: Marriage or Work?" *Journal of Marriage and the Family* 36 (Aug. 1974), pp. 492–97.

The effects of maternal employment upon sons are less clear. Although there is some pattern in the findings, the results have not achieved statistical significance. For this reason, the following should be considered more as hypotheses than as definite findings. One study indicates that lower-class sons of working mothers are least likely to name their fathers as the persons they most admire.[39] Since lower-class men are least able to support their families without assistance, the sons' low estimates may stem from the perceived inadequacy of the fathers rather than from effects of the mothers' employment. Both the mothers' employment and the sons' negative evaluations of their fathers may reflect lower-class conditions of life.

A second study found that the young sons of working mothers were more dependent and obedient, less self-reliant, less sociable, and more likely to seek succorance from adults.[40] Hoffman also found that the sons of working mothers are more dependent upon teachers,[41] and data from a study by Rouman suggest that sons of working mothers are more likely to be sent for counseling for withdrawal problems than for any other kind of problem.[42] Until further research modifies it, a tenable hypothesis appears to be that maternal employment is associated with adequate self-concepts and less traditional femininity among girls and with dependency, lack of aggression, and low achievement among boys.

Finally, the mother's attitude toward her employment appears to be important. Two studies show that when the mother is satisfied with her employment, the relationship between her and her children is likely to be warm and satisfying. There is some suggestion that mothers in this category may overindulge their children because they feel a little guilty about working. Among mothers who are dissatisfied with their employment, relationships with their children are less rewarding and the children are more likely to be burdened with too many household tasks.[43]

39. Elizabeth Douvan, *op. cit.* See also Karl King, Jennie McIntyre, and Leland J. Axelson, "Adolescents' Views of Maternal Employment as a Threat to the Marital Relationship," *Journal of Marriage and the Family* 30 (Nov. 1968), pp. 633–37.

40. Alberta E. Siegel, Lois M. Stolz, Ethel A. Hitchcock, and Jean Adamson, *op. cit.*

41. Lois W. Hoffman, "Mother's Enjoyment of Work and Effects on the Child," in F. Ivan Nye and Lois W. Hoffman, *eds., op. cit.*, pp. 95–105.

42. J. Rouman, "School Children's Problems as Related to Parental Factors," *Journal of Educational Research* 50 (Oct. 1956), pp. 105–12.

43. Elizabeth Douvan, *op. cit.* See also Doris K. Katelman and Larry D. Barnett, "Work Orientations of Urban, Middle-Class, Married Women," *Journal of Marriage and the Family* 30 (Feb. 1968), pp. 80–88; and Constantina Safilios-Rothschild, "The Influence of the Wife's Degree of Work Commitment Upon Some Aspects of Family Organization and Dynamics," *Journal of Marriage and the Family* 32 (Nov. 1970), pp. 681–91.

In summary, research contradicts the idea of significant differences between the children of working and nonworking mothers. Maternal employment operates in interaction with too many other variables to be studied alone. Scattered research indicates that there may be some relationships with juvenile delinquency at middle-class levels, that part-time maternal employment has a favorable effect upon adolescent children, and that the effects upon younger children may vary by sex. Any general conclusion that maternal employment is undesirable appears unwarranted.

Dual Career Families

A phenomenon that has received growing attention over the past few years is that of the dual career family. There is no one precise definition of the dual career family, but it seems to be mostly an upper-middle-class pattern in which the wife pursues an occupation, for which higher education is required and which has considerable personal salience for her, while the couple raises a family. Only small-scale studies of such families have been done to date, but careful studies have been completed both in England[44] and the United States.[45]

The studies agree that dual career families are not the result of any one conscious decision for the wife to continue her career after marriage and child-bearing. Instead, most of the women, even before marriage, consider their work important and depreciate being "just a housewife." By the birth of their first child, the wife is so committed to her job that modification of family roles seems more plausible than giving up her work.

One study of 14 dual career couples sought factors in the women's backgrounds that might have disposed them to this form of adjustment, with the following results. First, a high proportion were "only children," and the majority of the others were the oldest child in the family. Second, the mothers of these women often were employed while the girls were growing up, and many mothers, both employed and unemployed, were ambitious for their daughters. Third, tension in the home was common, centering, often, on the father. Miscellaneous other disturbing experiences during childhood also were reported.

44. Rhona Rapoport and Robert Rapoport, *Dual-Career Families*, Harmondsworth, Middlesex, England: Penguin Books, 1971.
45. Lynda Lytle Holmstrom, *The Two-Career Family*, Cambridge, Mass.: Schenkman Publishing Co., 1972.

Interestingly, no differences appeared between the backgrounds of the dual career husbands and the husbands in traditional families. Some husbands acquiesced in their wives' desires, saying, "I knew what I was getting into," or, more often, they were supportive, espousing principles of "fair play," or wanting their wives to be happy and fulfilled.[46]

Sometimes the theme is muted, and sometimes it is clear, but most studies agree that dual career families experience special strains, originating both outside and within the marriage. Outside pressures are felt primarily in two areas: first, husbands and wives are uncomfortable over the wife's having to delegate much child-rearing to sitters, day-care centers, schools, and so on; second, the demands of work and family are so great that social activities must be limited. The limitation of friendship circles does not appear to be particularly upsetting because the couple seek friends who also face severe time limitations. But relationships with the parental families are more troubling. Parents both resent the fact that their children's families do not have time for them and criticize the wives for apparent neglect of home and children.

Strains internal to the family are primarily of three sorts. First, there are problems of work overload for both husband and wife. Even with the husband assisting with housework and child care, the demands of two careers, meal preparation, cleaning, caring for and enjoying children, and so on, leave most spouses without the time and energy to perform all of their duties and responsibilities. Second, some persons experience confusion in relation to traditional definitions of masculine and feminine spheres. In extreme instances, this may lead to psychological or physical confusion, with accompanying frigidity or impotence. Finally, there are problems of role-cycling, associated with transition points in both career and family. The demands of the husband's career and the wife's career may conflict so that, for example, one must forego a sought-after promotion or transfer because of the potential interference with the other's career.[47] Child-bearing, too, is often delayed or timed not to coincide

46. A. C. Bebbington, "The Function of Stress in the Establishment of the Dual-Career Family," *Journal of Marriage and the Family* 35 (Aug. 1973), pp. 532–33. See also Ronald J. Burke and Tamara Weir, "Some Personality Differences Between Members of One-Career and Two-Career Families," *Journal of Marriage and the Family* 38 (Aug. 1976), pp. 453–59.

47. See R. Paul Duncan and Carolyn Cummings Perrucci, "Dual Occupation Families and Migration," *American Sociological Review* 41 (April 1976), pp. 252–61; and Benson Rosen, Thomas H. Jerdee, and Thomas L. Prestwich, "Dual-Career Marital Adjustment: Potential Effects of Discriminatory Managerial Attitudes," *Journal of Marriage and the Family* 37 (Aug. 1975), pp. 565–72.

with transitions in either partner's career. This may lead to having fewer children than the couple would like or having none at all.

We should not assume, however, that stress is higher in dual career families than in traditional families or, at least, it is not clear that *these* families could solve their problems by the wife giving up her career. Dual career wives state that they couldn't stand just to be housewives, or that they would "go mad" without their jobs. The dual career couples studied do not appear to have unstable marriages or even to be less happy than other couples. Perhaps the partners are unusually tolerant of stress, or perhaps they have simply accepted the strains of dual career living in order to escape, for them, the even greater strains of traditional living.

SUMMARY

This chapter focuses upon changes in marital adjustment as couples move through the child-rearing years, and beyond. Marital adjustment is seen as a process rather than a state, and the events of 5, 10, and 20 years after the marriage ceremony change it significantly. It is useful to conceptualize marriage as a set of mutually contingent careers in which couples may grow closer together or move farther apart.

Both longitudinal and cross-sectional studies of marital adjustment show a tendency for couples to grow farther apart with time. There is a gradual drop in marital adjustment scores, in marital satisfaction, in the frequency of sexual intercourse, and in the adequacy of marital communication. Nor are these changes simply a function of aging, for there is no comparable drop in personal adjustment scores. What happens may be conceptualized as a process of disenchantment in which the "goodness of fit" that prevailed between the couple at marriage gradually is lost. Not all marriages suffer this fate, however. A smaller percentage of marriages appears to improve in communication and empathy as time goes by.

Early studies showed most marriages to be somewhat male dominated, with the husband's power being greater at higher status levels. Husbands had more power in families with children, particularly during the child-bearing years. The husband's power fell off in retirement and old age.

One theory holds that the power of husbands and wives reflects the relative resources they bring to the marriage. Another theory holds that resources can only be evaluated in a particular cultural context: that norms concerning the distribution of power influence the way in which resources are used.

Recent studies show most marriages to have a fairly equal distribution of power, with some couples emphasizing autonomous decision making and others emphasizing joint decision making. Surprisingly, husband dominated marriages have about as many high happiness ratings as do equalitarian ones. Wife-dominated marriages have a much smaller percentage of very satisfactory relationships.

Studies of the roles that college students expect to play as adults show that virtually all women expect to be married, and that about half of them want both children and occupational careers. Women's expectations, in this respect, have changed markedly while men's expectations have changed very little. The potential for marital conflict is obvious.

The proportion of wives who work outside the home has been increasing irregularly over the past 30 years. The percentage of working wives drops off somewhat during the early child-bearing years and then reaches a high point when wives are between 35 and 65 years of age. Research shows that the gainful employment of wives is associated with the sharing of household tasks and conflict over marital roles.

Contrary to widespread belief, there appear to be few, if any, gross relationships between maternal employment and the adjustment of children. Carefully controlled studies have suggested a relationship between maternal employment and juvenile delinquency among middle-class children, but not among lower-class children. There is some evidence, also, that part-time maternal employment is positively correlated with the adjustment of adolescent children. Maternal employment appears to influence the self-concepts of both sons and daughters, but in different ways. The daughters of working mothers appear likely to develop adequate self-concepts, to make minimal distinctions between the household tasks deemed appropriate for men and women, and to anticipate employment themselves when they are older. The evidence concerning sons is less convincing but suggests that sons of working mothers have less admiration for their fathers, are more obedient, and less independent and self-reliant. An important variable is the mother's attitude toward her employment. When she is satisfied, the relationship between her and her children is likely to be warm and rewarding. When she is dissatisfied, the relationship with her children suffers.

Dual career families, in which the wife pursues a career instead of just having a job, appear to involve special strains, but no more, perhaps than the wives in these families would experience in more traditional roles.

Wives acknowledge some regret over having to delegate so much of the child-rearing function, and parental families resent not seeing more of their children and grandchildren. There also are problems of work overload, role confusion, and role-cycling.

SUGGESTED READINGS

Cromwell, Ronald E., and Olson, David H., *eds.*, *Power in Families*, Beverly Hills, Cal.: Sage, 1975. Provides a comprehensive review of the conceptual and methodological problems in studying family power.

Holmstrom, Lynda Lytle, *The Two-Career Family*, Cambridge, Mass.: Schenkman Publishing Co., 1972. A report of research on the life styles of two-career families compared to traditional one-career families.

Huber, Joan, *ed.*, *Changing Women in a Changing Society*, Chicago and London: The University of Chicago Press, 1973. Also published as the January 1973 issue of the *American Journal of Sociology*. Contains selections on female marital patterns in the United States and on the two-person single career.

Komarovsky, Mirra, *Dilemmas of Masculinity: A Study of College Youth*, New York: Norton, 1976. An in-depth study of Ivy League students that shows how traditional their role expectations are, both for their wives and for themselves.

Lopata, Helena Znaniecki, *Occupation: Housewife*, New York: Oxford University Press, 1971. A monograph reporting the findings of a series of studies of women in and around Chicago, and the ways in which they cope with the role of housewife.

Nye, F. Ivan, *et. al.*, *Role Structure and Analysis of the Family*, Beverly Hills, Cal.: Sage, 1976. A report of research that interprets data systematically in the context of various aspects of marital and parental roles.

Rapoport, Rhona, and Rapoport, Robert, N., *Dual-Career Families Re-examined: New Integrations of Work and Family*, London: Martin Robinson, 1976. Emphasizes dual-career families as one form of dual-worker families.

FILMS

Children of Change (Affiliated Film Board, Inc., 164 East 38th Street, New York, N.Y. 10016), 31 minutes. Discusses the problem of working mothers and their children in day-care centers. Reviews values of an effective day-care program for children.

A Family Affair (International Film Bureau, 332 S. Michigan Ave., Chicago, Ill. 01274), 30 minutes. The story of a middle-aged couple whose relationships are strained to the breaking point. Shows how the breaking up of a marriage can be averted with the help of a marriage counselor.

Joyce at 34 (New Day Films, 267 West 25th Street, New York, N.Y. 10001), 28 minutes, color. Joyce copes with her new baby while pursuing her career as a filmmaker. A startling and very personal statement of interest both to women and men.

Radcliffe Blues (American Documentary Films, 336 West 84th Street, New York, N.Y. 10024; or 379 Bay Street, San Francisco, 94133), 23 minutes. A woman speaks on women's rights, alienation, and radicalization.

QUESTIONS AND PROJECTS

1. What is meant by the phrase "marriage as a developmental process"? What are the implications for mate selection? How may marriage be conceived of as a set of mutually contingent careers?
2. What does research show about marital adjustment through the middle years? How does disenchantment describe what happens to most marriages? Do all couples decline in adjustment?
3. Are marital roles anticipated in adolescence and young adulthood? What expectations do people carry into marriage?
4. How does the power of husbands vary with socio-economic status and with parental status? How does it vary over the life cycle?
5. How common, relatively, are autonomous, syncratic, wife-dominant, and husband-dominant decision-making patterns? What are the relationships between them and marital satisfaction?
6. What factors appear to influence women to expect to have occupational careers? What do studies show about recent changes in women's role expectations?
7. How much change has there been in the expectations of men for their roles and those of their wives? What implications does this have for marital conflict?
8. What appear to be the major effects upon marital adjustment of the wife's working outside the home? What inferences, if any, can be made about cause and effect?
9. What does research show about the effects of maternal employment upon the adjustment of children? Are all of the effects of maternal employment known?

10. Take a poll of the class. Determine what marital-role expectations the students hold. Are there differences by sex? Are there differences by the work experience of the students' mothers?
11. What are dual career families? How do they differ from other families in which the wives work?
12. What special kinds of internal and external problems are experienced by dual career families? Would these people have fewer problems in traditional families?

FLORIGOLD
Indian River
FLORIGOLD

17
Divorce and Desertion

Paul Glick, senior demographer at the U.S. Census Bureau, says that, "if things continue the way they have, in addition to the 37 percent of first marriages that end in divorce, 59 percent of second marriages also will dissolve." . . .

Couples in the lower socio-economic strata account for an estimated 80 percent of the second divorces (at higher socio-economic levels, the second-divorce rate is closer to the 37 percent for first divorces. . . ."[1]

In a reversal of the past, apparently influenced by the feminist movement, more wives than husbands are now running away from home as a protest against their life roles, according to the nation's largest missing-persons search firm. . . .

The New York-based company reports that last year it was called upon to find 1,136 wives and 989 husbands; in no other year have women outnumbered men. The figures reflect a national trend, according to the firm's president. . . .

Based on his talks with runaways, Mr. Goldfader says the average man leaves home because of financial pressures or business frustration, but a woman runs away to get attention. "She's anxious to elevate herself from the role of cook, laundress and housekeeper," he says. "A couple of weeks after she's run away, she usually ends up in a menial job. . . . Reality hits her and she's ready to be found."[2]

Virtually everyone has read that the United States has the highest divorce rate in the world. In that bald form the statement is false, but that

1. *The New York Times Magazine*, Aug. 10, 1975, p. 13.
2. *The Gainesville Sun*, Feb. 24, 1975.

doesn't stop it from being repeated and reprinted. Perhaps this is because the statement is often intended to convey a feeling rather than to communicate a fact. The feeling is that divorce rates in the United States are so high as to threaten the existence of the family.

INTERCULTURAL PERSPECTIVE ON DIVORCE

When people evaluate American divorce rates, they usually compare them with the rates of other large nations. It should not be forgotten, however, that most of the world's societies are small, preliterate ones and that they have something to teach us, too, about the range of family practices that is consistent with the overall stability of the system.

As with other family practices, useful data on divorce in preliterate societies have been assembled by Murdock. He points out that all societies have provisions for ending marriages, and that divorce rates in about 60 percent of all preliterate societies are higher than those in the contemporary United States.[3]

Nor is there any particular relationship between divorce rates and other symptoms of social disorganization. High divorce rates can be, and are, associated with stable family systems where there are clear norms specifying what happens to husband, wife, and children after the divorce. It is generally provided that the husband and wife should be reabsorbed by their respective kin groups. The children continue to live with their lineage and do not suffer unduly from the separation of their parents.

Statements that the United States has the world's highest divorce rate generally have, as their referent, other large nations. Even within that context, however, the statement has not always been true. Some Moslem countries, for example, that still permit men to take up to four wives, and to divorce any of them simply by saying three times, "I divorce thee," have had extremely high divorce rates. In 1900, the divorce rate in Algeria (the only Moslem country for which reliable data were available then) was roughly four times as high as that in the United States. Algeria's rate has fallen since then, but a recent unofficial report indicates that, in 1970, Egypt had twice as many divorces (700,000) as marriages (325,000).[4] Pre-modern Japan also had high divorce rates associ-

3. George P. Murdock, "Family Stability in Non-European Cultures," *Annals of the American Academy of Political and Social Science* 272 (Nov. 1950), p. 197.
4. Reuters dispatch, Sept. 22, 1973.

ated with its patriarchal, patrilineal, extended family system. As in traditional China, divorce indicated that the young bride did not please her in-laws. As Japan urbanized, her divorce rate fell, a pattern opposite to that which occurred in the United States.

In summary, divorce rates vary drastically from one society to another, and, in the same society, they may vary drastically over time. There is no necessary relationship between divorce rates and either family or societal stability; high divorce rates may reflect family breakdown, or they may reflect societally prescribed ways of eliminating disruptive influences. In world perspective, the United States falls in the large group of societies having relatively high divorce rates. Striking increases in United States divorce rates have accompanied urbanization, industrialization, and the shift to a conjugal family system.

THE DIVORCE RATE IN THE UNITED STATES

The Historical Trend

Statistics on the frequency of divorce in the United States became available only about a century ago. These statistics, a few of which are presented in Table 17.1, show an inexorable rise both in the number and rate of divorces. In 1860, there were fewer than 8000 divorces in all of the United States. By 1900 there were 55,000 and, in 1976, there were over one million divorces.

Table 17.1. United States Divorce and Annulment Rates, 1920–1976

Year	*Number of divorces*	*Divorce and annulment rate per 1000 population*
1920	171,000	1.6
1930	196,000	1.6
1940	264,000	2.0
1946	610,000	4.3
1950	385,000	2.5
1960	393,000	2.2
1970	715,000	3.5
1976	1,077,000	5.0

Source: Historical Statistics of the United States, Colonial Times to 1957, Series B-29, p. 22; U.S. Bureau of the Census, *Statistical Abstract of the United States: 1972* (Washington, D.C.), p. 63; and National Center for Health Statistics, *Monthly Vital Statistics Report*, March 8, 1977, pp. 2–3.

Part of the increase in the number of divorces, of course, is to be accounted for simply by the growth of the population. It would be quite possible, in a growing nation, for the number of divorces to climb without there being any increase in the probability that any given marriage would end in divorce. The right-hand column of Table 17.1, however, shows that the number of divorces per 1000 population in the United States also has been climbing. In 1940, there were only 2.0 divorces per 1000 population. By 1976, the rate was 5.0.

The influence of War and the Economy

While the long-term trend in the divorce rate has been upward, the increases have not been uniform. The years 1930 and 1933 had lower rates than prevailed during the 1920s, and the years of 1945 and 1946 had higher divorce rates than either before or for nearly 30 years after that time. These fluctuations suggest the influences of wars and recessions that more complete statistics would show in detail.

Wars tend to be followed by sharp increases in divorce rates and then by a return to the level of the prewar trend. As early as the Civil War this was evident. There were 7380 U.S. divorces in 1860. In 1862, the number was down to 6230. In 1865, the number was 10,090 and the peak of 11,530 divorces was reached in 1866. The number of divorces then dropped off and did not reach the 1866 level again until 1871.

A similar pattern followed World War I. From 116,254 divorces in 1918, the number jumped to 141,527 in 1919 and to 171,000 in 1920. The number in 1921 was back down to 156,580 and dropped further in 1922. World War I also demonstrated that this is not strictly an American phenomenon. England, France, and Germany all had relatively greater increases in 1919 and 1920 than the United States. All three countries also experienced decreases in divorces during the early 1920s.

World War II saw fluctuations in the number of U.S. divorces, but gradually increasing numbers until 1946, when a total of 610,000 divorces was recorded. Today, over thirty years later, that figure has finally been surpassed. The divorce rate in 1946 was 4.3 per 1000 population. By 1950, the divorce rate dropped back almost to immediate pre-World War II levels, where it hovered until 1963. Since 1963, it has been on the rise again.

Explanations for these relationships between war and divorce rates are not difficult to find. A major factor is the large number of marriages contracted after short acquaintance. Such marriages probably would produce many divorces even without the effects of war. The war itself, however, separates many couples for long periods. In some instances, couples, who formerly were close, simply grow apart. In other cases, wartime separation merely establishes separate existences for couples whose marriages had been held together only by inertia. In addition, many lonely spouses are thrown together with persons of the opposite sex under conditions that encourage involvement. Relatively few of these persons institute divorce actions while the war is in progress, but many do so when the war is ended and readjustment must be achieved. Finally, the strains of postwar reunion themselves often are great. Some formerly stable marriages break under this additional strain.[5]

In addition to war, economic depressions also have marked effects upon divorce rates. The relative influences of a major depression and a major war are shown in Figure 17.1, which covers the great depression of the 1930s and World War II. The depression depressed divorce rates markedly, although not so much as World War II inflated them. Before the stock market crash in 1929 there were 201,468 divorces, or 7.9 divorces per 1000 marriages. At the depth of the depression in 1933 there were 40,000 fewer divorces and the divorce rate had dropped to 6.1.

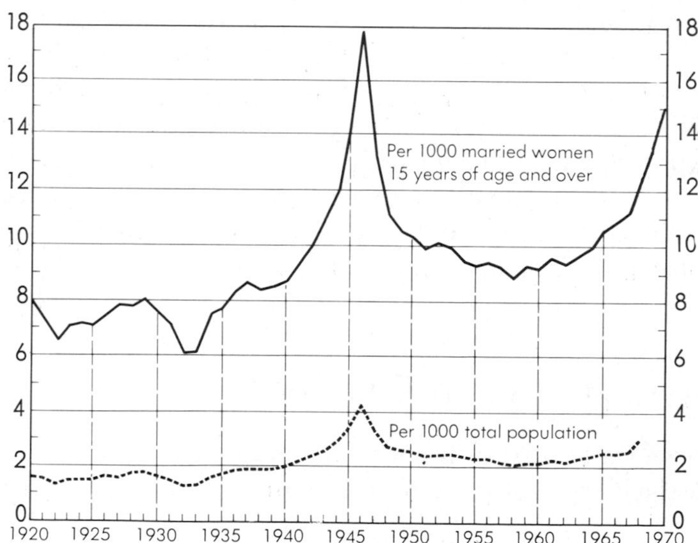

Figure 17.1. The influences of the Great Depression and World War II upon United States divorce rates

5. Reuben Hill, *Families Under Stress*, New York: Harper and Brothers, 1949.

From 1933 until the start of World War II, again both the number of divorces and the divorce rate climbed steadily.[6]

Explanations for the effect of depressions upon divorce rates are, again, not hard to find. Securing a divorce is costly and many people cannot afford it during a depression. Beyond that, divorce requires establishment of separate households, division of property, and establishment of specific terms for the support of children. These requirements tax most people's financial resources even during prosperity and often become prohibitive in bad times. Great financial hardship may draw together some couples who might otherwise become alienated, but, if it does, apparently the effect is short-lived. For, although divorce rates drop during the depression itself, they rise rapidly as the depression ends.

Present Status and Future Prospects

Popular concern with divorce rates often manifests itself in estimates of the probability that any given marriage will end in divorce. Just as the rate of divorce has been increasing, so have estimates of the probability of divorce for individual couples. In 1940, before World War II, there was 1 divorce for each 6 marriages contracted. There was 1 divorce for every 3.8 marriages in 1946, and by 1970 there was 1 divorce for every 3 marriages. Demographers estimate that, of 100 women who were 30 years old in 1971, approximately 30 to 35 will ultimately be divorced.[7]

We have already seen that the long-term trend in American divorce rates is upward, and, although predictions are hazardous, the prospect is that the upward trend will continue for some time. The number of divorces will continue to climb if only because the population is growing. In all probability the divorce rate will rise also.

THE DISTRIBUTION OF DIVORCE

The probability of divorce is not spread evenly throughout the population. The significance of this difference will be pursued in the next chap-

6. Paul H. Jacobson, *American Marriage and Divorce*, New York: Rinehart and Company, 1959, pp. 89–91.

7. Paul C. Glick and Arthur J. Norton, "Perspectives on the Recent Upturn in Divorce and Remarriage," *Demography* 10 (Aug. 1973), pp. 301–14. See also J. Lynn England and Phillip R. Kunz, "The Application of Age-Specific Rates to Divorce," *Journal of Marriage and the Family* 37 (Feb. 1975), pp. 40–46.

ter on remarriages. Here, we will analyze the influences of region, race, economic status, length of time married, and parental status upon divorce rates.

Variations by Rural-Urban Status and by Region

In the decennial census, information is secured on the current marital status of persons enumerated. These data show that divorced persons are overrepresented in urban and underrepresented in rural areas. In part, these data reflect a higher probability of divorce under conditions of urban living; the lesser likelihood of divorce under rural, particularly farm, conditions has been pointed out earlier. In part also, however, these statistics reflect a tendency for rural persons to migrate to urban areas before, during, or after a divorce. There is little place for divorced persons, particularly women, in a farm economy, whereas life in cities caters more to married and unmarried persons alike.

Divorce rates also vary by region, increasing from east to west. The divorce rate is lowest in the northeast, followed by the north central region, then by the south and, finally, by the west. Several factors help to account for these regional variations, but a full explanation does not exist. One factor undoubtedly is a difference in attitudes and values; something of a frontier tradition including rootlessness lingers on in the west. The age distribution of the population varies, with more younger, divorce-prone, persons being found in the west. Finally, the ethnic and religious composition of the population has something to do with it; Roman Catholics particularly are overrepresented in northern and eastern sections of the country.[8]

In a recent study, Fenelon offers another explanation of these variations. He suggests that divorce rates are a function of the social costs involved. States having a large number of migrants in their populations may be characterized by a lower degree of social integration and there may be fewer effective sanctions against divorce. Analysis of state and regional variations in divorce rates supports his hypothesis.[9]

8. See Paul C. Glick, "Marriage Instability: Variations by Size of Place and Religion," *The Milbank Memorial Fund Quarterly* 41 (Jan. 1963), pp. 43–55; and Kenneth L. Cannon and Ruby Gingles, "Social Factors Related to Divorce Rates for Urban Counties in Nebraska," *Rural Sociology* 21 (March 1956), pp. 34–40.

9. Bill Fenelon, "State Variations in United States Divorce Rates," *Journal of Marriage and the Family* 33 (May 1971), pp. 321–27. See also Henry Pang and Sue M. Hanson, "Highest Divorce Rates in Western United States," *Sociology and Social Research* 52 (Jan. 1968), pp. 228–36.

Variations by Race

Strange as it may seem, data on divorce rates by race are so inadequate as to render hazardous any unqualified generalizations about the relative rates of whites and blacks. The data come from two sources: from the decennial censuses, and from very incomplete reports made to the National Center for Health Statistics.

The decennial census data refer only to persons who are separated or divorced at the time of enumeration. Not only are these figures subject to error, but they do not include persons who have been divorced and remarried. For what they are worth, the figures for 1971 show that 3.4 percent of all nonwhite males were divorced while the percentage for white males was 2.8. The differences between white and nonwhite females were greater, with 5.6 percent of the nonwhite and only 3.8 percent of the white females reporting divorced status.

Data from the Divorce Registration Area are improving but still are woefully inadequate. The DRA is made up of 28 states in which local courts forward data on all divorces to their state health departments which, in turn, send systematic samples of these records to the National Center for Health Statistics. Unfortunately for our purposes, many of these records omit information pertaining to race. Very fragmentary data for the period from 1939 through 1950 suggest that divorce rates may have been higher among whites than among blacks until 1942, when the relationship appears to have been reversed and black divorce rates came to average 20 percent higher than those of whites.

Why these relationships should have changed over time requires explanation, and a plausible explanation is available. It appears likely that black divorce rates recently have come to reflect, more accurately than they did before, the actual rate of marital disruption. The factors described in Chapter 9 that encouraged the use of desertion among blacks as a solution to family problems probably held down the divorce rate.

There is evidence, too, that black divorce rates are more sensitive to economic conditions than are white rates. Blacks hold fewer middle-class jobs where employment is relatively secure, and are more likely to be laid off or fired during economic recessions. Jacobson, using divorce rates for Virginia, demonstrated that nonwhite divorce rates were higher than white rates during the prosperous period between 1918 and 1928. During the depression decade from 1929 through 1940, by contrast, nonwhite divorce rates were lower than those among whites. The same reversal occurred in Mississippi. Jacobson concludes that the upsurge in black divorce rates after World War II also was associated with economic prosperity. Higher incomes permitted blacks to hire lawyers and to file formal divorce proceedings.[10]

A sample survey of approximately 37,000 households by the Bureau of the Census, in 1975, confirmed that greater percentages of blacks than whites now experience divorce. Some 53 percent of nonwhite males and 64 percent of white males had been married only once.[11]

Variations by Socio-economic Status

At least four major studies have demonstrated an inverse correlation between socio-economic status and divorce rates. Regardless of the criterion of socio-economic status used, there are more divorces at the bottom of the structure, and the rate steadily declines as we move upward.

Hillman found that male private household workers and service workers had the highest proportion of divorces; laborers had rates nearly as high. The proportion of divorces dropped through the middle-class, white-collar occupations and was lowest of all among professionals, managers, and proprietors. Farming was in a class by itself. As might be imagined, the divorce rate among farm owners and farm managers was less than half that among proprietors, managers, and officials.[12]

In a study of 425 Detroit-area women who had been divorced from 2 to 26 months, Goode calculated an index of proneness to divorce by the husbands' occupational status. The results were consistent with Hillman's findings. Divorce rates were lowest at the top of the occupational structure, with professionals and proprietors contributing barely more than half their proportionate share. Not until we drop down to semiskilled and operatives did any group exceed its share. Finally, the un-

10. *Op. cit.*, pp. 102–3.

11. U.S. Bureau of the Census, *Current Population Reports*, Series P-20, No. 297, Oct. 1976, p. 2. For a penetrating analysis of the interrelationships among family stability and race, see Charles V. Mercer, "Interrelations Among Family Stability, Family Composition, Residence, and Race," *Journal of Marriage and the Family* 29 (Aug. 1967), pp. 456–60.

12. Farm laborers, interestingly, had high divorce rates like other laborers rather than low divorce rates like farm owners. See Karen G. Hillman, "Marital Instability and Its Relation to Education, Income, and Occupation: An Analysis Based on Census Data," in Robert F. Winch, Robert McGinnis, and Herbert R. Barringer, *eds., Selected Studies in Marriage and the Family*, New York: Holt, Rinehart, and Winston, 1962, pp. 603–8.

skilled had almost twice as many divorces as their share in the population.[13]

Goode's findings were confirmed in an independent study of 1434 Philadelphia divorce cases. Working from the divorce records, Kephart found that the upper occupational levels were underrepresented in divorce actions, the middle-level occupations were represented roughly in accord with their proportions of the population, and lower-level occupations were greatly overrepresented.[14]

Finally, Monahan analyzed 4449 divorce cases for Iowa and found evidence to support the three studies already cited. He found professional persons, officials, managers, and owners to contribute less than their share of divorces. The clerical and sales group contributed almost exactly their expected share, and laboring groups contributed up to four times their share. Farmers had the lowest rates of all.[15]

These four studies all used occupation as the index of socio-economic status. Goode and Hillman, however, also used education and income as indexes and found the same inverse relationship between these measures and divorce rates. When education is used, however, some striking anomalies appear. Hillman found that the relationships hold for white males only, and Goode found that when education is used, the relationships are reversed for blacks and whites. Among blacks, the higher the educational level up to college graduation, the higher the divorce rate. Again, blacks who actually finish college have low divorce rates, approximating those of blacks who have little formal education. It may be that blacks with more formal education are more likely to use attorneys and courts in the solution of their marital problems and are less likely to resort to desertion. The low divorce rates among black college graduates may reflect the next stage in this process: the eventual tendency for middle-class norms to have more salience than those associated with race.

The relationships between socio-economic status and divorce rates reflect differences in conditions of life at upper-, middle-, and lower-class

13. William J. Goode, *After Divorce*, Glencoe, Illinois: The Free Press, 1956, pp. 46–47. See also Irving Rosow and K. Daniel Rose, "Divorce Among Doctors," *Journal of Marriage and the Family* 34 (Dec. 1972), pp. 587–98.

14. William M. Kephart, "Occupational Level and Marital Disruption," *American Sociological Review* 20 (Aug. 1955), pp. 456–65. For a sophisticated analysis based upon 1960 census data, see Phillips Cutright, "Income and Family Events: Marital Stability," *Journal of Marriage and the Family* 33 (May 1971), pp. 291–306.

15. Monahan found Iowa farm laborers to have very low divorce rates, also. The conflict in findings here between Monahan's and Hillman's studies has not yet been reconciled. See Thomas P. Monahan, "Divorce by Occupational Level," *Marriage and Family Living* 17 (Nov. 1955), pp. 322–24.

levels. Although there is a widespread stereotype of carefree living at lower-class levels, the opposite situation exists. Lower-class people have more problems of all sorts. Divorce is one of them.

Variations by Length of Time Married

One of the hazards in tracing changes in divorce rates is that there may be apparent increases in yearly rates without there being any long-term changes in the proportion of the population becoming divorced. This may happen if the average duration of marriages to divorce shortens. Earlier divorces would cause the yearly rates to show temporary increases. Unfortunately, available data on length of marriage to divorce are too fragmentary to show conclusively what has been happening.

A second problem is that the duration of marriage to the date of divorce is not so useful a measure as is the duration of marriage to the time of separation. The period of separation before a divorce decree is granted may vary from only a few weeks to many years.[16]

Several early studies showed that divorce rates are higher in the early years of marriage and are highest among those who marry young. These studies also suggested that the first year of marriage is the peak year for separations, the third year shows the highest number of divorces being granted, and the mean length of marriage to divorce is longer, at least seven or eight years.[17]

A recent tabulation of data by the National Center for Health Statistics showed that, in 1973, the median interval from marriage to divorce was 6.6 years. Figure 17.2 shows the median interval for white men between first marriage and divorce by age at marriage, education, and income.[18]

The most recent study was based upon 77,491 California divorces in 1969. It also showed more divorces to be granted during the third year of marriage than any other, and an inverse relationship between age at

16. Thomas P. Monahan, "When Married Couples Part: Statistical Trends and Relationships in Divorce," *American Sociological Review* 27 (Oct. 1962), pp. 625–33.

17. Paul H. Jacobson, "Differentials in Divorce by Duration of Marriage and Size of Family," *American Sociological Review* 15 (April 1950), pp. 235–44; William M. Kephart, "The Duration of Marriage," *American Sociological Review* 19 (June 1954), pp. 287–95; and Thomas P. Monahan, "When Married Couples Part: Statistical Trends and Relationships in Divorce," *op. cit.*

18. Hugh Carter and Paul C. Glick, *Marriage and Divorce: A Social and Economic Study*, Cambridge, Mass.: Harvard Univ. Press, 1976, p. 430; and Paul C. Glick and Arthur J. Norton, "Frequency, Duration and Probability of Marriage and Divorce," *Journal of Marriage and the Family* 33 (May 1971), pp. 307–17.

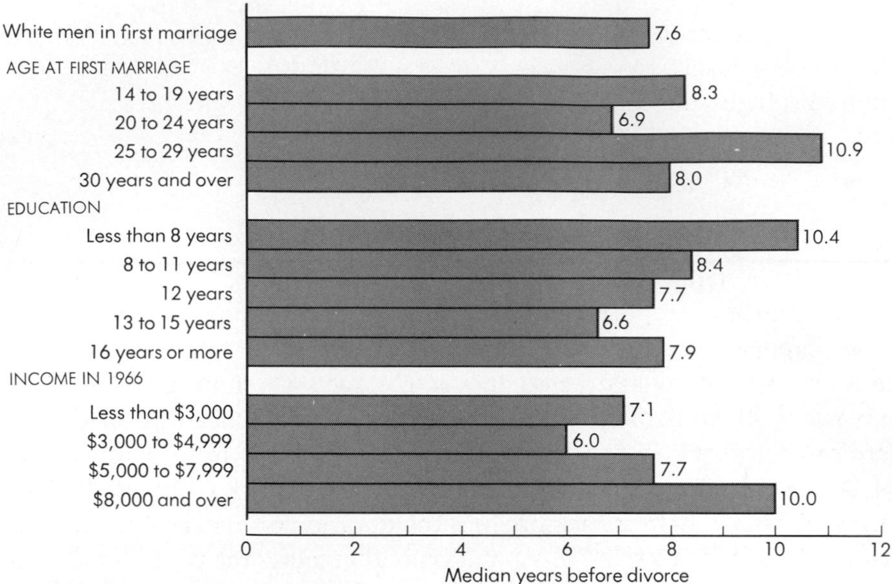

Figure 17.2. Median duration of first marriage for divorced white men by selected characteristics, 1960–1966

Source: U.S. Bureau of the Census, report from the 1967 Survey of Economic Opportunity.

marriage and the likelihood of divorce. Men marrying at age 18 and women marrying at age 16 were more than twice as likely to be divorced as those marrying ages 29 and 27.[19]

Variations by Parental Status

Crude statistics collected early in this century make it appear that the possibility of divorce was many times as great among childless couples as among couples with children. Cahen, for example, concluded that some 71 percent of childless marriages ended in divorce, while only 8 percent of marriages with children did so.[20] For some time, no one seriously questioned these extreme figures and the conclusion was widely accepted that childlessness and divorce are causally associated.

Gradually, however, flaws in the statistics became apparent. "Chil-

19. Robert Schoen, "California Divorce Rates by Age at First Marriage and Duration of First Marriage," *Journal of Marriage and the Family* 37 (Aug. 1975), pp. 548–55.
20. Alfred Cahen, *Statistical Analysis of American Divorce*, New York: Columbia University Press, 1932, p. 113.

dren" had been variously defined to refer to the number of children ever born to a marriage, the number of children living in the family, the number of minor children, the number of children affected by the decree, and so on. Moreover, it was discovered that the apparent childlessness of divorcing couples might be largely a function of the duration of marriage to divorce. Both childlessness and divorce are most common early in marriage; hence the relationship between them might be spurious.[21]

We do not know what the relationship between childlessness and divorce was several decades ago. Perhaps child-bearing was more of a deterrent to divorce then than it is now. We do know that the more refined the statistics become, the less of a relationship appears. And we do know that the proportion of divorces granted to couples with minor children in the home has been increasing fairly rapidly.

Both the number of children affected by divorce and the proportion of divorces involving children have been increasing. In 1948, for example, there were an estimated 322,000 children involved in parental divorces. By 1955, the number had climbed to 347,000 and, by 1965, it was 630,000. It should be remembered that these increases were occurring during a period when the number of divorces was relatively stable. This means that both the proportion of couples with children and the number of children per divorce have been rising.

From 1955 to 1965, it is estimated that the proportion of divorces involving children increased from 48 percent to 59.8 percent. The number of children per divorce ranged from one to eight or more (see Figure 17.3), and the percentages varied by region of the country. Sixty-nine percent of divorcing couples in the northeast reported children, compared to only 54 percent in the south.

Thus it seems quite clear that children are no longer—if they ever were—an effective deterrent to divorce. The effects of divorce on children will be dealt with in a later section of this chapter.

DESERTION

By its very nature, desertion is difficult to study. Deserting spouses do not register with the courts or any other official body. To the contrary, they seek to lose themselves in anonymity.

21. Thomas P. Monahan, "Is Childlessness Related to Family Stability?" *American Sociological Review* 20 (Aug. 1955), pp. 446–56.

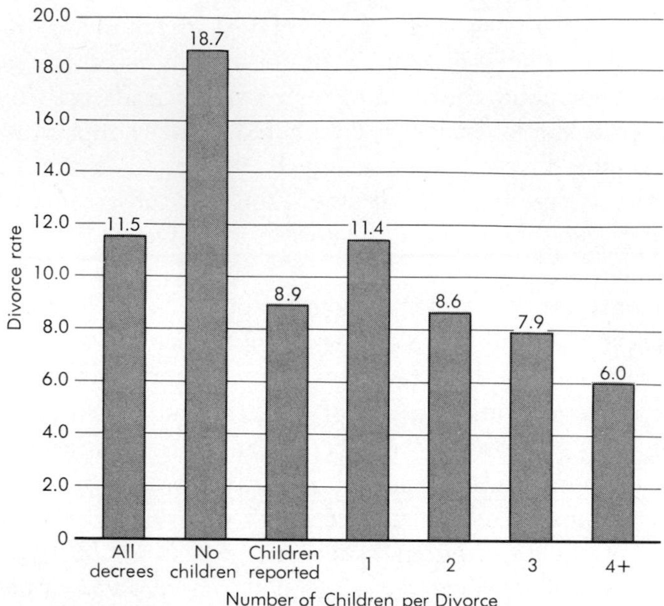

Figure 17.3. Divorce rate by number of children reported—per 1000 couples with a given number of children, the United States, 1960

Source: National Center for Health Statistics, *Children of Divorced Couples: United States, Selected Years* (Washington, D.C.), Series 21, Number 18, Feb. 1970, p. 3.

There is not even any clear definition of desertion. The Bureau of the Census uses the term *marital separations* and defines these as including "couples with legal separations, those living apart with intentions of obtaining a divorce, and other persons permanently or temporarily estranged from their spouse because of marital discord." Kephart estimates that the number of such separated couples runs into the millions, while Monahan estimates that at least three in every hundred married couples are truly separated, and another large group of couples live together in a state of extreme marital discord.

Basically, there are three sources of statistics on desertion in the United States: applications to social agencies for aid to dependent children; applications to courts for the support of wife and children by the husband; and divorce cases where desertion is presented as the legal ground for divorce. Statistics on aid to dependent children show that one and one-half million children may be receiving aid because their fathers are separated from their families.

Kephart and Monahan, working with data from Philadelphia, found that the occupational distribution in desertion cases is similar to that in divorce. Rates are highest in the unskilled and semiskilled occupations and decrease as we move up the occupational ladder. Second, desertion rates are higher among Catholics than among non-Catholics. This may be due to several factors. For one thing, Catholics are disproportionately represented in the occupational groups having the highest desertion and divorce rates. For another, the religious proscription of divorce for Catholics may force more Catholics into desertion as the only available alternative. Third, blacks are overrepresented and whites are underrepresented in desertion cases. This, of course, has roots in history and reflects the differential distribution of blacks and whites in the occupational structure. Finally, there are much more likely to be minor children present in the home in desertion cases than in divorce cases.

We have already indicated that the term "desertion" is used to refer to several different kinds of phenomena. At least three of them merit further discussion here.

One kind of desertion appears to be a lower-class phenomenon, associated with excess child-bearing. This is the kind of desertion that is sometimes referred to as "the poor man's divorce."[22] The deserting party usually is the husband and often the desertion occurs during or just after a pregnancy. The husband, unable to cope with his problems, simply leaves and does not return. This leaves his wife and children destitute and forces them to turn to the courts or to social agencies.

Historically, society has been ill-prepared to cope with this kind of desertion. Either social agencies assumed the support of the family—supporting them at a very inadequate level—or the courts sought to locate the husband and return him under criminal indictment. To bring the husband and father back in this fashion often made things worse. If reconciliation were not already impossible, the bitterness created by this situation often made it so. The husband might literally be put in jail until he made some token gesture toward supporting his family. In the meantime, he could not earn, his family was not better off, and the state was saddled with the expense of keeping him in jail. Soon after he was released from jail, he was likely to disappear again.[23]

The situation began to improve somewhat when the Family Location

22. This phrase is a misnomer. Desertion does not legally end a marriage and neither partner is free to remarry unless a divorce is subsequently obtained.

23. For an analysis of the ineffectiveness of sanctions, see Kenneth W. Eckhardt, "Deviance, Visibility, and Legal Action," *Social Problems* 15 (Spring 1968), pp. 470–77.

Service in New York got together with other groups to sponsor a uniform dependents' support law which has now been adopted in every state and territory.[24] These new laws permit the wife to go into a family court, instead of a criminal court, from which papers are sent to a corresponding court in the state where the deserting husband has been located. The second court then determines how much the husband can and should pay for his family's support, collects the money, and forwards it to the wife through the court in her own state. The husband and wife may also be urged toward reconciliation by referring them to counseling agencies in their own communities.

In 1975, a new federal welfare law required all states to establish programs to trace deserters, estimating that 99 percent of all deserters are men, and that at least half of them are financially able to support their wives and children. Deserted wives are urged to contact their state child-support agency first, and then to turn to the Federal Locator Service if that is unsuccessful. The federal agency uses information from Social Security files to attempt to obtain the absent parent's address, and can then garnishee the parent's wages to meet child support and alimony obligations. The program is too new to evaluate as yet, but it is quite controversial. On the one hand, it promises to reduce welfare rolls appreciably. On the other hand, it is accused of violating civil liberties by using the federal courts and the Internal Revenue Service's tax collection procedures.

If anything, this lower-class pattern of desertion may be becoming less common as living standards increase. A second widespread form of desertion has become more common over the past few decades. This "desertion" is to some degree fictitious and involves the use of desertion as legal grounds for divorce. Couples agree ahead of time to live apart to obtain the legal grounds. In Philadelphia, Kephart reported cases of "desertion" where the husband was simply living in a different apartment or building on the same street. In some one-third of Philadelphia desertion and nonsupport cases, the spouses were still living in the same household. A most striking finding was that, over the past 30 years, the number of new desertion and nonsupport cases in the courts was almost twice the number of divorces granted during that period. It appears likely that many of the nonsupport cases stemmed from the first kind of

24. Thomas P. Monahan, "Family Fugitives," *Marriage and Family Living* 20 (May 1958), pp. 146–51. See also Stan Skarsten, "Family Desertion in Canada," *The Family Coordinator* 23 (Jan. 1974), pp. 19–25.

desertion described above and that many of the desertion cases involved the use of "desertion" as preliminary to divorce.

The most striking development in desertion in the past 15 years is the growing numbers of women who have left their husbands and children. As indicated at the beginning of this chapter, the number of such cases has multiplied several times and now numbers in the thousands. Some of these women were trained for careers before their marriages, and simply decided that they wanted to return to their careers more than they wanted marriage. The largest proportion, however, are women who have devoted themselves to housekeeping and child-rearing, and have come to feel that they have lost their identity as persons. In some cases, they leave obvious clues to their whereabouts in what may be an unconscious effort to force their husbands to notice them, and to spend money seeking their return. In other cases, they disappear very effectively.

THE DIVORCE PROCESS IN THE UNITED STATES

The divorce process may produce as much strife within families as does divorce itself. Divorce law in the United States is state law and there are as many sets of laws as there are jurisdictions—51, including all the states plus the District of Columbia. Divorce law, and all of domestic-relations law, is state law because the United States Constitution does not grant the power to enact such law to the federal government. All powers not specifically granted to the federal government by the Constitution are reserved to the states.

Legal Grounds for Divorce

All states now sanction divorce. Until 1966, New York granted divorce for adultery only, but New York's grounds have been broadened to five: adultery, cruelty, abandonment, imprisonment, and living apart for two years after a formal separation. At the other extreme, Kentucky grants divorce on twenty legal grounds, and over the whole United States as many as forty different grounds are in use.

In spite of the variety of legal grounds available in most states, the overwhelming proportion of divorces have been granted either on grounds of cruelty or desertion. About 52 percent of all U.S. divorces have been granted on grounds of cruelty in some form or other. The laws of some states require that there must be extreme physical cruelty, while other laws specify only mental distress. In practice, the courts tend to interpret the term "cruelty" very loosely, and cruelty is widely used because it is a relatively unobjectionable ground for divorce.

About 23 percent of U.S. divorces have been granted on grounds of desertion, which, we saw in the last section, is often fictitious. Many couples live apart, but with knowledge of one another's whereabouts, in order to have grounds for divorce. Again, desertion is widely used because it is relatively unobjectionable.

The third most widely used legal ground for divorce, non-support, has been used in about 4 percent of all divorces. Adultery has been used in only about 1 percent of all cases.[25] Since adultery is ground for divorce in all states, and since New York previously granted divorce for adultery only, this is surprising. Many more marriages than this are adulterous, of course. And it appears likely that there has been adultery and that it is known in many cases where divorces are granted for cruelty or desertion. The use of adultery as grounds for divorce obviously carries a stigma that most couples try to avoid.

One more point is that there is little apparent relationship between the number of legal grounds for divorce and the number of divorces granted in a state.[26] The number of divorces granted appears more a function of the way in which laws are administered than of the laws themselves. This leads directly into consideration of the adversary system underlying the administration of United States law.

The Adversary System

In order for a divorce to be granted in most states, one spouse must bring charges against the other, which constitute legal grounds for divorce. Moreover, the spouse who brings the charges, the plaintiff, must not himself or herself be guilty of any offense that is ground for divorce. Thus, the law requires a guilty and an innocent party, a situation which seldom if ever obtains in marriage.

In truth, of course, people do not generally seek divorce because one

25. Paul C. Glick and Hugh Carter, *Marriage and Divorce: A Social and Economic Study*, Cambridge, Mass.: Harvard University Press, 1970, pp. 367–68.

26. Alexander Broel-Plateris, "Associations Between Marriage Disruption, Permissiveness of Divorce Laws, and Selected Social Variables," in Ernest W. Burgess and Donald J. Bogue, *eds., Contributions to Urban Sociology*, Chicago: University of Chicago Press, 1964, pp. 512–26.

of them has committed adultery or been cruel to the other; they seek divorce because they can no longer live together. By this time, it is likely that both spouses have treated one another in ways that constitute grounds for divorce and that both partners, if reluctantly, are agreed that a divorce should be sought. Yet, if it should be called to the attention of the judge that both partners have agreed to the divorce, this constitutes collusion and he is legally bound to deny the divorce.

In practice, the legal requirements are winked at. More often than not, the husband and wife agree to seek a divorce, their attorneys work out the terms, present a recommended settlement to the judge, and he accepts it with or without minor modification. Around 85 percent of U.S. divorces are uncontested; the defendant spouse does not appear in court and is assumed to be guilty by default.

The significance of the adversary system—beyond the fact that it involves judge, attorneys, and the couple in a tacit conspiracy to ignore the law—is that in spite of the efforts of all concerned to keep trauma to a minimum and to make the divorce as therapeutic as possible, it generates strife and bitterness. The husband and wife ordinarily have agreed that divorce is necessary but there are likely to be feelings of hurt, rejection, shame, and anger. The attorneys, in turn, are bound by legal ethics to obtain the best possible settlements for their clients. In addition to deciding which partner is to be charged with what offense, and how this is to be proved in court, bargaining must occur over the house, furniture, automobile, and so on. Custody and support arrangements have to be worked out for children, and it must be decided whether the wife is entitled to alimony. Before the negotiations are completed, what started out as an attempt by both partners to reach an equitable solution often has degenerated into bitter conflict. Virtually all authorities agree that much of the vindictiveness which has traditionally been associated with divorce is traceable to the hostilities engendered by the divorce process.

Beginning in 1969, with California, some states began doing something about it. The California legislation eliminated the term "divorce" and substituted "dissolution of marriage" to be granted on grounds of "irreconcilable differences" that have caused the irremediable breakdown of the marriage. The law also provides for the substantially equal division of property, and bases alimony upon the length of the marriage and the earning ability of both spouses.

Between 1969 and 1977, an additional seventeen states passed a single no-fault ground for divorce. Thirty other states, plus Puerto Rico and the District of Columbia, have added a no-fault ground to their existing grounds for divorce.[27]

It is still too early to know in detail how these laws will work, but some trends already are evident. First, and in spite of dire predictions to the contrary, three years' experience with the California law failed to show that it increased divorce rates. The divorce rate in California did increase but it failed to keep pace with the national average. Second, the administration of no-fault laws, so far, is quite uneven. Some judges accept the fact that the marriage is dead when one spouse testifies that he or she will no longer live with the other. Other judges still demand that detailed testimony be presented, in which specific acts that have destroyed the marriage must be recounted.

Another development which is intended to move more states in the direction of no-fault legislation was the promulgation by the National Conference of Commissioners on Uniform State Laws, of the Uniform Marriage and Divorce Act of 1970. This "act" is not a law, but provides a model for state legislatures to use in revising their laws.[28]

Migratory Divorce

People have long sought to get around the strict divorce requirements of their own states by traveling to other states or countries with more lenient laws. Reno, Nevada, has long been famed as a divorce center, as has Juarez, Mexico. Reno's popularity dropped after the passage of the new California law, and Mexico recently went out of the divorce business. Haiti and the Dominican Republic leaped into the breech, however, and the migratory divorce pattern goes on.

The problem (or the solution, if one happens to be seeking a migratory divorce) stems from the fact that divorce laws vary from one state to another and from the fact that the Supreme Court has held that the full faith and credit clause in the Constitution applies to domestic relations as well as to business contracts. This clause, which was designed to prevent people from escaping contractual obligations by moving from

27. Norman N. Robbins, "Have We Found Fault in No Fault Divorce?" *The Family Coordinator* 22 (July 1973), pp. 359–62; and Marie W. Kargman, "There Ought to be a Law! The Revolution in Divorce Law," *The Family Coordinator* 22 (April 1973), pp. 245–48. See also Gerald R. Leslie and Elizabeth McLaughlin Leslie, *Marriage in a Changing World*, New York: Wiley, 1977, p. 302.

28. Marie W. Kargman, *ibid*. For a critical analysis of the act, see Thomas P. Monahan, "National Divorce Legislation: The Problem and Some Suggestions," *The Family Coordinator* 22 (July 1973), pp. 353–57.

one state to another, holds that any legal status that accrues to a person by virtue of residence in one state shall be legally binding in any and all states to which he or she may subsequently move. As applied in this case, it means that people who are legally divorced in Nevada or elsewhere, must have their divorced status recognized by New York, or any other state to which they subsequently move.

Confusion arises when people take up residence in states with short residence requirements for divorce for the specific purpose of securing a divorce under that state's more lenient laws. The traffic between New York, with its stringent divorce laws, and Nevada, with its six weeks' residence requirement, has been widely publicized. Because there are many borderline cases and because no statistics are kept, it is not known exactly how much migratory divorce occurs. Jacobson estimates migratory divorces at somewhere between 3 and 5 percent of the total number of divorces.[29] In addition to Nevada and Idaho, disproportionately large numbers of divorces are granted in Florida; Alabama; Paris, France; and the Virgin Islands.

Most migratory divorces are binding simply because the parties agree to the divorce and no one challenges them. Occasionally, however, one spouse does bring suit in a court in the home state to have the migratory divorce secured by the partner declared invalid. A few cases have reached the Supreme Court, and it has held that courts in one state have the right to review court decisions in other states to determine whether those courts had jurisdiction under their own laws. The attempt obviously is to get away from establishing phony legal residence for purposes of divorce. The question has not yet been completely resolved. Most migratory divorces are binding simply because they go unchallenged. When suit is brought, most cases are resolved in state courts, and there is no unanimity of practice among these; certain migratory divorces may be accepted as binding in some states but not in others. Finally, the Supreme Court has not been consistent in its rulings. As a consequence, there are hundreds of thousands of people who have had migratory divorces whose marital statuses are potentially in legal jeopardy.

THE CONSEQUENCES OF DIVORCE

Most societies define divorce as undesirable, and the United States is no exception. On the one hand, there is the tendency to associate divorce

29. Paul H. Jacobson, *American Marriage and Divorce*, *op. cit.*, p. 109.

with a threat to family stability and to the larger society. On the other hand, divorce is assumed to have grave consequences for men, women, and children. The first part of this concern was dealt with earlier and requires no further treatment here. The second part—the presumed effects upon adults and children—has been extensively researched. We will first present the major findings of this research on the consequences for the marital partners, and then we will examine the alleged effects of divorce upon their children.

Consequences for the Marital Partners

A sensitive analyst of the effects of divorce upon marital partners, Willard Waller, brought to an early classic study the same combination of brilliant insight and lack of methodological rigor that we have witnessed in his studies of dating and marital adjustment. Waller focused upon the emotional aspects of adjustment to divorce and described a series of typical stages that many people go through.

First, he said, comes shock associated with the realization that one is actually being divorced. Although there may be intellectual understanding, separation and divorce frustrate deeply rooted habits quite painfully. What happens may be likened to the experience of an amputee who finds that the amputated limb still hurts. Dozens of times during the day, activities that were routine must be faced consciously and with nostalgia for the comfort and well-being that attended their performance in better days.

This disruption of habits is accompanied by ambivalence toward the partner and oneself. Self-preservation may demand that increased bitterness be felt toward the spouse and that he or she be blamed for the failure of the marriage. At the same time, the former partner may appear in some ways to be more desirable than before; even formerly disliked traits may come to be admired. An analogous ambivalence may be found in attitudes toward oneself. On the one hand, one's every action may be justified and held to demonstrate one's superiority to the former spouse. On the other hand, there may be nagging feelings of failure and a compulsive focusing of attention on what one might have done differently to avoid the beakup.

There is, of course, disruption of established sexual patterns. Some persons react by suppressing or repressing all sexual desire. This may or may not be associated with bitterness, generalized to all of the opposite sex. Many persons after the initial shock of divorce, however, go through a relatively promiscuous experimentation with sex that has overtones of revenge upon the spouse and some degradation of self. Casual affairs may represent some combination of these along with attempts to reassure oneself of one's desirability and sexual adequacy.

Finally, there is need to adjust to the loss of other relationships in addition to that with the former spouse, to make new friends, and to establish a new life. Alienation from the spouse is accompanied by alienation from many friends, some of whom have taken sides and all of whom serve as reminders of the relationship that is now dead. Without a spouse, one also becomes "a fifth wheel" at many social gatherings. Gradually one has to develop new friendships with people who do not know of the former relationship and whose circumstances of life are consistent with one's own.

The adjustment to divorce, according to Waller, is accompanied by much frustration and unhappiness. Gradually, however, the pains ease and new habits are developed. Gradually, new friends are acquired, and one's needs for love and affection are directed toward new partners. Some persons become permanently blocked at some stage in this process, but most eventually form new relationships that replace the old.[30]

In sharp contrast, methodologically, to Waller's analysis is a study, by Goode, of 425 Detroit-area mothers who had been divorced from 2 to 26 months. Goode sought to test hypotheses that (1) divorce is traumatic; (2) most divorcees are neurotic; (3) divorce often is secured for trivial reasons; (4) adequate readjustment following divorce is rare; (5) there are undesirable effects of the divorce upon children.[31]

Goode found that divorce is preceded by a long period of conflict and that the securing of a decree is the final result of a decision process that lasts for an average of about two years. One-third of the respondents reported waiting more than two years from the time they first seriously considered divorce before actually filing suit.

A paradoxical situation emerged in connection with attempts to discover which of the partners first wanted the divorce and which first suggested divorce. More often than not, the husband was the first to desire divorce, but the wife was the first to suggest it. Goode explains it this way. Men, by virtue of their relative dominance in the family, are more likely to come consciously to desire a divorce. This desire and the behaviors that lead to it tend to produce guilt feelings, however. As a

30. Willard Waller, *The Old Love and the New: Divorce and Readjustment*, Carbondale, Ill.: Southern Illinois University Press, 1967 (Originally published in 1930).
31. William J. Goode, *After Divorce, op. cit.*, pp. 15–17.

consequence the husband does not ordinarily press for divorce, but unwittingly assumes behavior that eventually forces his wife to ask for and insist upon divorce. He becomes disinterested and obnoxious. Sixty-two percent of the wives first suggested divorce, in 13 percent of the cases it was a mutual decision, and in 25 percent of the cases the husband first suggested divorce.[32]

This situation may be changing rapidly. A study of Florida divorces, for example, before and after the enactment of a no-fault divorce law, found a complete reversal in filing patterns. Between 1962 and 1971, when the traditional law was in effect, 62 percent of all suits for divorce were filed by women. In 1972 and 1973, however, after the new law was in effect, women filed only 36 percent of the suits while men filed 64 percent. Whatever "chivalry" influenced divorce filing behavior under the old system, may be giving way to the true expression of feeling and intent under the new laws.[33]

The Goode study also yielded data upon the trauma Waller found to be associated with divorce. The respondents were divided into high- and low-trauma groups on the basis of answers to questions concerning impact of the divorce upon sleeping, health, loneliness, work efficiency, memory difficulties, smoking, and drinking. Thirty-seven percent of the respondents showed little increase in symptoms and were classified as low-trauma cases. In about two-thirds of the cases, there was an increase in personal difficulty. Interestingly, the time of greatest difficulty was not at the time of or following the issuance of the divorce decree. The period of greatest trauma was the time of final separation. The divorce decree may announce the end of the marriage to the world at large, but the greatest personal crisis and the effective end to the marriage for the spouses, their kin, and their friends comes at the final separation.

Apparently, most women experienced little or no discrimination against themselves as divorced persons. Only 30 percent reported any discrimination at all, and the percentage declined steadily with the age of the woman.[34] By contrast, 54 percent of the women who had been divorced for 26 months had already remarried, and 50 percent of the re-

32. *Ibid.*, pp. 133–45.

33. B. G. Gunter, "Notes on Divorce Filing as Role Behavior," *Journal of Marriage and the Family* 39 (Feb. 1977), pp. 95–98.

34. William J. Goode, *After Divorce, op. cit.*, pp. 184–88. For a good summary of the literature on one-parent families, see Jane K. Burgess, "The Single-Parent Family: A Social and Sociological Problem," *The Family Coordinator* 19 (April 1970), pp. 137–44; and Benjamin Schlesinger, "The One-Parent Family in Canada: Some Recent Findings and Recommendations," *The Family Coordinator* 22 (July 1973), pp. 305–9.

mainder had steady dates. Over half claimed to have kept their old friends after the divorce, and most of the others had found new friends whom they believed to be equal to or better than their old friends.

Surprisingly, even the financial adjustment failed to bear out the belief that divorce works continuing hardship. In most cases, there was little property to be divided, and the wife got most of it. Where there was a house and furniture, the wife most often got them. The husbands were generally ordered to pay child support, but since their incomes often were low, the payments tended to be low also. About half of the husbands made support payments "always" or "usually," but 40 percent made them "rarely" or "never." As contact between the former spouses dwindled, support payments tended to become less regular.

On the average, the divorced women had almost as much income, from all sources, as their husbands had earned. Moreover, the women's incomes increased with the time since the divorce, most of which increase was associated with remarriage. There was, of course, a large difference in income between women who had remarried and those who had not. When the women's perceptions of their economic situations were considered, however, the differences were smaller. The remarried women judged themselves as better off than during their first marriages and better off than their objective financial situations indicated. Among those who had not been remarried, the tendency was to view their financial situations as worse than objective conditions indicated, but, even here, the financial attractiveness of the marriage continues to fade. More women come to believe that the period while they were separated from their husbands was better than either the time of the marriage or now.

Thus, Goode's analysis supports Waller's at some points and contradicts it at others. He did find that the majority of couples reach the decision to divorce only reluctantly over a long period of time; that for most of them there is considerable trauma involved; that a minority experience some discrimination and may be, for a time, almost without friends; and that there is some economic deprivation. On the other hand, Goode found that most divorcees kept their former friends or made other equally desirable friendships, that most quickly moved back into dating and remarriage, and that their estimates of their financial situations changed accordingly.

If divorce is a mixed blessing, there may also be problems in remaining married. Mathews and Mihanovich, for example, studied 984 Catholic respondents and found that couples who made low marriage-adjustment scores have more problems and more serious problems than those who made higher scores. Neither did they find that problems decrease with length of time married.[35] Landis found that the unhappily married, those who married young, those who are indifferent to religion, and those with more formal education are more likely to resort to divorce.[36]

Finally, Le Masters studied 36 marriages that had chronic conflict for at least ten years. He found personal disorganization in one or both spouses in 75 percent of the cases. Symptoms included alcoholism, psychosomatic illness, neurotic or psychotic behavior, occupational problems, and extramarital affairs. He found no evidence of improvement in the marriages over time, and found that husbands were more likely to suffer personality damage from their marriages than were wives.[37]

Landis has pointed out that another possible effect of divorce is to increase the likelihood of divorce in succeeding generations. He found that if neither set of grandparents is divorced, only 15 percent of their children become divorced. If one set of grandparents is divorced, 24 percent of the next generation is divorced. And, if both sets of grandparents are divorced, the probability of divorce in the next generation rises to 38 percent.[38] At first glance, these figures suggest that divorce within families is highly contagious. However, Peterson has correctly pointed out that these statistics should be regarded with caution until controls for social class are imposed. It may be that the marital failures of succeeding generations are more social class-linked than divorce-linked.[39]

Consequences for Children

There has been great public concern for the presumed effects of divorce upon children. Adults, knowing the trauma of divorce for themselves

35. Vincent D. Mathews and Clement S. Mihanovich, "New Orientations on Marital Maladjustment," *Marriage and Family Living* 25 (Aug. 1963), pp. 300–4.

36. Judson T. Landis, "Social Correlates of Divorce or Nondivorce Among the Unhappy Married," *Marriage and Family Living* 25 (May 1963), pp. 178–79.

37. Ersel E. Le Masters, "Holy Deadlock: A Study of Unsuccessful Marriages," *Midwest Sociologist* 21 (July 1959), pp. 86–91. See also William H. Clements, "Marital Interaction and Marital Stability: A Point of View and a Descriptive Comparison of Stable and Unstable Marriages," *Jounal of Marriage and the Family* 29 (Nov. 1967), pp. 697–702.

38. Judson T. Landis, "The Pattern of Divorce in Three Generations," *Social Forces* 34 (March 1956), pp. 213–16. See also Charles W. Mueller, and Hallowell Pope, "Marital Instability: A Study of Its Transmission Between Generations," *Journal of Marriage and the Family* 39 (Feb. 1977), pp. 83–93.

39. James A. Peterson, "Catastrophes in Partnership: Separation, Divorce, and Widowhood," in Seymour M. Farber, Piero Mustacchi, and Roger H. L. Wilson, *eds., Man and Civilization: The Family's Search for Survival,* New York: McGraw-Hill Book Company, 1965, p. 76.

and their peers, have assumed that children must suffer far more, that they must suffer a loss of emotional and financial security that could not help but make a deep impression upon their lives. Over the years too the number of children caught up in parental divorces has been increasing. The proportion of divorces involving minor children today hovers around 60 percent. Today, over one million children see their parents divorced each year.

Landis confirmed that the trauma experienced by children at the time of parental divorce is widespread. He studied 295 university students of previously divorced parents, finding, initially, that 112 were too young at the time of divorce to remember any trauma. Surprisingly, 19 percent of the remaining respondents had considered their families to be closely united before they learned of the impending divorce, and 24 percent reported no open conflict in the family. In only 22 percent of the cases was there constant open conflict between the parents.

The reactions of children to the divorce depended upon their previous evaluations of the parental marriages and their own security in their families. Over half of the children from openly unhappy homes reacted by thinking that divorce was best for all concerned. Over half of those who had believed their homes to be happy, on the other hand, reported that they were unhappy and upset. Two out of five of this group couldn't believe what was happening. After the divorce, the same split evaluation occurred between children who had thought their homes to be happy and those who knew them to be unhappy: those from apparently happy homes reported either no change in security and happiness, or a change to feeling less secure and less happy; respondents from unhappy homes reported shifts toward greater happiness and security.

Almost half of these youngsters (44 percent) reported that they felt "used" by one or both parents after the divorce. The parents played on their children's sympathy, tried to get information about the other parent, told untrue things about the other parent, and sought to involve the children in continuing quarrels.

Over the long haul, one effect of the divorce was to increase the feelings of closeness of the children to their mothers and to increase the emotional distance between them and their fathers. Undoubtedly this is associated with the mother's having custody. One cost of divorce for fathers, apparently, is loss of closeness with their children regardless of the nature of the situation that precipitates the divorce.

Finally, about one-fifth of the children experienced shame that their parents were divorced, and one out of six felt inferior to other children.

Some 15 percent talked to others as though their parents were not divorced or avoided the subject. One out of ten lied about the whereabouts of the other parent.[40]

Apparently there is foundation for the belief that children suffer trauma from their parents' divorce, just as adults do. So, also, is there reason to think that the trauma is related to the previously perceived quality of the family relationships: where the child has perceived the home to be happy, the trauma is great; where the home has been unhappy, trauma may be less conspicuous than relief that the conflict is over.

Goode's study of divorced mothers provides further data on this matter. He classified the mothers according to the trauma they experienced in connection with the divorce and then related the problems they had with their children to it. As expected, the greater the trauma, the higher the proportion of mothers who admitted that their children had been hard to handle. Eighty-one percent of the mothers admitted to worrying before the divorce about the effects upon the children. However, 55 percent reported no increase in problems afterwards. Eighteen percent said that the children were harder to handle during the separation or immediately following the divorce, 13 percent said they had been at their worst during the marriage itself, and only 14 percent thought that they were harder to handle at the time of interview.[41]

Goode also sought to determine whether the mothers thought their children better off or worse off following the divorce. The evidence, he concluded, indicated that the vast majority of mothers believed them to be better off. Three-fourths of the mothers who had remarried stated that their children were better off, and another 15 percent said that life was about the same. Only 8 percent thought that the children were worse off in the second marriage. Among women who had not remarried, 57 percent put their children in the care of relatives while they worked. Of the mothers who used outside help, 65 percent thought that their children received "excellent" care, 24 percent said that it was "good," 8 percent said it was "average," and only 4 percent acknowledged that it was "poor."

One series of studies has tended to show that broken homes contribute to juvenile delinquency. The Gluecks used matched samples of delinquent and nondelinquent youngsters, and found that 9 percent of the

40. Judson T. Landis, "The Trauma of Children When Parents Divorce," *Marriage and Family Living* 22 (Feb. 1960), pp. 7–13.
41. *Op. cit.*, pp. 317–21.

delinquents but only 6 percent of the nondelinquents had divorced parents. What was more surprising, however, was that homes where one parent had been widowed, or where the parents were separated, contributed even more significantly to the ranks of the delinquent.[42]

Although several studies confirmed the findings of the Gluecks, sociologists have been reluctant to draw firm conclusions about the relationship between divorce and delinquency for at least two reasons. First, both delinquency and divorce are heavily concentrated in lower socioeconomic strata; the apparent relationship between them may be largely spurious, with both stemming from other conditions of lower-class living. Second, there is a strong suggestion that family disorganization, rather than divorce, may be the crucial variable. The findings of the Gluecks regarding the effects of widowhood and separation suggest this. A study by Browning, of delinquent and nondelinquent boys in Los Angeles, led him to the same conclusion. He states that his findings "support the hypothesis that delinquents are as likely to come from disorganized but structurally unbroken homes as they are from broken homes."[43]

These results point to the fact that the negative impact of divorce upon children may be no greater than would be the effect of parents continuing to live together in an unhappy marriage. On the contrary, at least four studies have shown that unhappy, unbroken homes may have more deleterious effects upon children than do broken homes.[44]

SUMMARY

All societies provide for divorce. Divorce rates vary widely among societies, and there is no apparent relationship between divorce rates and other symptoms of societal breakdown. More than half of all preliterate

42. Sheldon Glueck and Eleanor Glueck, *Unraveling Juvenile Delinquency*, New York: The Commonwealth Fund, 1951.
43. Charles J. Browning, "Differential Impact of Family Disorganization Upon Male Adolescents," *Social Problems* 8 (Summer 1960), p. 43. For a careful analysis of such studies, see Karen Wilkinson, "The Broken Family and Juvenile Delinquency: Scientific Explanation or Ideology?" *Social Problems* 21 (June 1974), pp. 726–39.
44. Lee G. Burchinal, "Characteristics of Adolescents from Unbroken, Broken, and Reconstituted Families," *Journal of Marriage and the Family* 26 (Feb. 1964), pp. 44–51; Judson T. Landis, "A Comparison of Children from Divorced and Nondivorced Unhappy Marriages," *Family Life Coordinator* 11 (July 1962), pp. 61–65; Paul H. Landis, *The Broken Home in Teenage Adjustment*, Pullman, Washington: Agricultural Experiment Station Bulletin No. 542, June, 1953; and F. Ivan Nye, "Child Adjustment in Broken and in Unhappy Unbroken Homes," *Marriage and Family Living* 19 (Nov. 1957), pp. 356–61.

societies have higher divorce rates than does the United States, and some large nations have had higher rates also. Our divorce rate has been climbing steadily, however, and now it is the highest of any modern nation.

The long-term trend in divorce in the United States has been upward. The rate of climb has been unevenly affected by wars and depressions. Wars are followed by sharp increases in divorce rates and then by a return to the level of the prewar trend. Depressions depress divorce rates temporarily and then are followed by a rapid rise.

There are, currently, over one million divorces in the United States each year, or about 5.0 per 1000 population. The probability that first marriages currently being contracted will end in divorce is about one in three; the probability is somewhat higher in remarriages. The number of divorces is certain to continue to rise.

Divorced persons are overrepresented in urban areas. This reflects both the greater likelihood of divorce under urban living conditions, and a tendency for divorced persons to migrate to cities. Divorce rates increase from east to west across the country, reflecting differences in attitudes and values, and in the age, ethnic, and religious composition of the population. As blacks have come to rely less on separation, their divorce rates have been rising rapidly and now exceed those of whites. More blacks are found in the lower socio-economic strata, and there is an inverse correlation between economic status and divorce rates.

Studies show more separations during the first year of marriage than any other. The time lag from separation to divorce results in the peak number of divorces occurring from the second to the fourth year of marriage. The mean interval to divorce is longer, and is around seven to eight years. The length of marriage to divorce is longer in first marriages than in remarriages, and longer among blacks than among whites.

Refined statistics indicate less of a relationship between childlessness and divorce than formerly was believed to exist. There may be from one and one-half to two times the probability that a childless marriage will end in divorce, over a marriage with children. Both the number and proportion of divorces involving children have been increasing. The proportion of divorces in which children are involved is about 60 percent. Having children is no longer a very effective deterrent to divorce.

Desertion is an additional form of marital disruption and often is a prelude to divorce. Adequate statistics on desertion do not exist, but figures available suggest that the occupational distribution of desertion cases is similar to that in divorce, Catholics have higher rates than non-Catholics, and blacks have higher rates than whites. One form of desertion is found among lower-class groups and is associated with excess child-bearing. An increasing percentage of desertions may be fictitious, as couples use desertion as legal grounds for divorce. Finally, women deserting their husbands and children constitutes a relatively new problem.

Divorce law in the United States is state law. Legal grounds in the various states range up to 40 in number, with many divorces being granted on grounds of cruelty or desertion. These are widely used because they have little stigma associated with them, and their use tells us little about the actual causes of divorce. Most divorce law is administered through the adversary system, which again conceals the true causes of divorce and which creates bitterness between the spouses.

Since 1969, over half of the states have gone over to no-fault divorce systems, or have added no-fault grounds to their existing grounds. These seem to be reducing the trauma of the divorce process substantially although, as yet, the new laws are very unevenly administered.

Migratory divorces apparently number from 3 to 5 percent of all divorces. Although such divorces frequently involve the open flouting of state laws, most of them are valid because they go unchallenged. Some court decisions, however, have held that obviously migratory divorces are invalid, and the whole situation is in need of clarification.

The effects of divorce upon the marital partners include some trauma at the time and afterwards. There is a painful severing of former habits, ambivalence toward the partner and oneself, feelings of failure, interference with sexual patterns, and the need to form new relationships. Divorce seldom appears to be secured on frivolous grounds, and a long time generally elapses from the first serious consideration of divorce to the actual issuing of a decree. The evidence suggests that husbands more often than not desire the divorce first, but that they maneuver their wives into being the ones to ask for it. That situation may be changing. Studies of divorced women show that most do not feel discriminated against, most keep their former friends, most make an adequate financial adjustment, and most remarry.

Studies of unhappy couples who do not seek divorce indicate that their problems do not lessen with time, and that the partners suffer some personality damage. Statistics showing that divorce perpetuates itself in succeeding generations of the same families should be used with caution because of the possible contaminating influence of social class.

Divorce often produces trauma in children also. The effects are pronounced where the children have believed their parents' marriages to be happy. Following divorce, children tend to become closer emotionally to their mothers, who usually have custody, and to become more distant emotionally from their fathers. Where the parental home has been obviously unhappy, the children often experience relief when the divorce is final. Most mothers worry about the effects of divorce upon their children, but most experience no increase in problems after the divorce. Mothers who remarry generally believe their children to be better off in the second marriage, and those who have not remarried generally are satisfied with their child-care arrangements.

Studies have shown that broken homes and juvenile delinquency are associated. However, the correlation appears to be with all forms of broken homes, including those that are emotionally broken but structurally intact, and not just with divorce-broken homes. Predictions of dire effects of divorce upon children appear not to be warranted.

SUGGESTED READINGS

Bradway, John S., *ed.*, "Progress in Family Law," special issue of *The Annals of the American Academy of Political and Social Science* (May 1969). Contains articles on divorce, desertion, annulment, alimony, and the family court. An excellent reference source.

Epstein, Joseph, *Divorced in America: Marriage in an Age of Possibility*, New York: Dutton, 1974. A personal account, by an insightful man, of the social and personal factors leading up to his own divorce from a marriage of ten years. An unglamorized portrayal.

Rheinstein, Max, *Marriage Stability, Divorce, and the Law*, Chicago: University of Chicago Press, 1972. Analyzes the workings of a judicial system handicapped by obsolete divorce laws. Systematic use of intercultural data.

Weiss, Robert S., *Marital Separation*, New York: Basic Books, 1975. A personalized treatment of the processes by which marriages break down. Contains suggestions for easing the pain.

Wheeler, Michael, *No-Fault Divorce*, Boston: Beacon, 1974. An essentially journalistic account of the emergence of the no-fault divorce movement.

FILMS

Marriage Under Stress: The Causes of Divorce (*Time-Life* Films, 43 West 16th Street, New York, N.Y. 10011), 40 minutes. Shows the pressures that force couples apart. Discusses what happens when a marriage finally is over, including the chances of and problems in remarriage.

Mothers After Divorce (Polymorph Films, 331 Newberry Street, Boston, Mass. 02115), 20 minutes, color. Four suburban women with high-school-age children discuss their lives before and after divorce. They touch upon loneliness, careers, and child-rearing concerns.

Not Together Now: End of a Marriage (Polymorph Films, 331 Newberry Street, Boston, Mass. 02115), 25 minutes, color. Why a couple married and why they separated. Their lives and goals now that they are apart.

QUESTIONS AND PROJECTS

1. What is the relationship between the divorce rate in a society and the stability of the society?
2. How does the divorce rate in the United States compare to the divorce rates of preliterate societies? Of modern societies?
3. Describe the long-term trend in American divorce rates. Describe the influence of wars and depressions. What is the current divorce rate?
4. Analyze variations in divorce rates by rural-urban residence, region, race, socio-economic status, length of time married, and parental status. Try to account for the variations.
5. What patterns does desertion take in the United States? What does understanding of it contribute to our knowledge of family disruption?
6. What is meant by the adversary system in divorce? How does it complicate divorce for the persons involved? What is the relationship between causes of divorce and legal grounds for divorce?
7. What is no-fault divorce? How widespread is it? How does it differ from traditional divorce?
8. Analyze the impact of divorce upon the emotions, habits, and self-concepts of the marital partners.
9. What does research show about the way people decide to secure a divorce? What does it show about adjustment following divorce? What is the situation of unhappily married couples who avoid divorce?
10. What factor is related to the trauma children experience over their parents' divorces? What does research show about the problems of children following divorce?
11. What appear to be the relative effects of happy homes, unhappy unbroken homes, and broken homes upon children?
12. Arrange a visit to a local court where divorce cases are being heard. If possible, have the judge talk with the group about how he or she views the divorce cases moving through the court. Is he or she in sympathy with present legal procedures? What changes would he or she favor?

18
One-Parent Families and Remarriages

. . . In 1970 about one out of every eight children in the United States was a stepchild. Yet, nobody really knows what makes a good stepparent. There is only one rule most stepparents say they are conscious of: Do not be cruel and justify the wicked stepparent myth. But that is hardly enough to guide anybody through the hurly-burly of family life.

. . . Child psychiatrists [say] that there are some solid reasons why a stepparent may find it hard to love a stepchild. For example:

–The stepchild is a constant reminder of the parent's sexual intercourse with someone else (and may look and act like the absent partner as well).
–There is no legal bond between stepparent and stepchild. The stepparent has no parental rights and certainly no right of custody of a stepchild if the parent linking them dies or there is a divorce. . . .
–The lack of any clear incest taboo between stepparent and stepchild can make for uneasiness where a mother and her second husband live in close quarters with her sexy daughter (remember "Lolita"?), or a new wife is put into intimate proximity with her husband's grown son (as in "Desire Under the Elms"). . . .

An additionl source of strain . . . is money. Stepmothers . . . compete with their stepchildren for the father's income and inheritance as well as his love. . . . What is more, any group of half brothers and half sisters will have grandparents who belong to some and not others. This can mean that some children in a household can expect to be richer than others–a situation not always conducive to family harmony. . . .[1]

1. Brenda Maddox, "Neither Witch nor Good Fairy" *The New York Times Magazine*, Aug. 8, 1976, pp. 16, 18, 19. © The New York Times Company. Reprinted by permission.

This excerpt was taken from an article written by a woman about her own experiences with stepparenthood. It highlights some of the problems in some remarriages, although the total article from which the quotation was taken leaves one with the feeling that the author had coped well with her problems and probably had a pretty good marriage.

So little research on the quality of remarriages has been done as yet that we cannot compare their virtues and problems fully. A news release, early in 1977, presented a fairly positive picture:

> Stepfathers are as effective as natural fathers in their roles as parents, and the stepchildren are as happy as children who reside with their natural fathers, according to a study of "Stepfathers and the Mental Health of Their Children" made by a research team . . . at Western Behavioral Sciences Institute. . . .
>
> . . . children brought up in a home with a stepfather . . . also were found to be just as successful and as "achieving." The children in the study reported getting along well with their stepfathers, and the mothers agreed. . . .[2]

Remarriages, like first marriages, vary widely. Some are of young persons, although many are older. Some have children at the time of marriage, and some do not. Their strengths and their problems vary accordingly. Most people do not remarry immediately upon divorce or death of the spouse. Commonly, there is a period of living alone or of living with one's children but without a spouse.

CHANGING HOUSEHOLD PATTERNS

One of the most striking changes in living arrangements in the United States over the past two decades involves the increase in the number of households occupied by other than intact nuclear families. Some of this increase is of young adults who have not yet been married. Some of it involves the divorced and the widowed.

Delay in the Time of Marriage

During the first six decades of the twentieth century, the average age at marriage dropped for both men and women. In 1900, men averaged about 26 years of age when they first married, and women averaged about 22. By 1960, the median ages at first marriage had dropped to

2. *News Feature Service,* Alcohol, Drug Abuse, and Mental Health Administration, n.d.

22.8 for men and 20.3 for women. Then, during the 1960s and 1970s they began to climb. In 1976, the figures were 23.8 for men and 21.3 for women.

This upturn in the average ages at first marriage is reflected in larger proportions of young adults who are single. In 1960, for example, 28 percent of women aged 20 to 24 were still single; by 1974 the percentage had climbed to 40.[3] There was a comparable increase in the proportion of young single men. Several factors, one ideological and others demographic, helped account for this increase in singlehood.

A principal demographic factor was the increase in the proportion of young women attending college. From 1.2 million women in college in 1960, the figure jumped to 3.5 million in 1972. A second demographic factor was the so-called "marriage squeeze." This phenomenon arose from the fact that women tend to marry men who are two or three years older than themselves. The high birth rates of the post-World War II era created a temporary situation in which there was an excess of young women at the most marriageable ages. Still another factor was the increase in occupational opportunities for young women.

The chief ideological factor was the search for alternative life styles that grew out of the countercultural movement of the late 1960s and early 1970s. Many more young men and women elected to live together without marriage. The number of men under 25 years of age, for example, who reported that they shared their households with an unrelated female partner was 50 times greater in 1970 than in 1960. The number of women under 25 who reported sharing their households with an unrelated male increased 16.5 times during the same period. The actual numbers involved were fairly small: just over 22,000 male heads of household and almost 8000 female heads of household.[4] A U.S. census release in 1977, however, reported 1,320,000 unmarried persons living together in 1976.[5]

No one knows, yet, whether unmarried living together is likely to become permanent for a significant number of couples, or whether most of these people will eventually marry their current partners or someone else. Temporarily, at least, unmarried living together has helped to in-

3. Paul C. Glick, "A Demographer Looks at American Families," *Journal of Marriage and the Family* 37 (Feb. 1975), p. 17.

4. Paul C. Glick, "Living Arrangements of Children and Young Adults," *Journal of Comparative Family Studies* 7 (Summer 1976), pp. 321–33. See also Frances E. Kobrin, "The Primary Individual and the Family: Changes in Living Arrangements in the United States Since 1940," *Journal of Marriage and the Family* 38 (May 1976), pp. 233–39.

5. United Press International, Feb. 9, 1977.

crease the number and proportion of non-nuclear family households. A far greater increase in such households, however, has been created by the rapidly rising number of divorces.

ONE-PARENT FAMILIES

Families may be broken either through divorce or death. Widowhood will be analyzed in the next chapter, and we will concentrate upon divorce-broken families here.

Figure 18.1 shows the number of husband-wife, intact nuclear families and the numbers of female-headed and male-headed families in the United States. Intact nuclear families are by far the majority, 85 percent, but the number and proportion of one-parent families, particularly female-headed families has been increasing rapidly. Female-headed families constitute 12 percent of all families, while male-headed families make up only slightly under 3 percent. These figures are for all families, including both those with children in the home and those without.

The living circumstances of children are shown in Figure 18.2. The percentage of children under 18 years of age living with both parents is only 81 percent, while the percentage living in mother-headed families is 14 percent. Only slightly over 1 percent of children live in father-headed families. The remaining 3 percent, or so, either live with other relatives, non-relatives, or in institutions.

Two women economists who have studied mother-headed families in the United States emphasize the transitional nature of this phenomenon.

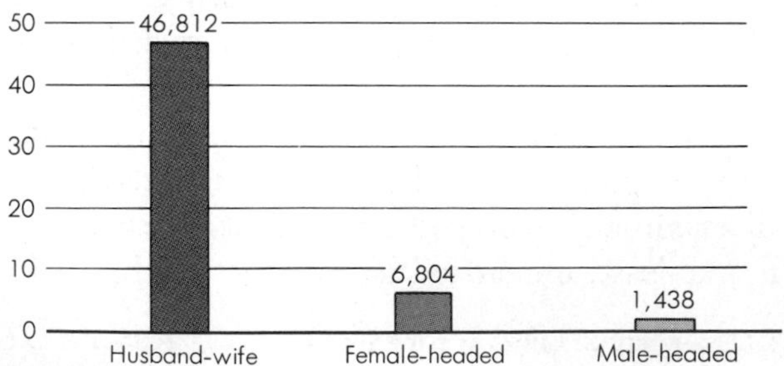

Figure 18.1. Husband-wife families, female-headed families, and male-headed families, 1974 (numbers in thousands)

Source: U.S. Bureau of the Census, "Household and Family Characteristics: March 1974," Series P-20, No. 276, *Current Population Reports,* Washington, D.C.

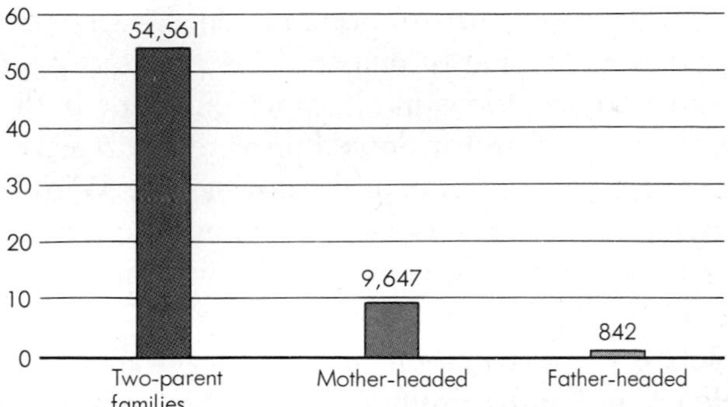

Figure 18.2. Number of children (in thousands) living in intact nuclear families, mother-headed families, and father-headed families, 1974

Source: U.S. Bureau of the Census, "Marital Status and Living Arrangements: March 1974," Series P-20, No. 271, *Current Population Reports,* Washington, D.C.

It is transitional in two ways. First the larger society is in transition in that, over the past decade, female-headed families with children have increased in numbers almost ten times as rapidly as have two-parent families. Second, it is transitional in the sense that living in female-headed families is usually temporary; it is a transitional stage between divorce (or widowhood) and remarriage.[6]

REMARRIAGES

There are many different kinds of remarriages. Some remarried couples are 20 years old, some are 40, and some are 60. In some cases, there are no children. In some cases, one partner brings children from the prior marriage, and in some both do. In addition, there may be children on one or both sides who live with the former spouse. The children may range from infancy to middle-aged adulthood and, eventually, there may be "your children," "my children," and "our children."

Types of Remarriages

The various types of remarriages that can be achieved through the use of previous marital status, presence or absence and age of children, age,

6. Heather L. Ross and Isabel V. Sawhill, *Time of Transition: The Growth of Families Headed by Women,* Washington, D.C.: The Urban Institute, 1975. See also Benjamin Schlesinger, "One Parent Families in Great Britain," *The Family Coordinator* 26 (April 1977), pp. 139–42.

and so on, are too complicated for full presentation. Either the bride or the groom may be single, previously divorced, or previously widowed, making eight possible combinations in all. Since either or both spouses may have been both divorced and widowed prior to the remarriage, the number of possible combinations is considerably larger. With so many combinations deriving from previous marital status alone, it is easy to see that dozens of variations would emerge if we were to add such elemental variables as children, age, economic status, and religion.

Two studies plotted the distribution of remarriages among the eight types for a Seattle group,[7] and a group of 2009 cases in a hypothetical community called Utopolis.[8] The highest percentages consistently involve at least one partner who was divorced previously. The largest number of cases was of the "single man–divorced woman" type. Almost equally numerous were marriages involving two previously divorced persons. "Divorced man–single woman" marriages came next, with no other type approaching these top three. At the other extreme, the lowest percentages involved persons who were previously widowed.

The Trend in Remarriages

Before 1900, the incidence of remarriage in the United States was low. About nine-tenths of all marriages were first marriages, and most remarriages involved widowed persons. As the divorce rate began to climb, the remarriage rate began to rise. More of the growing percentage of remarriage occurred among previously divorced persons.

Most of the change took place after World War I. In 1917, for example, 87.4 percent of all grooms entered marriage for the first time, 8 percent were widowed, and 4.5 percent were divorced. By 1960, only 77 percent of brides and grooms were entering marriage for the first time, about 6 percent were marrying after having been widowed, and between 16 and 17 percent were remarrying following divorce.[9]

The increasing remarriage following divorce is easy to understand,

7. Charles E. Bowerman, "Assortative Mating by Previous Marital Status, Seattle, 1939–1946," *American Sociological Review* 18 (April 1953), p. 171.
8. Jessie Bernard, *Remarriage: A Study of Marriage*, New York: Dryden Press, 1956.
9. Hugh Carter and Paul C. Glick, *Marriage and Divorce: A Social and Economic Study*, Cambridge, Mass.: Harvard University Press, 1970, pp. 82–83. For Canadian data, see Benjamin Schlesinger and Alex Macrae, "Remarriages in Canada: Statistical Trends," *Journal of Marriage and the Family* 32 (May 1970), pp. 300–303; and Paul Kuzel and P. Krishnan, "Changing Patterns of Remarriage in Canada, 1961–1966," *Journal of Comparative Family Studies* 4 (Autumn 1973), pp. 217–24.

but, at first glance, the declining proportion of remarriage among the widowed appears surprising. It does not, however, reflect a lesser tendency of the widowed to remarry, but a combination of the greater number of divorced people and the changing age composition of the widowed population. Increased longevity, particularly among males, tends to postpone widowhood to the older ages when remarriage is less likely.

The Incidence of Remarriage

There are two ways of stating remarriage rates, just as, in Chapter 13, we pointed out two ways of calculating mixed marriage rates. We may figure a remarriage rate for couples or a remarriage rate for persons.

Using data supplied by Glick, Bernard has stated the remarriage rate for couples as follows. Out of every 100 married couples, almost one-fifth involve remarriage for one or both partners. In 7 couples out of 100, both partners have been married before. In an additional 11 couples, one of the spouses has been married before. In all, 18 marriages out of 100 involve at least one remarried person.[10]

The incidence of remarriage among individuals is figured by taking the total number of remarried people in the 100 marriages–14 people in the 7 marriages where both partners are remarried, and 11 people who are remarried to formerly single persons–and calculating the percentage that the 25 remarried are of the total 200 people in the 100 marriages. This gives a remarriage rate of 12.5 percent for individuals. It should be kept in mind that remarriage rates figured on the basis of existing marriages understates the frequency of remarriage at the present time and the likelihood of remarriage in the future. It is estimated that between 20 and 25 percent of all persons marrying recently have been entering marriage for the second or subsequent time.

Race and Remarriage

At least two factors lead us to expect higher remarriage rates among blacks than among whites. First is the higher divorce rate among blacks; and second is the higher black death rate. Both factors should increase the proportion of blacks eligible for remarriage.

The expectation is borne out. According to the 1967 Survey of Eco-

10. Jessie Bernard, *op. cit.*, p. 45.

nomic Opportunity, approximately 30 percent of blacks had been married twice, compared with 17 percent of whites. Four percent of blacks, but only 2 percent of whites had been married three or more times.[11] As long as there are differences between the marital dissolution rate and death rate of blacks and whites, these differences will continue.

Age at Remarriage

Carter and Glick have presented statistics on age at remarriage. The median ages were 36.4 for men remarrying after divorce and 57.9 for widowers. Women averaged 34.7 years at remarriage following divorce, and widows averaged 53.2 years at remarriage.[12] Obviously, the remarrying population is considerably older than those who are marrying for the first time.

That remarriage generally involves older persons was confirmed by Bernard's study of 2009 remarriages in Utopolis. She found that the average age of divorced men at remarriage was 36.8 years and the average for women was 33.7 years.[13] Similar findings appear when the remarriages of widowed persons are considered, with the ages at remarriage being slightly older than in the case of divorced persons. Bernard's study showed widowed men to be an average of 45.4 years old and widowed women to be an average of 41.0 years old at remarriage.

Most remarriages involve men and women in their middle years. Although there are people remarrying at 20 and 25 years of age, most remarriages occur among people in their thirties and forties. We should at least entertain the hypothesis that the factors that lead them into remarriage are different from those motivating first marriages.

The Joint Effects of Age and Previous Marital Status

The remarriages of persons up to 35 years of age overwhelmingly occur following divorce. After 35, the proportion of remarriages involving widowed persons climbs rapidly, until beyond age 55 the number of such remarriages is far greater than the number following divorce. Of the total persons remarrying in 1959, about three-fourths had been divorced and one-fourth had been widowed. A slightly higher percent-

11. Paul C. Glick and Arthur J. Norton, "Frequency, Duration, and Probability of Marriage and Divorce," *Journal of Marriage and the Family* 33 (May 1971), p. 309.
12. Carter and Glick, *op. cit.*, p. 84.
13. Jessie Bernard, *op. cit.*, p. 11.

age of the men had been divorced and a slightly higher percentage of the women had been widowed.

Probabilities of Marriage and Remarriage

What may come as a surprise is that, at any age, persons who have been married before have higher probabilities of remarrying than single persons have of getting married for the first time! During the age period 20–24 the likelihood that a divorced woman will remarry is more than twice as great as the chance that a single woman will marry. At older ages, the differences gradually increase in favor of the previously divorced women. Sufficient cases to compare widows become available during the age period, 25–29. At that age, and for each succeeding age, widows are more likely to remarry than single women are likely to marry originally, but are less likely to remarry than divorcées are. The ages at which adequate cases for divorced and widowed men become available are slightly older than among women, but the same pattern is found. Divorced men have a greater probability of remarrying than do widowed men, and, age by age, single men have the lowest probabilities of all of marrying.

We cannot be certain of the reason for the greater probability of remarriage than of first marriage, but the following appears plausible. A developmental task facing people in adolescence and early adulthood is the necessity to establish relationships with the opposite sex that will, in time, lead to the emotional and physical intimacy that precede marriage. Divorced persons, even though their first marriages fail, have at least demonstrated ability to form relationships of some intimacy. Widowed persons have done this without the imputation of failure in the first marriage. Single persons, while they may be defined as being morally superior to and better adjusted than divorced persons, may not have achieved a heterosexual orientation adequate to eventuate in marriage. Moreover, with each increase in age beyond the early twenties, the chances that such an orientation ever will be achieved diminishes rapidly.

Divorced men have greater probabilities of remarrying, at every age level, than divorced women do. One study showed that more than 1 divorced man out of 3 in his early thirties remarried, while less than 1 woman out of 5 did so. Between the ages of 45 and 54, 1 divorced man out of 10 remarried, but only 1 woman out of 20 did so. Bernard has calculated the total remarriage rates of divorced men and women and comes up with the following probabilities. "Of 100 grooms in the 45–49 age bracket, 10 will remarry: of 100 brides in this age group, only 3–4 in 100 will remarry. The remarriage rate for men past 55 is five times that for women the same age."[14]

The explanations for this disparity are several. During the middle years, men need wives to help care for their homes and children. Where the situation is reversed and the women have the children, however, the opposite situation prevails; men are reluctant to assume the burden of women's children. Moreover, middle-aged women have to compete with the physical attractiveness of younger women. As we move into the older ages, the differential longevity of men and women begins to increase in effect. There develops a shortage of eligible men.

Statistics for Massachusetts and Iowa indicate that the traditional difference in remarriage rates for men and women is lessening.[15] If so, it may reflect two things. First, the trend toward smaller families may be lessening the deterrent effect of children upon the remarriage of women. Second, the trend toward equality between the sexes may be increasing the acceptability of those women as marital partners.

Interval to Remarriage

The interval between the ending of the first marriage and remarriage depends upon how the first marriage is terminated. The intervals for both divorced and widowed persons tend to be relatively short, but are considerably shorter in the case of divorce.

Jacobson reports that one-third of the women who remarry following divorce do so within one year. Almost half remarry within two years, and approximately two-thirds remarry within five years. He estimates slightly longer intervals for men, but that three-fifths of the men who remarry after divorce do so within five years.[16] Slightly shorter intervals are implied in Glick's findings, from survey data and from data collected by the National Office of Vital Statistics, that three-fourths of all divorced persons remarry within five years.[17]

Bernard's analysis of 849 divorced women and 809 divorced men in

14. *Ibid.*, p. 55. See also Alan Booth and Elaine Hess, "Cross-Sex Friendships," *Journal of Marriage and the Family* 36 (Feb. 1974), pp. 38–47.
15. Thomas P. Monahan, "One Hundred Years of Marriages in Massachusetts," *American Journal of Sociology* 56 (May 1951), pp. 538 39.
16. Paul H. Jacobson, *American Marriage and Divorce*, New York: Rinehart and Company, 1959, pp. 69–70.
17. "A Demographer Looks at American Families," *op. cit.*, p. 17.

Utopolis showed that the average intervals between first and second marriages were 4.6 years and 2.5 years, respectively. She also quotes, with approval, Landis's statement that "the large proportion of divorced persons who remarry so quickly makes one suspect that students of the family . . . have discounted too heavily the notion of the man on the street that most divorces take place so that one or both parties may be free to marry a person already selected."[18]

The interval from widowhood to remarriage varies both by sex and age. Widowers remarry sooner than widows, and the disparity increases with age. In Bernard's 2009 remarriages, the average interval was 3.4 years for 543 widowers and 6.2 years for 445 widows.

Courtship and Wedding Behavior in Remarriages

Hollingshead studied 900 couples, 715 of whom were being married for the first time and 185 of whom had at least one partner remarrying. The courtship pattern was determined, more than anything else, by whether the woman had been married before. Women who had been married before had courtships, before engagement, of about one year's duration. Where the woman had not been married before, the pre-engagement courtship lasted an average of almost a year and a half, irrespective of whether the man had been married before. Similarly, women who were remarrying were less likely to have a formal engagement, were less likely to receive an engagement ring, and, if engaged, were likely to be engaged for a shorter time.

Wedding behavior also varied more according to whether the bride was remarrying than according to whether the groom was remarrying. Only about 5 percent of remarrying brides had formal weddings, and only 20–25 percent had church weddings. Four-fifths of the first weddings were church weddings, and 45 percent of those where a previously married man was marrying a single woman were church weddings. In addition, there were fewer wedding guests and the wife's family was much less likely to pay for the wedding, if she were remarrying.[19]

18. Paul H. Landis, "Sequential Marriage," *Journal of Home Economics* (Oct. 1950), p. 626; as quoted in Jessie Bernard, *op. cit.*, p. 66.

19. August B. Hollingshead, "Marital Status and Wedding Behavior," *Marriage and Family Living* 14 (Nov. 1952), p. 310. See also Ersel E. Le Masters, "The Courtship of Older Persons," *The Midwest Sociologist* 20 (Dec. 1957).

THE SUCCESS OF REMARRIAGES

It is very difficult to estimate the success of remarriages. What criteria are we to use? Divorce rates? Duration of marriage to divorce? Marital-happiness estimates? Marital-adjustment scores? Achievement in other areas of life? There is no agreement on what good remarriages are, any more than there is agreement on what good first marriages are. In general, the data on success in remarriage are even scantier than those available for first marriages.

Divorce from Remarriage

An early study by Monahan, using data for Iowa for the years 1953–1955, reported divorce rates from second marriages to be twice as high as those from first marriages. Where one of the partners had been divorced twice before, the rate of divorce from the third marriage was higher yet.[20] This led to the conclusion that marital adjustment involves a rigorous selection process and that failure to make the necessary adjustments lessens the probability that they will be made in a second marriage. Failure a second time further lessens the probability of permanence in a third marriage, and so on. Monahan also found that the duration to divorce is shorter in second marriages than in first marriages, and is shorter yet in third marriages.[21]

The early Iowa data did not show the same high divorce rates for those who remarried following widowhood. In fact, divorce rates among the previously widowed were even lower than those from first marriages. Two possibilities were suggested. First, widowed persons often are reasonably well adjusted people whose prior experience with marriage was not too bad. While there are malcontents and bitterly unhappy people among the widowed, they are fewer than in the general population. Such persons may approach remarriage with values, attitudes, and skills that predispose them to satisfaction in their new relationships. Second, the divorce rate from remarriages of previously widowed persons must also reflect the older ages of such persons. Even remarried couples

20. Thomas P. Monahan, "The Changing Nature and Instability of Remarriages," *Eugenics Quarterly* 5 (June 1958), pp. 73–85.
21. Thomas P. Monahan, "The Duration of Marriage to Divorce: Second Marriages and Migratory Types," *Marriage and Family Living* 21 (May 1959), pp. 134–38. Remarriages also are more likely to be interreligious marriages. See Erich Rosenthal, "Divorce and Religious Intermarriage: The Effect of Previous Marital Status Upon Subsequent Marital Behavior," *Journal of Marriage and the Family* 32 (Aug. 1970), pp. 435–40.

who are unhappy are not so likely to seek divorce as younger persons would be.

Monahan's data on high divorce rates among the previously divorced were first seriously challenged by a national survey in 1967, which showed that the probability of divorce from all remarriages was quite low. Although these rates did not distinguish remarriages following widowhood from those following divorce, the small proportion of remarriages following widowhood is believed not to have affected the rates very much. In any event, divorce probabilities from all remarriages were lower than those from first marriages. Glick reasons that remarrying persons are more mature than when they married the first time, they may have exercised better judgment in the selection of the second partner, and they may make more effort in their second marriages.[22]

Adjustment in Remarriages

Three major studies have provided data on the quality of remarriages. Locke, in predicting adjustment by comparing happily married with divorced persons, secured data on 21 happily married persons who had remarried following widowhood and upon 146 divorced persons who had remarried. He tested the hypothesis that bereaved and divorced persons are less well adjusted in their second marriages than once-married are in their first marriages.[23] He reasoned that widowed persons in remarriages would idealize their former mates and find that their present mates suffered by comparison. The data, however, did not support this reasoning. Locke was forced to conclude that remarriages after widowhood are as happy as first marriages. He explained this finding as follows. Widowed and then remarried persons probably are highly adaptable or they would not have entered their second marriages; if they are more adaptable, then they should adjust to their second marriages in spite of idealization of the deceased spouse.

Turning to the marital adjustments of the 146 persons remarried following divorce, Locke found that approximately 45 percent rated their second marriages to be "very happy," and another 32 percent said they were "happy." A summary of his findings, along with comparable data from the Burgess and Cottrell and Terman studies of first marriages, is

22. Paul C. Glick and Arthur J. Norton, "Frequency, Duration, and Probability of Marriage and Divorce," *op. cit.*, pp. 314–15.
23. Harvey J. Locke, *Predicting Adjustment in Marriage: A Comparison of a Divorced and a Happily Married Group*, New York: Henry Holt and Company, 1951, pp. 298–309.

shown in Table 18.1. The 76.7 percent of the remarriages that were reported to be either very happy or happy is actually higher than Burgess and Cottrell found among Illinois couples, and nearly as high as Terman reported for California couples. The pattern is similar when the average and unhappy categories are considered. Locke concluded that divorced persons are fairly good risks for subsequent marriages.

Table 18.1. Marital happiness ratings in first marriages and remarriages

Happiness ratings	*526 Illinois first marriages*	*792 California first marriages*		*146 Remarriages*
		Husbands	*Wives*	
Very happy or happy	63.1%	82.5%	85.2%	76.7%
Average	14.4	12.9	9.2	12.3
Unhappy or very unhappy	21.5	4.6	5.6	11.0
Totals	99.0	100.0	100.0	100.0

Source: Ernest W. Burgess and Leonard S. Cottrell, Jr., *Predicting Success or Failure in Marriage,* New York: Prentice-Hall, 1939, p. 32; Lewis M. Terman, *Psychological Factors in Marital Happiness,* New York: McGraw-Hill Book Company, 1938, p. 78; and Harvey J. Locke, *Predicting Adjustment in Marriage: A Comparison of a Divorced and a Happily Married Group,* New York: Henry Holt and Company, 1951, p. 302.

Locke and Klausner also reported a smaller study comparing 47 divorced and remarried persons with 64 once-married persons in Los Angeles. They found that almost equal proportions of the remarried and once-married groups fell into "good" and "fair" marital-adjustment categories.[24] Interestingly, remarried men made lower adjustment scores than remarried women, contradicting Landis's assertion that women are poorer risks for remarriage than men are. Both of these comparisons were based upon fragmentary data, and research has yet to demonstrate whether men or women make better adjustment in remarriages.

The study by Goode of 425 Detroit mothers also yielded data on the quality of remarriages, in relation to the perceived quality of these same women's first marriages. Goode points out that his data on adjustment in remarriage are not definitive because none of these women had been remarried for longer than two years. He also emphasized that the most relevant comparison for previously divorced persons is not between the

24. Harvey J. Locke and William J. Klausner, "Marital Adjustment of Divorced Persons in Subsequent Marriages," *Sociology and Social Research* 33 (Nov. 1948), pp. 97–101.

quality of their remarriages and the quality of all first marriages but between their own first and second marriages.

A full 87 percent of the women in Goode's sample, who had remarried, claimed that their second marriages were "much better" than their first ones, and an additional 8 percent said that their second marriages were "a little better."[25] The high value placed upon their remarriages also was shown when they replied to the question, "Would you try to tell me how you think your life would be today, in general, if you hadn't got a divorce?" Eighty-two percent said that things would have been "worse" or "the same" as during the first marriage.

Finally, Bernard analyzed remarriages thoroughly in connection with her study of the entire remarried population in Utopolis. First of all, she points out that divorce is a learned pattern, and persons who have overcome the societal taboo and been through the experience once may be more likely to use divorce again if their remarriages do not measure up to high standards. According to this point of view, remarried persons may demand more from their new marriages and may more quickly dissolve them if their high expectations are not fulfilled. Thus, remarriages that survive may be relatively more satisfying than most first marriages.[26]

Many analyses of divorce and remarriage have emphasized the stability of basic personality characteristics and the apparent contribution of personality problems to divorce. When we talk about "the divorce-prone" this is what we mean. On the other hand, even if basic personality does not change—and this assumption is being more frequently questioned—the way in which personality is expressed in behavior certainly does change over time. Bernard analyzed three factors which may conduce to greater success in remarriages.

First, an unhappy first marriage may be painful, but contributes directly to the success of the second one. People learn, through divorce, something about what produced the failure of their marriages. At the simplest level, there are skills such as those involved in housekeeping and in earning a living. By the time of her second marriage, the wife is likely to be proficient at everything from cooking to budgeting. Similarly, her husband is likely to have achieved a stable occupational adjustment to which both he and the new wife are accommodated. Remarried persons are also likely to have increased their competence in interpersonal rela-

25. William J. Goode, *After Divorce*, Glencoe, Illinois: The Free Press, 1956, pp. 331–42.
26. *Op. cit.*, pp. 270–72. See also Norval D. Glenn and Charles N. Weaver, "The Marital Happiness of Remarried Divorced Persons," *Journal of Marriage and the Family* 39 (May 1977), pp. 331–37.

tionships, to have acquired more of such elusive qualities as maturity, wisdom, and tolerance. Although remarried persons may not compare favorably with the general population in these characteristics, they often are better prepared to make a success of their second marriages than they were to be successful in their first ones.

Second, failure in a first marriage often produces changes in motivation. Here we encounter a paradox. We have already stated that one divorce makes a second one easier and more acceptable. At the same time, failure in a first marriage appears to make many people determined and even desperate to succeed in the second one. We saw, in Chapter 15, how many couples with a history of failure in contraceptive practice become efficient family planners when they have had all of the children that they can stand. Similarly, men and women who remain basically committed to family life in spite of divorce may acquire a near all-conquering will to succeed in the second one. The motivation may be mixed: the will to achieve a stable family life and the will to remove the stigma of failure; but it may also be quite effective.

Third, and finally, the changes associated with aging may work to the benefit of partners in remarriages. Most persons, at the time of remarriage, have worked through—as much as they ever will—the rebelliousness and irresponsibility of youth. If people approaching middle age are unlikely ever to achieve the passionate commitment to one another of youth, they are more likely to accept one another as they are and not to view each flaw in one another as a catastrophe. The comfort and security that probably are more characteristic of marriage during the middle years may produce deep and lasting satisfaction.

Bernard also sought to acquire insight into success in remarriage by comparing marriages that were judged to be "extremely successful" with marriages reported to be either "below average" or "extremely unsuccessful." In general, she found conventionality, higher social class, lack of hostility toward the first spouse, favorable attitudes of children to the remarriage, favorable attitudes of parents to the remarriage, and favorable community attitudes to the remarriage all to be associated with success. Let us look briefly at these factors.

Both men and women who had entered first marriages before age 20 were less likely to be reported as successful in their second marriages. Bernard reasoned that the early first marriages might be conceived of as an index of impulsiveness or unconventionality that would work against success in remarriage also. In like fashion, persons who remarried immediately following divorce were behaving unconventionally, while those who waited at least a year before remarrying were behaving less impulsively. No interval before remarriage proved to be unfavorably associated with success in remarriage. Those persons who reported that their first marriages were successful (generally widows and widowers) were also more likely to be reported as successful in remarriages.

The measures of social class used included both education and type of occupation. Some college education of either husband or wife was associated with success in remarriage, while less formal education and working at clerical, skilled, semiskilled, and service jobs were unfavorable.

Hostility toward one's first spouse or toward the first spouse of the present mate was unfavorably related to success. The presence of such negative attitudes could reflect either continuing emotional involvement with the former partner or interference by the former spouse in the new marriage. In either case, the effects would be unfavorable. Friendliness toward former spouses was not associated with success in remarriage.

Custody arrangements for children of first marriages were not associated with the quality of the remarriage except where there was alternating custody between the parents. The adjustment of men also was affected unfavorably where their former wives had exclusive custody. As might be expected, the new marriages fared better where children of the former marriage were favorably inclined toward the new marriage and the new partner.

The importance of group support in influencing the success of remarriages was indicated by findings with regard to parental and community attitudes. Approval of the new marriage, both by one's parents and by the new spouse's parents, was associated with success; disapproval by either or both sets of parents was unfavorable. The same was true with community attitudes. In this case, however, there was a closer association between community approval of the woman's remarriage and marital success than between community approval of the man's remarriage and marital success.[27]

THE EFFECTS OF REMARRIAGE UPON CHILDREN

Among Bernard's 2009 remarriages, 60 percent of both men and women who remarried following divorce had children by their first marriages; among those who remarried following widowhood, from 75 to 80 percent had children by first marriages. The average number of children

27. William J. Goode, *After Divorce, op. cit.*, pp. 284–94, 355–60.

was between one and two. We shall summarize what sociologists have learned about the adjustment of children in the new marriage.

American attitudes toward remarriage are complicated by a widespread negative stereotype of stepparents. The "wicked stepmother," is prominent in fairy tales, and, for many people, the word "stepmother" calls forth an image of a cold, harsh figure who shows favoritism to her own children over those of her husband, and in relation to whom the usual emotions are fear and hatred. The folk characterization of the stepfather is less clear, reflecting the existence of greater numbers of stepmothers than stepfathers. When he does appear, the stepfather often is an aloof, unconcerned, intolerant person who puts up with his wife's children only because he must do so. With stereotypes such as these, and the recent emergence of remarriage as a large-scale phenomenon, it is not surprising that the literature on relationships between stepparents and stepchildren is scanty.

One of the earliest studies was Nye's study of 780 boys and girls in high school in the state of Washington. He compared children in broken, unhappy unbroken, and reconstituted families and found little evidence of special problems between stepparents and stepchildren. Instead, he found few differences in adjustment to broken homes, to homes with only one parent, and homes reconstituted through remarriage. In all three cases, the adjustment of children was better than in unhappy, unbroken homes. The conclusion was reached that "there are differences between the two categories of families, with the differences favoring the 'reconstructed' family including a stepparent, or the 'partial' family composed of one parent and child or children."[28]

A second study gathered data from 2145 junior- or senior-high-school students in Washington, Ohio, and North Carolina. Using affection for parents and stepparents and feelings of discrimination and rejection as criteria, this study supported the view that reconstituted families provide a less favorable environment for children than do intact families. The adjustment of children toward stepparents was poorer than toward the real parent of the same sex. Adjustment to stepfathers usually was better than adjustment to stepmothers. Moreover, stepparents more often were believed to discriminate, and stepchildren were more likely to feel rejected both by the natural parent and the stepparent.[29]

28. F. Ivan Nye, "Child Adjustment in Broken and in Unhappy Unbroken Homes," *Marriage and Family Living* 19 (Nov. 1957), pp. 356–61.

29. Charles E. Bowerman and Donald P. Irish, "Some Relationships of Stepchildren to Their Parents," *Marriage and Family Living* 24 (May 1962), pp. 113–21.

Although these studies are not directly comparable, there is no doubt that, if their findings do not conflict directly, at least they present quite different segments of reality. The hypothesis is suggested that children experience generally the best adjustment in intact homes, that there are more adjustment problems in reconstructed homes, and still more adjustment problems in unhappy but structurally intact homes.

This also is suggested by Burchinal's research in Iowa. He classified families into five types: unbroken families; broken families headed by the mother; and three types of reconstituted families—those consisting of fathers and stepmothers, those consisting of stepfathers and mothers, and those in which both parents had divorced and remarried. Measures of personality adjustment and social relationships were then compared among students in the five family types.[30] In general, the findings were of no striking differences in the adjustment of children in the five family types. There were no differences on personality measures, in participation in school or community activities, in school-grade point averages, in the number of schoolmates the respondent thought liked him or her, in attitudes toward school, or, among girls, how many of their schoolmates they liked. A few differences appeared. Students from unbroken homes were absent less often from school and those from broken homes were absent more often. It was also found that boys living with their fathers and stepmothers reported liking fewer of their schoolmates.

Goode points out that even when we establish a relationship between divorce and/or remarriage and certain personality or social characteristics of children we still have not determined that divorce and remarriage have any effect upon children. The problems, whatever they may be, may be caused by the same factors that predisposed the parents to divorce in the first place. The establishment of cause-and-effect relationships simply has not been done yet.

Goode's analysis indicated that most of the remarried mothers were satisfied with their children's adjustment. He concludes that remarriage tends to regularize the position of the children following whatever trauma was associated with the divorce and that, in most ways, reconstituted families are similar to unbroken families. Tensions between children and the new parent decrease with time.[31]

Another study of a random sample of remarried parents, their children, and stepchildren in Cleveland, Ohio calculated total Parent-Child

30. Lee G. Burchinal, "Characteristics of Adolescents from Unbroken, Broken, and Reconstituted Families," *Journal of Marriage and the Family* 26 (Feb. 1964), pp. 44–51.
31. *Op. cit.*, pp. 307, 339–41.

Relationship Scores. To the surprise of the researcher, 18 percent of the families rated "poor" on this scale, and 18 percent rated "good," while a huge 64 percent rated "excellent." Relationships among the two sets of children in these families were not quite as good, but 24 percent still rated "excellent," 38 percent rated "good," and another 38 percent rated "poor."[32]

The most recent study available compared 122 children in families with stepfathers with 2747 children living with their natural parents. Comparisons were made on 68 separate social and social psychological characteristics. In the words of the researchers, no substantial differences were found. Children's experiences in reconstituted families can be predominately positive, predominately negative, or mixed.[33]

Bernard reports on a study in which Bernreuter Personality Inventory scores were obtained for 59 young men and women who lived in families where there had been a remarriage. Since norms on this test are available for college students, the scores of the children of remarriages could be measured against those norms. On none of the three scores—stability, self-sufficiency, or dominance—did the children of remarriages differ from the general college population. When tests were made separately for remarriages following divorce and bereavement, again no differences were found. The data did not support the view that divorce leaves children more disturbed than does bereavement.[34]

Concluding that most remarriages are not harmful to children, Bernard explains this in terms of three factors: (1) the attitudes of the children to the remarriage; (2) the new parent as a salvaging force; and (3) the inherent resiliency of human nature. The Utopolis data showed that most children, whether the first marriage was broken by divorce or death, are in favor of the remarriage of the parent with whom they are living. Even adult children generally support their parents' remarriages. The only exceptions were found where custody of the children alternated between the parents, and where the remarriage of a father threatened the children's interest in his property.

The stereotype of the unfeeling stepparent was contradicted in the Utopolis data by both men and women who provided wisdom, love, and

32. Lucile Duberman, "Step-Kin Relationships," *Journal of Marriage and the Family* 35 (May 1973), pp. 283–92.

33. Kenneth L. Wilson, Louis A. Zurcher, Diana Claire McAdams, and Russell L. Curtis, "Stepfathers and Stepchildren: An Exploratory Analysis from Two National Surveys," *Journal of Marriage and the Family* 37 (Aug. 1975), pp. 526–36. See also E. M. Rallings, "The Special Role of Stepfather," *The Family Coordinator* 25 (Oct. 1976), pp. 445–49.

34. *Op. cit.*, pp. 306–11.

understanding to help their stepchildren compensate for the trauma of divorce. Interestingly, these effects were found more often in remarriages following divorce than in those following widowhood. The stepparent replacing a deceased parent was more likely to be resented than the stepparent replacing a divorced parent.

Finally, Bernard emphasizes the inherent toughness of the human organism. She points out that most persons, whether their parents' marriages have broken or not, undergo traumatic childhood experiences. Most persons cope effectively with them, and may even emerge stronger for them. Only when there is a compounding of such experiences is personality damage likely. It stands to reason that the effects of remarriage should be different in the lives of children whose lives otherwise are safe and secure, than in lower economic groups whose problems are compounded by minority-group status and social and personal pathologies of other sorts. Perhaps the greatest increases in our understanding of the effects of remarriage upon children will come when we are able successfully to control for economic status.

THE DYNAMICS OF REMARRIAGE

We have described remarriage analytically and statistically. When we are dealing with phenomena that we have been intimately exposed to over long periods of time, most of us can apply broad generalizations to the actual experiences of living men and women. When we come to remarriage, however, only a minority of college students have had direct, sustained experience. Remarriage, to most 20 year olds convinced that their own marriages will be successful and life-long, is about as academic as the family system of a preliterate society. To put some descriptive meat upon the statistical bones, let us look at the dynamics of remarriage.

The Dynamics of Courtship

Courtship among persons who are remarrying—particularly women—tends to be considerably shorter than among the young. Where a triangle situation existed before divorce, this may help explain the short courtship, but this is not the major explanation. First is the shorter courtships among remarrying women than among remarrying men. Stripped of its sentimental overtones, courtship may be described as convincing the woman to enter a sanctioned sex relationship. Where the woman is sexually inexperienced, this involves circumlocution; coquettishness is the order of the day. In remarriage, however, both the man and the woman know the woman to be sexually experienced. The man feels a freedom to approach her that would have been difficult before a first marriage. For the woman, the taboos upon sex have long since been overcome. She long ago adopted a heterosexual pattern and has little reason to fear sex now.

Not that courtship before remarriage becomes an orgy. Far from it. The tonicity and the erotic content of the relationship are likely to be lower than among the previously unmarried. The couple are older, and their sex needs—particularly those of the man—may be less frequent and less imperious than among younger people. The couple also have had enough experience to be better able to place sex in proportion to other aspects of marriage. Thus we have a paradox. Courtship before remarriage quickly becomes sexually explicit, and the percentage of couples who have intercourse is extremely high. Yet having had intercourse is not likely to lead to guilt or to alter seriously the probability of marriage. Sex, once a couple has had intercourse, is likely to occupy less of the time and attention of the couple than if they were younger.

Nor should sex be singled out as *the* area in which couples before remarriage are more intimate. They tend to anticipate most of the conditions of married life. While a young swain ordinarily takes most of his meals before seeing his girl, or ritually takes her out for a hamburger or a meal, older couples are likely to take a good portion of their evening meals, at least, together. Among other things, the man is looking for someone to cook his meals. The woman, who is used to cooking for a man, may find satisfaction in doing so and may use her culinary competence as an inducement to the man to marry her. She may also assume some responsibility for his clothing and his living quarters; doing laundry, mending, and even cleaning for him. In turn, the man often assumes some financial responsibility for the woman. He may buy groceries, he may buy clothing for her in a way that would be considered to be in bad taste if done by a younger man for a young woman. He may even make a regular financial contribution to her household.

Where there are children, they may figure prominently in the courtship. If marriage is to occur, the man and the woman must woo one another's children. Marriage may occur over the opposition of children, but it is unlikely and, in the eyes of both partners, undesirable. Consequently both partners are likely to move into quasi-parental roles in relation to any young children the other may have. These roles include efforts at the development of affection, but they also include everything from changing diapers, to bathing, to spanking, and to having the children accompany their parents on "dates."

There are many variations, of course. When the couples are younger and there are no children, their courtships may be virtually indistinguishable from those of persons marrying for the first time. At the other extreme, where there are grown children, particularly of the man, who fear the loss of property interests if he remarries, the courtship may be complicated by outside resistance. Among the divorced and widowed, also, are to be found people who want companionship, but are loath to remarry. Among them, the courtship may reach a plateau where one or both are relatively comfortable, and may remain there over a long time.

Remarriages, once decided upon, may come about more quickly and with less fanfare than first marriages. Weddings are less likely to be church weddings, guests usually are fewer, and the ceremony is more likely to be performed by a civil official. There is less aura of initiation into a new experience, and, although it may not be recognized, the role of the principals looms much larger in the remarriage ceremony. In first marriages, the emphasis is more on the ritual—upon the ceremony itself—and the young man and woman are somewhat dwarfed by the pomp and mysticism. In second marriages, by contrast, the ceremony often is viewed simply as giving sanction to a relationship that already exists or would exist, whether or not official provision were made for it.

The Dynamics of Marital Adjustment

Adjustment in remarriages is both like and unlike adjustment in first marriages. There is the need to establish new habits and roles. Adjustments must be worked out in each of the conventional areas—sex, inlaws, money, friends, religion, and so on. But there are differences too.

At least one of the partners is not a beginner—there is a storehouse of knowledge and experience upon which to draw. The spouses are likely to be older and to have worked through the authority problems that are so prominent in young adulthood. In some ways, at least, the man is more sure of his manhood and the woman is more sure of herself as a woman. But there are scars, too, resulting from the death or divorce that made the remarriage possible. And, usually, there are more people involved; in addition to the primary families of the new spouses, there may be up to two former spouses, and two sets of children. If nothing else, most remarriages are more crowded than most first marriages.

The initial adjustments probably are made more quickly in remarriages. As already described, quasi-marital and quasi-parental roles are likely to have been established before the ceremony. Too, the spouses are less threatened by the moods of their partners. Middle-aged people often know, as younger people seldom can, that the partner's being too tired to go out or to have sex or being just grouchy does not reflect upon oneself. On the other hand, what emotional crises do develop early in remarriages—and all of the conventional ones do to some degree—have more potential for disrupting the marriage. Paradoxically, remarried couples both adjust quicker and divorce quicker than first-married couples.

Sex Adjustment. The sex adjustment probably binds the pair together more comfortably than in first marriages. With the greater likelihood of sex before marriage, remarriages may be more selective; it is difficult to imagine middle-aged people entering a marriage when they think that the sex relationship will not be satisfactory.[35] Most sexual disabilities suffered by young wives probably are not experienced by older women in remarriages. Wives in remarriage are more comfortable with their own bodies and with those of men. They are not likely to be squeamish or easily offended; they are likely to sympathize with the sexual needs of their husbands when they are greater than the wives' own; and there is less likely to be a significant difference in sexual need. The man's needs typically have been declining with age,[36] while the woman's capacity has been increasing.

No figures are available on the frequency of marital intercourse by age and remarried status, but we might guess that, age for age, the frequency of intercourse is higher in remarriages than in first marriages. There are at least two reasons for this. First, at a given age level, the remarriages will be of shorter duration. Novelty gives stimulus to sexual participation, and in remarriages there has been less time for the novelty to wear off. Second, sexual participation in remarriage is less likely to suffer the debilitating effects of gross differences in sexual need and of being used as a focus for conflicts originating in other areas of marriage.

Social Life. In some other areas, remarriages are more likely to suffer

35. Benjamin Schlesinger, "Remarriage as Family Reorganization for Divorced Persons—A Canadian Study," *Journal of Comparative Family Studies* 1 (Autumn 1970), pp. 101–18.

36. That the sexual needs of men decline with age should not be overemphasized. Several studies have shown that many males remain sexually active well into old age. A survey by *Sexology* magazine reported that 70 percent of the married men over 65 years of age engaged in intercourse regularly. See William H. Masters and Virginia E. Johnson, *Human Sexual Response*, Boston: Little, Brown, 1966, pp. 248–49.

some disadvantage. The social life of remarried couples, for example, often has to undergo considerable reorganization. The specific patterns may vary according to whether one or both partners are being remarried, and whether the new marriage follows death or divorce.

In many instances, the new couple will encounter resistance from friends. Friends of a first-married man or woman, entering marriage with someone who has been married before, may think the match inappropriate and convey their distaste to the couple. Or the widowed person who has remarried may find that acquaintances interpret it as betrayal of the deceased spouse. Those who remarry following divorce are even more likely to encounter disapproval. Even the "innocent party" who did not want the divorce and who has been the object of sympathy may suddenly find himself or herself the object of disapproval. For the more aggressive partner in the divorce, or where there has been a triangle, there is almost certain to be censure from outsiders.

Most remarried couples attempt to cope, for a time, with the cool attitudes of their social groups, and some eventually win approval for the new marriage. Strains, however, are produced in the marriage. It is not pleasant to find oneself in disapproval by people whose opinions have mattered in the past. Whether the couple attempt to ignore such disapproval, or whether they acknowledge it openly, their relationship becomes a source of pain to them.

Most couples solve the problem to some degree by giving up some old friendships and making new ones among people who were not acquainted with the former marriage(s), and who accept the new relationship for what it is. It is not simple to do this, however. For the months or years that the change takes, remarried couples suffer some disability that most first-married couples do not. A significant number of couples find it necessary either to change jobs or to move away, or both, in order to escape the offended feelings of former associates.

Adjustment to Former Partners. In a real sense, the first marriage partners of the new spouses are parties to the remarriage also. Although they are not physically present, they intrude in subtle and not-so-subtle ways. Where one of the parties in the new marriage has been widowed, the spouse may find himself or herself competing with the former partner. Analyses of bereavement have indicated a tendency—particularly where the former marriage was happy, but even when it was not satisfactory—for the surviving spouse to build up an idealized image of the deceased partner. The earlier unpleasantnesses are forgotten while the good things are remembered, and the deceased spouse takes on an image larger than life. In remarriage, the new spouse, however desirable he or she may be, may be compared with this idealized image and found wanting.

In extreme cases, there may be numerous daily reminders of the former relationship. The new spouse may actually move into the home formerly shared with the deceased partner. Out of habit, he or she may occasionally be called by the former partner's name. Or there may be photographs of the former partner, unthinkingly displayed, or mementoes of the former life that are treasured to the distress of the new spouse. The competition with memories is particularly difficult, because the norms of our society hold that one should not feel animosity toward a deceased person. The new spouse must woo his or her partner away from memories without appearing to be doing so.

When the remarriage has followed divorce, one must cope directly with the former spouse rather than with memories. If the former spouse was the reluctant partner in the divorce, he or she may carry a torch and may literally be a rival in the new relationship. There are instances of former spouses waging, for months and years, battles to regain their partners. While the probability of the divorced spouse's being successful is small, considerable threat is likely to be felt by the new spouse.

Intrusion by the former spouse is likely, whether or not there remains emotional attraction, when there are children. If the new marriage has custody of the children, the former spouse usually must be permitted some entrée for visits. If the former spouse has custody, then he or she must be placated in order that continuing contacts with the children not be jeopardized. The necessity for such continuing contacts affords an aggrieved former spouse the opportunity to make demands that annoy the new partners and create strain.

Becoming a New Family. Adjustments in remarriages tend to be most complicated when there are children present from one or both of the preceding marriages. For Utopolis, Bernard found that 21.5 percent of the men and 23.4 percent of the women had children by a previous marriage, and in 5.6 percent of the cases both the new husband and wife had children. Following divorce, the typical situation was for a mother and her children to secure a new husband and father. Following widowhood, on the other hand, it was typically a father and his children who secured a new wife and mother.[37]

Marital adjustment may be viewed as a process whereby the separate value systems, attitudes, and habit patterns of the spouses yield to a new and joint way of life. That many people do not give up old patterns

37. *Op. cit.*, pp. 211–12.

easily is illustrated by the greater prevalence of conflict early in most marriages. In remarriages with children, the situation is more complicated because there are more people involved. Beyond that, the presence of other people, who may be drawn into alliances wittingly or unwittingly, may strengthen one's resistance to change and prolong the time required for adjustment to occur.

A wedding ceremony, by itself, does little to weld two families into one. Instead, what happens is that the two families take up common residence, but attempt unknowingly to continue their old ways of life. This is almost bound to bring them into conflict. It happens in different ways.

First, when there are children, they share with their natural parent a host of experiences and memories not shared by the other partner and his or her children. In normal conversation, and without any intent of so doing, one of the partners tends to be relegated to the role of outsider. He or she has not shared the common experiences, be they joyous, sentimental, or sad. The partner who is left out, unless he or she be exceptionally patient and wise, may react defensively. He may try to compete for the center of attention, he may retaliate by attacking the group or one of its members, or he may withdraw emotionally and set the family on an alienation course.

More directly, there is a tendency for alliances to develop within the family. Family ties are particularistic, and the special consideration that has grown up between a parent and children over the years is not easily extended to the new spouse and his or her children. Each partner justifiably feels that the other shows favoritism to his own natural children. It takes wisdom for the couple to realize what is happening and to prevent it from developing into a destructively rivalrous situation.

The potential for conflicts in reconstituted families is both greater and less than in first marriages. The tolerance that comes with age and experience must be balanced against the involvement of children in whatever conflict exists; the parents may be moved to greater wisdom by having jointly to deal with the demands made by their children, and, at the same time, the children may carry the fray with a vigor that only the young possess.

Just as earlier shared family experiences work against the solidarity of the new family, so does time and new experience work for it. For months, or years, customary remembrances go back to a time when this family did not exist. But eventually the shared experiences come to outweigh the separate experiences, and the group remembers the things that "we" did together or which happened to "us." Those "other things" happened a long time ago and no longer seem real or important.

Similarly, a new set of affectional relationships develops. A stepparent may come to be as cherished as the natural parent, and the relationship may draw special strength from the fact that it was worked out without the accident of birth. The stepparent, too, may cease to distinguish between my children, your children, and our children. The terms "Mom" and "Dad," and "son" and "daughter," may apply as naturally to sociological children as to biological ones. With or without benefit of legal adoption, a common family culture comes into existence.

At what point reconstituted families become more like than unlike original families it is impossible to say. It would be absurd to state that differences do not continue to exist. The relative strengths and problems of reconstituted and original families is a topic that is just beginning to be explored.

SUMMARY

Remarriages are not a homogeneous phenomenon. One or both partners may be remarrying. The remarriage may follow bereavement, or divorce, or both. There may or may not be children from one or both of the earlier marriages.

Until about the end of World War I, remarriage in the United States was uncommon, and most of it took place following widowhood. As divorce rates rose, however, so did rates of remarriage following divorce. Just after World War II, the remarriage rate for marriages was almost 20 percent, and that for individuals was about 12.5 percent. Remarriage rates are continuing to climb, and it is estimated that between 20 and 25 percent of all persons marrying recently have been marrying for the second or a subsequent time.

Living in one-parent families for a while commonly occurs between marital dissolution and remarriage. Mother-headed families are much more numerous than father-headed ones, and the number of such families has been increasing rapidly.

Men who are remarrying tend to be about 13 years older than men who are marrying for the first time; women who are remarrying are about 10 years older. The difference between the ages of bride and groom also is about twice as great in remarriages as in first marriages. Up to about 35 years of age, most remarriages follow divorce; after age 35, the number of remarriages following bereavement climbs rapidly.

Most divorced persons remarry. In fact, age for age, divorced persons have higher probabilities of remarrying than single persons do of marrying the first time. Again, age for age, widowed persons are more likely to wed than single persons are. Divorced persons have the highest probabilities of marrying, widows and widowers come next, and single persons have the poorest chances of all. Divorced and widowed men also have greater probabilities of remarriage than divorcees and widows do.

Intervals to remarriage tend to be relatively short, and to be shorter following divorce than bereavement. Up to three-fourths of divorced persons remarry within five years. Remarriages generally follow shorter courtships, more are civil ceremonies, and there is less pomp and formality than in first weddings. The fact of remarriage for the woman is more important in determining the type of courtship and wedding than is the remarriage of the man.

Early studies showed high divorce rates among couples who had remarried following earlier divorces, but not among those who had been widowed. More recent studies have challenged the notion that divorce reflects personality problems, however, finding that remarriages have lower divorce rates than first marriages.

Studies of adjustment among remarried couples yield different findings. Happiness ratings and marital-adjustment scores generally do not show remarriages to be less satisfactory than first marriages. The majority of remarried persons state that their second marriages are better than their first ones. Even if basic personality structure is not amenable to change, the way in which personality is expressed in behavior may change in second marriages. Three factors working to make second marriages successful are the learning which occurred during the first marriage, changes in motivation which follow an unsuccessful first marriage, and changes associated with increasing age and maturity.

Research into the effects of remarriage upon children indicates that adjustment is better than in broken homes or emotionally broken homes, but perhaps not so good as in happy, intact homes. Most remarried mothers report themselves to be satisfied with their children's adjustment, and personality testing of such children generally fails to show important differences between them and children from intact homes.

The dynamics of courtship and adjustment in remarriage differ from those in first marriages. Prior marital experience on the part of the woman changes courtship more than does that same experience of the man. Before remarriage, couples are more likely to be intimate sexually but may devote less attention to sex than first-marrying couples do. Also, before remarriage, couples may play quasi-marital roles in different areas of life and may assume quasi-parental roles as well.

Adjustment in remarriages is similar in many ways to adjustment to first marriages. There are the same general areas in which adjustment must be made, and the new couple must establish a common way of life. Adjustment differs from that in first marriages, too. Neither of the pair may be beginners and there may be more in-laws and children to be dealt with. Emotional crises may develop more quickly, and they may be resolved more quickly, or rapidly lead to divorce.

The reorganization of the couple's social life may be troubling initially. Some rejection by former friends often is encountered, and some frustration experienced. Part of the solution usually involves making new friends. Sometimes, too, the problem is alleviated by moving to a new location and/or taking a new job.

Then there are former marital partners who intrude on the new relationship. Deceased former spouses intrude symbolically, and divorced partners often intrude directly. Particularly where there are children from a former marriage, contacts must be maintained with the divorced spouse.

Adjustment in remarriages is most complicated when there are children present from a former marriage. The parent and his or her children inevitably share with one another more than they do with the new spouse. This can lead to rivalry or emotional withdrawal. In extreme cases, alliances may develop within the new family which threaten its solidarity. With time, however, these divisive forces tend to yield to the accumulating shared experience in the new family, and to the developing affectional relationships within it. Remarriages remain different from first marriages, but the nature of the continuing differences has not yet been analyzed adequately.

SUGGESTED READINGS

Duberman, Lucile, *The Reconstituted Family: A Study of Remarried Couples and Their Children*, Chicago: Nelson-Hall, 1975. A report of research by a scholar who is, herself, a member of a reconstituted family.

Engleson, James, and Engleson, Janet, *Parents Without Partners*, New York: E. P. Dutton, 1961. A Guide for divorced, widowed, or separated parents written by a remarried couple who had been members of the organization, Parents Without Partners, Inc.

George, Victor, and Wilding, Paul, *Motherless Families*, London: Routledge & Kegan Paul, 1972. Report of an English study that focuses on father-headed, one-parent families.

Ross, Heather L., and Sawhill, Isabel V., *Time of Transition: The Growth of Families Headed by Women*, Washington, D.C.: The Urban Institute, 1975. A detailed empirical analysis of the impact of rising divorce rates and government policy upon the growth of mother-headed families.

Simon, Anne W., *Stepchild in the Family: A View of Children in Remarriage*, New York: Odyssey, 1964. The author, who has been a step-grandchild, a stepchild, and a stepmother analyzes the problems encountered in remarriages that involve children.

QUESTIONS AND PROJECTS

1. Specify two different ways in which living in one-parent families is transitional.
2. The term *remarriage* refers to a number of different marriage types. Specify as many types of remarriage as you can.
3. What is the approximate incidence of remarriage in the United States? Specify the relationship between age and previous marital status to patterns of remarriage.
4. What intervals ordinarily occur between death of a spouse, or divorce, and remarriage? What are the probabilities that divorced and widowed persons will remarry as compared to the probability that single people will marry?
5. What differences exist in length of courtship and type of wedding between first-marrying and remarrying couples? Which has more influence—the previous marital status of the bride, or of the groom?
6. How does the divorce rate in remarriage compare with that in first marriage? What careful qualification needs to be made here?
7. What bases are there for thinking that any given person's adjustment in a remarriage may be different from his adjustment in the first marriage? What bases are there for thinking that it may not be different?
8. What does research show about the personality adjustment of children in remarriages compared with those living in intact families?
9. How are the dynamics of courtship before remarriage likely to differ from those which precede first marriages? Evaluate the statement that "remarrying couples are more likely to be preoccupied with sex."
10. Why is reorganization of the couple's social life often necessary after remarriage? How is this likely to come about?
11. How do former partners intrude upon the new marriage? What differences exist between remarriages following bereavement and those following divorce? What differences does the presence of children make?
12. What is the meaning of the phrase, becoming a new family, as applied to remarriages? What complications are likely to be encountered here? What factors operate in favor of the new marriage?

HAPPY
56

19
The Postparental Phase

. . . Of the 42 million married couples in the United States, little more than half have children at home; of these childless couples, more than two-thirds are in the post-parental category; that is, as many as 15 million couples. And of these, most would consider themselves middle-aged, not aged. . . .

From the standpoint of the individual, the newness of the problem of enjoying his life with his mate for that 20-year period before retirement will in part be mitigated and in part be aggravated by the fact that nearly his whole generation will be going through the experience simultaneously. The kinds of places that such couples like to go are likely to be crowded, as with the tourists who deplore the other tourists. On the other hand, to be free to go to parties, to travel, to have the opportunity to try new ventures without care of children to interfere, and while energy is still abundant, is a blessing that is somehow enhanced by sharing the discoveries with others similarly situated. . . .

Grandparenthood, especially for the grandmother—once in-law relations get straightened out—is still at moments almost an ecstatic experience. Esthetically it may be superior to parenthood, offering more of the joys with fewer of the problems, more perspective with less involvement. . . . Of course, if the generations are separated by geographical distance . . . the amount of time per week or year the grandmother can spend with her grandchildren is limited and sporadic. But she can be a grandmother for 20 to 30 years and thus recapitulate vicariously every phase of her grandchildren's development. She cannot, however, without sad consequences, directly take the place of their actual mother. And so the woman who becomes a grandmother at 45, as millions nowadays do, really does need to substitute some equally worthwhile and satisfying activity. . . .[1]

1. Nelson N. Foote, "New Roles for Men and Women," *Marriage and Family Living* 23 (Nov. 1961), pp. 326–27.

The article from which the quotation above was taken is titled "New Roles for Men and Women," and the patterns it discusses virtually did not exist a few decades ago. Increases in longevity and prolongation of the family life cycle have drastically altered the way of life of people from their mid-forties to their seventies and eighties.

If students will refer back to the discussion of the family cycle in Chapter 8, they will see that husbands and wives average less than 50 years of age at the marriage of their youngest child. There are, then, about 15 years before retirement and as long as 30 years before the marriage is broken by death. The postparental phase of married life is, on the average, as long as all the earlier stages put together.

CONTINUING MARITAL ADJUSTMENT

Not much has been written about relations between husbands and wives after the children have left home, and even less has been substantiated by research. It is widely recognized that the postparental phase gives couples the opportunity to rediscover one another and to do things that they could not do earlier because of the children. At the same time, it is feared that the parallel adjustments they have made during the child-rearing years perpetuate themselves after the children have gone. Husbands frequently are portrayed as becoming more engrossed in their work and less available to their wives. Wives, in turn, are described as lonely and frustrated in attempts to find new meaning in life. Women's clubs and civic duties are seen as providing less than satisfactory outlets.

Unfortunately, we have no information on the proportions of couples who follow different paths of adjustment. There are data, however, on the continuing trend of adjustment after the middle years. The most comprehensive data come from Blood and Wolfe's Detroit-area study and from a study of 312 Minneapolis-area families. Hill's study covered three generations of families and thus affords a unique opportunity to compare intergenerational patterns. The grandparent generation were between 60 and 80 years of age, the parents were between 40 and 60, and the married children were from 20 to 30 years old.[2]

Love and Companionship

It will be recalled that studies have shown a drop in marital adjustment and satisfaction, beginning early in marriage and continuing through the middle years. The Detroit data show that the process does not end dur-

2. Reuben Hill, *et al., Family Development in Three Generations*, Cambridge, Mass.: Schenkman Publishing Company, 1970.

ing the middle years, but continues through the postparental years and on into retirement.[3] Satisfaction with love in the relationship continues to decline steadily from a high point reached during the pre-school years, while satisfaction with companionship shows a modest increase after the children are gone. Thus, there is some basis for the idea that couples turn back toward one another when their children leave home. The most striking thing, however, is that the increase in companionship is so small. It is still lower during the postparental years than during the first 15 years of marriage.[4]

Power Relationships

Other changes accompany the gradual drop in satisfaction with love and companionship. The Detroit data on changes in the power relationship of husband and wife were presented in Chapter 16 and showed that the husband's power rises during the postparental but preretirement years, and then falls after he retires. The authors interpret this to mean that the gradual drop in the husband's power during the child-rearing years reflects his increasing preoccupation with his job rather than his family. After departure of the children, his power may increase again because of his wife's realization that he is likely to precede her in death. Still virile and fulfilling his role as breadwinner, his power is enhanced by the wife's realization that she may lose him. Retirement changes drastically the husband's status as income-provider, and removes much of

3. The magnitude of this decline should not be overemphasized. Havighurst, for example, has shown that the age period from 40 to 70 constitutes a plateau during which adjustment remains relatively constant. See Robert J. Havighurst, "The Social Competence of Middle Aged People," *Genetic Psychology Monographs* 56 (Nov. 1957), pp. 297–373. Other studies have shown that the postparental but preretirement period is more crucial in the adjustment of wives than of husbands. See Irwin Deutscher, "The Quality of Postparental Life: Definitions of the Situation," *Journal of Marriage and the Family* 26 (Feb. 1964), pp. 52–59.

4. The question of whether marital adjustment improves again in the retirement years has still not been answered satisfactorily. See Wesley R. Burr, "Satisfaction with Various Aspects of Marriage Over the Life Cycle: A Random Middle-Class Sample," *Journal of Marriage and the Family* 32 (Feb. 1970), pp. 29–37; Brent C. Miller, "A Multivariate Developmental Model of Marital Satisfaction," *Journal of Marriage and the Family* 38 (Nov. 1976), pp. 643–57; Boyd C. Rollins and Harold Feldman, "Marital Satisfaction Over the Life Cycle," *Journal of Marriage and the Family* 32 (Feb. 1970), pp. 20–28; Boyd C. Rollins and Kenneth L. Cannon, "Marital Satisfaction Over the Family Life Cycle: A Reevaluation," *Journal of Marriage and the Family* 36 (May 1974), pp. 271–82; and Graham B. Spanier, Robert A. Lewis, and Charles L. Cole, "Marital Adjustment Over the Family Life Cycle: The Issue of Curvilinearity," *Journal of Marriage and the Family* 37 (May 1975), pp. 263–75.

the prestige which attached to his occupational role. The husband's power during retirement is less than at any other time in the life cycle.

Hill's Minneapolis study provides data on power in relationships of young marrieds, their parents, and their grandparents (Table 19.1). In this case, the respondents were asked to specify who makes final decisions in different areas of decision making, and, at the same time, interviewers independently rated who did most of the talking, who exercised most influence, and who had the last word in the joint interview. The reports of the couples differed considerably from the interviewer evaluations.

Table 19.1. Family authority patterns, by generation, Minnesota families

Authority pattern	*Self-Reported*			*Observer Reported*		
	Grand-parent	*Parent*	*Married child*	*Grand-parent*	*Parent*	*Married child*
Husband-centered	22	12	15	34	24	41
Equalitarian	69	82	80	28	47	42
Wife-centered	9	6	5	38	29	18
Total	100	100	100	100	100	100
Number of families	94	100	107	74	90	96

Source: Adapted from Reuben Hill, *et al., Family Development in Three Generations,* Cambridge, Mass.: Schenkman Publishing Company, 1970, p. 48.

According to the couples themselves, the vast majority at each generation had equalitarian relationships. The respondents also indicate an increase in husband-centered and in wife-centered relationships in the parental and grandparental generations. Although the inference is that the power relationships change as couples move through the life cycle, it should be remembered that the data are cross-sectional; they come from three separate generations, not from the same couples through time.

The interviewers provide lower estimates of equalitarian relationships at each generational level. They also report substantial increases in wife-centered relationships at the parental and grandparental levels. Since Hill's data on the grandparental generation are not presented by retirement status, his findings cannot be compared directly with Blood's. Both studies, however, show shifts away from equalitarian norms among older couples and increasing power of the wife in later years.

Role Specialization

In one other area of marital role-taking, the Michigan and Minnesota studies provide roughly comparable data. Blood and Wolfe developed a measure of role specialization to determine the degree to which husband and wife share various tasks in maintaining a home and the degree to which they perform the tasks they deem most consistent with their sex roles. The data showed more sharing of tasks during the honeymoon than at any time thereafter. A large number of wives are working outside the home during this period. As wives move out of employment and into child-bearing, they begin to specialize in the traditionally wifely tasks. Husbands, freed from many domestic tasks, concentrate more on traditionally masculine tasks. This trend continues throughout child-rearing and into the postparental years. During the postparental years the trend continues, and the differentiation of marital roles reaches its peak during the retirement years.[5]

Hill sought not only to determine the degree to which men stick to traditionally manly tasks of earning a living, working in the yard, doing repair jobs, and so on; he developed measures of both role specialization and role conventionality. Role conventionality refers to men doing only what is traditionally man's work and women doing only what is traditionally woman's work. Role specialization refers to the degree to which there is shifting about in the performance of various tasks or the degree to which role differentiation is rigidly adhered to.

In Table 19.2, it can be seen that role specialization increases over the generations. High specialization increases markedly from the married child to the parental to the grandparental generation. Correspondingly, medium role specialization is more than halved over the generations.

When we look at role conventionality, the situation is more complicated. The number of conventional couples increases steadily from 17 percent in the married-child generation to 42 percent in the grandparental generation. However, unconventionality increases, too, in the older generations. The most unconventional pattern increases from 13 percent in the married-child generation to 26 percent in the grandparental generation. There is no satisfactory explanation for this latter finding. The fact that increased unconventionality is found in the pa-

5. This often is accompanied by feelings of loneliness on the part of wives. See Leland J. Axelson, "Personal Adjustment in the Post-parental Period," *Marriage and Family Living* 22 (Feb. 1960), pp. 66–68. See also Dennis K. Orthner, "Leisure Activity Patterns and Marital Satisfaction Over the Marital Career," *Journal of Marriage and the Family* 37 (Feb. 1975), pp. 91–102.

Table 19.2. Role specialization and role conventionality by generation, Minnesota families

Role specialization	*Grandparent percent*	*Parent percent*	*Married child percent*
High specialization, husband or wife always do certain household tasks	78	65	57
Medium specialization, spouses usually but not always do the same specified tasks	14	29	37
Low specialization, great shifting about, in who does tasks	8	6	6
Total	100	100	100
Number of families	99	100	107
Role conventionality			
Both conventional in doing sex-typed tasks, and combination where wife conventional, husband crossing line	42	21	17
Husband conventional and wife crossing line, and combinations where both cross line	33	62	70
Combinations of conventionality, line crossing and systemic role reversals	26	17	13
Total	100	100	100
Number of families	98	100	107

Source: Adapted from Reuben Hill, *et al., Family Development in Three Generations,* Cambridge, Mass.: Schenkman Publishing Company, 1970, p. 49.

rental generation, also, suggests that some couples may become increasingly flexible with time. In the grandparental generation, disabilities that come with infirmity or illness may produce role reversals in couples who, until then, have played conventional roles.

Marital Dynamics

The ways in which spouses relate during the postparental years may be as varied as those of early marriage and the middle years. There is continuity as couples move from one stage in life to another. There are differences, too, however, as the special problems of aging emerge.

There is reason to think that the transition to postparental status either may be smooth and uneventful, or it may be traumatic. Moreover, the transition may be unequally made by the partners; one partner may take things in stride and the other be thrown into an emotional tailspin.

At one extreme, some couples literally do "stay together for the benefit of the children." The marriage, or entrance into college, of the last child may signal the end of a long period of distasteful obligation. Divorce may soon follow; and experience attests to the fact that it may come as a shock to virtually unsuspecting children. Or, surprisingly, couples who have longed for the day when they might be free of marital bonds, find themselves immobilized when the opportunity finally appears. In spite of their professed wishes to be free, they may be sufficiently dependent upon one another that some other rationalization must be found for continuing the marriage. Essentially neurotic relationships may be clung to for the blend of pain and satisfaction that they bring.

At the other extreme is found an increasing proportion of couples who anticipate the day when they will be relieved of responsibility for children and thus free to enjoy the full fruits of whatever financial and other success life has brought. A diminishing proportion of couples define parenthood as the *prime* goal in life. Not that parenthood has been devalued, for few couples are content to do without it. But, increasingly, parenthood is viewed as occupying only one portion of the vigorous adult years—the ages from 20 to 45 or so.

And mixed with its joys are the seemingly unending frustrations of being tied down. Coping with baby-sitters, a continuous round of infectious illnesses, school schedules that discourage travel, the competing schedule demands of budding adolescents, financial demands for everything from braces to summer camps, to college expenses and weddings—some couples can hardly wait for the day when they may be free to indulge their own desires. Just a measure of privacy and quiet after hectic years of crowded family living may have overwhelming appeal—the opportunity to carry on uninterrupted conversation, to watch one's own favorite TV shows, and to have the daily schedule determined by one's own, instead of the children's, needs. Luxuries, from new clothes, to automobiles, to extended vacations, may be afforded. For couples in this situation, the postparental years may represent years of fulfillment rather than years of decline.

The postparental years are not without problems, of course. The data on continuing marital adjustment indicate a tendency for many spouses to live somewhat parallel rather than truly intertwined lives.

The Preretirement Years. The postparental years often appear more unsettling for wives than for husbands, because the marriage of children does not occasion drastic change in the daily routines of most husbands. They continue to spend much of their time at work. Moreover, assuming modest occupational success, these are rewarding years for men.

Their incomes, prestige, and power are at maximum. Even if the pain of "losing children" is severe, men have an escape into their work.

Their wives' situation is different. Women who formerly found that there were not enough hours in the day suddenly are burdened heavily with time. Only so much time can be devoted to the diminished demands of housekeeping. When the wife seeks to fill her time with attention to her husband, often she finds him physically and emotionally unavailable; his escape into work makes her feel more alone than ever. There are alternatives available to mothers whose children have flown the nest. Some seek fulfillment and escape in employment. And for some, this is quite successful. On the other hand, middle-aged women who wish to work face handicaps. They *are* middle-aged and have lost the fresh appeal of younger women. Moreover, they are likely to be untrained, or their earlier training is likely to have become out of date. As a consequence, the work available often is unskilled and poorly paid.

When the husbands' incomes are high enough that their wives are not tempted to seek employment, a combination of community service and an expanded social life often fill the hours. Many community agencies—the United Funds, the Red Cross, hospital auxiliaries, and many more—almost depend upon voluntary service. Then there are women's organizations in the churches, fund drives for worthy causes, and special community projects to absorb time and energy. And in the lulls, there are always shopping, lunch, and the ubiquitous bridge game. Some women thrive on this existence. Virtually everyone knows such women who are healthy, hearty, and content. Equally true, however, is the fact that community service and social life sometimes take on a compulsive quality that masks frustration. It is no accident that such women are a favorite subject of cartoonists.

Basic to women's problems at this stage of life appears to be the enforced recognition of age. It was pointed out earlier that women are regarded as most desirable somewhere around the age of 20, and that age brings decreasing attractiveness. When a woman's children marry, it not only deprives her of established routines and sources of emotional satisfaction, but also signals the end of the productive period of her life. Much has been written but, still, little is known about how women respond to aging during the middle years.

Some women—witness the clichéd joke about women who remain 29 for a decade or more—experience distress over aging quite early. It stands to reason that the transition to being over 40 is more difficult, and that seeing one's children begin their reproductive lives is more threatening yet. For women in the postparental years, the physical symptoms of the menopause reinforce feelings of becoming old and useless.

Even with these complications, research suggests that middle-aged women whose children have left home are happier and get more enjoyment out of life than women of similar ages who still have children at home. Data from six national surveys confirmed this to be the case.[6]

The Years Following Retirement. Most people face compulsory retirement from work at around 65 years of age. There are exceptions of course—professional people, farmers, and the self-employed, to mention a few. But, increasingly in the modern world, people work in large organizations with regular retirement policies.

The adjustments that couples make to retirement may not be as variable as the adjustments in earlier years, for, if nothing else, physical limitations are increasingly prominent. Then, too, the accumulating habit cage makes it less likely that there will be extreme deviation from earlier adjustment. Certainly couples vary in preparation for retirement. Some couples plan enthusiastically for retirement, just as some couples anticipate the marriage of their children so that they may have more time together and the opportunity to carry out long-delayed plans. Particularly when their income is adequate, retired couples may seek the good life. In genuine affluence, world travel is possible. On a more modest level, there still may be the winter cottage in Florida or California, and the summer place at a northern lake or in the mountains. Retirement may make it possible to make frequent and regular visits to children and grandchildren who now live in distant localities. It is also possible to leave again when the pleasures of the visit wane.

Other couples, of number undetermined, who have not the energy or income to live so well are content to stay in their old homes and not have to cope with the demands of other family members or with work. They may visit their children occasionally, or be visited by them. Disengagement from much of the world is the hallmark of such couples, who socially are becoming aged whether or not they are older chronologically than more active couples.[7]

For still other couples, retirement is filled with threat. Either the husband or wife, or both, may fear that the shaky equilibrium of their marriage will be upset by the adjustments that must be made when they are

6. Norval D. Glenn, "Psychological Well-Being in the Postparental Stage," *Journal of Marriage and the Family* 37 (Feb. 1975), pp. 105–10.

7. Elaine Cumming and William E. Henry, *Growing Old: The Process of Disengagement,* New York: Basic Books, 1961.

no longer out of the home for most of the day. And, although a steadily expanding proportion of retired couples has adequate income through social security, corporation retirement programs, and savings, retirement to some means severe economic deprivation. Problems of adjustment between husband and wife may be complicated by the threat of becoming dependent upon children or public agencies.

If the preretirement years are more often troublesome for the wife, those following retirement may be equally difficult for the husband. Men have their roles defined, more than anything else, by their status as breadwinners. Until retirement, most men achieve whatever self-respect they possess from their jobs. Their relationships with their wives are influenced by their success at work, and work often becomes an escape from full involvement in the family.

Upon retirement, all of this is changed drastically. In at least two ways, the retired man is faced with the necessity of making radical adjustments: adjustments in self-concept and adjustment in the daily routines of living. The threat to the husband's self-concept is of major importance and may also be the major determinant of how he adapts his daily routines following retirement. For many years, the man has had an ingrained concept of himself, as, for example, an executive, salesman, or clerk. Regardless of the relative prestige attaching to his occupation, the occupational identification has brought him self-respect at some level. He has had the strength and security that come from being useful.

Upon retirement, he is no longer executive, salesman, or clerk. In the eyes of his co-workers, his wife, and himself, suddenly he is old and no longer of great use. The assault on his self-concept is most likely to come from outsiders. Former friends on the job now exclude him, and no longer show him respect. He is now "old-timer," perhaps, to be patronized and not taken too seriously.

Of great importance is the attitude taken by his wife. If her conception of him remains what it was before, then the husband may hold on to his self-concept in spite of lack of support for it from other people. If, however, she is threatened by his retirement, or if she takes advantage of the opportunity to be hostile toward him, he must either capitulate or insulate himself against all outside opinions.

Many men struggle through severe ambivalence trying to find a new self-concept consistent with their retired status. The easiest time may be had by men of high status or expertise who continue to do some work even after retirement. Their situation is not greatly different from that of farmers, independent business people, and professionals who do not face absolute retirement at any particular age. Such people may be able to hold onto their occupational self-concepts into very old age.

A second alternative is to adopt a full-time leisure role. For those who can manage it, extravagant leisure such as foreign travel still affords high status. Occupational success makes such leisure possible, and one may conceive of oneself as a retired lawyer or banker rather than simply as a retired person. Full-time leisure may be more modest, but it is less likely to bring lasting satisfaction. The man who devotes himself to woodworking or gardening is likely to define himself and to be defined by others as just filling time—doing busy work rather than being truly busy.

A third alternative is to identify with old age itself. Some retired persons cease trying to hold onto earlier associations and confine themselves to relationships with other retired people. The men and women whose days center on the activities of Golden Age and Senior Citizens' Clubs provide the best example. While there may be macabre overtones in this adjustment, simple observation of these groups indicates that the organizations become a consuming interest for some members.[8]

Adjustments in daily routine are implied in these adjustments of self-concepts, but there is more to it than that. Before retirement, workers typically leave the house for eight or more hours each working day. Week-ends may be anticipated for the time to be spent together, but many couples are ready to return to their regular routines by Monday morning.

Retirement abruptly ends the work routines, and throws couples into the home on a 24-hour-a-day basis. Their only schedule for this kind of living is the usual, relaxed, weekend schedule that they can only tolerate for a few days at a time. Soon they become restive, the husband demands attention from his wife, perhaps seeking to aid her in her household tasks, or expecting her to defer to whatever projects around the home that he embarks upon. As he seeks to adjust both self-concept and routine to retirement, the stress seldom improves his disposition, and many wives find themselves living with men who are difficult to please.

Although the husband may be affected most profoundly by retirement, it often ushers in a crisis for the wife too. She may find herself trying to cope with a husband who makes impossible demands upon her time and her patience. He keeps the home in turmoil, disrupts her sched-

8. Some research has shown identification with old age to be associated with maladjustment. See Bernard S. Phillips, "A Role Theory Approach to Adjustment in Old Age," *American Sociological Review* 22 (April 1957), pp. 212–17.

ule and makes it impossible for her to get things done, and is constantly under foot. Even his efforts to assist with household tasks do more to disrupt her schedule than anything else.[9]

When the wife responds with annoyance, the husband's self-concept is threatened further, and acute conflict reminiscent of early marriage often emerges. Either partner may complain to their grown children, or to friends, and the family may appear on the verge of disruption. Seldom does disruption occur, however. Years of resolving crises have provided the stamina to handle this one, too, and at retirement there are few alternatives. Gradually, shifts in self-concept and routine occur, and most couples settle into new patterns with growing relief. As old age—with prospects for infirmity and death—draws closer, many couples become dependent upon one another as never before.

THE KIN NETWORK

Chapter 8 showed that married couples maintain a complex network of relationships with other kin. Within this network, relationships between parents and their married children are prominent. There is a comprehensive pattern of mutual aid in which the direction of flow is slightly more often from parents to children.[10] In Chapter 8 it was shown that mutual aid continues to 60 years of age or older, but the implications of there being three adult generations of the family were not systematically examined.

With postparental status often being achieved between 45 and 50 years of age, it follows that many families today have two living postparental generations. The younger of these generations is likely to be in full vigor and at the height of whatever financial success they will achieve; the older generation usually has passed the age of retirement. In Table 19.3, Hill presents data that specify the help given and received by all three generations in five areas—economic, emotional, household management, child care, and illness.

The parental generation stands at the center of the mutual aid net-

9. John A. Ballweg, "Resolution of Conjugal Role Adjustment After Retirement," *Journal of Marriage and the Family* 29 (May 1967), pp. 277–81.

10. One report shows retired parents giving more help to married children than they receive from them. See Gordon F. Streib, "Intergenerational Relations: Perspectives of the Two Generations on the Older Parent," *Journal of Marriage and the Family* 27 (Nov. 1965), pp. 469–76. See also Ethel Shanas, "Family-Kin Networks and Aging in Cross-Cultural Perspective," *Journal of Marriage and the Family* 35 (Aug. 1973), pp. 505–11.

Table 19.3. Help given and received in various areas by generation, Minnesota sample (in percents)

	Economic		*Emotional Gratification*		*Household Management*		*Child Care*		*Illness*	
	Gave	*Received*	*Gave*	*Received*	*Gave*	*Received*	*Gave*	*Received*	*Gave*	*Received*
Grandparents	26	34	23	42	21	52	16	0	32	61
Parents	41	17	47	37	47	23	50	23	21	21
Married children	34	49	31	21	33	25	34	78	47	18
Totals	100	100	100	100	100	100	100	100	100	100

* Some percentages do not add to 100 because of rounding.

Source: Adapted from Reuben Hill, *et al., Family Development in Three Generations*, Cambridge, Mass.: Schenkman Publishing Company, 1970, p. 67.

work. In four of the five areas, the parents give more aid than either the grandparental or married-child generations. Moreover, even in illness, the parental generation gives as much help as it receives. The married-child generation comes next, giving more help than it receives in three areas—emotional gratification, household management, and help in time of illness. As was also pointed out in Chapter 8, the married-child generation receives a great deal of financial help, and help with the care of children. The grandparents are mainly on the receiving end. Child care is not relevant for them, and in all other areas they receive substantially more assistance than they give.

Hill summarized these data by inferring ways in which each generation perceives its position and function in the family network. For the married-child generation there is both considerable giving and receiving. The parental generation is more affluent and supportive and occupies a kind of patron status in relation to the other generations. The grandparents are meager givers and high receivers. Theirs is almost a dependency status.

Three Generation Families

The kin network exists in spite of—or in consequence of—a trend toward the nuclear family as the basic residential unit. The traditional extended family has virtually disappeared from the American scene, and three-generation families—grandparents, parents, and children living together—typically are regarded as undesirable. Perhaps because of this, relatively little study has been devoted to either the frequency with which grandparents live with their children or what the adjustments are where doubling up does occur.

No nation-wide statistics are available to indicate how many parents live with their children. The census does estimate, however, the sharing of households with relatives generally. These statistics show that from 1910 to 1947 there was an increase in related families "doubling-up" in the same dwelling. In 1947, almost 10 percent of all families were sharing households with other families.[11] After 1947, the sharing declined again, and, by 1955, had dropped below the 1910 level. In 1955, some 3.5 percent of all married couples did not have households of their own; by 1975, the figure was 1.3 percent.[12]

11. Thomas P. Monahan, "The Number of Children in American Families and the Sharing of Households," *Marriage and Family Living* 18 (Aug. 1956), pp. 201–3.

12. U.S. Bureau of the Census, *Statistical Abstract of the United States: 1970*, Washington, D.C.

These statistics refer to the doubling-up of all family groups; not just the extent to which grandparents double up with their children and grandchildren. The census reported that there were 1,994,000 three-generation families in 1960, with only 1,245,000 of these involving a parent living with offspring and grandchildren.[13] The number of families who experience three-generation living *at some time* during the life cycle is considerably larger, and the proportion of aged persons who live with their children is substantial.

Carol Stone collected data from 5102 junior- and senior-high-school students in Washington, finding that only 318, or 6 percent, lived in households with one or more grandparents. She found that in more than half of these cases, the grandmother alone lived with the family; in one-fifth of the cases the grandfather lived with the family; and in only about 30 percent of the cases were both grandparents present. Thus, in only about 2 percent of the sample were there three-generation families.[14]

Koller, studying three-generation families in Ohio, found such small numbers that he resorted to studying them wherever he could find them, rather than drawing them systematically as a sample. In attempting to sample one community, he found that only 16 of 62 families could be classified as being concerned with three-generation living in any way. Moreover, those 16 cases were divided into three groups: those concerned with three-generation living in the past only; those living in three-generation families at the time; and those who expected to establish a three-generation household in the future. He also found that three-generation families do not last long. Most of them lasted from one to five years before the parent or parents died.[15]

As a proportion of all families, three-generation families are not numerous. When viewed from the standpoint of the grandparents, however, they are more common. Shanas estimates that a third of the old people, who have children, live with one child or another.[16] A U.S. census sample survey showed that one-fourth of married couples over 65

13. Hugh Carter and Paul C. Glick, *Marriage and Divorce: A Social and Economic Study*, Cambridge, Mass.: Harvard University Press, 1970, p. 159. See also Karen Kay Petersen, "Demographic Conditions and Extended Family Households: Egyptian Data," *Social Forces* 46 (June 1968), pp. 531–37.

14. Carol L. Stone, "Three-Generation Influence on Teen-agers' Conceptions of Family Culture Patterns and Parent-Child Relationships," *Marriage and Family Living* 24 (Aug. 1962), pp. 287–88.

15. Marvin R. Koller, "Studies of Three-Generation Households," *Marriage and Family Living* 16 (Aug. 1954), pp. 205–6.

16. Ethel Shanas, "Living Arrangements of Older People in the United States," *The Gerontologist* 1 (March 1961), pp. 27–29.

lived with their children, one-third of separated, divorced, and widowed men did so, and nearly one-half of separated, divorced, and widowed women did so.[17] The loss of a mate and increasing age make living with kin more likely. Thus, we may conclude that upwards of one-fourth of persons over 65 who have children live with their children. Most of these cases involve grandparents of advanced age, and three-generation living typically lasts only a few years.

The weight of opinion in the United States is against three-generation living. Speaking from a theoretical framework, Parsons states: "It is impossible to say that with us it is 'natural' for any other group than husband and wife and their dependent children to maintain a common household. . . . It is, of course, common for other relatives to share a household with the conjugal family but this scarcely ever occurs without some important elements of strain. For independence is certainly the preferred pattern for an elderly couple, particularly from the point of view of the children."[18]

Among the general population, from half to over 90 percent say that it is better for children to live separately.[19] Even among aged women living alone, more than half take this position. William Smith, using data from two Pennsylvania cities, reports that only 14 percent thought that it was a good idea for older persons to live with relatives, 50 percent said that it would work sometimes, and 35 percent stated flatly that it was "no good."[20]

One of the few studies reporting on three-generation living is Koller's study of 30 families in Ohio and Virginia. He reports that his respondents recognized such living as hazardous, requiring the virtues of diplomat, statesman, and saint. Oldsters, he says, who have had authority find it difficult to give up power to their children. Their married children, in turn, resent this intrusion upon their authority over their own lives and their children. Three-generation families were most likely to be created when the wife's mother moved into the home, and conflict between the two women over management of the home was common.

17. Ernest W. Burgess, "The Older Generation and the Family," in Wilma Donahue and Clark Tibbitts, *eds., The New Frontiers of Aging,* Ann Arbor: University of Michigan Press, 1957, pp. 161–62.

18. Talcott Parsons, "Age and Sex in the Social Structure of the United States," *American Sociological Review* 7 (Oct. 1942), p. 616.

19. Alvin L. Schorr, "Current Practice of Filial Responsibility," in Robert F. Winch, Robert McGinnis, and Herbert R. Barringer, *Selected Studies in Marriage and the Family,* New York: Holt, Rinehart, and Winston, 1962, p. 424.

20. William M. Smith, Jr., "Family Plans for Later Years," *Marriage and Family Living* 16 (Feb. 1954), pp. 36–40.

Sharp issue with the American bias against three-generation living, and with both the theoretical arguments and data in support of that bias, has been taken by Schorr. He points out that methodologically more adequate studies in England tend to challenge this view,[21] and that American data show only that three-generation living may cause problems, not that it necessarily does so.[22]

Schorr turns to the writing of Ernest Burgess, rather than to Parsons, for his interpretation of three-generation living. He quotes Burgess: "Where both parents and children elect to live together, the arrangement may work out more or less satisfactorily. Where the wife is working, the mother-in-law often takes on the major charge of the household responsibilities. She may be happy to function as a babysitter. . . . Although there may be some disagreements, these tend to be minor, and both generations report the relationship as satisfying."[23] Summing up, Schorr concludes that "there can be no question that there are potential strains when parents and adult children live together. But potential strains are inherent in any living situation—in work, in rearing children, in marrying. If technical and popular literature confined themselves to the strains intrinsic to each of these activities, would we conclude that we should give them up?"[24]

So the argument goes. Structurally, the American family has little place for aged parents. Apparently socialization, in this instance, works well, for the vast majority of older and middle-aged persons favor grandparents' maintaining their independence and living alone. Economic trends are consistent with this pattern. Social security, company retirement plans, and medicare, have gone far to remove the poverty which formerly accompanied old age. As more aging couples can maintain independence financially, more of them prefer independent living too.

On the other hand, there comes a time when people are forced to cope with decline and death. Couples in their fifties and sixties, and some in their seventies, may still be hale and hearty; but each passing year threatens emotional and financial security. Between 55 and 64, one woman out of five is a widow. Between 65 and 74, two-fifths are widows; and

21. Elizabeth Bott, *Family and Social Network,* London: Tavistock Publications, 1957, p. 218.

22. Alvin L. Schorr, *op. cit.*, p. 425. See also Sheila K. Johnson, "Three Generations, One Household," *The New York Times Magazine,* Aug. 19, 1973, pp. 24–31.

23. Ernest W. Burgess, "Family Living in the Later Decades," *The Annals of the American Academy of Political and Social Science* 279 (Jan. 1952), pp. 111–12.

24. *Op. cit.*, pp. 425–26.

past 75, 70 percent are widows.[25] Old people living alone are less likely to value their independence, and feelings of filial responsibility loom larger in their children. Even without death, illness or financial necessity frequently produce three-generation living. This produces strain. But, as Schorr points out, strain is inherent in living.

Parent-Child Dynamics

An implicit theme running through our discussion of adjustment in the preretirement and retirement years and through the analysis of the continuing kin network has been that these phenomena are progressive in character. It is one thing to talk of postparental couples in their forties and fifties, another with couples who have reached retirement age, and still another with couples who are aged. Perhaps nowhere is this more evident than in the changing relationships between parents and their adult children.

The parental generation stands at the center of the mutual-aid network. They give aid on a substantial scale. They conceive of themselves as powerful, independent, and interested in promoting their adult children's welfare. This orientation, still prevailing among parents who have reached approximately 69 years of age, was shown in Streib's study of 1500 families. He reports data from 1287 men who were married and still living with their wives. Seven hundred and forty-nine were retired, and 538 were still working.[26] Attitudes toward occupational achievement, upward mobility, mutual aid, and continuing close interpersonal relationships were studied.

Most of the parents acknowledged that it was important for their children to do well occupationally. They approved of their children going away to college and moving to remote locations when their jobs required it. They recognized that such moves threaten family ties, and they believed that children should not ignore their responsibilities to the parents. However, they were prepared to cope with these problems rather than stand in the way of their children's advancement. Parents who had retired were a little less likely than those who were still working to emphasize achievement norms, but the majority of both the retired and working groups did so.

25. *Statistical Bulletin*, Metropolitan Life Insurance Company, 47 (May 1966), pp. 3–4. See also Albert Chevan and J. Henry Korson, "The Widowed Who Live Alone: An Examination of Social and Demographic Factors," *Social Forces* 51 (Sept. 1972), pp. 45–53.

26. Gordon F. Streib, "Family Patterns in Retirement," *Journal of Social Issues* 14 (No. 2, 1958), pp. 46–60.

That the parents' assessment of their situation was realistic was indicated by the family experience of those whose children had achieved a higher level of occupational success than the parents had. Upward mobility appeared not to have adversely affected relationships between parents and children. The more successful children were more likely to keep in close touch with their parents, were more likely to offer financial aid, and were more willing to make sacrifices for their parents. Finally, when the parents were asked what they considered the children's major responsibility to the parents to be, the vast majority emphasized the maintenance of affectional and social ties over the offering of financial help. Here, however, we begin to see more clearly the effects of retirement and lowered income. Retired parents were more likely than parents who were still working to say that financial ties are as important as affectional ties. Moreover, the percentages who emphasized financial help, while still small, were greatest at the lowest income levels. In this, perhaps, we begin to see changes in parent-married child relationships as the parents move into old age.

The Glassers, working with a sample of persons about 70 years of age who approached a family service agency for help, concluded that their problems could be conceptualized as those of role reversal. Parents, they state, who must turn to their children for material aid are dependent upon their children much as the children were dependent upon them earlier. The children become like parents to their own parents, and the parents become like children of their own children. For many of both generations, this leads to role conflict and personal problems.[27]

The Glassers were working with a clinical population and warned that their findings might not apply to a general population. Data from a general population have been provided by Albrecht, who took a representative sample of parents over 65 years in a midwestern community. She found that 85 percent of the aging parents maintained roles associated with independence or responsibility, and that 15 percent showed dependence, distance, or neglect.[28] She further classified the parents into independent, responsible, dependent, and distant or lone groups.

The independent parents had allowed their children to become independent adults. They maintained close affectional and social relation-

27. Paul H. Glasser and Lois N. Glasser, "Role Reversal and Conflict Between Aged Parents and Their Children," *Marriage and Family Living* 24 (Feb. 1962), pp. 46–51.

28. Ruth Albrecht, "Relationships of Older Parents With Their Children," *Marriage and Family Living* 16 (Feb. 1954), pp. 32–35. See also Ruth Albrecht, "Relationships of Older People with Their Own Parents," *Marriage and Family Living* 15 (Nov. 1953), pp. 296–98; and Ruth Albrecht, "The Parental Responsibilities of Grandparents," *Marriage and Family Living* 16 (Aug. 1954), pp. 201–4.

ships with them, but neither dominated them nor were dominated by them. Most of these parents maintained separate households, but occasionally lived next door. Some had remarried in their later years and concentrated on their new marital relationships rather than upon their children. As a group, the independent persons were able to incorporate inlaws into the family without feeling threatened, maintained interests that gave them something in common with the younger generation, gave and accepted favors easily, and showed pride in their children.

By contrast, the responsible parents still maintained some responsibility for the second generation. In some large families, there still were adult children in the home after the parents had passed 65. Various other circumstances—the late adoption of a young child, remarriage and the acquisition of young stepchildren, prolonged education in preparation for a profession, and the return of offspring from the armed forces—combined to prolong parental responsibility in some families. Many of these were ethnic families in which traces of the old, large family system still survived. In others, there were hints of personality needs in the parents which caused them to hold on long after most parents had let go.

The dependent parents had suffered role reversals. They constituted only 6 percent of the parents and were, of course, older. Some maintained separate residences, and some lived with their children. Many had been widowed. The basis for their classification as dependent was that they required social attention, economic aid, or physical care from their children. They represented the ultimate stage in the family life cycle.

Finally, there were the lone or distant parents, widowed men and women who seldom see their children. There were more parents in this category—9 percent—than in the preceding one. Most of these people are in homes for the aged. Some feel deserted, and some, interestingly, resisted their children's efforts to care for them, apparently preferring life in the old people's home. Many of them had never had close relationships with their families, or these had been broken a long time ago. Since some of the children were stepchildren, we might entertain the hypothesis that here is a little recognized cost of remarriage.

GRANDPARENTHOOD

So far, little has been said about relationships between older couples and their grandchildren, or the significance of grandparenthood for marital and personal roles. The fact that relationships between grandparents and grandchildren are mediated through parents should not blind us, however, to the importance of these relationships.

The preparation for and reaction to grandparenthood often differ between men and women. They differ, too, according to whether grandparenthood is achieved relatively early in life or later on.

Some women, when grandchildren come early, are markedly ambivalent about them. When women marry around 21 and begin bearing children soon after, some may become grandmothers by 40, and many more by age 45. Where marriage of the daughter has been accompanied by threats to the mother's conception of herself as a young, attractive woman, the threat posed by grandparenthood may be even greater. Most people know grandmothers who refuse to be called grandmother and who insist that their grandchildren refer to them by pet terms of some sort. The status of the grandchild may be ignored by the grandmother, who concentrates, instead, on maintaining an image of herself as too young to have such a status.

Probably more often, middle-aged women find, in grandchildren, the opportunity to resume the maternal role directly, and to gain entrée to the lives of their children. Even before the baby is born, the grandmother-to-be reassumes a role of authority as she counsels her daughter or daughter-in-law on the management of pregnancy. In addition, she is permitted to buy clothing and other items for the new arrival, or to make some of them if she is so inclined.

Grandmothers frequently care for the new mother, her baby, and her family during the immediate postnatal period. After she returns to her own home, she is permitted and expected to continue a grandmotherly concern for the mother's well-being and the grandchild's care. Thus, grandmotherhood often is a major part of the middle-aged woman's solution to the loss of children through marriage. As grandmother, she acquires a new importance and usefulness. Moreover, she experiences again most of the joys of parenthood without having to cope with its exacting demands. Entering her children's homes as visitor and/or babysitter, she can indulge herself and her grandchildren; when her energy or her patience wane, she has simply to leave and go to her own quiet home.[29]

The adjustments made by grandmothers in their middle years do not change appreciably as they grow older. Unlike their husbands, many of them do not have to cope with retirement. They continue essentially the

29. Joan F. Robertson, "Grandmotherhood: A Study of Role Conceptions," *Journal of Marriage and the Family* 39 (Feb. 1977), pp. 165–74.

same roles into old age. Their care of grandchildren usually is welcomed, and they can slow the pace down gradually as their own physical and emotional needs dictate.

The status of grandfather, in middle age, has less impact. Some men resist the role of grandparent just as some women do, but it is likely to be less of a problem. Aging, during the middle years, does not present as much threat to men; indeed aging during this period often is associated with occupational and financial success. Moreover, the man's overwhelming identification with his job until retirement forestalls the role of grandfather being of major importance. Grandchildren may be a source of pride and pleasant diversions, but they do not stand at the center of things. Retirement brings great changes. Without jobs to claim their energy, many grandfathers identify more completely with their young grandchildren. They want to visit them, to take them for walks, to buy them things, and otherwise to participate in their care.

The role of older grandfather in American culture is essentially maternal. Unless the child's father is dead or absent, the grandfather is not an authority figure to his grandchild or the source of financial support. Instead, the grandfather baby-sits, plays with the children, and generally aids the mother in caring for them. Such a role is not likely to appeal to a younger man, and even the retired grandfather may have difficulty accepting it. On the other hand, the status of grandfather is envied, and grandfathers are permitted to display a tenderness and sentiment toward grandchildren not permitted to men in virtually any other circumstance. Both grandfathers and grandchildren often derive satisfaction from this relationship which is uncomplicated by any emphasis upon discipline.[30]

WIDOWHOOD

With few exceptions, the family life cycle ends in widowhood. Although young people seldom can imagine it, one partner is destined to live out the last part of life alone—at least without the marital partner. Moreover, the period of widowhood lasts, on the average, from 8 to 16 years.

For some 25 years, widows in the United States have been increasing by more than 100,000 per year, and the total number of widows is now

30. For a provocative discussion of emerging roles in grandparenthood, see Bernice L. Neugarten and Karol K. Weinstein, "The Changing American Grandparent," *Journal of Marriage and the Family* 26 (May 1964), pp. 199–204.

more than 9.5 million.[31] The disparity between the number of widows and widowers has been widening. Fifty years ago the ratio was about two to one; today it is five to one. Widowers are much more likely to change their status through remarriage, making widowhood in the United States an overwhelmingly feminine phenomenon.

That widowhood presents serious problems probably is obvious, but there are empirical data which verify this fact. Bellin and Hardt, for example, studying 1803 people over 65 in upstate New York, found that rates of mental disorder were higher among the widowed than among the still-married. These higher rates of mental illness were related not only to widowhood but also to advanced age, physical ill health, and other variables.[32] A report by Ilgenfritz based upon experience in a community guidance center also emphasizes that widows suffer from fears of being alone and from loss of self-esteem as women, in addition to the many practical problems related to living alone.[33]

Problems associated with widowhood are partly a function of increasing age, but not completely so. This was demonstrated in a study of almost 1000 people over 60 years of age in New York State. It found, first, that extensive association with friends is an important mechanism of adjustment to old age and widowhood. People over 70 who were still married were less likely to report high friendship participation than were younger married people. This decline did not occur among widowed men or women, however. In fact, older widowed persons often had more significant friendship associations than did younger ones.[34] How can this seeming paradox be explained?

The key was found in the status of widowed persons relative to that of others in their age group. Since friends tend to be about the same age, people who are widowed early find themselves with different experiences and interests than their fellows. Without the bonds of common experiences and interests, friendships suffer. With more advanced age, widowhood becomes common and it is the still-married people who

31. Associated Press, June 2, 1976.

32. Seymour S. Bellin and Robert H. Hardt, "Marital Status and Mental Disorders Among the Aged," *American Sociological Review* 23 (April 1958), pp. 155–62. See also Ira W. Hutchison III, "The Significance of Marital Status For Morale and Life Satisfaction Among Lower-Income Elderly," *Journal of Marriage and the Family* 37 (May 1975), pp. 287–93; Helena Znaniecki Lopata, "Loneliness: Forms and Components," *Social Problems* 17 (Fall 1969), pp. 248–62.

33. Marjorie P. Ilgenfritz, "Mothers on Their Own: Widows and Divorcees," *Marriage and Family Living* 23 (Feb. 1961), pp. 38–41.

34. Zena S. Blau, "Structural Constraints on Friendships in Old Age," *American Sociological Review* 26 (June 1961), pp. 429–31.

now are relatively deviant and isolated. Thus, whatever maladjustment is associated with widowhood is not a function of widowhood and advancing age alone but is also a function of the individual's position in a total social group. The individual's position in relation to other people of his or her age can make adjustment harder or easier.[35]

Widowhood for women is, in some ways, comparable to retirement among men. The death of the husband severely jolts the wife's image of herself. She is denied the opportunity to maintain her competence as companion to her husband and housekeeper for others. If she lives alone and remains active, she receives admiration from others. If she is not able to do this, her children are likely to offer her a home. This probably is the most common origin of the three-generation family.[36]

As already pointed out, three-generation families present problems for the younger generation of adults. They also present problems for the aging widow. The younger adults have established themselves in positions of authority in the family, and often they admit an aging widow in a subordinate and virtually functionless capacity. Patronized by their children and others, and denied opportunity to be useful, many aging widows deteriorate rapidly both in health and outlook. Some families are wise enough to recognize that aging parents need to retain their self-respect by being admitted to the household, if at all, as full and responsible partners. Under these circumstances it appears likely that many of the problems widely associated with old age in the United States may be avoided or at least ameliorated.

There is no escape. The life cycle of the family, as with the individual, must end in death. By this time, the family life cycle of the next generation usually is well along.

35. See Allen J. Watson and Vira R. Kivett, "Influences on The Life Satisfaction of Older Fathers," *The Family Coordinator* 25 (Oct. 1976), pp. 483–88.
36. For analyses of the roles of the widowed, see Felix M. Berardo, "Widowhood Status in the United States: Perspective on a Neglected Aspect of the Family Life-Cycle," *The Family Coordinator* 17 (July 1968), pp. 191–203; Felix M. Berardo, "Survivorship and Social Isolation: The Case of the Aged Widower," *The Family Coordinator* 19 (Jan. 1970), pp. 11–25; Bernard J. Cosneck, "Family Patterns of Older Widowed Jewish People," *The Family Coordinator* 19 (Oct. 1970), pp. 368–73; Jaber F. Gubrium, "Marital Desolation and the Evaluation of Everyday Life in Old Age," *Journal of Marriage and the Family* 36 (Feb. 1974), pp. 107–13; Carol D. Harvey and Howard M. Bahr, "Widowhood, Morale, and Affiliation," *Journal of Marriage and the Family* 36 (Feb. 1974), pp. 97–106; Jacqueline Johnson Jackson, "Comparative Life Styles and Family and Friend Relationships Among Older Black Women," *The Family Coordinator* 21 (Oct. 1972), pp. 477–85; and Benjamin Schlesinger, "The Widowed as a One-Parent Family Unit," *Social Science* 46 (Jan. 1971), pp. 26–32.

SUMMARY

Increasing numbers of couples have completed child-rearing and child-launching by 45 or 50 years of age. Most such couples remain vigorous, healthy, and alert. Although they may seem ancient to their children, they have a third of their lives ahead of them. Data show that the gradual drop in marital adjustment begun earlier continues into the postparental stage. The satisfaction that wives report with the love of their husbands declines steadily into old age. Companionship-satisfaction scores show a modest increase after the children are gone, suggesting that husbands and wives do turn back toward one another slightly.

Changes in power relationships occur, too, with husbands gaining in power up to retirement but losing it thereafter. Interviewer reports, more than self-estimates, emphasize the tendency for wives to increase in power as couples move into old age. The roles played tend to become more specialized with increasing age, men coming to play the traditional masculine role and women the traditional feminine role. Role unconventionality increases, too, with age. Many couples adapt flexibly to the limitations imposed by illness and infirmity. Some couples make the transition to postparental status uneventfully, while for others it is traumatic. Some unsatisfactory marriages break under the strain; others continue in neurotic interdependence. Increasing numbers of couples anticipate pleasantly their release from parental burdens and embark upon a life of relative leisure and companionship.

Adjustment, at this stage, often appears harder on women than on men. Women whose children have flown the nest may find themselves with too much time, with too few opportunities to use their energies, and confronted with a conception of themselves as old. A comparable crisis for men follows retirement. Husbands suddenly are deprived of their chief source of status; they define themselves and are defined by others as being old and useless. They face the necessity both of revising their self-concepts and of developing new daily routines. Some are able to develop a leisure role, and some come to identify with old age itself. Temporary conflict often develops between husband and wife until new definitions and routines are worked out.

The kin network at this stage may involve three adult generations—grandparents, parents, and married children. The parental generation stands at the center of the network, giving aid to the other two generations.

As grandparents become dependent, three-generation families appear. As a proportion of all families, three-generation families are not common; but the proportion of persons over 65 who live with their children is substantial. There is a bias against three-generation living, and data show that there often is conflict in such families. On the other hand, there is not evidence of more serious strains than in other family units at other stages of the life cycle. Most grandparents prefer to remain independent and emphasize the importance of their adult children being upwardly mobile. Both their expectations and actual experience show that upwardly mobile families are likely to be successful in maintaining close family ties and mutual aid. The older the grandparents become, the more likely they are to emphasize mutual aid.

Relationships between grandparents and parents are quite variable. Some grandparents are comfortable with their children's independence, and some seek to prolong dependence. Some grandparents become dependent in turn, and there may be a reversal of roles between the generations. In up to 10 percent of the cases, there may be estrangement and virtual loss of contact between the generations.

Relationships between grandparents and grandchildren also are variable. Some relatively young grandparents reject their grandparent status. More often, women use grandmotherhood to regain some of the maternal role. The role of grandfather becomes more prominent following retirement, when he, too, often assumes some responsibility for child care. These relationships may be satisfying to all three generations.

The family life cycle usually ends in widowhood. In extreme old age, widowhood often is problem-ridden. Evidence indicates, however, that the problems are a function of the total social situation, and not of aging alone. The widowed are, mostly, women who suffer then a drastic change of status comparable to that produced by retirement for men. Some widows carry on independently, and some quickly become dependent. According to the wisdom of the people involved, the final years in the life cycle may either be tragic or rewarding.

SUGGESTED READINGS

Atchley, Robert C., *The Social Forces in Later Life: An Introduction to Social Gerontology*, Belmont, California: Wadsworth Publishing Company, 1972. A new and comprehensive textbook in the field of aging.

Blau, Zena Smith, *Old Age in a Changing Society*, New York: New Viewpoints, 1973. Employs the concept of "role exit" to argue for the development of satisfactory associations among people who are relinquishing parental, work, and marital positions.

Butler, Robert N., and Lewis, Myrna I., *Aging and Mental Health*, St. Louis: The C. V. Mosby Company, 1977. Describes the processes of aging, analyzes treatment and prevention programs, and catalogs organizations and programs for the elderly.

Lopata, Helena Znaniecki, *Widowhood in An American City*, Cambridge, Mass.: Schenkman Publishing Company, 1973. Report of the findings of a series of studies of widows over 50 years of age in the Chicago area.

Woodruff, Diana S., and Birren, James E., *eds.*, *Aging: Scientific Perspectives and Social Issues*, Los Angeles: Ethel Percy Andrus Gerontology Center, 1975. An interdisciplinary analysis of the processes and problems of aging and of providing services to the elderly.

FILMS

Aging (NET Film Service, Indiana University, Bloomington, Ind.). Two elderly Jewish gentlemen, playing cards, reveal their attitudes toward life. Psychotherapist asserts that the greatest evil dealt to the elderly in modern times is the idea that an old person is functionless. Having an old person as a useful participant in a domestic situation is mutually beneficial to child, parent, and grandparent.

Passing Quietly Through (Grove Press Film Division, 53 East 11th Street, New York, N.Y. 10003), 26 minutes, black and white. Shows the death of an old man. Intense, but never mawkish or sentimental.

When You Reach December (Westinghouse Learning Corp., 100 Park Avenue, New York, N.Y. 10017), color. Details the plight of the elderly in nursing homes and those who live alone. Shows their fading health, dwindling money, and waning courage. Reports federal and state investigations of deplorable conditions.

QUESTIONS AND PROJECTS

1. What evidence is there to indicate the trend of marital adjustment during the postparental years? What is the trend with regard to wives' satisfaction with their husbands' love? With companionship?
2. Specify the changes that occur in power relationships between husband

and wife. What happens with regard to role specialization? How do you account for the changes in role conventionality?

3. Which partner usually experiences greater adjustment problems in the immediate postparental period? Why? What are these problems?
4. Which partner ordinarily experiences greater adjustment problems following retirement? Why?
5. In what two main areas must retired husbands make adjustments? What are some of the life styles adopted by retired men?
6. How are the wife's attitudes important in influencing the husband's adjustment to retirement? What problems are likely to be posed for her?
7. Describe the mutual-aid patterns typically existing among grandparents, parents, and married children.
8. What proportion of American families are three-generation families? What proportion of people over 65 live in such families? How long do they last? Do they have more problems than other families?
9. How do parents over 65 view relationships with their adult children? What values do they emphasize? How realistic are their expectations?
10. How may grandparenthood be dysfunctional for women? How may it be functional?
11. Describe the typical grandfather role for middle-aged men. For retired men. What is meant by the statement that "the grandfather role is a maternal role"?
12. What evidence is there that widowhood brings special problems? How do friendships play a part in the adjustment to widowhood?

Name Index

Subject Index

Photo Credits

Photo credits: *Chapter 1*, Jean Shapiro, © 1978. *Chapter 2*, UNICEF photo by Khopkar. *Chapter 3*, United Nations. *Chapter 4*, © René Burri, Magnum. *Chapter 5*, © Leonard Freed, Magnum. *Chapter 6*, Colonial Williamsburg. *Chapter 7*, New York State Historical Assc., Cooperstown. *Chapter 8*, © William Carter, Photo Researchers, Inc. *Chapter 9*, Barbara Pfeffer, Black Star. *Chapter 10*, Bob Fitch, Black Star. *Chapter 11*, © Diana Mara Henry. *Chapter 12*, © Eva Brandt, Photo Researchers, Inc. *Chapters 13* and *14*, Jean Shapiro, © 1978. *Chapter 15*, © Suzanne Szasz, Photo Researchers, Inc. *Chapter 16*, Harold M. Lambert, Frederic Lewis, N.Y. *Chapter 17*, Hilda Bijur, © 1978. *Chapters 18* and *19*, Jean Shapiro, © 1978.